The Good Skiing Guide 1989

THE GOOD SKIING GUIDE

Europe's 300 best
winter sports resorts

Edited by **Chris Gill**

Published by Consumers' Association
and Hodder & Stoughton

Which? books are commissioned and researched by
The Association for Consumer Research
and published by Consumers' Association
2 Marylebone Road, London NW1 4DX and
Hodder & Stoughton
47 Bedford Square, London WC1B 3DP

First edition 1985
New edition 1988

Consultant editor Adam Ruck
Research assistant Ray Lofting

Design Patrick Nugent and Val Fox
Maps David Perrott
Illustrations Jim Robins and Tom Cross

Front cover Kitzbühel, Austria

British Library Cataloguing in Publication Data

The good skiing guide: Europe's 300 best winter
sports resorts – 1989
1. Skis and skiing – Europe – Periodicals
I. Consumers' Association
796.93'094 GV854.8.E9

ISBN 0 340 43068 0

Typeset by Fox + Partners, Bath,
and PCS Typesetting, Frome

Printed and bound in Great Britain by
Pindar Print Ltd, Scarborough

Contents

Contributors

Sections of the *Guide* have been contributed by the following specialist writers:

Konrad Bartelski For several years Britain's only world-class downhill racer, now retired from competition

Martin Bell Bartelski's successor as the star of British ski racing, on whom high hopes are pinned

Alan Blackshaw Author of the *Penguin Guide to Mountaineering*

Mark Heller Author of many books about skiing, and recently retired ski-resort critic of *The Guardian*

David Goldsmith Freelance journalist, and Equipment Editor of *Ski Survey*, journal of the Ski Club of Great Britain

Nicol Glyn Physical fitness teacher, and author of the Ski Club of Great Britain booklet *Ski-fit*

Iain Peter Mountain guide and ski instructor at Glenmore Lodge National Outdoor Training Centre in Aviemore.

We should like to acknowledge the assistance of the Automobile Association in compiling parts of the Travel facts section.

Last but not least on our list of contributors are the hundreds of individuals – most but not all of them subscribers to *Which?* magazine – who have answered our various calls for help and have sent in their own reports on ski resorts, equipment, insurance claims, ski schools and tour operators. We have made full use of those reports, and are very grateful to have had them.

About this guide

This is the fourth edition of *The Good Skiing Guide*. It resembles earlier editions in aiming to help all skiers – beginners, 'intermediates' and experts alike – to get the most out of their skiing (with chapters on choosing equipment, get-fit exercises and so on), and in concentrating above all on one question: where to go skiing.

Ski resorts are changing more quickly than ever before, and the *Guide* has been thoroughly updated to reflect the developments of the past year. The great majority of the piste maps have required amendment to show new lifts and runs; and of course all the resort descriptions, factual details and verdicts have been brought up to date.

If you possess an early edition of the *Guide*, you will find this one greatly changed and expanded. Many more resorts are described in detail – some of them are new resorts, others are new to the British market, others simply new to us. Many resorts already in the original *Guide* are now given fuller treatment. We have also added new chapters on other aspects of skiing – an insight into downhill racing by British star Martin Bell, and our contribution to the important cause of making skiing even safer.

In a number of ways we have made the *Guide* easier to use. We have sent the resort index to the end of the book. We have rejigged the sequence of the resorts slightly without abandoning our conviction that the best order is a geographical one, with resorts that lie close to each other in the Alps placed close to each other in the *Guide*. We have split up into separate chapters some resorts which are essentially separate destinations, despite being linked by lift and piste. And we have restructured the major resort chapters, bringing together all the factual details for each resort in a box.

For the new reader, what matters is not how much this edition differs from last year's but how it differs from other sources of information about ski resorts. First, it is independent and thus impartial: we travel under our own steam, and prefer to ask holidaymakers rather than tourist offices or tour operators for their opinions of resorts. Secondly, it is consistent: we are a very small team, and we have a very broad recent experience of European resorts to draw on for comparative purposes. Thirdly, it is discriminating: by spelling out the drawbacks of each resort as well as its attractions, our descriptions highlight the differences between resorts instead of blurring them.

The *Guide* was born of a conviction that skiers planning a holiday lacked impartial, clear and relevant information, particularly about resorts. Its success confirms that belief, and gives us some confidence that we have gone the right way about filling the gap: reviewers have received the *Guide* warmly, and holiday skiers have bought the book in sufficient numbers to support annual publication. We have our critics, of course; some tourist offices have been distressed to find that their resort's write-up is not a good advertisement – which only goes to show how rarely they encounter any published reference to the drawbacks of resorts. We hope they will accept that our intention is to review critically, not simply to criticise, and forgive us for not deleting all references to lift queues.

Not everyone finds our maps as immediately comprehensible as the more widespread style of piste map – an artist's impression of a mountain landscape – but they are a unique aid in the difficult process of comparing ski resorts. Like any conventional map, they take a vertically downward view of the ground, showing its ups and downs by means of contour lines and shading. These maps do not distort many-faceted mountains to make them fit the picture, but show clearly whether runs face north, south, east or west. All but a couple of special maps are drawn to a single scale – so you can easily compare one ski area with another, for size at least. When comparing ski areas for difficulty, bear in mind that resorts differ in their understanding of 'easy' and 'difficult', and that the piste grades on our maps are those used by the resorts. We make it clear in the description of the ski area when we feel runs are incorrectly graded.

The information and judgements the *Guide* contains are largely the result of our own inspection trips. But we are well aware that some aspects of a resort are not easy to judge on brief working visits, and the *Guide* has been greatly strengthened by the observations of the many correspondents who have sent in reports on their own holiday experiences. The more of these reports we receive, the more useful the *Guide* will be. Towards the back of the book is a checklist that shows how you can be most helpful.

A book calling itself *The Good Skiing Guide* ought to be selective, and it is; it might be expected to include 'good' resorts and to exclude 'bad' ones, but it doesn't. There is no such thing as a 'bad' resort. Every ski resort can properly claim to be good for someone – which is why, despite pleas from several major resort tourist offices to be left out, only one or two very minor resorts which appeared in earlier editions have been dropped from this one. We have included the resorts which we think have the biggest claims on your attention (for a wide range of reasons) if you are choosing a holiday with an open mind.

On the other hand, do pause and reflect before you write to ask why we seem so unenthusiastic about the slopes where you had that wonderful afternoon's skiing in March 1986. Try though we may (and we do), it is inevitable that reports like ours, which aim to find faults where they exist, will seem negative compared with what you might read elsewhere – or compared with what you might write about your own favourite places. We know that skiing is tremendous fun, that the Alps in winter are entrancing, and that any ski resort is a fabulous place on the right day. We could have prefaced each resort entry with a statement to that effect; but we hope that saying it once is enough.

Introduction

With this fourth edition of the *Guide*, we have reached something of a turning point in its development. Up to now, we have concentrated most of our energies (or, rather, most of our research budget) on gaining first-hand experience of the resorts we are aiming to describe. We are in little doubt that the investment has paid off: the clear comparative evaluation of all of Europe's major resorts, which is the foundation of the book, would not otherwise have been possible. This is particularly true of our evaluations of the skiing itself, of which judgements are notoriously subjective. But we have always been conscious that there are aspects of resorts which the small research team of the *Guide* cannot properly assess. The standard of ski tuition, discussed later, is one of them – but there are others. We have always sought the views of skiing holidaymakers on such things, but we are now making arrangements to do so on a larger scale and on a continuing basis.

The chapter after this one announces the formation of the Good Skiing Association, and spells out how we see it working. The rest of this Introduction also touches on a number of matters on which we hope readers will contribute views or experiences in the interests of making the *Guide* more useful.

Run for your life

Not long ago, ski runs divided clearly into two kinds. There were pistes, where most skiers spent their time (marked and patrolled runs, usually machine-prepared to make skiing easy, and subject to closure when conditions were poor) and there was skiing outside those runs – off-piste. Whether off-piste runs were recognised routes, or improvised by individual skiers or their guides, there was no doubt that those skiing them were doing so at their own peril.

But things are no longer so simple. It is now common for the maps of lifts and runs issued by resorts (which we and most British skiers, at least, call piste maps) to show runs which are not pistes. Sadly it is not at all common for the maps to explain precisely the status of these non-pistes – and that status can vary widely.

For example, French resorts routinely show runs which they call *itinéraires*, which may or may not be explained. Some of these *itinéraires* are marked (roughly) on the ground, others are not. In Davos/Klosters, in Switzerland, there are 'difficult and not marked' runs (which are presumably patrolled) and 'marked but not controlled' runs. Looking back through our files, we find that runs in Obergurgl (Austria) which once were mysteriously labelled 'Schiroute' have recently become explicitly identified as skiable 'only with guide or instructor'. The map from nearby Sölden shows a black dotted 'Wilde Abfahrt' from the top of the skiing, and an unexplained red dotted run lower down.

We complained in last year's *Guide* about developments in St Anton, where the famous and wonderful black runs on the Valluga, which are what draw good skiers to the resort, are now classified not simply as off-piste runs but as 'high-touring routes'; a high-touring route is defined as requiring extensive mountain experience and expert guidance, and is not marked, protected or patrolled. Between this category and ordinary pistes there is another set of runs classified as 'ski routes' – clearly defined as having markers at longer intervals than ordinary runs; being protected from avalanche; being groomed occasionally, in parts; and (the major factor distinguishing such a route from a piste) being unpatrolled. We persist in the belief that this is a fundamentally wrong-headed way to deal with the hazards presented by runs which are served by major lifts and attractive to thousands of skiers who are not and never will be ski-tourers. But there is no denying that the resort authorities have done what they set out to do with admirable clarity.

An alternative approach which has some merit is that adopted by Val d'Isère/Tignes, whose map marks the points of departure of off-piste runs (labelled *hors piste: sous la responsabilité du skieur*) but not their course. The clear implication is that you will need to get someone to show you the way down. But in practice, of course, there is the temptation on heavily skied off-piste routes to just follow other skiers' tracks. And if St Anton has two species of non-piste, does the skier assume that all of Val d'Isère's non-pistes are equivalent to one of those varieties? If so, which?

It seems to us that skiing off-piste is becoming a less and less specialised business, being undertaken by more and more skiers no longer satisfied by increasingly crowded pistes. If this is so, it is going to become more and more important to eliminate confusion in the minds of skiers about the risks of undertaking particular runs. What is needed is a simple, standard set of definitions of off-piste runs – preferably consisting of no more than two varieties. Those adopted in St Anton seem to us a suitable model, despite the fact that they have been applied in that resort in a counter-productive way.

Bindings recalled

We're all used to the notion of cars and domestic appliances being recalled by the makers because of safety defects; now, it's happening with ski equipment. Last winter two binding manufacturers, Look and Tyrolia, found it necessary to recall several of their models in the USA (where binding makers are often sued for compensation by injured skiers). The Look recall was extended to Britain, the Tyrolia one was not – but both seem worth drawing attention to.

The Look problem affected their new range of bindings which feature upward-releasing toe units – models XF, XG, ZL, ZP and ZR. It is possible for the release adjustment (the large screw on the front of the toe unit) to work loose, allowing the binding to release more easily. A rubber 'O' ring can be fitted to prevent this happening. If you bought a set of these bindings before February 1988 it would be worth taking them back to the shop for a check.

The Tyrolia bindings which are suspect are the 480, 290, 280, 190, 180 and 170, and the junior models 80 and 90. On these models, the boot flange is held down by plastic lugs which are distinct from the main components of the binding, and in a contrasting colour; lugs which are coloured white, grey, blue or black are apparently liable to break – those coloured red are not. If you have bindings like this, you can either try to convince the suppliers that they have a duty to rectify a fault which has not yet manifested itself, or you can simply keep a close eye on the lugs in future. Neither alternative is very satisfactory; perhaps it is not too late for Tyrolia to do the proper thing and encourage retailers to make the necessary modifications.

Accessible lifts

At last, there are signs that before long skiers will no longer have to find £50 to £200 in foreign currency on day one of the holiday to buy a lift pass: the number of resorts which accept credit cards in payment is steadily growing. This is not something that tourist offices are likely to advertise, or even own up to if we ask them – so if you notice a resort which offers this facility do please let us know, and we'll include the fact in our resort fact-boxes from now on.

Thumbs up

A great many skiers damage a thumb at one time or another. It is one of the most common skiing injuries, and although it is usually not serious (you tend to carry on skiing despite the fact that you're unable to grip one of your ski poles properly) it can cause its share of misery – not least when the skiing is over and you have to return to pen-pushing, typing or wielding a spanner.

It's not surprising that the thumb has a hard time: while the fingers are curled around the ski pole in a fairly streamlined fashion, the thumb sticks forward, waiting to be wrenched back when (as is often the case in a fall) the inside of your 'fist' makes contact with the ground. So it's good to see that equipment manufacturers are beginning to provide this vulnerable extremity with some protection: Marker, the binding makers, have brought out a new style of pole handle which incorporates a shield curving around the front of the knuckles and over the thumb. Independent tests in Germany have shown that the device works; the only problem is the price – a hefty £39 a pair. The importers are Badger Sports, Unit 1, Alliance Road, London W3 0RA ✆ 01-993 7433.

Paradise spoilt

One of the hazards of compiling a guide such as this is the natural tendency to focus on the negative aspects of ski resorts. It is the negative aspects, more often than not, which prompt people to write to us out of the blue about their holiday experiences; and, it must be admitted, the process of choosing where to go next (particularly for a group of mixed ability) is often one of minimising the negatives rather than maximising the positives. So perhaps it is sensible to preface the remarks that follow by saying that Val d'Isère is one of our favourite resorts, and one about which we are very ready to enthuse.

More than most areas, it is thoroughly good for all grades of skier, provided you go to the right parts and are not ashamed to take lifts back to the valley if necessary. But the resort authorities are spoiling this paradise, for novice skiers at least, by negligence in two matters. The first is erratic piste grading, about which we have a mounting file of complaints. The second, which is perhaps not unrelated, is slack piste maintenance – and particularly maintenance of green and blue runs. Val and Tignes have plenty of easy skiing, and what's more it is easy skiing which normally provides good snow, unlike much of the 'easy' skiing in resorts of under one-third the altitude. But nothing so affects the delicate, slow-growing confidence of novice skiers as the constant fear of encountering steep pitches which seem to them unskiable. Green runs with mogul fields are a contradiction in terms, yet reports make it clear that such runs were to be found in Val and Tignes last winter. Novices should stay away until the resort authorities get their act together.

Scandalous schools

For many British skiers who get only one or two opportunities a year to practise their skills, going skiing means going to ski school. And if all or most of your skiing time is spent in school, it's clearly crucial to the success of your holiday that the lessons should go well. Generally, they do: the majority of the reports we have on file are favourable. There are of course exceptions: there are bound to be better-than-average and worse-than-average instructors in any school, and (let it be admitted) there are bound to be pupils who will interpret an unsatisfactory week's skiing in terms of unsatisfactory tuition, whatever the root cause. Most of our ski school files tell a mixed story, and result in an inconclusive final report in the *Guide*.

But some of the files leave little room for doubt that there is something amiss in the management of the ski school. Even the most prestigious and affluent of resorts may run its school incompetently.

The prime example of this is Zermatt. Its ski school is widely held to be as poor as its scenery is magnificent, its skiing is challenging and its cost of living is high. In early editions of the *Guide* we said as much, but had little direct evidence to support the accepted view. Last year, however, we spelt out some recent criticisms from reporters to the *Guide*. In preparing this edition, as usual, we sent a copy of last year's entry to the resort tourist office and invited their comments. The result? A letter from the resort's marketing manager expressing the view that 'your opinion about the ski school is too bad'.

Our response to this is to print below the latest report we have received, dated April 1988.

'My first instructor (class 3) tested us and divided us into two groups. He chose me for his own group. I kept up with the group all morning (all we did was follow the instructor, there was no instruction), and never lagged behind or fell, but suddenly he turned to me and said I would have to go into class 2. The rest of the class were astonished and told me not to go, because I was of the same standard as the rest. However, I didn't want trouble, and at lunchtime I joined a class 2 group. This was extremely slow and boring.

'The next day I got delayed by enormous lift queues on my way to join this group, and they went without me; fortunately, I spotted the other class 3 group, and the instructor allowed me to join them. He kept his eye on me, but as I did not lag behind (again it was simply follow-my-leader, no instruction), he said I could stay. But during the morning he very rudely and unkindly told two other women in the group that they would have to go into a lower class, and at lunchtime he said the same to a 15-year-old girl, who became upset by this. He said I could stay. But I had befriended the girl, and so I opted to go with her.

'The class 2 group we joined was in the hands of Marcus (a shepherd, and very old – almost toothless). Again, we followed him down and got no tuition. The next day, when we met for the afternoon session, Marcus said he had to leave us for just a minute; we presumed he was going to the loo. Forty minutes later, we concluded that he had abandoned us. Luckily, the head of the school was around, heard of our plight and arranged for another instructor to take over. Still no actual instruction was forthcoming.

'The next morning, Marcus failed to turn up at the school meeting point. By this time I had revealed that I was a journalist, and I think it was because of this that we were finally given a good instructor (who was told to leave his original class to someone else). We completed the week successfully with this instructor – he actually did some teaching, and incidentally said that we were of good class 3 standard.'

Clearly, such a story might not mean much in isolation. But supported as it is by complaints from others about individual problems of the kind this reader faced *en masse*, it cannot be ignored. Our advice to the Zermatt authorities is to give their ski school a thorough shake-up. And our advice to holidaymakers planning to take lessons is to forget Zermatt until there is evidence that results have been achieved.

Ski schools are of course one of the aspects of ski-resort quality which can be evaluated only by holidaymakers, and so one of the main items on the agenda of the Good Skiing Association.

Passing thoughts

Imagine that you are the proprietor of a ski lift installation in Les Deux-Oeufs. Over the hill on which your lifts are planted is another resort, Le Grand-Plat. Each resort has 10 lifts and 5,000 visitor beds, and charges visitors 500 francs for a week's use of the local lifts. One day, your opposite number over the hill rings up and suggests that your two resorts should enter into an arrangement to allow visitors to each resort to buy a joint pass, covering all the lifts of the whole Oeufs-sur-le-Plat area, for a larger-than-normal price – 600 francs, say. He reckons that perhaps half of your visitors would pay the 20 per cent extra for access to twice the skiing, which means that your revenue could be expected to increase by 10 per cent, and your operating profit by a much larger amount. What are you going to do? The answer is simple: laugh all the way to the Banque de Savoie.

To put it another way: all other things being equal, big lift installations, for access to which skiers will happily pay large amounts, are much more profitable than small ones. Or rather they may be. We have become used to the idea that big ski areas mean big prices, but it is not always so. An analysis of the pass prices of the major resorts in the *Guide* reveals that there are some substantial areas which charge modest prices. The average price of a six-day pass in all our major resorts (at June 1988 exchange rates) is close to £63; among the resorts with pass prices well below that – around £52 – are Söll, Wagrain and Mayrhofen. All of these Austrian resorts give access (indirectly in the case of Mayrhofen) to a lot of skiing, and seem markedly better value than some averagely expensive resorts such as Niederau. Austrian resorts are not all cheap, but none is notably expensive – Ischgl and the Arlberg region (Lech, St Anton) are dearest at nearly £70.

French pass prices dominate the middle ground, and seem to offer excellent value, particularly at a time when other French prices (eg for meals and drinks) are high. The Portes du Soleil resorts of Avoriaz and Morzine are right on the average, while passes for most of the big ski areas of the Tarentaise – La Plagne, Les Arcs, Val d"Isère and Tignes – cost only a few pounds more (and less than those for much more limited places such as Obergurgl, Courmayeur and Saas Fee).

Just about the only rule to emerge from this study is that Swiss resorts are almost all expensive. Only Arosa, Andermatt and Villars manage to stay just below the average, while at the top of the scale are Flims (£79), Zermatt (£85) and Verbier – way out in front at £96, only failing to break the £100 barrier because of the current strength of the pound. We have left out of this comparison the Italian resort of Sauze d'Oulx, about which we have found it impossible to obtain reliable information – last year the resort was quoting astronomical pass prices but we understand they have been trimmed. Other Italian resorts are to be found dotted through the price range.

Skiing low-down

Leaving aside the fact that some of the resorts most popular with British skiers are located in the valley bottom, we are not as a whole used to the idea of using valley towns as a base for skiing. Even those who have discovered the advantages of going skiing by car tend to stay in a ski resort. But valley communities with no skiing of their own have clear attractions – mainly that they are cheap, that they have a life of their own (as of course do some ski resorts), and that you are better off not spending your nights half-way up one mountain if you are going to descend it each morning on your way to ascend another.

A report from two readers very satisfied with their fortnight in Austria shows how it can work. Nigel S and Julie P rented an apartment in the village of St Martin am Tennengebirge, 60km south of Salzburg, well placed for access by motorway to the large number of resorts covered by what is claimed to be Europe's most wide-ranging ski pass – the Top Tauern Skischeck. Among the resorts it covers are Obertauern, Schladming and Wagrain (all major resorts in our terms). The other main areas involved are Zauchensee-Flachauwinkel-Kleinarl (a three-valley system just to the south of the Flachau-Wagrain-St Johann one); Radstadt-Altenmarkt (at the bottom of the road up to Obertauern);

Filzmoos-Neuberg (north of Radstadt); and the Lungau region on the south side of the Niedere Tauern, of which Mauterndorf, Weisspriach and St Margarethen are the major resorts.

Using the Top Tauern pass, Nigel and Julie visited a different area each day for a week – emerging particularly impressed by Filzmoos ('very scenic, easy skiing, deserted') and Zauchensee ('excellent, uncrowded lift system, super interlinked ski area'). In the second week they bought day passes and explored other areas – the Hochkönig area, including Dienten and Muhlbach ('excellent, and worth a week of anybody's time – very quiet, very cheap and incredibly scenic'); Werfengen ('modest but interesting skiing, lots of cheap mountain huts, no English voices'); and Dachstein west ('an unexpected treasure – long easy runs).

Last resorts

To judge by the experience of the readers whose finds are revealed above, a tour of Salzburgland's resorts should be high on the agenda for the coming winter's *Guide* inspections. Where else? Nearby Bad Kleinkirchheim, close to the Yugoslavian border, is increasingly popular (at least with tour operators). Analysis of package holiday programmes suggests that other resorts which may merit inclusion for the first time or more detailed treatment include Châtel, Kirchdorf and Valloire. We get the occasional letter promoting the claims of the German resort of Garmisch. If international exchange rates stay as they are, the pressure to include the best of the American resorts will be irresistible. Why not let us know what resort coverage you would most like to see added or expanded in the next edition? We do not claim to operate a democracy, but we can certainly be influenced by readers' views.

Snow wonder

It is only three seasons since we encountered our first snow cannon, on the lower slopes of Schladming. So erratic has the winter weather been since then, and so powerful an attraction has 'guaranteed' snow become, that major resorts without significant snow-making machinery will soon be in a minority.

Snow-making does not, of course, 'guarantee' snow. The process provides precipitation, but it requires nature to provide the low temperatures to turn the drizzle that is projected over the slope into white stuff. Nevertheless, it clearly has a value, particularly for high resorts which can, up to a point, depend on being cold from December onwards but cannot count on snowfall. And even for low resorts, snow-making offers some hope of keeping pistes in reasonable condition when they might otherwise degenerate into packed ice.

But this is theory; and our limited experience of artificially produced snow over the last couple of seasons leaves us in some doubt about its real value. We have found it being applied when natural snow was plentiful, and we have found it making precious little impression when natural snow was virtually absent. Before we embark on the laborious and expensive task of marking snow-making installations on the *Guide's* piste maps, we invite readers' guidance: is snow-making now an important factor in resort choice? Or is it mainly window-dressing? Write and tell us about your experiences.

Age concerns

'Please put much, much more in your guide about taking children skiing – in general, and in terms of the suitability of different resorts for kids. Especially ski school.' This plea comes from the mother of a four-year-old (a 'keen and confident skier') who was reduced to misery by his kindergarten instructor at Courchevel. We have had such letters before, and confess to a readiness to file them under 'I' for 'Idealistic but Impossible Ideas'. What we have lacked is the motivation to tackle the difficulties (which are considerable). But no more. The recent arrival of an editorial offspring puts these matters in a rather different light.

'Family holidays' is one of the headings under which we assess resorts, with the results reflected in the verdicts at the head of each major resort chapter, and in the comparative chart which precedes all those chapters. But we are told, by those better placed than ourselves to know, that this is not enough. What is crucial, says one correspondent, is to know what there is to amuse children when the weather closes in. The success of ski-kindergarten arrangements, says another, depends on how the supervisors respond to fatigue (in the children, not in themselves). Cold chair-lifts (of all things) have ruined the holiday happiness of a third. If you have experience of taking children skiing, and if you think there are realistic ways in which the *Guide* could help people like you to choose where to go, tell us.

At the other end of the spectrum, we are persuaded that we have not been doing what we can to inform senior citizens of the opportunities which exist in some resorts for saving on the cost of lift passes (and other expenses). We have made a modest start this year by including in our fact-boxes the information that resorts put out routinely in the literature they send us. For the future, we shall be actively soliciting information on this front, and awarding Senior Citizens a heading of their own in our fact-boxes.

Scholarly expeditions

School skiing trips are big business – they now constitute one of the major segments of the British skiing market. Yet the number of tour operators in the business is tiny, compared with the number selling ordinary holidays; and, what's more, a good proportion of that tiny number are not competitors but are part of a single group. School party holidays are something that **Frank Barrett** of the *Independent* has taken a particular interest in, so we asked him to give us a clearer picture. Here's his report.

School trips continue to form a substantial part of the skiing business. In winter 1987–88, for example, it's estimated that while the adult skiing market amounted to nearly 400,000 holidays through travel agents, a further 200,000 school children bought trips direct from specialist schools operators.

While the school skiing business is big in terms of volume, in recent years for many operators it has not always been particularly lucrative. In the 1970s, the business grew regularly every year, but recently, with the long-running industrial action by teachers ruling out extra-curricular activities, and the introduction of the new GCSE syllabus, ski holidays have been dropped by many schools.

Even for those schools continuing to take ski trips, there are other difficulties. The main problem has been that an increasing number of state schools are unable to take school trips during term time. This means that during the Christmas, spring half-term and Easter holidays the schools' demand for ski holidays exceeds supply. In contrast, demand during the off-peak times of January, February and March is negligible, limited to a handful of private schools.

The package holiday business depends for its financial success on a steady, regular flow of business over the whole 17-week winter season – charter flights and hotel bedrooms cannot be contracted only for the popular times. School skiing companies have been finding it increasingly difficult to cope with the 'trough' periods.

The result has been a gradual amalgamation of the main school skiing specialists into one conglomerate. At the centre of this conglomerate is Schools Abroad. From its formation in 1972, Schools Abroad rapidly outstripped the opposition by bringing to the schools holiday market a forceful style of marketing that had until then been restricted to the Mediterranean package holiday business. Before the arrival of Schools Abroad, the major school travel companies were more 'gown' than 'town' in their approach to marketing; one company, for example, insisted that all its employees were graduates (these days anyone in a travel company with an A-level is counted an intellectual).

Schools Abroad's sophisticated sales techniques quickly gave it a substantial share of the school skiing market. Following its acquisition by the Granada group in 1987, the company had the funds to take over rival operators and also establish new brands. The group now consists of not only Schools Abroad but also Travelaway, Hourmont, Schoolplan and SkiSet.

The group is better placed to make money out of the schools business through economies of scale – the more bookings it handles, the better the rates it can negotiate with airlines and hotels. As the same group also runs adult programmes including Skiscope, Snowbird and Hourmont, it is better able to fill the trough periods.

The Granada/Schools Abroad conglomerate holds a dominant share of the schools market – at least 50 per cent, which in tour operating terms is practically a monopoly (Thomson, the leader in ordinary packages, has nothing like this proportion). But the group's chief executive, Peter Hopkins, argues that his group's dominant position doesn't prevent other companies from entering the business and acquiring market share. 'For example, Snow World has built up a programme of 15,000 in the past few years – and other significant independent companies include STS and SkiBound,' says Mr Hopkins.

But with the wide spread of school skiing holidays available from the Granada group's various programmes – from upmarket holidays by air to cheap-and-cheerful trips by coach – any new company is likely to find it tough to find a niche. And the difficulties are compounded by a curiously fierce loyalty among the schools to particular tour operators. This loyalty can be partly explained by the rewards offered to regular bookers – free or reduced-price 'inspection visits' supplied to party organisers who reach certain booking targets. For teachers on relatively low wages, the prospect of a free or reduced-price holiday for themselves, their friends and relatives is obviously an alluring one.

The new aggressive style of selling school skiing holidays is raising other anxieties. There are fears that the hard sell of the brochures could persuade inexperienced party leaders to select resorts that offer the best prices rather than the most suitable environment and skiing conditions for their party. The main operators have a skilled army of sales reps regularly touring the schools: for teachers whose time is already heavily under pressure, the smooth promises and impressive offers can prove extremely tempting – whether or not the trips on offer actually meet the needs of pupils.

A frequent complaint from school party organisers is that they seem to suffer last-minute changes to flights and even ultimate destinations more often than those buying normal adult skiing holidays – the implication being that operators are happier to muck about with the travel plans of children (and teachers travelling at no cost) than with those of ordinary package-buyers, who will prove readier to complain.

School party organisers also fear that tour operators are paring down accommodation costs unreasonably. Many party organisers complain of overcrowded bedrooms where three, four or sometimes five beds are squeezed into a space where there seems barely enough room for one. The overcrowding of rooms and the wooden construction of many elderly resort hotels present a fire-risk which worries many teachers (though this is not a problem to which the operators are insensitive).

Such is the grip that the specialist operators have on the schools market that many party organisers don't realise the possibilities for arranging a trip themselves. One of the most efficient ways of doing this is through an exchange with a school situated in one of the main Continental skiing areas – the French Alps, for example. For as little as £150 per child, a school party can have a three-week trip involving not only skiing but also opportunities to improve their French and develop their understanding of life abroad.

Advice on do-it-yourself exchange trips is available from the School Journey Association (48 Cavendish Road, London SW12 0DH ✆01-675 6636) which for an affiliation fee of £5.75 offers advice and special school travel insurance. Advice on contacts leading to exchange visits can be had from the Central Bureau for Educational Visits and Exchanges (Seymour Mews House, Seymour Mews, London W1H 9PE ✆01-486 5101).

Associated ideas

As we have noted in the Introduction, the foundation of the *Guide* (and of its standing as the most authoritative English-language guide to Europe's ski resorts) is its careful, consistent and comparative assessments of resorts, and in particular of the skiing to which resorts give access – an aspect of which the *Guide* can claim to provide a uniquely clear view. We plan gradually to extend that foundation in one direction or another (by adding new resorts to the book), and we are prepared to underpin it (by revising our views of known resorts) when the ground underneath subsides; but it is basically in place and doing its job. As a result, we feel able now to devote more attention to the many other factors which go to make a resort ideal for one skier and quite inappropriate for another.

This is not to say that our resort assessments are going to pay less attention in future to the nature of the skiing available; on the contrary, the skiing remains to our mind the first aspect to be considered when choosing a resort. It is simply an acknowledgement of the fact that the *Guide* has weaknesses as well as strengths, and of the belief that we now have the opportunity to tackle those weaknesses. We particularly want to improve the information we give about ski schools, lift queues, piste marking and maintenance, kindergartens, mountain restaurants, après-ski, hotels, apartments, shopping, non-skiing facilities and so on. And this aim implies a change in methods – or at least a change in the emphasis placed on different methods.

The main approach we have used in producing the early editions of the book, when we were laying the aforementioned foundation, has been to visit resorts ourselves. Our secondary source of evidence has been reports from holidaymakers, which we have solicited through appeals in *Which?* magazine as well as through the pages of the *Guide*. We now propose to shift the focus.

We shall still be visiting ski resorts, of course – not only in order to continue broadening the book's coverage, but also to make sure that we stay in touch with resorts that we already know. We do not underestimate the pace of change in ski areas, and we intend to continue to evaluate those areas primarily by inspecting them ourselves. But we shall now be looking for much more help from holidaymakers, who are better placed than our inspectors to sample and judge ski schools, lift queues and sleigh rides, for example.

Over the last four years we have had what might be described as a healthy trickle of reports. Some have been from regular correspondents who keep us posted on their every move; others have been isolated letters from readers who may have seen one of our appeals when they had an hour to spare. A review of last season's reports has led us to conclude that we face three main problems in making more use of holidaymakers' reports.

First, we aren't getting enough reports; even if the reports we get were evenly distributed across all the resorts in the *Guide*, there would still be important aspects of resorts on which we would lack sufficient evidence to pronounce clearly. But the second problem is that the distribution of reports is, not surprisingly, uneven; as a result we are often very short of reports (and sometimes entirely short of reports) on certain resorts – and not always the unimportant resorts you might expect. Thirdly, reports vary a great deal in two ways: how valuable the information is that they contain, and how clearly that information is conveyed.

We propose to tackle these problems by forming a loose association of *Guide* readers, so as to give us a framework within which we can, to a degree, control the flow and the quality of the reports we get.

Anyone is welcome to enrol as a member of the Good Skiing Association, simply by writing to us. Once you have done so, we shall expect you to be willing to do two things: first, to summarise your skiing credentials – what kind of skier you are, where you have skied and so on; secondly, to reveal to us your skiing plans for the coming season. You will receive a copy of an occasional bulletin summarising the latest information we have on resort developments, on package holidays and on equipment. On the basis of what you have told us, and of any previous reports we have had from you, we shall then ask individual members to help with the next edition by providing a report on a specified resort that they are planning to visit. We shall prepare a list of specific queries about the resort, based on earlier reports and information received from the tourist office. Members who agree to help – and who eventually deliver the goods – will in due course receive a copy of the next edition of the *Guide*, in which they will find their contribution acknowledged.

Any member who has not been specifically commissioned will still be welcome to contribute a report, and the better such reports are, the more likely it is that you will be asked to undertake a full report the following season. But unprompted reports will not automatically earn a copy of the next edition – that would amount to signing a blank cheque.

If you have sent in a resort report in the past, you should get a letter from us before the season starts, setting out what we already know about you and asking if you would like to be considered a member. If you are interested but don't hear from us, or if you have not so far sent in a report, please write to Dept HM, Consumers' Association, FREEPOST, 2 Marylebone Road, London NW1 4DX.

THE 300 BEST SKI RESORTS IN EUROPE

The heart of the *Guide* starts here. In this 330-page section, we describe and assess the 300 or so ski resorts in Europe which, one way or another, have the biggest claims on your attention – either because of their own qualities or because they give access to excellent skiing belonging to neighbouring resorts.

We have arranged the resorts not in national or alphabetical order, but geographically – so that resorts which are close together on the ground are close together in the book. We are aware that some people like to decide first which country to go to, and then to choose within it – and our geographical order *will* be a bit painful if pasta and Chianti are your main priorities. But countries other than Italy form almost solid blocks of the book, and the geographical order has the great advantage that it allows you to consider sensibly the several shared ski areas which cross boundaries both alphabetical and national – chief among them the Portes du Soleil (France/Switzerland), the Milky Way (France/Italy) and the Matterhorn area, between Zermatt (Switzerland) and Cervinia (Italy). Even where there is not shared skiing, there is sense in choosing your resort in the knowledge of what other resorts nearby have to offer. The skier who likes to explore can easily run up against borders – from the Chamonix valley in France, for example, the sunny slopes of Courmayeur in Italy lie only half an hour away, through the Mont Blanc Tunnel. If you want to know what lies over the hill, you need only look over the page.

To find a resort by name, turn to the **index** at the back.

To find the resorts of a particular region, turn over the page to the **list of chapters**, which is in geographical order, or look at the **location maps** starting on page 44.

To find a resort to suit your needs, turn first to the **verdicts chart** starting on page 37, which summarises the pros and cons of the major resorts covered by the *Guide*.

Resorts chapter by chapter

The resorts are grouped into short chapters which are ordered geographically. First, north-east Italy is dealt with from east to west; then the sequence goes through the Alps in an anti-clockwise sweep via Austria and Switzerland to France – taking in further parts of Italy on the way. After the most southerly resort in the French Alps come chapters on the Pyrenees; then Scotland; and finally Eastern Europe.

Major resorts – those which attract a lot of British visitors or which have undeniably major ski areas – are covered in detail, with information on lift passes, ski school and so on, as well as a full description of (and judgements on) the resort; the names of these resorts are printed in **bold type** below. Minor resorts, which are summarised in a few lines (or even a few words) in the *Guide*, appear in ordinary type below – very minor ones are not listed here at all. The skiing of each major resort (and of most minor resorts linked in to a major area) is described in detail, and shown on a map; the key to these maps is on page 50.

The chapters on Scotland and Eastern Europe do not quite fit the same pattern. Each contains a general review of the style of resort to be found in those areas, as well as detailed observations on the main resorts. You will find some general remarks on Pyrenean resorts in a separate short chapter before the first of the detailed reports on those resorts.

In the list below, recognised names of ski areas are given in *italic type* after the resort names. Where an area bridges two chapters, we have applied the label to both with the addition of a suffix 1 or 2.

Choosing your resort

Choice of resort may not be the most important reason for the success or failure of a holiday – luck with the weather and snow, and perhaps with companions, is probably more decisive – but it is one aspect of the holiday over which you have some control. Every ski resort is somebody's ideal resort; on the other hand, none suits everyone. In this chapter our aim is mainly to provoke thought about what constitutes your own ideal – so that with the help of the main resorts section of the *Guide* you can arrive at your own short-list. But we also offer a short-cut to that short-list: at the beginning of the resorts section is a six-page comparative chart summarising our verdicts on all the major resorts covered by the *Guide*.

The time-of-year factor

The general pros and cons of different skiing months are outlined in 'A Skiing Primer'. The shifting patterns of weather and crowds affect resorts in different ways: timing of a holiday should weigh heavily in the balance when choosing your resort.

Going skiing **before Christmas** means going before the skiing season is properly under way. Choose a large, well-known resort popular with good skiers. Val d'Isère has a famous pre-Christmas downhill race, is lively and as reliable for snow as anywhere. A few resorts (Verbier and St Anton are the best known examples) are popular places for pre-season ski courses known as Wedelkurse or Cours de Godille. The resorts offer all-in packages of accommodation, lift pass and ski school just as they do at other low-season periods. There is an undeserved mystique about these courses, which are in fact no more than an intensive course of ski school which can be undertaken by fit skiers of all standards.

If you are going skiing over **Christmas/New Year** mainly in order to be away from home for the festivities, then resort charm and specific choice of hotel count for a lot. Little Austrian resorts such as Alpbach and Serfaus have a delightfully festive atmosphere at this time of year and are justifiably popular, despite their limited skiing. In general, lower resorts which have a permanent as well as a casual population are attractively Christmassy. Skiers who have had snowless skiing over the holiday in the few years may be tempted to aim high – though lack of precipitation has often been the problem. Those who do so shouldn't be surprised to find bleak, low-visibility conditions if the weather is more traditional. They must also be prepared to find not much of a Yuletide atmosphere – though a jovial chalet party can make up for that. One clear advantage of a high, purpose-built resort is shorter queues, because of better-organised lifts.

Some long-established Swiss resorts have a special appeal; the

British have been spending Christmas in resorts such as Wengen and Mürren for over half a century, and there's still nowhere more suitable for living out your own Christmas-card idyll – beautiful old log-cabin chalets, no cars, and magnificent scenery.

Continental skiers stay at home in **January**, unless tempted on to the slopes by good weather at the weekend. Keen British skiers, lured to the Alps by keen British package prices, should go to places with a big British trade – such as Val d'Isère, Sauze d'Oulx, Verbier and Söll – if they want to be sure of finding much life in the resort.

Although recent winters have not conformed to the pattern, January has traditionally been expected to bring more than a fair share of blizzards. In these conditions, medium-altitude resorts with plenty of skiing below the tree-line come into their own, because visibility is better among trees and the slopes are sheltered from wind – so lifts are less likely to be closed. In general the Alpine tree-line is at about 1800 to 2000m; resorts such as Kitzbühel and Söll in the Austrian Tirol offer a full 1000 metres of skiing (measured vertically) in more-or-less friendly woodland surroundings. Chair-lifts and drag-lifts are less prone to closure than cable-cars, but riding them can be bitterly cold. The ideal is to have a choice of kinds of lift.

January is a tempting time to visit big-name resorts notorious for their lift queues. If you have a week of good weather, you'll get very fit and be an immediate convert to January holidays. With a car, you could even sample several such resorts in one trip, fixing up hotel or guest-house accommodation as you go – you'll have no trouble finding a bed.

You can hope to find decent skiing wherever you go in **February**; but you must expect crowds. The French, Swiss and Germans have holidays during the month. The concentration of French holidays is particularly heavy, and although the French resorts are better able to cope than most, the roads leading to them (the Tarentaise resorts in particular) are not. The national tourist office can tell you which particular weeks to avoid each year.

For a holiday in **early March**, it is advisable to choose a resort with plenty of skiing above 2000m on slopes facing north and east. In high resorts you can be pretty sure of snow and reasonably hopeful of good snow; conditions are often excellent for exploring off-piste. (Many of the lower Austrian resorts, on the other hand, offer low-season prices for March, because they are regarded as increasingly risky for snow as the month progresses.)

To be confident of finding decent skiing in **late March** or **April** you have to go high – as a rule of thumb, you need slopes in the range 2500m to 3500m, and preferably north-facing. The resorts which can provide such slopes are few, with the result that skiers are concentrated in those resorts and the crowds at Easter are the worst of the season – particularly in France, where many of the reliable late-season resorts are to be found.

The tail end of the season in the Alps is often the time when cconditions are at their best in Scotland; in the depth of winter the weather is often discouragingly bad, while in spring the sun is not so strong as to ruin the snow.

The ability factor

It's important that your choice of resort takes account of the kind of skier you are. We've called this the ability factor, but it's actually rather broader, embracing your skiing appetite as well as aptitude.

The first requirement of a resort for **beginners** is that it should have a gentle nursery slope on which to take those first faltering steps on skis. It should ideally not be much of a slope at all (part of it should be completely flat); it should be big enough to cope with however many beginners there are, and it should not be part of a piste used by other skiers on their way down the mountain. It should have a gentle, slow lift, not one which non-nursery skiers are tempted to use. It should get some sunshine, and there should be a bar close by.

Most resorts have such slopes beside the village, at the foot of the main ski slopes. If the nursery slopes are high up, beginners face the cost of getting to and from them each day. On the other hand, high-level nursery slopes are usually sunnier than village ones; they are usually more convenient for mid-day meetings with other skiers; and they are extremely valuable if snow is in short supply in the village – the lower the resort is, the more likely this is, especially late in the season. Many purpose-built resorts have achieved the best of both worlds by siting themselves high up, with excellent wide-open nursery areas immediately at hand. Alpe d'Huez, Sestriere and Isola 2000 are spectacularly good in this respect.

Nursery slopes are for the first few days only. For a painless graduation to real skiing, you need easy, unthreatening pistes – graded green in those resorts which sensibly adopt four categories of run – on which to build up confidence. Many resorts which have perfectly good nursery areas – Selva, for example – are very uncomfortable places for a near-beginner because they lack such runs. It is equally important to bear in mind that not all beginners are dedicated piste-bashers by the end of their first week. Some don't take to skiing at all, and throw in the towel (and their crippling hired boots); others find skiing all day a bit exhausting, and like to mix skiing with other things. So it's important to consider the charm factor, and the non-skiing factor – dealt with later in the chapter.

Fashionable resorts with enormous ski areas, where lift passes and ski hire are expensive, are wasted on most beginners. Affluent beginners – or beginners joining parties of more experienced skiers – need not avoid them altogether. But some big-name resorts which appeal strongly to good skiers are best avoided for your first trip – see our comparative chart.

We know of only one resort where **intermediate** skiers will not find skiing suitable for their ability: La Grâve, in the southern French Alps, has a gondola lift which serves 1500m vertical of totally unprepared, unpatrolled, unmaintained and steep mountainside. In all other resorts most of the pistes will be negotiable under good snow conditions by plucky (and that does not mean fearless or reckless) intermediates. Plenty of them ski around the toughest skiing resorts in the Alps without a qualm. These resorts do not provide very much scope for relaxing, flattering skiing – you have to enjoy a challenge, and be prepared to take a lift down if you're not up to it.

Many intermediate skiers are keen and adventurous without relishing the challenge of difficult skiing, and the modern resorts with big ski areas have bred a species of skier for whom variety in skiing is very much the spice of life. These piste-freaks look for resorts where 'you can ski for a week without doing the same piste twice'; and provided you're not too literal about it there is now quite a range of resorts which conform to the specification. Many are modern French resorts in the Tarentaise or the northern Alps. Piste tourism at its most beautiful is to be found in the majestic scenery around the Sella Group in the Dolomites. In all these areas, no very difficult runs have to be skied in the course of skiing from resort to resort. Our comparative chart identifies several other traditional resorts with extensive skiing areas where intermediates can cover lots of ground without terrifying themselves. And the *Guide*'s piste maps are in a way tailor-made for the intermediate piste-basher, who can now see at a glance what a resort means when it claims to possess 'le plus grand domaine skiable du monde'.

We hesitate to prescribe what the **expert** skier should look for in a resort – we imagine that anyone who is expert at negotiating steep slopes will also have become expert at identifying them, and at figuring out what other resort characteristics are desirable. But our comparative chart shows which resorts we would turn to first for tough skiing and for off-piste skiing.

Any grade of skier may have an interest in the quality of the **ski-school**. In the *Guide*'s resort assessments, we have drawn what conclusions we can about individual ski schools from our experiences, but it is impossible to generalise except in a few respects. First, standards within any one school are likely to vary widely, and schools with long-standing reputations (such as those of Kitzbühel and St Anton) are no exception to this. Secondly, it's important for most skiers that they are taught in English; this means not only that the instructor must speak English well, but also that there must be enough English-speakers wanting tuition to justify the creation of an English-speaking class – and that means going to a resort with a big UK holiday trade. Thirdly, it doesn't matter how skilled the instructor is if there are 20 people in the class – your progress will be slow, or nil. We've paid particular attention to class size in our resort reports but, as you'll see, there are precious few resorts which do not at some time or another permit classes of ludicrous sizes.

The access factor

Holiday-makers who are used to a 30-minute ride from package airport to package hotel in their summer resorts get a bit of a shock when they first go skiing. Coach transfers of less than two hours are exceptional. Most of the very easily accessible resorts are in two areas – close to Geneva, where France, Switzerland and Italy meet, or in the eastern Austrian Tirol, within easy reach of Munich airport by motorway. Resorts in Western Austria and Eastern Switzerland are all much further away from either Munich or Zurich. Most Italian resorts involve very long airport transfers – some as long as eight hours, even without delays; the exceptions are the resorts in the extreme west of the country, which are about two hours from Turin. Enthusiastic supporters of resorts in the Tarentaise region of the French Alps – Méribel, Val d'Isère and so on – admit that the transfers are a drawback. In theory the journey from Geneva takes four hours or so, culminating in tortuous climbs from the valley to the high resorts – but weekend traffic jams can double the theoretical journey times. New road-building for the 1992 Olympics should solve the problem at long last.

If you're going by car, don't pay too much attention to slight differences in distance to resorts; winter weather (in the Channel as well as the Alps) and holiday traffic are more likely to determine how long the journey takes. But some of the differences are not slight: it's an appreciably longer-than-average journey to Italian resorts east of Milan, to St Moritz, and to southern French resorts – especially Isola 2000 and its neighbours, which are best reached via Nice.

In the 'Travel facts' chapter we list the major resorts which have railway stations. Many can be reached with only one or two changes of train, and some can be reached with no changes at all – Aviemore, Badgastein and St Anton, which is outstanding in this respect: you can board a train at Victoria after lunch, and disembark next morning about 100 yards from the cable-car station which gives direct access to some of the best skiing in the world.

The convenience factor

Most skiers would like to have ski lifts going up from their front door and pistes coming back down to it. Most would also like to spend their holiday in a community rather than a holiday camp. But it is very rare to find a village or town which is ideally placed as a skiing base *and* has grown up naturally for some other reason. St Anton is one example – a travellers' rest at the foot of the Arlberg Pass, and coincidentally at the foot of excellent ski slopes. Its village centre is a very convenient base for skiers. Obergurgl is another – a high village which might have been purpose-built, but didn't need to be. In most other traditional resorts, you need to choose your location with care, and with one eye firmly on the public transport system.

If the convenience factor really matters, though, you will almost certainly be better off choosing a modern resort which has been designed solely for skiers. Convenience is not just a question of getting around; planned resorts, provided they are sufficiently remote, can in theory achieve an approximate balance between the supply of uphill transport and the demand for it. Although resort developers make no money out of blissfully uncongested lifts, many purpose-built resorts have managed to put this theory into reasonably effective practice; what's more, many have also managed to plan lift and piste networks so as to avoid bottlenecks.

Skiing convenience dictates a style of building and a resort layout which have little in common with real communities. In most ski areas there is one situation which makes a more convenient base than any other, and the logical plan is one which concentrates skiers there. The landmarks of the first purpose-built resort, Sestriere, show the logic in action: tall, round towers full of very cramped accommodation.

Some small resorts – Puy St Vincent, Isola 2000 – consist of little more than one single-building complex, with flats, shops, bars, restaurants and resort offices under one roof. The walking you have to do is along carpeted corridors, the lift queues are to get to and from the 32nd floor. They're a bit like ocean liners – except that low standards of finish and maintenance have made them more like troop ships than the QE2. But a single such unit cannot simply be expanded to accommodate any number of skiers, or to service any size of ski-area. Thus, in the much larger resort of La Plagne (which claims to sell more lift passes than any other resort), half a dozen clusters of buildings are scattered far and wide, high and low, around an enormous skiing area – including a couple of old hamlets far below the main resort centres which stand high up in the wide snow-fields above the tree line.

There is no shortage of skiers who welcome the effortlessness of holidays in these new resorts. There are keen skiers who are obliged to take their holidays in high season, when many resorts cannot handle the crowds; they ski hard, value the lift system which enables them to do so, and are not too bothered about après-ski or sleigh rides. Then there are skiing families, who find that the freedom and economy of the apartment formula suits them and their pockets well, and that many of the new resorts (especially in France) are the most relaxing places to take children.

Needless to say, resorts such as these do not suit everyone; one man's convenience food is another man's junk. Non-skiing activities (day-time and night-time) are rarely as fully developed as in traditional resorts. What they lack more than anything else is life, the feeling of being a community, which by definition they are not. Hoteliers, shop-keepers and ski instructors are foreigners hired for the season or commuters from the valley, who leave the place deserted in the evening except for holiday-makers at a loose end, who may search in vain for a café with some local atmosphere.

Other big resorts have been developed differently, to have some resemblance to a real village – in overall structure even if not in style. It is no coincidence that these resorts – of which Méribel is the clearest example – are ones where you need to take care about where in the village you stay, just as you do in traditional resorts.

It may not be possible to give a new resort the vitality of an established community, but it is possible to build one which is both convenient and appealing – provided it is not also required to be large. That, at least, is the conclusion we draw from the example of Valmorel, recently developed not far from the Three Valleys. Its designers have obviously set out to synthesise an Alpine village atmosphere, and if the buildings mature rather than decay as they age, that objective seems likely to be achieved.

In many ways the most successful of the big purpose-built resorts is one of the first – Courchevel. It is no beauty, but under snow its ugliness is not obtrusive and it is much less shoddy than many younger resorts. It has a lively centre, with comfortable hotels (it pre-dates the great self-catering boom), restaurants and varied nightlife. Chalets and more hotels are spread around the mountainside in a broad horseshoe so that nearly everyone can get to and from home on skis. The terrain is such that the skiing around the resort itself is spacious and very easy, and snow is usually reliable at resort level. For bad weather there is good skiing below the resort among the woods. Queues build up at the main lift departure point, but there are alternative ways into the system. The only thing it isn't easy to do in Courchevel is economise.

The crowds factor

You don't have to be a super-keen skier to prefer skiing in a resort which is relatively free of lift queues; they are boring, tiring, often stressful, and disruptive of the best-laid plans. Tourist offices like to produce statistics giving the ratio of resort beds to lift capacity in persons per hour, but these figures rarely tell you what you need to know about queues – and can be highly misleading. The *Guide's* resort reports contain what concrete information we have about queues in recent seasons, but it is also helpful to have an appreciation of what makes a resort more likely or less likely to suffer from bad queues in high season.

A resort will be relatively queue-free if it is small (relative to its skiing area) and remote from centres of population; or if it has a lift system without bottlenecks (a shortage of lifts leaving the resort is the usual problem – and most of the resorts which don't suffer from bottlenecks are purpose-built ones); or if it attracts a high proportion of non-skiers and cross-country skiers; or if it doesn't attract many people at all. A few examples will serve to show how these factors operate in practice.

Obergurgl is very popular, and its lift system which depends on single-seater chair-lifts is not the ultimate in efficiency; it often has good snow when other places are short. But it very rarely has lift queues, because it is a very small place and, equally important, it is remote. Valmorel is small and rarely gets crowded; other resorts in its neighbourhood are much more powerful magnets. Val d'Isère is large and very popular, but remote and very well served by lifts from the valley floor – altogether, three cable-cars, three chair-lifts, a gondola and now a very efficient underground funicular. Even before this latest addition, queues were rarely serious, except in bad weather when higher lifts are closed by wind.

Famous, large resorts which provide inefficient access to excellent skiing areas normally have substantial queues. Kitzbühel is a prominent example: a fashionable, international resort with a lot of visitor beds, easy access from Munich in southern Germany and a quite inadequate access lift from the town to the main ski area. In Cortina d'Ampezzo the ratio of beds to lift capacity (especially capacity from the resort) is also discouraging; but queues are usually not serious, because so many people do things other than skiing, and because many skiers are late starters in the morning.

The queueing for lifts in most of the long-established resorts is in fact not the problem it used to be, now that new lifts have relieved their notorious bottlenecks. But the result of all this efficiency is that the pistes in many resorts are becoming crowded, instead of the lifts; this is just as unpleasant and much more dangerous. At least in the Chamonix Valley (where the hostility of terrain and ecologists have for years combined to frustrate initiatives to alleviate the queueing problem), when you do get to the top of the mountain you don't have to ski all the way down in a crowd, as you often do on the Grande Motte in Tignes.

The accommodation factor

Most skiers choose the style of their holiday accommodation before considering where to look for it – indeed many skiers go to the same sort of accommodation year after year. Such single-mindedness predetermines to some extent your choice of resort.

Nearly all package holidays in Italy and Austria employ **hotel** accommodation. In most Italian resorts there are plenty of cheap, mostly very simple hotels and guest-houses, which make other forms of accommodation look expensive. Cheap as they are, not all these places represent good value, unless your requirements are minimal. The Pensione Turistica in Courmayeur, for example, until recently featured one bath and one shower for 26 beds; we understand that matters have now improved. Most of our reporters' disappointment with hotels has come from Italian holidays. Most Italian resorts have one or two large, comfortable hotels; few of these are stylish or cheaper than comfortable hotels in other countries.

In Austria (and in most of the Dolomite resorts – which are in many ways more Austrian than Italian) the standard of hotel accommodation is high and uniform. Not only are most hotels well-kept, clean and comfortable, but also they tend to be attractive (outside and in) and welcoming. For many of our reporters, the attraction of a particular hotel is a powerful reason to return to an Austrian resort which they might otherwise desert. Lots of not-very-luxurious Austrian hotels have saunas and pools. In (and near) the largest and most famous resorts, such as Kitzbühel and St Anton, many package operators offer cheap holidays in simple bed-and-breakfast accommodation (the prefix 'Haus' often indicates this); even the simplest are usually attractive and adequately comfortable. In most skiing regions of Austria there are lots of small villages within easy driving distance of skiing, where almost every family takes in bed-and-breakfast guests.

In traditional Swiss and French resorts there is a much greater variety of style, standard and price of hotel accommodation, ranging from very simple boarding houses, where ski-bums cram several to a room and live very cheaply, to simple family hotels and (mostly in Switzerland) large, expensive palaces which are almost self-sufficient resorts in themselves. In the new purpose-built resorts there are usually few hotels, and not much of a range of comfort and cost. Courchevel is one of the few purpose-built French resorts with a lot of hotels, some of them very comfortable and expensive.

There are **self-catering** chalets and apartments for rent in most resorts, but the majority of self-catering package holidays are in French resorts, mostly purpose-built. Shopping facilities, more important for self-caterers than other skiers, are usually good and convenient, but demand for them in the early evening is heavy, and prices are of course higher than in valley-bottom *hypermarchés*. It is quite possible to arrange self-catering holidays in other resorts – write to the local tourist offices for information, and get hold of the Interhome brochure for the country you're looking at; if nothing else, it will give you a clear idea of the possibilities.

Verbier and the French Tarentaise resorts are the great homes of the **chalet** holiday, and now of the 'club' or 'jumbo' chalet which has sprung off from the original animal; all are very fashionable among gregarious young and not-so-young keen skiers who like the staffed chalet formula. Chalets are also to be found (usually in smaller numbers) in a few other Swiss and Italian (mainly Dolomite) resorts, and in a very few Austrian ones. The cost of chalet holidays doesn't vary much from country to country, which makes them a particularly attractive way to holiday in Switzerland and France, and not very attractive in Italy and Austria. Our resort verdicts pick out the small number of resorts where there is a wide range of chalet holidays on offer.

The charm factor

Keen skiers who piste-bash themselves to exhaustion every day may well scorn the idea that the style, looks and diversions of a ski resort could make any difference to them. But for most people the very word 'Alpine' has connotations of Christmas-card charm, and an Alpine holiday with no trees, no log cabins, no jingle bells, and no skaters – only bare rock and snow and concrete – adds up to a sadly incomplete holiday. Resort charm has seven major ingredients.

A year-round community – probably a village, but sometimes a town, with a life independent of skiing; preferably farming buildings and hamlets dotted around the valley and hillsides. This is most easily found in Austria, where many ski resorts have grown out of farming communities, at relatively low altitude. It is not a matter of prettiness, more a matter of people – a sense of place, of character.

A picturesque setting – not too enclosed, with some woodland. The beauty of the mountain scenery is a major contribution, for example, to the appeal of Zermatt and St Moritz. It is an even greater element of the appeal of the Dolomites. Not all high mountain scenery is particularly beautiful – on the contrary, it is often merely bleak, hostile and monotonous. Resorts in balcony settings half way up the flanks of wide, deep valleys benefit from broader, longer views and usually more sunshine than resorts at the bottom of valleys, which may be better placed for multi-directional skiing; examples are Crans-Montana, Sauze d'Oulx, Wengen and Mürren – surely the most beautifully set ski resort of all.

Absence of cars – or at least an absence of busy through-routes; preferably snowy streets. Here most high, remote resorts naturally have the advantage. Most purpose-built resorts restrict or banish cars; and most car-free resorts are purpose-built – the main exceptions are Zermatt, Saas Fee, Mürren, Wengen and Serfaus.

Traditional winter sports activities – horses and sleighs, walkers, outdoor skating and curling, tobogganers, cross-country skiers to give the place something other than the brutal downhill atmosphere. Most

often found in long-established winter sports resorts, mainly in Switzerland (St Moritz and Arosa among others). Seefeld is a departure from the pattern – in Austria, and mainly of recent development.
Decent mountain restaurants – plentiful in number, with outside terraces for good weather and mountain-refuge-style (rather than cafeteria-style) interiors for bad weather. Long-established resorts, and especially ones popular for summer walking, tend to be well and attractively catered for – Klosters, Zermatt, Courmayeur, the Dolomites, Gstaad, even Sauze d'Oulx.
Dignified clientele – resort not dominated by rowdy international youth. Undoubtedly the popularity of resorts such as Sauze d'Oulx, Mayrhofen, Söll, Val d'Isère, St Anton with rowdy young people, not necessarily British, spoils the atmosphere for others.
Chalet-style buildings – with balconies and pitched roofs. In Austria, not only are many resorts attractive old villages, they have also been developed in a carefully pseudo-traditional style; very few – not even resorts which grew from almost nothing, such as Obergurgl and Zürs – are eyesores. Not all 'traditional' resorts can claim this, especially in Switzerland: Davos, Arosa, Crans-Montana, even St Moritz, can rival any purpose-built resort for architectural bleakness.

The non-skiing factor

The needs of non-skiers are largely covered under the charm factor. For variety of spectacle as well as variety of activity, there is no beating the Engadine (St Moritz and its surroundings); part of its great appeal is the scope it offers for escaping the paraphernalia and mechanics of a modern ski resort to explore beautiful wooded valleys where no skiers (or at least no Alpine piste skiers) venture.

Many people like to get out of the resort for a day to go shopping or sightseeing, or simply for a change. Resorts near Innsbruck are the very good for this, with plentiful day-trips to Innsbruck and to the various places of interest, cultural and material, over the Brenner Pass in Italy. Non-skiers in the Dolomites not only have these interesting excursions within reach, they can also do their own Sella Ronda spectacular by public bus and can just about fit in visits to Venice or Verona. By contrast, a non-skier in one of the resorts of the French Tarentaise region – Val d'Isère or Méribel, say – is practically confined there for the duration of the holiday.

The family factor

Properly speaking, there is not a separate family factor. If you are taking children skiing, you will want to take account of the matters we have considered under charm, convenience, ability, access (long coach transfers can be a nightmare with children), non-skiing and accommodation. But there remains the distinct question of how resorts actually look after children. In general, the most recent generation of purpose-built resorts aims for family business, and the skiing requirements of beginners, and especially junior beginners, are very well looked after. Parents can dump their offspring for the day or half-day in trained hands and enjoy their own skiing. See our comparative chart at the beginning of the resorts section. Consider also where you will want to spend your skiing day, and how far away it is from the nursery areas.

The snow factor

Good snow is an important element in a satisfactory skiing holiday; in general, where you should go to find it varies with the time of year, and that factor is dealt with at the beginning of the chapter. But with most resorts there is always a risk that the snow at a normally dependable time of year will turn out to be disappointing, and if you're prepared to travel out of high season it's tempting to think that you can avoid this risk by fixing your holiday at the last moment and going to a resort which is doing well in the snow reports published in the newspapers.

There are two kinds of published snow reports. Resort tourist offices issue figures for the depth of snow on the upper and lower slopes; even if these figures were reliable (which they are not) they would give only a crude idea of the snow cover. Much more valuable are the reports sent by the Ski Club of Great Britain's representatives (based in about 30 Alpine resorts). These incorporate the figures, but add brief comments which are very illuminating once you learn to read between the words. The Club has to tread carefully in order to provide helpful information while meeting its obligation to the resorts, which sponsor the reps in the expectation that having a rep in town will attract British skiers. So the comments (which are often telexed by the tourist office) have to be delicately written if conditions are poor: 'Good skiing above 2,500 metres' and 'Good skiing on upper slopes' are favourite ways of describing wash-out conditions on the lower slopes.

Naturally, reps vary in how they handle these difficulties, and in how they perceive snow conditions. Some resort officials take a much closer interest in the reports than others, too. So resort-to-resort comparisons are unlikely to tell you much. But you can certainly use the reports to build up a general picture of which broad areas of the Alps are in favour with the great snowmaker in the sky, and which are out.

A further problem is the inevitable delays involved in getting the reports published. At best, a snow report can tell you where you ought to have been yesterday. Even if you decide on a week-end departure on the basis of a report in Friday's paper, the report may well relate to conditions early in the week, which means that by the time you are on skis the report will be nearly a week old. In a week snow conditions can change dramatically – particularly late in the season.

Since the 1986–87 season, the *Independent* has carried not only daily snow reports from the Ski Club but also (on Saturday mornings) a general review of snow conditions, drawing on all the available sources. Since it is prepared by the Editor of the *Guide*, it is not for us to say whether this innovation is any advance; but it has been widely imitated by other national papers.

The cost factor

For most people, the cost of a skiing holiday can be broken down into three parts – your package of transport, accommodation and perhaps meals; your skiing 'overheads' (equipment, lift pass, tuition); and incidentals (drinks, meals other than those included in the package).

Our studies of package holiday prices lead us to the not very helpful conclusion that it is difficult to generalise about which resorts or which countries are cheap and which expensive, and still more difficult to generalise about which places offer good and bad value for what you pay. So much depends on the particular deal assembled by the tour operator that even such plausible assertions as 'Italy is less expensive than Switzerland' should not be accepted without question – there are, for example, catered chalet holidays to be had in very respectable Swiss resorts at distinctly modest prices.

Overhead costs vary very widely between resorts; they are not so much the result of fundamental economic characteristics of different countries as of the place in the market that different resorts occupy – though of course exchange rates (and rapid changes in those rates) can have a marked effect on comparisons. Nevertheless, it is broadly true that most skiers going to Switzerland or France should expect to spend more than those going to Austria or Italy – and much more than those going to Spain, Andorra and eastern Europe. There are places in Switzerland and France where a modest budget can be made to suffice, but they are in the main not internationally known.

The most expensive Swiss resorts (Verbier or Zermatt) may charge three or four times as much as the cheapest downmarket resorts for lift passes, ski school tuition and equipment hire, making a difference of perhaps £150 to the total cost of a week's holiday.

Incidental costs too vary widely from the cheap-and-cheerful to the dear-and-dignified resorts. The differences are surprisingly difficult to pin down – a problem to which we are according a high priority over the coming winter (see the introductory pages of the *Guide*).

Major resort verdicts

The charts on the next six pages show our verdicts on the attractions and drawbacks of Europe's major resorts, as an aid to making your own shortlist. The chapter on 'Choosing your resort', starting on page 25, explains what we mean by some of the less obvious concepts used here, such as *Alpine charm* (apologies to Pyrenean Barèges), *chalet holidays*, *family holidays* and *skiing convenience* (which does not refer to the number of high-altitude loos, as one miffed resort tourist officer thought it did). The chapter also explains some of the seasonal variations, which the tables cannot convey. These are especially important when considering such matters as *lift queues* (good for queues means queues are rare), *après ski* and *resort-level snow* (which refers to the likelihood of snow in the village and on the runs down to it). Some resorts are low and unreliable for snow in and around the resort but have high, absolutely reliable glacier runs; this is why we have a separate *late holidays* category.

Do not rely exclusively on the chart for resort selection. Use it as a short cut to the resort chapters, which explain and sometimes qualify the verdicts. Also remember that there are plenty of good smaller resorts described in the *Guide* but not in this chart.

For most aspects of a resort we employ a simple scale of three unashamedly subjective judgements – good, bad and average. But for some aspects, where the distinction between average and poor has little meaning, we use only the good rating. These include *ski touring* (which means climbing on skis, not travelling around various resorts by car), *off-piste skiing* or direct *rail access* (in which we include resorts such as Verbier and Les Arcs, where the station and the village are linked by cable-car).

By a *big ski area*, we mean a large, linked lift network making it possible to cover lots of ground without removing your skis, as exemplified by the Trois Vallées resorts. By *easy runs* we mean not nursery slopes but long easy runs which can give near-beginners and timid skiers some variety and satisfaction. In assessing how good or bad a resort is for *tough runs*, we have concentrated on whether a resort as a whole is likely to appeal to skiers who relish a challenge. By good for *not skiing*, we do not mean useless for skiing (as an even more miffed tourist officer thought), but good for a non-skiing holiday. The *sunny slopes* category refers to ski areas well-endowed either with south-facing slopes or with both east- and west-facing ones.

Resorts rated good for *easy road access* are ones which are not too far from the Channel *and* which present no local difficulties for drivers. To be judged good for *freedom from cars* a resort must also not be over-run by other vehicles – such as Zermatt's electric taxis.

Major resorts
our verdicts summarised

★ good
○ average
● bad

	Easy runs	Big ski area	Tough runs	Off-piste skiing	Ski touring	Lift queues	Mountain restaurants	Beautiful scenery
Adelboden	○		○			○	○	
Alpbach	○		●			○	○	
Alpe d'Huez	●	★	★	★		○	○	★
Andermatt	●		★	★	★	●	●	
Les Arcs	○	★	★	★		★	●	★
Arosa	★		●		★	○	○	
Avoriaz	○	★	○			○	●	
Badgastein	●	★	★			●	○	
Barèges	○	★	●			○	●	
Bormio	●		●			○	★	
Cervinia	★	★	●			●	●	
Chamonix	●		★	★	★	●	●	★
La Clusaz	○		○			○	★	★
Cortina d'Ampezzo	○		●			○	★	★
Courchevel	★	★	○			★	○	
Courmayeur	●		●	★	★	○	★	★
Crans-Montana	★	★	●			○	○	★
Davos	★	★	○	★	★	●	○	
Les Deux Alpes	○		★	★		○	●	★
Engelberg	○		○			○	○	
Flaine	★	★	●			○	●	
Flims	○	★	●			○	○	
Gstaad	★	★	●			○	★	

	Late holidays	Sunny slopes	Nursery slopes	Skiing convenience	Cross-country	Summer skiing	Resort-level snow	Not skiing	Family holidays	Alpine charm	Freedom from cars	Apres-ski	Short transfers	Easy road access	Rail access	Chalet holidays
	○	★	○	●	★		○	○		★	○	○	○	○		
	●		★	●			○	○	★	★	○	★	★	★		
	★	★	★	○			★	●	★	●	●	○	○	★		
	○		●	●			★	●		★	○	●	○	○	★	
	★	★	○	★			★	●	★	●	★	●	●	●	★	
	○	★	★	●	★		★	★		○	●	○	○	●	★	
	○		★	★			★	●	★	●	★	●	★	○		
	○		●	●			●	★		●	●	★	○	○	★	
	●	★	○	○			●	●		★	○	○	★	○		
	●		○	○		★	●	★		○	●	○	●	●		
	★	★	★	○		★	★	●		●	●	○	○	○		
	★		●	●	★		●	○		○	●	★	★	★	★	
	●		○	●	★		○	○		○	●	○	★	★		
	●	★	★	●	★		○	★		○	●	○	●	●		
	○		★	★			★	●	★	●	○	★	●	●		★
	○		●	●	★		○	○		★	○	★	★	★		
	●	★	○	●	★		○	★		●	●	○	○	★	★	
	○	★	○	●	★		★	★		●	●	○	○	○	★	
	★	★	○	○		★	★	●		●	●	★	○	○		
	○		○	●	★		●	★		★			★	★	★	
	★		★	★			★	●	★	●	★	●	★	○		
	●	★	○	●	★		●	○		○	○	●	○	○		
	●		○	●	★		●	★		★	○	○	○	★	★	

Major resorts
our verdicts summarised

★ good
○ average
● bad

	Easy runs	Big ski area	Tough runs	Off-piste skiing	Ski touring	Lift queues	Mountain restaurants	Beautiful scenery
Hintertux	○		●			○	○	★
Ischgl	★	★	○		★	●	○	★
Isola 2000	○		●			○	○	
Kitzbühel	★	★	○			●	★	
Klosters	○	★	○		★	●	★	
Lech	★		●			○	●	
Lenzerheide	★	★	●			○	○	
Livigno	★		●			●	●	
Madesimo	●		★			○	○	
Madonna di Campiglio	★	★	●			○	★	★
Mayrhofen	○		●			●	○	
Megève	★	★	●			○	★	★
Méribel	○	★	○			★	○	
Montgenèvre	★	★	●			○	●	
Morzine	★	★	●			○	★	★
Mürren	●		○			○	○	★
Niederau	★		●			○	○	
Obergurgl	★		●		★	★	○	
Obertauern	○		○	★		○	○	
La Plagne	★	★	○	★		○	●	★
Saalbach	★	★	●			○	★	
Saas Fee	○		○		★	●	○	★
St Anton	●	★	★	★		●	○	

Late holidays	Sunny slopes	Nursery slopes	Skiing convenience	Cross-country	Summer skiing	Resort-level snow	Not skiing	Family holidays	Alpine charm	Freedom from cars	Apres-ski	Short transfers	Easy road access	Rail access	Chalet holidays
★		●	●		★	★	●		○	○	●	○	○		
○	★	●	○			○	○		★	○	★	●	○		
○	★	★	★			★	●	★	●	★	●	○	●		
●		○	●			●	★		★	●	★	★	★	★	
○	★	○	●	★		○	○		○	○	●	○	★	★	
○	★	○	○			★	○		★	○	○	●	●		
○	★	○	●	★		○	★		○	○	●	○	○		
★	★	★	●			★	●		●	●	★	●	●		
○		○	○			○	●		○	○	●	●	●		
●	★	★	○			○	●		○	○	○	●	●		
○		○	●			●	★		○	○	★	★	★	★	
●	★	○	●	★		●	★		○	●	★	★	★		
○	★	●	○			★	●		○	○	●	●	●		★
●		○	★			★	●		○	○	●	○	○		
●		○	●	★		●	★		○	●	○	★	★		
○		○	○			★	○	★	★	★	●	○	○	★	
●		★	○	★		●	○	★	○	○	○	★	★		
★		○	○			★	●	★	★	○	★	●	●		
○	★	★	★			★	●		●	○	●	○	●		
★	★	★	★			★	●	★	●	★	●	●	●		
○	★	○	○			○	○		★	○	★	★	★		
★		★	●			★	○	★	★	★	○	●	●		
●	★	●	●			○	●		○	○	★	○	★	★	★

Major resorts
our verdicts summarised

★ good
○ average
● bad

	Easy runs	Big ski area	Tough runs	Off-piste skiing	Ski touring	Lift queues	Mountain restaurants	Beautiful scenery
St Johann in Tirol	★		●			○	★	
St Moritz	○	★	○			●	★	★
Sauze d'Oulx	○	★	●			●	★	
Schladming	★		●			○	○	
Seefeld	○		○			○	○	
Selva	○	★	○			●	★	★
Serfaus	★		●		★	○	○	
Serre-Chevalier	○	★	○	★		★	●	
Sölden	○		○			●	○	
Söll	○	★	●			○	○	
La Thuile	★	★	●			★	○	★
Tignes	○	★	★	★		★	●	
Val d'Isère	★	★	★	★		★	●	
Valmorel	○		○			★	●	
Val Thorens	○	★	★	★		○	●	
Verbier	●	★	★	★	★	●	○	★
Villars	★		●			○	○	★
Wagrain	★	★	●			○	○	
Wengen	★	★	●		★	○	○	★
Zell am See	★		○			○	★	
Zell am Ziller	★		●			○	○	
Zermatt	○	★	★	★	★	○	★	★

Late holidays	Sunny slopes	Nursery slopes	Skiing convenience	Cross-country	Summer skiing	Resort-level snow	Not skiing	Family holidays	Alpine charm	Freedom from cars	Apres-ski	Short transfers	Easy road access	Rail access	Chalet holidays
●		○	●			●	○		○	●	★	★	★	★	
★	★	●	●	★		★	★		○	○	★	●	●	★	
●	★	○	●			●	●		○	●	★	★	○		
●		★	●	★		●	○		★	○	○	★	★	★	
○		○	●	★		○	★		○	○	○	★	★	★	
●		★	●	★		○	★		○	●	★	●	●		★
○	★	★	●	★		○	○	★	★	★	○	○	●		
○		★	●	★		●	●		●	●	○	○	○		
★		●	○		★	○	●		○	○	★	●	○		
●		○	●			●	○		○	○	★	★	★		
○		○	★			○	●		●	○	●	★	○		
★		○	★		★	★	●		●	○	●	●	●		
★	★	○	●		★	★	●		●	○	★	●	●		★
○	★	★	★			★	●	★	★	★	●	○	○		
★		★	★		★	★	●		●	○	●	●	●		
○	★	○	●			○	●		○	○	★	○	★	★	★
●	★	○	○	★		○	★		○	●	○	★	★	★	
●		○	○	★		●	●		○	●	○	★	★		
●		★	●			○	★	★	★	★	○	○	○	★	★
●		○	●	★		●	★		○	●	★	★	★	★	
●	★	★	●			●	○		○	●	○	★	★	★	
★		●	●		★	★	★		★	○	★	●	●	★	★

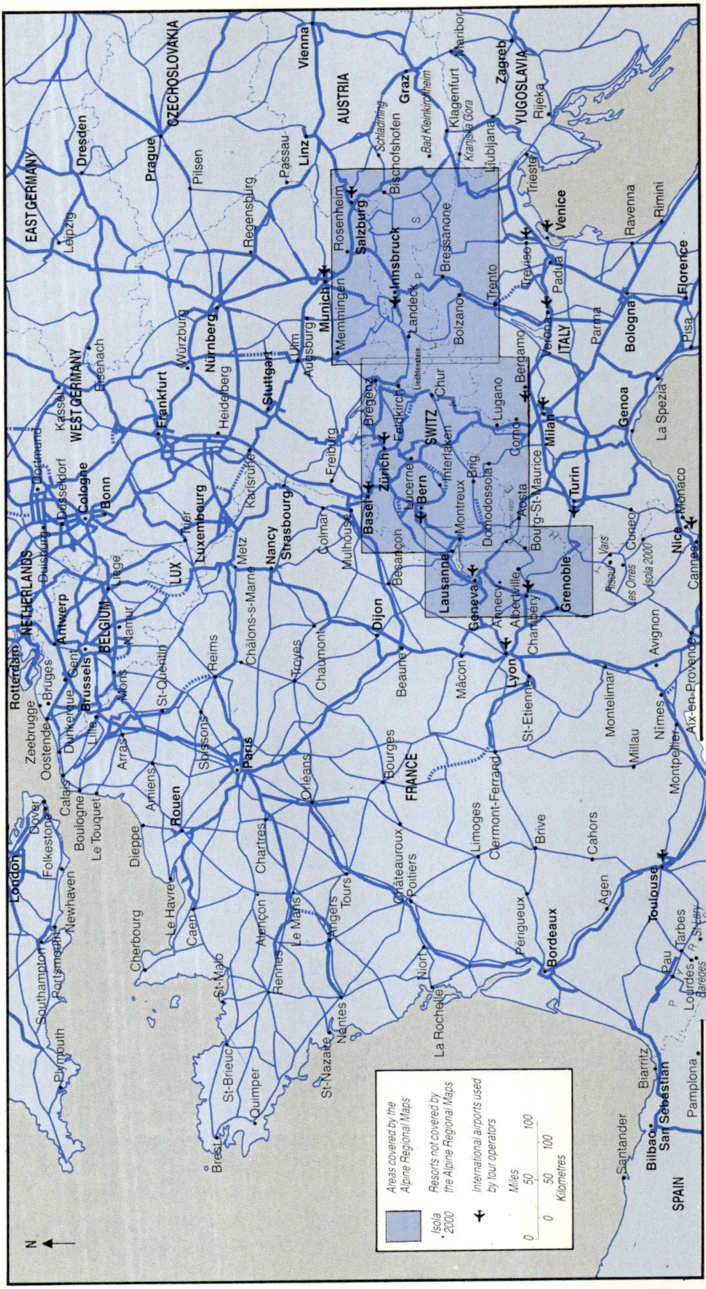

Areas covered by the Alpine Regional Maps
Isola 2000 Resorts not covered by the Alpine Regional Maps
International airports used by tour operators
Miles 0 50 100
Kilometres 0 50 100
N
EAST GERMANY
WEST GERMANY
CZECHOSLOVAKIA
AUSTRIA
YUGOSLAVIA
NETHERLANDS
BELGIUM
LUX
SWITZ
ITALY
FRANCE
SPAIN
ANDORRA
London
Dover
Folkestone
Newhaven
Portsmouth
Southampton
Plymouth
Rotterdam
Zeebrugge
Oostende
Bruges
Antwerp
Gent
Brussels
Dunkerque
Calais
Boulogne
Le Touquet
Lille
Mons
Namur
Liège
Duisburg
Dortmund
Düsseldorf
Cologne
Bonn
Kassel
Eisenach
Leipzig
Dresden
Prague
Pilsen
Regensburg
Passau
Linz
Vienna
Frankfurt
Würzburg
Nürnberg
Heidelberg
Stuttgart
Karlsruhe
Ulm
Augsburg
Munich
Memmingen
Rosenheim
Salzburg
Bischofshofen
Schladming
Graz
Bad Kleinkirchheim
Klagenfurt
Kranjska Gora
Maribor
Zagreb
Ljubljana
Rijeka
Trieste
Innsbruck
Landeck
Bressanone
Bolzano
Trento
Treviso
Venice
Padua
Verona
Parma
Bologna
Ravenna
Rimini
Florence
Pisa
La Spezia
Genoa
Milan
Bergamo
Como
Lugano
Chur
Liechtenstein
Feldkirch
Bregenz
Zürich
Lucerne
Interlaken
Bern
Basel
Brig
Domodossola
Montreux
Aosta
Bourg-St-Maurice
Turin
Lausanne
Geneva
Annecy
Albertville
Chambéry
Grenoble
Vars
Risoul
Les Orres
Isola 2000
Cuneo
Monaco
Nice
Cannes
Luxembourg
Trier
Metz
Nancy
Strasbourg
Colmar
Mulhouse
Freiburg
Besançon
Dijon
Beaune
Mâcon
Lyon
St-Etienne
Montelimar
Avignon
Aix-en-Provence
Nîmes
Montpellier
Millau
Perpignan
Châlons-s-Marne
Reims
St-Quentin
Arras
Amiens
Soissons
Troyes
Chaumont
Paris
Rouen
Dieppe
Le Havre
Caen
Cherbourg
St-Malo
St-Brieuc
Brest
Quimper
Rennes
Alençon
Chartres
Orléans
Bourges
Le Mans
Angers
Tours
Nantes
St-Nazaire
Châteauroux
Poitiers
Niort
La Rochelle
Limoges
Clermont-Ferrand
Brive
Cahors
Périgueux
Agen
Bordeaux
Toulouse
Tarbes
Pau
Lourdes
Barèges
St-Lary
Baqueira-Beret
La Molina
Formigal
Biarritz
San Sebastian
Bilbao
Santander
Pamplona

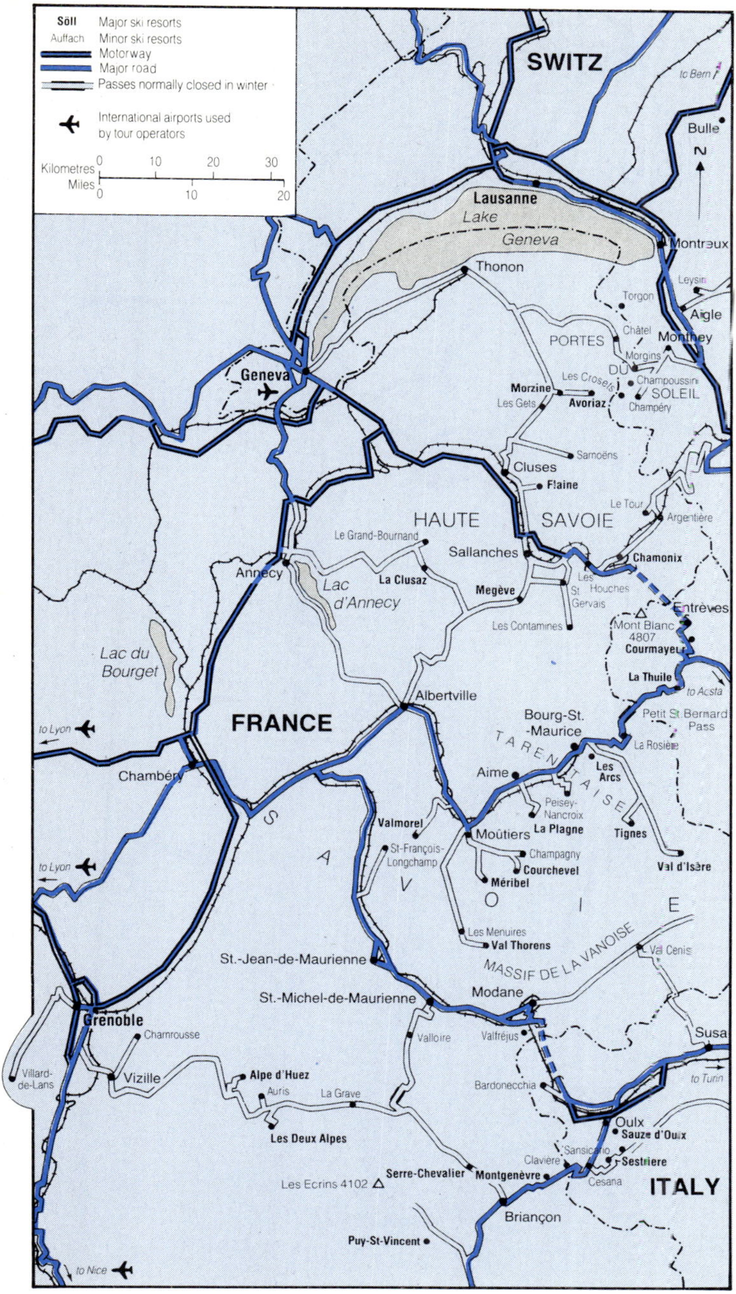
Söll Major ski resorts
Auffach Minor ski resorts
Motorway
Major road
Passes normally closed in winter
International airports used by tour operators
Kilometres 0 10 20 30
Miles 0 10 20
SWITZ
to Bern
Bulle
N
Lausanne
Lake Geneva
Montreux
Thonon
Leysin
Torgon
Aigle
Châtel
Monthey
PORTES DU SOLEIL
Morgins
Champoussin
Les Crosets
Geneva
Morzine
Les Gets
Avoriaz
Champéry
Samoëns
Cluses
Flaine
Le Tour
Argentière
HAUTE SAVOIE
Le Grand-Bornand
Sallanches
Chamonix
Annecy
La Clusaz
Lac d'Annecy
Megève
Les Houches
St Gervais
Entrèves
Les Contamines
Mont Blanc 4807
Courmayeur
Lac du Bourget
La Thuile
to Aosta
Albertville
Bourg-St.-Maurice
Petit St Bernard Pass
to Lyon
FRANCE
TARENTAISE
La Rosière
Chambéry
Aime
Les Arcs
Peisey-Nancroix
Valmorel
La Plagne
Tignes
Moûtiers
St-François-Longchamp
Champagny
Val d'Isère
to Lyon
Courchevel
Méribel
SAVOIE
Les Menuires
Val Thorens
Val Cenis
St.-Jean-de-Maurienne
MASSIF DE LA VANOISE
Modane
St.-Michel-de-Maurienne
Susa
Grenoble
Chamrousse
Valloire
Valfréjus
to Turin
Villard-de-Lans
Vizille
Alpe d'Huez
Auris
La Grave
Bardonecchia
Oulx
Les Deux Alpes
Sauze d'Oulx
Sansicario
Clavière
Sestriere
Cesana
Serre-Chevalier
Montgenèvre
Les Ecrins 4102
ITALY
Briançon
Puy-St-Vincent
to Nice

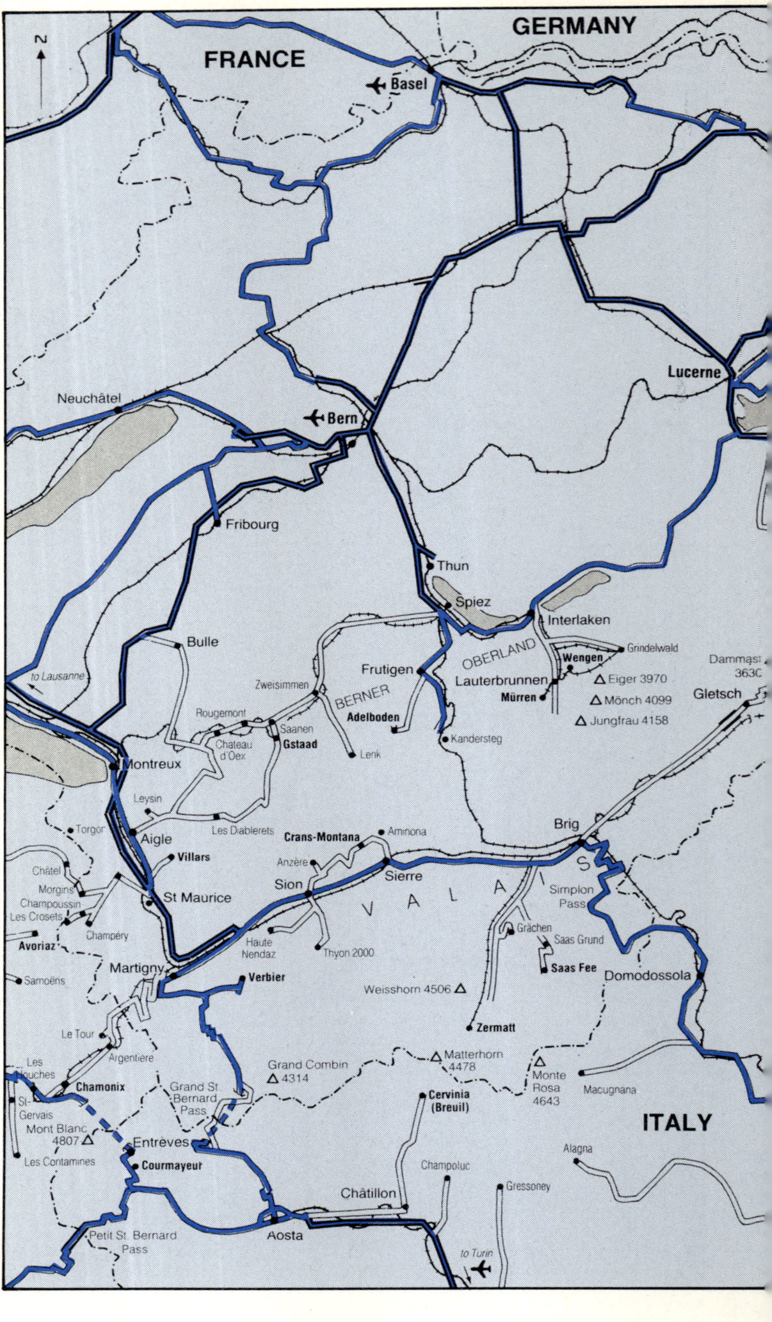

N
GERMANY
FRANCE
Basel
Lucerne
Neuchâtel
Bern
Fribourg
Thun
Spiez
Interlaken
Bulle
OBERLAND
Grindelwald
Wengen
Frutigen
Lauterbrunnen
Eiger 3970
Mürren
Mönch 4099
Jungfrau 4158
BERNER
Adelboden
Zweisimmen
Rougemont
Saanen
Gstaad
Chateau d'Oex
Lenk
Kandersteg
Dammast 3630
Gletsch
to Lausanne
Montreux
Leysin
Torgon
Aigle
Les Diablerets
Crans-Montana
Aminona
Villars
Anzère
Sierre
Brig
Châtel
Morgins
Champoussin
Les Crosets
St Maurice
Sion
V A L A I S
Simplon Pass
Champery
Avoriaz
Haute Nendaz
Thyon 2000
Grächen
Saas Grund
Saas Fee
Martigny
Verbier
Samoëns
Domodossola
Weisshorn 4506
Le Tour
Zermatt
Argentière
Les Houches
Chamonix
Grand Combin 4314
Matterhorn 4478
Monte Rosa 4643
Macugnana
St-Gervais
Grand St. Bernard Pass
Cervinia (Breuil)
Mont Blanc 4807
Entrèves
ITALY
Les Contamines
Courmayeur
Alagna
Champoluc
Gressoney
Châtillon
Aosta
Petit St. Bernard Pass
to Turin

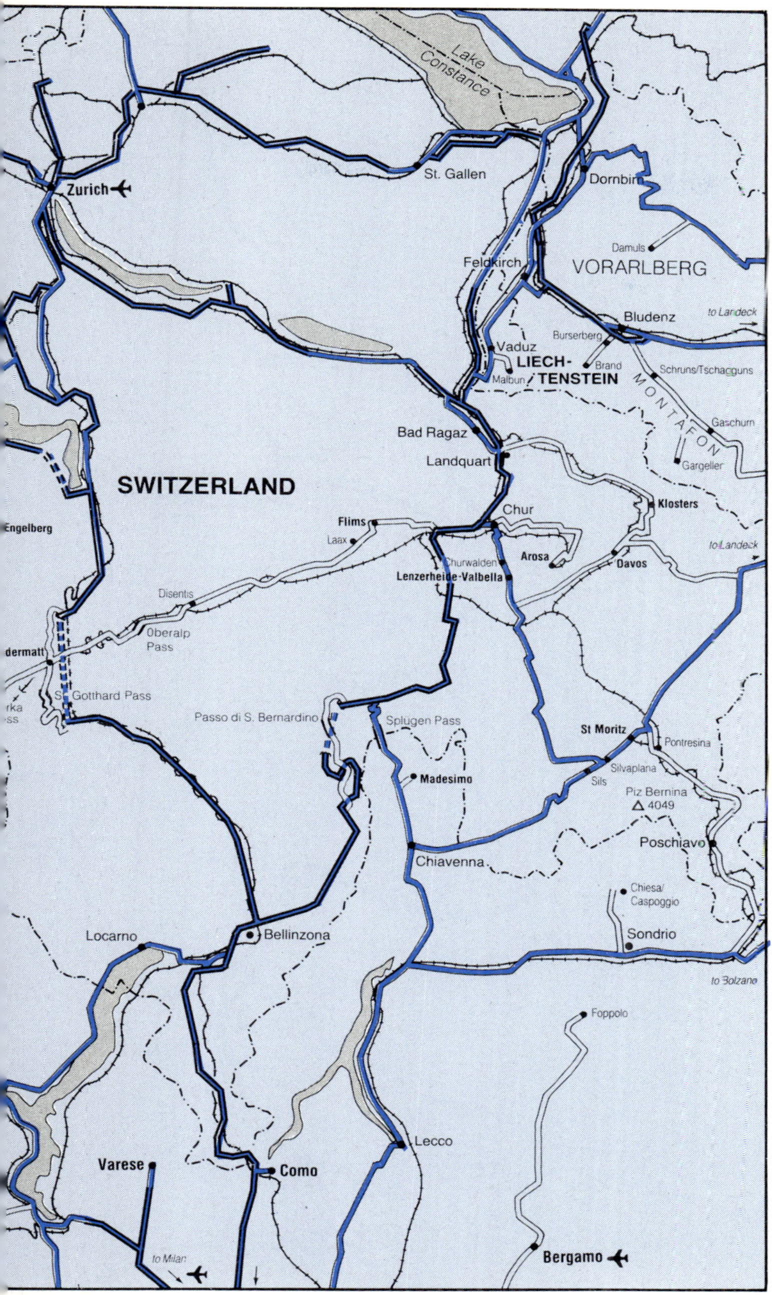
Lake Constance
Zurich
St. Gallen
Dornbirn
Damuls
VORARLBERG
Feldkirch
Bludenz
to Landeck
Burserberg
Vaduz
LIECHTENSTEIN
Malbun
Brand
Schruns/Tschagguns
MONTAFON
Gaschurn
Gargellen
Bad Ragaz
Landquart
SWITZERLAND
Klosters
Chur
Flims
Laax
Arosa
Churwalden
Lenzerheide-Valbella
Davos
to Landeck
Engelberg
Disentis
Oberalp Pass
Andermatt
St Gotthard Pass
Passo di S. Bernardino
Splugen Pass
St Moritz
Pontresina
Silvaplana
Sils
Madesimo
Piz Bernina
4049
Poschiavo
Chiavenna
Chiesa/Caspoggio
Sondrio
Locarno
Bellinzona
to Bolzano
Foppolo
Lecco
Varese
Como
to Milan
Bergamo

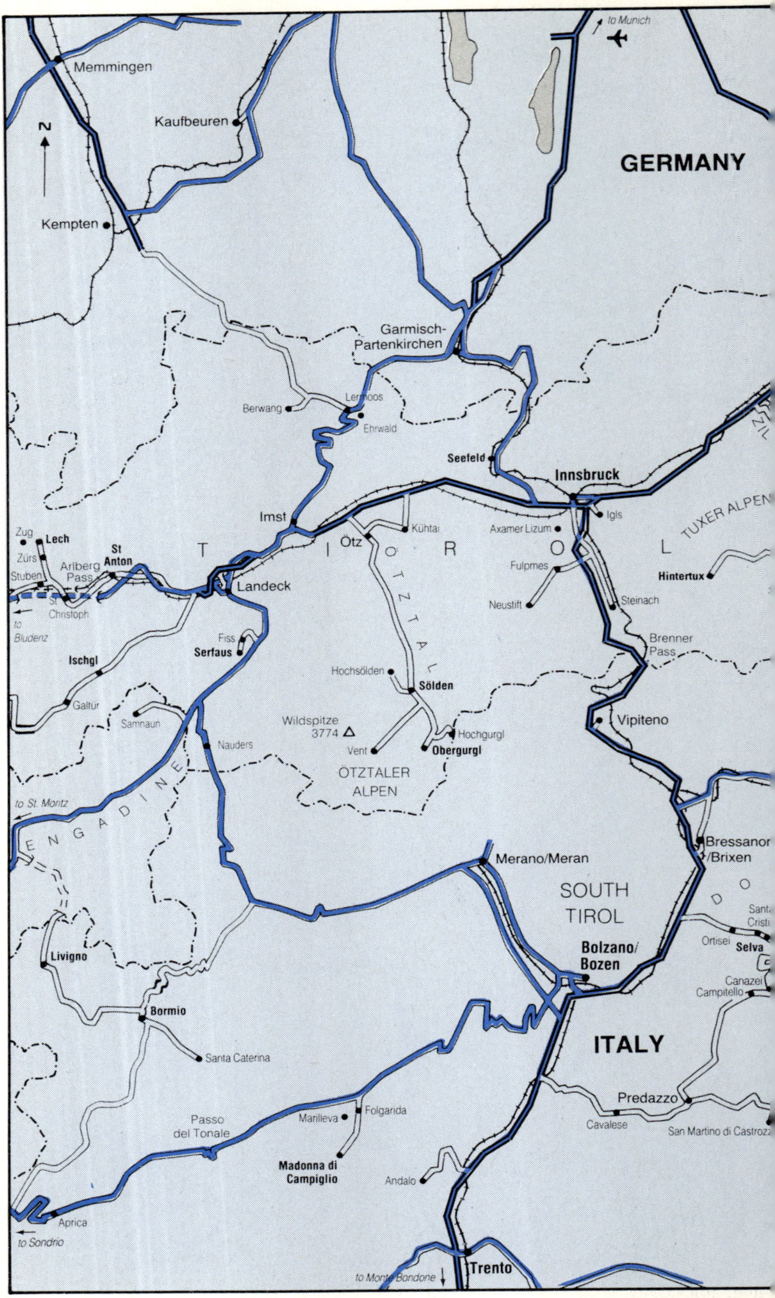
to Munich
Memmingen
Kaufbeuren
N
GERMANY
Kempten
Garmisch-
Partenkirchen
Berwang
Lermoos
Ehrwald
Seefeld
Innsbruck
Igls
TUXER ALPEN
Imst
Zug
Lech
Zürs
Stuben
Arlberg Pass
St Anton
St Christoph
to Bludenz
T I R O L
Ötz
Kühtai
Axamer Lizum
Fulpmes
Neustift
Hintertux
Landeck
Steinach
Brenner Pass
Fiss
Serfaus
Ischgl
Galtür
Samnaun
ÖTZTAL
Hochsölden
Sölden
Wildspitze
3774
Vent
Hochgurgl
Obergurgl
Nauders
ÖTZTALER
ALPEN
Vipiteno
to St. Moritz
ENGADINE
Bressanone
/Brixen
Merano/Meran
SOUTH
TIROL
Ortisei
Selva
Bolzano/
Bozen
Canazei
Campitello
Livigno
Bormio
Santa Caterina
ITALY
Predazzo
Cavalese
San Martino di Castrozza
Passo
del Tonale
Marilleva
Folgarida
Madonna di
Campiglio
Andalo
Aprica
to Sondrio
to Monte Bondone
Trento

Rosenheim
Salzburg
Scheftau
Söll
St Johann in Tirol
Wörgl
Itter
Ellmau
Going
Fieberbrunn
Niederau
Oberau
Westendorf
Kirchberg
Kitzbühel
Auffach
Bischofshofen
Filzmoos
SALZBURG
Saalbach
Hinterglemm
Alpbach
WILDSCHÖNAU
St Johann im Pongau
Flachau
to Schladming
Pass Thurn
Zell am See
Wagrain
KITZBÜHELER ALPEN
Kaprun
Dorfgastein
Obertauern
Zell am Ziller
Gerlos
Mayrhofen
Bad Hofgastein
AUSTRIA
Badgastein
Böckstein
EAST TIROL
Lienz
Brunico/Bruneck
La Villa
San Cassiano
Corvara
Gruppo Sella
Cortina d'Ampezzo
Arabba
Marmolada
Belluno
Monte Cavallo
to Venice and Treviso

Reading a resort entry

Resorts in the Guide are divided into 'major' resorts and 'minor' ones. These categories are not meant to indicate the size or the absolute worth of any resort. Alpbach, although small, is a 'major' resort because it attracts a great number of British skiers for very good reasons; Les Menuires, which has much bigger and better skiing, is a 'minor' resort because it has a very limited appeal.

In the chapter starting on page 56, for example, Selva is the major resort. Its name is picked out in large type, and is followed by a list of verdicts – the things it is 'good for' and 'bad for'. The summary chart starting on page 37 compares the verdicts for different resorts.

Below the verdicts is a list of minor resorts covered by the chapter and then a general summary of the area. Then follows a detailed description of the major ski area, including the skiing of minor resorts provided it is part of (or at least linked to) the major area. After that comes a description of the major resort village or villages, with details of ski school and so on. Finally there are brief descriptions of the significant minor resort villages in the area; if their skiing is separate from that of the major resort, this is where it will be described.

The skiing area of each major resort (and linked minor resorts) is shown on a map. All but a couple of these maps are specially drawn to a consistent scale, and use colour tints to show height above sea level – see the key below. The arrows on the runs indicate the resorts' own gradings, not our assessment of difficulty. The maps are meant to help you compare resorts, not to find your way around the mountains.

Both the text and the maps are based on the 1987–88 ski season; but where a new lift is virtually certain to be in place for the 1988–89 season we have included it.

Two final points of clarification. When we say a resort is good for lift queues, we don't mean that it's a resort where queues are easy to find; we mean that from the queuing point of view it's a good resort. When we talk about a run of 1600m vertical, we don't mean a mile-high precipice; we mean that the bottom is 1600m lower than the top.

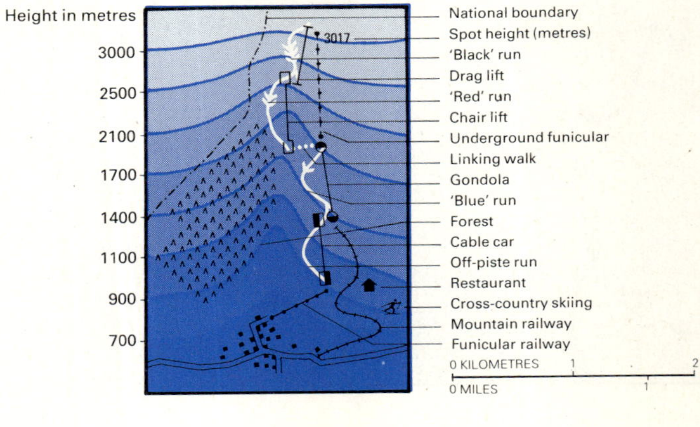

Ageing beauty

Cortina d'Ampezzo Italy 1230m

Good for *Nursery slopes, mountain restaurants, beautiful scenery, sunny slopes, cross-country skiing, not skiing*
Bad for *Tough runs, skiing convenience, late holidays, short airport transfers, easy road access, freedom from cars*

Cortina is Italy's most fashionable ski resort and, unlike many Dolomite resorts, thoroughly Italian in atmosphere and style. It is one of the most remote resorts for visitors from north and west, and although it is very cosmopolitan the bulk of its clientèle is cosmopolitan Italians. It hosted the 1956 winter Olympics and ranks with St Moritz and Chamonix as one of the most complete wintersports resorts in the world. Its downhill skiing includes some of the best nursery slopes anywhere and a few long, challenging runs for good skiers, all in dramatically beautiful scenery. Much of the most recent development of the resort was generated by the Olympics, and it is showing its age. It is a large sunny town in a wide valley with separate skiing areas spread around the surrounding mountains, and travelling between them is tiresome.

Cortina has a very glamorous reputation which may deter skiers who look to Italy for informal, cheap holidays. For a short high season (New Year and mid-February) there are plenty of beautiful people to match the shop windows, but it is not an exclusive or uniformly expensive resort: there are plenty of small, attractive, not outrageously expensive hotels, and simple, friendly bars full of character as well as the expensive restaurants and nightclubs. A recent reporter was 'very impressed by the helpfulness and friendliness of virtually everybody', which makes a change.

The resorts ringing the Sella massif are within reach by car, and one lift pass covers all of them (and a great many other Dolomite resorts).

The skiing top 2930m bottom 1220m

The skiing is typical of the Dolomites in being broken up by cliff faces. There are excellent open fields of very easy runs and a few steep and narrow gullies which verge on the extreme. Between the two there is a variety of intermediate skiing, and longer runs than in any of the other Dolomite resorts. The main Tofana skiing area is west of the town, served by two stages of a three-stage cable-car. On the other side of the large resort the Staunies and Faloria areas are just about linked, despite the road between them, and provide a few interesting runs. A long way out of town, by Passo Falzarego, are several lifts which do not add greatly to the quantity of skiing available, but are well worth visiting for a change of spectacular scenery.

The bottom station of the **Tofana** cable-car is a long walk from the centre of the resort. Between the resort and Col Druscié (1774m) the cable-car goes over gentle woodlands and open fields with wide, easy trails complicated only by several danger points where piste crosses rough roads with unobtrusive warnings for skiers and drivers which are easily missed. Snow conditions often make these home runs more difficult than they are graded (blue/green). The second stage of the cable-car climbs an impressively steep and rocky mountain side to Ra Valles, in the middle of an excellent sheltered bowl of intermediate runs between 2828m (the top of the sking on this side of the valley) and 2216m. The top section of the cable-car serves no skiing but is popular for sun-bathing and limitless views. Near the bottom of the bowl there is a breach in the rock which allows skiers a narrow path down; there is a fairly steep south-facing stretch in the middle of this, and timid skiers should take the cable-car down in poor conditions. The run ends up at the bottom of the Pomedes chair-lifts, about 100m lower than Col Druscié, which is set on a little peak. You get up to it by skiing on down to another chair-lift which itself has an interesting short black run underneath it. The Pomedes chair-lifts, which can usually be reached by car, add an excellent series of more-or-less direct runs, including a couple of genuine blacks and the spectacular downhill race-course which starts down a narrow *canalone* between massive pillars of rock. There is also a very long circuitous blue trail from the middle station. The Pomedes runs and lifts link up via long, panoramic woodland paths with the splendid open skiing above Pocol and Lacedel – a vast area of very easy and nursery slopes, usually referred to by the general name of Socrepes, hardly ever plagued by fast skiers.

A cable-car goes up to **Faloria** from the ring road, the first stage over flat ground, the second over a cliff to 2120m. There are no runs under the cable-car, but an area of short intermediate runs beyond it, including several challenging pitches. You can ski through attractive woods to the Tre Croci road at Rio Gere, either directly from Faloria, or with less effort by means of a little-used red run from Tondi.

On the other side of the Tre Croci road are south-facing slopes which are served by a slow and long chair-lift going up to the foot of the cliffs of the Cristallo massif. The run back down is wide and easy. A two-stage gondola climbs to **Staunies**, one of the steep and narrow chutes so characteristic of the Dolomites. The run under the top section starts narrowly and steeply, faces south and is often unskiable. Its beauty is rather spoilt by lift pylons. If it is open, do not go up the top section of the lift unless you are prepared to ski down – you may not be allowed to ride down. The way back to Cortina is a long, easy piste beside the Tre Croci road. There is no link with the extensive area of easy runs served by a number of lifts beneath **Mietres**.

An isolated two-stage chair-lift (1900–2400m) beside the road up to Falzarego serves the intermediate runs of **Cinque Torri**, surrounded by beautiful scenery; the slopes face north and are little skied, so snow conditions are usually good.

One of the Dolomites' extremely dramatic cable-cars soars up a cliff face from Passo Falzarego (2105m) to **Lagazuoi** (2746m). The run back down is mostly blueish in difficulty with a short red section in the middle.

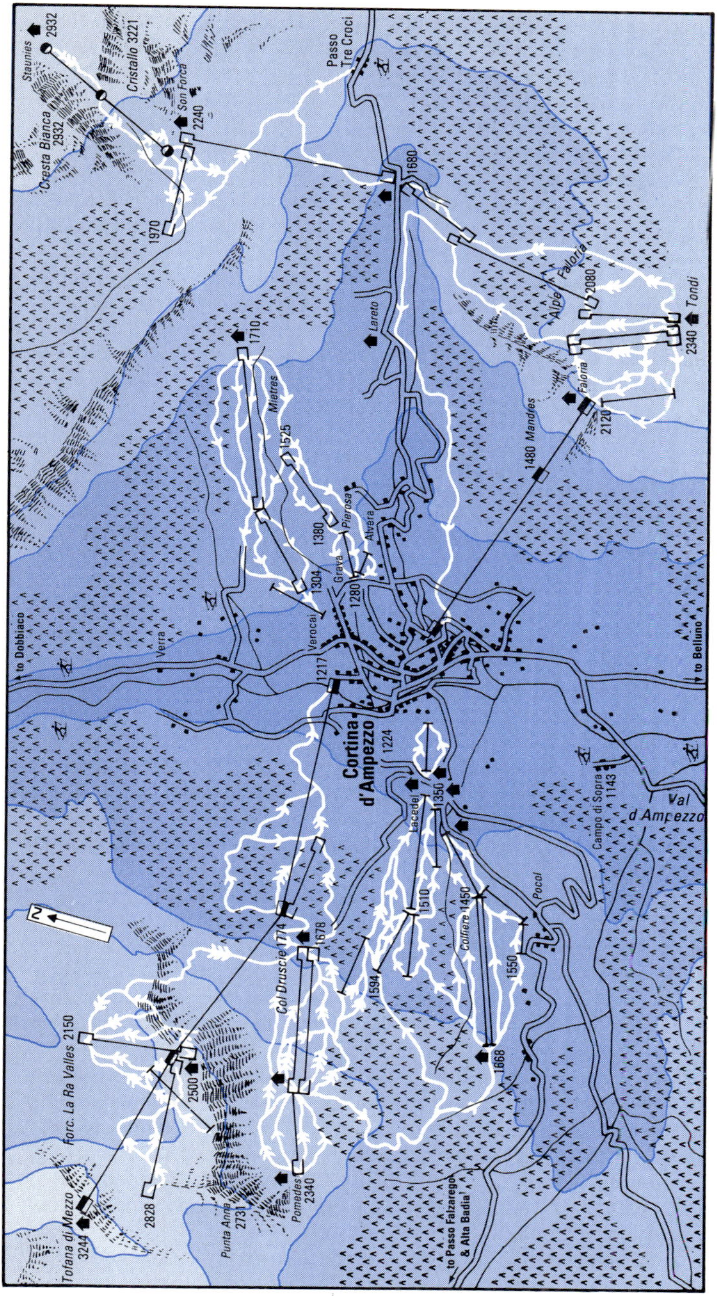

Staunies 2932
Cristallo 3221
Cresta Bianca 2932
Son Forca 2240
Passo Tre Croci
1680
1970
Lareto
Alpe Faloria
2080
Tondi
2340
Faloria
2120
1480 Mandres
1710
Mietres
1525
1380
Pierosa
Alvera
Grava
1280
1304
Verocai
1217
to Dobbiaco
Verra
to Belluno
Cortina d'Ampezzo
1224
Lacedel
1350
Campo di Sopra 1143
Val d'Ampezzo
Pocol
1510
Colfiere 1450
1594
1550
1668
Col Druscie 1774
1678
Forc. La Ra Valles 2150
2500
2828
Tofana di Mezzo 3244
Punta Anna 2731
Pomedes 2340
to Passo Falzarego & Alta Badia
N

Much more worthwhile is the run down the back to Armentarola, near San Cassiano in the Alta Badia (see the Selva chapter). This is an 11km run of no great technical difficulty, but wild and exceedingly beautiful, and punctuated by restaurants. There are buses from Cortina and Armentarola to Falzarego.

Mountain restaurants are plentiful in all the skiing areas, mostly excellent and not particularly expensive. There are particularly delightful restaurants at Pomedes, Col Druscié and Tondi. There are several expensive restaurants for serious gastronomic lunches near the Socrepes lifts, notably El Camineto.

Cortina's skiing is very far from being a unified system, and getting from one place to another can be extremely time-consuming. But morning **queues** for the Tofana cable-car are not as serious as you might expect (Cortina skiers are notoriously late risers). A recent visitor found a complete absence of up-to-date piste maps, and of any piste marking apart from patchy directional signposting.

The resort

Cortina is a handsome small town of 8,000 inhabitants set in a beautiful broad bowl, a busy crossroads with plenty of through, as well as local, traffic. The attractive main street, Corso Italia, is sheltered from this as a pedestrian precinct, and traffic streams around a central one-way circuit. There are lots of very stylish shop windows and elegant people strolling up and down in the early evening. Outside the centre the resort spreads widely up and down the valley, with comfortable chalets beside the main road out towards Dobbiaco, and some development across the river on the hill which climbs more steeply up towards Falzarego.

The ski-bus service consists of three buses circling anti-clockwise continuously between the two cable-cars, leaving many parts of the resort unserved. There are other, less frequent buses from the centre to outlying ski-lifts, now covered by the lift pass. Having a car is extremely useful, although parking in the centre is difficult.

Accommodation consists of a great variety of hotels from international conference comfort to very simple, and large numbers of private apartments and chalets, usually empty. The most attractive hotel is the absolutely central, comfortable Poste (✆4271), right at the heart of fashionable Cortina life. Also comfortable, central and stylish, but cheaper, is the Ancora (✆3261). Two small, attractive chalet hotels within walking distance of the main cable-car are the Capannina (✆2950), with a well-reputed restaurant, and the inexpensive Barisetti (✆2491). Although its position is not convenient, the Menardi (✆2400) is highly recommended – attractive, friendly, medium price; the ski-bus passes within easy walking distance. The Montana (✆3366) and the 'simple and friendly' Olimpia (✆3256) are among the cheapest and most central B&B hotels. The Fiames (✆2366) is a very simple hotel, placed conveniently for the cross-country trails.

Après-ski is very varied, but evenings are generally quiet outside high season. There are a dozen discothèques, and numerous bars with a lot of character – the Poste hotel bar being the smartest rendezvous in the early evening. There are also several excellent restaurants outside hotels, notably the Meloncino, and the very expensive Toula, both beside the road up towards Falzarego, and in hotels (the Capannina and the Da Beppe Sello). A reporter recommends the Buca da Diavola pizzeria – 'central and full of character'. Occasionally there is an ice disco on the Olympic rink, and evening bobsleigh practice to watch. The Mietres chair-lift serves a toboggan run.

The **cross-country** trails are long and beautiful and varied, although Fiames is a long way from central Cortina and the trails do not link with any of the Alpine skiing areas. One very long trail follows the old railway track to Dobbiaco. There is a marathon in early February, ending in the Corso Italia. For **non-skiers** there are good walks along the valley and to restaurants in the skiing area. Excursions are easily arranged around the Dolomites and to Venice. The resort is varied, interesting and colourful, with an excellent skating rink.

Nursery slopes (and long green runs for early post-nursery stages) are excellent. Most beginners use the very extensive area above the Falzarego road at Pocol. The Pierosa and Mietres area is equally broad and gentle and even more secluded – but it is also isolated.

The main **ski school** has an office in the centre of the resort, and a meeting place for adult beginners at the Socrepes lift. A recent report speaks well of the school.

Cortina d'Ampezzo facts

Lift payment

Passes Superski Dolomiti Pass covers all lifts in an enormous area. Local pass for Cortina area available. Passes include local bus services.
Cost 6-day Superski pass L159,400.20% off in low season.
Children 30% off up to 14.
Beginners Coupons.

Ski school

Classes 9.30–noon or noon–2.00.
Cost 6 days (mornings only) L130,000. Private lessons L32,000/hr.
Children Ski kindergarten at Pierosa/nursery area – no non-ski kindergarten.

Cross-country skiing

Trails Extensive trails, total length 74km, of varying difficulty (graded green, red and black) in the valley north of Cortina, with a base and ski school and equipment rental facilities at Fiames (5km from Cortina).

Not skiing

Facilities Artificial ice-rink (skating/curling), swimming, tennis, saunas, sleigh rides, riding, ski-bobbing, 6km walking paths, tobogganing, museum art gallery, cinemas.

Medical facilities

In resort Fracture clinic, doctors chemists, dentists.
Hospital Pieve di Cadore (30km).

Getting there
Airport Venice; transfer 3hr.
Railway Calalzo (30km) or Dobbiaco (32km); frequent buses.
Road Via Munich, Brenner, Dobbiaco; chains occasionally needed.

Available holidays

Resort beds 4,500 in hotels; 18,000 in apartments.
Package holidays Pegasus (Ht), Small World (Ch)

Further information

Tourist office ✆(436) 3231. Tx 440004. Fax (436) 3235.

Super-scenery Dolomiti

Selva Italy 1550m

Good for *Big ski area, beautiful scenery, nursery slopes, cross-country skiing, mountain restaurants, après-ski, chalet holidays, not skiing*
Bad for *Skiing convenience, late holidays, short airport transfers, lift queues, easy road access, freedom from cars*

Linked resorts: Ortisei, Corvara, Canazei, San Cassiano, Arabba, Colfosco, Campitello, Santa Cristina, La Villa

For most British skiers, skiing in the Dolomites means skiing in the area around the massive Gruppo Sella, Europe's Table Mountain. The Sella Ronda is the name of the trip round the mountain. It is piste tourism at its most spectacular, with as much of the enjoyment coming from the dramatic spectacle of the landscape as from the skiing itself.

The Dolomites typically have gentle lower slopes surmounted by vertical cliffs, which means a large proportion of easy runs and a few extremely steep, narrow chutes between towers of rock, with few runs between the two extremes. Although the peaks are high, not much skiing takes place near the tops, and the range of altitude is not great. A more important reservation is that the Dolomites have an extremely erratic snow record. The area seems to inspire extremes of love and hate, and luck with the snow is probably the main reason. But the snow-making network is now very extensive, and early last season we were impressed by the amount of good skiing at a time when natural snow was in extremely short supply.

Although the Sella region is entirely in Italy, holidays there have very little Italian about them. Much of the area was Austrian until 1918 (many villages have dual names as a result) and the area as a whole is dominated by car-borne visitors from Germany. Nightlife consists of beer-swilling and tea-dances to the sound of zither and squeeze-box. Standing slightly apart from most of the German-speaking Dolomites is the Val Gardena (Gröden), and particularly its main town of Ortisei, where the Ladin dialect and crafts are proudly perpetuated.

It is not an area of big resorts. Accommodation is spread widely around the valleys in hamlets at the foot of the slopes or in complete isolation – clean, simple B&B houses and new chalet-style hotels. The Val Gardena does have two large resorts. Ortisei (St Ulrich) is a long-established town of considerable charm, detached from the main Sella Ronda circuit. The major resort is Selva (Wolkenstein), a good base for exploring the region, but a disappointingly characterless and inconvenient roadside resort. There are long and challenging runs on the local slopes, and both après-ski and accommodation are plentiful and varied.

In some ways the most convenient base for moderate skiers is Corvara, the most major of the minor resorts in the Alta Badia region, with its infinity of blue runs. For good skiers the choice destination is Arabba, with its big, steep, north-facing non-Dolomitic mountain.

The Sella Ronda can now be skied in either direction. Either way, it consists predominantly of easy blue runs; the red sections are not very severe, but poor snow conditions may make them difficult – there is no escaping south-facing slopes at some stage. The tour involves about 20km of uphill transport, and 26km and 4000m vertical of skiing. It takes about five hours, not allowing for queues or rests. Getting between resorts by car is not much quicker than by lift and piste.

The skiing top 2950m bottom 1225m

Ortisei: Alpe di Siusi A cable-car from the southern edge of the town scales a very steep wooded mountainside. The only run down is a red-graded track engineered into the face, with netting to protect skiers from long drops. The cable-car delivers you to Punta Mesdi (2006m), on the rim of the remarkable Alpe di Siusi (Seiseralm) – a broad, high, gently sloping basin which claims to be the biggest alp (in its sense of high pasture) in the Alps. Behind Punta Mesdi there is an extensive, confusing and incompletely linked arrangement of short drags and chair-lifts which make it just about possible to ski down to a collection of hotels at 1850m and join up with some longer lifts on the other side of the basin with a top station of 2238m. Nearly all the skiing is extremely gentle, and getting from lift to lift involves walking.

The Alpe di Siusi is an idyllic area for the under-confident and for those who enjoy pottering around in beautiful mountain surroundings, with sleigh rides, extensive cross-country trails, walking paths and dozens of hotels and restaurants dotted around the spacious sunny slopes. From the top of the gondola, beneath the towering silhouette of the triple-barrelled Sasso Lungo, it is possible to ski (and walk) across to Monte Pana above S Cristina.

Ortisei/Santa Cristina: Seceda Two lifts from the edge of the town give access to south and south-west facing slopes with long runs which often lack snow and are little skied. The two-stage cable-car to Seceda may involve long waits for a quorum to assemble, even in high season. The top section scales an impressive cliff to the main skiing area – south-facing slopes above the Col Raiser and S Cristina offering open intermediate skiing and advanced sunbathing, with several very welcoming restaurant chalets. Below Col Raiser there is a single easy run down to the edge of S Cristina; it is also possible to ski (off-piste) to the edge of Selva. The long run back to Ortisei skirts the rock face with a narrow path and runs on through woods easily and prettily.

Santa Cristina: Monte Pana This small community of hotels and restaurants is reached by road or chair-lift from S Cristina, with a fan of nursery lifts and a chair-lift which serves two short woodland runs (black and red) which in themselves hardly merit a detour. There is no marked run down to S Cristina.

Santa Cristina/Selva: Ciampinoi Cable-cars from the edge of S Cristina and the centre of Selva give access to this splendid skiing

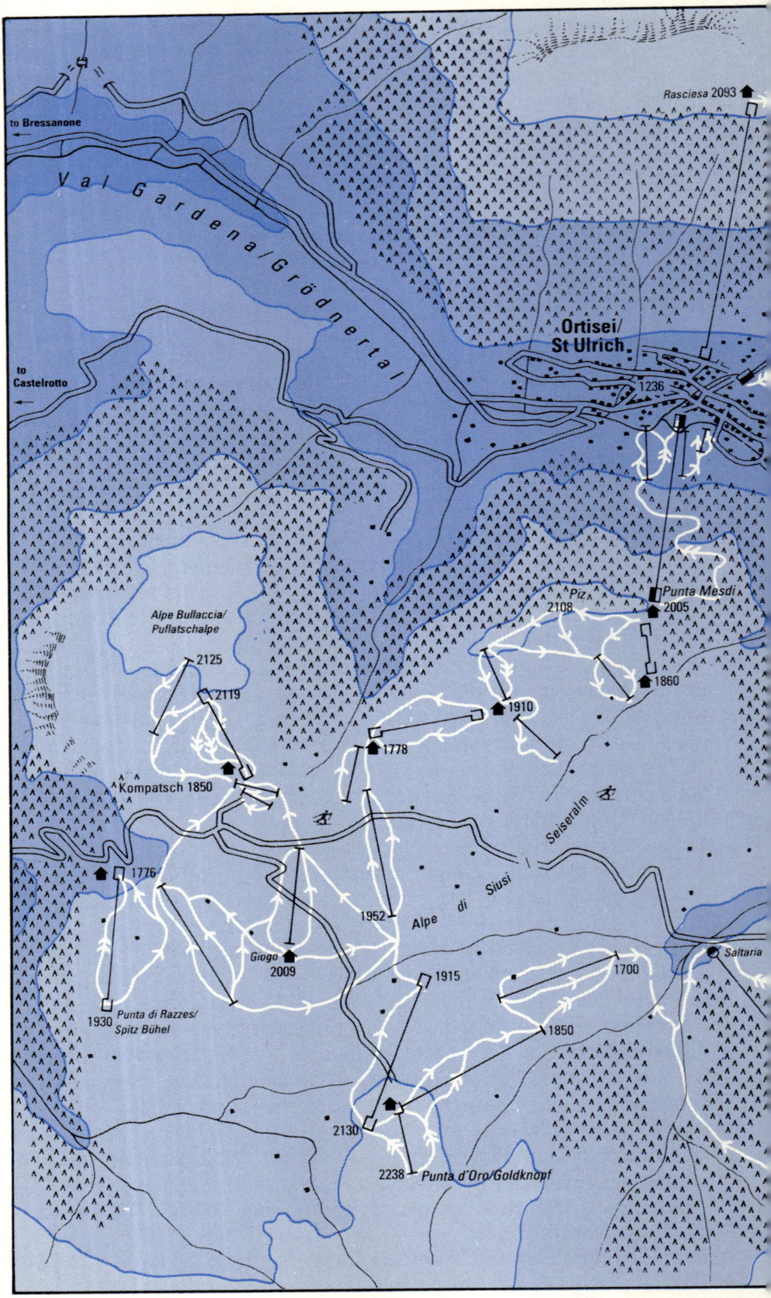

to Bressanone
Val Gardena/Grödnertal
to Castelrotto
Rasciesa 2093
Ortisei/
St Ulrich
1236
Punta Mesdi
Piz
2108
2005
1860
1910
1778
Alpe Bullaccia/
Puflatschalpe
2125
2119
Kompatsch 1850
Seiseralm
Alpe di Siusi
1776
1952
Giogo
2009
1915
1700
Saltaria
1930
Punta di Razzes/
Spitz Bühel
1850
2130
2238
Punta d'Oro/Goldknopf

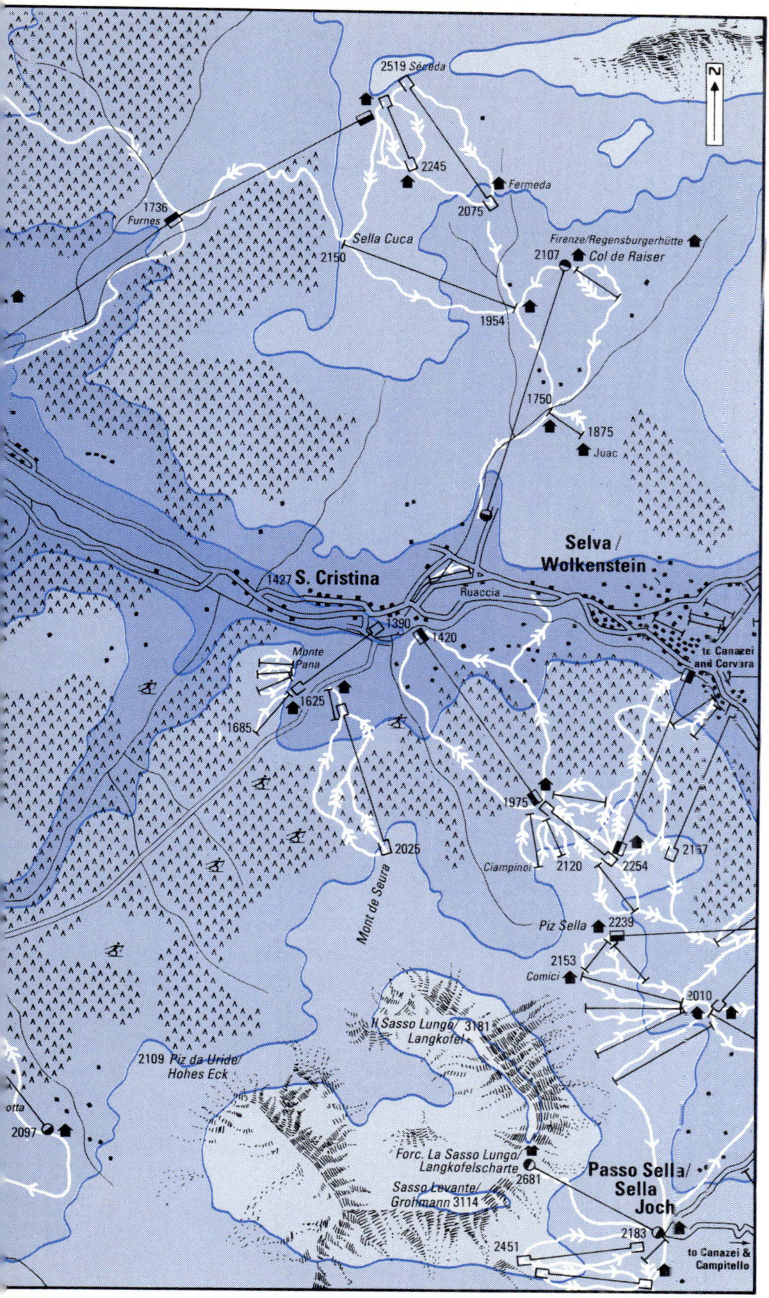
N
2519 Séceda
2245
Fermeda
2075
1736
Furnes
Sella Cuca
2150
Firenze/Regensburgerhütte
2107
Col de Raiser
1954
1750
1875
Juac
Selva /
Wolkenstein
1427 S. Cristina
Ruaccia
1390
1420
to Canazei
and Corvara
Monte
Pana
1625
1685
1975
2025
Mont de Seura
Ciampinoi
2120
2254
2157
Piz Sella
2239
2153
Comici
2010
Il Sasso Lungo/ 3181
Langkofel
2109 Piz da Uride/
Hohes Eck
2097
Forc. La Sasso Lungo/
Langkofelscharte
2681
Passo Sella/
Sella
Joch
Sasso Levante/
Grohmann 3114
2183
2451
to Canazei &
Campitello

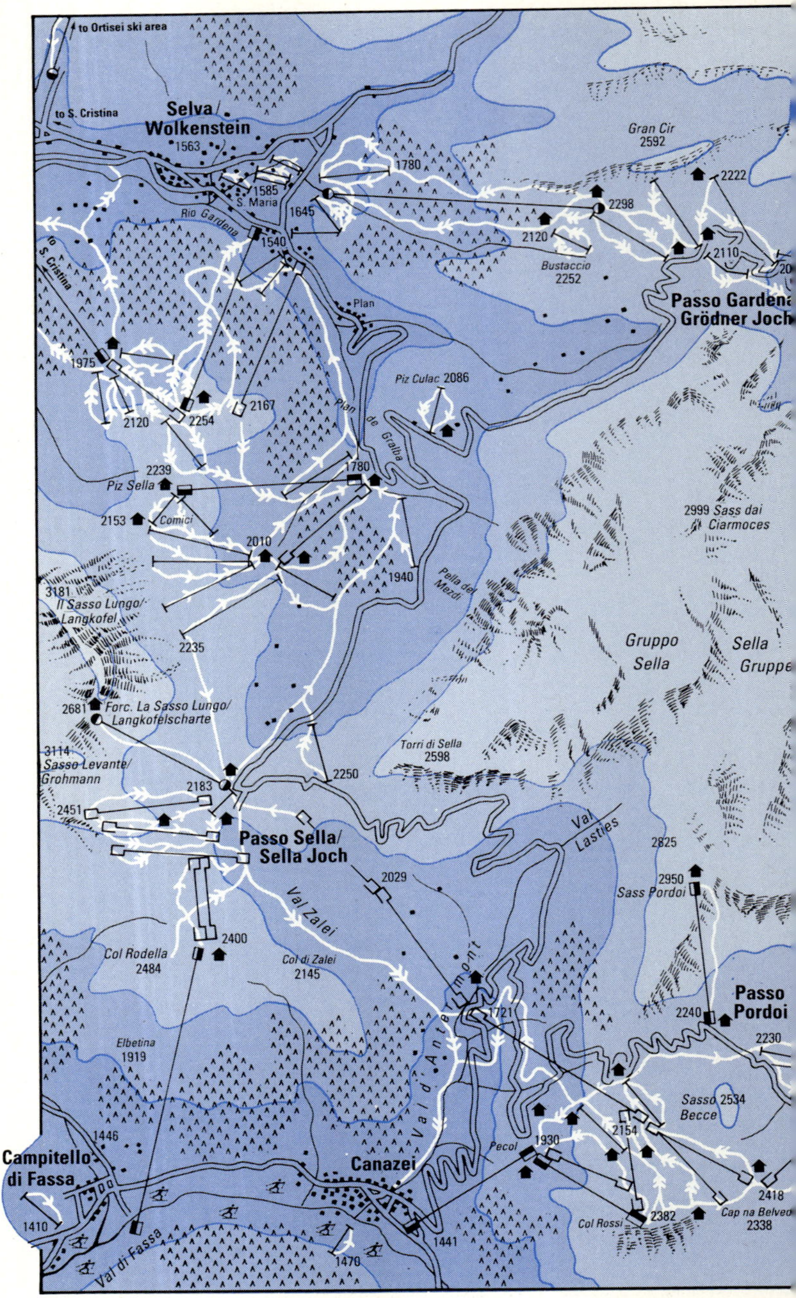
to Ortisei ski area
to S. Cristina
Selva/
Wolkenstein
1563
1585
S. Maria
1645
1780
Gran Cir
2592
2222
2298
2120
Bustaccio
2252
2110
Rio Gardena
1540
to S. Cristina
Plan
Passo Gardena
Grödner Joch
1975
2120
2254
2167
Piz Culac 2086
Plan de Gralba
2239
Piz Sella
1780
2153
Comici
2010
1940
2999 Sass dai Ciarmoces
Pella del Mezdi
3181
Il Sasso Lungo/
Langkofel
2235
Gruppo
Sella
Sella
Gruppe
2681
Forc. La Sasso Lungo/
Langkofelscharte
Torri di Sella
2598
3114
Sasso Levante/
Grohmann
2250
2183
2451
Passo Sella/
Sella Joch
Val Lasties
2825
2029
2950
Sass Pordoi
Val Zalei
2400
Col Rodella
2484
Col di Zalei
2145
Passo
Pordoi
2240
1721
2230
Elbetina
1919
Sasso 2534
Becce
2154
1446
Campitello
di Fassa
Canazei
Pecol
1930
2418
Cap na Belvedere
2338
1410
Col Rossi
2382
1441
1470
Val di Fassa

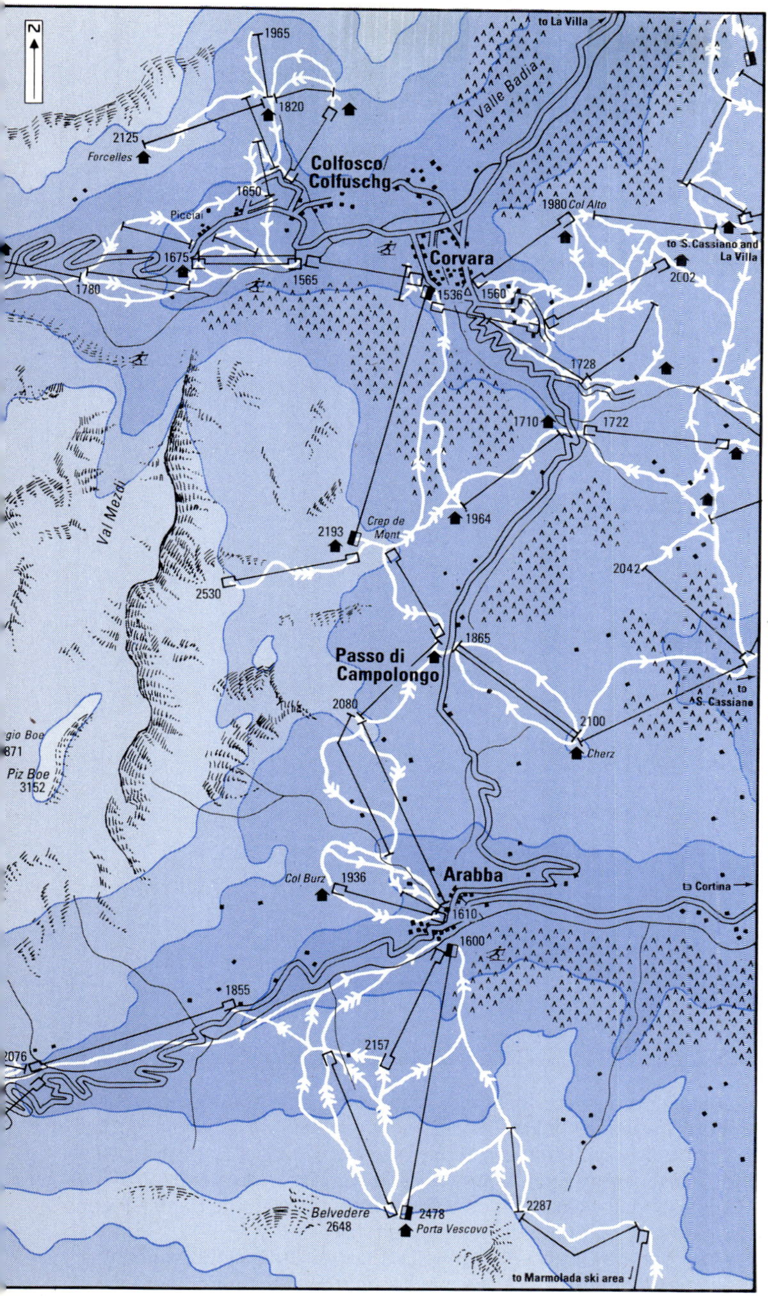
N
to La Villa
Valle Badia
1965
1820
2125
Forcelles
Colfosco/
Colfuschg
1650
Pìccìai
1980 Col Alto
to S.Cassiano and
La Villa
Corvara
1675
1565
1536
1560
2002
1780
1728
1710
1722
Val Mezdì
1964
2193
Crep de
Mont
2530
2042
Passo di
Campolongo
1865
to
S. Cassiano
2080
2100
Cherz
gio Boe
871
Piz Boe
3152
Arabba
Col Burz
1936
to Cortina
1610
1600
1855
2076
2157
Belvedere
2648
2478
Porta Vescovo
2287
to Marmolada ski area

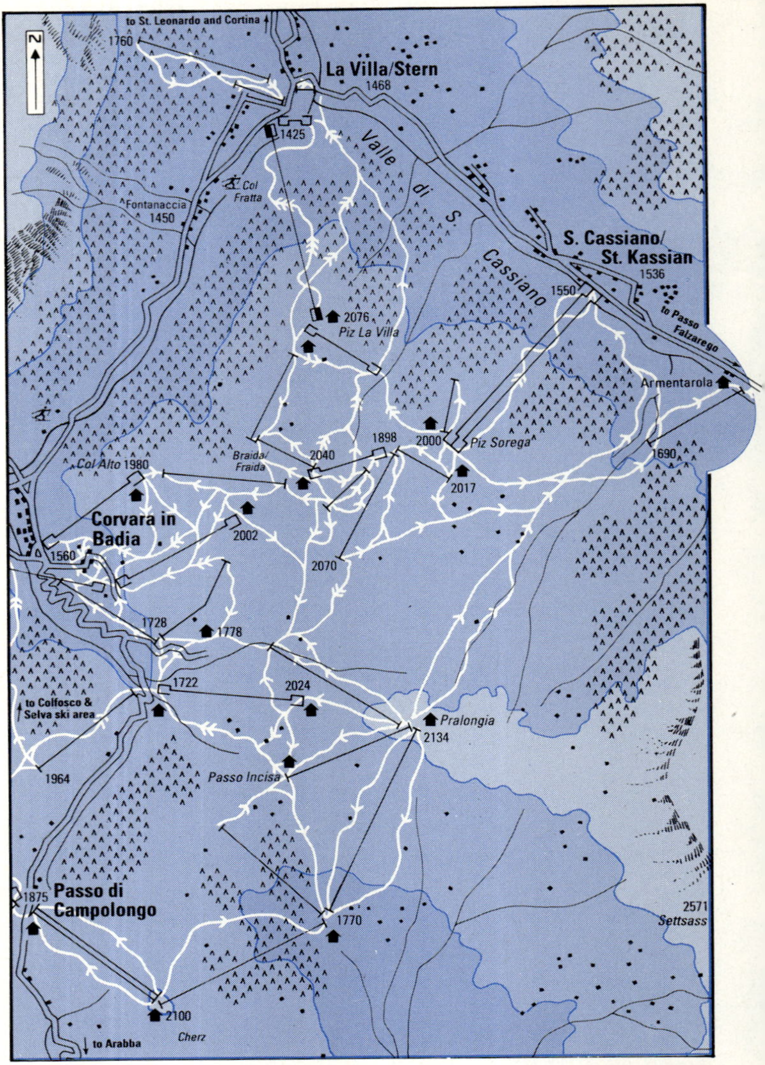

mountain, with a spray of broad, long, challenging north-facing runs cut through the woods below its bald, rounded peak, windswept and often treacherously icy. There is no easy way down, except on the top half of the S Cristina run. From Ciampinoi and from Piz Sella at the top of the Plan de Gralba skiing it is possible to ski round to Monte Pana – though this pleasant ski-ramble is not easy to follow.

Selva: Plan de Gralba/Passo Sella Plan de Gralba (1780m) can be reached either by bus in a few minutes from Selva, or via Ciampinoi.

The skiing route gets a lot of sun, is rarely in good condition, and is usually crowded, which adds to the difficulty of negotiating the ice and stones and roots. It is quite steep enough for long falls. The Ciampinoi chair-lift very usefully cuts out queuing and the most awkward slope. Plan de Gralba is a roadside skiing service area with one network of short, easy intermediate runs linked to another higher, bleak and windswept one above the Sella Pass between 2200m and 2500m. The landscape above Plan de Gralba is pleasantly wooded, with restaurants and an outdoor ice bar. Unfortunately the peaks of the Sasso Lungo block out the sun early in the afternoon. There is a very easy run beside the road to Selva, skirting the Ciampinoi mountain. The link from Plan de Gralba to Passo Sella is called Rock City or the Moon Walk – a track through a chaos of enormous boulders which does indeed involve some walking. It finishes at the foot of the Sasso Lungo bucket lift, which climbs to a refuge in a narrow breach between two pinnacles. The notorious run back down is steep and narrow – not exceedingly difficult in good snow, but a dangerous slope on which to fall. Much less often skied and less steep is the beautiful run down behind the mountain to Monte Pana. New lifts have completed the link in both directions between Passo Sella and the Canazei skiing via Lupo Bianco (1721m), a roadside restaurant.

Selva: Dantercepies The Dantercepies gondola goes from the top end of Selva to 2298m above Passo Gardena, serving a couple of long and satisfying red runs back to Selva and a more challenging narrow unofficial run between the pylons – splendid skiing in good snow.

Colfosco From the top of the Dantercepies lift a very long, very gentle run drops down to the lifts and pistes of Colfosco, much of it a straight schuss. The last kilometre to Corvara is almost flat; many skiers take the chair-lift in both directions. Set apart from this main skiing thoroughfare, the little village of Colfosco has its own nursery area and a few attractive runs above it between 2125m and 1650m, served by a series of drag-lifts. This is a secluded ski area with enjoyable intermediate runs and a particularly delightful sun-soaked bar among the trees at the top. We saw no sign of a black run down from the top to the road above Colfosco, as indicated on some maps.

Corvara: Boe On the western side of the road over Passo Campolongo a chain of lifts provides connections to and from Arabba. The runs to Arabba face south and tend to be icy in the mornings; apart from this there is no great difficulty about the skiing, although most of it is graded red. The long run down to Corvara beneath the Boe cable-car is wide and fast. The blackness of the run down from the top chair is mainly to do with its being unprepared.

Corvara: Alta Badia The bulk of Corvara's skiing is the wide area east of the Campolongo road which Corvara shares with the smaller villages of La Villa and San Cassiano. The not very high, round-topped, wooded mountain is covered with little drags and chair-lifts and what seems like an endless number of very gentle runs, individually short but adding up to a great deal of skiing. The main problem is that in a number of places the pistes have to be walked. The great exception is the excellent north-facing black run above La Villa of nearly 700m vertical – there is also a challenging red variant (both have artificial snow). At the other end of the web of lifts and runs, the area around Pralongia and Cherz is always uncrowded. This provides an alternative, slower way to and from Arabba.

Arabba The attraction of this small area is a series of long, steep, north-facing runs on a wide, fragmented mountainside served by a cable-car which climbs nearly 900m from the village to the Porta Vescovo (2478m). Arabba tends to get very crowded, especially when conditions elsewhere are generally poor. A two-stage chair-lift has been installed to relieve the cable-car and to enable moderate skiers to proceed towards Pordoi without tackling the slightly daunting slope, often icy and stony, at the top of the cable-car. The grading of the runs back down to Arabba varies from map to map. They are in fact all excellent, challenging descents – the Ornella blue run has an impressive 25° pitch. The top station of the cable-car commands a magnificent view southwards to the grand, glacier-covered northern flank of the highest mountain in the Dolomites, the Marmolada (3344m), which provides some summer skiing and exhilarating long runs in winter. A chain of lifts gives access via Passo Padon to the sunny slopes above Marmolada's resort, Malga Ciapela. They are covered by the lift pass, but the Marmolada (rarely open before February) isn't.

Passo Pordoi As well as being the link between Arabba and Canazei, Pordoi has a cable-car which climbs very steeply up to 2950m. This is the only lift which penetrates the fortifications of the mighty Gruppo Sella. It serves no pistes, but several notorious runs. The obvious one is the Forcella, under the cable-car. This faces due south and includes a narrow, steep top section which must very often be dangerously icy or bare, as we found it. Longer off-piste routes include the Val Lasties down to near the Lupo Bianco restaurant and lifts; and the Val de Mesdi, the great adventure which involves a 45-minute walk across the massif, before entering a very long, enclosed north-facing valley which drops, steeply in parts, down towards Colfosco.

Canazei The local skiing is confined to the open, not very large, north-west-facing bowl above Pecol (1933m), reached either by road or by cable-car. The top of the skiing is 2426m, so runs served by the fan of lifts up to the rim of the bowl are not long. They are mostly of intermediate difficulty with a couple of short nursery lifts. There is a long, gentle but often unskiable descent to Canazei via Lupo Bianco.

Mountain restaurants are one of the great joys of skiing in the Dolomites. There are plenty of them (except at Arabba), the views are beautiful and most are welcoming, with generally reasonable prices.

In season there may be serious lift queues at various points on the circuit – notably in the morning at Selva (Ciampinoi cable-car and Dantercepies gondola), S Cristina, Canazei and Corvara, and again in the late afternoon at Selva and Arabba. The Porta Vescovo at Arabba gets particularly crowded in the late morning and early afternoon, especially when conditions elsewhere in the region are poor. The return from Corvara to Selva is a very tedious series of lifts, often with queues for each one.

The resort

Selva is a long, shapeless village which suffers from having grown along the road. From the centre it extends far down towards S Cristina with an uninterrupted succession of shops and hotels, and chalets spreading back from the road. It is mostly modern and has no very obvious village character, but the style of building is generally attractive, and when full in winter it is a lively place, with the western wall of the Sella group providing a magnificent fiery sunset backdrop. Snow permitting, it is possible to ski back from Ciampinoi and Dantercepies to within easy reach of most parts of the village.

Most skiers make full use of the valley bus services – frequent between Ortisei and Selva and Plan de Gralba, less so up to the passes to link up with services in other valleys. The competition for places is tough and a recent reporter resorted to daily taxis to Plan de Gralba – not too expensive if shared. There are no evening buses.

Selva lacks the charm factor, but in most respects the Val Gardena as a whole is excellent for **cross-country** and **non-skiers**.

Accommodation is mainly in modern comfortable hotels, none of

Selva facts

Lift payment

Passes All lifts (except Marmolada) covered by Superski Dolomiti pass, but no bus services. Various local passes available.
Cost 6-day Superski Dolomiti pass L159,400. 20% off in low season.
Beginners Coupons.
Children 30% off under 14.

Ski school

Classes 3hr, mornings only. Full-day excursions twice a week.
Cost 6 days L125,000. Private lessons L27,000/hr.
Children Ski kindergarten, ages 4–12, 9.30–4.00, 6 days with lunch, lifts and lessons L230,000. Non-ski kindergarten, ages 2–4, 10.00–4.00, 6 days L150,000.

Not skiing

Facilities Natural ice rink, swimming/sauna/solaria (hotels open to non-residents), sleigh rides, curling, bowling alley, extensive walking paths around Selva and above S Cristina and Ortisei, ski-bob on most runs.

Cross-country skiing

Trails 12km trail in Vallunga with abbreviations to create shorter trails. 2km easy trail at La Selva (on edge of resort). Over 40km trails at Alpe di Siusi.

Medical facilities

In resort Fracture clinic, doctors, chemists.
Hospital Bolzano (42km).
Dentist Ortisei (7km).

Getting there

Airport Munich, Treviso or Milan; transfers about 5hr. Verona, about 4hr.
Railway Chiusa (27km); frequent buses.
Road Via Munich, Brenner, Bressanone; chains occasionally needed.

Available holidays

Resort beds 4,000 in hotels, 3,500 in apartments.
Package holidays John Morgan (Ht Ch), Mark Warner (Cl), Small World (Ch)

Further information

Tourist office ✆(471) 75122. Tx 400359.

them very stylish, and simple B&B houses; staffed chalet accommodation is offered by a few companies. The Aaritz (✆75011) and Antares (✆75400) are comfortable, expensive hotels near the Ciampinoi cable-car. Even better placed for access to both Ciampinoi and the Costabella chair-lift are the comfortable, functional Laurin (✆75105), the Genziana (✆75187) and the large and fairly simple Stella (✆75162). But about the best location of all is across the river, near the very useful Ciampinoi chair-lift, where several inexpensive B&B hotels include the Somont (✆75090) and the Eden (✆75028); the more comfortable Savoy (✆75343) is just by the lift and has a restaurant.

Après-ski is one of Selva's main advantages over the other mostly small and peaceful resorts in the Sella area. There are several discothèques (reporters recommend the Club Stella), one or two places with live music, and plenty of bars and inexpensive restaurants.

Nursery slopes are excellent – a wide open area with snow-making machines near the resort centre and beneath the Dantercepies lifts. Unfortunately the slopes and lifts are often busy with skiers in transit.

We have no reports on Selva's **ski school**.

Minor resorts

Ortisei 1240m

The main town in the Val Gardena is charming but not convenient as a base for keen Alpine skiers, and is neglected in winter, at least by the British. But the Alpe di Siusi, reached either by road from Castelrotto or by cable-car from Ortisei, is unbeatable for beautiful walks, sleigh rides and cross-country skiing at high altitude. Ortisei is also well placed for excursions to the Adige Valley reaching as far as Verona.

The town centre is by-passed by the main valley road, but this busy highway still has to be crossed on foot to get to and from the ice rink and Alpe di Siusi cable-car. The main street is a long one and includes a short, fairly steep hill between the church and main square and bus terminal. As in Selva, staying in Ortisei usually involves quite a lot of tiresome walking. Ortisei nightlife is less lively than Selva's, but there are some good bars and restaurants, especially the delightful Zur Traube/all'Uva, and a discothèque. A local passion is ice hockey; there are often evening league matches. Most of the many hotels in the centre of the resort are simple, except for the smart and expensive Adler (✆76203). Opposite it is the Posta (✆76392), a large, solid, central old village hotel. The Snaltnerhof (✆76746) is simple, inexpensive and welcoming, and very well placed beside the main bus stop. The Alpe di Siusi offers varying degrees of retreat. The main community is Kompatsch, at the top of the road up from Castelrotto, where there are several hotels, a ski school with kindergarten and a skating rink. Two large, comfortable and secluded hotels are the Floralpina (✆72907) at the S Cristina end and the Sonne (✆76377) near the top of the cable-car from Ortisei.

Tourist office ✆(471) 76328. Tx 400305.

Arabba 1600m

A small and attractively unspoilt village in the Italian-speaking sector of the Sella region, Arabba is the best resort in the area for good and adventurous skiers, thanks to its excellent home slopes and to the ease of access to the Marmolada and Cortina. There is nothing much to do except ski, eat, drink and sleep, apart from one discothèque (recommended by one visitor). There are a few hotels and a number of B&B houses, some of which are used for British 'chalet' holidays. The Sport Hotel Arabba (✆79321) is the most comfortable hotel. The Posta (✆79105) is simpler, cheaper, older and more friendly.

Tourist Office ✆(436) 79130. Tx 440823. **Package holidays** Beach Villas (Ch Sc), Small World (Ch).

Corvara 1550m

The main resort of the Alta Badia area and probably the best location on the Sella Ronda for skiers who want a lot of open skiing and the best chance of good snow conditions close at hand. Selva and Arabba are easily reached and the most remote segment of the available skiing (Canazei) is the least interesting for intermediate skiers.

The village is a characterless sprawl of modern chalets and chalet-style hotels large and small, spread across a large area beside the roads down from the Gardena and Campolongo passes. The centre and most convenient place to stay is near the Col Alto chair-lift (for access to the Alta Badia) which is a manageable walk from the Boe cable-car (for Arabba) and the scene of most of Corvara's limited après-ski. This usually includes dancing (at tea-time and in the evening) at the Posta (✆836175), the biggest, smartest and most central of the hotels (pool and sauna). The Veneranda (✆836127) and Fortuna (✆836043) are much smaller and less expensive and are also conveniently placed. There is a short cross-country track between the Boe cable-car and Colfosco and an ice rink with facilities for curling.

Tourist office ✆(471) 836176. Tx 401555.

Colfosco 1650m

A small holiday village which has grown up beside the road between Corvara and the Gardena Pass with easy access to Selva and Corvara and a small skiing area of its own (including a good nursery area) beside the village. There are a couple of plush, modern, expensive hotels at the top of the village of which one, the Kolfuschgerhof (✆836188), boasts a swimming pool and squash court. Most hotels are more modest; the Centrale (✆836118) is large and comfortable and, as it sounds, well placed for skiing and also for après-ski.

Tourist office ✆(471) 836145. **Package holidays** Small World (Ch).

San Cassiano 1537m

A small roadside village in typical Dolomite style with a lot of mostly new chalet buildings, largely consisting of hotels and B&B houses. San Cassiano has some of the best of the local skiing for beginners and timid skiers who can enjoy the very long, easy runs down to the village itself from Pralongia and from Piz Sorega before venturing further afield. The Rosa Alpina (✆849500) is a large, comfortable, modern

hotel (with pool) at the centre of the village and the focus of après-ski (live bands afternoon and evening). There are some cross-country possibilities at Armentarola, a cluster of quiet hotels and restaurants about 1km east. Cortina is less than an hour away via Valparola and Falzarego passes – a spectacular drive through a rocky wilderness.
Tourist office ✆(471) 849422. **Package holidays** Small World (Ch).

Canazei 1440m

Canazei is a large, noisy village in the Italian-speaking Val di Fassa, cut through by the busy main road. It is the only real alternative to the Val Gardena for skiers wanting varied off-slope activities and plenty of nightlife. Its local skiing is inconvenient and limited, but once on the slopes (only by the cable-car, which is a long walk from the resort centre, and often crowded), it doesn't take long to reach Arabba.

The village centre is an attractive jumble of busy narrow streets with some rustic old buildings as well as new hotels and shopping precincts which have sprung up with the Dolomites' tourist boom. There are plenty of bars, restaurants and evening entertainment (mostly hotel-oriented), with discos and jokey contests. There is a large public pool/sauna, a natural ice rink beside an attractive wooded playground in the centre, and a long chain of cross-country trails (mostly easy) along the shady side of the river. The Val di Fassa hosts a 70km X-C marathon (the Marcialonga) between Canazei and Cavalese; some stretches of the course are open only at the time of the race.

In the centre, the Croce Bianca (✆61111) is a long-established hotel, substantial and comfortably refurbished. The Bellevue (✆61104) is better placed for the cable-car. The Laurin (✆61286) is on the wrong side of town for skiing purposes, but is otherwise attractive.

Two hotels offer greater skiing convenience. The comfortable and friendly Bellavista (✆61165) is at Pecol, near the top of the Canazei cable-car. Higher up (2100m), the inexpensive 80-year-old Pordoi (✆61115) is somewhat spartan. It has a new self-catering annexe with pool and sauna.
Tourist office ✆(462) 61113. Tx 400012. **Package holidays** Intasun (Ht).

Campitello 1440m

Canazei's close neighbour is a quieter and much smaller village, its centre set back from the main road, an attractive collection of old buildings beside a stream running down into the main river. Its ski-lift is a new cable-car from beside the road to the Col Rodella above the Sella Pass. The Fedora (✆61597) is a comfortable hotel beside the cable-car station. There are adequate shopping facilities in the village, and we are informed that there is nightlife, too, in the Fummelbunker, which roughly translated means the Grope Hole. There are secluded nursery slopes in the valley, conditions permitting, and an ice rink near the river. There are no pistes down to Campitello; returning via the cable-car is much more relaxing than struggling back through Canazei.
Tourist office ✆(462) 61137. **Package holidays** Intasun (Ht), Pegasus (Ht).

White Madonna

Madonna di Campiglio Italy 1510m

Good for *Beautiful scenery, mountain restaurants, nursery slopes, easy runs, big ski area, sunny slopes*
Bad for *Tough runs, late holidays, easy road access, not skiing, short airport transfers*

Linked resorts: Marilleva, Folgarida

Madonna di Campiglio is a large, comfortable, fairly quiet modern resort in the western Dolomites which attracts well-heeled Italian skiers, few from abroad and hardly any from Britain. The atmosphere is more villagey than in most modern resorts and the building style is attractive and harmonious, which is rare for an Italian ski resort, as is the high standard of accommodation. Madonna's setting among thick pine woods beneath the jagged turrets of the Brenta mountains is a splendid one. The slopes on either side of the resort are steep, but most of Madonna's skiing is different – typical of the Dolomites in taking skiers over long distances through beautiful scenery, past tempting refuges, on gentle runs with a limited range of altitude (there is little skiing above 2000m). Lift queues are rarely a problem except at weekends and when snow is scarce, and there is a good nursery area.

Marilleva and Folgarida do attract some British custom. Despite lower prices, they are less appealing than Madonna, sharing neither the beauty of its surroundings nor its freedom from queues. Skiing home, especially to Marilleva 900, is often impossible.

The skiing top 2510m bottom 1512m

Madonna's skiing is mostly on broad, well-prepared avenues between trees. Most of it is sheltered, sunny and spectacular. Snow on the runs down to the village is not very reliable. There are four main lift departures, three of them within walking distance of the centre.

The **Pradalago** lifts open up the widest area of skiing, linking up with Folgarida and Marilleva. Access is either from the resort via the Pradalago cable-car (soon to be doubled up with a chair-lift) or by chair-lift from Camp Carlo Magno. Runs back down follow the route of the chair-lifts, and include a very gentle black, with a maximum gradient of 18°. The link to Marilleva and Folgarida consists of straightforward up and down, open and wooded skiing past the Lago delle Malghette to Monte Vigo, which is the parting of the ways to the other resorts. The **Marilleva** side includes three linked, not very fearsome black runs from over 2000m down through the woods to the bottom station of the Pian del Grum gondola. The bottom section, from 1400m to 900m, is often unskiable. The more direct route to 1400, via Panciana, is easy and very busy. On the **Folgarida** side there is one tough black mogul-track (28°)

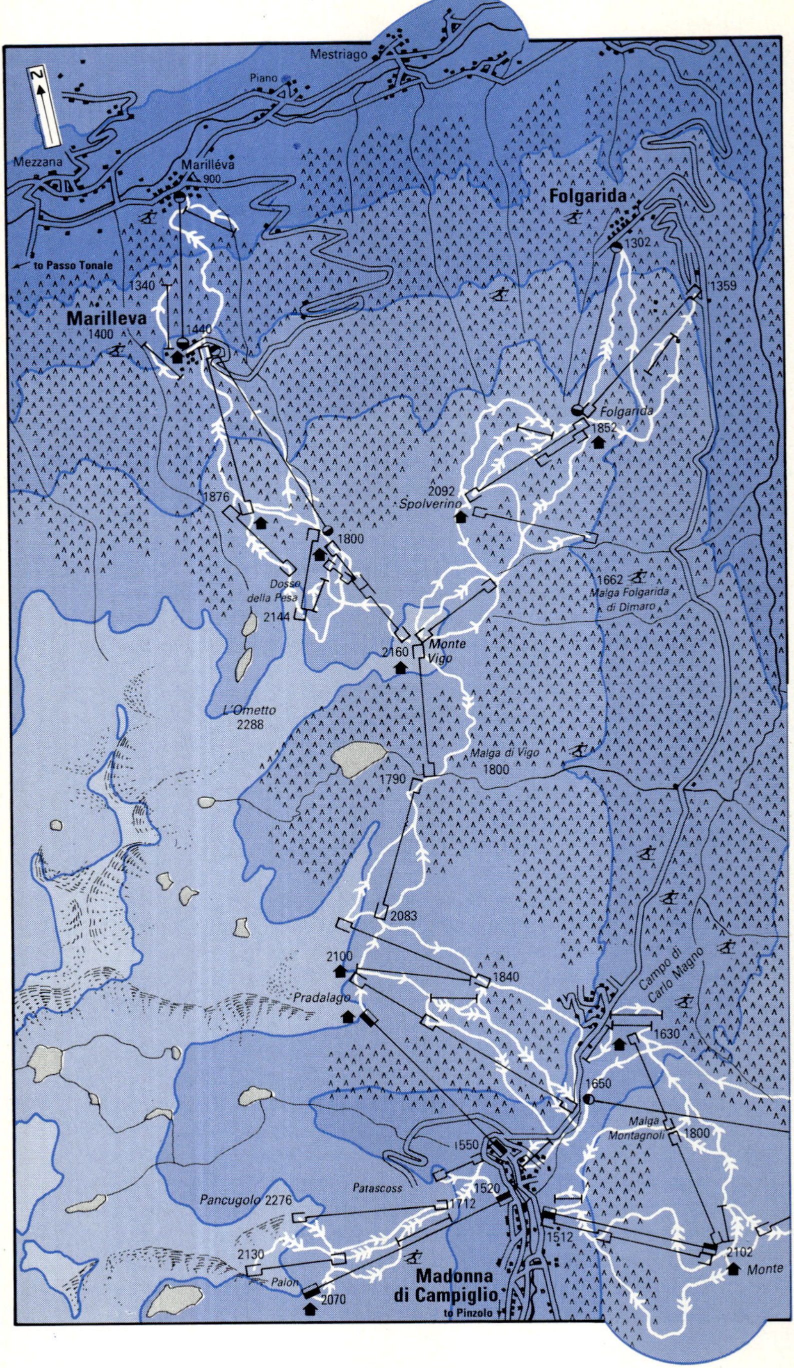
N
Mestriago
Piano
Mezzana
Marilléva
900
to Passo Tonale
1340
Marilleva
1400
1440
Folgarida
1302
1359
Folgarida
1852
2092
Spolverino
1876
1800
Dosso della Pesa
2144
1662
Malga Folgarida di Dimaro
2160
Monte Vigo
L'Ometto
2288
Malga di Vigo
1800
1790
2083
2100
1840
Pradalago
Campo di Carlo Magno
1630
1650
Malga Montagnoli
1800
1550
Patascoss
1520
Pancugolo 2276
1712
1512
2102
Monte
2130
Palon
2070
Madonna di Campiglio
to Pinzolo

below the profusion of green and blue runs between upper Folgar da and Spolverino. The runs back to Madonna are not difficult.

Of the other three ski areas, the largest is **Groste**, reached indirectly from the village via the Spinale cable-car or directly by a powerful new gondola starting opposite the Pradalago chair. The top station is the departure point for three touring routes. The runs are beautiful, easy, open and long, with a gentle blue-green route from the top to Campo Carlo Magno. The flat path back to the resort is not always skiable.

Monte Spinale can be reached either by cable-car and parallel chair-lift from near the ice rink, or by chairlift from Campo Carlo Magno. Runs back down to the resort are tricky, poorly marked and unreliable for snow, but there are gentler north-facing runs down through the woods to Carlo Magno and an easy red link with the mid-station of the Groste cable-car. The **Cinque Laghi** skiing, Madonna's racing hill, is served by cable-car from the western side of the resort. A short red run down from the cable-car top station links to the Tre Tre chair-lift. The runs are not exactly jet black, but provide plenty of challenge and no easy way down.

Madonna and its linked resorts are very well supplied with **mountain restaurants** – many of them tablecloths and waiters, and real kitchens with chefs. The Nube d'Oro below Spinale, the Rifugio Giorgio Graffer at Groste, and the Panciana above Marilleva are recommended. The Rifugio Spinale is not.

In general the Madonna half of the lift system works well, with few

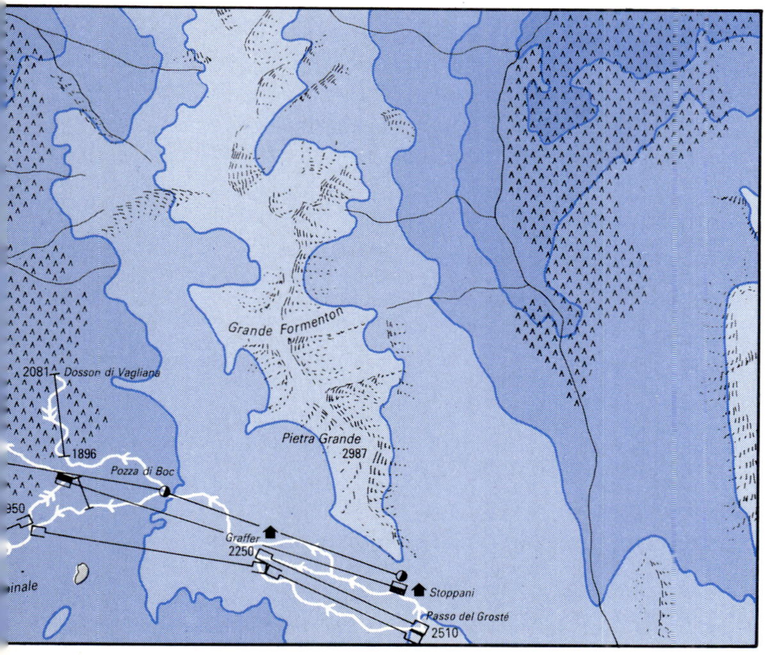

serious **queues** except when snow conditions are poor (when Groste becomes crowded – though the new gondola should help here). A good piste map, complete with contours, is available if you insist. From both Folgarida and Marilleva 1400 very efficient lifts (six-seater gondolas and four-seater chairs) serve narrow skiing areas, and pistes and restaurants tend to be very crowded; congestion at Monte Vigo, the one point where the ski areas meet, is inevitable – especially late in the day. The key chairlift back from Madonna to Monte Vigo has apparently been upgraded to a three-seater. For keen skiers, the limited coverage of the weekly pass is frustrating.

The resort

Madonna's situation does not ideally suit skiers. It has grown up along the road and river about half a mile to the south of a wooded pass, and 150 vertical metres below it. In winter a street on the other side of the river is used to form a long one-way circuit, but even this cannot prevent traffic jams along the main street at weekends. At the centre of the resort between the two axes is an attractive pedestrian precinct with tempting *pasticcerie* and smart, towny shops. Nearby is a frozen lake used for skating, motor-cycling and even American football.

A car is useful in the resort if your hotel is at the southern end, but

Madonna facts

Lift payment

Passes 'Skirama' day pass covers all Madonna, Folgarida, Marilleva lifts except Carlo Magno nursery lifts. 6-day pass covers all Madonna lifts and is valid for one weekday (two with a 7-day pass) in Marilleva/Folgarida.
Cost 6-day pass L154,000. 8% off in low season.
Children Reduction on 6/7 days for up to age 14.
Beginners Payment by the ride.

Ski school

Classes 2hr/day, 9.00–11.00 or 11.00–1.00.
Cost 6 days L87,000–L99,000. Private lessons L29,000/hr.
Children Ski kindergarten ages 4–13, 10.00–1.00, 6 days, L113,000. No non-ski kindergarten.
Special courses Ski-touring.

Cross-country skiing

Trails At Campo Carlo Magno, easy–moderate, 5km and 10km. Patascoss, 13km, easy.

Not-skiing

Facilities Skating, swimming.

Medical facilities

In resort Doctor, fracture clinic, chemist.
Hospital Tione (30km).
Dentist Pinzolo (13km).

Getting there

Airport Verona; transfer 3hr; Milan about 5hr.
Railway Male; about 1 hr by bus; Trento 2hr.
Road Via Innsbruck, Brennner, Trento; chains may be needed.

Available holidays

Resort beds 4,000 in hotels, 26,000 in apartments.
Package holidays Snowcoach Holidays (Ht)

Further information

Tourist office ✆(465) 42000. Tx 400882. Fax (465) 40404.

otherwise inessential. A ski-bus (free if you use 'White Week' arrangements) links the bottom lifts stations including Campo Carlo Magno every 20 minutes. There are buses to Folgarida.

Accommodation is in private apartments and numerous hotels, many of them modern, comfortable and expensive. Hotels in the centre, such as the Majestic (✆41080), the stylish St Hubertus (✆41144) and the Miramonti (✆41021) ('excellent food, resident pianist') are withing easy walking distance of the lifts. The Spinale (✆41116) is cheaper than most and quietly situated at the foot of the Spinale lifts. Reporters praise the copious food and friendly service.

Après-ski is varied, but outside holiday periods (when there are lots of young Italians around) the atmosphere is subdued and the many bars and restaurants do better business than the expensive discos.

The resort does not offer much for **non-skiers**. Excursions to Venice, Innsbruck and Lake Garda are advertised. **Cross-country** trails in the woods around Campo Carlo Magno and the mid-station of the Cirque Laghi lifts are very pretty.

Nursery slopes in Madonna and around the mountains are numerous and generally good, provided there is enough snow at resort level. The best area is Campo Carlo Magno, near the road from Madonna to Folgarida. It is pleasant, spacious, sunny and quiet, unlike the smaller nursery slopes in the centre of the resort. For times of snow shortage there is a small nursery area at Groste.

There are seven **ski schools**, all officially accredited, and with standard hours and prices. Proximity to your accommodation is probably the most important criterion. The only report we have is of a drunken torchlit descent from Pradalago – 'the highlight of the holiday'.

Marilleva 900m and 1400m Folgarida 1300m

Marilleva is a small, split-level, purpose-built resort. The lower level, Marilleva 900, is in the main valley near the village of Mezzana on the Tonale road. There is not much more to it than a large hotel complex at the foot of the often bare runs and the inefficient gondola linking it to Marilleva 1400. When snow is plentiful there is plenty of scope for cross-country skiing along the valley. The core of the more stylish upper resort is a huge, low-lying concrete block very close to the ski-lifts, with hotels, apartments, pool and sauna, restaurants and bars, mostly under one roof. Folgarida is an older and more random collection of simple, inexpensive hotels and bars. Its position beside the road up to Campo Carlo Magno and Madonna makes it a better base than Marilleva for skiing and especially après-ski excursions.

Tourist offices Marilleva ✆(463) 77134; Folgarida ✆(463) 96113.
Package holidays Marilleva: Hourmont (Groups) (Ht Ap), Hourmont (Schools) (Ht), Schoolplan (Ht), Snowcoach (Ht); Folgarida: Hourmont (Ht), Snowcoach (Ht).

Dolomite backwater

San Martino di Castrozza

Italy 1450m

San Martino, one of the largest and southernmost Dolomite resorts, has a chic reputation which is now quite unfounded, and is an attractive, all-Italian resort, neglected internationally but far from negligible in terms of skiing and entertainment value. Our two reporters found that the friendliness of the resort outweighed its disadvantages, notably the layout – it is built along the road which descends steeply to the south of Passo Rolle – and the disjointed nature of the skiing. The setting is open and sunny, amid forests beneath the towering pinnacles of the Pale di San Martino, among the most spectacular of all Dolomite peaks. The village is neither offensive nor charming. Around the church and river bridge is a cluster of shops, bars and hotels – many of the older ones distinctly dowdy. The Orsingher (✆68544) is one of the most comfortable, a large modern chalet building beside the road.

There are four ski areas, of which only one is within walking distance of the centre. At the top of the village, where there are good nursery slopes and a kindergarten, a chair-lift to **Col Verde** (1930m) serves blue and red runs back to the resort. The spectacular cable-car to **Rosetta** (2639m) serves an adventure run down to Col Verde.

Tognola, below the resort, is the most popular area, and the long gondola from Fratazza (1400m) to the splendid sunny belvedere of Alpe di Tognola (2165m) is often crowded, as are the runs through the woods – long, broad and satisfying trails, ranging from meandering blue to direct, not very severe black. Behind Alpe di Tognola is a wide open basin of gentle skiing (1900m to 2200m) served by several drags.

Ces is a quiet area to the west. A slow chair-lift leads to Malga Ces (1617m), a clearing with a couple of nursery lifts, also accessible by car. A second chair-lift, to Punta Ces (2231m), serves the main slope, which offers some good varied skiing, on and off the piste, open and wooded. The pistes (red and black) are not very difficult for their categories. The café terrace at Punta Ces gives splendid views.

Passo Rolle is 9km from San Martino, a high, open and sunny area of mostly easy intermediate runs on both sides of the pass between 1880m and 2300m. The steep Paradiso drag-lift serves a variety of more challenging runs down more or less directly beside it.

Pleasant and varied as it is, the local skiing is unlikely to satisfy good, keen skiers for more than a few days, and San Martino is too far from the rest of the Dolomite skiing for excursions to be practical. There is an easy cross-country circuit at San Martino and good long trails at Passo Rolle. The resort is well suited to non-skiers: beautiful walks, ice rink, riding. The ski-bus service is essential, adequate, and free to lift pass holders. Après-ski is mostly confined to hotel bars.

Tourist office ✆(439) 68101. Tx 401543.

Lombard North Central

Bormio Italy 1225m

Good for *Summer skiing, mountain restaurants, not skiing*
Bad for *Easy runs, tough runs, resort-level snow, late holidays, easy road access, short airport transfers, freedom from cars*

Separate resort: Santa Caterina

Bormio, host of the 1985 skiing World Championships, is a small town in a remote corner of Lombardy at the foot of the Stelvio pass which separates Italian Italy from Germanic Dolomite Italy and serves some of the best summer skiing in the Alps. Bormio's history as a spa goes back to Roman times, and the old centre is old, unaffected and very Italian, with a greater variety of everyday shops, cafés and restaurants tucked away in the back-streets than in most ski resorts, and good open-air markets. The skiing that matters is on one tall mountainside whose slopes provide long to very long runs, mostly intermediate. New lifts and a battery of snow cannons have helped to relieve the associated problems of queues and not being able to ski down to the valley, but have not opened up any new skiing on what is by today's standards a narrow skiing area. Bormio is often presented as a resort for advanced skiers and as a pretty little mountain village; those who go with those expectations will be disappointed.

The lift pass covers Santa Caterina, a pretty nearby village with more reliable snow, less queuing and an area of intermediate skiing which is a match for Bormio's when snow low down is poor. A car is handy for exploring the other skiing areas. The road to Livigno (also covered by the lift pass) has been improved, but is still long and often requires chains. Reaching Bormio by road via Milan is very time-consuming.

The skiing top 3012m bottom 1225m

The north-west-facing slopes of the tall Monte Vallecetta rise evenly from the riverside near Bormio to its 3148m summit just above the top of a two-stage cable-car from the edge of town. The middle station is Bormio 2000, an upper mini-resort, usually accessible by car (a car park separates the two stages of cable-car). An alternative access route is by gondola to Ciuk, followed by chair-lifts or a long drag. When conditions permit there are very long runs from top to bottom, up to 14km and nearly 1800m vertical. On the open top half alone the runs are long and satisfying, but the range of difficulty is limited; the easy runs are a bit tough for skiers just off the nursery slopes, and only when they are icy do the more difficult ones (two short blacks) excite skiers hungry for a challenge. Immediately below the top cable-car station and to the west of the pistes, a fairly steep, wide and sunless bowl provides excellent off-piste skiing when conditions are safe. Check that the

Ornella drag-lift is working before embarking on the lower section.

Most skiers spend the day on the top half of the mountain, and the wide, undulating trails through the woods below Ciuk are little used except in bad weather and for skiing home in the afternoon, when they are crowded. The Stelvio downhill course starts steeply just above La Rocca and runs down past Ciuk to near the bottom of the gondola 1000m below. This fine run is a legacy of the World Championships, as are snow-jets beside 9km of the lower slopes.

On the other side of town a worthwhile new ski area has been created by the building of new lifts on the north-facing slopes above the small resort of Val di Dentro, linking up with those above Oga and Le Motte, facing west. There are not many runs, but a worthwhile vertical drop of 800m and 900m vertical metres on the two sides. The Bormio lift pass no longer covers Val di Dentro.

Mountain restaurants are plentiful, considering the limited size of the ski area, and several reporters commented on good food, even in the self-service restaurant at Bormio 2000.

Queues for both sections of the cable-car can usually be avoided, except when the bottom runs are unskiable. Several of the drag-lifts were not working when we visited recently on a fine, busy weekend; the Nevada lift is steep and very long; the Graziella is a more important link and even longer. The piste map and signposting are unhelpful.

The resort

The outskirts of the town, much less attractive than the centre, include numerous modern hotels along the road at the foot of the slopes between cable-car and gondola station. This is the most convenient location for skiers' **accommodation**, within 10 or 15 minutes' walk of the old centre. Of the hotels near the cable-car, the Nevada (✆902491) is recommended by a regular visitor, and the Ambassador (✆904625) is friendly and welcoming. The Cima Bianca (✆901449) is an inexpensive, attractive and convenient B&B hotel. In the centre the Posta (✆904753) and Astoria (✆904541) are both comfortable and attractive. A reporter who stayed at the Girasole (✆904652), isolated at Bormio 2000, enjoyed being able to take advantage of cheap full-board terms; a big effort is made to provide entertainment for residents. A half-hourly bus does a circuit of the town, and there is a less frequent service to S Caterina.

Après-ski is generally quiet, but there are a few discos and a wide range of bars and restaurants outside hotels. Organised outings may include the excellent Baiona restaurant, beside the road up to Bormio 2000. Many skiers enjoy easing their joints in the thermal baths.

Bormio offers a lot to the **non-skier**, with new thermal and sports facilities generated by the World Championships (a bus ride from the centre), and is itself interesting. Reporters recommend the excursions to Livigno and St Moritz. The **cross-country** trails in the Val di Dentro are more reliable for snow than those around Bormio itself.

Nursery slopes are at Ciuk and Bormio 2000, the first being larger

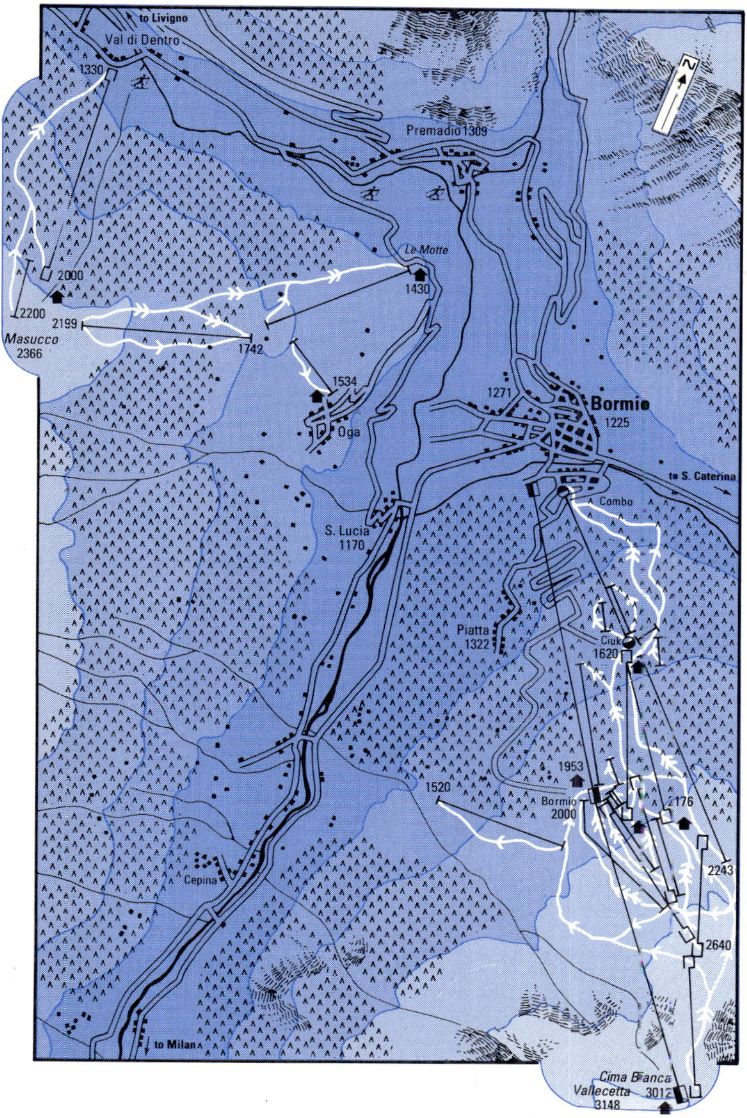

and more tranquil, but sometimes short of snow. These are good areas, but the lack of village nursery slopes is a disadvantage. There s not much very easy skiing for the post-nursery stages.

Prices of the five recognised **ski schools** vary slightly. English-speaking instructors are numerous. Several reporters commented on the helicopter excursion to the Vallecetta and off-piste run to S Caterina, long but not difficult.

Santa Caterina 1750m

S Caterina is a quiet little resort in the pretty, wooded Valfurva, a dead-end in winter when the exciting road over the Gavia pass is closed. When snow conditions are good, adventurous skiers based here are tempted to take the regular buses down to Bormio, but when snow is in short supply the traffic flows the other way, and weekend queues can occur. The local skiing is on the north-east-facing slopes of the Sobretta between the village and a top station of 2725m. The higher slopes are fairly steep and graded black, but most of the skiing is intermediate, with a beautiful long run round the mountain behind Cresta Sobretta, and good wide woodland trails including the women's World Championship downhill course. There is a good but often overcrowded nursery area with restaurants above the woods and an easy way home via the Gavia road. There is some attractive cross-country skiing (up to 10km) in quiet surroundings beyond the resort, and skating on the natural rink. Night-life is limited.

Tourist office ✆(0342) 935598.
Package holidays Enterprise (Ht Sc), Global (Ht Sc), Neilson (Ht), Pegasus (Ht Sc), Schoolplan (Ht), Ski Travelaway (Ht).

Bormio facts

Lift payment

Passes Area pass (2, 6, 7, 13 or 14 days) covers Bormio, Santa Caterina, Livigno. Day and half-day pass for Bormio only.
Beginners Coupons or lift pass.
Cost 6-day pass L130,000. 25% off in low season.
Children 20% off, under 12.
Summer skiing Extensive area at Stelvio Pass (20km), 2760m to 3420m.

Ski school

Classes 2hr or 4hr per day.
Cost 6 days (12hrs) about L70,000. Private lessons L27,000/hr.
Children Ski kindergarten (Sertorelli), 6 days (12hr) L115,000.
Special courses Racing, ski touring, helicopter skiing.

Not skiing

Facilities Two museums, library, cinema, thermal baths, swimming, sauna, sports hall, indoor tennis, clay pigeon shooting, mini-golf, ski-bob, skating, toboggan run.

Cross-country skiing

Trails 10km trails near resort (easy). More difficult trails (up to 25km) in Val di Dentro.

Medical facilities

In resort Hospital, doctors, chemists, dentists.

Getting there

Airport Milan (200km); transfers 4½hr.
Railway Tirano (40km); regular buses.
Road Via Mont Blanc Tunnel, Milan, Sondrio; chains rarely needed. Via Livigno; chains often needed.

Available holidays

Resort beds 3,500 in hotels; 12,500 in apartments.
Package holidays Enterprise (Ht Sc), Global (Ht Sc), Intasun (Ht Sc), Neilson (Ht), Pegasus (Ht Sc)

Further information

Tourist office ✆(342) 903300. Tx 314389. Fax (342) 904696.

High skiing, low spirits

Livigno Italy 1820m

Good for *Nursery slopes, easy runs, resort-level snow, late holidays, sunny slopes, après-ski, duty-free*
Bad for *Skiing convenience, tough runs, lift queues, Alpine charm, short airport transfers, easy road access, mountain restaurants, not skiing, freedom from cars*

Livigno is a very strung-out series of villages in a long, wide, high and exceedingly remote valley – a lost world to which the easiest access from mother Italy is the 2290m pass from Bormio, over an hour's drive away. British skiers face airport transfers of over six hours in which to build up a thirst for Livigno's much-vaunted duty-free drink.

The high and wide slopes along both sides of the valley above the resort provide a lot of uncomplicated intermediate skiing for a long winter season. In good weather and good snow it is splendid; in bad weather 'Piccolo Tibet', as Livigno is known locally, is extremely bleak. Whatever the weather, the lift system is very poorly conceived and skiing usually involves a lot of legwork as a result. The village is old and interesting, but recent development has spoilt most of its charm.

Thanks to a road tunnel from Switzerland, Livigno is no longer seriously inaccessible to motorists. Having a car is handy in the resort and for excursions: the lift pass covers Bormio and Santa Caterina, and St Moritz is easily reached for a day's skiing or just a look at how the other wintersports half live.

The skiing top 2800m bottom 1816m

Skiing takes place on both flanks of the valley, now covered by a shared pass. Although there are many more lifts on the south-east-facing side of the valley, most of them are short nursery drags, and the north- and west-facing Mottolino slopes above the winding road to Bormio offer a similar amount of skiing. Most of the skiing is above the tree-line, and only one lift is enclosed.

The two-stage **Lago Salin** gondola from the southern end of town spans the longest slopes in the ski area, a wide open, south-east-facing mountainside with several possible variations of the run back down, none of them severe, although snow is often difficult on the lower slopes, which are fairly steep and poorly marked. Behind the top station is a quiet area of short runs beside the Federia drag-lifts, with reliably good snow. A very long and gentle blue run northwards along the mountain ridge links up with the Costaccia chair-lifts above the northern end of the resort (S Maria), which serve a small area of shorter wooded runs, often worn.

The **Mottolino** skiing, reached by one drag-lift near the edge of the

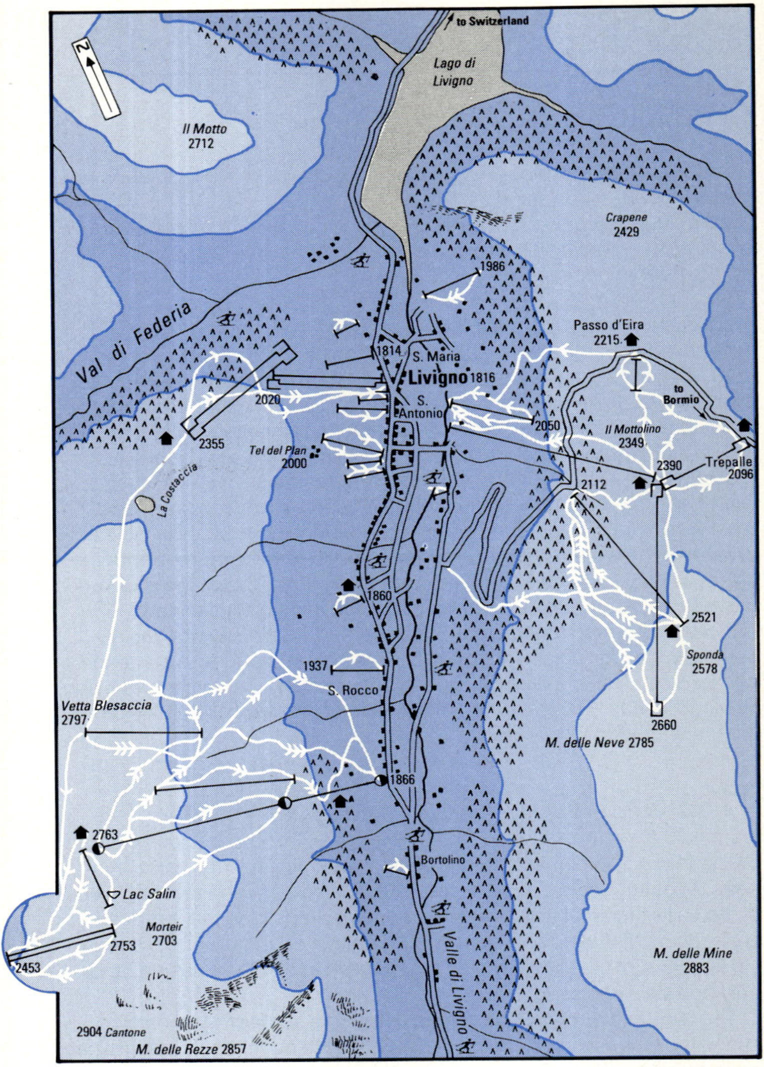

resort or from various points along the Bormio road, consists of intermediate runs complicated only by poor signposting and by the road itself which cuts awkwardly through the skiing area (the drag-lift crosses it by bridge). Lifts are inadequate but there is plenty of space and usually good snow on the upper runs which include a very easy one along the top ridge. The wide slope above Trepalle (little more than a few houses, including a bar, beside the road) faces east, and the red run beneath the chair-lift can be quite a challenge at the end of a sunny day. There is tempting off-piste skiing below the Monte della Neve, but it is difficult to stay within reach of lifts.

For Italy, Livigno is not well equipped with **mountain restaurants** – they are no more than adequate in number, and unremarkable in style.

The main problems with lifts are the difficulty of getting to them, and the **queues** for the Mottolino ones, especially the steep Sponca crag. The Lago Salin bucket has been replaced by a six-seater gondola, so efficient that you have to queue to leave the top terminal. Three piste maps are needed.

The resort

Originally three separate communities (Santa Maria, San Antonio and San Rocco) spread out along the western side of the long flat valley, Livigno is now an unbroken three-mile straggle of hotels, bars, garages and duty-free supermarkets. They are interspersed by many beautiful old buildings and barns full of animals, but there is no real old village centre. Spirits cost from £3 a litre, petrol is about half the normal Italian price and there are small savings to be made on some ski equipment – though to be sure of making a saving you need to be very well informed on prices at home.

The main road (a surprisingly busy thoroughfare between Italy and Austria) by-passes the southern end of the village (San Rocco) but central San Antonio is a very busy road junction. Because of the road tunnel and the duty-free goods, Livigno is one of the few Italian resorts outside the Dolomites to attract many German skiers (for holidays and shopping day-trips). They all come by car, and daytime traffic nuisance is considerable.

Accommodation is mostly in hotels along the resort's single axis. Style and comfort vary greatly. The Alpina (✆996007) is the original village inn, central, comfortable and inviting. Nearby, the Bivio (✆996137) is quieter and very attractive, with sauna and pool. Some hotels have been built on the other side of the valley at the foot of and alongside the Bormio road. The lower ones are within striking range of the Mottolino lift. From most locations in the northern half of the village it is not far to the Costaccia access lifts or to a nursery lift that makes it possible to ski across to them, but the bus is useful for access to the Lago Salin lift unless you stay in Livigno's deep south (San Rocco, which is very quiet for après-skiers) – as it is for crossing from one flank of the skiing to the other. The bus is free but reported to be elusive in the middle of the day.

Après-ski is bar-oriented, inexpensive and lively, but far from riotous. There are not many restaurants other than in hotels.

For **non-skiers** there are few diversions except drinking and regular excursions to St Moritz and Bormio. The **cross-country** trails are convenient, running along the valley beside the village, and at this altitude are reliable for snow.

Nursery slopes and lifts cover a large expanse of the lower slopes on the western side of the resort. They are open and gentle, and easily accessible from accommodation in the main strip of village, with bars close at hand, including the Bar Scuola, the lively headquarters of the main ski school.

There are four **ski schools**, all officially recognised, and all operating classes at similar times and similar prices. Torchlit descents are organised weekly.

Livigno facts

Lift payment

Passes General pass covers all lifts at Livigno, Bormio, and S Caterina and Val di Dentro, and local ski-bus, except for day-pass (Livigno only). Limited passes available.
Cost 6-day pass L120,000. 25% off in low season.
Children 20% off, under 12.
Beginners Coupons.

Ski school

Classes 2hr/day, 9.00–11.00 or 11.00–1.00.
Cost 6 days L60,000.
Children No kindergartens.
Special courses Racing, video, ski touring, monoski, surfski.

Cross-country skiing

Trails 30km green and 10km red trails along valley floor.

Not skiing

Facilities Skating, sauna, ice driving, snow buggies.

Medical facilities

In resort Doctor, dentist, chemist.
Hospital Sondalo (60km).

Getting there

Airport Munich, Innsbruck or Zurich are most easily reached, but most packages use Milan – transfers 6hr plus.
Railway Tirano; bus to resort 3hr.
Road Via Munich, Innsbruck, Landeck, Zernez; chains may be needed; toll tunnel open 8am to 8pm. Alternative route via Bormio; chains often needed.

Available holidays

Resort beds 4,700 in hotels, 3,200 in apartments.
Package holidays Edwards (Ht), Enterprise (Ht Sc), Global (Ht Sc), Inghams (Ht Sc), Intasun (Ht Sc), Neilson (Ht Sc), Pegasus (Ht Sc), Ski Falcon (Ht Sc), Ski NAT (Ht), Ski Young World (Ht Sc), Skiworld (Ht Sc), Thomson (Ht Sc)

Further information

Tourist office ✆(342) 996402. Tx 350400.

Expensive, at the price

Aprica Italy 1181m

Aprica at its best can offer some good intermediate skiing with runs of over 1100m vertical from top to bottom. But by all accounts it is not very often at its best, and the reports we have received make depressing reading, giving an impression of standards lower than prices. Most of the disadvantages of Italian skiing are here gathered together.

The arrangement of the resort, which extends for about a mile along a road pass east of Sondrio, is unappealing, and there is no attractive old centre. There are three neighbouring ski areas on the same mountainside, but they are not well linked, there is no ski bus, and the general lift pass is expensive. Accommodation is mostly drab. Several reporters found the locals were unfriendly and uninterested in foreign visitors. Others complained of primitive sanitation in the mountain restaurant and a low standard of equipment for hire (and refusal to repair hire equipment without payment). The resort is quiet except at weekends, when it becomes overcrowded.

The skiing, on the south side of the road, mostly consists of trails through woods, intermediate in standard (including the black runs). There is a string of short lifts on the lower slopes above the village which are useful for getting from one end of the resort to the other. The Baradello lift system, at the eastern end of the resort, consists of only three lifts, a cable-car followed by a pair of drags up to 1975m. The runs, graded green to black, exaggerate the variety of the skiing. You can ski across the lower slopes using the nursery lifts (except at lunchtime), or off-piste from the top station, to the bigger and more interesting Palabione lift system.

The Palabione system attracts most of the weekend crowds. A combination of gondola, chair-lifts and drags (in three stages) reach a top station of 2309m, with the chance of long runs down to the village when snow conditions are good. Most of the skiing is pleasantly undemanding, with occasional narrow and crowded sections through the trees. The long Benedetti black is nowhere more than about 22°. The Palabione lifts share a local pass with the small but smartly equipped Magnolta lifts, not far away but awkward to reach on skis. An efficient gondola climbs to a new restaurant building and sun-terrace at 1945m, with a long, wide and fairly steep run (about 25°) directly underneath the lift to the resort. Above the restaurant a chair-lift serves a short run gentle enough for near-beginners, high and uncrowded.

There is a good indoor swimming pool, a natural ice rink, and a cross-country trail on the other side of the pass from the Alpine skiing area. Tour operators usually organise trips to St Moritz and Livigno. Two hotels conveniently placed for the Palabione lift are the San Lorenzo (✆746185) and the nearby Baitone Belviso (✆746095).

Tourist office ✆(342) 746113. Tx 312126.
Package holidays Hourmont (Ht), Ski Travelaway (Ht).

Can a lone run suffice?

Madesimo Italy 1550m

Good for *Tough runs*
Bad for *Easy road access, short airport transfers, après-ski, not skiing, easy runs*

Of all the remote Italian resorts hidden away near the Swiss border, Madesimo is one of the least accessible, but one of the most tempting for good skiers. Its skiing issues a challenge in the form of one of the most notorious descents in the Alps, the Canalone – not a reference to the pasta-like state of legs at the bottom of the run, but to its dauntingly steep, gun-barrel form. The vital statistics of the ski area (over 1300m vertical) show impressive length as well as pitch. But the reality disappointed us. The skiing is steep enough to be challenging, and the Canalone itself is wild and beautiful as well as a stiff technical challenge. But one run doesn't make a skiing holiday. Adventurous skiers may find the area limited after a few days (it is not very suitable for off-piste skiing), and inexperienced ones may find quite a lot of the skiing unpleasantly difficult. Those most likely to enjoy the skiing are sporty intermediates who have not acquired a taste for the freedom offered by much more extensive ski areas – typically school parties, of which Madesimo attracts quite a few.

Like many Italian resorts, Madesimo comes to life at weekends in fine weather. Italians drive up in large numbers despite (or perhaps because of) the hair-raising access road. On a Friday you may have to wait for a quorum before the cable-car will run; next day you may face a long queue for a drag-lift.

The village claims to be an 18th-century health resort, but does not seem old, and most of the buildings are apartment blocks around a large tower hotel. The feature of Madesimo most consistently picked out as memorable by reporters is the beauty and drama of the coach transfer from Milan – an epic of Wagnerian dimensions. Madesimo is quiet in the evenings, another attraction for school party-leaders.

Motta, a tiny community on the open hillside above Madesimo, is reached only by snow-cat from the larger resort or directly by cable-car from the lower village of Campodolcino. Although very close to Madesimo and its skiing, Motta is not connected with it.

The skiing top 2890m bottom 1550m

Madesimo's skiing is spread along the west-facing flank of mountainside above the village, with a wide network of runs lower down but increasingly rocky and hostile ground higher up around the Pizzo Groppera, accessible only by cable-car and only just skiable. Behind Groppera are two more lifts opening up a friendlier north-east-facing

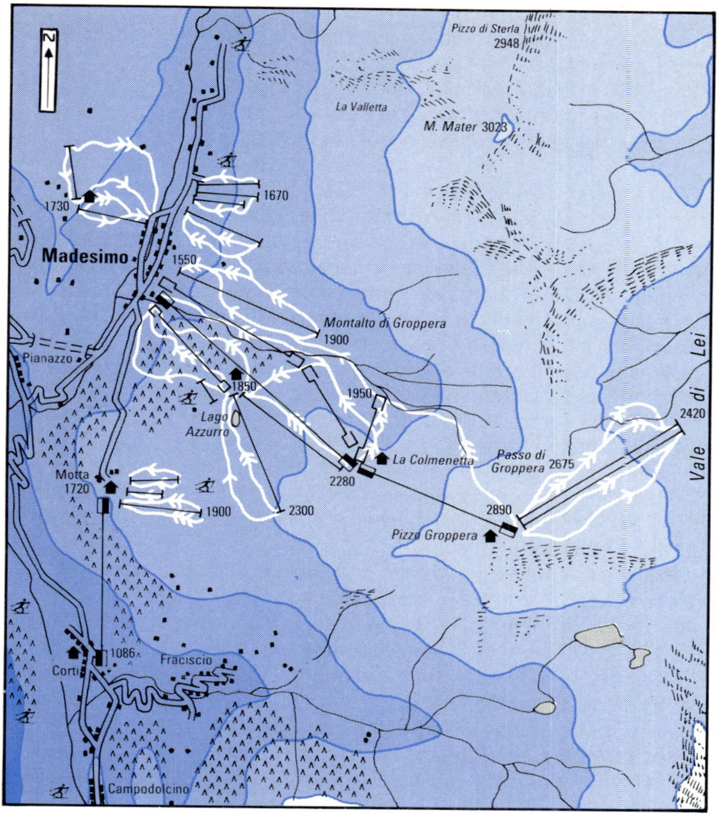

mountainside which keeps snow late into spring. There are two lifts on the western side of Madesimo, behind the Andossi hotel. We have no evidence that these are ever used.

At the north of the village is a series of parallel drags which have some easy skiing but more importantly offer a way for those staying at that end of the resort to get to the main lifts in the village centre. The final and longest drag is to Montalto, and from here you can with luck find a path across into the heart of the skiing – an attractive variety of good long runs, open ground above Lago Azzurro, woodland below it. This area is accessible from the village by the main cable-car to La Colmenetta (2280m) or by a chair-lift beside it; the slopes face west, and ice can make the staple intermediate runs unpleasant, especially where they converge on a short steep slope at the bottom.

From Lago Azzurro you can see across the open hillside to a huge gilt statue of the Madonna, gesticulating as if imploring a snowfall on skiers' behalf, beside Motta's three short drag-lifts. Despite being very close to each other on the same slope, they serve runs varying from very easy (green) to moderately steep (black). Motta has the attraction of morning sunshine, but is quite a plod (an attractive walking or X-C trail) across from Lago Azzurro. The Colmenetta Est drag-lift above Lago Azzurro serves two pleasant, open intermediate runs.

The mid-station of the cable-car stands at the top of steep slopes which provide some tough skiing, especially beside the very steep Colmenetta Nord lift – no piste, though one is marked on the map.

The top cable-car section to Pizzo Groppera climbs over a very steep, very rocky and menacing mountain face which looks unskiable. But there is a very long gully to one side which is almost permanently in the shade. This is the Canalone, a much-feared run which is everything a famous black run should be – long, consistently steep (before the gentle run-out at the end, the run takes only 1.85km to drop 724m) and dramatic. A long funnel it is, but for most of its length not an unpleasantly narrow one, and in good snow conditions it is negotiable by many less-than-expert skiers. Being the only way down the mountain except by lift, lots of brave intermediates ski it.

The reverse of Groppera is a beautiful open side of the Valle di Lei, which drops steeply down to a reservoir. The drag-lifts give just under 500m vertical of varied intermediate pistes and off-piste skiing between them. Snow conditions are nearly always more pleasant on this side, but it can be extremely cold.

Mountain restaurants are few and not very attractive, except for the refuge at Lago Azzurro, a good sunbathing spot which gets very crowded when the resort is busy. As well as the main restaurants there are a couple of drinks stands in Valle di Lei and at Piano dei Larici.

There are serious weekend **queues** for the top section of the cable-car giving access to the Valle di Lei and the Canalone, and for the Valle di Lei drag-lifts. During the week the cable-car may run infrequently, and it is prone to closure because of wind. On a recent January visit, we found both stages of the cable-car closed on a fine day, for no reason other than the emptiness of the resort.

The resort

Madesimo is set high up in a narrow valley. The surrounding slopes are wooded but the overall impression of the landscape is not the most welcoming, in winter at least. The village stretches thinly a long way (over half a mile) up the dead-end valley from the centre. Although there are not large numbers of British skiers in Madesimo, at off-peak times there are few others, so the impression is of a larger number. Several reporters commented favourably on the helpfulness, quality and cheapness of ski shops, both for hirers and purchasers.

Because of the arrangement of the lifts, having **accommodation** at the top end of the village isn't too much of an annoyance for skiing (and it is a great advantage for beginners), but it is inconvenient in the evening. Of the central hotels near the main cable-car and chair-lift departure stations, La Meridiana (✆53160) is an exception to the norm in being friendly, cheerful, and obviously decorated and looked after with pride; some bedrooms are small. The Cascata et Cristallo

Madesimo facts

Lift payment

Passes Area pass covers all lifts including Motta. Day and afternoon passes available.
Cost 6-day pass L120,000. 20% off in low season.
Beginners Coupons.
Children No reduction.

Ski school

Classes 2hr mornings only.
Children No kindergartens.
Cost 6 days L75,000. Private lessons L25,000/hr.

Cross-country skiing

Trails 5km at north end of village. 3.5km at Lago Azzurro/Motta.

Not skiing

Facilities Natural ice rink (skating until 11pm), ski bobbing, bowling, 15km of paths, cinema, swimming/ sauna/ solarium, toboggan run.

Medical facilities

In resort Chemist, doctor and fracture clinic.
Hospital Chiavenna (20km).
Dentist Chiavenna (20km).

Getting there

Airport Milan; transfer at least 4hr.
Railway Chiavenna (20km); daily buses to resort.
Road Via Chamonix/Milan. The last 20km are difficult; chains often required.

Available holidays

Resort beds 700 in hotels, 1,500 in apartments.
Package holidays Global (Ht Sc), Schoolplan (Ht)
Further information
Tourist office ✆(343) 53015. Tx 312216.

Prices are approximate.

(✆53108) is a larger, convenient alternative with its own pool and sauna. The big Grand Hotel Torre (✆53234) is no longer modern or luxurious but is still spacious – almost eerily so out of season.

There are several good cafés for **après-ski** teas. Later on, get-togethers organised by tour operators offer the best chance of a lively evening – snow-cat rides, tobogganing, fondue and sangria evenings are usually offered. The discothèques are quiet during the week despite free entrance. Outstanding among the restaurants are the expensive Osteria Vega, over two centuries old and looking it; and the Dogana Vecchia, also old and attractive but a long way from the centre. The ice rink is open in the evening.

Madesimo is not good either for **cross-country** or **non-skiers**. The toboggan run, supposedly open morning, afternoon and evening, was not in evidence when we visited. Tour operators usually offer excursions to St Moritz (a long day-trip) and to delightful Chiavenna.

The central **nursery slope** by the Meridiana is small and the larger ones at the northern end of the village are used for access to the ski area. Madesimo is not ideal terrain for near-beginners progressing from nursery to piste.

We have mixed reports of the **ski school**, but at least some good ones, with special commendation for detailed after-hours video analysis sessions: 'useful and amusing, if deflating'.

Paradise reinvented

Schladming Austria 750m

Good for *Nursery slopes, Alpine charm, easy runs, cross-country skiing, short airport transfers, easy road access, rail access*
Bad for *Skiing convenience, late holidays, resort-level snow, tough runs*

Linked resorts: Rohrmoos, Haus in Ennstal

This world-famous ski racing town became familiar to Sunday afternoon television viewers before it started attracting British holiday skiers – a process which is sure to gather momentum, to judge by the enthusiasm of our reporters, though for the moment it remains popular mainly with Viennese and other Austrian skiers. Schladming is the furthest east of Austria's major skiing centres and the only one in Styria, and differs from the Tyrolean norm in giving the attractive impression of being an ordinary old town with a life of its own, independent of tourism; as well as wooden chalets with painted shutters there are sober old stone buildings, including a splendid medieval town gate.

The town lies in the middle of a broad valley on a main east-west road and rail route. To the north are the spectacular rocky peaks of the Dachstein, the highest in the eastern Alps, with summer skiing (Alpine and cross-country) on its very gentle expanse of glacier. But Schladming's skiing, forming the heart of what is called the Skiparadies, is on the gentler wooded foothills of the Tauern mountains to the south of the Ennstal – long, broad runs through woods from around 2000m to the valley at 750m. It offers a great deal of intermediate skiing, but it is split into four separate areas and there is a pronounced lack of variety in their many blue and red runs.

There are further substantial areas of skiing within easy reach by car at high, purpose-built Obertauern and the resorts in the valleys around Wagrain (see separate chapters), all of it covered by what is claimed to be the most extensive lift-pass in Austria.

Rohrmoos is a straggling community with no village focus, but a near-ideal location for beginners, on an extensive, gentle open shelf, elevated slightly above Schladming, at the foot of one of the main skiing areas; it is the slopes around Rohrmoos to which our 'Good for easy runs' verdict refers. Haus is a quiet rustic village offering direct access to the most easterly major ski area.

The skiing top 2105m bottom 750m

The four mountains lined up on the south side of the valley are for practical skiing purposes quite separate – the two mountains in the centre of the range and closest to Schladming, Planai and Hochwurzen, are linked awkwardly by chair-lift and not at all by piste, and the lifts which one day will link Planai to Hauser Kaibling and Hochwurzen to Reiteralm are not imminent. Most of the slopes face north and provide good, long red runs which are difficult to distinguish from one another; there is also some added skiing on the east- and west-facing flanks, at higher altitudes. The ski-bus service (including routes going up into the skiing) is essential for adventurous skiers without cars; it is covered by the lift pass.

For skiers based in Schladming, the closest skiing is on the **Planai**, served by a recently improved two-stage gondola to 1894m from the edge of town, a manageable walk from the centre. The middle station (Kessleralm) of the gondola can be reached by car; a chair-lift runs in parallel with the top half of the gondola. Beyond the top station of the gondola are open east-facing slopes served by drag-lifts – good, sustained runs, with moguls in places, but not particularly steep. There are snow-making machines on the lower slopes of the Planai, but all the same these slopes are often icy as well as steep.

The **Hauser Kaibling** (2115m) lies above the village of Haus to the east. The main access is by means of a gondola from a huge car-park beside the main road (a long walk east of the village) to a big congregation area half-way up the mountain, also reachable by bus. Motorists can drive up to the eastern edge of the system (Knappl, 1100m) to avoid queues. Beyond the gondola, a series of three drags is necessary to reach the minor peak of Krummholzhütte, also reachable directly by a small and inefficient cable-car from the top of Haus. A gentle path leads from here along the side of the mountain to the Gipfellift, serving a black slope of no particular difficulty unless it is icy, and on to a remote area of gentle skiing at Kaiblingalm, with two short drags, no crowds, excellent snow and a friendly restaurant. The snag is the very long walk back. The Gipfellift also gives access to a short, well marked and very popular off-piste route down to the lifts at the eastern extremity of the system – slightly awkward at the top and quite steep, with moguls, but not terrifying.

Hochwurzen offers several long red runs between 1100m and 1850m served by two steep drags and a chair-lift, and an extensive network of easy and beginners' slopes around the village of Rohrmoos – and below it down to the western edge of Schladming. There is a long toboggan run from top to bottom of the Hochwurzen, on a hairpin road alternately reserved for buses and toboggans.

The westernmost of the four local ski areas is the **Reiteralm**, with skiing from 1860m to the banks of the Enns over 1000m below. Access is either by gondola from the edge of Gleiming village or by chair-lift from an isolated riverside lift station across the valley from the hamlet of Pichl, more convenient for motorists. The skiing is spread over a wide area, with yet more long woodland trails as on the other mountains, and more of red than of blue difficulty.

Mountain restaurants are adequate in number and generally attractive. Among the most attractive are those at Mitterhausalm, at the foot of the Märchenweise lift and Onkel Willi's Hütte on Planai; Krummholzhütte on Reiteralm; and Eiskarhütte on Reiteralm.

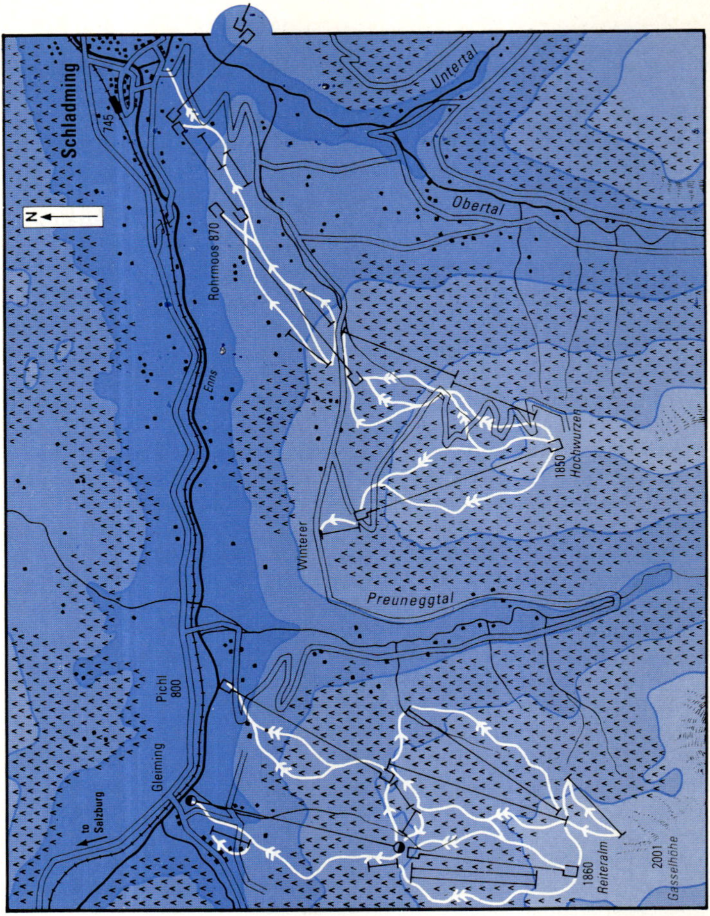

The resort

Schladming is a fairly compact town, with most of its shops and a good many of its hotels, restaurants and bars concentrated around the attractive, broad main street, the Hauptplatz.

Most of the **accommodation** is in private rooms, guest-houses and hotels. The most desirable place to stay, about the most convenient and among the most expensive, is the charming Alte Post (✆22571) in the Hauptplatz. The Sporthotel (✆23240) is recommended by a reporter as 'everything one could ask for on an activity holiday': as well as comprehensive sports facilities of its own, it is next to the swimming pool and ice rink. At the western end of the centre is the jolly, more modest Gasthof Zum Zottenhuber (✆22468); and for lower prices still a

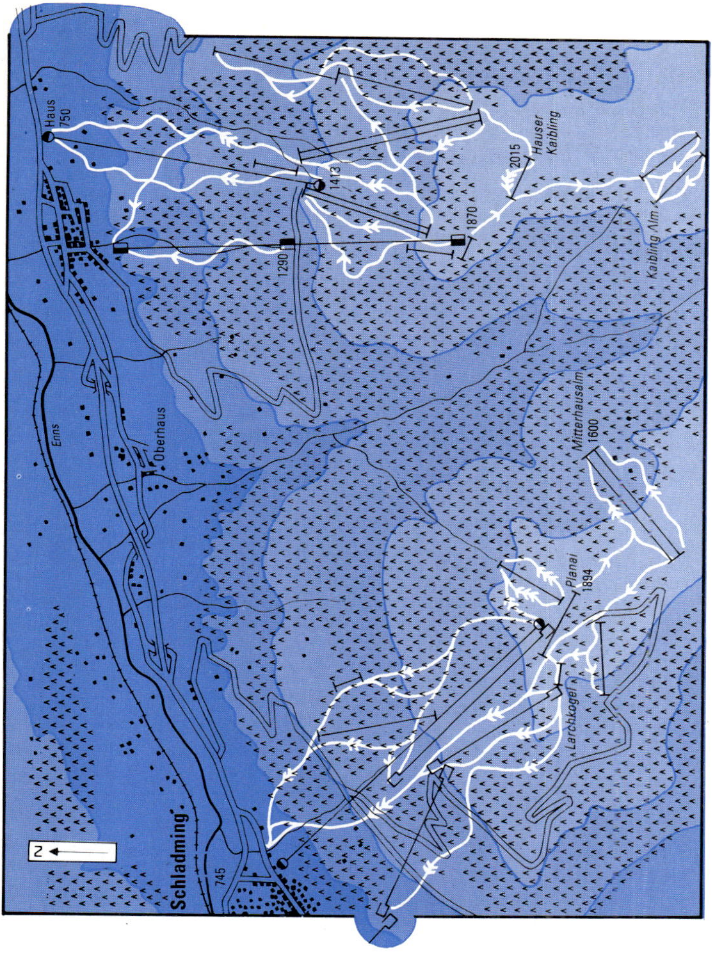

reporter recommends the simple Mayer (✆22128), just off the western end of the Hauptplatz.

Reports suggest that the town is better for tea-time and early evening **après-ski** than in the small hours, although there are one or two discothèques, and live music in some of the bars.

The good sports facilities, easy access to mountain restaurants, amiable town and good excursion possibilities (eg by train to Salzburg) make Schladming a sound bet for **non-skiers**. And for **cross-country** skiers there is enormous scope.

Rohrmoos consists almost entirely of **nursery slopes**, and beginners should not consider starting elsewhere. As well as the conventional **ski schools** (of which there are several) there is a group of Ski Guides offering Ski Safaris for good skiers.

Schladming facts

Lift payment

Passes Skiparadies pass covers all Schladming lifts and buses; available for any period from half-day upwards. Local day and half-day passes available; also Top Tauern Skischeck pass for 6 or 7 days covering many areas.
Cost 6-day pass AS1,250. 12.5% off in low season.
Beginners Lift pass.
Children 35% off, under 15; further reduction when accompanied by a parent buying a full-rate pass.

Ski school

There are separate schools at Schladming, Rohrmoos, Pichl and Haus. Details are for Schladming.
Classes 2hr morning and afternoon.
Cost 5 days AS880. Private lessons AS350/hr.
Children Classes as adults. Ski kindergarten, age 4 up, 5 days with meals AS1,300.
Special courses Racing, ski-touring, powder skiing.

Medical facilities

In resort Hospital, doctors, chemists, dentists.

Cross-country skiing

Trails Long trails down the valley to Pruggern and beyond. Higher, more interesting trails from Rohrmoos: 4km easy, 6km medium, 17km medium up Obertal, 32km medium up Untertal.

Not skiing

Facilities Swimming, sauna, toboggan run (road up Hochwurzen), tennis, curling (Schladming, Rohrmoos and Haus), skating (natural rinks, Rohrmoos and Haus), bowling.

Getting there

Airport Salzburg; transfer about 1½hr.
Railway Main-line station in resort.
Road Via Munich and Salzburg; chains normally unnecessary.

Available holidays

Resort beds 3,300, mainly in hotels and pensions.
Package holidays Crystal (Ht), Intasun (Ht Sc), Neilson (Ht), Schoolplan (Ht), Schools Abroad (Ht), Skiscope (Ht), SkiSet (Ht), Thomson (Ht), Vacations (Ht Cl)

Further information

Tourist office ✆(3687) 22268. Tx 38276.

Rohrmoos 870m

This diffuse satellite village has easy skiing to and from many hotel doorsteps. Among its many good-value hotels and guest-houses are the Austria (✆61444), well placed at the point where the lower gentle slopes of Rohrmoos meet the steeper slopes of Hochwurzen proper. The smarter Schwaigerhof (✆61426) has a good position on the edge of the pistes, and is one of the few places with a pool. We have favourable reports of the ski school and kindergarten.

Tourist office ✆(3867) 61147. **Package holidays** Included in Schladming list.

Haus in Ennstal 750m

Haus is a quiet village with its farming origins still in evidence – though it has quite a lot of holiday accommodation. There are a couple of shops and cafés, and a gentle, open nursery slope between the village and the gondola station. The smart and relatively pricey Hauser Kaibling (✆2378) is one of the two or three hotels with a pool. The Gasthof Reiter (✆2225) is a fine old chalet, much cheaper. Steger's Gasthof 'Zur Herrschaftstaverne' is brightly lit and modern, but in traditional style.

Tourist office ✆(3686) 2234. Tx 038254. **Package holidays** Intasun (Ht).

Take the high road

Obertauern Austria 1740m

Good for *Resort-level snow, sunny slopes, skiing convenience, nursery slopes, off-piste skiing*
Bad for *Not skiing, Alpine charm, après-ski, easy road access*

Until quite recently, the Niedere Tauern – the mountains at the eastern extremity of the Austrian Alps that separate Villach and Klagenfurt in southerly Carinthia from northerly Salzburg – were all but impassable in winter. Now, a motorway tunnel goes through the mountains, and the only point in the chain where they drop below 2000m is no longer an important pass. Obertauern, built right on the summit of the pass, is not a mightily important ski resort either, at least for British skiers. But it is interesting, and may become more popular as its unusual blend of qualities become more widely known. Obertauern is a high, modern village which exists almost entirely for skiing, and which has densely mechanised slopes allowing skiers to do complete circuits, in either direction, of the mountain bowl surrounding the village. Such a thing may be common in France, but not in Austria.

Although the village is high, the skiing does not go much more than 500m higher – so although it is an excellent February resort it may not be a very satisfactory April one. Our map makes it evident that the area is not very extensive, either. But there is more to it than there is to most ski areas of such a size – partly because it is quite steep and heavily mogulled (at least around the rim of the bowl), partly because it crams in a lot of lifts and partly because the terrain is interestingly varied. For reasons we explain below, our map shows all the runs as easy ones. They are not: the skiing suits all grades of skier, except those 'experts' who prefer steep moguls to deep snow.

The resort has some non-skiing sports facilities, and is not as hideous as many French purpose-built resorts. But it is no beauty, and the setting is bleak and many lifts close when the weather turns bad. Après-ski, as in most such remote places, is limited.

A car is not of much use in Obertauern, and although the access road is a good one it often requires chains. But taking a car opens up the possibility of making wide use of the Top Tauern Skischeck lift pass, giving access to Schladming and many other resorts.

The skiing top 2313m bottom 1640m

Obertauern's piste map places heavy emphasis on the lifts and runs which constitute the clockwise and anticlockwise circuits of its skiing, marking them prominently in red and green respectively. This convention, coupled with an almost vertically downward view of the resort, makes the map admirably effective. But neither on the map nor

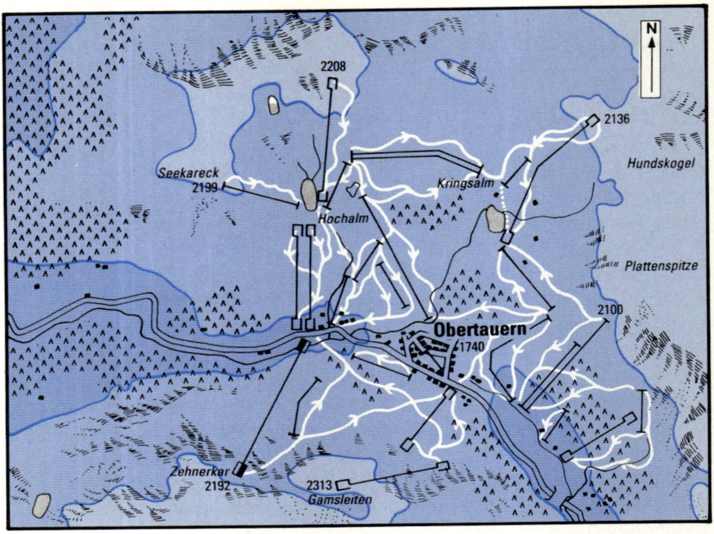

generally on the ground are the pistes graded for difficulty. Since our own piste maps follow resort gradings, and since our piste-grading arrows indicate not only the difficulty of pistes but also their downward direction, we have marked all the runs in the area with a single arrow. *Do not* take this to mean that all the runs are easy. If you are not confident of your ability to ski moderately steep pistes, explore the skiing only with an instructor or with skiers who already know it.

The skiing circuit is concentrated on the north side of the resort, spread around a broad, undulating, largely treeless bowl ringed by rocky peaks. Around the bowl there are four main lifts going up to points near the rim. Two of them go up to about 2200m from more-or-less the same point at Hochalm (1940m) – the Seekareck drag-lift over a steep east-facing slope, and the Panorama chair-lift over a more varied south-facing one. As the altitudes suggest, neither run is long, but both are challenging and entertaining, often with moguls. The chair also gives access to a longer, gentler run down to Kringsalm.

The Hundskogel chair-lift serves a slightly longer slope offering a choice of routes down – a moderately steep piste away from the lift on the north side, and off-piste routes more directly down on its south side. The Plattenkar drag-lift goes up from a point just below the village, to 2100m under the Plattenspitze, giving a good intermediate run of 400m vertical. Beyond this drag, a little further down the pass, the Schaidberg double chair-lift serves the steepest run on the north side of the resort, but also gives access to a short drag gentle enough to be used as a high-altitude nursery. An easy roundabout way back to the valley is apparently available.

Supplementing these lifts going up to the outer edges of the skiing are lifts and pistes linking one with another. These offer less experienced skiers plenty of scope, and a clockwise circuit of this northern part of the area need not involve any of the higher, more difficult runs. But the pistes of most interest to timid skiers are the easy, open runs across the middle of the bowl, served by drag-lifts including the long Zentral lift from just below the village.

On the south side of the resort, the mountains rise more immediately, keeping the village in shade for much of the day in mid-winter. The major lift is the Zehnerkar cable-car, climbing over 500m from the western extremity of the village and giving access to a long, moderately testing run branching to various points along the pass. The lower Gamsleiten chair-lift serves a straightforward piste across the mountainside to the foot of the cable-car, which is part of the clockwise circuit, and more challenging ones back to the base. The upper Gamsleiten chair-lift serves an unpisted run from the high point of the system. When we visited there was a sign in German at the foot of the lift warning that you are not allowed to ride down on the chair; what it did not explain was the reason you might want to – which is that the only run is seriously steep, particularly in the middle section.

Mountain restaurants are more than adequate for an area where there is such easy access to village restaurants, though one widely experienced reporter felt prices were high. The Seekarhaus at Kringsalm is particularly cosy, with waitress service.

Recent reports say that **queues** are minimal – even in high season – with the exception of the Zehnerkar cable-car, which can be bad all day and forms a blockage on the anticlockwise circuit. Even at off-peak times the short Seekar button lift just below Kringsalm restricts the clockwise flow.

The resort

The main part of the resort is spread along the road gently dropping down to the east from the summit of the pass, where there is a big open parking area. There are buildings dotted along lanes off the road on the north side, and there is a distinct cluster where these lanes rejoin the road on the west side of the village. There is a much smaller community some way down the road to the west, at the foot of the twin chair-lifts to Hochalm and the cable-car to Zehnerkar. A lot of the buildings are in chalet style, but without the conviction the Austrians normally manage in lower, more comforting settings. The result is a village which is neither offensive nor charming to the eye.

Nearly all the **accommodation** is in hotels and guest-houses, few of them cheap by Austrian standards. Location is not critical, but a good compromise position for skiing both sides of the road, for swimming and tennis and for evening atmosphere is close to the foot of the Gamsleiten chair-lift. Closest of all is the very smart Gamsleiten (✆286). Across and up the road a little, the neat Gasthof Sailer (✆328) is simpler and cheaper. Given a car, our inclination would be to stay 6km down the pass in Tweng, at the cheap and cheerful Gasthof zur Post (✆(6471)225).

Our brief low-season inspection visit gave us precious little evidence about the **après-ski** life of Obertauern, but it seems safe to say that what little there is will pivot around hotel bars, of which over 15 claim to offer music and dancing.

The **non-skiing** sports facilities are good, provided you want to swim or play tennis: more traditional winter sports are not in evidence. The **cross-country** skiing trail in the heart of the sunny bowl covers quite interesting terrain but lacks scenic variety. The very long trails of the Tauernloipe can be reached from Untertauern, 9km down the road.

The **nursery slopes** are excellent. There is a short, gentle drag-lift in the heart of the village, just north of the road, and another rather longer one on the lower slopes at the east end. There is an even longer one parallel to and just south of the road, though it is shaded for much of the day in mid-winter. The high Gamskarlift, at the top of the steep Schaidberg chair-lift, is anything but shaded.

The **ski school** arrangements are as different from the Austrian norm as the resort itself, with three apparently competing schools in different locations. We lack reports on this stimulating set-up.

Obertauern facts

Lift payment

Passes One pass covers all lifts; available for any period from half-day, including 1½ and 2½ days. Top Tauern Skischeck pass also available covering many other areas.
Cost 6-day pass AS1,215; 14% off in low season.
Beginners Points cards.
Children 35% off, under 14.

Ski school

There are three schools: Skischule Seekarhaus, Skischule Krallinger Obertauern Süd, and Ski ON – Skischule Obertauern Nord. Their prices are similar.
Classes 2hr morning and afternoon.
Cost 6 days AS950. Private lessons AS380/hr.
Children Ski kindergarten, age 4 up, 6 days with lunch AS1,450.
Special courses Powder, moguls, racing, acrobatics, ski-touring.

Cross-country skiing

Trails 6km loop from top of village into downhill ski area.

Not skiing

Facilities Swimming, tennis.

Medical facilities

In resort Fracture clinic, doctor, dentist, chemist.

Getting there

Airport Salzburg; transfer about 1½hr.
Railway Radstadt (20km); connecting buses and taxis. Also direct bus service from Salzburg station.
Road Via Munich and Salzburg; chains often needed.

Available holidays

Resort beds 4,800, mainly in hotels and *pensions*.
Package holidays Austro Tours (Ht), Thomson (Ht), Vacations (Ht)

Further information

Tourist office ✆(6456) 252. Tx 67560.

Inoffensive Pongau

Wagrain Austria 900m

Good for *Big ski area, easy runs, cross-country skiing, short airport transfers, easy road access*
Bad for *Tough runs, late holidays, resort-level snow, not skiing, freedom from cars*

Linked resorts: St Johann im Pongau, Flachau

The success of the French resorts operating under the Trois Vallées banner has not gone unnoticed elsewhere, and any ski area which can claim to offer linked skiing in three or even four adjacent valleys is now likely to want to climb aboard their bandwagon. Each of the major Alpine countries now offers such a ski area, and Austria's is the *3-Täler-Skischaukelland* in the Pongau region, south of Salzburg. The skiing is much more modest in scale, and is practically devoid of challenge for the expert, but by Austrian standards is undeniably an extensive system. Wagrain is the Méribel of the area, ideally placed for full exploration of the skiing. It is a busy village, not created for skiing and not exceptionally charming in Austrian terms, but pleasant and adequately convenient. St Johann is more widely sold by UK tour operators, but is linked in to the western extremity of the skiing only via its satellite of Alpendorf. Flachau at the eastern end is scarcely sold at all in Britain, but has a great deal of holiday accommodation and is in some ways the most attractive of the three resorts.

The skiing

Wagrain sits in a valley with ski-lifts rising on either side. Those to the east approach the ridge of Griessenkareck, on the shoulder of the Saukarkopf; on the far side of it is Flachau and its suburbs, with a range of lifts on the same mountains but none on the other side of its valley. To the west of Wagrain is a slightly lower but more complicated mountain, the Sonntagskogl, which is fragmented at altitude by two mini-valleys. There are lifts and pistes on the St Johann side of this mountain, but they stop short of the town at the slightly elevated community of Alpendorf. St Johann has some further, separate skiing of its own on the Hahnbaum, closer to the town.

The lifts for **Griessenkareck** start from a spacious suburb of Wagrain (Kirchboden), a few hundred metres east of the centre. The first stage is a chair-lift; the second is a 12-place gondola which gives access to the skiing over on the Flachau side. From the top you can also ski a little bowl, provided with two drags, beneath the Saukarkopf; the drag towards the Saukarkopf summit serves a short, moderately challenging north-facing slope, graded black.

All the runs from Griessenkareck are broad swathes through the woods, of intermediate difficulty. The reds are not difficult, and the blues are not the simplest of blues, but the gradings do separate the more difficult from the less so. There are no really easy ways down to Flachau or to its outposts of Moadörfl and Reitdorf, but there are chair-lifts which we presume may be ridden down – and apparently a new gondola is planned.

The **Sonntagskogl** side of Wagrain's skiing is reached by an efficient six-seater gondola starting from a roadside station a little way out of the town and going up to Grafenberg. Most of the easy slope underneath it can be skied repeatedly by using chair- and drag-lifts rather than returning to the village. Stretching westward from Grafenberg is an attractive, open landscape of minor ridges and troughs with lifts making the necessary skiing links and serving additional north-facing runs on the Sonntagskogl. There is little here to challenge the good skier, but the skiing is not trivially easy on the runs down to Sonnalm, or on the attractive run from Hirschkogel down to the bottom of an isolated drag-lift. The run down to Alpendorf (above St Johann) is graded red, but it is not an intimidating run and requires only a moderate amount of confidence. From Alpendorf a new lift system, comprising a six-seater gondola and a four-seater chair-lift, runs up to the Strass Alm below

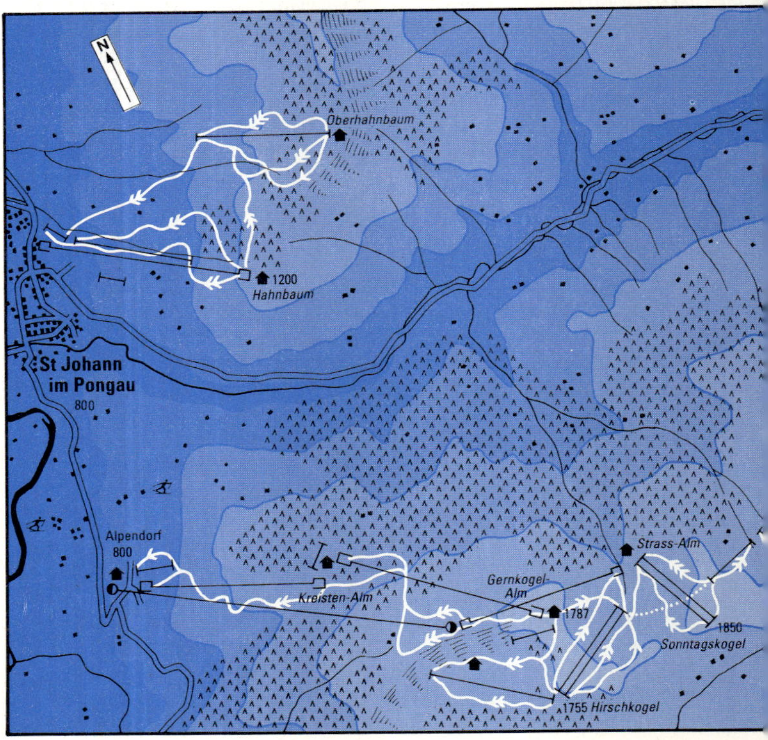

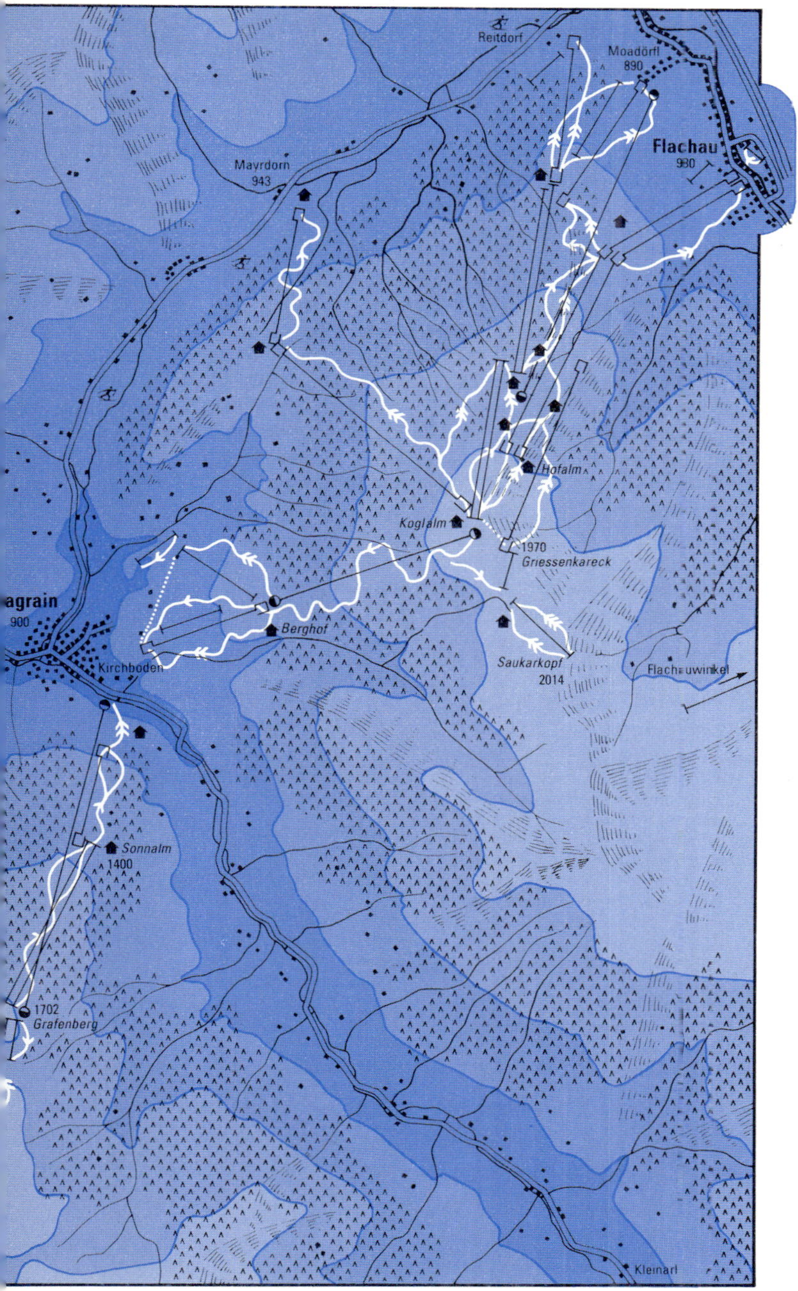
Reitdorf
Moadörfl
890
Flachau
930
Mayrdorn
943
Hofalm
Koglalm
1970
Griessenkareck
Berghof
Saukarkopf
2014
Flachauwinkel
agrain
900
Kirchboden
Sonnalm
1400
1702
Grafenberg
Kleinarl

Sonntagskogl, duplicating the existing chairs toward Gernkogel-Alm.

There are plenty of **mountain restaurants** all over the ski area except in the middle of the Sonntagskogl; the easy slopes above Flachau are peppered with places.

High-season lift **queues** have been serious at times, though there are several major new lifts this year. (The piste map wrongly showed some of these lifts last year.)

The resort

Wagrain is a tight, compact and busy little place with a fair amount of traffic on the minor road from St Johann to Flachau and Radstadt running through on the north side. Fortunately the village has been able to develop away from this road, along the dead-end road up the valley to Kleinarl, and into the fields at the foot of the Griessenkareck lifts and pistes. Location within the resort is not critical; there is a free ski-bus linking the centre and the lift station every 20 minutes.

Most of the **accommodation** is in modern, chalet-style hotels, *pensions* and private houses. In the centre, the Wagrainerhof (✆8204) is the smartest place, and not very expensive. Simpler and more atmospheric places include the Gasthof Grafenwirt (✆8230) and the modest Gasthof Steinwirt (✆8209). The simple Gasthof Kalkofen (✆8206) is well placed at the foot of the Griessenkareck lifts.

Wagrain facts

Lift payment

Passes Single pass covers all lifts in Wagrain, St Johann and Flachau; available for any period from half-day. Top Tauern Skischeck also available, covering Obertauern, Schladming and many other ski areas as well as this one.
Cost 6-day pass AS1,105; 15% reduction in low season.
Beginners Points cards.
Children 40% off, under 15.

Ski school

Classes 2½hr morning and 2hr afternoon.
Cost 5 days AS930. Private lessons AS380/hr.
Children Ski kindergarten, age 4 up, 9.30–3.30, price as ski school plus AS85 for lunch.
Special courses On request.

Cross-country skiing

Trails The Tauernloipe network amounts to 120km of trails.

Not skiing

Facilities Curling, toboggan run, sleigh rides, air-gun shooting gallery, swimming (in hotel).

Medical facilities

In resort Doctor, chemist, dentist.
Hospital Schwarzach (15km).

Getting there

Airport Salzburg; transfer about 1½hr.
Railway St Johann (8km).
Road Via Munich and Salzburg; chains sometimes needed.

Available holidays

Resort beds 3,800, mainly in hotels, *pensions* and private rooms.
Package holidays Thomson (Ht).

Further information

Tourist office ✆(6413) 8265. Tx 67563.

Après-ski is mainly traditional, with musical events organised by the resort, and evenings part-way up the mountain at the Edelweiss hut followed by a toboggan ride home. There is dancing in at least one of the central hotels (the Wagrainerhof).

Wagrain is rather too small to be a particularly good place for **non-skiers**, though there are limited sports facilities and other diversions; but excursions to Salzburg are easily arranged. It is a much better resort for **cross-country** skiers; a trail starting at Kirchboden links with the very extensive Tauernloipe network.

Flachau 930m

Flachau is very much a holiday village – a spacious, relaxed place with chalets and apartment blocks spreading along the valley and up the slopes away from its somewhat nebulous centre. There are countless comfortable, modern and quite big chalet-style hotels and guest-houses. The central Reslwirt (✆216) is mid-priced, and partly old and traditional in style. Flachau is well placed for the long, widely varying Tauernloipe cross-country trails, and there are walks, toboggan runs and sleigh rides. Après-ski activity includes traditional musical events and three or four discos in hotels. The nursery slopes are excellent: a very gentle area in the village, separated from the main pistes (its only drawback that it is shaded early in the morning in mid-winter) and more extensive and slightly steeper areas at the foot of the main slopes.

Tourist office ✆(6457) 214. Tx 67698.

St Johann im Pongau 800m

St Johann is a town rather than a village, with a thriving existence independent of skiing. The Hahnbaum skiing starts close to the centre: it has a nursery lift at the bottom, but there is a much better nursery area – gentler, more spacious and with better snow – part-way up the mountain (reached by bus). The nursery slope at Alpendorf is uncomfortably steep for beginners. Alpendorf is nothing more than a hillside collection of chalet-style hotels and guest-houses, of which the Sonnhof (✆6171) is ideally placed between the nursery drag and the Gernkogel chair-lift. The Gasthof Oberforsthof (same owner and same ✆) just across the road has a bit more traditional style about it, and a modest pool. There are short cross-country trails near Alpendorf and down in the valley bottom. The resort as a whole offers cleared walks, tennis and squash, skating and curling on natural rinks, toboggan runs and sleigh rides. There are traditional après-ski events (some of them in Alpendorf), and half a dozen discos.

Tourist office ✆(6412) 6036. Tx 67502.
Package holidays Global (Ht), Ski Lovers (Ht), Snow World (Ht), Tentrek (Ht Hm).

No rest cure

Badgastein Austria 1080m

Good for *Big ski area, tough runs, après-ski, not skiing, rail access*
Bad for *Skiing convenience, easy runs, lift queues, Alpine charm, nursery slopes, resort-level snow, freedom from cars*

Linked resort: Bad Hofgastein
Separate resorts: Dorfgastein, Sportgastein

Badgastein is one of three widely differing resorts in a long and beautiful valley in western Salzburgerland. Dorfgastein, just inside the narrow gateway into the valley, is an unspoilt rustic village near a lot of pleasant intermediate skiing. A few miles upstream, Bad Hofgastein is a spacious and comfortable spa without any grandiose pretensions. Badgastein itself is one of the most ponderously grand of spa resorts, but in a remarkable setting – stacked on a steep hillside at the head of the valley. The river cascades down between the hotel blocks at the heart of the resort, which is still rather sedate and formal, though now more dependent on the conference than the *Kur* business. A second Badgastein has grown up for skiers – a sprawl of hotels and apartment buildings beside the railway station and main ski-lift departure, and on up the valley from there. It is not at all beautiful, but practical and increasingly full of young people, and lively in the evenings.

Lift links between Badgastein and Bad Hofgastein have created one of Austria's major ski areas – big and varied, with very long and mainly challenging runs from top to bottom. Although a few blue trails wind across the slopes, these mountains are in general best suited to experienced skiers. Problems are not confined to the pistes – some of the drag-lifts are intimidating, too.

In Badgastein, parking space is inadequate and driving is hazardous, but having a car is very useful for making the most of the skiing and après-ski. It is quite a long drive to any other major resorts.

The skiing top 2686m bottom 850m

In addition to the main ski area on the western side of the valley between Badgastein and Bad Hofgastein, there are three other separate areas, all less crowded and in different ways very attractive. The Graukogel slopes above Badgastein are few, but long and satisfying for good skiers. Sportgastein has some good runs in a very different style: high altitude, open ground and no resort development. And the friendly skiing shared by Dorfgastein and Grossard adds greatly to the area's appeal for leisurely skiers.

From a milling concourse of car park, ski school meeting-place and nursery area squeezed between the steep mountain and Badgastein station, a two-stage gondola climbs to the **Stubnerkogel** (2246m), a tangled junction of lift arrivals at the top of a long ridge. The alternative chair and drag-lift route, which was always slow and steep, has even less to commend it now that the gondola has been upgraded to a six-seater. The east-facing runs to Badgastein provide good, tough skiing with a mixture of open ground above half-way and woods below – mostly graded red, but difficult when conditions are poor. There is a blue run winding down the mountain, but this too is often icy and crowded. The open top half of the slope gives plenty of opportunity for skiing off-piste between the runs. The west-facing back side of the ridge is broken ground with some impressive rocky drops and gullies, and skiing options down to Jungeralm are limited; the piste tends to be crowded. There is more space and some good off-piste skiing beside the steep Hochleiten drag-lift. The north-facing runs down into the Angertal provide some of the best skiing in the region. From Jungeralm a long, undulating black run drops directly through the woods. The alternatives are to traverse to and fro on the 'Skiweg' from Jungeralm, or take the famous, much more satisfying red run from Stubnerkogel.

From the Angertal, a chair and drag-lift go up over south-facing slopes to the **Schlossalm** skiing – also accessible by funicular railway starting a long walk from Bad Hofgastein. This is a very spacious basin above the tree-line providing a lot of similar intermediate runs, not very long and mostly easier than on the Stubnerkogel. For good skiers the main interest is the beautiful long run round the back of the mountains, reached either from Hohe Scharte (2300m) or from Kleine Scharte (2050m). In good snow the run goes to the bottom of the railway, an 8km descent of 1450m vertical. There are no very easy ways down to the bottom of the mountain, and snow conditions are often poor on the lower slopes and on the south-facing runs down into the Angertal.

The thickly wooded, north-west-facing slopes of **Graukogel** are served by a slow two-stage chair-lift. This is the local racing hill and, apart from one easy run round the top of the mountain, all the trails are challenging variants of the direct descent under the chairs of 900m vertical. Not all of them are prepared. Snow conditions are as good as you'll find locally, and the surroundings and views are delightful.

Sportgastein is a valuable asset if snow elsewhere in the valley is poor – when (unusually) it can become crowded. The high, narrow, dead-end valley is empty and undeveloped save for a couple of restaurants. A chair and then a drag go up from 1600m to Kreuzkogel at 2686m, most of it above the trees and facing west. The top half may be exposed and cold, but usually has good snow on its gentle runs. The great attraction to good skiers is the long north-facing off-piste run over the back down to the tollgate above Böckstein (where you catch a bus). The slopes beneath the chair-lift are steeper, with some good off-piste skiing among the thinly scattered trees as well as a stiff red run.

A long and very slow chain of lifts (chairs and drags) links the skiing of **Dorfgastein** and **Grossarl** via two neighbouring hilltops, Fulseck (2033m) and another Kreuzkogel, which give runs of over 1000m vertical. Although most of the runs are classed red, this is basically friendly terrain and few of the runs are steep, except the black direct descent to Dorfgastein. The Grossarl side is mostly gentle with long,

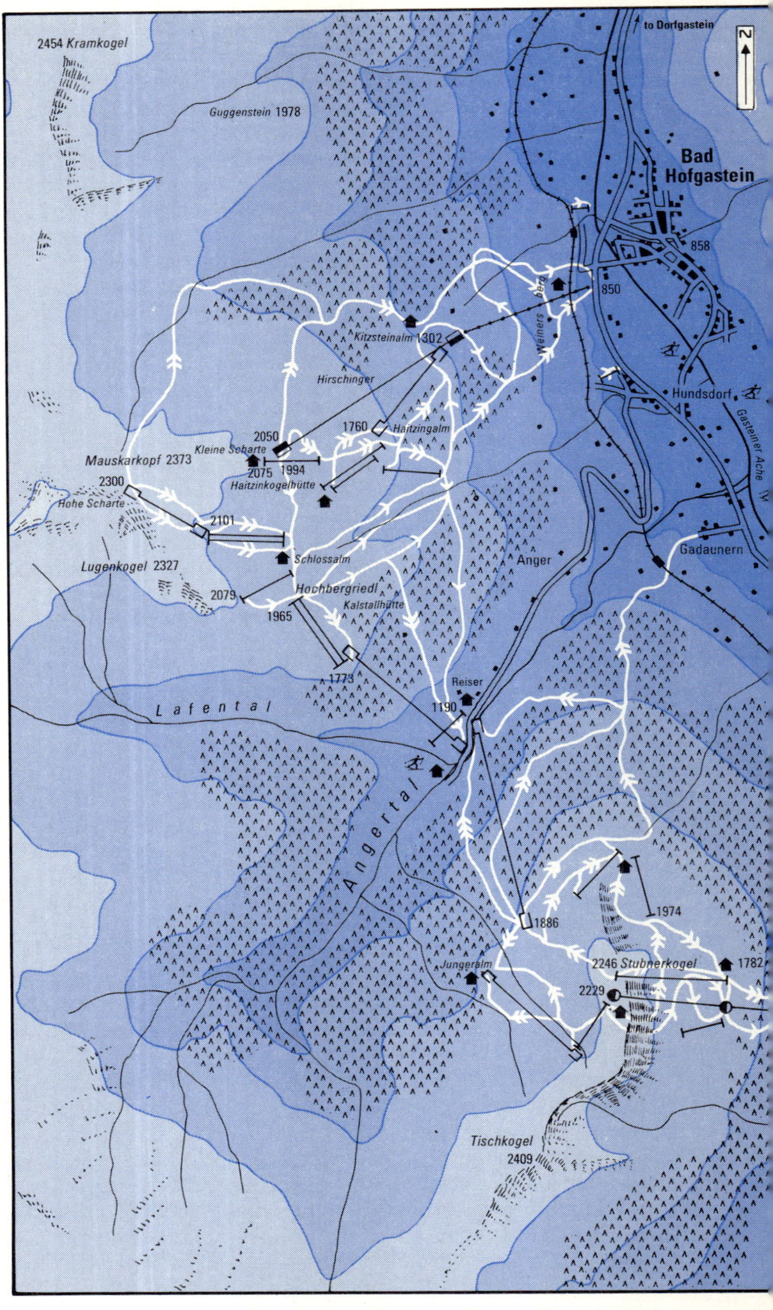
2454 Kramkogel
Guggenstein 1978
to Dorfgastein
N
Bad Hofgastein
858
850
Weiners Berg
Kitzsteinalm 1302
Hirschinger
Hundsdorf
Gasteiner Ache
1760
Haitzingalm
2050
Kleine Scharte
Mauskarkopf 2373
2075
1994
Haitzinkogelhütte
2300
Hohe Scharte
2101
Schlossalm
Lugenkogel 2327
Anger
Gadaunern
2079
Hochbergriedl
Kalstallhütte
1965
1773
Reiser
1190
Lafental
Angertal
1974
1886
Jungeralm
2246 Stubnerkogel
1782
2229
Tischkogel
2409

wide runs through the woods and some easy off-piste skiing among the trees. After the crowded and often icy slopes of Stubnerkogel, intermediate skiers may welcome this attractive pastoral landscape.

Mountain restaurants are plentiful and generally pleasant, with charming alternatives to the big cafeterias at the main lift stations. Stubnerkogel now has a new restaurant at the top. There are several very attractive huts on the lower slopes of the Stubnerkogel and of the Schlossalm. Although most piste maps do not mark them, there are restaurants dotted around above Dorfgastein and Grossarl.

The six-seat gondola must have relieved the serious **queues** for access to Stubnerkogel which formed at peak times, but we have no high-season reports to confirm this. The Bad Hofgastein funicular remains inadequate; the alternative is to go via the Angertal.

The resort

Badgastein is built in a cramped, claustrophobic position on the steep wooded slopes which abruptly close the southern end of the Gastein valley. The main road and railway by-pass the resort centre, which is more simply negotiated by the steep footpaths and staircases than by car. The focus of the resort is a smart new complex including hotel,

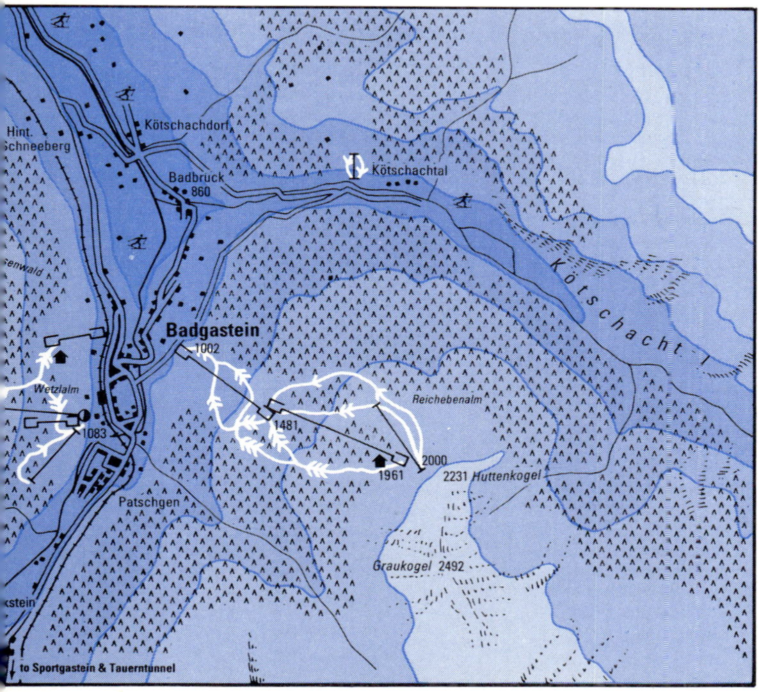

shopping precinct, casino and conference hall projecting from the hillside beside the waterfall. In the vicinity there are shop windows, coiffeurs and tea shops for those with expensive tastes. The upper level (a steep but short walk away) is a rather ordinary collection of unfashionable spa hotels, which attract skiers in winter because of their convenient location, and newer accommodation which has grown up there for the same reason. Bus services link the village centres and main lift stations reasonably efficiently, but only in the daytime.

Accommodation is mostly in hotels, of which there are hundreds in the valley, many of them with hot and cold running radioactive water. Among the hotels at the top of the resort, within easy walking distance of the Stubnerkogel lifts, the new Bärenhof (✆3366) is the most comfortable and expensive. The Krone (✆2330) and the Goethehof (✆2717) are ideally placed but very uninspiring middle-range hotels. Much more charming and in a quieter position is the simple Fischerwirt (✆2231). In the centre, the Straubinger (✆2012) is not in the grand league but handsomely traditional; the map of Europe was redrawn in room seven, so they say. The Grüner Baum hotel (✆2516) or Hoteldorf deserves special mention – an idyllic, self-contained tourist colony in the beautifully secluded setting of the Kötschachtal, with

Badgastein facts

Lift payment

Passes Gastein Superskischein pass covers all lifts, buses and trains. Day, half-day and 'hourly' tickets available.
Children 40% off under 14.
Cost 6-day pass AS1,400; 15% off in low season.
Beginners Coupons, and some limited passes for a few nursery lifts.

Ski school

Classes 2hr morning, 3hr afternoon.
Cost 6 days AS1,150. Private lessons AS360/hr.
Children Ski kindergarten, ages 2–7, 6 days with meals AS1,200. Non-ski kindergarten, ages 2–3, 9.00–5.00, 6 days AS900.

Not skiing

Facilities Natural ice rinks (skating/ curling), swimming/ sauna/ gym, thermal baths, sleigh rides, riding, toboggan runs, ski bob, tennis, squash, bridge, chess, bowling, casino, museum, theatre, concerts, 35km cleared paths.

Cross-country skiing

Trails Of varying length and difficulty along the main valley floor between Bad Hofgastein and Badbruck (over 20km), around Dorfgastein (12.5km) and Sportgastein (over 20km); also at Böckstein, Angertal and Kötschachtal.

Medical facilities

In resort Numerous doctors, dentists, chemists.
Hospital Schwarzach (25km).

Getting there

Airport Salzburg; transfer about 2hr. Also Munich.
Railway Main-line station in resort.
Road Via Munich; chains rarely needed.

Available holidays

Resort beds 6,000 in hotels, 1,000 in apartments.
Package holidays Austro Tours (Ht), Made to Measure (Ht), Skiscope (Ht)

Further information

Tourist office ✆(6434) 2531. Tx 67520.

accommodation of varying comfort in a number of buildings.

Après-ski is very varied. In the centre there are quiet tea rooms, plush hotel bars with formal dancing, and a casino. The big hotels put on live shows (fashion displays, beauty contests, cabaret). For less formal entertainment, there is a handful of discothèques, and a number of pubs, simple bars and restaurants, mostly around the station. Lots of young and old go out at night, and the atmosphere is usually lively.

Although Badgastein itself is not an ideal base, the valley as a whole has an excellent amount and variety of **cross-country** skiing. There are lots of things for **non-skiers** to do apart from inhale radon; there are long and beautiful walks in the woods above Badgastein and along the eastern flank of the valley towards Bad Hofgastein.

Nursery slopes at the foot of the Stubnerkogel, Angertal and Bad Hofgastein lifts are rather cramped, and there are not many runs suitable for skiers making the transition from nursery slopes to pistes. The area as a whole is not good for beginners.

There are **ski school** offices near the main lift stations at Badgastein (Stubnerkogel), Bad Hofgastein and Dorfgastein. Reports are mixed. There is now an alternative for skiers who want to be led around the slopes but not formally taught – the *Ski-gäste-guides*.

Bad Hofgastein 870m

Bad Hofgastein has neither the inconveniently steep and dark setting nor the stodgy grandeur of Badgastein; it is smaller but still a sizeable resort, spread along the broadest part of the valley. The Kitzstein funicular is inconveniently distant, and the resort is not very ski-oriented: it attracts lots of non-skiing visitors who potter about in the very agreeable, spacious sunny surroundings. It is a good base for the valley's walks and cross-country trails, and busy skating and curling rinks complete the winter scene. There is an outdoor, naturally-heated swimming pool, and a new sports centre (tennis and squash). Evenings are quiet. The most convenient hotels for skiers are the mostly new ones lining the road from the centre to the river. The Kärnten (✆711) is well-placed, large and comfortable. Less convenient are the simpler and prettier hotels on the village square – Zum Boten (✆416) and Kaiser Franz (✆742).

Tourist office ✆(6432) 6429. Tx 67796. **Package holidays** Austro Tours (Ht).

Dorfgastein 835m

Dorfgastein is a charming, villagey resort, untouched by the depressing influence of spa-hood. Horses and carts clatter along the narrow, arcaded main street past the old church, more often taking local folk about their business than taking tourists for jaunts. There are several well-kept, friendly and comfortable medium-priced hotels in the centre; the Steindlwirt (✆2190) and Kirchenwirt (✆251) are two of the larger hotels, typically comfortable although without much character. The ski-lift departure is at least a 5-minute walk from the village; the Gasthof Schihäusl (✆248) stands at the foot of the slopes. Dorfgastein does not lack bars, music and animation in the evening.

Tourist office ✆(6433) 277. Tx 67737.

Beside the seaside

Zell am See Austria 750m

Good for *Easy runs, not skiing, mountain restaurants, après-ski, easy road access, short airport transfers, cross-country skiing, rail access*
Bad for *Skiing convenience, resort-level snow, late holidays, freedom from cars*

Separate resort: Kaprun

Zell am See enjoys a splendid textbook setting on a gentle promontory where a mountain stream flows into a lake. The town predates tourism by many centuries and its car-free old centre has great charm. But Zell now sprawls far beyond the centre; as a sizeable town on a main road and rail thoroughfare, it is very different from what many British skiers expect of an Austrian ski resort (unless they are used to Kitzbühel).

Zell is busy all the year round and has most of the ingredients of an all-round winter resort: pistes steep and gentle, good nightlife, a vast network of cross-country skiing, lots for non-skiers to do, and even a snow guarantee in the form of glacier skiing half an hour's drive away on the Kitzsteinhorn. But the ingredients do not blend perfectly. The town is separated from one access lift by the main road and from the main ones by over a mile. Most of the skiing is either very easy or fairly challenging, and the glacier is not much of a compensation for the poor-snow risk inherent in Zell's altitude – its skiing is not very interesting and, as it is also the snow guarantee for many other low resorts, tends to be prohibitively crowded when snow is scarce.

Kaprun has a small ski area of its own, but is mainly of interest as the closest resort to the glacier and as a base for cross-country skiers.

The skiing top 1965m bottom 750m

The two arms of a mountain horseshoe rise gently from the ends of the lake to the rounded peak of Schmittenhöhe, giving long easy runs, especially along the southern limb. Steeper wooded slopes facing south, north and east drop down from Schmittenhöhe into the pit of the bowl, providing some challenging skiing. There would be good off-piste skiing, but in the interest of the trees little is allowed.

From close to the resort centre a gondola goes up to the southern limb of the horseshoe, and from the suburb of Schüttdorf a new six-seater gondola does likewise. A third lift station is in the pit of the bowl, about 2km from the centre of Zell. One of the two cable-cars from here goes directly to (indeed into) the Schmittenhöhe Berghotel, where an elevator delivers you to the sunny summit plateau.

Behind the summit is a small area of pleasant intermediate runs, of varying difficulty. Turning right at the top takes you along a flattish ridge to a sunny area, also reachable via the other cable-car from the valley

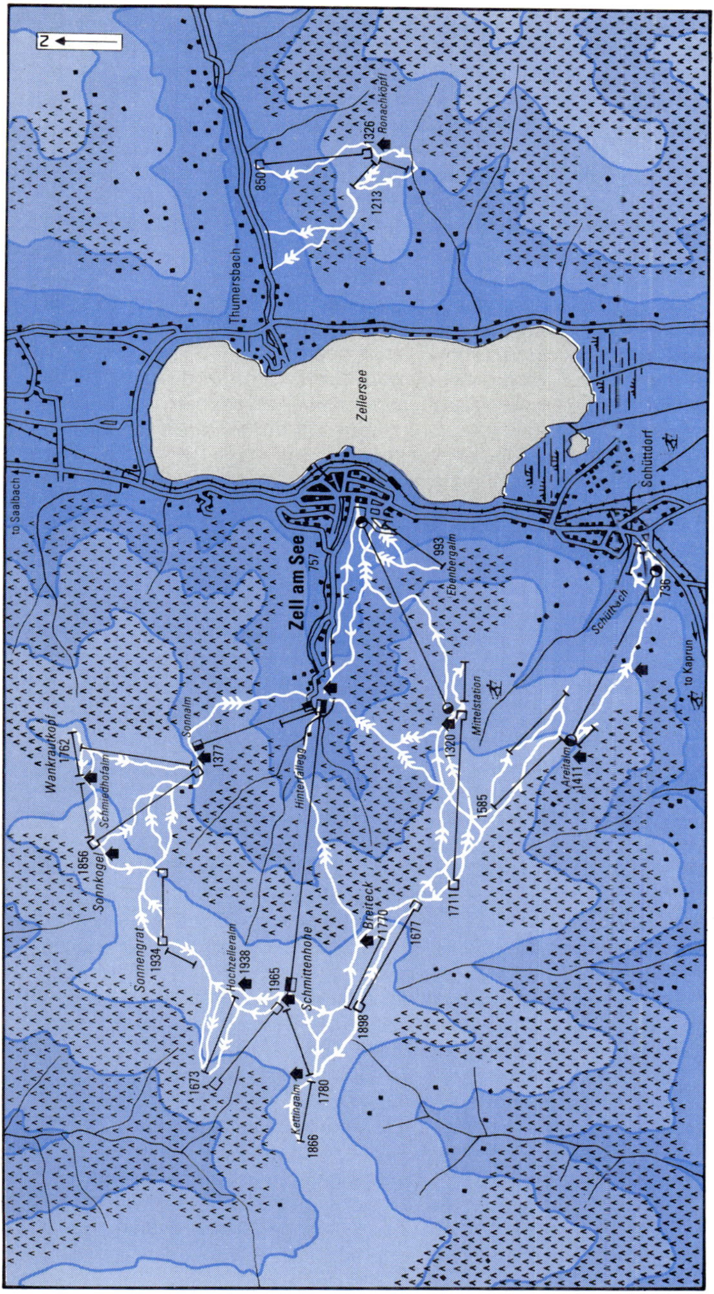
N
Ronachkopf
1326
850
1213
Thumersbach
Zellersee
Schüttdorf
to Saalbach
Zell am See
757
993
Ebenbergalm
736
Schüttbach
to Kaprun
Mittelstation
1320
Areitalm
1411
1585
1711
Sonnalm
1377
Hinterfeldegg
Wankrautkopf
1762
Schmiedhofalm
1856
Sonnkogel
Sonnengrat
1934
Hochzelleralm
1938
1965
Schmittenhöhe
Breiteck
1770
1677
1898
1673
Kettingalm
1780
1866

to Sonnalm. None of the skiing here is at all difficult; the black run below Sonnalm is no steeper than 25°, but it does get very worn and icy or slushy. Lifts and pistes link Sonnalm with Schmittenhöhe.

South of Schmittenhöhe there is a succession of gentle, broad, sunny pistes along the horseshoe ridge. A right fork takes you to Areitalm, where the gondola from Schüttdorf arrives; the pleasant intermediate piste to Schüttdorf doesn't keep its snow for long and ends steeply. Taking the left fork brings you to the top of the gondola from Zell. At two points on the horseshoe, black pistes branch off into the bowl. These soon steepen into fine long runs, challenging but not too intimidating for adventurous intermediates (the steepest is from Breiteck, about 28°). Other runs to the bottom stations are less steep, but get more sun. The Ebenberglift, little used except for slalom practice, gives a splendid view of the town, and a short, fairly steep run.

There are quite a number of **mountain restaurants** around the ski area, most of them in pleasant surroundings and sunny positions.

In high season there are long **queues** all day for the Schmittenhöhe cable-car, and even the efficient gondola access lift from the town has morning queues. The Sonnalm route up to Schmittenhöhe is slow.

The resort

Zell is a town rather than a village, with shops catering for the needs of residents and the whims of summer tourists rather than just for skiers. Post buses run regularly though not very frequently to the lifts.

Accommodation is in hotels, some in the centre, others in the quieter streets towards the lake and the north end of the town. For après-ski the centre is the best base. The Traube (✆2368) is a comfortable, friendly small hotel in the pedestrian zone, with an atmospheric bar/restaurant. A long way up-market is the very smooth Neue Post (✆3773). Most people will find better value in the charming and inexpensive Alte Post (✆2422), close to the gondola station. For skiing purposes there is much to be said for staying close to the cable-car station. The Schwebebahn (✆2461) is the obvious choice, but expensive. Staying in dreary Schüttdorf puts you close to cross-country trails, tennis and riding facilities – and gives easy access to the skiing if you're based close to the gondola.

There is plenty of **après-ski**, at least in season: restaurants at every price level, bars, discos, *Weinstüberl*, tea-dancing, and the standard 'evenings' – Tyrolean, fondue, zither, tobogganing.

The extent of **cross-country** trails in the valleys around Zell is enormous; Kaprun hosts a famous marathon race. There is lots for **non-skiers** to do, with very good sports facilities, and easy access by train to Salzburg. When the lake is frozen (from New Year to mid-February in a good year) you can walk across to Thumersbach.

There are **nursery slopes** at the bottom cable-car station and more at Schüttdorf, but the snow is often in poor condition. Beginners then go up by gondola or chair to higher nursery lifts.

The **ski school** is used to British pupils and English is widely spoken.

Kaprun 770m

Kaprun is a spacious, pleasant, but characterless holiday village with a splendid sports centre, a range of après-ski, kindergarten and shops. The local skiing on the Maiskogel consists of easy-intermediate runs (facing roughly east) served by a chain of drag-lifts starting near the village and a cable-car starting quite a way out. A further couple of drags going up to 1737m serve less straightforward north-facing runs at the top. The Kitzsteinhorn skiing (2450m–3029m) is reached by cable-car or funicular starting several miles up the valley. It is an exposed area of predominantly easy-intermediate skiing, without great variety of terrain but with some tough blue runs. The interesting red to the middle station of the underground funicular ends in a tiring push along the plastic floor of a virtually flat tunnel.

Tourist office ✆(6547) 8643. Tx 6/6763.
Package holidays Austro Tours (Ht), Crystal (Ht Sc), Global (Ht).

Zell am See facts

Lift payment

Passes Area pass covers all lifts in Zell and Kaprun, and buses between. Minimum period 3 days. Also local passes, including day, half-day and 'hourly' ones.
Cost 6-day pass AS1,360. 15% off in low season.
Children 35% off, under 15.
Beginners Coupons, or limited pass.
Summer skiing Extensive near Kaprun.

Ski school

Classes 2hr morning and afteroon.
Cost 6 days AS950. Private lessons AS380/hr.
Children Ski kindergarten, ages 4–10, 10.00–4.00, 6 days AS950. Non-ski kindergarten, ages 4–11, 6 days AS480.
Special courses Ski-touring.

Cross-country skiing

Trails Easy and medium loops totalling 200km on the valley floor and 2.3km at middle station of Zellerbergbahn. Also very long trails along the Salzach valley east and west of Kaprun.

Not skiing

Facilities Swimming, sauna, solarium, riding, tennis, skating, fitness centre, toboggan runs, bowling, plane flights, sleigh rides, shooting range, curling, squash.

Medical facilities

In resort Doctors, chemists, dentist, fracture clinic.

Getting there

Airport Salzburg is closest, Munich more commonly used by operators transfer about 2½hr.
Railway Station in resort.
Road Via Munich; chains rarely needed.

Available holidays

Resort beds 8,200 in hotels, 800 in apartments.
Package holidays Austro Tours (Ht), Blue Sky (Ht), Club 18-30 (Ht), Crystal (Ht Sc), Enterprise (Ht), Global (Ht Sc), Horizon (Ht), Inghams (Ht), Intasun (Ht), Neilson (Ht), Schoolplan (Ht), Ski Lovers (Ht Ch), SkiBound (Ht), Snowcoach Holidays (Ht), Thomson (Ht Hm)

Further information

Tourist office ✆(6542) 2600. Tx 66617.

Discreet charm

Saalbach Austria 1000m

Good for *Easy runs, big ski area, sunny slopes, mountain restaurants, après ski, Alpine charm, easy road access, short airport transfers*
Bad for *Tough runs*

Linked resorts: Hinterglemm, Leogang

The essentially friendly mountains of the Kitzbühel Alps are familiar territory to British skiers, who have long formed a large part of the winter clientele of such resorts as Alpbach, Söll and Kitzbühel. The two resorts of the east–west Glemm valley, at the eastern extremity of the range, are at least as worthy of our attention, combining as they do a fairly successful replication of Austrian Alpine village charm, an extensive network of easy and intermediate skiing which links the two resorts and the two sides of the valley with almost French efficiency, and adequately varied non-skiing diversions – and all this amid pleasant though unspectacular scenery. As our cautious choice of words implies, the area is a compromise, and it is unlikely to suit those who seek the ultimate in rustic village charm, riotous nightlife or challenging skiing. But it is a very smooth confection.

Saalbach and Hinterglemm are 4km apart but growing towards each other – and as part of their campaign to capture the 1991 World Championships the resort authorities have now declared themselves a single resort called Saalbach Hinterglemm. But the distinction is one which shouldn't be forgotten when choosing where to stay. Saalbach, the first village you come to, is considerably more established and rounded as a resort, as well as bigger and more sophisticated.

Zell am See is close, and may be of interest to skiers in search of a bit more challenging skiing. The Kitzsteinhorn glacier is within reach by car or bus.

The skiing top 2096m bottom 929m

Spread along both sides of the valley, the interlinking lifts enable you to ski comfortably from either village to the other, or to perform a circuit of the valley – hence the area's 'Ski Circus' label. The south-facing slopes are mostly open and undemanding, but can deteriorate rapidly in good weather, especially low down, despite snow-making machinery. The north-facing slopes provide a few more challenging runs.

Austria's largest cable-car rises 1000m from the centre of Saalbach to the eastern summit of the **Schattberg**. Behind the peak is some fairly easy skiing on the sunny slopes served by two drag-lifts and a beginners' lift, and below the cable-car is a fine 4km black north-facing run to the village which is never excessively steep (about 29° at its steepest), and can be tackled by adventurous intermediates. The easy alternative is a delightful long round-the-mountain blue run through the woods to Vorderglemm, where a cable-car now makes the link with the Wildenkarkogel slopes on the other side of the valley. The third option is to turn right towards a connecting lift up to Schattberg West, at 2096m the top of the lift system. The black grading of the runs between the two summits is misleading: this crucial link in the circus holds no terrors. There is then a fine wide 5km red run down to Hinterglemm, partly open and partly wooded, and often busy.

From nearby, parallel double and single chair-lifts rise over 1000m in two stages to the summit of **Zwölferkogel** at 1984m. There are two-drag lifts and some fairly easy skiing on the open south-east facing slopes near the top. The main run back to Hinterglemm is a broad intermediate piste facing north-east, with steeper and easier variants. The alternative is to take an unpatrolled back-of-the-mountain route directly into the Glemm valley, which presents no serious difficulties until the steep final section where most skiers stick to a narrow zig-zag path. This route connects with the **Hochalm** lifts on the north side of the valley, serving a range of broad, smooth pistes, all graded red, though only the more direct runs justify the grading. From the top you can traverse across to Hinterglemm, or use the series of drags north of the village on **Reiterkogel** to progress along the valley. You can also traverse in the opposite direction from Hasenauer to Hochalm. This whole area has wide intersecting pistes of varying intermediate steepness, but with little challenge.

There are lifts from Saalbach back up these south-facing slopes on Bernkogel, and onward to **Kohlmaiskopf**, embarking on another area criss-crossed by intersecting pistes and paths, with some worthwhile intermediate runs, eventually bringing you to **Wildenkarkogel**, also accessible by the new Schönleiten cable-car from Vorderglemm, where the easy run from Schattberg finishes. From the top you can traverse westwards towards Saalbach, or take a connecting lift to the **Leogang** ski area, on the north side of the ridge. The upper Leogang slopes have wide, open pistes ideal for most intermediates, and the runs down to the village are also fairly straightforward.

Absent from the otherwise admirable piste map, **mountain restaurants** are profusely distributed around the slopes. Particularly attractive or good-value ones include the Westgipfel Alm, the Panorama Alm and the Thurner Alm. The Bergstadl, at the Westgipfel mid-station, has lunchtime dancing.

Moderate **queues** develop in the morning peak period on the main exits from Saalbach – up to a half-hour wait for the cable-car. Queues at Hinterglemm are usually shorter. Minor bottlenecks can occur on the connecting lifts on the south-facing slopes.

The resort

Saalbach is almost entirely a post-War development, though built very much in the traditional Austrian village manner. The traffic-free central zone is pleasantly compact, with shops, restaurants and hotels lining

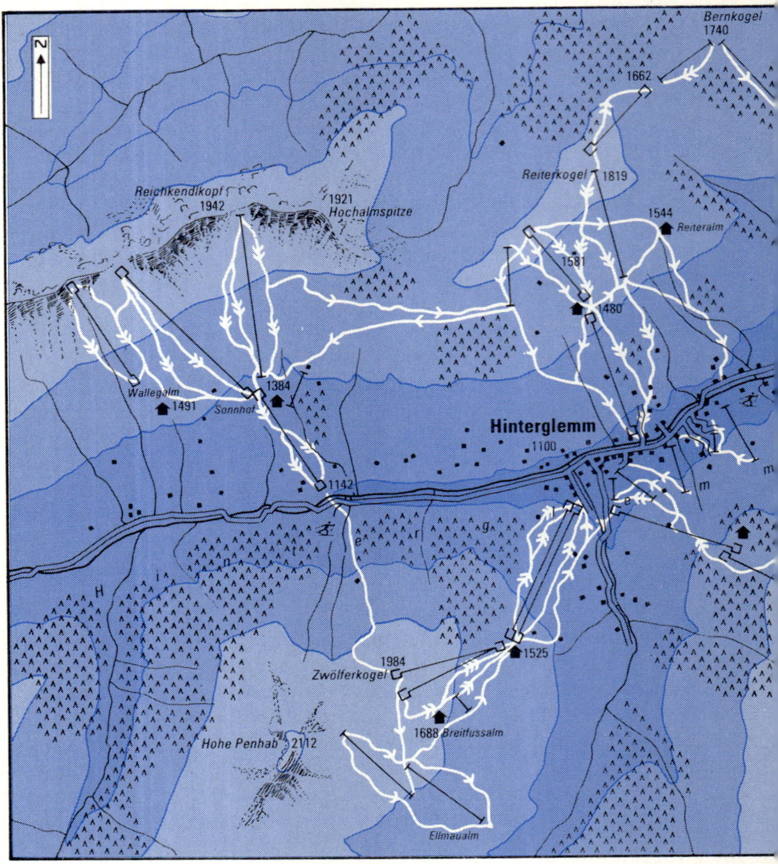

the steepish, narrow main street leading past the onion-domed church and square. The atmosphere is lively and friendly, though not rowdy.

Day-time buses run every 20 minutes (and more frequently at morning and afternoon peaks) between Vorderglemm, Saalbach and Hinterglemm, supplementing the much less frequent post bus. There are plenty of taxis to cope with the post-skiing queue overflows and for evening transport along the valley. A car is no great advantage.

Accommodation includes a mixture of stylish, modern hotels (chalet-style rather than concrete blocks) and cheaper guest-houses, many of which straggle out along the main road on either side of the village. It's well worth staying near the centre if you can, close to the lifts and the main life of the village, and in many cases you can ski right back to the front door. Recommended hotels in the upper price range include the Ingonda for plushness and good food (✆7334), the Saalbacher Hof for all-round service (✆7111) and the Neuhaus for proximity to lifts and for value for money (✆7151).

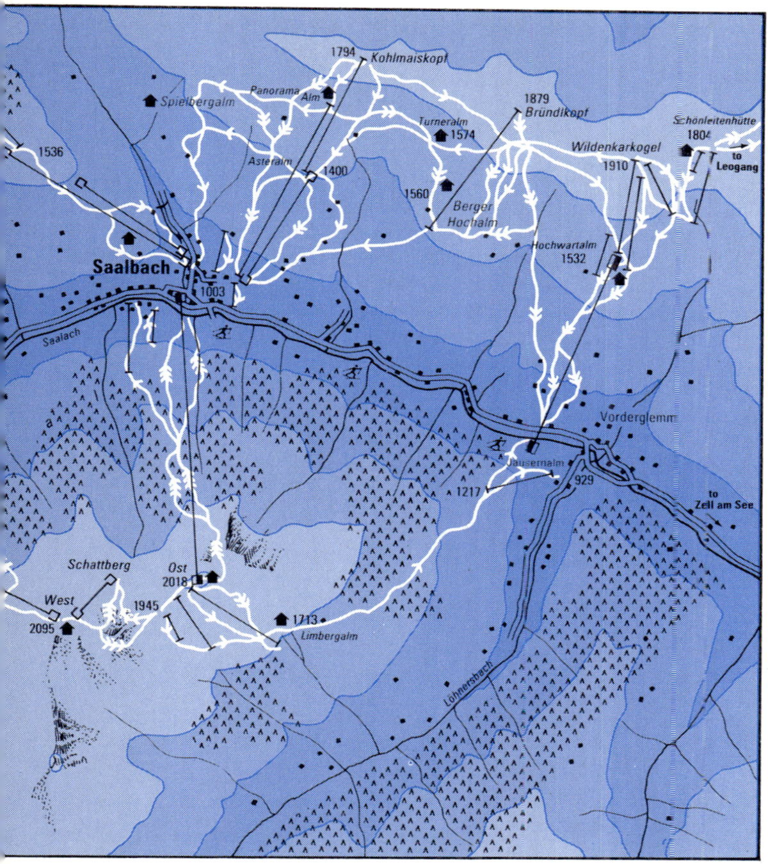

Après-ski is lively from late afternoon onwards. Several hotels and bars have tea-dancing and are usually packed. Tobogganing outings to and from the delightful Spielbergalm are organised, and recommended. There's plenty to do later on too, with a variety of discos, live bands and a choice of bars with rock or more traditional Austrian music.

Both **cross-country** trails are along the flat floor of the valley and are overshadowed by the Schattberg and Zwölferkogel respectively. More extensive opportunities can be found by taking a 35-minute bus ride to Zell am See. Although these are not ideal resorts for **non-skiers**, there is plenty to do on days off. There is a good public pool and sauna, but many hotels have their own.

The **nursery slopes** at Saalbach are central and gentle but south-facing, and deteriorate badly as the season progresses. Beginners must then use the open slopes on Bernkogel (the top section is admirably flat) or Schattberg.

Our most recent report on **ski school** (from pupils at different levels) complains of large class size, little English spoken and not much of any other language: 'he just skied on ahead.' A small breakaway group of instructors now operate as the Saalbacher Ski-Guides, taking non-beginners around the slopes without formal tuition. We have an enthusiastic report of this service.

Hinterglemm 1100m

Although Hinterglemm has also stuck to the proper Alpine style in most of its development, it has achieved a less satisfactory result than Saalbach. The road along the valley runs through the centre, and even though it goes nowhere it interferes with both safety and atmosphere. There are big apartment blocks at the west end of the village, which are rather out of things but close to the sports centre (tennis, skating). The nursery slopes are extensive, free from passing traffic and north-facing – but get relatively little midwinter sun. The Haus Wolf (✆3460) is recommended by a reporter as a 'good, convenient but expensive' hotel. Hinterglemm has its own all-day kindergarten.

Tourist office As Saalbach. **Package holidays** Austro Tours (Ht), Crystal (Ht), Global (Ht), Horizon (Ht), Inghams (Ht Sc), Intasun (Ht), Ski Lovers (Ht), Thomson (Sc).

Saalbach facts

Lift payment

Passes Single pass covers all local lifts including Leogang; passes for over 5 days valid for swimming pool. 'Hourly' day pass available, with refund if handed in after 2, 3 or 4 hours. **Cost** 6-day pass AS1,390. 25% off in low season. Two-stage reductions for senior citizens.
Children 39% off under 16, 54% off under 11.

Ski school

Classes 2hr morning and afternoon.
Cost 6 days AS950. Private lessons AS380/hr, AS1,520/day.
Special courses Racing, Alpine touring, 'alternative' skiing.
Children Same times and prices as for adults; lunchtime care/meal for ages 4 up, AS90/day. Ski kindergarten, age 3 up, 10.00–4.00, 6 days with lunch AS1,200.

Not skiing

Facilities Swimming (free for holders of 6-day or longer lift passes), sauna, solarium, tennis, tobogganing, bowling, sleigh rides, skating, curling.

Cross-country skiing

Trails 8km from Saalbach to Vorderglemm, 10km trail from Hinterglemm to Lengau.

Medical facilities

In resort Doctor and dentist.
Hospital Zell am See (18km).

Getting there

Airport Munich; transfer about 3hr. Salzburg 1½hr.
Railway Zell am See; regular buses.
Road Via Munich; chains rarely needed.

Available holidays

Resort beds 14,000 in hotels, 2,000 in apartments.
Package holidays Austro Tours (Ht Ch), Crystal (Ht Sc), Global (Ht), Horizon (Ht), Inghams (Ht), Intasun (Ht), Neilson (Ht), Thomson (Ht), Vacations (Ht Ch)

Further information

Tourist office ✆(6541) 7272. Tx 66507.

Place of Streif

Kitzbühel Austria 760m

Good for *Easy runs, big ski area, mountain restaurants, après-ski, Alpine charm, not skiing, easy road access, rail access, short airport transfers*
Bad for *Lift queues, skiing convenience, late holidays, resort-level snow, freedom from cars*

Linked resorts: Kirchberg, Jochberg, Pass Thurn

Linking lifts and runs to form a ski 'circus' is no longer the novelty it was when they first created one at Kitzbühel. As modern circuses go this one is low, with the result that its lower slopes are often icy, and washed out long before spring; and it suffers from lift bottlenecks – not least in Kitzbühel itself, where the queues are some of the worst (and worst-behaved) in the Alps. But with those provisos it is a very attractive skiing area, possessing a delightful mixture of friendly woodlands (with chalet restaurants playing jolly Tyrolean tunes) and open upper slopes commanding magnificent views – a surprise, considering the altitude. The snow is often good, and the shared skiing of Kitzbühel and Kirchberg makes an impressive ski region by all but the most testing standards – though the Ski Safari linking with Jochberg and Pass Thurn can hardly be called big game, and little of the skiing is tough.

Kitzbühel is a substantial town on a main road and rail thoroughfare. It is one of the oldest and most famous of Austrian ski resorts, and along with Lech and Zürs one of the most fashionable. Unlike the other two, it is large and not exclusive, and attracts large numbers of British skiers – particularly young ones, whose presence can be very obvious on the streets and in the bars.

There are several quieter villages which give the chance to enjoy the skiing, without having to submit to the tumult of the town – Kirchberg most important among them. Although rustic by Kitzbühel's standards, it is nevertheless a large, busy resort. If you want a haven of tranquillity, Kirchberg is not it. But it is certainly more attractive as a base than bargain hotels 'near' Kitzbühel, which in terms of skiing and après-skiing convenience are a long way from anywhere.

Taking a car has the undoubted benefit of being independent of the bus system, but this may be outweighed by the hellish difficulty of driving and parking – and other major resorts within reach for day trips are not particularly tempting.

The skiing top 1995m bottom 760m

The skiing is in three main areas. Kitzbühel and a 25-minute walk separates two of them – Horn and Hahnenkamm (which links Kitzbühel with Kirchberg). The third, above Jochberg and Pass Thurn, can almost

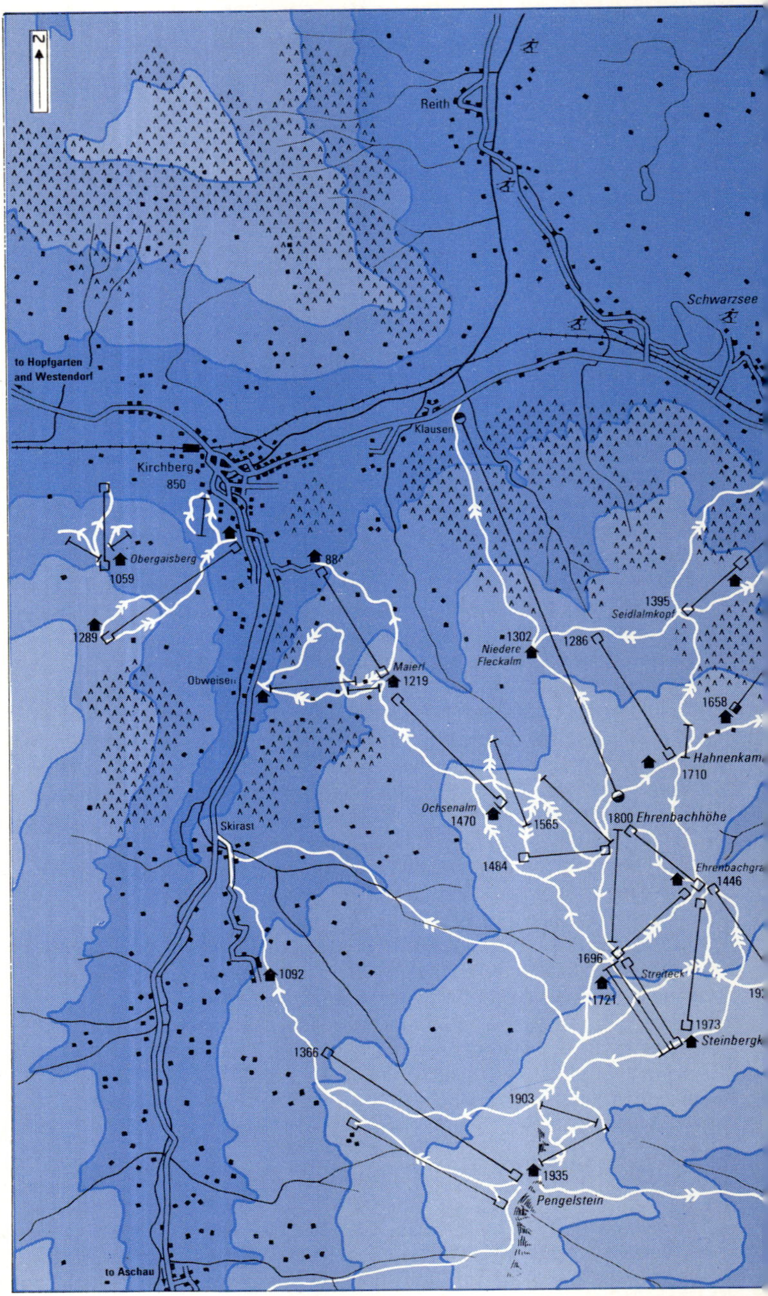
N
Reith
Schwarzsee
to Hopfgarten and Westendorf
Klausen
Kirchberg
850
Obergaisberg
1059
1289
884
1395
Seidlalmkopf
1302
Niedere Fleckalm
1286
Maierl
1219
Obweisen
1658
Hahnenkam
1710
Ochsenalm
1470
1565
1800 Ehrenbachhöhe
1484
Skirast
Ehrenbachgra
1446
1696
Streiteck
1721
1092
1973
Steinbergk
1366
1903
1935
Pengelstein
to Aschau

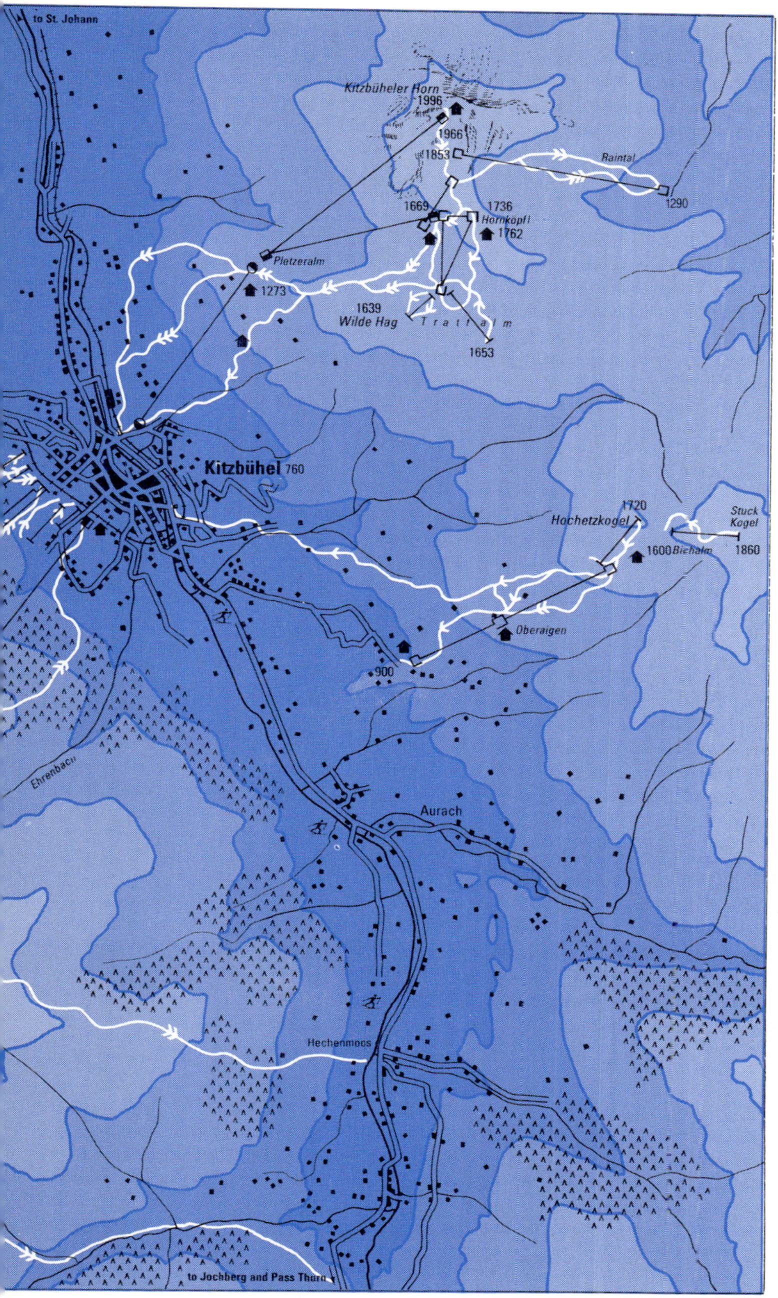
to St. Johann
Kitzbüheler Horn
1996
1966
1853
Raintal
1290
1669
1736
Hornkopfl
1762
Pletzeralm
1273
1639
Wilde Hag
Trattalm
1653
Kitzbühel 760
1720
Hochetzkogel
Stuck Kogel
1600 Biehalm
1860
Oberaigen
900
Ehrenbach
Aurach
Hechenmoos
to Jochberg and Pass Thurn

be reached on skis from the Hahnenkamm – via the 'Ski Safari'. Kirchberg adds a fourth small area of its own.

The **Kitzbüheler Horn** is a big and beautiful mountain, its peak rising over 1200m from the valley floor and giving tremendous top-of-the-world views. For the skier, it's less good than it looks: the runs are rather limited, and much easier than they are graded except when conditions are bad – which towards the bottom means quite often, since they face mostly south-west. The skiing is reached (after a non-trivial walk from the town centre across the main road, river and railway) by a lengthy combination of gondola and cable-cars – one to the Horn itself, the other towards the lower Hornköpfl, nearby.

Most flanks of the Horn are steep and rocky, which explains the lack of a lift link with nearby St Johann. At the top there is no obvious alternative to the single piste, which soon branches to give access to the Raintal bowl on the back of the mountain. Although the runs are black and red, there isn't much to this area (the red is almost a schuss). Beyond a briefly dense network of short lifts and mostly easy runs around the Trattalm (a good post-nursery area), the run back down to Kitzbühel dutifully splits into black, red and blue. The black isn't steep, but may present a stern test of skating ability. The red is exhaustingly flat for a long way at the bottom.

Just along the hill, the little-used Bichlalm lifts above the hamlet of Aurach serve limited straight-up-and-down pistes facing south-west, and an off-piste route to Fieberbrunn.

The **Hahnenkamm** is the site of the world's most feared downhill race (see 'Competitive edge'), but most of the runs are easily managed by intermediates, as long as the snow is good. It is more easily reached from the centre than the Horn, but still a five-minute walk. Direct access is by cable-car over a steep mountainside to an open ridge about 900m above. The preferable alternative (in all but the worst weather) is to take the two Streifalm chair-lifts, thus avoiding not only the cable-car queue but also some plodding at the top. There are a couple of good, long, northish-facing runs back to the town from the Streifalm, the most direct being the downhill race-course. For a brief period after the race the course can easily be identified and less easily skied.

The Hahnenkamm gives access to the heart of the skiing which Kitzbühel shares with Kirchberg, a few miles round the mountain. It offers lots of variety, some good off-piste runs, and some very long and beautiful pistes. There is an easy run down into the Ehrenbachgraben dip where more queues build up for the chair-lifts which fan out from here. The skiing here, beneath Steinbergkogel, is the most challenging in the region – a genuinely black 500m drop, facing north, with a number of variants and often big moguls. From the top of the ridge there are apparently good off-piste runs, a long run down through the woods to Hechenmoos and an easy connection to the Pengelstein. On the north-western flank of Pengelstein there are now two chair-lifts (one an efficient four-seater) serving open easy runs which continue down to a bus stop beyond Kirchberg. There is also an unpatrolled route (which involves some initial walking) down to Aschau.

Above Kirchberg the Ehrenbachhöhe is a busy meeting place, with several hotels and restaurants around the summit (there's quite a bit of walking). There are easy connections to and from Hahnenkamm skiing, and long runs down north-west-facing slopes to Kirchberg (mostly gentle) and down the north-facing slope to Klausen (with more scope for challenge and off-piste adventure), served by a six-seater gondola.

Kirchberg has its own small ski area on the Gaisberg – a modest slope, now sensibly graded red, notable mainly for a lack of crowds.

A very long, easy run from Pengelstein forms the main link in the Ski Safari chain; the bottom half goes along a road through woods – very slow, but beautiful. Then it's ten minutes' walk (or a taxi) to the lifts at **Jochberg** (920m to 1728m), of which you have to take nine in order to complete your Safari to the slopes above **Pass Thurn** (1265m to 1995m). A simple network, mostly of drag-lifts but with a couple of double chairs, serves mostly easy, wide open skiing with beautiful views from the top lifts towards the distant Kitzbüheler Horn, and with one stiff mogul-field to provide a change from gentle cruising. Recently added lifts make it possible to retrace your steps as far as Jochberg, but from there you still have to take the bus to Kitzbühel.

Mountain restaurants are liberally scattered around the slopes and peaks of the area; they're not much more expensive than the national average, and in several cases attractive, welcoming and sunny. A reporter recommends the hut on run 25 just above Klausen for low prices despite waitress service. The Hanglalm hut above Pass Thurn is jolly and quite good value. The best value is said to be at Trattenbachalm, also above Pass Thurn, and the worst at the Alpenhaus on the Horn.

Kitzbühel is large, easy to get to, and fashionable. The result is lift **queues** wherein, as one reporter put it, 'you really feel your capital outlay trickling away.' Exits from the town (especially the Horn gondola) are the main (but by no means the only) bottlenecks, with waits of over an hour not uncommon – an early start is the solution, we're told.

The resort

Kitzbühel is set splendidly between its main ski areas, spreading across a wide and busy junction of valleys. It is a large and colourful old town enclosed by walls and, less prettily, by main roads and a loop in the railway. The old town with its twin-towered church, cobbled streets and gaily painted houses is one of the few ski resorts you might choose to visit just for a look. Shopping is sophisticated and international. The centre is, by day at least, traffic-free, but only at the cost of a complicated and nearly always congested one-way ring-road system, which doesn't prevent traffic seriously impairing the quality of Kitzbühel life throughout the season – for drivers and pedestrians alike. Getting from the centre of town to either ski area involves crossing the railway line and a long walk or slow bus ride. The day-time buses around the resort and to other villages in the ski area are efficiently organised, though stretched at peak times. The service is complicated by the one-way system and hampered by the traffic. For the evening, there are plenty of taxis.

Accommodation consists equally of hotels large, comfortable and expensive, and guest-houses cheap and simple, with little in between. The town has spread far beyond the old core, and because of the far-reaching coverage of the lift pass lots of (mostly cheap) accommodation which is a long way from Kitzbühel itself is sold under its name. Because skiing on the Horn is of secondary interest, the best location is either in the old centre (certainly the most attractive place to stay) or near the Hahnenkamm lifts, most people's starting point for the skiing, and where the nursery slopes are. The central Tiefenbrunner (✆2141) is expensive and fashionable, but reportedly no longer well run. The Maria Theresia (✆4711) is recommended for 'first-class cuisine'. The Haselsberger (✆2866) is cheaper than most and convenient for the Hahnenkamm, as is the comfortable Montana

Kitzbühel facts

Lift payment

Passes Kitzbühel, Kirchberg, Jochberg, Pass Thurn, Aschau and Bichlalm lifts (and linking buses) are covered by one pass. Day passes are cheaper the later you buy them. Also 'hourly' tickets, which give a refund when handed in, and passes for any 5 days in 7, or 10 in 14.
Cost 6-day pass AS1,390. 18% off in low-season (includes late March).
Beginners Coupons (not on all lifts).
Children 50% off under 15. Also cheap coupons. Free skiing if under 1.10m (3ft 7in).

Ski school

Classes 2hr morning and afternoon.
Cost 6 days AS950. Private lessons AS1,785/day.
Children Classes, ages 3 up, adult times and prices; lunch AS70/day. Non-ski kindergartens: ages 1–3, AS350/day including meals; ages 2½–5, 6 days AS1,100 including meals.
Special courses Wedel, slalom, racing, off-piste.

Cross-country skiing

Trails 14km trail to and from Hechenmoos (medium), 20km of loops around Reith (mixed), 3km at Schwarzsee (easy). Instruction and free guided excursions (thrice weekly) available.

Medical facilities

In resort Hospital, doctors (including specialists), chemists, dentists.

Not skiing

Facilities Local museum, open-air ice rink (curling/skating), swimming (free to holders of lift-passes), sauna, solarium, riding, sleigh rides, wildlife park, tennis, squash, fitness centre, toboggan run, ski bobs.

Getting there

Airport Munich; transfer about 2hr. Daily public buses.
Railway Main-line station in resort.
Road Via Munich; chains rarely needed.

Available holidays

Resort beds 8,000 in hotels, 500 in apartments.
Package holidays Austro Tours (Ht), Best Skiing (Ht Ch Hm), Bladon Lines (Ht Ch Cl Hm), Blue Sky (Ht), Club 18-30 (Ht), Crystal (Ht), Edwards (Ht), Enterprise (Ht), Global (Ht Hm), GTF Tours (Ht Hm), Horizon (Ht), Inghams (Ht Sc), Intasun (Ht), Made to Measure (Ht), Mark Warner (Ch), Neilson (Ht Hm), Schoolplan (Ht), Ski NAT (Ht), Ski Team (Ht Hm), Skiworld (Ht), Snowcoach Holidays (Ht), Tentrek (Ht Hm), Thomson (Ht Hm)

Further information

Tourist office ✆(5356) 2155. Tx 5118413.

(✆2526). Two regular visitors recommend the family-run Mühlbergerhof (✆2835), a B&B on the edge of town, not far from the skiing.

Après-ski is extremely lively and varied, from the horrifically crowded Londoner pub (of which we do not see the attraction) to the Casino (jacket, tie and passport). There are plenty of tea-bars, tea-dancing, discothèques, smoky dives, and more traditional musical venues, and organised outings. A reporter recommended the Mockingstube, near the Hahnenkamm lift, for happy-hour bargains. Restaurants are varied, the Tenne (cabaret, band) most fashionable.

Although Kitzbühel is low and its surroundings rather built up, its **cross-country** trails are good and the guided excursions recommended. **Non-skiers** will find a great variety of things to do. Operators organise regular excursions. The museum is recommended.

The **nursery slopes**, across a broad area at the bottom of the Hahnenkamm, are no more than adequate – rather a thoroughfare, and often short of snow; there is a smaller but better one further away, beyond the Streifalm lifts. Both mountains have easy runs to move on to.

We have had mixed reports, over recent years, of the **ski school** and its famous Red Devils. Most of our latest reports are damning, repeating earlier observations of instructors mainly interested in skiing, and of large class sizes. One observer came to the view that 'most of the instructors did not even seem to be good skiers themselves'. But one pupil received 'very good, detailed tutoring'.

Kirchberg 850m

Kirchberg is a busy village 5km from Kitzbühel, centred on a road junction, with river and railway nearby. It shares some of its more interesting neighbour's problems, as well as its skiing – it is full of traffic, and its lifts are a bus-ride away from the centre of the village. The idea that you can do Kitzbühel on the cheap by staying in Kirchberg is misguided, but it is an attractively lively resort in its own right, and has long been popular among British skiers with no taste for the glamour of Kitzbühel. It has plenty of good traditional Tyrolean nightlife, good facilities for cross-country skiing (not only along the valley to Westendorf but also a short, difficult loop at higher altitude), long cleared paths, tobogganing, skating and curling (natural rinks), tennis, squash, sleigh rides and swimming, and plenty of organised excursions. If staying on B&B terms, be prepared for queues and early closing in the village restaurants. Most of the hotels and guest-houses are in the centre, though there are a handful by the lift departure for Ehrenbachhöhe. There are nursery slopes at that same place, and both skiing and non-skiing kindergartens. Among the most charming of the town hotels is the mid-priced Gasthof Unterm Rain (✆2298), on the Kitzbühel road.

Tourist office ✆(5357) 2309. Tx 51371.
Package holidays Austro Tours (Ht), Enterprise (Ht), Horizon (Ht), Hourmont (Ht), Inghams (Ht), Intasun (Ht), Neilson (Ht), Ski Lovers (Ht Ch), Skiworld (Ht Sc), Thomson (Ht), Top Deck (Ht Cl Sc).

Round the Horn

St Johann in Tirol Austria 650m

Good for *Easy runs, mountain restaurants, après-ski, short airport transfers, easy road access, rail access*
Bad for *Tough runs, late holidays, skiing convenience, resort-level snow, freedom from cars*

Separate resort: Fieberbrunn

St Johann is a substantial, bustling valley town, just over the hill from Kitzbühel. The hill in question is the Kitzbühelerhorn, and the mainly gentle skiing of St Johann covers a north-facing wooded shoulder of it, from the modest height (even by local standards) of 1700m all the way down to various points along the valleys.

Proximity to Kitzbühel should not be taken to indicate similarity. St Johann has little of the gloss of its famous neighbour, and none of the fashionable following. Its appeal (like its skiing, which suits beginners and early intermediates well) is much more straightforward – it is a pleasant chalet-style setting for a lively and quite varied winter holiday at reasonable prices.

Only a few miles up the road from St Johann, but seemingly much further from the bustle of the busy junction of main roads and valleys, lies the small village of Fieberbrunn, covered along with St Johann by the regional lift pass. When skiers argue about snowfall, it always seems to be the name of lowly little Fieberbrunn that crops up to illustrate the point that higher does not always mean snowier. We have not attempted to substantiate the theory that this is in fact as well as name a *Schneewinkl* – a snow-pocket – but our own experience is, as they say, not inconsistent with that theory. We skied there a couple of seasons ago when snow was generally good in this corner of Austria, and found conditions even better than in neighbouring resorts – no doubt partly because Fieberbrunn's slopes were less heavily skied.

The skiing top 1700m bottom 680m

After some years of apparent torpor, the resort authorities in St Johann seem to have come very much awake. A large installation of snow-making machinery (still a rarity in Austria, although increasingly common in France) should this season be in operation on the village run from Angeralm. Equally important is the opening last season of a six-seater gondola to the top of the skiing, replacing the old funicular and cable-car combination. The new lift goes up from a point close to the valley station of the old funicular all the way to Harschbichl at 1700m. From this point, runs fan out down three gentle rounded ridges, separated by wooded glades, some of them splitting and linking further down the mountain. Practically all the skiing on the top half of the

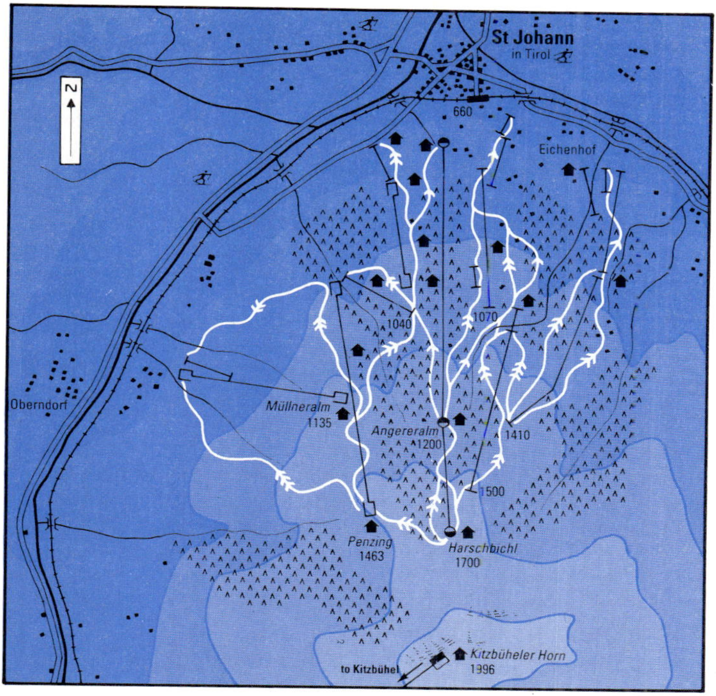

mountain is graded red, and properly so. These are good intermediate slopes, pleasantly varied and occasionally challenging. Most runs can be extended to the valley, but there are plentiful drags and chair-lifts on most of them to allow red-run skiers to stay high and leave blue-run skiers in peace lower down. The long Penzing chair is now a fast four-seater, making its red run particularly attractive for energetic skiers.

The bottom sections of the runs are all easier, and constitute excellent terrain for building the confidence of near-beginners. The main run back to the village has the additional attraction for nervous novices of involving no tricky lifts (served as it is by the first stage of the gondola). What's more, the slope is littered with restaurants.

Only one black run is marked on the piste map – a pleasant long run almost from top to bottom of the hill on the west side – and its grading is an exaggeration. There is a moderately steep, sunny pitch part-way down, where poor snow can make things tricky for a few yards, but the run is otherwise easy, and manageable by many skiers who normally baulk at reds. It may be closed, even in high season, for racing practice.

The choice of reasonably priced and welcoming **mountain restaurants** is very wide. Practically every piste has a hut at the top or bottom, or part-way down, or all three – in one run down from Harschbichl to the village it is possible to include no less than eight restaurants. Several of the restaurants are also hotels.

Judging by the report of a 1988 high-season visitor, the new lifts have done the trick, and **queues** are not a problem at village level or up the mountain. The system of lifts and pistes fanning out down a conical mountain is not prone to bottlenecks.

The resort

St Johann is at a junction of valleys, rivers and roads, and has a railway line running through; the centre is a triangle neatly defined by this railway on the south side and by the two rivers which meet to the north. The ski slopes are across the railway line, and there are spreading suburbs outside these boundaries on all sides. The main road from Kitzbühel bypasses the centre. It is an old town much developed, and a popular summer resort as well as a winter one. These facts would lead you to expect a town with a bit of character and life, and St Johann has both. But it is not particularly pretty or charming.

A free ski-bus serves the main lift station, so your location within the resort is not critical. But there is something to be said for being on the skiing side of the railway, or at least on the town side of the two rivers.

Most of the **accommodation** is in hotels, *pensions* and private

St Johann in Tirol facts

Lift payment

Passes Single pass covers all lifts; available for all periods from half-day. Schneewinkl pass (day or 6-day) also covers Fieberbrunn and other small resorts.
Cost 6-day pass AS1,100; 10% reduction in low season. Schneewinkl pass AS1,200.
Beginners Points card, and half-day passes for nursery drag-lifts.
Children 40% off, under 15.

Ski school

Classes 2hr morning and afternoon.
Cost 6 days AS950. Private lessons AS850/half-day.
Children Classes as adults. Kindergarten with ski instruction from age 4, 9.30–4.30, prices as adults; lunch available.
Special courses Racing, ski-touring, surf, acrobatics.

Getting there

Airport Munich; transfer about 1½hr.
Railway Main-line station in resort.
Road Via Munich; chains rarely needed.

Cross-country skiing

Trails 74km total – easy, medium and difficult trails both on east and west sides of the town.

Not skiing

Facilities Swimming, sauna, solarium, fitness room, massage, tennis (4 courts), skating (natural rink), curling, sleigh rides, riding, plane joy-rides, air-gun range, toboggan run, 40km cleared paths, bowling.

Medical facilities

In resort Hospital, doctors (including specialists), dentists, chemists.

Available holidays

Resort beds 6,000, mainly in hotels, pensions and private rooms.
Package holidays Austro Tours (Ht Ch), Crystal (Ht), Enterprise (Ht), GTF Tours (Ht Hm), Horizon (Ht), Hourmont (Ht), Inghams (Ht), Intasun (Ht), SkiBound (Ht), Thomson (Ht)

Further information

Tourist office ✆(5352) 2218. Tx 5124117.

rooms. Among the smarter hotels, the Dorfschmiede (✆2323) is attractively rustic, in parts at least, and in a good compromise position just on the town side of the railway. The much cheaper Gasthof Bärer (✆2308) is right in the centre on the Hauptplatz; it is a popular aprés-ski meeting place, and reportedly very comfortable.

The **après-ski** scene is lively, with such dignified proceedings as Mr and Miss St Johann competitions, as well as charming old bars and restaurants (the Speckbackerstub'n is reportedly a good example) and towny tea-rooms. There are youth-oriented discos as well as more traditional musical venues.

For **non-skiers** St Johann has a wide range of sporting activities, and is ideally placed for excursions to Kitzbühel, Innsbruck and Salzburg. The resort is an excellent base for **cross-country** skiers, who have a choice of long trails of all degrees of difficulty on two sides of the resort. A new cross-country centre (the Koasa-stadion) has been built just across the main road, with changing rooms and waxing facilities – plus deck-chairs and a 'cross-country bar'. The ski-bus calls at appropriate points for langlaufers as well as downhillers.

The gentle pistes coming down to the village and its outposts have excellent **nursery slopes** at the bottom, provided there is snow. We have no recent reports on **ski school**.

Fieberbrunn 800m

Fieberbrunn's village centre is set back from the road and has the usual ingredients of Tyrolean charm: clean and cheerful hotels and guest-houses, a pretty church and a very jolly après-ski atmosphere (tea-dancing and beauty contests) in the Alte Post and one or two other bars, with Dutch visitors much in evidence. Overall the resort is small, but it is also highly inconvenient – strung out along the road for over a mile but at no point within walking range of the main ski area. A few chair- and drag-lifts cover a small and very attractive, lightly wooded mountainside between the base station near the road at about 800m and the bald Lärchfilzkogel (1655m), with a chair-lift on the slopes beyond this peak reaching 1870m. There are several long, very easy runs, some easy off-piste skiing on the open eastern side of the mountain, and steeper north-facing slopes dropping from the summit down into a wide and empty valley. An unpisted route makes it possible to ski back to the nursery slopes on the edge of the village. Ski tours between Fieberbrunn and the Kitzbühel valley are popular. Returning by train is not difficult. There is a swimming pool and an indoor ice rink near the railway station at the northern end of the village, all-day kindergartens, and a free ski-bus.

Tourist office ✆(5354) 6304. Tx 51560. **Package holidays** Blue Sky (Ht), Enterprise (Ht), Global (Ht), Schoolplan (Ht).

Grossraum: space available

Söll Austria 700m

Good for *Short airport transfers, après-ski, easy road access, big ski area*
Bad for *Tough runs, late holidays, skiing convenience, resort-level snow*

Linked resorts: Scheffau, Going, Ellmau, Brixen, Hopfgarten, Itter
Separate resort: Westendorf

Like nearby Kitzbühel, Söll shares with several less well-known neighbours a broad ski area which is spread around a pleasantly wooded, mostly round-topped ridge – more hilly than mountainous in Alpine terms. The area's name is Grossraum, which (literally translated) means big space, and it is a fair summary. The skiing is friendly in general, with lots of villages dotted along the broad low valleys below. Söll is the main centre, particularly for British visitors: although still definitely a village, it attracts very large numbers of package holiday-makers from the UK – especially (to quote one reporter) 'the young singles fraternity for whom skiing is secondary to nightlife' and whose nightlife usually ends with a lot of noise in the village streets at a late hour. With the introduction of a big gondola access lift, this season should see an end to the queues to get out of the valley which have spoilt Söll for many skiers in the past.

Set low, and beside a main road very near the motorway system, Söll is admirably accessible both for motorists and for air travellers. Having a car can be very valuable for skiing excursions and for going to glacier areas (Stubai, Hintertux) when local conditions are poor.

There are dozens of other holiday villages giving access to the Grossraum. Of those close to the skiing, Scheffau is the most charming, and probably the best base for exploring the whole ski area; Ellmau is closer to lifts but less well placed for the area as a whole; quiet little Itter is also on the same side of the main road as the ski area, and now has an access lift; the village of Going is peripheral for skiing, but has charm and regulars who swear by it; Hopfgarten, on the south-west side of the area, is young and lively, with good but south-facing runs. Westendorf is a charming and civilised resort with its own separate ski area, deservedly popular with inexperienced skiers and now covered by the Grossraum lift pass.

The skiing top 1827m bottom 621m

The Grossraum ski region is spread around broad, medium-altitude mountains separating two wide valleys. One side consists of north-facing slopes above Söll, Scheffau, Ellmau and Going, the other of south-facing ones accessible from Hopfgarten and Brixen im Thale.

The skiing above Itter, between Söll and Hopfgarten, faces west.

For most people, **Söll**'s skiing starts with a long walk from the village centre to the lifts (there are ski-buses, but few and far between). A new eight-seater gondola goes up to Hochsöll, an open but not very flat shelf, with a few short drag-lifts on the easier slopes at the foot of the impressively steep Hohe Salve, reached by chair-lift. Runs down from this beautiful, panoramic peak (with church and restaurant on top) are not easy and include a genuinely black run down the face. Apart from these the most interesting runs are the long descents through the trees from Hochsöll to Söll, an excellent red and a more roundabout 'family run' blue, both of which can be treacherous or unskiable when icy – as they not infrequently are.

The easiest ways down from the Hohe Salve are on the western flank of the mountain down to Rigi above **Hopfgarten**. In good conditions these runs can be extended a long way (1200m vertical) down to Hopfgarten itself, over interestingly varied terrain. From Rigi there are easy runs round to Hochsöll and a run down to **Itter**, which now has a lift back up from the valley. From Thennwirt, below Rigi, a chair-lift makes the connection with the south-facing slopes at Kälbersalve and thus with the wide area of almost flat lifts and runs around Filzalm above **Brixen**. The runs (including a black) down to Brixen are excellent, given good snow; but don't count on it. There are more direct routes down to this area from Hohe Salve, but they are either steep or likely to be icy, or both. If heading for the skiing of Brixen or Scheffau from Söll, the prudent approach now is to cut out Hohe Salve by taking the recently built cable-car from Hochsöll to the east of it (though some leg-work is involved). This cable-car and the chair-lift above it have opened up a worthwhile new area of skiing on the north-east flank of Hohe Salve, as well as improving Söll's connections with other resorts in the Grossraum area.

From Filzalm there are easy although time-consuming connections over gently-rounded knolls (Zinsberg and Eiberg) to the top of Scheffau's skiing at Brandstadl. Runs down to **Scheffau** are long open trails through the woods, steep and fast enough to be a challenge, but wide enough to be easily manageable. The alternative is to ski further along the ridge to Hartkaiser, for runs down to **Ellmau**, where lower-slope lifts link up with the skiing of **Going**, below Astberg (1267m). Getting back to Söll from these places means retracing your steps. Many skiers prefer to ski these parts of the system by taking the valley bus in the morning or the evening. Several reporters have found that Scheffau has better snow conditions than Söll.

Mountain restaurants were generally considered by reporters to be adequate but not exciting. Those at Hochsöll are often crowded.

The new Söll gondola will doubtless relieve the serious **queues** to get into the skiing from there, as the recently built one at Brixen did. Whether Hochsöll will now become more of a bottleneck remains to be seen. The system as a whole is not queue-free – any drag-lift which forms a link in the east-west chain is likely to attract them. Hopfgarten's chair-lifts are rarely over-subscribed.

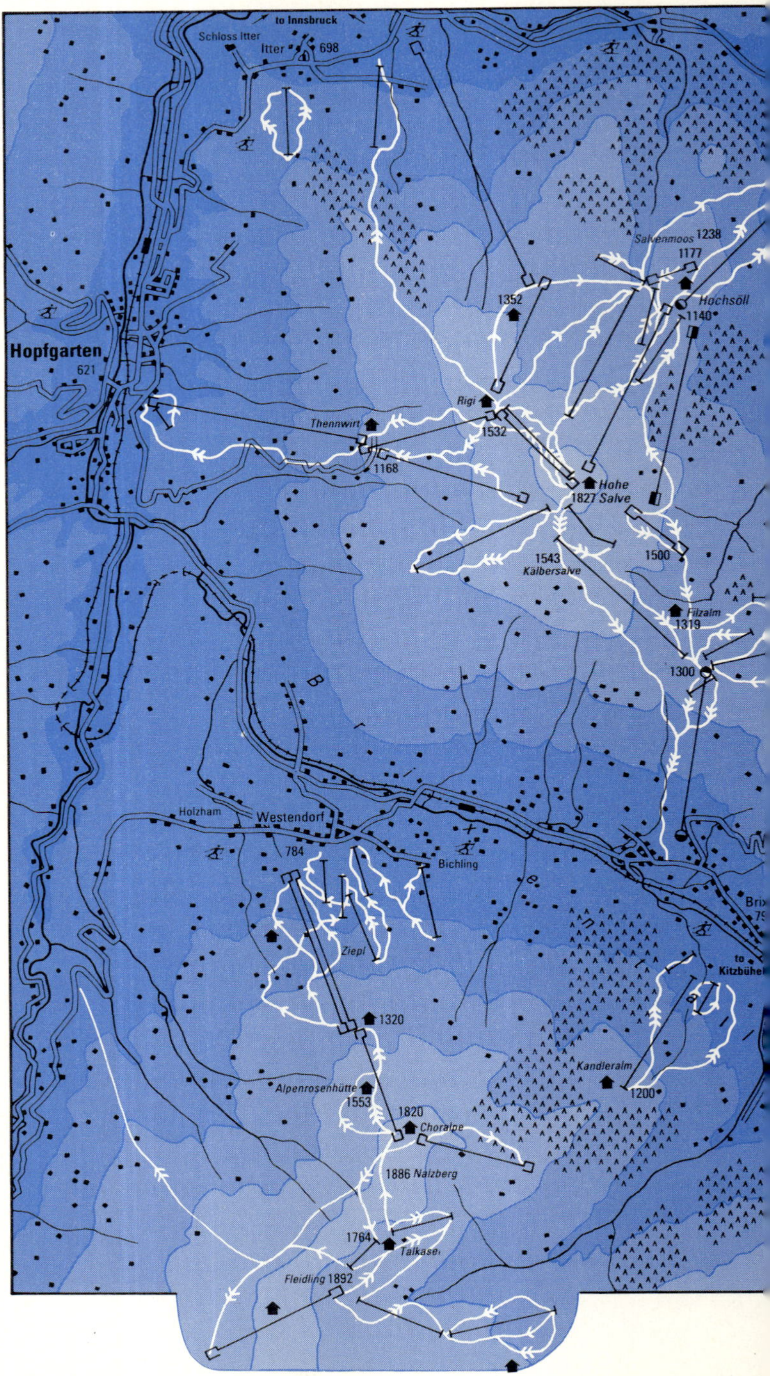
to Innsbruck
Schloss Itter
Itter 698
Hopfgarten
621
Salvenmoos 1238
1177
Hochsöll
1140
1352
Rigi
Thennwirt
1532
1168
Hohe
1827 Salve
1500
1543
Kälbersalve
Filzalm
1319
1300
Holzham
Westendorf
784
Bichling
Brixental
Ziepl
1320
Kandleralm
1200
Alpenrosenhütte
1553
1820
Choralpe
1886 Nalzberg
1764
Talkaser
Fieldling 1892
to Kitzbühel

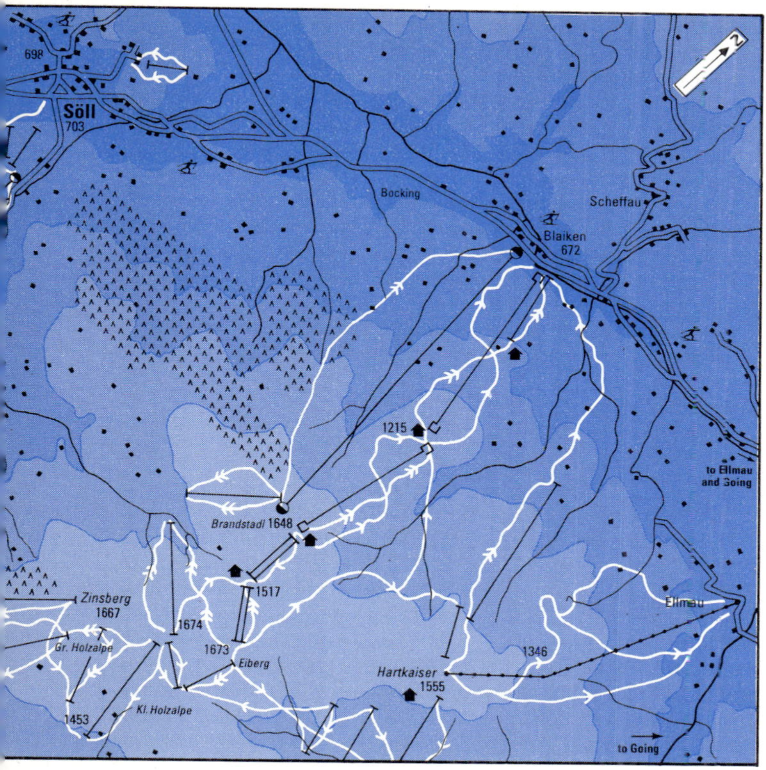

The resort

Söll is not a very large village but it has spread considerably across its wide valley. The buildings are attractive, in a neat neo-Tyrolean way, but do not add up convincingly to a village with any real character. A main road by-passes the village, between it and the ski slopes, which are a long walk or a bus or taxi-ride away. (Several reporters were in central hotels on full board terms, and regretted it.)

Accommodation is in hotels, mostly simple but satisfactory. The Post (∅5221) is an attractive old hotel right in the centre (of the nightlife as well as the village). The Eggerwirt (∅5236) and Austria (∅5213) are quieter central alternatives. There are several hotels lining the nursery slopes; the Ingeborg (∅5223) and Eisenmann (∅5258) have received favourable reports.

With so many young British around, many of them on B&B terms, **après-ski** activity is predictably lively (nearly all reporters remarked on the very crowded thrice-weekly folk-singing evenings at the Hotel Post and on the Whisky Mühle disco for up-to-date chart sounds). There are all sorts of organised evening amusements, from bowling to zither performances. Queues are common for restaurants as well as for lifts.

The **cross-country** trails, on the valley floor, look satisfactory to our untutored eye, but one reporter pronounces them uninteresting. The resort is not very exciting for **non-skiers**, but the swimming pool (with a heated outdoor section) is highly recommended. There are lots of organised excursions.

Söll's **nursery slopes** are beside the chair-lift departure – open fields between the bottom of the wooded mountain and the village. They are splendidly wide and near-horizontal, but often short of snow, when the gentle slopes at Salvenmoos have to be used. There are always lots of people around, and often lift queues.

We have approving reports of numerous colonial **ski-school** instructors with better-than-Austrian English.

Scheffau 750m

Scheffau is poorly placed for skiing, a little way up the wrong side of the valley. But for many visitors the rustic seclusion of the spacious village more than compensates. Hotels and pensions are dotted around in the pastures, but there is also a recognisable village centre, where the old Gasthof Maikircher (✆8102) offers good-value accommodation. There is an adequate sunny nursery slope close to the village.

Tourist office ✆(5358) 8137. **Package holidays** Crystal (Ht), Edwards (Ht), Enterprise (Ht), Intasun (Ht), Thomson (Ht).

Ellmau 820m

Ellmau is not a big place, but it is the most towny of the Grossraum resorts, with more shops and bars than elsewhere. The centre is compact, but the resort sprawls widely between the valley station of the main lift on the west – a funicular to Hartkaiser – and an enormous area of nursery slope spreading across to Going on the east. Recent reports speak well of the ski school teaching and the lack of lift queues – and of the friendly Pension Christoph (✆2154). There is a 4km toboggan run.

Tourist office ✆(5358) 2307. **Package holidays** Best Skiing (Ch Ht Hm), Club 18-30 (Ht), Crystal (Ht), Enterprise (Ht), Inghams (Ht), Intasun (Ht Hm), Neilson (Ht Hm), Schools Abroad (Ht), Skiscope (Ht), SkiSet (Ht) Ski NAT (Ht Hm), Thomson (Ht).

Going 800m

Going is a charming rustic village with the Goinger Bach flowing through between its mellow old chalets. Its mountain, Astberg, is low and connected to the rest of the Grossraum skiing only at resort level (Ellmau). One reporter who wishes he had discovered Going (and skiing) 60 years ago warmly recommends the Retthäusl (✆2782).

Tourist office [TL](5358) 2438. **Package holidays** Enterprise (Ht).

Westendorf 790m

Westendorf is a small village in the Brixental near Kitzbühel, within sight of the Grossraum skiing but not linked to it. The local skiing is a small area of mostly easy runs, reached by a chair-lift or a new gondola from the good, broad nursery slopes at the edge of the village (about five minutes' gentle walk from the centre). It is pretty skiing on broad, mostly woodland pistes and snow-covered roads, and suits inexperienced or leisurely skiers very well. Westendorf attracts numerous British (and Irish) skiers, but even more Dutch. In general it is a very friendly village, with plenty of nightlife both imported (Andy's Tavern) and traditional (the Café Angerer and Kegelbahn bar), and some excellent hotels – the Schermer (✆6268), Mesnerwirt (✆6206), and Jakobwirt (✆6245) are highly recommended by reporters. There is also good, cheap B&B accommodation. Tables need to be reserved for evening meals in the village restaurants. The Mesnerwirt is said to offer the best value.

Tourist office ✆(5334) 6230. Tx 51237. **Package holidays** Crystal (Ht), Enterprise (Ht), Global (Ht Hm), Horizon (Ht), Intasun (Ht Hm), Neilson (Ht), Thomson (Ht Hm)

Other Grossraum resorts

Itter 700m

Tourist office ✆(5335) 2670. **Package holidays** Best Skiing (Ht Hm), Crystal (Ht), Enterprise (Ht), Horizon (Ht), Ski NAT (Ht).

Hopfgarten 620m

Tourist office ✆(5535) 2322. **Package holidays** Crystal (Ht), Enterprise (Ht), Tentrek (Ht Hm).

Brixen 800m

Tourist office ✆(5334) 8111. **Package holidays** Hourmont (Ht).

Söll facts

Lift payment

Passes Grossraum pass covers all lifts, and the Scheffau–Hopfgarten bus. Day and half-day passes, and limited area passes (eg Söll only) available.
Cost 6-day pass AS1,140.
Beginners Coupons.
Children 25% off, under 15.

Ski school

Classes 2hr morning and afternoon.
Cost 6 days AS950. Private lessons AS320/hr.
Children Ski kindergarten, ages 5–14, 9.30 to 4.15, 6 days with lunch AS1,290.
Special courses Guided Grossraum tours.

Cross-country skiing

Trails 100km of easy runs between Söll, Scheffau, Going and Ellmau. Instruction available.

Not skiing

Facilities Swimming (indoor/outdoor pool), sauna, solarium, natural ice rink (skating, curling), riding, sleigh rides, floodlit toboggan run, bowling, rifle range.

Medical facilities

In resort Doctor, dentist, chemist.
Hospital Wörgl (13km), Kufstein (15km).

Getting there

Airport Munich; transfer about 2hr. Salzburg; transfer about 1½hr.
Railway Wörgl (13km) or Kufstein (15km); bus to resort.
Road Via Munich; chains rarely needed.

Available holidays

Resort beds 1,400 in hotels, 2,800 other.
Package holidays Best Skiing (Ht Ch Hm), Blue Sky (Ht Hm), Club 18-30 (Ht), Crystal (Ht), Edwards (Ht), Enterprise (Ht), Global (Ht Hm), Horizon (Ht), Inghams (Ht), Intasun (Ht Hm), Neilson (Ht Hm), Ski Falcon (Ht), Ski NAT (Ht Hm), Ski Team (Ht Hm), Thomson (Ht)

Further information

Tourist office ✆(5333) 5216. Tx 51216.

For want of a better name

Niederau Austria 830m

Good for *Easy runs, nursery slopes, cross-country skiing, family holidays, short airport transfers, easy road access*
Bad for *Tough runs, late holidays, resort-level snow*

Separate resorts: Oberau, Auffach

Wildschönau is a savage-sounding name, but it is attached to an area of mainly amiable skiing on low, mostly wooded mountains south of the Inn valley, between Alpbach and Söll – highly popular with British tour operators and, evidently, with British skiers. The area embraces several resorts, all of them very small. Niederau is the main one on the British market; it is a sprawling village at the foot of one of the two small main ski areas, its modern hotels and guest-houses built in traditional style but with no central focus. As Tyrolean villages go, it is not particularly appealing – 3but it can be convenient, with skiing to some hotel doors.

The valley road climbs gently beyond Niederau to a low col on which sits Oberau, a more established village with its own nursery slopes and an attractive community atmosphere. Beyond it, around a bend in the valley, is Auffach, a tiny but growing village with a gondola up to the Schatzberg (1900m). This mountain adds greatly to the skiing available in the Wildschönau, but taken as a whole it is still a very limited area.

The skiing top 1900m bottom 830m

The skiing immediately above **Niederau** is in two small areas, each reached initially by a chair-lift from the valley. You can ski from the higher Lanerköpfl to the lower Markbachjoch.

The chair-lift for Lanerköpfl leaves from the western extremity of Niederau. The runs from it are graded red, and one of them is given the status of skiroute, which we hope is an excuse for not grooming the run rather than not patrolling it. In practice they are both good intermediate trails through the trees. The top drag-lift to Lanerköpfl itself serves a short slope which is not a lot steeper, but is graded black.

From the top an easy-intermediate run, with some leg-work involved, links with Markbachjoch, where, beyond the hotels and restaurants and linking lifts, there are two drag-lifts serving a sunny open slope, correctly graded blue. From the lower of these two easterly lifts, a run goes through the trees down to a drag on the lower slopes above an outpost of the village, or on to the village itself. A central section is sensibly graded red, but the run as a whole is harmless. Steeper runs come down directly from the top of the main Markbachjoch chair-lift out of the village. There is a black skiroute variant on the attractive main red run, but it is not difficult. Nor, in terms of steepness, is the route down under the chairs.

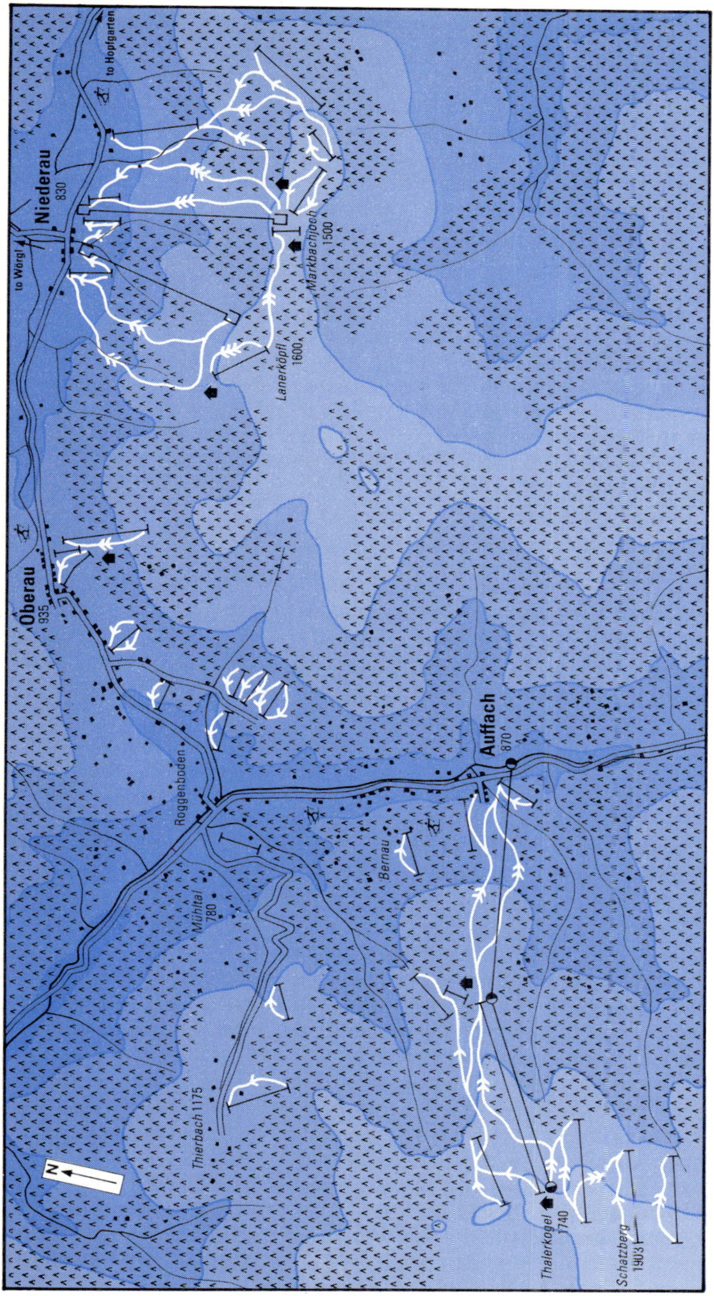
to Hopfgarten
to Wörgl
Niederau
830
Markbachjoch
1500
Lanerköpfl
1600
Oberau
935
Roggenboden
Auffach
870
Bernau
Mühltal
780
Thierbach 1175
Thalerkogel
1740
Schatzberg
1903
N

Our exploration of the skiing above **Auffach** was limited by very poor visibility, in which only one thing was clear: signposting of the links between the upper lifts is inadequate. The gondola goes up from a busy car park area south of the village. Its top section is duplicated by a very long drag-lift. Three parallel drags on the high open flank of the Schatzberg serve easy slopes of around 200m vertical and give access to long off-piste runs to the valley, outside the piste network. The slope under the gondola is properly graded red – much of it is easy, but occasional pitches are moderately steep (or seemed so in the fog). Some piste maps show a blue alternative on the top section, but it was not conspicuous. At the top and middle stations there are worthwhile drag-lifts on the northern flanks of the mountain which do serve easy runs, but there is no genuinely easy way back to the village.

Many skiers have lunch in the village, but there are adequate **mountain restaurants** in both main ski areas – including a jolly little hut on the west side of Markbachjoch.

At ski school time (morning and afternoon), **queues** for the village lifts are reported to be 'terrible'; at other times the system seems to function reasonably well.

The resort

Niederau spreads across the gentle north-facing slope at the foot of its skiing, with no very clear distinction between village and not-village. All the buildings have a veneer of chalet style applied, but it is a thinner one than in some other Tyrolean resorts. Location is not critical – it is not a huge place – but the ideal would be between the two chair-lifts.

Most of the **accommodation** is in hotels and guest-houses, with which our reporters have no complaint. The smartest in the village (there are also hotels up the mountain) is the big, comfortable, central Austria (✆8188) – 'without doubt the place to stay,' says a recent reporter. The Vicky (✆8282) is one of the pivots of the nightlife. A little further from the lifts is the Sonnschein (✆8353), in the view of one recent reporter the best in town – 'food very good, service excellent'.

Small though it is, the village does not lack lively **après-ski** in its cafés, bars and discos, largely based in hotels.

Non-skiers who are not content to potter along gentle paths between the villages will find the Wildschönau limited. The **cross-country** trails linking the villages are attractive and varied, and those beyond Auffach at Schönanger are peaceful and pretty.

There are **nursery slopes** right next to the village which represent a reasonable compromise between sunniness and snow reliability. Views on the **ski school** are generally favourable – 'excellent English-speaking tuition', says the latest.

Oberau 935m

Oberau is a friendly little village with no direct access to the main ski areas (which are served by a free ski-bus). It has good broad nursery slopes close to hand and slightly further away, along the hillside

Niederau facts

Lift payment

Passes Wildschönau pass covers all lifts in Niederau, Oberau, Auffach and smaller villages.
Cost 7-day pass AS1,310.
Beginners Points cards.
Children 30% off, under 15.

Ski school

Classes 2hr morning and afternoon.
Cost 6 days AS950. Private lessons AS310/hr.
Children Ski kindergarten, age 3 up, 9.30–4.30, AS280/day with lunch.
Special courses Ski-touring.

Cross-country skiing

Trails Over 35km in total, linking the villages and beyond Auffach at Schönanger.

Medical facilities

In resort Doctor, chemist.
Hospital Wörgl (7km).
Dentist Oberau (3km).

Not skiing

Facilities Curling, skating (natural rink), sleigh rides, toboggan runs, riding, sauna, solarium, cleared paths, bowling (in hotels).

Getting there

Airport Munich; transfer about 1½hr.
Railway Wörgl (7km).
Road Via Munich; chains rarely needed.

Available holidays

Resort beds 2,900, mainly in hotels and *pensions*.
Package holidays Enterprise (Ht), Global (Ht), Horizon (Ht), Intasun (Ht), Schoolplan (Ht), Ski NAT (Ht), Thomson (Ht)

Further information

Tourist office ✆(5339) 8216.

towards Auffach, at Roggenboden. And it has one short intermediate piste above the main nursery slopes, served by a drag-lift. The resort attracts elderly walkers and cross-country skiers as well as downhill beginners. The Gasthof Bergland (✆8250), about 1.5km out, is not luxurious but highly recommended for food and service.

Tourist office ✆(5339) 8255. Tx 51139.
Package holidays Club 18–30 (Ht), Enterprise (Ht), Inghams (Ht), Ski Sutherland (Ht), Snowcoach Holidays (Ht), Thomson (Ht).

Auffach 870m

Auffach has developed relatively little as a resort, despite its convenience for the major lift in the area. It consists mainly of a fairly tight gathering of chalets around the church, and a line of hotels and guest-houses along the road beyond the gondola station. There is also an elevated outpost at Bernau, with its own nursery lifts and cross-country loops. The Auffacherhof (✆8837) is a comfortable modern chalet hotel, convenient for the gondola and moderately priced. There is a toboggan run from the middle station of the gondola to Bernau.

Tourist office ✆(5339) 8980.
Package holidays Enterprise (Ht), Thomson (Ht).

Is love at first sight blind?

Alpbach Austria 1000m

Good for *Alpine charm, family holidays, après-ski, easy road access, short airport transfers*
Bad for *Tough runs, late holidays, skiing convenience*

Alpbach is a small village in attractive although unspectacular mountainous country between Kitzbühel and Innsbruck. Its skiing area is inconveniently located, and is limited in extent, variety and challenge. Yet Alpbach is one of the best-loved of Austrian resorts, with a special corner in the affections of many British skiers who return year after year to meet their friends, both locals and regular visitors like themselves. Among so many picturesque little Tyrolean villages, Alpbach stands out as one of the prettiest of them all, and it wins visitors over from the moment they arrive (unless they arrive at the same time as a great many other people, when their appreciation of the charms of the village may be inhibited by one of the small-scale traffic jams to which it is prone). It is a particularly good place for a family holiday at Christmas, and for beginners, who stand to benefit more than most skiers from its welcoming, charming atmosphere.

As our map makes clear, the ski area of Alpbach is modest in scale – basically only two main mountain slopes, neither measuring more than 4km from top to bottom as an intermediate skier flies. It will not suit the piste-basher reared on the *domaines skiables* of northern France. But no one should make the mistake of dismissing it as being suitable only for beginners. Provided skiing the same pistes repeatedly does not worry you, there is plenty of interest to be found in Alpbach's several red runs and couple of short blacks. And the lift system, which has already been improved appreciably in recent years, takes a leap forward this season with the installation of a big gondola.

Having a car in Alpbach seems rather anti-social, but many visitors (including not a few British visitors) take one; it does help you get to and from skiing, both locally and further afield – expeditions are possible westward to the Zillertal (Mayrhofen, Hintertux and so on) and eastward to Söll or even beyond to Kitzbühel. If staying in Inneralpbach a car is very useful for après-ski purposes.

The skiing top 1890m bottom 830m

Apart from a small nursery area beside the village, all Alpbach's skiing is on the slopes of the Wiedersbergerhorn, which means a short bus ride to and from the resort at each end of the day (and at lunch time for anyone with a village rendezvous).

The usual starting point is the Achenwirt lift station, beside the road up from Brixlegg. A six-seater gondola has now replaced the chair-lifts

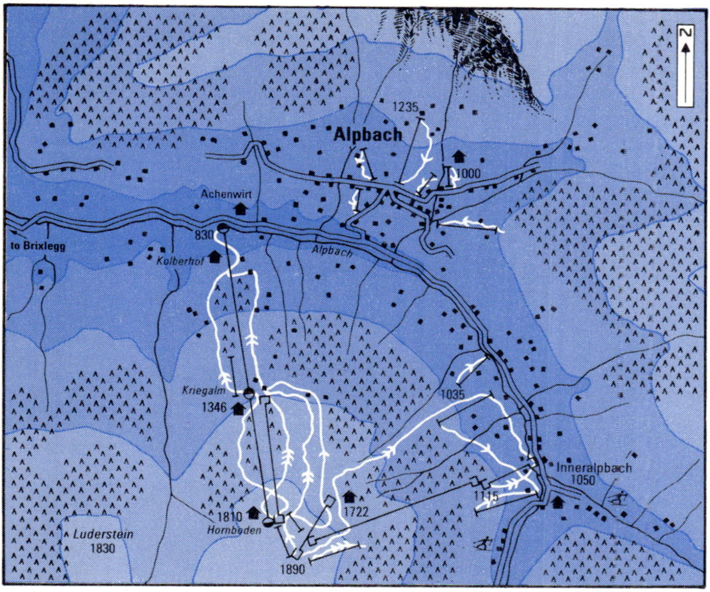

going up from here across wooded north-facing slopes to Hornboden. There are broad trails down either side to the Kriegalm half-way station, including a race-course marked black, and on down to the bottom to give an excellent long, fast course of over 1000m vertical – used by British racing clubs for annual competitions. Around Hornboden the views are splendid, the terrain is open and gentle, with several short drag-lifts suitable for near-beginners. But this area does not lack steeper slopes, both down the Brandegg drag-lift (marked black) and down the short but efficient three-seater Gmahbahn, which a couple of years ago replaced the old drag-lift up the top bowl to the east of Hornboden. There is an easy blue run (mostly pathway) down as far as Kriegalm, but no further. Lifts from Inneralpbach join up with the skiing above Hornboden and serve a long, not very tough red run back down.

A single off-piste route is marked on the lift map, from the top of the Brandegg drag to Inneralpbach. Conditions are not off-piste for long, and neither this nor the added possibility of skiing over the hill to Hygna (buses back) make Alpbach a resort which can safely be recommended to ski adventurers.

There are several **mountain restaurants**; the self-service one at Hornboden is often crowded; better prospects are to be found at the new Gmah restaurant, just down from the top of the mountain on the eastern side, or down in the valleys at Achenwirt and Inneralpbach.

The old chair-lifts up from Achenwirt to Hornboden were prone to serious **queues** in the mornings, but the new gondola should put paid to that problem. Old hands will be relieved to know that the long, steep drag-lift on the Inneralpbach side was replaced by a chair-lift a couple of seasons ago, improving this alternative way into the main skiing area. The new Gmahbahn chair-lift on top has greatly increased the uphill capacity at altitude.

The resort

Alpbach is a small village in a sunny position set on a hill, but compact enough for that not to matter too much, even in ski boots. At the heart of the village is its spotlessly clean green-and-white church, surrounded by traditional chalet buildings large and small. Tradition is a very evident part of Alpbach life, especially at Christmas and New Year, which is when many of Alpbach's family regulars prefer to visit. A good many such regulars are British; there is even a British ski club, the Alpbach Visitors, based in the resort. Shopping is limited; the Spa supermarket is reportedly competitive, but one reporter on a self-catering holiday regretted the lack of a butcher.

The bus to Achenwirt runs frequently enough for the needs of the small village; that to Inneralpbach is less frequent.

Accommodation is mostly in hotels, with a wide variety of comfort and cost between simple B&B houses and spacious, very comfortable hotels. The centre of the village is the most convenient for the ski-bus, but location isn't a serious worry. The most comfortable hotels are the expensive Böglerhof (✆5227) and Alphof (✆5371), both with swimming pools – the Böglerhof ideally placed for the ski-bus and nursery slopes,

Alpbach facts

Lift payment

Passes Covers all lifts and ski-bus from Alpbach. 5% off in low season. Day and half-day passes available.
Cost 6-day pass AS990.
Beginners Coupons.
Children 25% off under 15.

Ski school

Classes 2hr morning and afternoon.
Cost 6 days AS950. Private lessons AS315/hr.
Children Ski kindergarten, ages 4–6, 9.30–4.00, 6 days with lunch AS1,500. Non-ski kindergarten, ages 3–6, 9.30–4.15, 6 days with lunch AS990.

Cross-country skiing

Trails 17km of trails near Inneralpbach. Instruction available.

Not skiing

Facilities 20km of cleared paths, swimming, skating, curling, sauna/massage, sleigh rides, toboggan run.

Medical facilities

In resort Doctor and chemist.
Dentist Reith(6km).
Hospital Wörgl (28km).

Getting there

Airport Munich, 2hr; Innsbruck, 1hr.
Railway Brixlegg (10km).
Road Via Munich; chains rarely needed.

Available holidays

Resort beds 700 in hotels, 1,700 in apartments.
Package holidays Blue Sky (Ht), Enterprise (Ht), Global (Ht Ap Sc Hm), Inghams (Ht), Ski Sutherland (Ht), Ski-plan (Ht Hm), Thomson (Ht)

Further information

Tourist office ✆(05336) 5211. Tx 51380.

the Alphof quite a walk from the village centre. Among less expensive, more informal hotels, reporters recommend the Post (✆5203) – 'especially friendly Christmas Eve dinner, Birdy Pub noisy late at night' – the Messnerwirt (✆5212) and the Jakober (✆5223) – all very friendly and central, and the last an important hub of the British après-ski scene. Keen skiers may prefer to stay in Inneralpbach – 'very quiet, ideal for families' – or even at Achenwirt, where the old Gasthof Achenwirt (✆5202) has simple rooms above its panelled *stube*. But if you're that keen you probably shouldn't be considering Alpbach at all.

Après-ski has typically Tyrolean ingredients – notably the Tyrolean Evening itself, plus sleigh rides, skating and curling, very lively tea-time bars in central hotels, and a couple of discothèques. Reporters staying on B&B found little variety of restaurants – most are in hotels.

Cross-country skiers should stay in Inneralpbach. The trails are low and not entirely reliable for snow, but very attractive. **Non-skiers** can enjoy plenty of attractive walks, although not many within rendezvous range of skiers, and a wide choice of interesting excursions (Salzburg, Kitzbühel, Innsbruck, and over the Brenner Pass to Vipiteno in Italy). The public swimming pool is good, but a long walk from the centre of the village, as is the ice rink.

The **nursery slopes** close to the village centre are very good, being sunny and offering a variety of terrain from flat to slightly challenging. When snow is short, as it may be on this south-facing shelf, beginners are taken up to Hornboden.

We have generally favourable reports on the **ski school**; the instructors were especially commended for making the best of the very difficult conditions early last season, when skiing was restricted by lack of snow, and the tuition was reported as 'excellent, in good English. Guides are available for day ski tours (with skins).

Hard sell

Zell am Ziller Austria 600m

Good for *Sunny slopes, nursery slopes, easy runs, short airport transfers, easy road access, rail access*
Bad for *Tough runs, late holidays, resort-level snow, skiing convenience, freedom from cars*

Zell is a large village in the Ziller valley, downstream of Mayrhofen. It is a fairly unremarkable, traditional village where life and tourism are not wholly ski-oriented, lent some charm by the little steam train running through its centre and the Ziller round the edge, and by the interesting, ornately decorated Baroque church. It is a relatively quiet place, with nightlife which is neither sophisticated nor riotous nor particularly entertaining in the traditional Austrian way. Like Mayrhofen, Zell does not have skiing on its doorstep – the mountain is on the far side of the broad valley, reached by bus, and has no runs to the valley floor.

To sum up, Zell has not much to be said for it and quite a lot to be said against it. And yet tour operators continue to sell Zell successfully, and we have reports from skiers who are not only happy to go back but are actually planning to do so. They say the village and its ski instructors are friendly, prices are reasonable and the skiing is satisfactory without being threatening.

The skiing top 2264m bottom 930m

Zell's skiing is on two quite separate mountains. Very much the major area is Kreuzjoch-Rosenalm (the former the name of the peak on whose flanks the skiing takes place, the latter the name of the congregation area at the heart of the system); access is a short bus-ride away, across the valley. The minor area is Gerlosstein-Sonnalm, starting a long bus-ride away at the elevated hamlet of Hainzenberg. The Kreuzjoch skiing is sunny, and some of it directly south-facing. Gerlosstein is much less sunny, and often has better snow.

The Kreuzjoch gondola starts from a huge car park complex close to the Zillertal highway. It goes up over piste-less farmland to Wiesenalm – for practical purposes the base of the skiing. (The cable-car going up in parallel with the gondola stops 300m lower down.)

The left-hand chair-lift from Wiesenalm goes to Rosenalm – a sunny, open, flat area above the trees which forms a natural meeting point for pistes and lifts in all directions. Facing north-west below it are two nursery drag-lifts; above it are the three lifts on which many skiers spend their time. The new Kreuzjochbahn chair-lift looks interesting on paper, serving a new black run which merges with the easy red run beside the Torljoch drag. The terrain between the two drag-lifts is quite varied, allowing some choice of steepness, but there is nothing of dark

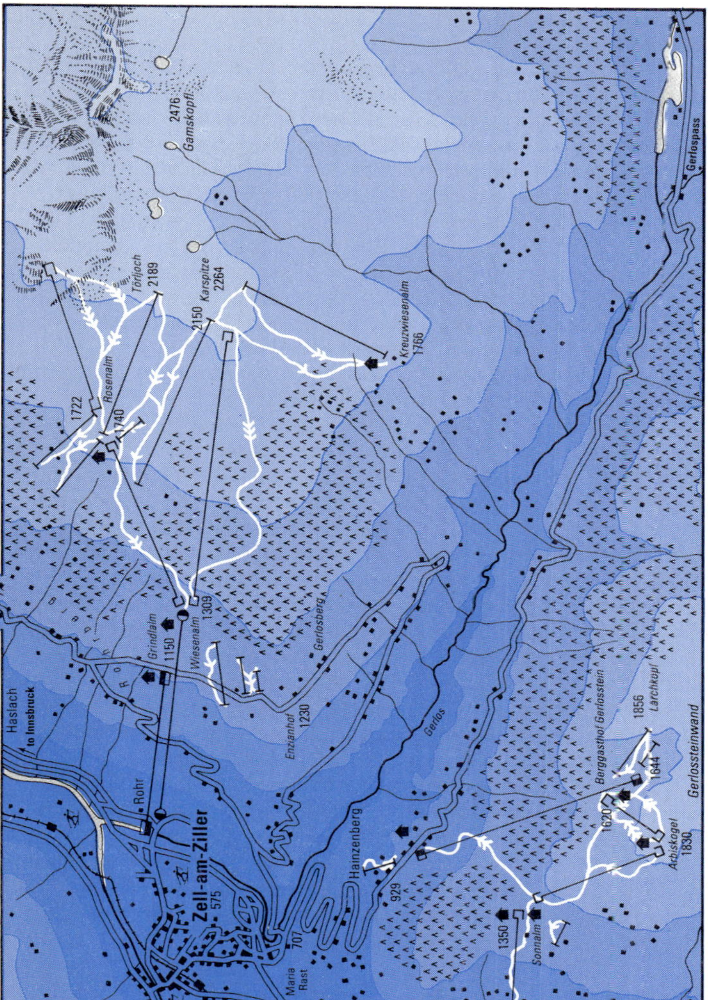
Haslach
to Innsbruck
Rohr
Zell-am-Ziller
575
Ziller
Maria Rast
707
Grindlalm
1150
Wiesenalm
1309
Enzianhof
1230
Gerlosberg
Gerlos
Hainzenberg
929
1722
Rosenalm
1740
Törljoch
2189
2150
Karspitze
2264
Kreuzwiesenalm
1766
2476
Gamskopfl.
Gerlospass
1350
Sonnalm
Ramsau
604
Schwendau
to Mayerhofen
Berggasthof Gerlosstein
1620
1644
1856
Lärchkopf
Arbiskogel
1830
Gerlossteinwand
N

red difficulty. Areas which start out off-piste are skied to become modest mogul-fields.

The right-hand Karspitz drag gives access to a similarly varied and attractive south-facing slope down to Kreuzwiesenalm – an admirable spot for sunbathing but not a place where snow lasts for long. The Karspitz drag also connects with Zell's one black run, also served by the Sportbahn chair-lift from Wiesenalm. The dimensions of this lift (length about 3.5km, height gain about 800m) give some clue to the nature of the run which winds its way through the woods from the top of it to the bottom: it is not generally steep. For most of its length it is a splendid easy intermediate course deserving no more than a blue grading, but blissfully free of traffic because it is marked black. There is a steepish final section which may also be icy, but this can be avoided by joining the zigzag path down from Rosenalm to Wiesenalm.

The alternative way down from Rosenalm to Wiesenalm is a red piste which can be difficult at the top when snow is in short supply.

The main lift at Gerlosstein is a modest cable-car from close to the Zell–Gerlos road at Hainzenberg up to a sheltered bowl underneath the rocky wall of the Gerlossteinwand. In the bottom of the bowl are two drag-lifts, one fairly short, the other very short, serving easy beginners' slopes. Going up from the cable-car station is a short but steep chair-lift to the top of this area at Arbiskogel, where there are tremendous views of the high peaks at the head of the Zillertal. Short, moderately challenging runs go back down to the pit of the bowl, the black perhaps graded thus because of its inferior snow. On the shoulder of the mountain a good long red run goes down first to Sonnalm (where a chair-lift effects the return to Arbiskogel) and then on down to Hainzenberg – a total of 900m vertical, with plenty of variety en route. The valley village of Ramsau has a single chair-lift up to Sonnalm; the off-piste route back down is rarely skiable for very long.

Both areas are adequately equipped with **mountain restaurants**, which are mostly self-service places in token chalet-style. There is a jolly hut on the piste down from Rosenalm to Wiesenalm.

There must be peak-time **queues** for the Kreuzjoch gondola, despite its efficiency. The Rosenalm nursery lifts are often oversubscribed. The Gerlosstein cable-car mainly comes under pressure when skiers are diverted from Kreuzjoch by poor snow conditions.

The resort

Zell sits to one side of the flat-bottomed Zillertal, in a bend in the Ziller, which at that point flows close to the eastern wall of the valley. The centre is quite compact, between the river and the railway line, but its chalet-style buildings spread along the roads out. And there is quite a lot of development across the river bridge, along the road skirting the foot of the Zellerberg. Since skiing means taking buses wherever you stay, location is not of prime importance.

The **accommodation** is mostly in hotels and guest-houses, of a generally high standard. In the centre, the modern Tiroler Hof (✆2227)

Zell am Ziller facts

Lift payment

Passes Zillertal pass covers all lifts in Zell, Mayrhofen, Hintertux and several other resorts; available for periods of 4 days or longer. Zell pass available for shorter periods.
Cost 6-day pass AS1,160, 18% off in low season.
Beginners Lift pass.
Children 40% off, under 15.

Ski school

Classes 2hr morning and afternoon.
Cost 6 days AS950. Private lessons AS320/hr.
Children Ski kindergarten, age 4 up, ski school hours, 6 days with lunch AS1,350. Non-ski kindergarten, ages 3–6, 9.00–3.30, AS160/day.
Special courses Monoski, snowboard, ski-touring.

Cross-country skiing

Trails 24km locally, 15km further afield.

Not skiing

Facilities Curling, skating (natural rink), sleigh rides, sauna (in hotels), tennis at Kaltenbach (8km).

Medical facilities

In resort Doctors, dentist, chemist.
Hospital Schwaz (30km).

Getting there

Airport Munich; transfer about 2hr.
Railway Branch-line station in resort.
Road Via Munich; chains rarely needed.

Available holidays

Resort beds 5,000.
Package holidays Neilson (Ht), Ski Falcon (Ht Hm), Snowcoach Holidays (Ht), Thomson (Ht)

Further information

Tourist office ✆(5282) 7165. Tx 0533979.

is one of the pivots of the nightlife, and its small suites are good value for families; tables are shared when necessary. Reporters particularly recommend the Neuwirt (✆2209) – 'excellent value, unbelievably helpful proprietor' – and the Zellerhof (✆2612) – 'excellent menu, particularly breakfast', 'superb food, first-class service'.

The village's **après ski** is not a strong point, and hinges around hotel bars and three or four discos – including ones in the cellars of the Tiroler Hof and Zellerhof – and a few informal restaurants. Tour operators organise events – Tyrolean evenings, bowling – but it does not add up to a scene of great animation. Not much happens in the village at tea-time but there are one or two good café/cake shops.

Zell is neither good nor bad for **non-skiers** – it is well placed for excursions by road or rail (eg to Innsbruck) and has some sports facilities, but the village is not a captivating place. Lunch-time meetings with skiers are no problem (at Wiesenalm). There are long, sunny, flat **cross-country** skiing trails along the valley.

The **nursery slopes** at Rosenalm are excellent in themselves, though they tend to be crowded. Getting to and from them costs money as well as time and effort.

We have no very recent reports on **ski school**, which meets at both Rosenalm and Gerlosstein, but earlier reports are uniformly favourable.

End of the lines?

Mayrhofen Austria 630m

Good for *Not skiing, après-ski, easy road access, rail access, short airport transfers*
Bad for *Tough runs, lift queues, skiing convenience, resort-level snow*

Hintertux Austria 1500m

Good for *Late holidays, summer skiing, beautiful scenery, resort-level snow*
Bad for *Nursery slopes, skiing convenience, après-ski, not skiing, tough runs*

Other resorts: Finkenberg, Lanersbach

Mayrhofen is one the great British favourites in Austria. It enjoys a splendid setting enclosed by the steep wooded walls of the Zillertal (a busy, touristy valley of which Mayrhofen is the main focus), its hotels are clean and comfortable, there is lots to do off the slopes and plenty of evening life in the bars. Its popularity must rest on these things (and on the reputation of the ski school, particularly its caring for young children), because the large, towny resort is only moderately attractive and its skiing is far from ideal – being limited in variety for experienced skiers and yet awkward for the inexperienced, who have to take cable-cars to and from skiing. These are important drawbacks in the era of purpose-built resorts, and in the past reporters have been almost unanimous in recommending Mayrhofen only to inexperienced skiers and in remarking on the length of the lift queues.

But improvements have been made, and more are planned. The Zillertaler Superskipass opens up enormous possibilities within day-trip range; school hours are designed to relieve the pressure on the main lifts up to and back from the skiing; and new lifts have been built giving speedier access to the main ski area from other points in the valley. The real breakthrough may come in 1989–90, when the main lift out of Mayrhofen is trebled in capacity.

Mayrhofen does not suffer the snow problems common to many other low Tyrolean resorts, because most skiers have to spend most of their time on the sunny slopes at the top of the ski area; so although it is hardly an ideal late-season resort – its skiing does not reach 2300m – it is not merely an early-season resort either.

South of Mayrhofen the Zillertal splits into three small glacier valleys and the Tuxertal – a high, narrow valley, very different from the broad Zillertal. Several small resorts line the road up to and along it. Just above Mayrhofen, Finkenberg is a cramped village sharing Mayrhofen's main ski area, the Penken. Vorderlanersbach and Lanersbach have plans to link up with the same lift system, and already

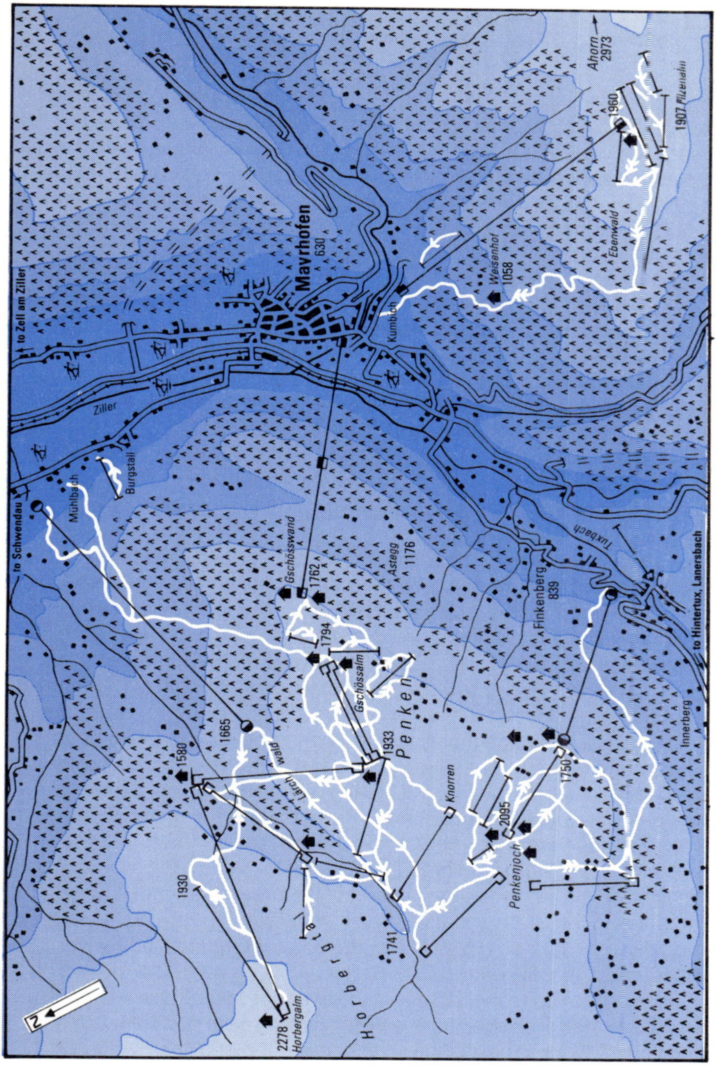

have interesting skiing of their own. Near the head of the valley lies Hintertux, a quiet and rather sunless spa blessed with one of the best glacier ski areas in the Alps. On several visits we have been impressed by the extent, beauty and variety of the skiing (with much more challenge than is common on glaciers) and the relative lack of queues even in fine weather. There are half-hourly buses up to Hintertux (covered by the Zillertal lift pass), but having a car is a great advantage for keen skiers wanting to make the most of the region.

The skiing top 3250m bottom 640m

Mayrhofen skiing is on two separate mountains enclosing the Zillertal with their steep, wooded walls. The main skiing is on the Penken, reached by cable-car from the resort centre or by gondola from Schwendau (a bus-ride away to the north) or from Finkenberg (to the south). The Ahorn, on the other side of Mayrhofen, is accessible only by cable-car from a point which is a long walk from the centre of the village. For all these lifts (except Finkenberg's) there is a regular but often over-subscribed ski-bus, covered by the lift pass.

The **Ahorn** faces mainly west, but so gentle are the slopes around the top of the cable-car that orientation doesn't matter much. This is an excellent open, spacious beginners' area, with a broad and beautiful panorama. There is one run down from the upper slopes to the bottom, the top of it served by drag-lift. This trail through the woods is graded red, but only as far as a restaurant (served by occasional buses). The steeper, but not extreme, bottom stretch is officially off-piste.

For most skiers, Mayrhofen skiing means the **Penken**. The notoriously crowded cable-car climbs over an unskiable wooded mountainside to a shelf at the top of the trees; chair-lifts starting an awkward distance from the top of the cable-car (the lift planned for 1990 will go further) then go up to Penkenjoch. From Penken there is a long ungraded run, some of it difficult, down to the bottom of the Horberg gondola: excellent skiing for good skiers in good snow. The main skiing area consists of a relatively narrow band of open and lightly wooded skiing on the north and south sides of the wide ridge that peaks at the rounded Penkenjoch, where there are merry ice bars and restaurants. The runs are short and mostly more red than blue, with easier ones (and some nursery slopes) back along the ridge towards Penken. A new easy run links Penken and the top of the Horberg lift, allowing inexperienced skiers to take the gondola down at the end of the day. The area has been extended by several new lifts on the sunny Gerent side of the Horbergtal, up to 2278m, the top of Mayrhofen's skiing. Apart from the sunshine, the interest of the area is the unpisted run underneath the chairs, relatively long and steep (about 27°), usually mogulled and littered with bodies. There is a red run back down to Finkenberg, mostly path.

At the entrance to the Tuxertal, and at about 1300m, **Lanersbach** and **Vorderlanersbach** share a wide skiing area in two halves, linked in both directions. The skiing is pleasantly open and uncrowded and includes enjoyable, fast and fairly long runs between 2300m and about 1450m. Runs down to both villages are easier and more reliable for snow than those to Mayrhofen. There are no runs down through the farms under the Vorderlanersbach chair-lift, but the skiing above the tree-line (up to 2500m) is wide, open and mostly gentle. It is possible to ski off-piste from there to the Penken area.

The foot of the **Hintertux** ski area is about half a mile from the edge of the village. A slow gondola and chair-lift climb in parallel over woods to Sommerbergalm, a sunny platform with restaurants and a small area

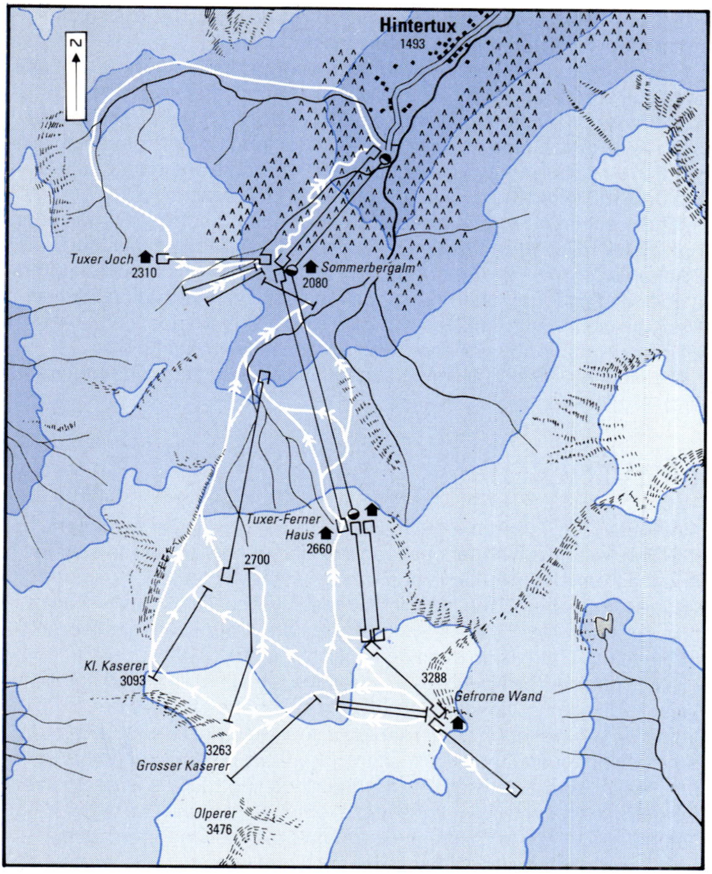

of easy east-facing skiing directly above it, beneath the Tuxerjoch. The main glacier area is separated from Sommerbergalm by a shallow gorge. Its runs are long and the ride up beside the glacier to Gefrorene Wand ('deep-frozen wall') is slow and cold. A new three-seater chair-lift on the back of the mountain has opened up 350m vertical of sunnier skiing. There are easy runs across the glacier near the top and down to Tuxerfernerhaus, but the skiing is less uniformly easy than on many glaciers, with fairly tough runs on the western side and below glacier level – over 30° in places. A short T-bar returns to Sommerbergalm, from which point the obvious run down is an ungraded route, easy to follow and not very steep, but narrow in places and often in difficult condition. The much more attractive alternative for experienced skiers is to take the Tuxerjoch chair-lift and then traverse an unnervingly steep slope to gain access to the beautiful run down the bowl of the Schwarze

Pfanne – off-piste, but heavily skied and not difficult. There is said to be good off-piste skiing on and off the glacier.

The Penken is well equipped with **mountain restaurants**, which are plentiful, sunny and good, though often crowded after ski school. Crowds are even more of a problem on the Ahorn, where there is only one restaurant. Going down to the resort for lunch is not something you want to do if you can avoid it. Hintertux restaurants are inadequate for the demand when there is good weather in high season.

The problem of serious **queues** for Mayrhofen's cable-cars has been only partly relieved by the installation of another gondola up to the Penken skiing (at Finkenberg) and by a ski school scheme which offers a choice of morning, afternoon or all-day lessons. Even when the new Penken cable-car is installed in a year's time, the queues for the Ahorn lift may persist. And ever-improving access to Penken can only increase the considerable high-season congestion there (in restaurants and on pistes, as well as on lifts).

Mayrhofen

Mayrhofen is traditional in style and not totally given over to tourism, but the long, wide main street between the market place near the station and the Penken cable-car is busy and touristy and there is not much village atmosphere. The main valley road by-passes the resort centre and, although there are always plenty of cars around, congestion isn't unpleasant. There is no evening public transport.

Accommodation is mostly in attractive, traditionally styled hotels (with traditionally clad staff), and nearly all reports we have are favourable. One reporter had stayed in four different cheap B&B houses and found them all excellent. There are a couple of hotels by the Penken cable-car station – the Sporthotel (✆2205) is large and very full of British tourists (residents and evening revellers). The large Neuhaus (✆2203) is calmer and generally rated by reporters as the best hotel in the resort, within easy reach of the ski-bus. We particularly liked the Kramerwirt (✆2615) a refurbished old hotel with lots of charm, and the new, very attractive Elisabeth (✆2929) just off the main street. The Neuhaus and Elisabeth both have their own pools, as does the St Georg (✆2793), also recommended by one reporter.

Après-ski is very lively. There are venues for traditional live music as well as deafening discothèques, and Tyrolean, tobogganing and sleigh-riding evenings are regularly organised by operators. Hotel bars see most of the après-skiing custom, though they are not very atmospheric; the Sporthotel's is packed from early evening.

One **cross-country** skiing reporter was well pleased with the long valley floor trails, but they are mostly easy and not reliable for snow cover. Mayrhofen is a good place for **non-skiers**, although the pool is small and the natural ice unreliable. Walks are good, and there are plenty of attractive excursions, within the local area and further afield to Innsbruck, Salzburg, and Italy (Cortina and Vipiteno). Non-skiers can reach sunny mountain restaurants on both sides.

Nursery slopes on the Ahorn are excellent – sunny, high, and pleasantly free from bombers on skis. But even without them the slopes, lifts and restaurant are often crowded, as is the cable-car up and down. The small nursery area on the Penken, often used by the adult ski school, is more convenient for meeting up with other skiers.

The **ski school** is Mayrhofen's pride and joy – especially the ski kindergarten, started by a local and international racing family (Spiess) in the late 1950s, when it was the first of its kind. Arrangements for children are excellent – they are looked after all day, and jump the queue for the cable-car to Ahorn. Reports on adult ski school are generally favourable (English spoken, serious attitude), but we have heard of large classes ('no more', says the tourist office) and of a beginner's dissatisfaction at the inefficient selection process at the beginning of the week. The recently introduced system of half-day (am or pm) classes is now to be complemented by a full-day 'Ski Total' option.

Mayrhofen facts

Lift payment

Passes Zillertal pass covers Mayrhofen, Finkenberg, Hintertux, Lanersbach, Zell am Ziller, Gerlos, Ramsau, Fügen, Hochfügen, Kaltenbach, plus post buses and the railway to Jenbach, and is available for periods of over 3 days. The Mayrhofen local pass, for shorter periods, does not cover the Finkenberg access lift.
Cost 6-day Zillertal pass AS1,160. 20% off in low season.
Beginners Lift pass needed.
Children 40% off under 15.
Summer skiing See Hintertux.

Ski school

Classes 2½hr morning or afternoon, or 2hr both morning and afternoon.
Cost 6 half-days AS790. 6 full days AS950. Private lessons AS320/hr.
Children Ski kindergarten, ages 4–12, 9.00–4.00, 6 days with lunch AS1,400. Non-ski kindergarten, 8.00–5.00, 6 days with lunch AS1,140.
Special courses Ski touring trips.

Not skiing

Facilities Natural ice rink, bowling, riding, sleigh rides, swimming, sauna, jacuzzi, 45km paths, hang-gliding, para-gliding, squash, tobogganing, 3 fitness centres.

Cross-country skiing

Trails 20km of easy trails along valley floor to Zell am Ziller. One trail floodlit 6pm to 10pm. Instruction available.

Medical facilities

In resort Doctors, dentists, chemist.
Hospital Schwaz (40km).

Available holidays

Resort beds 8,000, mostly in hotels and pensions.
Package holidays Best Skiing (Ht Ch Hm), Blue Sky (Ht Hm), Club 18-30 (Ht), Crystal (Ht), Enterprise (Ht), Global (Ht Hm), Horizon (Ht), Inghams (Ht), Intasun (Ht), Neilson (Ht Hm), Ski Falcon (Ht Hm), Ski NAT (Ht Hm), Ski Team (Ht Hm), Ski-plan (Ht Hm), Snowcoach Holidays (Ht), Thomson (Ht)

Getting there

Airport Munich, 2½hr; Innsbruck, 1hr.
Railway Local-line station in resort.
Road Via Munich; chains rarely needed.

Further information

Tourist office ✆(5285) 2305. Tx 533850.

Hintertux 1500m

Hintertux is a small spa, without much village atmosphere, at the head of the Tuxertal. Mountains rise steeply to the east, west and south, leaving the village in the shadow for much of the day in mid-winter. Cars and coaches on their way to and from the glacier ski area detract from the charm of the village, as they do all along the Tuxertal. Shopping is limited and there is no bank. Apart from an indoor spa pool, walks and a good toboggan run down from the Bichlalm restaurant, there is little for **non-skiers** to do, and Hintertux's **nightlife** is also quiet, with just a few cafés, a couple of bars with dancing, and bowling in one of the hotels near the lift station. **Cross-country** skiers are better catered for, with a long and reliably snowy trail down the valley.

There are a few **hotels** around the village's single square, and a couple at the foot of the lifts about half a mile away, the obvious base for downhillers to choose for convenience. The Rindererhof (✆501) is comfortable and has a sauna and use of the pool in the big spa hotel Kirchler in the village. Its neighbour, the Neu Hintertux (✆318), has bowling and more elaborate facilities (steam bath, sauna, whirlpool and solarium). Buses are free for anyone staying locally.

Hintertux has no **nursery slope**. There is a **ski school**, about which we lack reports. It offers children's classes, but the all-day kindergarten is at Lanersbach, quarter of an hour away by bus.

Hintertux facts

Lift payment

Passes Local passes for periods up to 3½ days, covering all Tuxertal lifts or Lanersbach lifts only; also available for 3 out of 6 and 6 out of 10 days. Zillertal pass for longer periods – see Mayrhofen chapter.
Summer skiing Extensive; 6 lifts, 2600 to 3250m.

Ski school

Classes 2hr morning and afternoon.
Cost 6 days AS950. Private lesson AS320/hr.
Children All-day ski kindergartens in Lanersbach; from age 4, 9.00–4.30, 6 days including lunch and lessons AS1,410, AS810 if parent also taking instruction. Non-ski kindergarten in Lanersbach, from age 2.

Cross-country skiing

Trails 23km trails along valley between Vorderlanersbach and Madseit (about half a mile away).

Not skiing

Facilities Thermal pool and sauna, 20km walks, tobogganing, bowling.

Medical facilities

Hospital Schwaz (56km).
Doctor and chemist Lanersbach (5km).
Dentist Mayrhofen (17km).

Available holidays

Resort beds About 1,000 in hotels and guest-houses.

Getting there

Airport Munich; transfer 3hr. Innsbruck; transfer 1½hr.
Railway Station in Mayrhofen (17km).
Road Via Munich; chains may be needed

Further information

Tourist office ✆(5287) 6060. Tx 533155.

Olympic fame

Innsbruck Austria 575m

This historic city at the cross-roads of western Austria is not what most European skiers expect of a ski resort but, having twice hosted the Olympics, Innsbruck is a thoroughly equipped winter sports town, with an interesting range of downhill and cross-country skiing within easy commuting range on the (often over-subscribed) free bus services. This is a familiar routine for American skiers, for many of whom Innsbruck is a major port of call. The city is an excellent base for excursions (notably to Italy), eating and drinking is cheap by skiing standards and evening entertainment is quite varied.

The most challenging skiing is on the steep and often unfriendly south-facing slopes served by the cable-cars from the edge of Innsbruck, but a greater extent and range is found on the south side of the valley, above small resorts covered by a joint lift pass. **Igls** (893m) is traditionally the most popular, with sedate hotels and tea shops (but also some busy bars), beautiful walks and the Olympic bob-run, which is open to fearless members of the public. The skiing mainly consists of the downhill race-course where Klammer skied himself into legend – a nicely varied north-facing red run beneath the Patscherkofel (2247m). There are easier variants, and some off-piste skiing among the trees.

On the other side of the Brenner motorway, **Axamer Lizum** (1600m) is a characterless ski station – a couple of hotels and a huge car park -- in the middle of the most interesting local skiing, beneath the neighbouring peaks of Hoadl (2343m) and Pleisen (2236m). Weekend queues for the lifts can be a problem, but the skiing is extensive and varied, mostly above the trees, and includes a splendid long easy black off the Pleisen down to Axams (874m). Across the narrow valley, a chair serves a not-too-severe black run and links up with the long, easy, sunny pistes above the charming, unspoilt village of **Mutters** (830m).

Slightly further away, with a separate lift pass, the long Stubaital has two main ski areas. Above the small resort of **Fulpmes** (937m), but not directly accessible from it, there is excellent skiing in a sheltered bowl between Sennjoch (2224m) and the Schlickeralm (1616m), including some tough unpisted runs and a small, sunny nursery area. The access chair-lifts are slow and often crowded, and the run down to the car park is often worn bare. 18km beyond the jolly village of **Neustift** (993m) is a large area of glacier skiing, with lifts from Mutterbergalm (1728m) up to 3200m, open all year. In winter there are long runs, not all of them easy, down to the mid-station at 2300m, and a tough, unpisted route down to the base station. When snow elsewhere is short, queues are long.

Innsbruck tourist office ✆(5222) 25715.

Package holidays Fulpmes: Alpine Tours (Ht Sc), Ski Sutherland (Ht). Igls: Austro Tours (Ht), Inghams (Ht), Neilson (Ht), Ski NAT (Ht), Thomson (Ht). Innsbruck: Made to Measure (Ht). Mutters: Ski Sutherland (Ht). Neustift: Alpine Tours (Ht Sc), Austro Tours (Ht), Crystal (Ht).

Take your time

Seefeld Austria 1200m

Good for *Cross-country skiing, not skiing, rail access, easy road access, short airport transfers*
Bad for *Skiing convenience*

To prevent the suspension of diplomatic relations with the tourist office of this popular resort, we are no longer flippantly branding Seefeld as 'Bad for downhill skiing'. But let us be clear: if downhill skiing is your main priority, Seefeld is the last major resort in this guide you should think of visiting. The plain fact is that the terrain around Seefeld is admirably suited to the Nordic sport, and less to the Alpine one. It provides some pleasant skiing for beginners and for undemanding intermediates who are content with a limited skiing terrain set in attractive scenery. There are a couple of black off-piste runs, but they do not amount to enough to satisfy the adventurous skier. It would take no more than a day or two to exhaust the downhill possibilities. But the resort complements its skiing attractions with a range of non-skiing facilities second to none, and has thus secured its popularity with affluent elderly Germans. If such facilities are an important part of your winter holiday, Seefeld may sensibly be included in your short-list – provided you are not also looking for genuine (as opposed to synthetic) Alpine charm or for fashionable companions on the slopes. Seefeld is not Kitzbühel: it has been very deliberately developed over recent decades in typically thorough Tyrolean style for a particular purpose, which it meets admirably. Several reporters have thought prices high by Austrian standards.

The skiing top 2074m bottom 1180m

There are two quite separate skiing areas. The Rosshütte to the east is for the more serious skier, while the Gschwandtkopf is a low conical peak south of the village centre, used principally by the ski school. The two are connected to each other, and to other points in the village, by a free circular ski-bus service in each direction, starting at 9.30am. Seefeld disdains the dawn rush for the slopes, and anyone on skis much before 10am is something of an early bird.

The skiing at **Gschwandtkopf** is chiefly concentrated on a broad, north-facing slope which rises for 300m between thick woods, starting from just beyond the sports centre. Of the two parallel chair-lifts rising up the centre of the slope only the left-hand one goes to the top, but the summit can also be reached by a combination of shorter lifts – there are three T-bars besides the chairs, all more or less parallel. The runs back down form a single slope on which even the most timid intermediate can happily find a safe course, but on which steeper sections can be

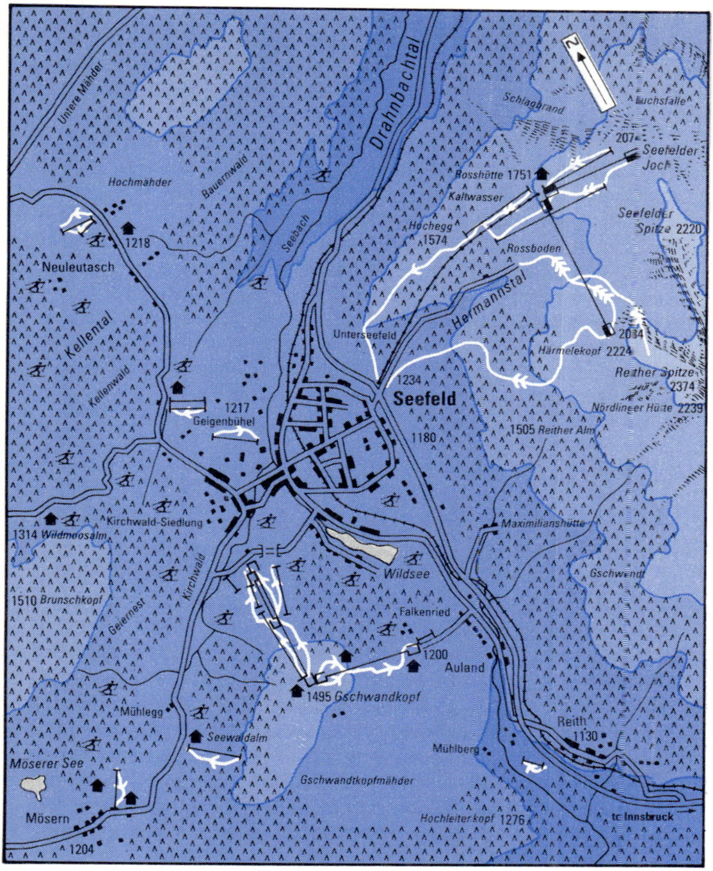

found. On one side of the slope you can test your skill on a coin-in-the-slot timed slalom course. The summit of the Gschwandtkopf can also be reached by a chair-lift from the neighbouring village of Reith, on the eastern side of the mountain. The single run down this side is very pleasant and slightly more demanding.

The starting point for the **Rosshütte** ski area is on the eastern edge of the village beside the by-pass, about 1km from the centre. A funicular railway follows a fairly gentle gradient for about 3km up to the Rosshütte (1750m). Queuing is not usually a problem here, but outside peak hours the service may be no better than half-hourly. There are some easy blue runs served by a couple of drag-lifts on the wide area of piste around Rosshütte, or you can take a short cable-car to the summit of the Seefelder Joch (2074m) with some fine views at the top. A parallel drag-lift also goes almost to the top. A couple of good, though shortish, red runs bring you back to Rosshütte. From here the long path back through the woods to the foot of the railway is an almost flat schuss. Adventurous skiers will want to take the small cable-car from Rosshütte which travels high across the Hermannstal to a shoulder of the Harmelekopf at 2000m. A short climb to the left then gives access to a couple of steep off-piste runs straight down the sides of the valley until you're forced to follow the flat valley floor back to the railway. The conventional route down from the Harmelekopf descends the shoulder as a nice open red run (watch for worn areas near the top) until it reaches the trees and becomes another schuss.

There are adequate **mountain restaurants** at top and bottom of the Gschwandtkopf, and at Rosshütte. There are plenty of sun-terraces, as much for the benefit of non-skiers as skiers – though you have to pay for a seat. The Rosshütte is particularly popular for basking.

The lift system presents no particular problems with **queues** during the week. Expect weekend invasions from Munich in good weather, with queues for the nursery lifts as well as the funicular.

The resort

Seefeld spreads across a broad plateau a few hundred metres above (and a few km to the north of) the Inn valley. There are wooded hills (they can hardly be called mountains) to the south and west, and the more pronounced peaks of the Seefelder Spitze and Reither Spitze to the east. Much of the resort's area is rather suburban-feeling, and the village centre proper is entirely to the south-west of the railway station. The streets forming the central cross-roads are traffic-free, and lined by comfortable, neat hotels and by tourist shops of a kind unseen in more single-minded ski resorts. Because skiing does not rule the lives of visitors, there are always plenty of people about – but the place remains calm and quiet, with voices never raised above a murmur. The human traffic is most concentrated in the street leading to the splendid sports centre on the south-west edge of the town, where there are countless curling and skating rinks.

There is all sorts of **accommodation** in abundance. Location should be considered with some care, according to how you plan to spend your time. The central area is convenient for the sports centre, and it's only a short walk out to the ski-bus route. Right on the central crossroads is the friendly old Tiroler Weinstube (✆2208), more affordable than the Post and the smart Alpenhotel Lamm nearby. There are several hotels between the crossroads and the sports centre. If money is no object, the big Klosterbrau (✆2621) has most of the facilities you could want under one roof. Further along, the Sonneck (B&B only, ✆2387) and next-door Batzenhäusl (✆2285) are a quarter the price. The suburbs to the west are better placed for cross-country than those to the east, between the railway and the by-pass. There is an attractive enclave of exclusive hotels (Astoria, Lärchenhof) to the north of the centre, close to the Geigenbühel nursery slopes. It's neither easy nor particularly relevant to find accommodation close to the main ski-lifts; if that's the way you're thinking, go elsewhere.

There's quite a good variety of **après-ski**, from tea-dancing to discothèques and a casino which one report calls 'stuffy'. But it is not a boisterous resort; young Brits who wish it was are to be found making the best of it in a simulated pub.

With thousands of skiers striding along scores of trails, ranging from eight-lane motorways across the plateau to stiff forest tracks, **cross-country** skiing appears to be the major activity in Seefeld. But is it? Quite possibly more people spend their time **not skiing** at all, but skating to Strauss, or curling, or wallowing in the 'fantastic' pool, or taking long walks. The resort is well placed for excursions to Innsbruck and further afield (over the Brenner to Italy).

There are short beginners' lifts at the foot of the Gschwandtkopf slopes, but the **nursery slopes** proper are on either side of a separate little hill, Geigenbühel, on the north-east fringe of the village. They have a bit more variety of gradient than many, including very gentle bits.

Reports of the **ski school** are uniformly favourable, with some glowing comments on standards of cross-country teaching.

Seefeld facts

Lift payment

Passes Area pass covering all lifts is for minimum of three days. Limited day passes also available. Lifts can be paid for by the ride.
Cost 6-day pass AS1,280. 15% off in low season.
Beginners Day passes or coupons.
Children 25% off under 14.

Ski school

Classes 2hr morning and afternoon.
Cost 6 days AS950. Private lessons AS300/hr.
Children Ski kindergarten, ages 4 up, 8.30–5.00, 6 days with meals AS1,400, without meals AS950. Non-ski kindergarten, ages 3 up, 9.30–13.00, 5 days without meals AS350. Private arrangements can be made for whole-day care.

Not skiing

Facilities Swimming, saunas, 60km of paths, toboggan run, curling, skating, sleigh rides, tennis, bowling, riding.

Cross-country skiing

Trails Totalling 200km, from the Lenerwiese (2.5km, easy) to the Olympia (25km, difficult).

Medical facilities

In resort Doctor, dentist, chemist.
Hospital Innsbruck (20km).

Getting there

Airport Munich, 2hr; Innsbruck, 1hr.
Railway Main-line station in resort.
Road Via Munich; chains rarely needed.

Available holidays

Resort beds 4,500 in hotels, 2,500 in pensions and private rooms, 1,500 in apartments.
Package holidays Austro Tours (Ht), Blue Sky (Ht), Crystal (Ht), Enterprise (Ht), GTF Tours (Ht Hm), Horizon (Ht), Inghams (Ht Sc), Intasun (Ht), Snowcoach Holidays (Ht), Thomson (Ht)

Further information

Tourist office ✆(5212) 2313. Tx 533452.

Proud relic

Obergurgl Austria 1930m

Good for *Late holidays, Alpine charm, après-ski, ski touring, lift queues, resort-level snow, easy runs, family holidays*
Bad for *Tough runs, short airport transfers, easy road access, not skiing*

Obergurgl is a tiny, high village with an awkward, bitty network of chair-lifts and drag-lifts which don't add up to a large skiing area, even when you count neighbouring Hochgurgl. It became famous in the days when skiing was much closer to what we now call ski touring; for that purpose, the top of the Ötztal with its 21 glaciers is, as it has always been, a superlative area. Not surprisingly, given the altitude, the immediate surroundings of the resort are bleak; but the resort has charm; it has not gone for growth and it is a real, inhabited village, and not merely a mountainside service area for skiers – which is what most resorts at this height are, and exactly what Hochgurgl is. All visitors agree that Obergurgl is a very friendly place, with a jolly evening atmosphere; you can't help seeing the same faces each day, and to a degree each year. The combination of snow reliability, village charm and lack of crowds puts Austria's highest parish closer to paradise than other ski resorts in more ways than one.

Obergurgl is a very remote village at the head of the Ötztal, nearly 50km from the main road west of Innsbruck. Only Sölden is within easy reach for a day out, and the road up from there is slow and narrow and prone to closure – though less so than it used to be, thanks to new avalanche barriers. Long delays are reported.

The skiing top 3035m bottom 1911m

The skiing areas of Obergurgl and its satellite Hochgurgl together cover a high, wide, north-west-facing area of the southern end of the Ötztal, and can usually be relied on to have good snow from early December to late April. But not always; we found the top slopes bare and unskiable in supposedly safe February, because of wind. Avalanche danger can also be a problem, closing lifts and, occasionally, the road up to the resort. The skiing is practically all above the tree-line and intermediate in difficulty, and consists of three small areas split up by the valleys beneath peaks and glaciers. Hochgurgl's one area offers the greatest vertical drop, and has the extra variety of a wooded hillside between Hochgurgl and Untergurgl. Obergurgl's two sectors have greater off-piste potential and steeper runs (none of them long) near the top of the lifts.

From the middle of Obergurgl, a two-seater chair takes you over gentle slopes to the **Gaisberg** area – attractive short intermediate runs

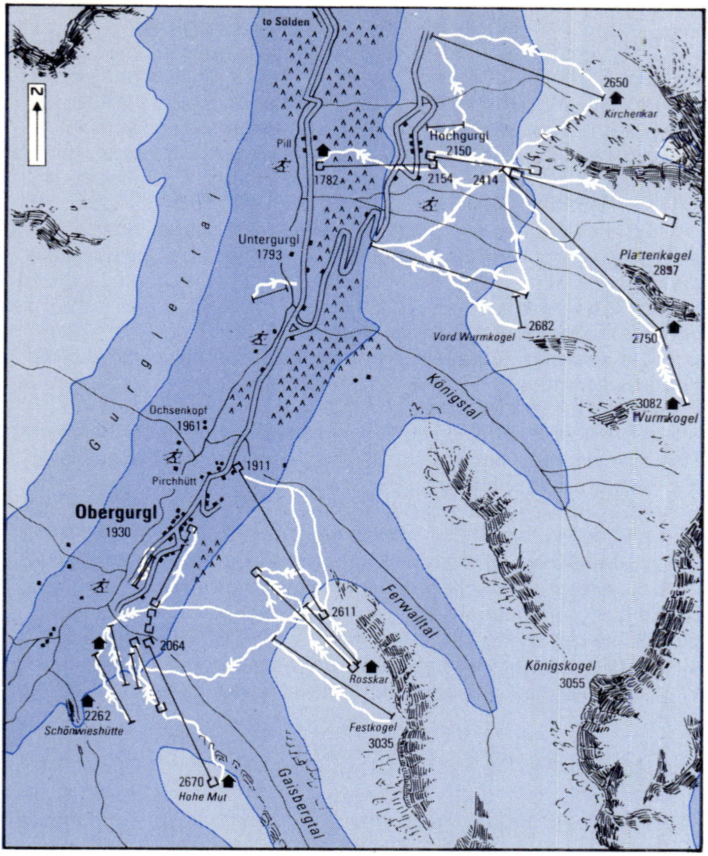

(categorised red but not difficult) among a scattering of trees, down to the popular Steinmann restaurant, and a couple of short, steeper gullies under the Nederlift. The long single chair-lift to Hohe Mut has an attractive restaurant and sun terrace at the top, and magnificent views out over the glaciers. The only run down from here is officially off-piste. In good conditions it is not exceedingly difficult, although it is narrow and fairly steep in places; but the terrain is rocky, and poor snow cover may be unannounced.

The single-seater **Festkogel** chair-lift starts from the cluster of hotels at the entrance to Obergurgl, a long walk from the centre although reachable (with some poling) on skis from the upper part of the village by the ice rink. This lift climbs in the shade of a steep wall to a plateau with a new restaurant and short practice drag-lift and a longer drag up to the highest point of Obergurgl's skiing. The only runs down to the bottom are another two off-piste marked routes of moderate difficulty – good long runs down the flank of a beautiful valley. There are several pistes under the long twin Rosskar chair-lift – none of them particularly severe – and an easily manageable run across to Gaisberg.

Hochgurgl's skiing is mostly very gentle, on a broad, open mountainside above the resort; there is a short drag-lift on the glacier at the very top (Wurmkogel) with a black run, but it should be graded red. The powerful new Schermerspitz chair-lift, which goes up from the same point as the lower Wurmkogel lift, serves a new red piste which is said to be 'splendid – wide, curving and well prepared'. On the south side of the area is a long drag-lift with a short second section above it, serving another good red – by the standards of this area, long and varied, with moguls on the bottom half in the woods leading down to a car park on the road up to Hochgurgl. There is another good, fast piste through the woods under the chair-lift from Untergurgl which is the main way into the Hochgurgl skiing for visitors.

There are few **mountain restaurants**, and most skiers lunch in the village, where there are hotels with sun terraces. Of the restaurants on-piste, the Hohe Mut does not open until late in the season and the attractive Steinmann is usually very crowded. At Hochgurgl there are several restaurants near the top of the system. The Wurmkogel hut is friendly, attractive and warming, with marvellous views into Italy. The Schönwieshütte, a 20-minute ski and walk from the top of the Sattellift, is heartily recommended by one reporter ('another world').

Because Obergurgl is so small and remote, **queues** are hardly ever a problem except at ski school departure time, and when bad weather closes higher lifts. Some chairs are single-seaters. Queues for lift passes are bad on Monday mornings. The main limitation of the lift system is the lack of links between the three areas. For a small and not very efficiently mechanised ski area, the lift pass may seem expensive.

The resort

Although traditional in style, Obergurgl is not a picturesque, colourfully painted Tyrolean charmer. A 19th-century guidebook refers to 'a hamlet composed of wretched cowherds' huts, with a church on an eminence'; things have not changed much, except that the hamlet is now composed not of wretched huts but hotels – some comfortable, others simple – offering a not insignificant 3,000 beds. The clientele is predominantly German, with a minority of faithful British visitors. A ski-bus runs to and from Untergurgl (for Hochgurgl skiing). The Gurgls are generally very unsuitable for **cross-country** skiers and **non-skiers**, and excursion possibilities are limited.

For a small village, Obergurgl is not compact, and location of **accommodation** is important. There are basically three clusters of buildings. The first is at the entrance to the village – convenient for the Festkogel lift, but otherwise unappealing. Clustered above the old village around the skating rink are comfortable, modern and quite expensive hotels – the Austria (✆282) is the most attractive of them, with sauna, jacuzzi, turkish bath and massage. These hotels are easy enough to ski back to, but it is a stiff walk up from the village centre – 'exhausting, long and dangerous,' says one report. In the centre there's more of a mixture. The dominant building is the comfortable Edelweiss

Obergurgl facts

Lift payment

Passes One pass covers all lifts, and local ski-bus. Day passes available.

Beginners Lift pass or coupons.
Cost 6-day pass AS1,440. 15% off in low season.
Children About 40% off, under 15.

Ski school

Classes 2hr morning and afternoon.
Cost 6 days AS950. Private lessons (two people) about AS1,600/day.
Special courses Ski touring.
Children Ski kindergarten, ages 6–10, 9.00–12.00, 2.00–4.00, and non-ski kindergarten, ages 3–5, 9.30–12.30, 1.30–4.30, 6 days AS930. No lunchtime care.

Cross-country skiing

Trails 10km between Obergurgl and Untergurgl. Small loop at Hochgurgl.

Not skiing

Facilities Natural ice rink (open in the evenings) and hotel pools, saunas, whirlpools; bowling.

Medical facilities

In resort Doctor.
Hospital Innsbruck (102km).
Dentist Sölden (15km).
Chemist Sölden (15km).

Getting there

Airport Munich; transfers about 4½hr.
Railway Ötz (48km); regular buses.
Road Via Ulm, Munich or Basel; chains often necessary.

Available holidays

Resort beds 2,800 in hotels, 90 in apartments.
Package holidays Bladon Lines (Ht Ch), Crystal (Ht), Horizon (Ht), Inghams (Ht), Made to Measure (Ht), Neilson (Ht), Ski NAT (Ht), Ski-plan (Ht), Thomson (Ht)

Further information

Tourist office ✆(5256) 258/353. Tx 05/34457.

(✆223). Most UK tour operators use the cheaper, smaller guest-houses. The Wiesental (✆263) is about the cheapest of them – friendly, lively and well placed. So too, although slightly less cheap, are the Gamper (✆238) – 'good food, convenient' – the Josl (✆205), the Fender (✆316) and the Jennewein (✆203). Curiously, overbooking seems to be a persistent weakness of Obergurgl hoteliers. Hochgurgl, a modern development beside the road over to Italian Merano (closed in winter), has little to recommend it.

Après-ski is very jolly in a traditional Tyrolean way, ('... great – we did the conga through the hotel'), mostly bar and hotel-keller oriented. But the dedicated disco piste-basher will soon tire of the lack of variety. In the old centre there are several bars, animated at tea time (sometimes with tea-dancing) and later, some of them with live music. Reports are generally enthusiastic.

There is a wide, flat **nursery slope** in the village with a small tow beside it, and plenty of scope for easy après-nursery skiing, especially above Hochgurgl, so even beginners may find a lift pass economical.

Reports on the **ski school** are generally though not entirely favourable. Many very beautiful and not too arduous day-trip ski tours can be made at any time in the season, and from March onwards tourers can undertake the famous Ötztal Rundtour, which takes about a week. Information is available from the ski school or from its leader Herr Giacomelli (✆251).

Handy Hoch

Sölden Austria 1380m

Good for *Après-ski, summer skiing, late holidays*
Bad for *Lift queues, nursery slopes, not skiing, short airport transfers*

Linked resort: Hochsölden

Sölden is a long-established, large and lively resort for which we find it hard to work up much enthusiasm, despite its undoubted qualities. The skiing area is extensive and varied, spread along the high (and in places steep) western wall of the Ötztal, and on paper is impressive – a big new gondola replacing the old cable-car going to over 3000m, and glacier areas offering some very good summer skiing. Unfortunately the skiing served by the gondola is limited (at least for most people, most of the time), the summer and winter ski areas are not linked and the glacier lifts do not open until spring. The rest of the skiing is not so outstanding that Sölden can be counted among the top sporty ski resorts, nor so outstanding that it outweighs the disadvantages of the resort itself – a long, main-road straggle with no charm, redeemed only by vibrant nightlife (in high season, at least). Not all reporters agree with these conclusions, but most do – and point out the attractions of staying up at Hochsölden: reliable snow, no queues and, for a mini-resort, a jolly atmosphere.

The skiing top 3056m bottom 1377m

Sölden's skiing area is in two linked sectors, south and north, split by the deep Rettenbachtal (where the road up to the summer ski fields has been built). Although both sectors are directly accessible from the edges of Sölden (served by a regular ski-bus), the northern area is usually referred to as the Hochsölden ski area, the southern one as Sölden's skiing. The skiing is extensive, with a healthy vertical drop of about 1600m from the gondola top station, 1350m from the top above Hochsölden. It is varied in difficulty, and is partly open, partly wooded. There are some wide open, easy slopes above Hochsölden and a few black runs but these are hardly worthy of the name. Most of the slopes are east-facing.

The new gondola (opening this season) goes up to the **Sölden** skiing area from the southern end of the resort, where there is a large car park. There are open slopes around the middle station with a couple of drag-lifts, one of them taking you to a beautiful, long and usually empty run down to the Gaislachalm (where there are several restaurants) and on down a gentle woodland trail to rejoin the main piste to Sölden at Innerwald. The main run down from the middle station is red, can be icy, and tends to be crowded at the end of the day. Once you get to know the lower slopes it's usually possible to find a route down through the

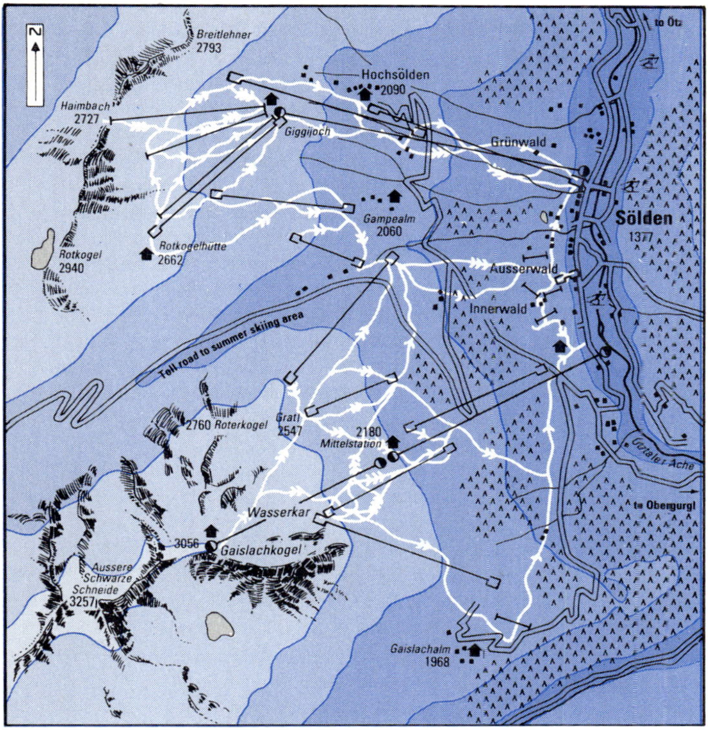

back gardens to most parts of the village. Roads are a hazard.

The top section of the gondola climbs over 850 metres steeply to the rocky Gaislachkogel peak, where there is a round panoramic restaurant. The bowl underneath the cable-car is very steep and has up to now had no marked piste, only a 'wilde abfahrt' which must be very exciting when conditions are right. (It was closed when we visited and we have no reports from others.) The normal run from the top station gives beautiful views, but only at the top does it justify its red grading.

Of the two pistes down into the Rettenbachtal to link up with Hochsölden, the one from the middle gondola station is an easy path and can be pursued as far as Sölden. The run down beside the long Stabele chair-lift is more difficult, and being north-facing often has very good snow. There are some good off-piste possibilities around here, but the underlying terrain is rocky. From the Rettenbachtal there is a more difficult run down to Innerwald and Sölden.

From the northern edge of Sölden a long chair-lift (over 20 minutes) climbs directly to **Hochsölden**, and a gondola which is the more popular way in the mornings goes slightly higher to the Giggijoch. Above this gondola there is a wide open expanse of gentle mountainside. There is a steeper area between Hochsölden and the Haimbach, but the runs marked black are not fierce. The runs to

Hochsölden are graded blue and black, but are fairly red in practice.

From the Rotkogelhütte there are superb views over to the glacier skiing areas and a beautiful, sunny long run down to the Rettenbachtal via the Gampealm restaurant. This run may be a bit much for inexperienced skiers; if so they will not be able to get across to the Sölden skiing, nor down to Sölden, except via the blue to the gondola station. The black next to that blue is another over-graded run.

There are several large, not very attractive **mountain restaurants** in the obvious places, and a few more charming ones, notably the Gampealm and Rotkogelhütte. Gaislachalm reportedly suffers from disorganised service.

The serious high-season **queues** to get out of Sölden will presumably be relieved by the new gondola. At other times, and in most other places, the system works well. Skiing access is queue-free for Hochsölden residents. Some lifts close for lunch, and most close at an early hour in the afternoon.

The resort

Sölden stretches for miles (literally) along the Ötztal valley floor, and the river and the main road run through the village. Although most buildings are traditional in style, the long, wide main street has no particular

Sölden facts

Lift payment

Passes All lifts and the ski-bus are covered by the general lift pass. Day passes available, and 'hourly' cards with refunds when you hand them in.
Cost 6-day pass AS1,570. 15% off in low season.
Beginners Coupons.
Children 40% off, under 15.
Summer skiing Large area up to 3250m, 10 lifts. Season starts when winter skiing stops.

Ski school

Classes 2hr morning and afternoon.
Cost 6 days AS950. Private lessons about AS1,500/day.
Children Ski kindergartens at Sölden and Hochsölden, ages 3–8, 9.00-4.30, 6 days with lunch AS1,400.

Getting there

Airport Munich; transfers at least 4hr; Innsbruck 2hr.
Railway Ötz (30km): frequent buses.
Road Via Ulm, Munich or Basel; the road from Ötz rarely requires chains.

Cross-country sking

Trails Along valley floor near Sölden and at Zwieselstein on road towards Obergurgl (16km, easy).

Not skiing

Facilities Sauna, solarium, swimming, fitness centre, skating, curling, bowling, riding, toboggan run, tennis, rifle range, cinema.

Medical

In resort Doctor, dentist, chemist.
Hospital Innsbruck (87km).

Available holidays

Resort beds 3,700 in hotels, 200 in apartments.
Package holidays Blue Sky (Ht), Crystal (Ht), Horizon (Ht), Inghams (Ht), Neilson (Ht), Ski-plan (Ht Hm), Thomson (Ht)

Further information

Tourist office ✆(5254) 22120. Tx 0533247. Fax (5254)243519.

character or focus. In high season the resort is extremely busy, with a daily influx from smaller villages in addition to Sölden residents. Visitors come from many countries, the majority being German. Traffic is a hazard along the main street and parking is often difficult along the main road and in lift car parks. As well as the ski-bus, there are two buses daily between Sölden and Hochsölden.

Accommodation is nearly all hotels and guest-houses. Skiers should choose to stay at either end of the town; the northern end is better for inexperienced skiers, for access to Hochsölden skiing.

In season there is a wide variety of lively **après-ski** action (cafés, live bands, discothèques) and lots of packaged evening outings. After skiing there is a disco at Innerwald in the Café Philip until 6pm, when the chair-lift down to Sölden closes. The most popular organised event is a jeep ride from the Alpenland and Silbertal up to the Gaislacha m for *Glühwein*, dancing and/or dinner, followed by a 6km toboggan ride back.

The main valley is not very attractive for **cross-country** skiing. Although there are some sporting facilities, it is not really a **non-skier's** resort either, and there are no cleared mountain paths for walkers

The village **Nursery slopes** are not very satisfactory: Innerwald, a short chair-lift ride from Sölden, has a nursery area which goes without sun for much of the day, and often has poor snow conditions. But most beginners are taken to the slopes above the Giggijoch gondola, which are very much better.

Reports suggest that **ski-school** is good but often too widely shared – in groups of as many as 17. The kindergarten is said (by an onlooker) to be 'fun, instructive and safe'.

Hochsölden 2090m

Hochsölden, reached by road or chair-lift from Sölden, stands over 700m higher, above the trees. There is more of a village atmosphere than in many such resort satellites, despite the fact that there are only a couple of shops, no bank, no more bars and restaurants than there are hotels, and in the evening there is almost nowhere to go. But you don't have to go anywhere to have a party, and the regulars of the Hotel Hochsölden make very merry from around 5pm onwards. The only access to Sölden in the evening is by taxi. The hotels are traditional and fairly simple. We have good reports of the Alpenfriede (✆2227): 'friendly, welcoming, good food; the sort of buffets you see in the brochures and never believe.' Although the easy slopes above Giggijoch are not far away, the ledge drops sharply to Hochsölden, making things difficult for beginners. A recent visitor found skiing down to the resort more challenging than the Haimbach black run. The resort's lift (the Rotkogel chair) has been extended downwards and given extra capacity. We have good reports of the ski school.

Package holidays Horizon (Ht), Thomson (Ht).

West Tirol: small resorts

Lermoos, Berwang, Vent, Kühtai, Nauders Austria

Among the many small resorts west of Innsbruck not covered in other chapters, a handful are worth describing briefly.

The Zugspitze is an impressive bulky peak a few miles north of the Inn valley, towering 2000m above a basin of flat pastures and forming the border with Germany (the major German resort of Garmisch-Partenkirchen lies just on the other side). In the right conditions there is a superb 20km run from the summit to the pretty village of **Ehrwald** (1000m) at the foot of the mountain. Ehrwald also has a pleasant red run of its own from the Ehrwalder Alm, reached by ski-bus and chair-lift. The bus also links with Biberwier and Lermoos; most of the downhill skiing in the area is on other mountains above these villages.

Biberwier (1000m) has a modest installation of drags and chair-lifts serving north-facing slopes on the Schachtkopf (1642m), but the main resort of interest to British skiers is **Lermoos** (1000m), a pleasant but undistinguished village, directly across the once-marshy basin (the 'moos') from the Zugspitze. It has easy and intermediate runs of over 1000m vertical, mostly facing north-east, on the Grubigstein, served almost entirely by chair-lifts. One goes up from each end of the long village across open, gentle lower slopes – admirable terrain for near-beginners – to the middle station at 1350m, where there is a big and adequately pleasant restaurant. Only one chair-lift goes up from this meeting point – a recipe for queues, in principle – and all the higher pistes are red, with the occasional variant stretch graded black (but not steep). The runs are satisfactory but unremarkable; many intermediate skiers spend their time skiing repeatedly the double chair-lift reached from the top of the main access lift and going up to much the same altitude (2060m). The piste map when we visited was laughably inaccurate, showing pistes where there were ski-routes, ski-routes where there was nothing, and nothing where there were pistes. Snow and cloud prevented our verifying that there are splendid views across the basin to the Zugspitze, and forced us to research in depth the merits of a delightful little chalet restaurant reached by ski-route signposted off to the left of the main pistes.

The village sprawls over quite an area; the most attractive location is close to the church square at the foot of the Hochmooslift (the left-hand lift, looking up). The cheap little Pension Pechtl (✆2898) has the prime position at the foot of the chair-lift, but even the relatively swish Post und Alte Post (✆2281), with ozone-pool, sauna etc, admirably positioned on the church square, cannot be called expensive. The Hotel Edelweiss (✆2214) has been highly praised by one reporter. There is abundant cross-country skiing on the floor of the basin and in the valleys leading off it, several cleared paths, horse-drawn sleighs, (as there are in Ehrwald), a natural ice rink, and a good sports centre (with tennis and pool) at Ehrwald. Evening entertainment is muted and traditional, including such things as curling competitions, toboggan runs and slide shows.

A few miles to the west is a separate ski area centred on the attractive little village of **Berwang**, in an out-of-the-way and slightly elevated position at 1340m. Its skiing is small and without challenge – blue and easy red runs of 300m or 400m vertical at the most – but has the added interest of taking you to the valley village of Bichlbach (1075m) and, in the opposite direction, to the even more secluded hamlet of Rinnen (1285m).

South of the Inn valley, **Vent** is a small village high up (1900m) in its own beautiful valley, which branches off the Ötztal between Sölden and Obergurgl. As a base for ski touring, it is excellent – it is one of the terminal points of the Ötztal Rundtour. For downhill skiers there is only a chair-lift followed by a drag, with wide open intermediate skiing on either side of the lifts back down to the village. There are also two beginners' lifts. Vent is a friendly little place, with one discothèque and a couple of other bars.

Kühtai is also very high (2020m), also close to the Ötztal, and also mainly of interest for the access it gives to ski tours (in particular, excellent day-tours), not in the Ötztal Alps but in the Stubai Alps, which stretch away to the south. There are nine ski-lifts; the pistes served by them cover the spectrum of difficulty, at least on paper, but are not long (less than 500m vertical) and hold no particular interest apart from the altitude of their base. The village consists of a score of hotels and pensions, and little else; it is not a cheering place in a blizzard. Cross-country skiing trails total 20km.

Nauders (1400m) is a spacious, traditionally styled village in a remote setting where Austria, Switzerland and Italy meet. Here, too, there is plenty of scope for short ski-tours, but there is more extensive downhill skiing as well. Apart from an excellent open nursery area near the village, the skiing is far enough away for the ski-bus to be essential. The main area is high and spread widely around an impressive circus of mountains (facing north and west), but offers surprisingly few good runs. There are short, easy and intermediate runs at altitude, and an exposed but otherwise enjoyable red run served by a chair-lift to 2700m. There are wide, easy paths back to the bottom, and some off-piste skiing in the woods under the gondola. Across the road to Italy, a slow chair-lift serves the wooded Mutzkopf (1812m) – a pretty knoll with a long gentle 'Familienabfahrt'. There is good cross-country skiing, with a claimed total of 80km of varied trails, some linking up with trails in Italy, and including a small loop in the woods near the top of the main gondola. Non-skiing facilities include indoor tennis, swimming and sauna at several hotels, and coach excursions to St Moritz and Italy (Merano). Après-ski is typically Tyrolean, with live bands in several hotels.

Tourist offices Lermoos ✆(5673) 2401, Berwang ✆(5674) 8268, Kühtai ✆(5239) 222, Vent ✆(5254) 8193, Nauders ✆(5473) 220.

Package holidays Ehrwald: Crystal (Ht), Hourmont (Groups) (Ht). Lermoos: Blue Sky (Ht), Crystal (Ht), Enterprise (Ht), Thomson (Ht). Kühtai: Ski Sutherland (Ht)

Let the train take the strain

Serfaus Austria 1430m

Good for *Alpine charm, easy runs, sunny slopes, nursery slopes, family holidays, ski touring, cross-country skiing, freedom from cars,*
Bad for *Tough runs, easy road access, skiing convenience*

Separate resort: Fiss

Serfaus works hard to be a family-favourite resort, with all the qualities of charm and friendliness that are associated with winter in the Tirol. The village is attractive, with a mixture of traditional chalet-style buildings old and (mostly) new, and the accommodation is nearly all of a high standard. It claims to be the only traffic-free ski resort in Austria, and certainly comes close. (Cars are allowed in only for the purpose of reaching your hotel in the first place and, thanks to a smart underground railway running the length of the village, there is no need for the electric taxis found in Swiss pedestrianised resorts; but the cars silently littering the village for the duration of their owners' holiday seem an unnecessary eyesore.) There is plenty of après-ski and the skiing, although devoid of challenge to the expert, is high and extensive by the standards of charming Austrian villages. The separate ski area of nearby Fiss (a much more ordinary village, popular with local weekenders) is every bit as good as that of Serfaus – in some ways better, at least for good skiers.

Having a car is of no great value in traffic-free Serfaus unless you want to go on excursions to other resorts. Going to Samnaun is a very attractive idea, since it gives relatively queue-free access to the very good skiing shared with Ischgl, and duty-free shops.

The skiing top 2745m bottom 1430m

The skiing extends in a chain of lifts up and down a series of treeless ridges to the west of the resort. The slopes face east and west, with no really long runs.

There are three lifts up the wooded hill behind Serfaus to the sunny plateau beside the Alpkopf – a gondola and a small cable-car to a vast restaurant building at Kölner Haus, and a chair-lift directly to the Alpkopf. A new high-capacity gondola is promised for the 1988-89 season. The plateau is a good open area for sunbathing, with short drag-lifts for near-beginners. Parallel drag-lifts to Plansegg serve a modest red and a long, roundabout blue run which is ideal for building up confidence. There are several long, not very difficult runs through the trees back to Serfaus.

From a depression just beyond Kölner Haus a chair-lift climbs quite steeply to Lazid, serving Serfaus's two most difficult runs; these are not very long (400m vertical), and the steeper Nordabfarht scarcely deserves its black grading. There are a couple of drag-lifts serving fairly easy slopes either side of Lazid, which is also the departure point for the rest of the skiing – down into, and up out of, two further high, shallow valleys. The lifts serve no particularly exciting skiing (again, the one black run available could be graded red, and the layout of the system does not encourage off-piste diversions), but it is a scenically splendid trip. It is a good area for short, easy ski-tours.

Mountain restaurants are adequate and sunny; two at Kölner Haus (accessible to non-skiers) and two others up at the end of the ski area at Masneralp. One of them is a mountain refuge off the piste.

When the resort is full (at New Year and in February) there have been morning **queues** for the various lifts leaving the top of the village, and at Kölner Haus. The new gondola opening this season should help with the former, but may accentuate the latter. Beyond Kölner Haus, cold is the main problem – none of the high lifts is enclosed.

The resort

Serfaus sits on an open, sunny ledge looking out south-eastwards over the Inn Valley south of Landeck. The village is quite long and narrow in plan, but not too much of a straggle, with the skating rink, church and nursery area in the centre. It is a bit of a hike up the hill to the main ski-lifts from here, and the alternative of using the underground railway often involves a tedious wait (it is a single train, shuttling back and forth between the lifts and the car parks at the entrance to the village).

Nearly all the **accommodation** is in modern, comfortable, attractive, chalet-style hotels and pensions with balconies. The Cervosa (✆6211), with pool, and the Maximilian (✆6255) are about the most spacious and comfortable hotels, neighbours centrally placed above the nursery area. The Alte Schmiede (✆6492) is less expensive, attractively decorated, friendly and within easy walking range of the lifts; there is a cosy, woody bar downstairs.

Après-ski is lively, attractive in setting and mostly traditional in style. After skiing the Postbar is full (tea-dancing is rumoured), and later on it is the setting for dancing to traditional Alpine music. For a younger atmosphere the best places are the bars and discos under the Hotels Rex and Astoria – and perhaps the new Patschi's Pub near the gondola station.

The **cross-country** runs between Serfaus and Fiss are not convenient for rendezvous with other skiers, but the longer wooded runs around Alpkopf are; this area is secluded, and gives beautiful views. The range of **non-skiing** activities is not enormous, but the village is a pleasant enough place in which to spend time.

Serfaus is good for beginners and especially children, with a delightful **nursery slope** and playground area in the village itself. There is also a good, high beginners' area around Kölner Haus.

We have no recent reports on **ski school**; but, despite the lack of British visitors, the resort claims that over half its instructors are English-speaking. The school organises tours to nearby peaks.

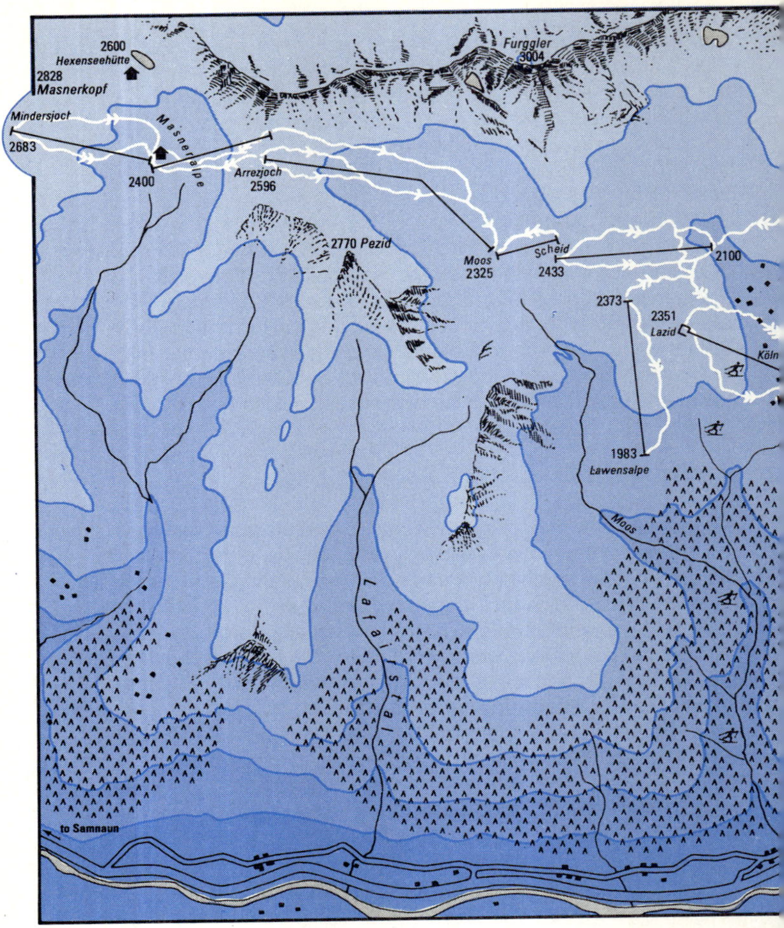

Fiss 1440m

From Fiss you don't travel so far on skis as you do from Serfaus, but in other ways the skiing, spread round a bowl and over the back of its rim, offers more satisfying pistes. They are mostly south-facing, and good snow conditions tend not to last long in fine weather. The main bowl is not particularly large, with a top station of 2426m (the Fisser Joch, reached by two-stage gondola), but there are some good open runs down to the village from here giving 1000m vertical, and they are in general steeper than at Serfaus. There is also a very good black run down through the woods on the west of the village, served by the separate Waldlift drag. From two points on the western side of the Fiss skiing area it is possible to ski down to Serfaus, but there is no lift back up. There are several recently added lifts behind the Fisser Joch with intermediate north-facing runs, and skiers who embark on the long

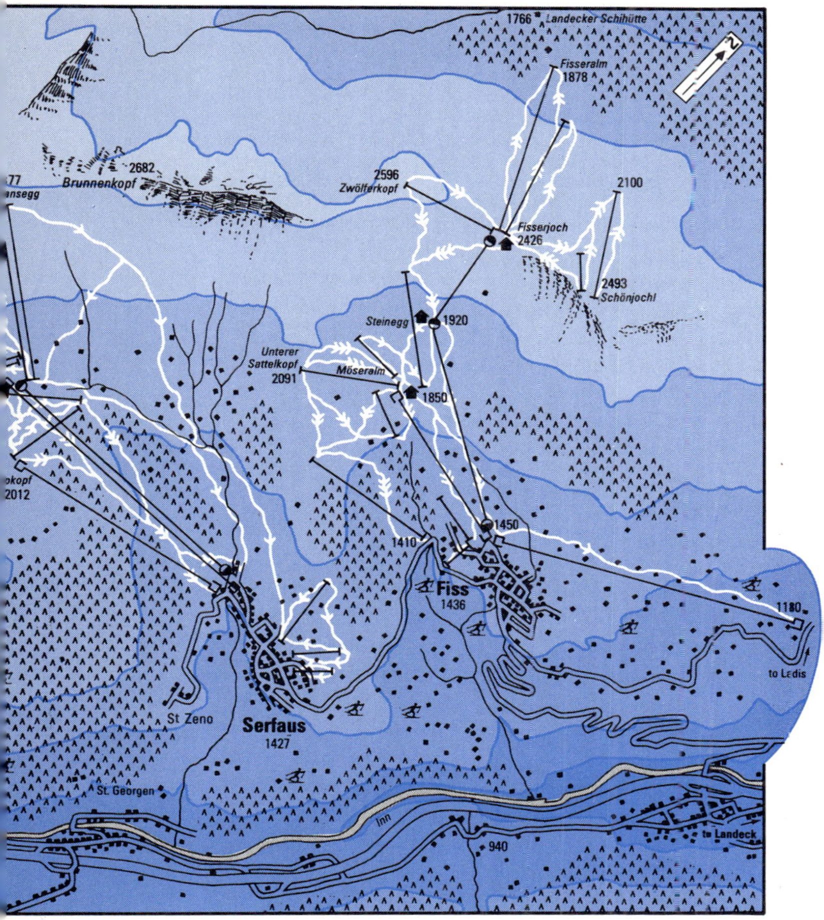

unprepared descent from Schönjochl to Ladis (1180m) can return by the two-stage chair-lift which also serves a long, easy blue piste across the mountainside from Fiss to Ladis.

Fiss is a quiet, traditional-style village of chalets old and new. The bulk of the accommodation is in good-value pensions and B&B places, with just a few hotels. The best-located hotel for skiing, at the top of the village close to the main lifts, is the small, friendly Cores (✆6417); the bigger, glossier Fisserhof (✆6353), at the bottom of the village, is handy for the nursery slope and the Waldlift, and has a pool. There is occasional traditional Tirolean evening entertainment, a handful of bars and cafés, a toboggan run from the mid-station of the gondola, and cross-country skiing of all grades. The ski school organises short tours, for example to the Furgler (3004m) above Serfaus.

Tourist office ✆(5476) 6441.

Serfaus facts

Lift payment

Passes Serfaus only (pass entitles holder to free one-day Fiss voucher; otherwise Fiss is separate). Day and afternoon pass available. Non-consecutive 3- and 10-day passes.
Cost 6-day pass AS1,275. About 20% off in low season.
Children About 40% off, under 15.
Beginners Coupons.

Ski school

Classes 2hr morning and afternoon.
Cost 6 days AS950. Private lessons AS400/hr.
Children Ski kindergarten, ages 4–14, 9.00–5.00, 6 days with meals AS1,330. Non-ski kindergarten, ages 2–7, 9.00–4.30, 6 days with meals AS780.
Special courses Racing; one- and two-day ski tours.

Not skiing

Facilities Natural ice rink, public pools in three hotels, sauna, solarium, sleigh rides, tobogganing. Cable-car runs one evening a week for toboggan riders.

Cross-country skiing

Trails About 30km of marked and graded trails (blue and red) in two main areas, including easy 1km loop at entrance to village and moderately easy 2½ km loop near Kölnerhaus. Longest trail 13km. Instruction available.

Medical facilities

In resort Doctor.
Hospital Landeck (30km).
Chemist and dentist Ried (14km).

Getting there

Airport Munich; transfers about 4hr.
Railway Landeck (30km); daily buses.
Road Via Munich and Garmisch, or via Ulm or Basel and Feldkirch; chains occasionally necessary.

Available holidays

Resort beds 1,700 in hotels, about 500 in apartments.
Package holidays Inghams (Ht), Ski Sutherland (Ht)

Further information

Tourist office ✆(5476) 6332. Tx 58154.

Bordering on the ideal

Ischgl Austria 1400m

Good for *Big ski area, après-ski, Alpine charm, beautiful scenery, ski touring, easy runs, sunny slopes*
Bad for *Nursery slopes, lift queues, short airport transfers*

Linked resort: Samnaun (Switzerland)
Separate resort: Galtür

The recipe for a perfect resort might mix the skiing and snow reliability of Val d'Isère and Tignes with the village charm of Alpbach – the best aspects of French and Austrian skiing – with the drinks prices of Livigno thrown in for good measure. Ischgl comes closer than most resorts to fitting this recipe. It is an old Tyrolean village high in the remote and beautiful Paznaun valley at the foot of a vast skiing area. And it almost has the good measure thrown in – you can ski over to duty-free Samnaun (in Switzerland) for bargain shopping whenever the drinks cupboard runs dry. Despite these powerful claims on our attention, Ischgl is not well known in Britain; but it is far from undiscovered and teems with German and Swedish skiers (and après-skiers) throughout the season. Low-season non-skiers should be warned that most of the village is sunless in January.

Ischgl's skiing contains few severe runs, but plenty are difficult enough for most skiers and satisfyingly long and varied; several sectors are suitable for off-piste skiing. The lifts are smart and modern, far superior to the Austrian norm, but not free of serious bottlenecks at times. One sure way to avoid the peak season crowds is to ski at Galtür, a peaceful and very friendly little village at the head of the valley, long known as an excellent ski touring base and perhaps soon to be better known by those who prefer to ski downhill than up. With a couple of new lifts Galtür has doubled the size and added greatly to the variety of its small ski area and it has recently joined the select list of Alpine heli-skiing resorts.

Ischgl is a rather isolated resort, but skiers with cars can make expeditions to St Anton. A car is otherwise of no great advantage.

The skiing top 2872m bottom 1250m

The Silvretta consists principally of the splendid slopes above Ischgl; long descents through woods to the village and a series of high, rocky bowls above with plenty of open, easy pistes. A long mountain crest which forms the Austro-Swiss border is reached by lift and easily breached on skis in a number of places, opening up a less extensive but no less beautiful Swiss ski area above Samnaun. The slopes on the Ischgl side face north-west and west; on the Samnaun side mainly south and east.

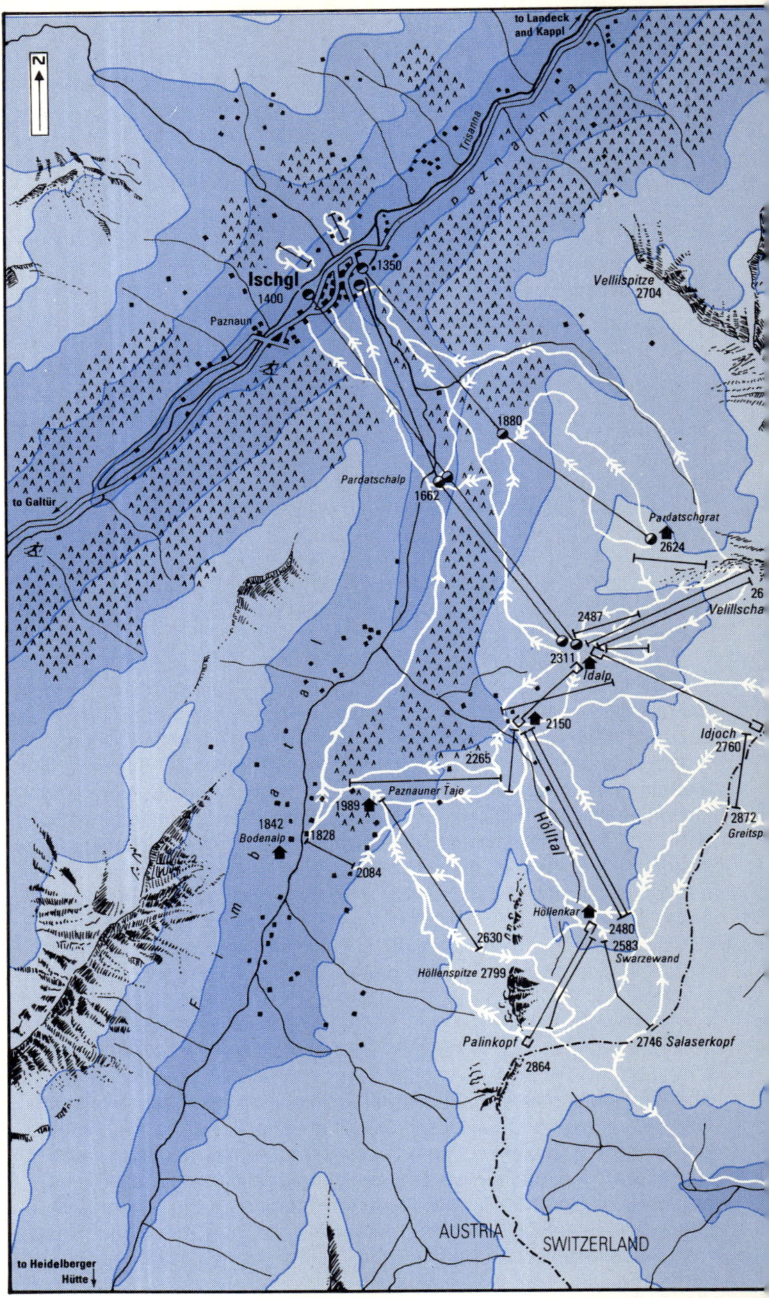
N
to Landeck and Kappl
Trisanna
Paznaun
Ischgl
1400
1350
Vellilspitze
2704
to Galtür
Pardatschalp
1662
1880
Pardatschgrat
2624
26
Velillscha
2487
2311
Idalp
2150
Idjoch
2760
2265
Paznauner Taje
1989
2872
Greitsp
1842
Bodenalp
1828
2084
Fimbatal
Höltal
Höllenkar
2480
2583
Swarzewand
2630
Höllenspitze 2799
Palinkopf
2746 Salaserkopf
2864
AUSTRIA
SWITZERLAND
to Heidelberger Hütte

From Ischgl there are lift departures at both ends of the village, to Idalp, a broad, sunny, open plateau with a ski school, restaurants, hotel and nursery slopes, and to the Pardatschgrat above Idalp with runs back down to Ischgl or an easy connection with the rest of the lift system via Idalp.

The runs down to Ischgl from Pardatschgrat are about the best in the area for good skiers, some of them giving an uninterrupted and demanding 1200m vertical across open slopes and then through woodland. Splendid as these runs are, it is unfortunate that there are none graded easier than red – and one of the reds on the map is deservedly graded black on the mountain. In the late afternoon they can get very crowded, and when they are icy the lower parts of these runs can be extremely hazardous and unpleasant.

At Idalp there are lots of lifts going all over the place around a fairly shallow, unevenly shelving, rocky bowl with good, easy runs including a few nursery slopes. For better skiers this is not a place to linger, but a staging post with links to other areas. Vellilscharte offers one of the most beautiful and least skied of all the descents to Ischgl, down a

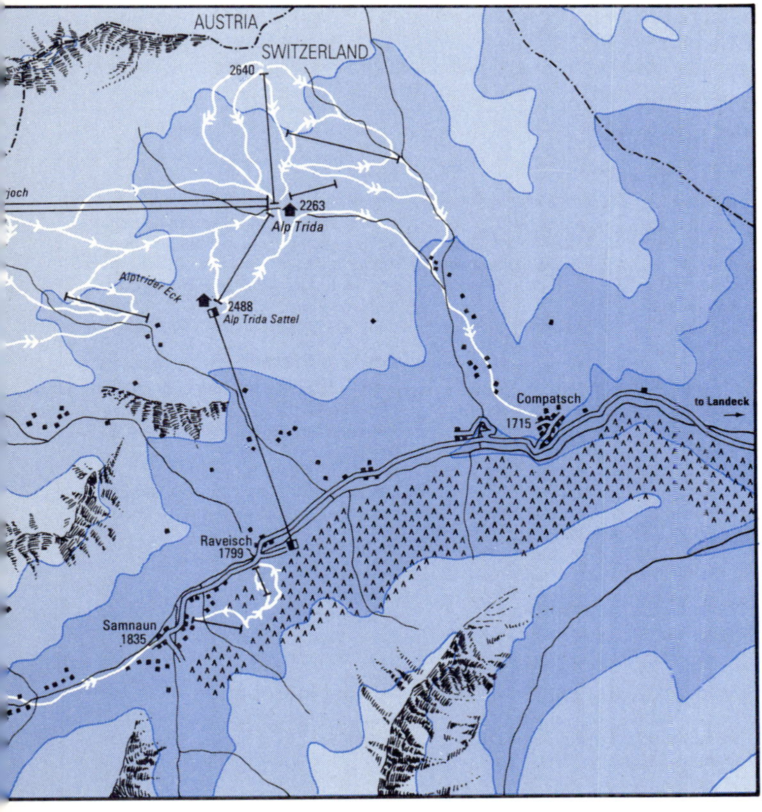

valley of its own; it is not always open. From Idjoch, there are easy runs down into the sunny Swiss Alp Trida and a long panoramic traverse to the narrow Hölltal beside Idalp. The lifts up the Hölltal serve a variety of short runs, and also give access to some of the best skiing in the region. Behind Palinkopf (the high point of the system) is some excellent open skiing with runs marked black – not extreme but the most challenging of the high runs – and the best local off-piste possibilities. This sector is particularly beautiful – sunny in the afternoon, with two very attractive restaurants.

The run down a Swiss valley to the scattering of woods around Samnaun can be reached from any of the three lifts near Palinkopf. It is long, and extremely beautiful, but not very interesting skiing, being mostly wide and gentle (unless you start from the Schwarzwand drag). The absence of lifts, which adds greatly to the joy of the run, is due to be remedied before long.

After a visit to Samnaun's duty-free shops (which helpfully sell small backpacks) it is an awkward ski beside the road or a short ski-bus ride to the cable-car at Raveisch. The cable-car delivers you to the southern upper rim of the beautiful Alp Trida basin, with its wide open, easy and intermediate skiing. The run down from the Alp Trida restaurant ends up at Compatsch, further than walking distance from Raveisch. From Alp Trida a double T-bar links up with Idalp and Ischgl via Austria's highest

Ischgl facts

Lift payment

Passes The Silvretta pass covers Ischgl, Kappl, See, Galtür and Samnaun lifts, and local buses. Slightly cheaper pass for Ischgl/Samnaun lifts.
Cost 6-day pass AS1,540. 15% off in low season.
Children 40% off, under 15.
Beginners Lift pass.

Ski school

Classes 2hr morning and afternoon.
Cost 6 days AS950, private lesson AS700/2hr.
Special courses Wedel course; off-piste courses. Ski touring.
Children Ski kindergarten, ages 4–15, 10.30–4.00, 6 days with lunch AS1,310. Non-ski kindergarten at Idalp, ages 3–6, 9.30–3.45, 6 days with lunch AS720.

Cross-country skiing

Trails 25km Ischgl/Galtür/Wirl graded blue. Instruction available.

Medical facilities

In resort Doctor, chemist.
Hospital Zams (near Landeck).
Dentist See (20km).

Not skiing

Facilities 24km cleared walks, swimming (Silvretta-Center and some hotels), skating, curling, sleigh rides, toboggan/ mini-bob runs, sauna/ solaria, turkish bath, bowling, shooting, local museum (in Mathon), tennis (Galtür) and squash (Hotel Solaria).

Getting there

Airport Munich; transfer about 4½hr. Also Zurich.
Railway Landeck (30km); frequent buses.
Road Via Basel or Ulm, then Feldkirch. The road up from Landeck is not difficult, but chains may be needed.

Available holidays

Resort beds 5,500 in hotels, 300 in apartments.
Package holidays Bladon Lines (Ht), Enterprise (Ht), Inghams (Ht), Neilson (Ht), Thomson (Ht)

Further information

Tourist office ✆(5444) 5266/5318. Tx 58148.

customs post, but even this cannot prevent late-afternoon queues.

There are two very attractive, sunny **mountain restaurants** around Bodenalp; otherwise merely adequate, large, new restaurants in most of the obvious places. Alp Trida is a huge sun-trap, and its large restaurant has an outdoor bar. The absence of duty is not noticeable in restaurant prices; they are in Swiss francs but schillings pass. There are several places for lunch in Samnaun itself.

If the area has one great drawback, it is lift **queues**. You can travel round the shared ski circus only in one direction, and as nearly all skiers are based in Ischgl there are often queues to get out of Ischgl in the morning and out of Samnaun in the early afternoon, and congestion on pistes down to Ischgl at the end of the day. The morning rush has been eased by the recent addition of another gondola (and there may be long queues for the main Silvrettabahn when there is no queue for the other two), but the problem is an inherent one. The only solution is to start from Samnaun.

The resort

Ischgl is an old village which has developed in a smart and harmonious way with a high standard of new building and accommodation and a generally high price level. The centre is by-passed by the main road and is tightly packed, bustling with activity in the early evening. The village has grown up in the shadow (literally, in January) of the steep, wooded mountainsides which are now the ski slopes. Parts of it are hilly, and there are several staircases and steep paths which can be very hazardous when icy.

A bus service between Ischgl and Galtür runs infrequently, and not in the evening. There are also regular buses to Landeck and points between (including Kappl).

Ischgl as a whole is now quite large, but most **accommodation** is conveniently placed for one or other of the two lift departures. The Solaria (✆5205) is about the nicest of the hotels, with a beautiful wooden interior and good facilities for residents (squash, sauna). The Post (✆5233) is very central. There are no cheap hotels in the resort – and few cheap places to eat, either.

Après-ski is excellent, with a good choice of traditional music ('endless accordions', says a reporter) and tea dancing, sophisticated live music shows, and one or two very contemporary discothèques of the kind to be found wherever young Swedes go. Café Christine is a particularly popular disco. A reporter recommends the Kitzloch restaurant. Fondue expeditions to the Heidelberger Hütte (an hour by snow-cat) are organised most evenings.

The **cross-country** skiing along the dark valley floor is not very interesting, inconvenient for meeting up with others, and quite often interrupted because of avalanche danger. We saw cross-country activity in the much more attractive upper section of the Fimbatal, reached by gondola or on foot. There is plenty for **non-skiers** to do, with very good fair-weather walks (up to the mountain restaurants at

Bodenalp and beyond), good sports facilities (mostly at Galtür) and a new conference and leisure centre with various hot bathing facilities. The mountain restaurants accessible by gondola are charmless. Excursions to Innsbruck are often organised.

Nursery slopes are at Idalp – open, sunny, with refreshments close at hand. In general though there are much better places than Ischgl for beginners (Galtür is one), especially given the cost, the queues and the awkwardness of runs down to the resort.

Ski school meets at Idalp, with classes starting at the civilised hour of 10.30. We have no reports on the standard of instruction. The school organises excursions on skins in what is one of the best ski touring areas in the Alps.

Samnaun 1840m

Samnaun is one of those anomalous communities in high, remote, dead-end corners of a country (in this case Switzerland) which has stayed alive thanks to duty-free status. It is not exactly booming – little more than a large cluster of shops and hotels with no more vitality than a supermarket – and it is hardly the place for a winter holiday unless the price of spirits (SF10 to SF15 a litre) is an all-important consideration. Petrol is also very cheap, but ski equipment, cigarettes and scent are less so. The resort's attraction is that you can ski the Ischgl circus without the rush-hour for lifts and crowds on-piste. There is a 10-km cross-country trail, a ski school which organises ski-tours, and a kindergarten at Alp Trida. Access by car is from the Inn valley south of Landeck, not far from Serfaus and Nauders.

Tourist office ✆(84) 95154. Tx 74869.

Galtür 1590m

Compared with Ischgl, Galtür is a peaceful little mountain village. It enjoys a sunnier position at the head of the valley but is further away from its ski-lifts, which are at Wirl, a long walk or a short bus-ride away. There are avalanche slopes on both sides of the village, which is quite often cut off from both Ischgl and Wirl. There are hotels and cheerful bars, some with tea-dancing, both in Galtür and beside the lifts at Wirl. Galtür is a good base for cross-country skiers (45km of trails, very reliable for snow) and an even better one for ski-tourers, for whom the scope in the Silvretta range is enormous. Heli-skiing can be arranged by the drop (about £30), by the day, or by the week (including accommodation at the very comfortable Alpenhotel Tirol (✆440)). There is an ice rink and a surprisingly smart new sports centre (swimming pool, squash, tennis, bowling) open till midnight, its pool free to holders of a Silvretta lift pass bought in Galtür. Even after the addition of new lifts on Vorarlberg territory above the Kopssee (1850m), Galtür's ski area is by no means vast. But there are no queues and the new chair-lift has added 500m vertical of north-facing slopes (including some off-piste skiing, useful for those preparing for a heli-ski adventure) to the varied east-facing pistes above Wirl, which also has nursery slopes and a kindergarten.

Tourist office ✆(5443) 204. **Package holidays** Enterprise (Ht), Ski Sutherland (Ht).

Alpine watershed

St Anton Austria 1300m

Good for *Tough runs, big ski area, sunny slopes, off-piste skiing, easy road access, rail access, après-ski, chalet holidays*
Bad for *Easy runs, lift queues, nursery slopes, skiing convenience, not skiing, late holidays*

Linked resorts: St Christoph, Stuben

The Arlberg is not a province or a mountain but a pass, where the waters of western Europe (the Rhine) are divided from those of the eastern Danube. In this century the Arlberg has given its name to a once-revolutionary style of skiing and the ski school which taught it, and to a magnificent ski region spread on both sides of the pass. On the western (Vorarlberg) side are Lech and Zürs, Austria's two most exclusive resorts and the subject of the next chapter. On the Tyrolean side (and separate for practical skiing purposes), St Anton is a teeming thoroughfare with a privileged place in skiing history, and a resort where many a proud skier, flattered by other, gentler ski-fields, discovers that there is more to the sport after all.

Austrian resorts are renowned for village charm and warmth of welcome rather than the extent and challenge of their skiing. St Anton stands out as the main exception – a big-time resort with slopes to rival the best of France and Switzerland. As the home of Hannes Schneider's famous Arlberg ski school, St Anton has the image of a resort for the dedicated technical perfectionist. Its runs offer what is arguably the greatest variety of difficult skiing of any resort. The village has lost most of its charm under the influence of the hordes of young people who swarm in from all over the world. It seems the antithesis of a Tyrolean ski resort. And, although heavy traffic has been reduced by a new road tunnel and lift queues by new lifts, there are still as many who abhor St Anton as adore it. But it should be judged against the places with which it competes for business – Val d'Isère, Verbier and the like. It then emerges as inconvenient in many ways, but full of character, far from unattractive, and very good fun after dark. It does lack very high ski-fields and many of its slopes get a lot of sun, but the resort now has plenty of snow-making machinery to prolong the life of the lower slopes and is anyway well known for abundant snowfalls. In 1988 this reputation was reinforced by exceptional depths of snow (in excess of 4 metres) on the upper slopes in the latter part of the season – producing a massive (and fatal) avalanche through the eastern fringe of the village, as well as excellent late-season skiing.

St Anton has far too many cars, and parking near the centre is always difficult; but a car is handy for après-ski if you aren't staying centrally, and for making the most of the Arlberg skiing.

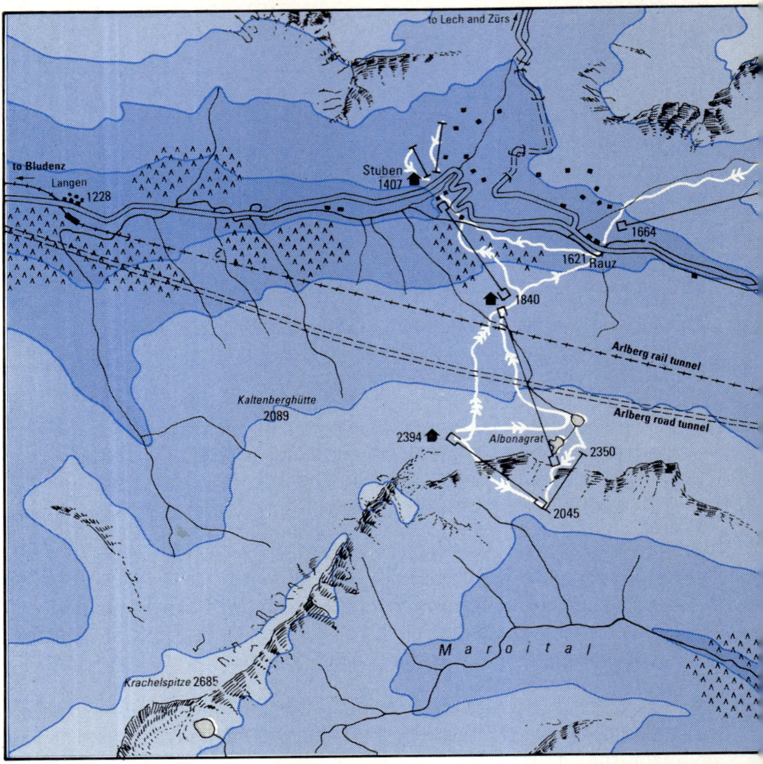

The skiing top 2650m bottom 1304m

Skiing at St Anton means skiing in the aura of the famous Valluga (2811m), a fine peak to the north of the village. There are many separate slopes of mountain, facing mainly south-east and west, and numerous ridges, bowls and subsidiary valleys. Many of the pistes are steep and challenging, and whereas many resorts have to invent black runs to appeal to good skiers, St Anton has to contrive blue runs in order not to discourage the timid. On the other side of the main road, facing the Valluga, St Anton has a separate ski area – the Rendl, which is sunny and not too difficult. A third area – the Albona, above Stuben on the other side of the Arlberg Pass – is (unlike Rendl) reachable on skis from the Valluga; the slopes are bleak, steep and sunless, but often have better snow conditions than anywhere else.

St Anton is a connoisseur's area for off-piste skiing, and every descent variant, however rarely skiable, has its name. It is an area which improves as you get to know it (especially since the resort now treats its high, challenging runs as off-piste itineraries – which means no grooming, no patrols and, in many cases, no marking). Many of the

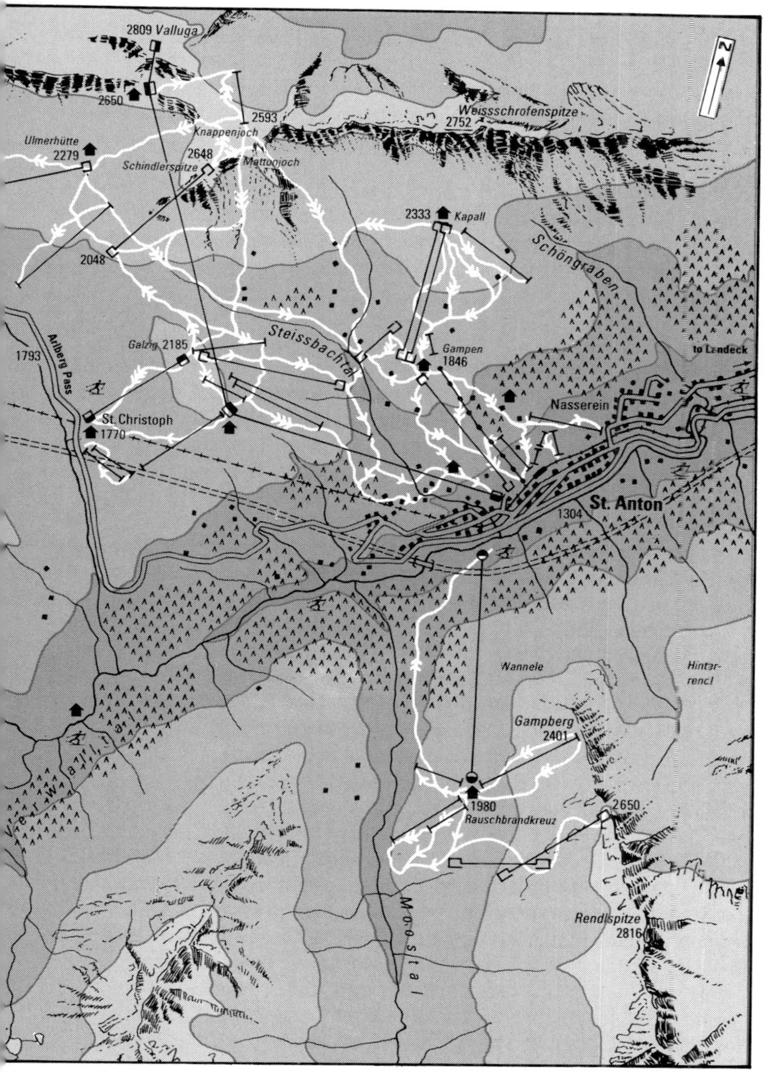

main runs above St Anton get a lot of sun, and tend to be icy in the mornings during clear, cold weather; always challenging, they can become treacherous.

The long **Rendl** gondola starts an awkward distance from the resort centre – further than a gentle stroll, but not so far that it really seems worth shoving to get on the village bus, as you often have to. The gondola top station is set on a west-facing slope below a rocky ridge. Benefiting from sunny afternoons, the Rendl and its restaurant terrace get very full on a fine day. Around the gondola station are a few short drags and across the slope two new chairs going up to 2650m – the top of the area until the planned second stage of the gondola is built. The runs on the top half of the mountain are open, and suitable for intermediate skiers. There is only one main run down to St Anton – a long red run, good in the right conditions, but which gets very crowded in the late afternoon, and is often icy and/or worn as well. For good skiers the Rendl offers much more excitement off-piste than on; there is a lot of space on the open shoulder of the ridge below Gampberg, and a very alluring secluded bowl behind it; the awkward woodland path out of the bowl is easy to miss, and crucial.

Valluga and Kapall are the two aspects of the main skiing area to the north of St Anton, either side of the long Steissbachtal, which provides an easy (blue) run down to St Anton from each mid-station. Snow conditions on the lower runs, below Galzig and Gampen, are now much more reliable thanks to a battery of mobile snow cannons. **Kapall** is the smaller and less crowded area, mostly sunny and south-facing. Most of the runs are intermediate and graded red or blue. The blue runs, for example under the chairs from Kapall to Gampen, may unpleasantly surprise intermediates, and the most direct descent to the resort is the course of the famous Arlberg-Kandahar Downhill race. Below Gampen there are some good bump sections down through the trees. The run to the Rodelhütte and Nasserein is one of the most interesting, but not well signposted. Beside Kapall, facing east and often keeping better snow than elsewhere, is the short Schöngraben drag-lift with fairly easy pistes beside it, and off-piste runs into the Schöngraben valley – some of the most beautiful, least terrifying and most skied in the area.

The **Valluga** is one of the big names in skiing. The first stage of lifts from both St Anton and St Christoph is to the rounded knoll of Galzig (2185m), with pistes down in all directions and a maze of chairs, cable-cars and tows arriving at different points of the hilltop. There are drag-lifts at the top with easy runs beside them, and an easy but attractively varied run down to St Christoph. The rest of the slopes of Galzig are steep, and provide some very challenging skiing, notably the Osthang – a long, steep mogul-field through trees towards the resort. Remarkably, this is now St Anton's only black run accorded the status of piste. Numerous staple unpisted runs from Galzig include slopes of 30–35° above St Christoph and down into the Steissbachtal (north-facing).

The second section of the cable-car from Galzig takes a spectacular course, high above the Steissbachtal to a first ridge, then across another bowl to the Vallugagrat, a shoulder below the Valluga itself. From here a tiny cable-car goes up to the rocky peak (for sightseeing purposes).

The direct descents from Vallugagrat are stern, south-facing slopes down into the Steissbachtal, with two famous unprepared runs – Mattun (also accessible from Kapall), a vast bowl with countless variations, and Schindlerkar, which is shorter, narrower and steeper (about 30°). Both consist of large moguls which seem to go on and on. They get a lot of sun, and after a warm afternoon and a cold night should be left well alone until the ice softens up. It is usually possible to avoid the steep part of Schindlergrat by traversing to the Grat chair-lift after the relatively gentle first half of the run. The most exciting off-piste skiing can be seen below the cable-car and the chair-lift, and a glance on the way up will be enough to put most skiers off.

For most skiers, the beginning of skiing from the Valluga is the easy cruise from the Vallugagrat to a small drag-lift. The easier runs are round the back – a moderate run with a single awkward pitch of 25° down to the Ulmerhütte, and from there either easily round to the Steissbachtal and to St Anton, or on to Rauz, over the road and down to Stuben. Rauz is no more than a chair-lift station beside the road, but a very useful back-door-entry to the Valluga, often resorted to by St Anton skiers and day-trippers from Lech/Zürs as a Galzig by-pass. It links up with the Schindlergrat chair-lift, which takes you to much the same skiing as the Valluga cable-car.

From **Stuben** a long and cold two-stage chair-lift climbs the steep north-facing slopes of the Albona. Wind often makes it unpleasant, but in the right conditions there is some exhilarating steep powder and piste skiing. At the top you can restore circulation in the bar, or beside the short Sonnleiten south-facing chair-lift. There is one run suitable for intermediates down to Rauz, and a steeper off-piste descent to St Christoph. A great excursion is the run down to Langen – unmarked except by the warning sign at the outset and not easy to follow, but a beautiful mixture of terrain. Equally beautiful and often more sheltered is the run via the Maroital (much of it through thick woodlands) ending up at a restaurant in the Verwalltal, a long walk from St Anton.

Mountain restaurants are adequately spread around the slopes, and there are a few memorable ones, notably the Rodelhütte above Nasserein and the Ulmerhütte – one of the oldest mountain restaurants in the Alps, one of the most malodorously plumbed, and one of the best for sunset panoramas. These huts, and the Krazy Kanguruh just above the resort, get extremely crowded, and service is often without a smile.

Skiing the Valluga is no longer the nightmare it used to be, but long **queues** still form at the Galzig cable-car, and a ticket-reservation system operates on the Valluga cable-car. The best way round these delays is to catch a bus to Rauz. Lifts and pistes in the Steissbachtal get very crowded – though the installation of a new four-seater chair-lift from the valley up to the Kapall chairs will help. The lack of marked pistes at high altitude severely restricts skiing possibilities in bad weather.

The resort

St Anton is a natural staging post at the bottom of the Arlberg pass road; mountains drop steeply down to the village from both north and south sides. There is room for the village to be by-passed by the main road – but only just, and a number of St Anton's hotels are in effect roadside ones. This main road is not nearly as busy as it used to be, now that the Arlberg tunnel has been constructed, but it is still noisy. Squashed uncomfortably between road and railway is the long, narrow resort centre. Its mixture of hotel buildings old and new, cafés, shops and hot-dog stalls is not the most picturesque in Austria, but the main street is colourful, traffic-free and always bustling. The village has grown into an inconvenient straggle, with chalets and hotels lining the road down to neighbouring villages. Nasserein is a not very convenient suburb where where many UK operators send their clients.

There are buses between St Anton centre and St Jakob via Nasserein, and in the other direction to Mooser Kreuz, at the top of the resort. They are often overcrowded, especially between the centre and the Rendl lift station. There is no evening service. Post buses go to St Christoph, Zürs, Lech, Stuben and Langen.

Accommodation is varied in comfort, style, cost and desirability of location. The last is important, and skiers lucky enough to stay in the attractive, expensive Post (✆22140) and Alte Post (✆25530) or the numerous more down-to-earth central B&B hotels will be the envy of less privileged skiers stuck half-way between the resort centre and Nasserein or up above the resort on the steep hill down from the Arlberg Pass. Other central hotels often used by UK operators are the Rosanna (✆2400), the Sporthotel (✆3111), the very attractive

St Anton facts

Lift payment

Passes Arlberg Pass covers all St Anton, Lech and Zürs lifts and buses within St Anton. Area day and half-day passes available.
Cost 6-day pass AS1,530. 15% off in low season. Reduction for senior citizens.
Beginners Day and half-day passes valid only for certain lifts – one for beginners, one with greater scope.
Children 40% off, under 15.

Ski school

Classes 2hr morning and afternoon.
Cost 6 days AS950. Private lesson AS1,600/day (4hr).
Special courses Wedel courses, off-piste, helicopter skiing.
Children Ski kindergarten, ages 5–14, 9.00–4.30, 6 days with lunch AS1,570. Non-ski kindergarten, same times, ages 5–14 same price, ages 3–5 free.

Cross-country skiing

Trails About 40km along main valley going beyond St Jakob, and in Verwalltal. Marked but not graded.

Medical facilities

In resort Fracture clinic, doctors, dentists, chemist.
Hospital Zams (20km).

Not skiing

Facilities 20km of cleared walks, hotel swimming pools/ sauna/ massage, tennis, squash, natural ice-rink (skating/ curling), sleighs, museum, tobogganing, ski bob, bowling.

Getting there

Airport Zurich; transfer about 3½hr. Also Munich.
Railway Main-line station in resort.
Road Via Basel or Ulm, then Feldkirch. The Arlberg Pass is occasionally closed and often requires chains; the toll-road-tunnel rarely presents difficulties.

Available holidays

Resort beds 5,200 in hotels, 700 in apartments.
Package holidays Activity Travel (Ch), Bladon Lines (Ht Ch), Horizon (Ht), Inghams (Ht), John Morgan (Ch), Made to Measure (Ht Hm), Mark Warner (Ch), Neilson (Ht Hm), Ski Club of GB (Ht), Ski West (Ht Ch Sc), Small World (Ch), Supertravel (Ht Ch), Thomson (Ht)

Further information

Tourist office ✆(5446) 22690. Tx 58335. Fax (5446) 253215.

Schwarzer Adler (✆2244) and the less expensive Kristall (✆2848). Eastwards along the valley there is ample scope (except in peak season) for skiers with a car to stay within range of St Anton, often very cheaply and comfortably. Chalet accommodation in and (mostly) around St Anton is also easily available. Several reporters found that being able to deposit skis and boots at the bottom of the Galzig lift took a lot of the discomfort out of the daily march to and from skiing.

Après-ski is extremely lively and varied, with mountain restaurants where skiers linger until dark; bowling; meals around the fire and tobogganing down from the Rodelhütte; lots of bars and tea rooms along the main street full to bursting from late afternoon (tea-dancing can usually be found) until late; lots of restaurants and cheap snack bars; live bands, noisy pick-up joints and discothèques. Several reporters commented unfavourably on the presence of large numbers of rowdy young Swedes. Nasserein has a few bars and restaurants.

Although there are long **cross-country** trails (the Verwalltal is much prettier than the main valley trail beside road and railway), and lots of **non-skiing** activities, St Anton is emphatically a resort for keen skiers.

Despite a couple of new lifts, **nursery slopes** are not very good, and even if they were St Anton would be no place for a beginner. Nasserein is the usual place where learners are confined, and there are small nursery lifts at Galzig and Gampen and on the Rendl.

St Anton's **ski school** has a reputation second to none, and many keen, proficient skiers who would scorn instruction anywhere else come to St Anton for this reason. Instructors often stay with classes over lunch, acting as guides to bars and restaurants. Whether the school's reputation is still justified is a controversial issue; there are certainly plenty of critics, suggesting that the school is more sensitive to the needs of strong skiers than the fears of timid ones. Many skiers find the timetable, with classes ending at 3pm, awkward.

Stuben 1410m

Stuben is a very small village beside the road on the western side of the Arlberg pass. It is dark, cold and windy, but one of the most convenient places to stay for getting around the Arlberg skiing, especially if you have a car. Rauz is nearby, for queue-free access to St Anton skiing, and Lech and Zürs are also close. There are buses in each direction. Stuben has its own skiing, described above, and also some excellent sunny nursery slopes on the other side of the road from the village (a drawback for toddlers). The village is quiet but does boast some traditional nightlife and has a few friendly hotel bars and restaurants.

Package holidays Ski Total (Ht Ch).

St Christoph 1780m

A few yards on the Tyrolean side of the Arlberg pass, St Christoph is no more than a few hotels and restaurants beside the road, among them the massive, smartly renovated and pricey old Hospiz. It is a bleak place to be when the blizzards howl, and is not recommended as a holiday base despite direct access to the Valluga by means of the little cable-car which carries a modest 250 skiers an hour to Galzig.

Package holidays Inghams (Ht).

Get stuck in

Lech Austria 1450m

Good for *Easy runs, resort-level snow, Alpine charm, sunny slopes, getting marooned*
Bad for *Tough runs, easy road access, mountain restaurants, short airport transfers, getting marooned*

Linked resort: Zürs

The deep, steep bowl which divides the Arlberg's two major ski areas could be spanned, but has not been. No doubt this is in order to keep the St Anton riff-raff out of the high seclusion of Lech and Zürs – the smart, expensive, showy winter hideaways of rich and royal, with a national split (for Lech) of 60% German visitors, 20% Austrian, 2% British, and at least 95% swathed in furs. The two resorts share a skiing area which is varied, extensive and open but not well mechanised and (despite piste maps peppered with black runs) not as suitable for good piste skiers as for intermediates and beginners. Liberal use of artificial snow means the slopes are as immaculately groomed as the visitors.

Of the two resorts, Lech is the older, larger and more attractive by far – an established village with good cross-country skiing, delightful walks and other sports facilities, and moderately lively in the evenings. Zürs is little more than a large group of expensive modern hotels above the tree-line along the road to Lech. Oberlech is a car-free scattering of chalets and hotels in the middle of sunny, gentle ski-fields above Lech the resort and linked to it by cable-car – an attractive base for families with small children. It has more accommodation than Zug, a very picturesque hamlet a mile or two from Lech up a pretty dead-end valley.

Lech and Zürs are only a few miles from the major east-west road and rail link between Austria and Switzerland, but they are very awkward miles. Until the turn of the century, the villages could be reached from the Arlberg pass road only by a narrow and hazardous path, and were cut off all winter. Even now there are times when the Flexenpass is blocked for days on end. Parking in the village streets is difficult, restricted and ruthlessly policed. Having a car is a great help for good skiers who are likely to be drawn to St Anton.

The skiing top 2450m bottom 1445m

Lech and Zürs share a skiing area spread over three mountains; you can get around all three on skis, but only clockwise, which means crowds of people all going the same way at the same time. Although the valleys are not wide, the connections across them are not perfect. Zürs is high, with all its skiing above the tree-line, while Lech has a more attractive arrangement of gentle lower slopes among woodland and open ground above. Zürs is particularly well known for off-piste skiing,

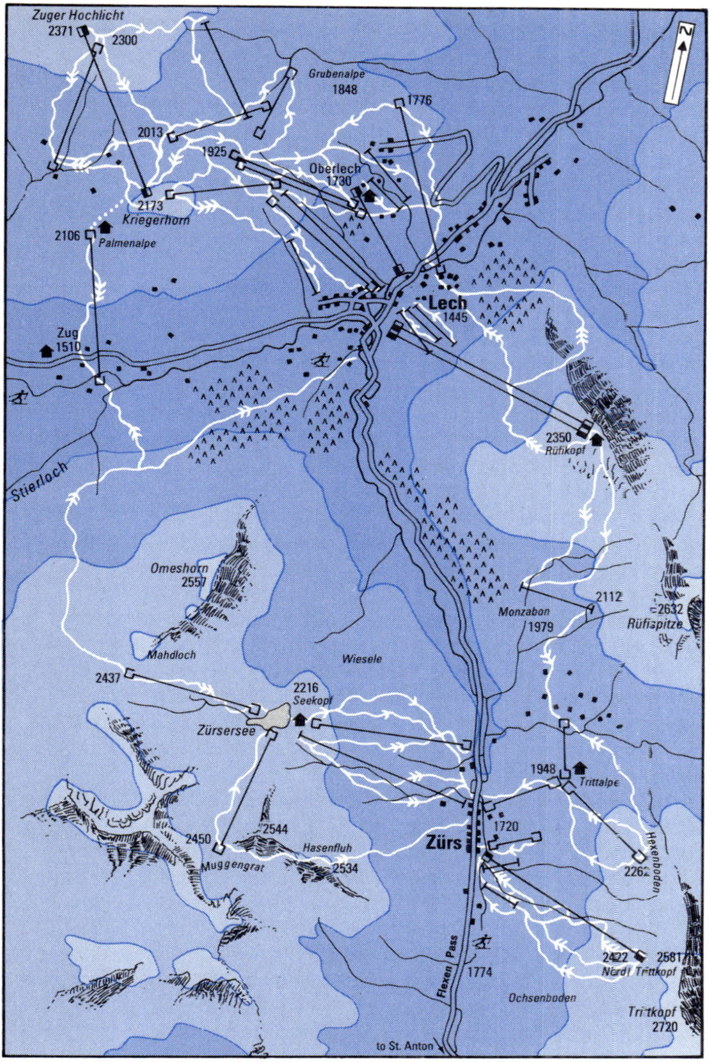

for which there are large, reasonably safe open spaces, although no especially fearsome runs to compare to St Anton's.

The **Rüfikopf** cable-car scales an impressive wall from the centre of Lech, too steep to be skied directly but with long, beautiful and difficult unprepared runs, often closed after heavy snowfall, in several directions – either down to Lech via the Wöstertäli or down the shoulder of the Rüfikopf to the woods by the road from Zürs. Long, beautiful pistes traverse across to the Hexenboden skiing above Zürs.

Lech's main skiing area, on the other side of the river, is contrastingly open and mostly gentle, though the slopes immediately above the village (sunny, but equipped with snow machines to compensate) are uncomfortably steep for near-beginners. From different parts of the village several lifts serve the slopes between Lech and **Oberlech**. The cable-car has no piste back to the bottom, only a toboggan run. Above Oberlech, lifts and pistes are spread in a wide, fragmented basin below the peaks of the Kriegerhorn and the Zuger Hochlicht, the two linked by a spectacular cable-car. There are easy and intermediate motorway pistes in all directions, but also some tough runs, especially from the Kriegerhorn – a couple of short, steep pistes down towards Lech and to the Steinmähder chairs, and a beautiful long south-facing slope down to Zug, steep but not dauntingly so, where new snow soon deteriorates. Off-piste skiers can traverse for miles from the Zuger Hochlicht to ski down either to Oberlech or Stubenbach or even Warth; most itineraries involve a lot of walking between bits of skiing. In the other direction the open slopes beside the Steinmähder chair-lift are much favoured after a new snowfall. From the bottom a beautiful long gully schuss (often closed because of avalanche danger) leads round to Zug.

The skiing above Zürs is also split into two areas by the village, and the west-facing slopes are themselves split except at the bottom. The long **Hexenboden** chair-lift serves fairly ordinary intermediate pistes, with plenty of off-piste opportunties when the snow is right. The **Trittkopf** cable-car climbs higher and offers much more demanding runs, with some difficult and renowned off-piste descents reached by long traverses. The most difficult to reach is the run down to Stuben, which involves skiing over a gallery that protects the road. Beside Hexenboden there is a link lift for skiers coming from Lech or for those who have skied the north-facing off-piste slopes from Hexenboden down into the Pazieltal.

The east-facing **Seekopf** slopes are served by a long drag-lift from above the centre of the village near the Zürserhof, and a road-side chair-lift out of the village. At the north end of the sector there is one long, fairly easy run down to the village with some off-piste descents accessible by a short climb, ending up on the road between Lech and Zürs. On the other side of the lift there are a couple of more difficult pistes, graded red and, as elsewhere, off-piste variants around the hillside. From Zürsersee (just below the Seekopf) a chair-lift climbs a secluded north-facing bowl behind the Hasenfluh; its easy piste usually has good snow. The alternative is to go over the back and drop down into a steep bowl and on to a beautiful out-of-the-way run, manageable for intermediates, back to Zürs. The other chair-lift from Zürsersee gives access to superb long runs behind the Omeshorn to Lech and Zug, on and off the piste, with no machinery in sight.

Mountain restaurants are surprisingly inadequate for such long-established and fashionable resorts. The Palmenalpe restaurant above Zug gets very crowded. The best places for lunch are Zug (several restaurants, mostly quite a walk from the pistes), and Oberlech, where again there is plenty of choice; the 14th-century Goldener Berg at the top of Oberlech might be captivating were it not so crowded.

The lift system has traditionally suffered from serious **queues** when the resorts are full, as they are for most of the season. One of the traditional blackspots on the clockwise Zürs-Lech circuit, the lift from below Zürs to Seekopf, is now a 4-seat chair and (equally importantly) has a squad of attendants to encourage skiers to fill all four seats; we found high-season queues negligible as a result. The Rüfikopf cable-car out of Lech has now been doubled up, which should have greatly diminished the notorious early-morning queues there. But be warned: the bottom station includes the most elaborate set of queue-concealment devices yet seen in the Alps. There is no relief in sight for other bottlenecks – notably the chairs from Zürsersee to Madloch-Joch, out of Zug and up the Zuger Hochlicht – and it would scarcely be surprising if new log-jams now manifest themselves. The Trittkopf cable-car continues to be over-subscribed in the afternoon when it gets the sun. Helicopter lifts are available.

The resort

Lech is a pleasant, sunny village with a church in the middle, and a covered wooden bridge over the water where sleigh horses take shelter from the elements. There are trees and old buildings, and the modern expansion of the resort has been unobtrusive; chalet-style hotels line the main street, next to the river, and smaller chalets are dotted around.

There are regular but not frequent post buses connecting Lech, Zug, Zürs, Stuben, Langen and St Anton.

Accommodation is mostly in comfortable and expensive hotels. The village is fairly compact, and the location of accommodation is not very important, except for the very lazy. To do Lech in style the hotels to choose are the Post (✆2206), a beautiful traditional hotel in the centre; the Arlberg (✆2134), modern, plush, central and spacious; or the Tannbergerhof (✆2202), the centre of Lech's gaudy social life. There are numerous less formal hotels, and some rented chalet accommodation, but nowhere is cheap. Rooms are often very hard to come by in high season. Oberlech has several comfortable hotels near the cable-car station, and chalets spread widely around the hillside. The main attraction of staying here is to avoid ski-school crowds on the Schlegelkopf lifts out of Lech itself, and to be away from traffic. One of the most attractive and friendly hotels is the Sporthotel Petersboden (✆2438), known for its piste-side Red Umbrella bar.

Après-ski is a serious and smart business: Lech après-skiers prefer to put their hair up rather than let it down. The Tannbergerhof has made itself the hub, with a very popular pavement bar in the afternoon, and a disco tea-dance following shortly afterwards; there is live music later on, here and in several other hotels. Dining and dancing out at Zug (by sleigh) and Oberlech (cable-car up, toboggan or walk down if you miss the last cable-car at 1am) are popular.

Lech is an attractive place for **cross-country** and **non-skiers**, mainly because it is so pretty. Walks and X-C trails are not remarkably extensive but are well suited to those wanting to meet up with skiers.

Lech facts

Lift payment

Passes Arlberg pass covers all St Anton, Lech, Zürs lifts but not buses. Passes available for day, half-day, and 4 non-consecutive half-days.
Children 40% off, under 15.
Cost 6-day pass AS1,530. 15% off in low season.
Beginners Limited pass covering a few lifts, by the day. Adventurous second-week skiers need an area pass.

Ski school

Classes 2hr morning and afternoon.
Cost 6 days AS1,100. Private lessons AS1,550/day.
Children Ski school, age 3½ up, 9.00–4.00, 6 days AS1,020 (meals extra). Ski kindergarten, age 2½ up, 9.00–4.00, 6 days with meals AS1,440.
Special courses Helicopter drops, guided off-piste skiing, paragliding, surfing.

Not skiing

Facilities 25km of cleared paths, toboggan run (Oberlech), natural ice rink (skating/curling), sleigh rides, tennis, squash, hotel swimming pool, saunas.

Cross-country skiing

Trails 25km of trails along valley to Zug and beyond. Graded easy. Instruction available.

Medical facilities

In resort Fracture clinic, doctor, chemist.
Hospital Bludenz (40km).
Dentist St Anton (15km).

Getting there

Airport Zurich; transfer about 3½hr.
Railway Langen (15km); buses connect with international trains.
Road Via Ulm or Basel, then Feldkirch; chains are routinely needed, and the Flexenpass is liable to closure.

Available holidays

Resort beds 5,750 in hotels, 250 in apartments.
Package holidays Austro Tours (Ht), Inghams (Ht), John Morgan (Ch), Made to Measure (Ht Hm), Ski Sutherland (Ht), Supertravel (Ht Ch)

Further information
Tourist office ✆(5583) 2161. Tx 052 39123.

The main **nursery slopes** are at Oberlech and are in all respects excellent – there are also very gently slopes above the village on the Rufikopf side. Once off the nursery slopes inexperienced skiers will find plenty of scope for building up speed and confidence. We lack recent reports of teaching standards in the **ski school**.

Zürs 1720m

Zürs conforms to traditional Austrian architectural style, and is not the eyesore such a place would be in the French Alps, but apart from the broad snow-fields above the resort and the elegant visitors, there is nothing attractive about it. There are few shops, and nothing much seems to go on outside the confines of the many comfortable hotels, and a few bars and restaurants. Zürs is not even a particularly convenient place – although it is small, the lifts are awkwardly dotted around; one reporter complained of 'constantly tramping about the village from one lift terminal to another'. There are adequate nursery lifts near the bottom of the Trittkopf cable-car.

Tourist office ✆(5583) 2245. Tx 5239111. **Package holidays** Made to Measure (Ht Hm), Ski Sutherland (Ht).

Brand loyalty

Brand Austria 1040m

Brand is a straggling village near Bludenz in a beautiful valley beneath the mighty Scesaplana. Its skiing is of minor interest, and by Austrian standards the village is not particularly charming – it has no real centre, and its layout is not ideal for skiing. But many beginners, timid intermediates and children enjoy the skiing; some excellent hotels offer good value for money, and although there isn't a great range of nightlife, the atmosphere is friendly and lively.

Chair-lifts from two extremities of the village climb over steep, unskiable wooded slopes to an area of open, sunny, easy skiing between 1600m and 1900m, with a small nursery slope and several restaurants. The only long runs are down from Palüdhütte to the top end of the village (snow cover unreliable), and the beautiful Lorenzital run, reached from the top station, occasionally closed because of avalanche danger. Snow conditions permitting, you can prolong the Lorenzital all the way down to the bottom of the Niggenkopf chair-lift, giving 900m vertical. The north-facing flank of the Lorenzital offers some good off-piste skiing. There is a good nursery slope facing north on the other side of the village, a long walk from the rest of the skiing.

Valley-floor cross-country runs are good. There are shorter loops in the Lorenzital at about 1500m, accessible from the Niggenkopf, and a strenuous off-piste cross-country tour (up to 15km) from the Lorenzital. There is a small natural ice rink, swimming pools and saunas in several hotels, indoor tennis courts, bowling, and 10km of cleared walks. Three mountain restaurants are accessible to non-skiers. Bludenz and Feldkirch, a very attractive old town, are easily reached.

Après-ski is in hotels, except the self-explanatory Britannia Pub (darts and Saturday's football scores chalked on a blackboard). The Scesaplana is about the only dance spot, at tea time and later. Its buffet evenings are recommended by reporters.

Welcoming and comfortable hotels are one of the things that take visitors back to Brand. The Hämmerle (✆213) is attractive, comfortable and well placed, not far from the Niggenkopf lift. Reporters enjoyed excellent food, including a buffet breakfast, and very good service (fruit in the bedroom and a bottle of wine for the return journey). The Lagant (✆285) is also close to the Niggenkopf – 'pool, views, food all excellent'. The Sporthotel Beck (✆306) is a better compromise location for those wanting access to the nursery slopes, and has a good pool/sauna, charming service, and hearty food.

The nearby hamlet of **Bürserberg** has few lifts (only a chair and three drags) but they serve a worthwhile extent of mostly easy, mostly wooded, skiable mountain between 900m and 1800m; it is covered by the Brand lift pass and linked by bus several times a day.

Tourist office ✆(5559) 201. Tx 052470. **Package holidays** Austro Tours (Ht), Inghams (Ht Sc).

Montafon multiplier

Schruns, Tschagguns, St Gallenkirch Gaschurn, Gargellen Austria 700m–1430m

The Montafon is a large skiing region south of Bludenz in the Austrian Vorarlberg, spread along a long and populous valley which is a busy tourist thoroughfare in summer but a dead end in winter. The many villages along the valley have got together to share a lift pass covering all the local skiing and public transport between the scattered areas. Pretty little Gargellen, tucked away in a secluded side valley, joins in the arrangement, which has transformed the Montafon from a bitty region of limited appeal except to ski tourers and German weekenders into a bitty region of considerable appeal to skiers who want varied intermediate skiing and don't mind taking buses to get to it.

Even more than most Austrian resorts, the Montafon is dominated by Germans, especially the ski areas most accessible to day-trippers (Schruns and Tschagguns). Gargellen was a great favourite in the early days of package tours to Austria, but now the area attracts few British skiers, and we have had few reports. The few have recommended the area for its broad, open, well-mechanised intermediate skiing with the chance of long runs down to the valley when the snow is good at these low levels. Reporters also appreciated the friendliness of the villages, by no means the most picturesque in Austria (they all straggle), but less affected by tourism than most. Schruns is the most convenient base for those relying on buses to get around, as the two relevant bus services are Schruns–Partenen (the village at the end of the road in winter) and Schruns–Gargellen. Close scrutiny of the timetables is needed if you're planning day-trips between Gargellen and Gaschurn/St Gallenkirch, but they can be managed. Gaschurn and Gargellen are the most charming resorts, and the least subject to the weekend influx.

The main resort in the valley is **Schruns** (700m), a busy little market town and spa beside the river, accessible by train from Bludenz. Schruns' skiing is the Hochjoch, reached by a long two-stage cable-car from near the town centre over wooded slopes to Kappell (1850m), where a good nursery area is cordoned off from other skiers. Above Kappell a chain of chair-lifts opens up a large area of open easy skiing beneath rocky crests behind the Kreuzjoch (2350m). There are some more taxing runs down to Kappell including a possible 11km run for nearly 1700m vertical if snow is good enough to ski down to the base station. Slopes face north and north-west. The centre of Schruns is car-free and shopping is attractively varied. There is plenty for non-skiers to do, including skating and curling, a local museum, a reading room, sleigh rides, and indoor tennis and swimming at the large, central Hotel Löwe (✆3141) which is also the focus of Schruns après-ski.

Schruns almost merges with its smaller neighbour **Tschagguns**, on the other side of the valley. There are two small ski areas, neither of them immediately accessible from the village. The larger is Golm

(1000m to 2085m), which has some entertaining open intermediate skiing, including a friendly women's downhill course, above the mid-station of a quaint open-topped funicular.

Higher up the valley, skiing consists of the M-shaped Silvretta Nova system, created by the integration of the north-east-facing slopes above the neighbouring villages of **St Gallenkirch** (880m) and **Gaschurn** (1000m) via the Novatal which divides them. There is lots of space and lots of easy ground to cover on the broad slopes. Lifts reach 2200m at both ends of the system, with a couple of tougher runs and some good off-piste skiing above Gaschurn. Busy lifts have been duplicated in most places, and Gaschurn's queues have been cut by a long new six-seater gondola. There is an easy (but over-used and often worn) run down to the valley at Gaschurn. St Gallenkirch has access lifts at either end of the long village, but the only pistes down to the valley are under the Garfrescha chairs at the southern end. Reporters have commented that the Gaschurn hotels used by British operators are inconveniently placed, so far from the skiing that the bus is essential. Gaschurn has a tennis hall.

Gargellen (1430m) is a miniature resort (it has only 750 guest beds) tucked away beneath the Madrisa in a secluded side valley away from the main Montafon thoroughfare. It is an old British family favourite, mainly thanks to the very high standard and the friendliness of the Hotel Madrisa (✆6331), the main village institution, now expensively modernised but still very handsome. It is the centre of Gargellen après-ski, has a good nursery slope in the back garden, a ski hire shop, swimming pool, fitness room and children's play area.

Gargellen's skiing on the north-east-facing Schafberg is small but attractively varied. There are easy open slopes at the top of the system between 2000m and 2300m, a beautiful long easy run round the mountain from the top to the Gargellenalp mid-station restaurant (1733m), a short blackish route under the chair-lift to the same point, and some good off-piste skiing nearby. Runs down through the woods to the edge of the straggling village are friendly, and snow at resort-level is much more reliable than in the main valley.

The Montafon has long been famous as an excellent base for ski tours (and, recently, heli-skiing) in the beautiful Silvretta and Rätikon mountains which separate Austria and Switzerland. Tourers strike out from the top of the lifts above Gaschurn, Tschagguns and Gargellen, where the favourite and least arduous excursion is over to Switzerland via the Antönierjoch and down into the beautiful, notoriously avalanche-prone valley of St Antönien. This is only a short bus and train ride away from Klosters whose Madrisa lifts lead back towards Gargellen via the Schlappinerjoch. The skiing is not difficult, the uphill sections are not long, and the resorts honour one another's lift passes. The Silvrettasee (1950m) above Partenen is the best starting point for more serious tours in the Silvretta peaks and has high-altitude cross-country skiing.

Tourist offices Gaschurn ✆(5558) 8201; Schruns ✆(5556) 2166; Tschagguns ✆(5556) 2457; St Gallenkirch ✆(5557) 6234; Gargellen ✆(5557) 6303.

Package holidays Schruns: Austro Tours (Ht); St Gallenkirch: Austro Tours (Ht); Gargellen: Inghams (Ht,Sc), Made to Measure (Ht), Ski Sutherland.

Ski-running in the old-fashioned way

Davos Switzerland 1560m

Good for *Big ski area, off-piste skiing, ski touring, cross-country skiing, resort-level snow, not skiing, sunny slopes, rail access, easy runs*
Bad for *Alpine charm, lift queues, skiing convenience, freedom from cars*

Klosters Switzerland 1130m

Good for *Big ski area, ski touring, mountain restaurants, sunny slopes, cross-country skiing, easy road access, rail access*
Bad for *Lift queues, après-ski, skiing convenience*

If skiing has its magic mountain, it is the Parsenn above Davos, where the ski pioneers of the 19th century discovered a large range of long and beautiful descents in all directions. These runs have not been bettered: for skiers with a taste for long, leisurely outings involving frequent stops at mountain huts and a train-ride home, the Parsenn is in a league of its own. Those who have become used to systematic lift arrangements may well be disappointed – though they may find consolation on one of the four or five less crowded ski areas scattered around this extensive region.

The two resorts which share the Parsenn have little else in common, apart from affluence and long-standing British connections. Davos is one of the big towns of Alpine skiing, and with its square, block buildings it is no beauty; for Swiss Alpine charm, look elsewhere. Already established as a health resort before recreational skiing was invented, it took to the new sport quickly. It was in Davos that a funicular railway was first built especially to carry skiers and it was here that the first drag-lift was installed. Ironically, that invention has in the long term helped other resorts to develop new Parsenns which have eclipsed the original – leaving Davos to look increasingly to cross-country skiers and conference delegates for its business.

Thanks largely to the patronage of Prince Charles, Klosters has an exclusive image. It is quite attractive, and smaller than Davos – a place to spend months of the winter in the seclusion of your chalet. Its skiing is curious, with exciting and very beautiful runs spread across an enormous north-facing mountain served by hardly any lifts. Up to now, the result has been very serious queues for the cable-car out of the village. But the enlargement of this lift last season – coupled with major improvements up the mountain – has done much to make Klosters queue-free.

A car is helpful in making the most of the separate ski areas – though parking near the lifts is difficult – and (as if the local skiing were not sufficient) for expeditions to St Moritz and Lenzerheide. Arosa and Gargellen (in Austria) are more easily reached on short ski-tours Frequent buses (oversubscribed in high season) link Davos Dorf and Platz from early morning until late in the evening, with more occasional services running Wolfgang–Parsennbahn, Platz–Teufi and Dorf–Pischa. In Klosters, daytime buses every half hour serve Gotschna and Madrisa lifts and points between. There are buses from Serneus about every hour, and frequent trains linking all the ski areas except Pischa.

The skiing top 2844m bottom 813m

The core of the skiing is the Parsenn/Weissfluh area above Davos Dorf, which links up with Strela above Davos Platz and the Gotschna area above Klosters Platz. Most of the lifts are on the Davos side of the mountain, but Klosters has the north-facing slopes and more than its fair share of good skiing. There are four other separate ski areas which offer excellent skiing with much less crowding. The Jakobshorn, the other side of Davos, has excellent challenging runs and very good off-piste skiing when conditions are right. The Rinerhorn, above Glaris, has a good range of skiing giving a drop of over 1000m. The other two areas are off our maps: Madrisa, above Klosters Dorf, is excellent for sunshine, uncomplicated skiing and tours over to Austria and back; Pischa is a little-skied open mountainside with good off-piste potential.

From Davos Platz the **Strela** skiing is reached by a steep funicular to the sunny Schatzalp, where there is a large and comfortable old hotel. From here, there is a toboggan run down to Platz, a path for walkers and skiers down to Dorf and off-piste skiing for adventurers. Above the Schatzalp, the east-facing open bowl below the Strela Pass consists of mainly easy skiing down the middle, and some steeper runs. These lifts are used less for the skiing they serve directly than for access to many famous old ski-tours – both on the Davos/Glaris side of the range and down to Arosa over the other side – and as a back-door way into the Parsenn ski area, via a cable-car and drag-lift to Weissfluhjoch.

This is the major lift junction above Davos and the point of arrival of the **Parsenn** funicular railway from Davos Dorf. There are enormous possibilities in three directions: first, back towards Davos Dorf – south-east-facing slopes, gentle on the top half, steeper and often icier lower down. Secondly, the extensive, open, mostly easy motorway pistes behind the Weissfluhjoch, the heart of Parsenn skiing (now with a much enlarged cable-car from Parsennhütte); for good skiers there is an excellent run, steep in places, from the Meierhoftälli drag-lift to the railway at Wolfgang. And thirdly, tremendously long runs (10km to 15km), open at first and then wooded, to the villages of Klosters, Serneus, Saas, Küblis and even beyond, to Landquart. Unless you take the cable-car to the top of the Weissfluh none of the runs is particularly difficult – easiest is a simple blue via Cavadürli to Klosters, trickiest is a moderate red to Serneus. The mountain is basically north-facing and snow is pretty reliable, though the lower slopes may well be bare or patchy. In between the various runs, there is some tough off-piste skiing

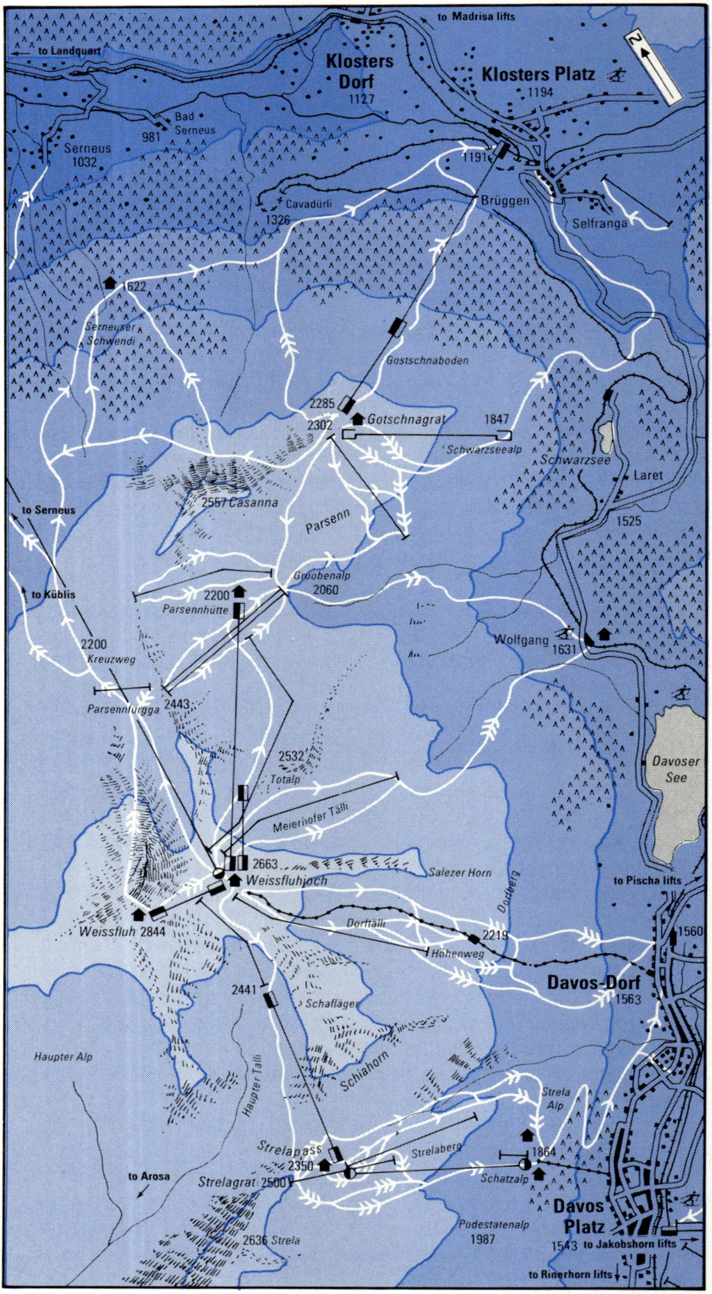
to Madrisa lifts
to Landquart
Klosters Dorf
1127
Klosters Platz
1194
Bad Serneus
981
Serneus
1032
1191
Cavadürli
1326
Brüggen
Selfranga
1622
Serneuser Schwendi
Gotschnaboden
2285
2302
Gotschnagrat
1847
Schwarzseealp
Schwarzsee
Laret
2557 Casanna
Parsenn
to Serneus
1525
Grüobenalp
2060
2200
Parsennhütte
to Küblis
Wolfgang
1631
2200
Kreuzweg
Parsennfurgga
2443
2532
Totalp
Davoser See
Meierhofer Tälli
2663
Weissfluhjoch
Salezer Horn
Dorfberg
to Pischa lifts
Weissfluh 2844
Dorftälli
2219
1560
Höhenweg
Davos-Dorf
1563
2441
Schaflager
Haupter Alp
Schiahorn
Haupter Tälli
Strela Alp
Strelapass
2350
Strelaberg
1864
to Arosa
Strelagrat 2500
Schatzalp
Davos Platz
Podestatenalp
1987
2636 Strela
1543
to Jakobshorn lifts
to Rinerhorn lifts

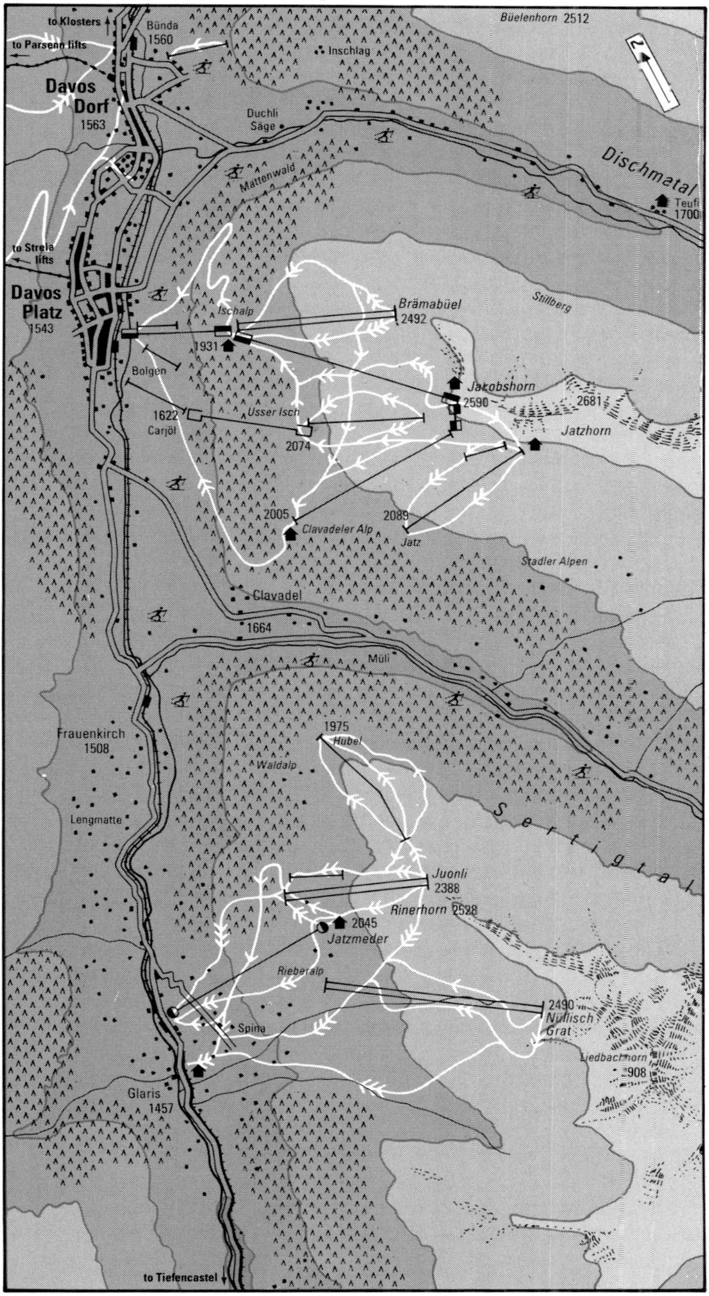
to Klosters
to Parsenn lifts
Bünda
1560
Inschlag
Büelenhorn 2512
N
Davos
Dorf
1563
Duchli
Säge
Mattenwald
Dischmatal
Teufi
1700
to Strela
lifts
Davos
Platz
1543
Ischalp
Brämabüel
2492
Stillberg
1931
Bolgen
Jakobshorn
2590
2681
1622
Carjöl
Usser Isch
2074
Jatzhorn
2005
Clavadeler Alp
2089
Jatz
Stadler Alpen
Clavadel
1664
Müli
Frauenkirch
1508
1975
Hubel
Waldalp
Sertigtal
Lengmatte
Juonli
2388
Rinerhorn 2528
2045
Jatzmeder
Rieberalp
2490
Nüllisch
Grat
Spina
Glaris
1457
to Tiefencastel

in the woods. Last season an extremely long gondola was opened, going from Schifer (1560m) across these previously unmechanised ski-fields to Weissfluhjoch – making it possible to ski the top part of the Serneus run repeatedly, and at the same time detracting considerably from the attractions of skiing it at all.

The two-stage **Gotschnagrat** cable-car from near Klosters Platz railway station is the only lift to the Parsenn from Klosters. There are runs of varying difficulty back towards Klosters. The direct run back down to the Gotschnaboden mid-station is the Gotschnawang (or simply Wang) – a slope of awesome steepness, dropping about 500m, which was notorious even before the avalanche last season which killed one skier and seriously injured another in the company of Prince Charles. Media reports at the time placed the accident on the Wang, despite the fact that the run (which is categorised as a piste, though it is not marked) was closed all season – a not unusual state of affairs. It seems more likely that the party was off-piste between the Wang and the next run along, Drostobel. This is a magnificent black run – long, steep, but nothing like as intimidating as the Wang, and much safer. On the other side of Gotschnagrat there is an easy traverse across to the Parsennhütte and some very easy runs beside the Parsennmeder drag-lift. Underneath the neighbouring Schwarzsee chair-lift is a black run which often consists of formidable moguls. The red run from the bottom of the chair-lift takes you through the woods and to a not very convenient fringe of Klosters Platz.

The very sunny, south-west facing **Madrisa** bowl above the Saaseralp (1880m) is reached by gondola from Klosters Dorf. Most of the skiing is above the tree-line, and includes a good nursery area near the Saaseralp and some long runs from the top of the Madrisa lift (2542m), including an unprepared black run to Saaseralp and the beautiful Schlappin run all the way down a wooded valley to the village, marked black but not difficult. This run is joined by a similar black going down directly from Saaseralp, but the wooded lower slopes below Saaseralp are otherwise not skied, and timid intermediates take the lift down. From this area you can make a day-tour round the Madrisa, over to Gargellen in Austria; the skiing is not particularly difficult, but a guide is recommended (as well as a passport).

A cable-car serves the whole south-west-facing slope of **Pischa** (1800m to 2485m). There is a simple array of parallel drag-lifts above the tree-line with very sunny, mostly intermediate runs beside them, and some more difficult descents through the trees. There is easy off-piste skiing beside the runs and some much more adventurous possibilities behind the Pischahorn and along the shoulder down to the Klosters road at Laret.

Jakobshorn is the most extensive alternative to the Parsenn/Weissfluh skiing, and the most handy from Davos, with access from near Platz station. Above the tree-line there is a wide range of long, mostly intermediate runs, facing roughly west, below the peaks of Jakobshorn and Brämabüel. Both are fairly steep at the top. There is gentler skiing in the sunny, west-facing bowl above Clavadeleralp. The woodland paths back to Davos Platz are not appealing, but there is always the cable-car. The steep, north-facing descent from the Jakobshorn to Teufi in the Dischmatal (nearly 900m below) is one of the best off-piste runs in the area. If you tackle it, take advice.

Rinerhorn is a small area of west- and north-west-facing slopes. Early risers will be pleased to hear that the old, cold chair-lift up to Jatzmeder has been replaced by a six-seat gondola. There is nothing very special about the pistes above the trees, but there are enough runs down to the valley to make this a good area in poor visibility. We cannot confirm claims that this area is a powder-snow paradise. About 20 minutes' climbing gives access to the steep, north-facing side of the Sertigtal. There is some less extensive off-piste skiing between the two sets of drag-lifts above Jatzmeder, and a long run down to Glaris, reached from the Nüllischgrat drag-lift.

There is an adequate number of **mountain restaurants**, but most of the high ones, notably at the top of the Jakobshorn and at Weissfluhjoch, are very cheerless. Outstandingly attractive are the delightful *schwendis* in the woods on the way down to Klosters and nearby villages, and a number of restaurants in the valleys around Davos (at Teufi, Clavadel, Sertig, Glaris and at the bottom of Pischa), which fit in well with many skiers' itineraries.

Both resorts get very crowded in peak season, and the main access lifts have traditionally suffered from very serious **queues**. The recent lift improvements seem certain to have relieved the pressure in Klosters, but will have had precious little effect on Davos.

Davos

Davos is set in a spacious, flat-bottomed junction of valleys beside a lake. The town is a through-route, and often unpleasantly congested with traffic. Buildings are square, grey, concrete and mostly undecorated. Platz is perhaps slightly uglier than Dorf, but has the better shopping and après-ski. Fortunately there is plenty of space nearby where you can find peace and quiet in beautiful surroundings, and a few outlying hamlets with accommodation and easy access to the railway (Wolfgang and Glaris).

Accommodation is in hotels large and small, simple and luxurious, throughout Platz and Dorf. Central Platz is more convenient – an easy walk to the station, and to the lifts for Strela and the Jakobshorn. The Belvedere (✆21281) is the traditional grand hotel, these days part of a chain and more expensive than stylish. Of the well-placed hotels, the Alte Post (✆35403) is cheerful and reasonable in price. The Meisser (✆52333) is well placed, with the attraction of being off the main road through the resort, and less expensive than most of its neighbours.

Après-ski is not particularly chic, but there is a variety of bars, restaurants and well-attended dance spots. Some of the most attractive and least expensive eating places are outside Davos – evenings at Teufi (reached by car or sleigh) and Schatzalp (last train down at 11pm) are particularly recommended. There is evening skating several times a week at Dorf; Platz has hockey matches, cinemas, and occasional cultural events at the conference centre.

Although not a picturesque resort, Davos is large and well equipped with **non-skiing** facilities, including an enormous natural rink – 'the equivalent of several football pitches' according to one reporter. Gentle walks were the order of the day for the consumptives who first patronised Davos, and it is still an excellent place for walkers – quiet valleys with attractive restaurants, and a few higher paths. **Cross-country** skiing is very popular, with long and attractive valley runs.

Although Davos is not really an ideal place for beginners, the **nursery slopes** beside Davos Platz at the bottom of the Jakobshorn are adequate. Klosters has a good sunny nursery area on the Madrisa at Saaseralp, and a few small lifts beside Klosters Dorf.

Davos is a celebrated area for short ski-tours, and the **ski school** organises group excursions according to conditions and demand from February onwards.

Klosters

In Klosters, Platz and Dorf are separate villages, Platz very much the centre of skiing and social life – a recognisable village centre, with a number of hotels and shops. Both villages are spread along beside the busy through-road and railway, enclosed in a narrowing wooded valley which admits little sunlight in midwinter.

Accommodation consists mostly of private chalets, with some hotels in both villages. Platz is the more convenient base, with a number of comfortable and expensive hotels around the main street near the station and cable-car. The Alpina Aparthotel (✆ 41233) is a very smart neo-rustic chalet, the Chesa Grischuna (✆42222) is smaller, older and more desirable. The small Wynegg (✆ 41340) is warm, welcoming and about as cheap you'll find, though its situation on the road toward Davos is not ideal.

Après-ski is quiet. The most attractive places for tea are up the mountain, though in Platz there are several congenial bars. More sophisticated visitors gravitate to the piano bar below the Chesa Grischuna, or to the Casa Antica or the Funny Place at the Aaba hotel – about the only recognisable discos. In Dorf the Madrisa Bar is nice for traditional music, dancing and décor. For eating out the Chesa Grischuna is the most attractive place, the Wynegg has the best atmosphere – by appointment to HRH PoW.

Klosters does not have the **non-skiing** facilities of Davos, but it is a more attractive place to spend time, and has beautiful walks and **cross-country** skiing trails. The straggling lay-out along the road is a bit of a drawback – though you can get away up the Vereinatal.

We have no recent reports on **ski school**. Guides are available for ski-tours, the most common being the excursion to Gargellen.

Davos facts

Ski school

Classes 2hr morning and afternoon.
Cost 6 days SF150. Private lessons SF44/hr, SF195/day.
Children Classes, ages 4–12, 10.00–12.00 and 2.00-4.00, 6 days SF112 without lunch. Kindergarten, Davos Dorf and Platz, ages 3–10, 9.00–5.00, 6 days with lunch SF132.
Special courses Off-piste, ski-tours.

Cross-country skiing

Trails About 75km of trails along the main valley between Glaris and Wolfgang, and up the Flüela, Dischma and Sertig valleys. Dogs allowed between Davos Platz and Glaris; small illuminated loop between Platz and Dorf. Runs graded easy or medium.

Not skiing

Facilities Over 60km cleared walks mostly at valley level, natural and artifical ice rinks, curling, fitness centre, tennis, squash, swimming, sauna, toboggan run, riding, hang-gliding, sleigh rides, cinema, museums.

Medical facilities

In resort Hospital, doctors, chemists, dentists.

Available holidays

Resort beds 6,000 in hotels, 14,000 in apartments.
Package holidays Inghams (Ht Sc), Kuoni (Ht), Made to Measure (Ht Sc), SkiGower (Cl), Swiss Travel Service (Ht)

Further information

Tourist office ✆(83) 35951. Tx 853130.

Getting there

Airport Zurich; transfer about 2½hr.
Railway Station in resort centre.
Road Via Basel/Zurich; chains may be needed from Klosters.

Klosters facts

Ski school

Classes 2¼hr morning and afternoon.
Cost 6 days SF138. Private lessons SF180/day, SF40/lesson (50mins).
Children Classes, ages under 13, times as adults, 6 days SF120. Ski kindergarten, ages 3–6. Non-ski kindergarten, ages 2–5. Both 9.15–4.30, 6 days with lunch SF108.
Special courses Ski touring.

Cross-country skiing

Trails About 40km of trails, between Serneus and Dorf, and in the Vereinatal above Platz. Near Platz a small loop for X-C with dogs, illuminated one evening a week.

Not skiing

Facilities Natural ice rink (night skating once a week), saunas, pools in hotels, squash/fitness centre, sleigh rides, toboggan run, 30km of cleared walks (mostly at valley level).

Medical facilities

In resort Doctors, chemists, dentist in resort.
Hospital Davos.

Available holidays

Resort beds 2,000 in hotels, 6,600 in apartments.
Package holidays Made to Measure (Ht Sc)

Further information

Tourist office ✆(83) 41877. Tx 853333.

Lift payment

Passes General pass covers all Klosters and Davos lifts, the railway in the whole region and buses within the two resorts. Also valid in Gargellen (Austria). Available only for 3 days or more. Also a confusing variety of passes for areas or combinations of them, with or without railway, for half-day and longer periods – some with an option of 8 non-consecutive days.
Cost 6-day pass SF190.
Children 40% off, under 16.
Beginners Coupons. Free lift for ski school pupils at Klosters Dorf.

Skiing isn't everything

Arosa Switzerland 1775m

Good for *Easy runs, not skiing, cross-country skiing, ski touring, nursery slopes, sunny slopes, resort-level snow, rail access*
Bad for *Tough runs, skiing convenience, easy road access, freedom from cars*

Of the large, long-established, traditional winter sports centres of Switzerland, Arosa is one of the less widely known in Britain, and for dedicated skiers one of the less interesting. The ski area is high and sunny, but it is not large and most of the runs are not long, and neither the village nor the winter clientele is particularly beautiful. Nevertheless Arosa commands the loyalty of many regular visitors (mostly Swiss and German, but with the British coming third), and it is an excellent place for a varied winter holiday, with some of the most beautiful mountain walks, cross-country trails and sleigh rides in the Alps, and very good ice rinks; nearly half of Arosa's visitors don't ski. But there are drawbacks: the very awkward layout, in two separate parts – the main centre (Obersee) and the higher old village of Innerarosa – plus development along the steep road linking the two; and the ugliness of Obersee's square grey buildings.

The road up to Arosa is tricky, parking and driving in the village is strictly controlled and difficult, and a car isn't much use except for expeditions to Lenzerheide or (more likely) Davos and Klosters.

The skiing top 2653m bottom 1745m

Arosa's ski area consists of two facets of the bowl at the head of the valley which, although linked by a lift, seem separate because of the distance between the main lifts and pistes at opposite ends of the resort, and because of the gullies that split up the mountainside. An unusual feature of the area is crossing paths with non-skiers. There are runs for ski-bobs and toboggans, cleared walking trails across most of the ski area, and sleighs carrying tourists from Maran up to Tschuggen and down to Innerarosa. On a fine day the ski-fields present a rare and attractive picture of a traditional winter sports recreation area.

From Obersee, a two-stage cable-car climbs from near the station and lake to Tschuggen – a broad, sunny plateau above the tree line, also accessible by chair and tow from Innerarosa – and on to the impressive **Weisshorn** (2653m), which has the steepest slopes in the ski area. One run from the top is black, but not very severe except when the south-facing slopes have frozen overnight, and there are some short, steep off-piste pitches between the rocky outcrops down the flanks of the Horn. The other pistes are mostly intermediate and easy. Off-piste skiing is limited to brief forays between the trails except for the

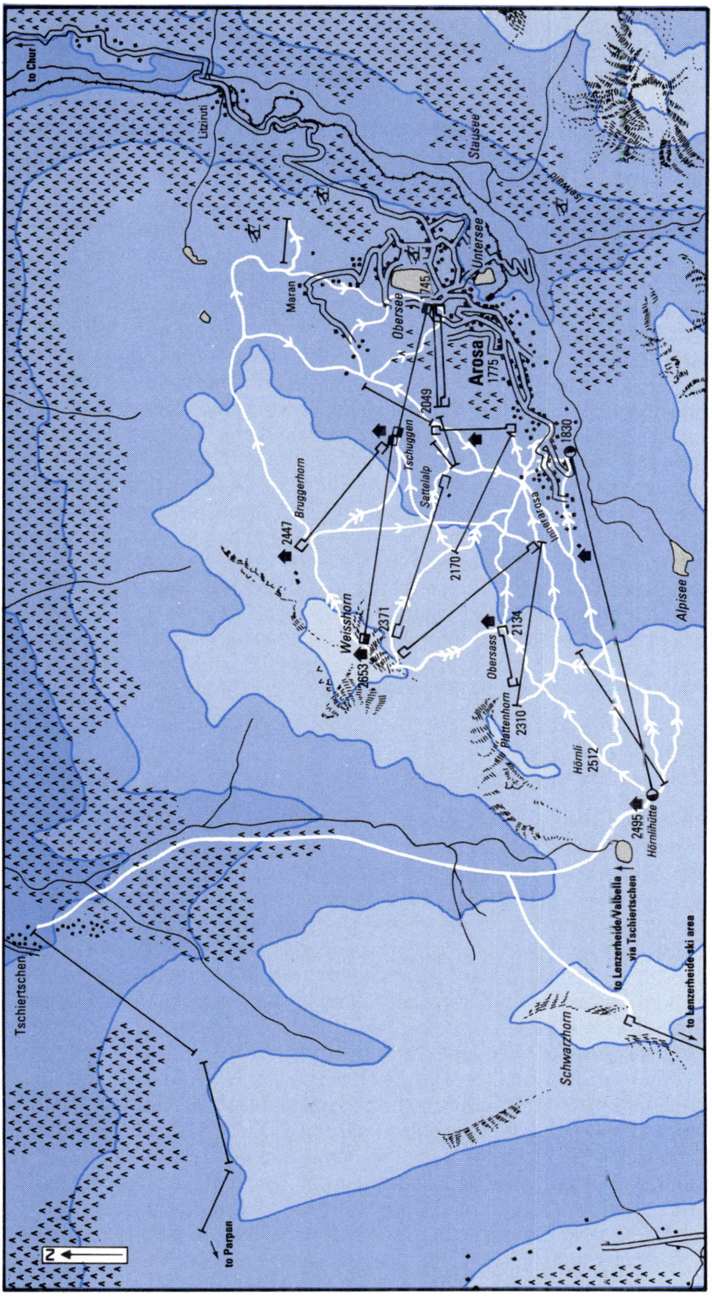
to Chur
Litzirüti
Stausee
Untersee
Obersee
1745
Maran
Arosa
1775
2049
Tschuggen
Sattelalp
1830
Bruggerhorn
2447
Innerarosa
2170
Weisshorn
2371
2653
2134
Obersass
Alpisee
2310
Plattenhorn
Hörnli
2512
2495
Hörnlihütte
to Lenzerheide/Valbella via Tschiertschen
to Lenzerheide ski area
Schwarzhorn
Tschiertschen
to Parpan
N

steep (and in some cases very difficult) runs off the back and the sides of the Weisshorn, which involve long excursions – to Tschiertschen, Litziruti and Chur. From the top of the Bruggerhorn chair-lift, a long motorway run flanks the mountain and descends to Maran, an uphill suburb of Arosa. Below Tschuggen is the only part of the Arosa ski area which is wooded; there are two runs to Obersee, one directly under the lift, the other easier and more roundabout, via Maran.

You can also ski from Tschuggen to Innerarosa and link up with the **Hörnli** side by means of the Plattenhorn drag lift (the adjacent Bänkli chair-lift assures the connection the other way round). The east-facing slopes of the Hörnli are mainly served by a long gondola (now a six-seater) which starts an inconvenient distance from Innerarosa. The pistes are open, wide and undemanding. From the restaurant on the ridge at the top you look down into an inviting bowl and hidden valley. It is a beautiful ski excursion with a marked but not groomed run of no great difficulty down to the woods and along the flank of the mountainside to the little ski village of Tschiertschen. Provided you set out early you can go on from there to Lenzerheide, and ski back either via the Hörnli or down the beautiful, remote off-piste run past Älplisee.

Mountain restaurants are adequate. The sunny restaurant at the top of the Hörnli has a friendly atmosphere, and being accessible on foot is a popular target for non-skiing hikers and their dogs when the weather is fine. At Tschuggen there is a restaurant and open-air bar.

Although limited, the lift system in general is not prone to serious **queues**. Half-hour waits for the Hörnli gondola should be a thing of the past now that its capacity has been improved. But the Weisshorn cable-car must still be expected to attract crowds.

The resort

Arosa is remotely set at the head of a beautiful steep wooded valley at the end of a long, winding 20 miles from Chur. At the bottom, the main centre of the resort is built, in very plain style, around a small lake (Obersee) with the railway and Weisshorn lift station nearby. From here the village climbs along, above and below the road, for about a mile to Innerarosa, which is the old village up in the sunny pastures – pleasant, but with no central focus. There is not much traffic (there is a midnight-to-6am car curfew), but the road is often icy and hazardous for walkers. Buses run every 20 minutes between Innerarosa, Obersee and Maran (hourly service at night, until 2am).

Accommodation is mostly in hotels varying widely in size and degree of comfort. Obersee is the best location for resort facilities; well-placed hotels include the quiet, comfortable Derby (✆311027), the large Posthotel (✆310121), and the very simple, friendly Vetter (✆311702). Innerarosa is better for access to the skiing and is more open, sunny, and attractive. The Hold (✆311408) is very conveniently placed at Innerarosa; simpler and much less expensive than its palatial neighbour the Kulm (✆310131). Lots of hotels are along the road between the two centres, which has little to recommend it.

Après-ski is varied (floodlit langlauf, evening bus for tobogganers, chess competitions after tea in the Cristallo, ice hockey matches to watch), but far from uproarious for dancers. The Kursaal is the liveliest, most youthful disco. Most restaurants are in hotels; a very cheerful exception is the Waldeck – the ice-hockey team's local.

Arosa is very good for **non-skiers**, with an impressive catalogue of other sports facilities and entertainments, and outstanding high-level paths (with benches). It is equally good for **cross-country** skiing. Trails are in two areas – the easy runs and longer Prätschalp one starting from the main cross-country centre at Maran, and the more demanding Isla runs in the woods below Obersee, across the railway. Dogs are allowed on the beginners' loop on the lake. There are buses from Obersee to Maran and Isla. There is not much scope for meeting up with downhill skiers.

Nursery slopes are adequate. Tschuggen is a broad sunny plateau with refreshment close at hand, and good for meeting up with other skiers. There is another nursery area at Maran.

There is a great variety of day tours to Davos, Klosters and Lenzerheide, which can be arranged through the **ski school**.

Arosa facts

Lift payment

Passes Area pass covers all lifts and bus. Half-day and day passes available.
Cost 6-day pass SF145. Senior citizens 15% off.
Beginners Coupons. Free baby-lift at Innerarosa.
Children 30% off, under 16.

Ski school

Classes 2hr morning and/or afternoon.
Cost 6 days SF145. Private lesson SF40/hr.
Children Ski kindergarten (Pinocchio Club), ages 3–8, 9.30–noon and 2.00–4.30, 6 days SF110. Non-ski kindergartens at Hotel Park and Hotel Savoy for ages 3–8, 9.00–5.00, SF102/132.
Special courses Ski touring.

Not skiing

Facilities Sleigh rides, over 30km of cleared walks, riding, artificial and natural skating and curling rinks (weekly beginners' sessions), ski-bob, toboggan runs, swimming (in hotels), sauna, massage, tennis, squash, bridge, chess, bowling, fitness centre, cinema, concerts.

Cross-country skiing

Trails 7½and 5½km trails at Isla, 8km at Prätschalp plus 6km extension, 2 x 2km loops at Maran, 1km at Obersee. 2km loop floodlit until 9.00. Instruction and off-trail guided excursions.

Medical facilities

In resort Doctors, dentist, chemist, fracture clinic.
Hospital Chur (30km).

Getting there

Airport Zurich; transfer 3hr by rail.
Railway Station in resort (Obersee).
Road Via Basel, Zurich and Chur. The last 30km is narrow, tortuous and difficult; chains often necessary.

Available holidays

Resort beds 5,700 in hotels, 5,300 in apartments. **Package holidays** Kuoni (Ht), Made to Measure (Ht Sc), SkiGower (Cl), Swiss Travel Service (Ht)

Further information

Tourist office ✆(81) 311621. Tx 851671.

If you're passing through...

Lenzerheide-Valbella

Switzerland 1500m

Good for *Easy runs, not skiing, cross-country skiing, big ski area, sunny slopes*
Bad for *Après-ski, tough runs, skiing convenience*

Linked resort: Churwalden

If you haven't heard of Lenzerheide and Valbella, do not fear: you are not alone. Although they share a large skiing area in a famous skiing region, and are popular with the Swiss for family holidays, they have largely escaped international attention. The area has considerable attractions – as well as the extent of the skiing, it can fairly claim excellent cross-country possibilities, no shortage of non-skiing activities, pleasant scenery and a civilised atmosphere. But the extent of the skiing area cannot disguise its lack of variety. And the villages themselves are not particularly attractive or convenient.

The originally distinct villages lie at either end of a lake in a wide, attractively wooded pass running north–south, with high mountains on either side. The road linking them is an important thoroughfare, which in itself reduces the area's appeal for people with small children and has encouraged the two villages to spread along the valley until they have almost merged. Their comfortable chalets sprawl across the valley too; and the result is a straggling, lifeless sort of place with more of the feel of a suburb than of a living village or a jolly resort.

Two other smaller villages come into the ski area, both used mainly by weekend visitors. Parpan is hardly more than an old hamlet beside the road up from Chur, Churwalden a larger village appreciably lower down, with its own little ski area.

Having a car is handy for getting to and from skiing, and for evening entertainment; it also gives the chance of some excellent day-trips – St Moritz, Arosa, Laax-Flims, Davos and Klosters are all within range.

The skiing top 2865m bottom 1230m

The skiing is in separate areas on either side of the inconveniently wide pass. Both have about half woodland and half open skiing terrain; the Danis/ Stätzerhorn area to the west is more extensive, and gets the sun in the morning; the Rothorn to the east is higher, more beautiful, more interesting but more crowded, and gets sun in the afternoon. There are no particularly difficult pistes, although the Rothorn cable-car opens up some off-piste skiing. Runs down to the two villages (or as near to them as they go) are in general gentler than the higher slopes, and suitable for inexperienced skiers, except in poor snow conditions – which are said to be not unusual.

The essential components of the **Rothorn** skiing are the two stages of the large cable-car which climbs from a point beside the lake, well away from both villages, to the peak about 1400m above. The panorama from the top is magnificent; the Rothorn drops away in awesome rocky faces, limiting the skiing possibilities to one main piste behind the main crest, through a wooden gallery, then over a ridge giving a choice of descents (red and not-very-severe black) to the lifts above Parpan and back to the cable-car mid-station at Scharmoin. In terms of length or difficulty there is nothing very special about this run, but it does make a change from the local straight-up-and-down pistes.

From Scharmoin there is a choice of several gentle, winding descents through the woods taking you back either to the bottom station or to the edge of Valbella or Lenzerheide. There are several drags around Scharmoin, the longest linking with the sunny Schwarzhorn chair-lift, high above Parpan. If tempted by the open, not very steep unpisted hillsides below the chair-lift, be warned that you risk ending up stranded somewhere between Parpan and Churwalden.

The best off-piste run goes from the Rothorn to Lenzerheide via the beautiful Alp Sanaspans; it is long and demanding, with no escape once begun except the variant back to the middle station which involves a steep and exposed drop over a rocky ridge separating Sanaspans from the main skiing area.

Various excursions are possible from the Rothorn area into the next valley. You can embark on an enormous circuit via Arosa and Tschiertschen by skiing from the Rothorn via Älplisee (a serious off-piste run) or by first walking round the narrow bowl which divides the top of the Schwarzhorn from Arosa's Hörnli. But most skiers opt for the direct run down from the Schwarzhorn to Tschiertschen – a very beautiful, easily identified and usually easy semi-piste. Lifts bring you back to the slopes above Churwalden. From here it's a long and almost flat traverse to reach Parpan (for a lift back up on the Rothorn side) or down to Churwalden (for a lift up the other side of the valley). In either case you have only paths to follow.

Compared with the Rothorn and its neighbour the Lenzerhorn, the **Scalottas/ Danis/ Stätzerhorn/ Pradaschier** peaks are not impressive, but the rather featureless open hillsides below them have been easy to develop for skiers: a long network of parallel drag lifts makes it possible to cover a lot of ground, even if there is precious little difference between one piste and another. Conditions permitting, you can ski just about anywhere – so you can have fun when the snow is fresh. The skiing is mostly intermediate, and the couple of runs categorised black are not particularly terrifying. Runs home through the trees are mostly straightforward, but aiming for Lenzerheide from Scalottas you can end up in back gardens or on gritted roads. A new triple chair-lift is due to be installed on these slopes for the 1988–89 season, apparently replacing the drag up to Tgantieni.

The skiing of **Churwalden** is separated from the rest by a steep, densely wooded north-facing hillside, which is not easily skiable. A long, cold chair-lift makes the connection with Parpan, and good skiers have fun off-piste under it. The other way round is the gentle path which

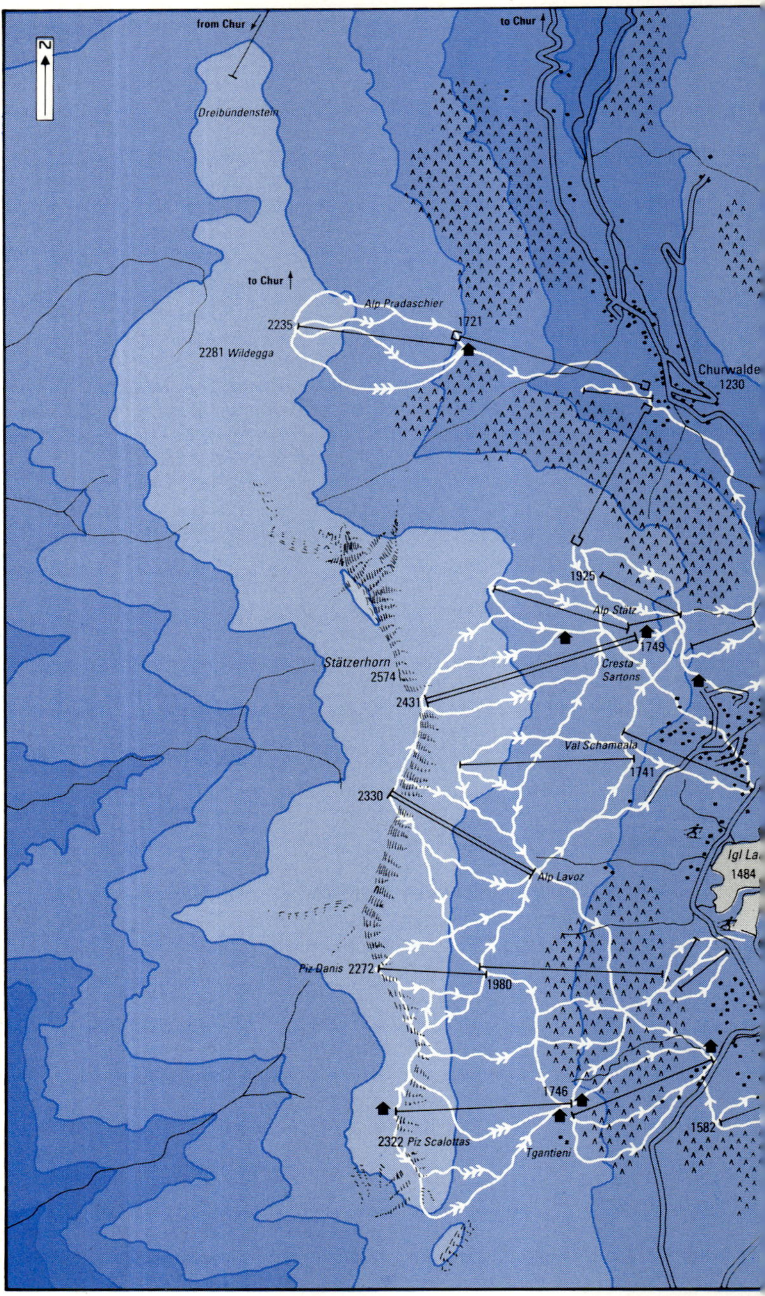
from Chur
to Chur
N
Dreibündenstein
to Chur
Alp Pradaschier
2235
1721
2281 Wildegga
Churwalden
1230
1925
Alp Statz
1749
Cresta
Sartons
Stätzerhorn
2574
2431
Val Schameala
1741
2330
Igl La
1484
Alp Lavoz
Piz Danis 2272
1980
1746
1582
2322 Piz Scalottas
Tgantieni

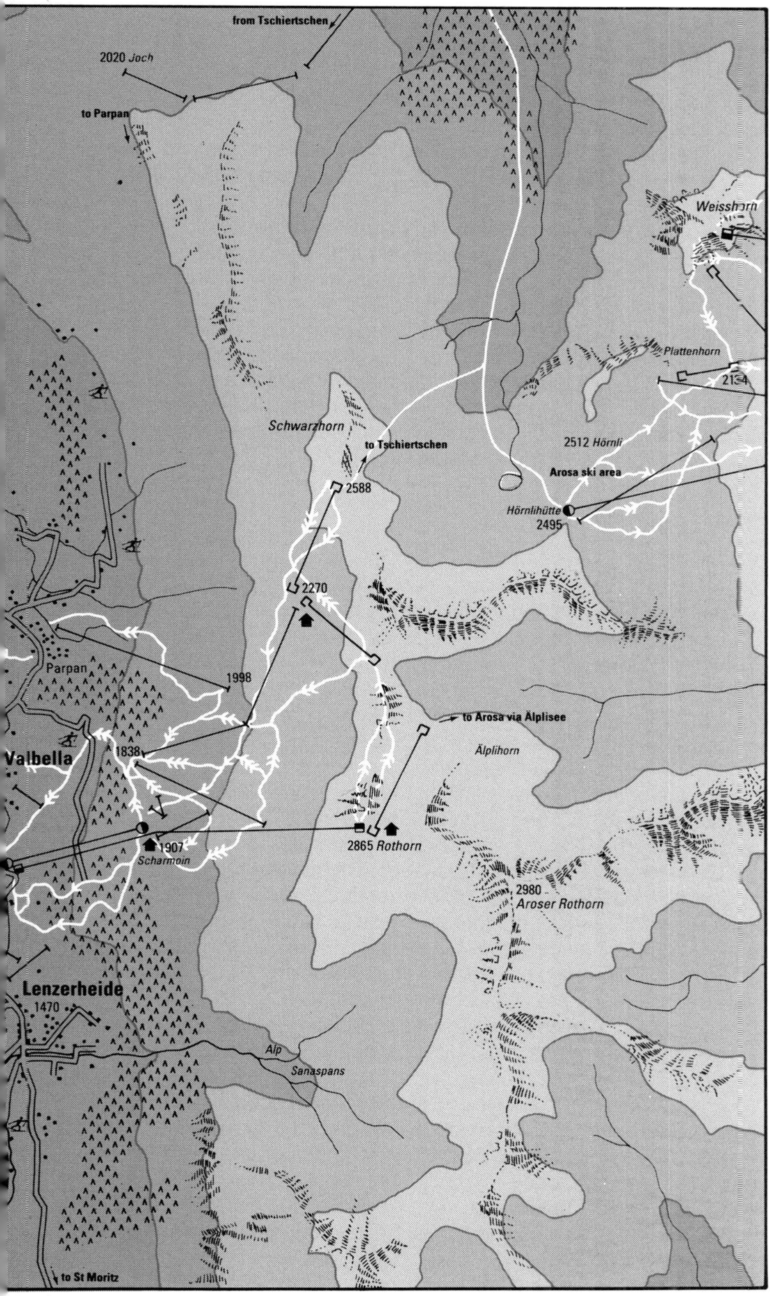
from Tschiertschen
2020 Joch
to Parpan
Weisshorn
Plattenhorn
2134
Schwarzhorn
to Tschiertschen
2512 Hörnli
Arosa ski area
2588
Hörnlihütte
2495
2270
Parpan
1998
to Arosa via Älplisee
Älplihorn
Valbella
1838
1907
Scharmoin
2865 Rothorn
2980
Aroser Rothorn
Lenzerheide
1470
Alp
Sanaspans
to St Moritz

skirts the bottom of the hill from Parpan, beside the road. Churwalden's other lifts provide a descent of 1005m back to the village. But from the top the great excursion is to head off northwards along the hill tops for about 2km, to the Dreibundenstein (2174m), at the top of a chain of lifts up from the town of Chur, and then ski down as far as snow permits. At 595m, Chur is very low; but there is a cable-car up to 1170m, so you can get down to the town even when snow conditions don't allow you to do it on skis.

There is a good range of sunny **mountain restaurants** on the Danis side, all (except the refuge at the top of Scalottas) about half-way up, around the tree-line. On the Rothorn side there are adequate facilities at half-way and top stations of the cable-car.

Long **queues** build up for Rothorn lifts especially at weekends. The lift system relies too heavily on short drag-lifts, making access to the Danis side, in particular, slow and tiresome (though the new Tgantieni chair will help here). Lift departures are sited to keep weekenders out of Lenzerheide, not to make life convenient for Lenzerheiders. The Scalottas drag-lift is very long and steep.

The resort

Lenzerheide is the major centre of development, and consists of a long main street (the main through-road) at the foot of the Rothorn slopes, with some style-less modern development below the road to the west. On the main street there are some attractive old buildings, but as a whole the place has no particular charm. Valbella has even less identity than Lenzerheide, being no more than a large community of hotels and holiday homes, but it is in some ways a better base; it is less of a roadside strip, and gives direct access to the western ski area at least.

There are buses effectively linking the villages and lifts, and you need them for crossing from one side of the skiing to the other; they run on time, but the times are widely separated. **Accommodation** consists of apartments and hotels in both villages. The most attractive and best-situated of the numerous hotels in the centre of Lenzerheide is the simplest and cheapest – the friendly Danis (✆341117), where people come to drink and play cards in the evening. From the hotel you can walk up to the Dieschen lift and from there ski down to the Rothorn cable-car station. Some way out of the resort, the Guarda Val (✆342214) is outstanding – splendid old wooden buildings, expensive and comfortable and with a good restaurant, but remote. La Palanca (✆343131) is attractive and well placed for the Scalottas lifts. The Dieschen (✆341222) is simple and friendly, with a good restaurant; you can ski down to the Rothorn lift station directly from the hotel. In Valbella the best choice is the Chesa Rustica (✆343078) close to the Danis lifts and just off the main road.

Après-ski is very quiet, even in Lenzerheide – a couple of tea-rooms, a few restaurants, a disco and some cheek-to-cheek live music in one hotel that we observed.

Non-skiers are well provided for, especially for skating and curling (a free lesson is offered). There is a smart sports centre at Dieschen. **Cross-country** trails are very good – long, mostly fairly easy, in linked sectors along the pass, through attractive woods and round the lake; and there is excellent scope for more adventurous excursions on wide open slopes above Parpan and Churwalden on the eastern side, and in the Danis Alpine skiing area – good for restaurant access.

There are several adequate **nursery slopes**, all at the bottom of the mountains (except for two baby lifts beside the Rothorn middle station). The best area is the gentle lower slope at Churwalden.

One reporter went on a pre-season wedel course at the **ski school** and was very disappointed by it.

Lenzerheide facts

Lift payment

Passes Available for whole ski area (including buses, but not Arosa, Chur or Tschiertschen lifts) or for smaller parts of it (inconveniently split).
Cost 6-day area pass SF176.
Children 15% off, under 16.
Beginners Coupons. One free lift for children at Scharmoin.

Ski school

Classes Swiss Ski Schools in Lenzerheide and Valbella. Independent Caselva School in Valbella. All 2hr morning and afternoon.
Cost 5½ days SF125, with 7-day lift pass SF265. Private lessons SF45/hr.
Children Caselva Ski kindergarten, age 4 upwards, timetable as for adults, SF108/week; non-skiing kindergarten, age up to 7, at Hotel Valbella Inn and Schweizerhof (Lenzerheide), 9.00–6.00 with meal SF126/week.
Special courses Off-piste, racing, freestyle, cross-country and ski-tours.

Getting there

Airport Zurich; transfer about 2½hr.
Railway Chur; frequent buses.
Road Via Zurich; chains may be required.

Cross-country skiing

Trails 42km of trails of all grades including those at Lantsch and Parpan. The Luziuswiese (1km) and Kleinersee (1km) at Lenzerheide are floodlit from 7.00–9.45. Tours and instruction at all three centres.

Not skiing

Facilities 30km of cleared walks, toboggan runs (one floodlit), sleigh rides, natural and artificial rinks for skating and curling, swimming pools, fitness centre, sauna, solarium, tennis, squash, ski-bob pistes.

Medical facilities

In resort Doctors, dentist, chemists, fracture clinic.
Hospital Chur (17km).

Available holidays

Resort beds 2,700 in hotels, 11,000 in apartments.
Package holidays Inghams (Ht Sc), Kuoni (Ht Sc), Made to Measure (Ht), Ski Club of GB (Ht), Swiss Travel Service (Ht)

Further information

Tourist office ✆(81) 341588. Tx 851700.

In with the Inn crowd

St Moritz Switzerland 1800m

Good for *Beautiful scenery, big ski area, resort-level snow, not skiing, cross-country skiing, après-ski, mountain restaurants, rail access, sunny slopes, late holidays*
Bad for *Skiing convenience, nursery slopes, easy road access, short airport transfers, lift queues*

Linked resort: Celerina
Separate resort: Pontresina

The official line is that you don't have to be rich to enjoy St Moritz. You certainly don't have to be much richer than you need be to enjoy other large, fashionable Swiss resorts, and many skiers who never give St Moritz consideration are making a mistake. The scenery is wonderful – the infant river Inn fills a succession of beautiful lakes against a backdrop of 4000-metre peaks with glaciers draped on their shoulders; the non-skier and cross-country skier are better catered for than almost anywhere else; and, for a resort which became fashionable because of its scenery and climate, the skiing is surprisingly good, provided there is snow in this dry and sunny corner of the Alps. And the undisputed queen of wintersports resorts is still a fascinating place for seeing the idle rich on display and the not-so-idle rich at play. Its main drawback is the resort itself – more of a town than a village, disappointingly ugly and inconvenient. Skiers keener on sport and mountain (as opposed to human) scenery may prefer to stay in Celerina, a quiet village centrally placed for the various ski areas and with direct access to the main Corviglia/Piz Nair sector.

The British began wintering in St Moritz before skiing became a sport, and the resort still revolves as much round tobogganing and riding on the frozen lake as it does around skiing – despite being among the highest of Alpine resorts, with excellent late-winter skiing, its real season ends early because the ice starts to thin and the toboggan runs close in late February or early March. Old hands say that St Moritz has lost its style, as the original core of well-to-do British has been replaced by Continentals and Americans, trying to behave in the same way but succeeding only in behaving wealthily. Certainly the Palace, most expensive of the luxury hotels, seems merely flashy. But the Carlton and the Kulm still have the quiet formality, the card tables, the worn leather and the heavy jowls of London clubs, and the St Moritz Tobogganing Club still seems defiantly British.

All approaches except that from Austria involve high passes – the Julier pass (from Chur) is kept open but is often snowy. The past lives on in the special train service from London, and rail is the best means of access (apart from flying to nearby Samedan). St Moritz is also one terminus of the Glacier Express, which runs to Zermatt via Andermatt – a spectacular journey.

The skiing top 3300m bottom 1720m

The upper Engadine skiing is spread widely around the two valleys which meet at Celerina just below St Moritz. There are wide open sunny slopes to flatter tan-conscious intermediates; steep and gentle descents through woods; long, steep pitches with walls and bumps; excellent glacier skiing with superb views; and lots of scope for long off-piste excursions which few skiers exploit. But these different kinds of skiing are found on four widely separated mountains.

Corviglia is the sunny south-facing mountain immediately above St Moritz. The funicular railway from the top of Dorf and the cable-car from the edge of Bad give access to wide open slopes with a series of drag-lifts serving not very varied intermediate runs, the most direct only moderately challenging. The only clear piste to the valley is the blue from Signal to the cable-car station at Bad. The cable-car up to Piz Nair gives access to off-piste runs down the Suvretta valley towards Bad, and to long and beautiful pistes down to Marguns. This bowl, reached more directly from Corviglia, offers long runs both easy and challenging down from Trais Fluors and Glüna. The new Piz Grisch chair-lift has widened the possibilities from the latter. The run down to Celerina is narrow and awkward in places.

The **Corvatsch** area, similarly, is accessible from both ends at valley level and consists of a band of connected drag-lifts above the tree-line serving intermediate skiing, with a single cable-car climbing much higher. But the skiing is more varied and challenging – especially from the top station, where the snow is nearly always excellent and the views, across to the glaciers of Piz Bernina, even better. The direct piste is an exhilarating sustained slope, either bumpy or hard and very fast, with an extraordinary view back up to a sheer blue ice wall at the end. The less direct route is manageable by most intermediates. Another great joy is the beautiful long run through the woods to St Moritz Bad, via a secluded mountain hut. There is good off-piste skiing; one reporter was pleased to find the various runs down to Champfér, Surlej and (more adventurously) into the Roseg valley so little used.

A piste down from Corvatsch mid-station connects with the **Furtschellas** skiing above Sils via a long chain of lifts stretching across rocky mountainsides. At the other end there are some excellent long runs from Furtschellas itself to the isolated base station. Although not precipitous, none of the runs on the lower half of the mountain is easy.

A single long cable-car goes up from the Bernina pass road to the magnificently situated hotel, restaurant and sun-terrace of **Diavolezza**, amidst marvellous glacier scenery. There is an easy open slope beside a drag-lift at the top, and a straightforward long intermediate run back down under the lift. The great attraction is the much-skied off-piste run over the back, across the glacier and through woods to Morteratsch. It involves some walking, and there are narrow passages between big holes and an awkward icy drop to negotiate at the end of the glacier; these should not deter reasonably competent skiers from enjoying a beautiful tour for little effort.

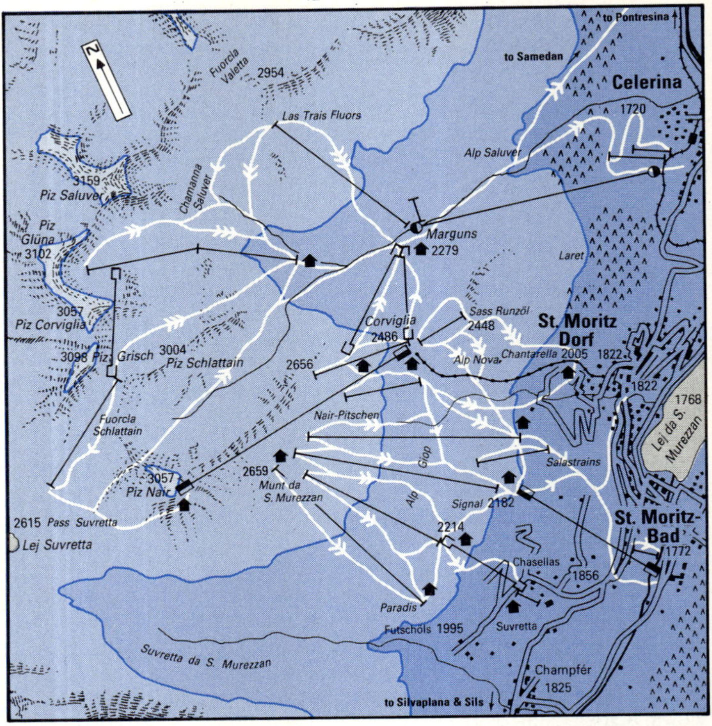

Lagalb is a consistently steep conical mountain opposite Diavolezza which presents long runs from top to bottom – ranging from very challenging (the direct route, initially steep and usually very bumpy) to only moderately so. A run from the top station links up with a couple of drag-lifts at the Bernina pass.

Reporters tell us that **Muottas Muragl**, between Celerina and Pontresina, is worth a visit for beautiful views and a good lunch. There are a few short, sunny, easy runs near the top of a funicular and one run down through the woods, intermediate except for one steep section. **Alp Languard** is directly accessible from Pontresina; it has a nursery area and a long T-bar, often closed because of avalanche danger, serving a red run.

Mountain restaurants on Corviglia are plentiful and varied, from anonymous self-service cafeterias to very attractive chalets. On the Corvatsch side only the Fuorcla Surlej and Hahnensee (Lej dals Chöds) restaurants have any charm. Prices are high.

Large areas of skiing depend on few lifts, especially the cable-cars, where there are often long **queues** despite the high proportion of non-skiers in the resort. The Sils cable-car is reported to be queue-free – but there may be half-hour queues for Piz Nair even in January (which is busy by Swiss standards). Easter is another peak.

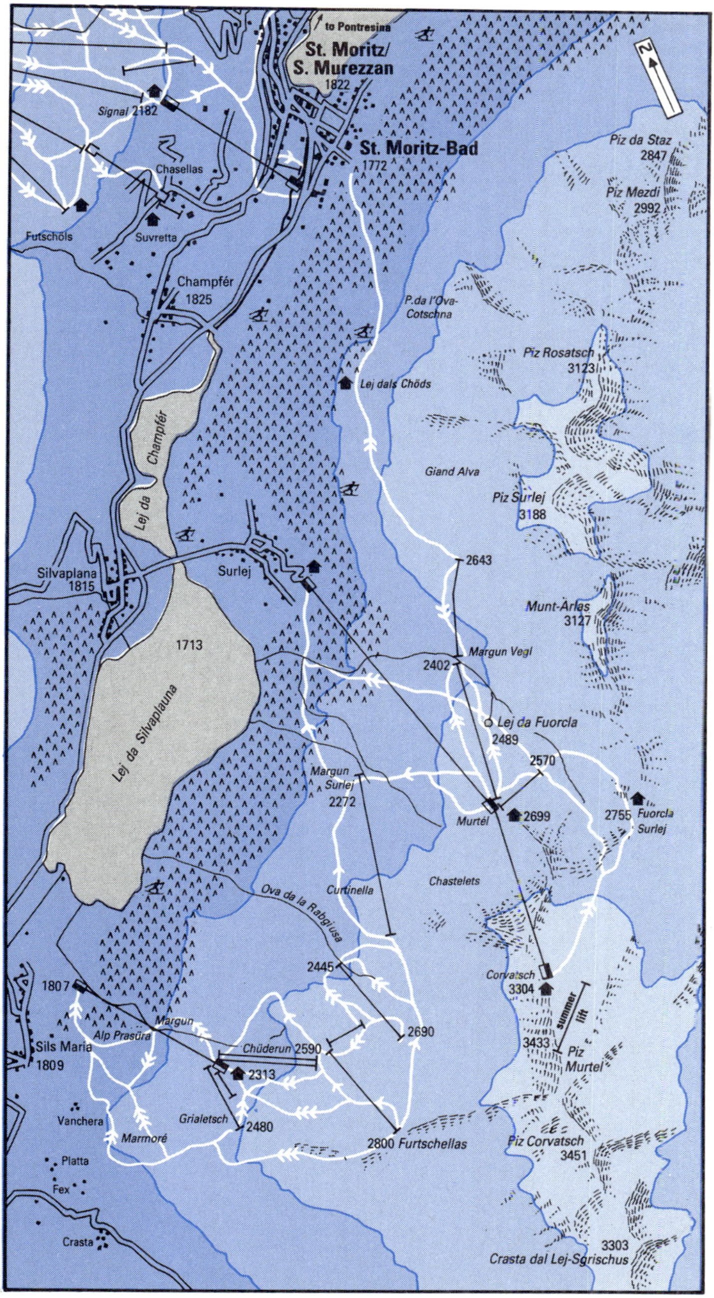
to Pontresina
St. Moritz/
S. Murezzan
1822
N
St. Moritz-Bad
1772
Signal 2182
Chasellas
Suvretta
Futschöls
Champfér
1825
Piz da Staz
2847
Piz Mezdi
2992
P.da l'Ova-
Cotschna
Piz Rosatsch
3123
Lej dals Chöds
Lej da Champfér
Giand Alva
Piz Surlej
3188
2643
Silvaplana
1815
Surlej
Munt-Arlas
3127
1713
Margun Vegl
2402
Lej da Silvaplauna
Lej da Fuorcla
2489
2570
Margun
Surlej
2272
Murtèl
2699
2755
Fuorcla
Surlej
Chastelets
Curtinella
Ova da la Rabgiusa
2445
Corvatsch
3304
summer
lift
1807
2690
Margun
Alp Prasüra
Chüderun
2590
3433
Piz
Murtel
Sils Maria
1809
2313
Vanchera
Grialetsch
2480
Marmoré
2800 Furtschellas
Piz Corvatsch
3451
Platta
Fex
Crasta
3303
Crasta dal Lej-Sgrischus

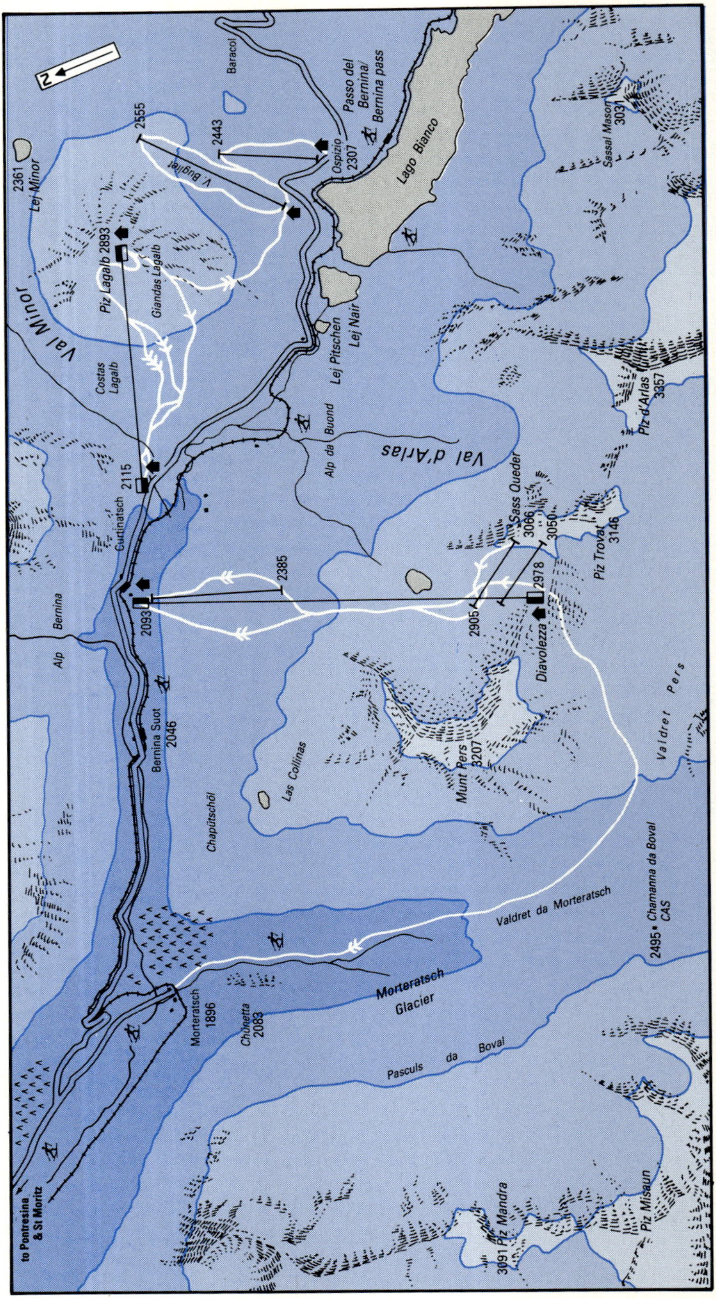
N
Baracol
Passo del Bernina/ Bernina pass
Ospizio 2307
Lago Bianco
2443
2555
V. Bugliet
2361 Lej Minor
Val Minor
Piz Lagalb 2893
Giandas Lagalb
Costas Lagalb
2115
Curtinatsch
Lej Pitschen
Lej Nair
Alp da Buond
Val d'Arlas
Sassal Mason 3031
Piz d'Arlas 3357
Sass Queder 3066
3050
Piz Trovat 3146
2385
2093
2978
2905
Diavolezza
Alp Bernina
Bernina Suot 2046
Las Collinas
Munt Pers 3207
Valdret Pers
Chapütschöl
Valdret da Morteratsch
2495 Chamanna da Boval CAS
Morteratsch Glacier
Morteratsch 1896
Chünetta 2083
Pasculs da Boval
3091 Piz Mandra
Piz Misaun
to Pontresina & St Moritz

The resort

St Moritz is a resort of parts. **St Moritz Bad**, the spa part, is spread out beside the lake on the valley floor without shape, style or animation. There are good although not especially smart shopping facilities. The cross-country track passes through, and there is direct access to Corviglia. **St Moritz Dorf** is tightly packed on the steep hillside to the north of the lake, beneath the ski slopes of Corviglia. This is fashionable St Moritz, more like a town centre than a village. Bulky Victorian hotels loom over the lake – exclusive worlds of their own, at the heart of high society; outside them and the expensive shopping precincts, St Moritz is not particularly smart or attractive. Nor is it convenient – distances on foot are considerable and parking is difficult. From the top of the resort a road winds down an attractive wooded slope, following the course of the Cresta and Bob runs to the edge of the quiet, spacious village of Celerina. In general, trains and buses serve skiers well, but the bus service between Bad and Dorf is often oversubscribed. There are no evening buses, and trains stop at about 10pm. Parking is difficult in Dorf – there is a multi-storey park.

Accommodation is spread out around the two component parts of town. Most of St Moritz's hotel beds are in four- and five-star hotels. For

St Moritz facts

Lift payment

Passes Oberengadin pass covers all lifts and public transport; available for periods from 1 day and for 5 or 10 non-consecutive days. Also local day, half-day and longer passes.
Cost 6-day pass SF190.
Beginners Two nursery lifts included in ski school cost. Otherwise coupons.
Children 25% off, under 16.

Ski school

Classes 2hr morning and afternoon.
Cost 6 days SF168. Private lessons SF50/hr.
Children Ski kindergarten, ages 4–12, 9.00–4.00, 6 days SF324 with lunch and sleigh ride. Non-ski kindergarten, SF33/day.

Cross-country skiing

Trails 150km in Engadine area; 30% easy, 50% middling, 20% difficult. 1.6km easy trail at Bad is floodlit.

Medical facilities

In resort Doctor, dentist, chemist, fracture clinic.
Hospital Samedan (6km).

Not skiing

Facilities Sleigh rides, ice rink, curling, swimming, sauna/solarium, skeleton toboggan run, hang gliding, riding, golf, tennis, squash, bobsleigh run, 120km cleared paths, museum, plane joy-rides, spa cures, English films, aerobics.

Getting there

Airport Zurich; transfer about 3½hr. 3 flights daily Zurich–Samedan (6km – air taxis from there).
Railway Main-line station in resort.
Road Via Zurich, Chur; chains often needed on Julierpass.

Available holidays

Resort beds 6,000 in hotels, 6,500 in apartments.
Package holidays Club Med (Ht), Kuoni (Ht), Made to Measure (Ht), SkiGower (Cl), Swiss Travel Service (Ht), Thomson (Ht)

Further information

Tourist office ✆(82) 33147. Tx 852-29. Fax (82) 32952.

ski-lift convenience the best locations are on the edge of Bad near the Signal lift – where the secluded Chesa Sur L'En (✆33144) is a luxurious old chalet, beautifully decorated and furnished – or high up in the centre of Dorf. The Steffani (✆22101) is one of the most attractive of the smaller hotels, with a pool; simpler, but still comfortable, B&B hotels in the centre are the Eden (✆36161) and the Languard (✆33137). The Sonne in Bad (✆33527) is large, adequate, styleless and inconveniently located, but cheap by local standards.

Most of the stylish **après-ski** is hotel-based, with formal dress requirements in several establishments – including the Palace Hotel's King's Club disco, where photographers and bouncers crowd the door. The Steffani is a popular, rather more casual and less expensive venue for drinking and dancing. There are a few simple, honest restaurants on the main square in Dorf, and in Bad. Do not be taken in by the 'Casino', which is a tacky bar with dancing and strip-shows.

The frozen lakes and side-valleys make up one of the most famous and beautiful **cross-country** areas in Europe, and the annual 42km marathon attracts over 10,000 entrants. St Moritz is also a spectacular destination for **non-skiers** both active and inactive. There are long and beautiful walks to restaurants in the skiing area (Corviglia) and up the Roseg and Morteratsch valleys, with only cross-country skiers and chamois for company. In season, there are lots of spectator sports. The tonic effect of the high and dry 'champagne climate' is famous.

Nursery slopes are not very satisfactory, there being very little available space on the valley floor except at Celerina at the foot of the Marguns gondola. Most St Moritz beginners start on slopes at Corviglia around Chantarella and Salastrains where there is a beginners' merry-go-round; when snow conditions are good they can progress to long easy runs in this sector, but often the transition is an awkward one.

We have one recent, laudatory report of the **ski school** – 'good English, took a lot of trouble'.

Pontresina 1800m

All the activity in St Moritz attracts most of the non-skiing and après-skiing custom from the other villages around – Celerina, Silvaplana and Sils – which are quiet resorts for families who come to the area (not all on high budgets) to ski or simply to enjoy the beautiful surroundings. Pontresina is much more developed, and does feel and look like a self-sufficient resort, albeit a sedate one. Although it is closer than St Moritz to some of the best skiing (Diavolezza and Lagalb) there is no significant skiing from the village itself. Many traditionalists return annually to the great comfort and considerable charm of Pontresina hotels, and appreciate being at a distance from the glitter and hubbub of St Moritz. The Steinbock (✆66371) and Engadinerhof (✆66212) are very comfortable and attractively traditional hotels on the single main street. It is one of the best locations in the region for cross-country skiers, and also has a good skating/curling rink and pool.

Tourist office ✆(82) 66488. **Package holidays** Club Med (Ht), Made to Measure (Ht), SkiGower (Cl), Swiss Travel Service (Ht).

New in to the arena

Flims Switzerland 1100m

Good for *Big ski area, sunny slopes, cross-country skiing*
Bad for *Tough runs, skiing convenience, late holidays, après-ski, resort-level snow*

Linked resorts: Laax, Falera

Take a long-established, sedate, year-round resort, better known for its sunshine and woodland walks than for its skiing and little known at all in Britain, and graft on to its modest lift system a huge new network of mechanisation opening up a vast interconnected ski area, and you have the strange hybrid phenomenon that is Flims and Laax and the White Arena ski area which they share – extensive, varied, beautiful, intelligently conceived, and smartly equipped. Unfortunately the resorts aren't ideal bases for skiers, and don't fit in with the brave new image of the modern ski-circus. But, provided you don't mind the identity problem, the inconvenience, and the peculiar ugliness of the local place-names, Flims and Laax have a lot to offer.

Flims lies on a wooded hillside near the foot of the mountains which form the northern wall of the Vorderrhein valley. Hundreds of metres beneath the wooded shelf on which the resorts stand, the river cuts through a rocky gorge. The railway follows it, but the main road runs through Flims. Although the mountains climb high they are not steep, and the valley is so wide that the setting is open, spacious and sunny. Flims is split into two separate parts – Dorf and Waldhaus.

Laax, 5km away, is smaller and more attractive, with a modern purpose-built satellite at Murschetg. The rustic farming hamlet of Falera adds yet another alternative style of base.

There are no other major resorts very close to Flims, but with a car day trips to Arosa and Lenzerheide are possible. A car is handy for evening expeditions, too.

The skiing top 3020m bottom 1080m

The skiing area extends over a very broad section of the northern wall of the valley. It faces mainly south-east, but is broken up by a number of deep gullies and tributary valleys whose flanks face south-west and north-east. Most of the ski area is very sunny, and the runs down to the resorts cannot be relied upon late in the season. The terrain is varied, with long woodland runs on the lower slopes, open ground above and a small area of glacier skiing at the top. There are few very steep slopes around, but good skiers will enjoy many runs which make up in length what they may lack in technical difficulty – the World Cup Downhill course starts little more than half-way up the mountain.

The Flims entrance to the ski area is on the edge of Flims Dorf. Of the

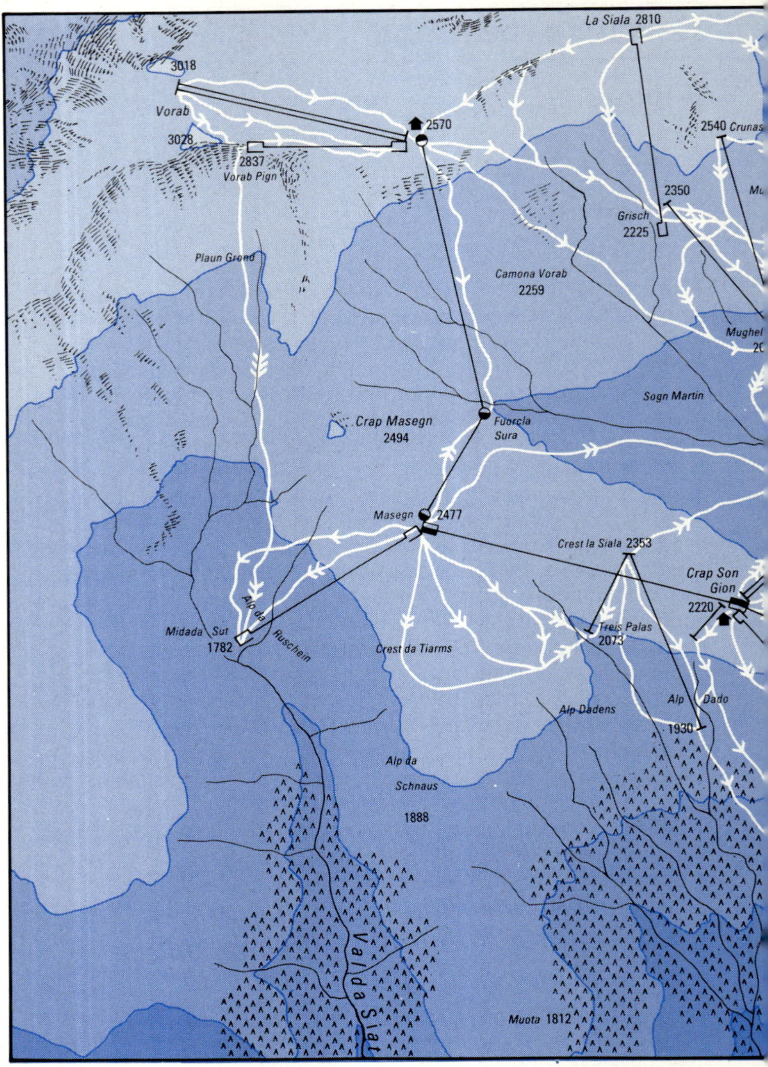

two main lifts, the more important for Flims's pistes is the chair, now upgraded to a three-seater. The runs beneath this lift and the gondola to Startgels are mostly easy, and the red runs from Naraus hold no terrors, apart from frequently inadequate snow cover. There are usually a lot of people around though, because the cheaper restricted Flims day-pass covers only this area.

For good skiers, the main attraction of Flims's skiing is the descent from **Cassons**, reached by cable car from Naraus up over the cliffs of

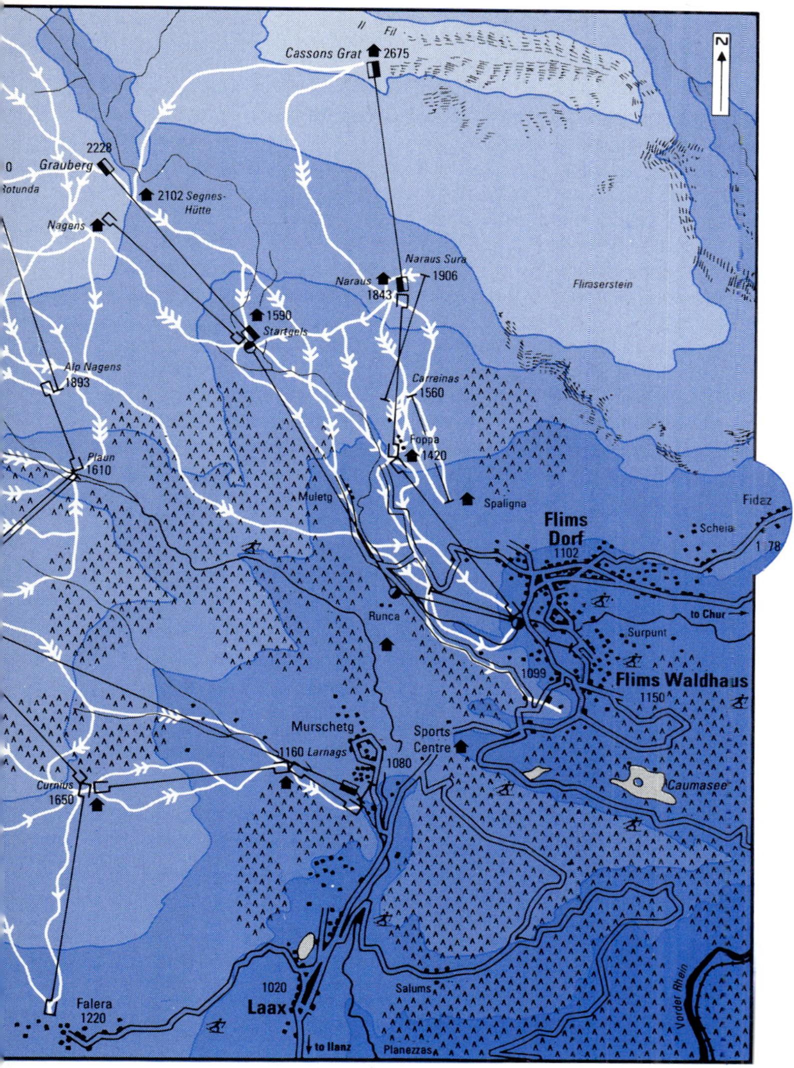

the Flimserstein. There is an annoying walk up behind the top station, but the view is splendid, as is the direct black descent back to Naraus – a fairly steep, wide open 800m face, paradise in good fresh or spring snow conditions. Only the gentler bottom half ever has a prepared piste. The alternative red run is less satisfactory, with one rather steep section near the beginning followed by a walk up to the Segnes-Hütte; it is now 'partly and intermittently prepared', whatever that means.

Flims' skiing is connected to the **La Siala** area, between Flims and

Laax, by a cable-car from Startgels to Grauberg and a triple chair-lift to Nagens. The runs back down to Startgels are good, challenging ones. Most of the skiing on La Siala consists of long, open, featureless pistes, but the top chair-lift serves long, beautiful runs, mixing motorway with moguls, down to Grauberg.

From La Siala there are connections with Laax skiing either by traversing to (or from) the Vorab glacier restaurant, or via Plaun at the bottom of a steep-sided valley with lifts up either side. The awkward bumpy paths down to Plaun are categorised black, and lots of skiers take the chair down. The other side of the valley is much more satisfactory, with longer runs down from Crap Sogn Gion to Plaun – one black, two red, and often good off-piste skiing.

Crap Sogn Gion (St John's Hill) is where the vast but still inadequate cable-car from Murschetg arrives. A series of three chair-lifts (the top one a new four-seater) make the same journey without queues, but more slowly. The run under the cable-car from Crap Sogn Gion is the downhill course – a magnificent trail, cutting a broad swathe through the woods, with a vertical drop of over 1000m. There are other gentler descents, through Curnius under the chairs, and down to Falera, whose chair-lift is a useful back-door way into the lift system.

The cable-car to **Crap Masegn** doesn't climb much but gives access to good, long, open runs down to Alp Ruschein, which are usually

Flims facts

Lift payment

Passes The White Arena pass covers all lifts and buses between Flims, Laax and Falera; available for all periods, including 8 non-consecutive days. Limited day-pass for lower Flims lifts (as far as Startgels and Naraus).
Cost 6-day pass SF198.
Beginners Passes or payment by the ride for Flims nursery lifts.
Children 50% off, 6–16.
Summer skiing Small area of about 400m vertical on Vorab glacier; 3 lifts; small summer cross-country piste.

Ski school

Classes 2hr morning and afternoon.
Cost 5 days SF135. Private lessons SF100/½ day.
Children 25% off. Ski and non-ski kindergartens, ages 3–6, 9.30–5.00, 5 full days SF100. Non-ski kindergarten, ages 3–10, 9.30–5.00, 5 full days without lunch SF100.

Medical facilities

In resort Doctor, chemist, dentist.
Hospital Ilanz (11km).

Cross-country skiing

Trails Total length of trails 60km, from 2.5km to 20km; 2km floodlit trail; cross-country centre and school at Surpunt.

Not skiing

Facilities 60km of cleared paths, swimming/sauna in hotels, indoor and natural ice rinks, tennis, riding school, sleigh rides, curling, toboggan runs, ski-bob, bowling.

Getting there

Airport Zurich; transfer about 2hr.
Railway Chur (17km); frequent buses.
Road Via Basel/Zurich ; chains rarely necessary.

Available holidays

Resort beds 4,000 in hotels, 13,000 in apartments.
Package holidays Made to Measure (Ht Sc), Ski Club of GB (Ht), Ski Sutherland (Ht), Swiss Travel Service (Ht)

Further information

Tourist offices Flims ✆(81) 391022. Tx 851919.

deserted and often good for off-but-near-the-piste skiing. In the other direction a gondola goes down into a gulley then up again to the bottom of the **Vorab** glacier, which offers gentle skiing with reliably flattering snow, accessible to all. For good skiers, and even strong intermediates, the great attraction of the Vorab is the run which drops over a saddle near the top down into an empty and beautiful valley. The run is marked black, but the short steep beginning is not as steep as all that, and the rest is mostly glorious, wide-open, fast cruising for over 1000m vertical to Alp Ruschein.

The old part of the ski area, above Flims, is well provided with attractive old **mountain restaurants**, many of them accessible to walkers. On the Laax side there are just a few large, functional service areas, at obvious points. A happy exception is the piste-side chalet at Larnags.

The improved chair-lift out of Flims has relieved the serious rush-hour **queues** there, says the tourist office. We await verification. The Murschetg cable-car and chairs cannot cope with the demand they face in the mornings (the Falera chair-lift is relatively queue-free). But once up the mountain there are rarely any significant queues. Get up, as they say round here, with the larks.

The resort

Flims Dorf is the original village, long and spread out along a busy main road in a rather characterless way. The base lift station is at the western edge of the village. Half a mile or so further south, Waldhaus, with no ski-lifts of its own, is the traditional resort – a large cluster of hotels among the trees and beside the main road. Waldhaus is quiet and comfortable, Dorf livelier, more like a small town than a ski resort. Both stretch down the hill below the road in a suburban, residential way with a few hotels mainly of interest to cross-country skiers. The daytime regional post bus serves Flims, Murschetg and Laax well, and there are less frequent services to Fidaz and Falera.

Accommodation consists mainly of comfortable hotels and self-catering apartments in chalets. The best location for skiing accommodation is on the edge of Dorf, where a few medium-priced hotels are within easy walking range of the lift station – the lively, modern Albanasport (✆392333), Meiler (✆390171), Bellevue (✆393131), and the attractive, modern chalet-style Garni Curtgin (✆393566); small, quiet, friendly, and immaculately kept. The Crap Ner (✆392626) is the most comfortable hotel in Dorf; it is very inconveniently situated, but one reporter says it provided 'the best skiing food I've ever had'. In Waldhaus, the Parkhotel (✆390181) is a world of its own, with a number of different buildings spread around the grounds. The Waldeck (✆391228) is a smaller, smart newish hotel by the main road, with neat and tidy rooms and a comfortable restaurant that prides itself on its fish. The hotel Surpunt (✆391169) is outstandingly well-placed for cross-country skiers. The Fidazerhof (✆391233) is remote (in a little community of chalets above Dorf), restful and comfortable.

Après-ski is generally muted. In Flims Dorf the meeting place for young people is the Albana pub. Across the road, the Hotel Meiler offers a more conventional mixture of tea upstairs and dancing, in theory at least, downstairs (afternoon and evening). Most restaurants are in hotels; the Parkhotel has several of varying styles. The Foppa chair-lift facilitates fondue evenings up the mountain, and toboggan rides home.

Both Flims and Laax cater very well for **cross-country** skiers and **non-skiers**, with long walks and trails through beautiful woodland scenery and up into the skiing area. Flims has more scope than Laax. A sports centre has been opened between the two.

There are good wide **nursery slopes** beside Flims Dorf, and another nursery lift at the top of the Startgels gondola. There is a small nursery slope at Murschetg, and an easy open slope high up at Crap Sogn Gion. Skiers with a few days' experience will find plenty of scope. We lack recent reports on the **ski school**; there is now a specialised paraski school, based in Falera, for those who need help with unweighting.

Laax 1020m

Laax has emerged as a ski resort only recently. It is unaffected by the development of the ski area, mainly because the lifts are further than a walk away. Much the nicest hotel is the Posta Veglia (✆(86) 34466); old, charming, with a warm and lively atmosphere and reasonable prices – for rooms and in the restaurant, the *stübli* and the piano bar. While old Laax has stayed as it was, Murschetg has grown into a spanking new resort complex, most of which is at least convenient for the slopes (although a major element of it, the Happy Rancho complex, is a tiresome walk down the hill). At the foot of the pistes is the expensively neo-rustic Signina (✆(81) 390151). Like Flims, Laax is a good resort for walkers and cross-country skiers (Murschetg is linked to Flims by cross-country trail), and offers free skating on the village pond as long as the ice holds.

Of the other communities dotted around the sunny hillsides, **Falera** is the most important; it is a sleepy old village with farming smells and noises and just a couple of hotels, reached by narrow road. Falera has the great advantage of direct access to the main lift system; the Encarna (✆(86) 33344) is a central, simple hotel.

For skiing convenience and queue avoidance you can stay up the mountain in the modern and very well appointed Crap Sogn Gion Berghotel (✆(81) 392193; panoramic views, pool/sauna, bowling).

Tourist offices Laax ✆(86) 34343. Tx 856111. Falera ✆(86) 33030. **Package holidays** Made to Measure (Ht).

Gemsstock gem

Andermatt Switzerland 1445m

Good for *Tough runs, Alpine charm, off-piste skiing, rail access, resort-level snow, ski touring*
Bad for *Easy runs, nursery slopes, skiing convenience, lift queues, mountain restaurants, not skiing, après-ski*

Andermatt is full of character. It is one of the most important places in Switzerland for mountain military service, but retains a lot of simple Alpine charm, and the skiing on the mighty Gemsstock can be as exciting and challenging as anywhere. There is also some good skiing for near-beginners, but there is not a large network of lifts, and bad weather or heavy weekend queues can make skiing practically impossible. Once much favoured by British skiers, Andermatt is now neglected by all but a faithful few. Over fine weekends and Christmas and Easter, it is very full of local Swiss and Italians, but most of the time the resort ticks over very slowly and seems to be threatening to stall. It is a celebrated centre for ski touring.

Oberalp and Furka passes are closed in winter, but cars can usually be put on the train for access to resorts in south-east and south-west Switzerland. The famous Glacier Express train, running between Zermatt and St Moritz, calls at Andermatt.

The skiing top 2965m bottom 1445m

There are four ski areas along the flanks of the Urseren valley, between the Furka and Oberalp passes. The two main ones lie at either end of Andermatt, the two smaller and less popular areas south-west of Andermatt at the villages of Hospental and Realp.

The **Gemsstock** is Andermatt's big hill, climbing steeply from the south-western edge of the village to a peak over 1500m higher. The lift system is simple and incapable of accommodating large numbers of people: there is a two-stage cable-car and a couple of lifts around the middle station (at Gurschen) where the mountainside flattens out a little to provide a small area suitable for intermediates. Above and below this the runs are moderately or very demanding. The steep slopes face north and keep their snow well; but avalanche danger can close large areas after snowfalls. From the top station, which gives magnificent views, you can traverse to a beautiful red run around the shoulder of the mountain, with a moderately steep section followed by a long path back to the middle station. Or you can tackle the runs down the front of the Gemsstock which offer 800m vertical, almost all of it severe. There are numerous variants down the one bowl. The snow sees almost no sun, and when it is fresh it is a good skier's dream. The top half is rugged terrain – some glacier, a lot of rocks, no trees. It is too steep for piste machines. Apart from the hazardous off-piste skiing in this bowl, there are very long off-piste runs in other directions from the top station, ending up either at the St Gotthard pass (the Guspis run), near Hospental (Felsental) or at Andermatt via the beautiful Unteralptal. None of these should be undertaken without a guide. The bottom half of the main face is hardly more friendly than the top; there is a single long and challenging run, less steep than the top section, but a genuine black with pitches of nearly 30°. It sees heavy traffic at the end of the morning and afternoon, and snow conditions are usually much less good than on the top half of the mountain.

From Andermatt station, a short train ride up towards the Oberalp Pass, or a ride on the new chair-lift (sited beside the barracks, more for the convenience of soldiers than holiday skiers) brings you to **Nätschen**, where three drag-lifts serve a small sunny area of mostly easy, south-west-facing pistes. There is plenty of space for skiing off-piste between the top station and the railway line. There are two ways down to Andermatt: the easy main piste mostly following the path of the road (closed in winter) and a direct descent (not pisted) more or less under the chairs. This starts gently, but becomes much steeper towards the village; difficult snow very often adds to the problems.

Above the village at **Hospental**, on the south side of the valley, there are just two lifts towards the Winterhorn – a chair over the steeper, scrub-covered lower half of the mountain, followed by a drag serving open blue runs. The lifts, which are long enough to give very worthwhile skiing, are rarely crowded. **Realp** (1538m), several miles further away, has a little-used drag-lift, suitable for beginners and near-beginners.

There are not many **mountain restaurants** to tempt you to stay high for lunch – a fairly basic one near the Gemsstock mid-station and two sunnier restaurants at Nätschen.

The Gemsstock cable-car is usually crowded at weekends; we have reports of two-hour **queues** at Easter. At other times it runs according to demand and the bottom half closes for an hour at midday. In the past, the resort has not gone in for piste grading, either on maps or on mountain; but the latest piste plan shows grades, somewhat exaggerating the variety of the areas other than Gemsstock.

The resort

Andermatt is the main settlement in the high, flat-bottomed Urseren valley. Although initial impressions of grim barracks, stony-faced guards and steep bare hillsides may be off-putting, closer inspection reveals Andermatt to be a very attractive village. It stretches along a single, sharply bent main street between the two ski areas; the old compact heart of the village (which gets little sun) has little traffic and a mixture of buildings, some dilapidated hotels of faded grandeur, others garishly colourful and some attractive old chalets. There is no public transport within the resort, and none is necessary. Having a car is no more than a luxury, saving some walking and a few train rides.

Accommodation is nearly all in hotels (or barracks). Nowhere is

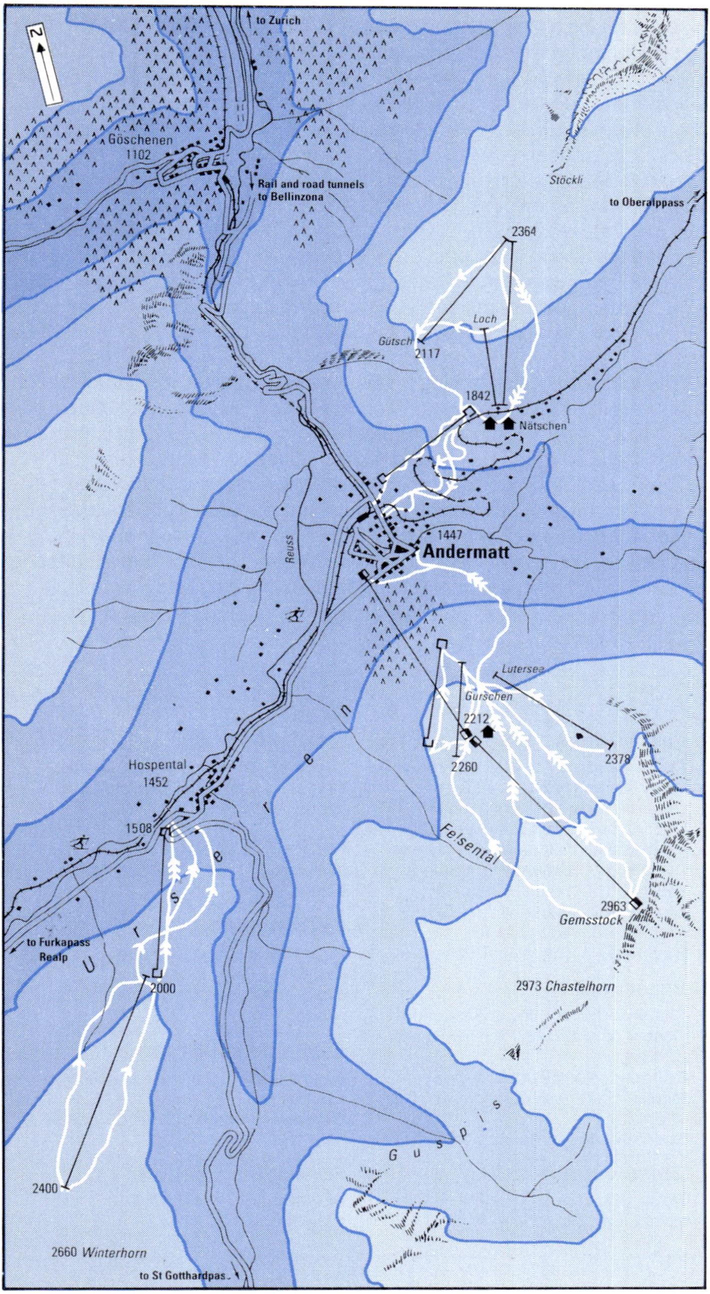
N
to Zurich
Göschenen
1102
Rail and road tunnels
to Bellinzona
Stöckli
to Oberalppass
2364
Loch
Gütsch
2117
1842
Nätschen
1447
Andermatt
Reuss
Lutersee
Gurschen
2212
2260
2378
Hospental
1452
1508
Felsental
2963
Gemsstock
to Furkapass
Realp
U r s e r e n
2000
2973 Chastelhorn
G u s p i s
2400
2660 Winterhorn
to St Gotthardpass

ideal for all the skiing. For the Gemsstock, the Aurora (✆67663) is most convenient. The Drei Könige und Post (✆67203) is a big, solid, chalet-style building in the centre without much atmosphere. The neighbouring Gasthaus zum Sternen (✆67130) is the most attractive old wooden chalet in Andermatt – cheap, fun, and a popular meeting and eating place. The Ochsen (✆67420) also does inexpensive B&B. The Bergidyll (✆67455) is a comfortable chalet-style hotel near the station; friendly family management, good breakfasts.

Après-ski revolves mainly around bars; ; some, like the Restaurant Tell and the Sterner, are packed with locals and soldiers. Others, like the Ochsen pub (hosted by a Swiss-American ski freak), are popular with skiers. There are a couple of bars with more expensive drinks and some music, and one disco. Restaurants, apart from the friendly Tell, are in hotels.

The wide, flat valley makes an ideal easy **cross-country** track which rises less than 100m over 9km. The trail is graded into green, blue and red loops – referring more to length than difficulty. Andermatt is not recommended for an active **non-skiing** holiday.

Andermatt has little in the way of **nursery slopes**, but for near-beginners the long run down from Nätschen to Andermatt is excellent.

Ski school meets by the station, and has a few English-speaking instructors. The well-known local guide Martin Epp is now more often to be seen in Wengen; another local skier and climber, Alex Clapasson, runs weekly off-piste and touring courses throughout the winter (✆67144)..

Andermatt facts

Lift payment

Passes Area pass covers all Urseren valley lifts and the train. Passes for separate parts available. Weekly Oberalp pass gives seven separate day-passes for local areas, including Disentis (not covered by Urserental pass) and 50% reduction on trains.
Cost 6-day Urserental pass SF149.
Children 33% off up to 16.
Beginners Coupons or lift pass.

Ski school

Classes 2hr morning and afternoon.
Cost 6 days SF143. Private lessons SF43/hr.
Children 20% off adult rates, 4½–12. Minder for non-skiing children in resort (✆67479).
Special courses Touring, off-piste.

Cross-country skiing

Trails 20km of easy and medium trails along most valley floor.

Not skiing

Facilities Open-air skating, curling, saunas, cinema (English films), fitness centre, toboggan run.

Medical facilities

In resort Military hospital, doctor, dentist, chemist.

Getting there

Airport Zurich; transfer about 2hr.
Railway Station in resort.
Road Via Zurich; chains may be needed.

Available holidays

Resort beds 650 in hotels, 800 in apartments.
Package holidays Made to Measure (Ht)

Further information

Tourist office ✆(44) 67454. Tx 868604.

Titlis wonder

Engelberg Switzerland 1050m

Good for *Not skiing, cross-country skiing, Alpine charm, easy road access, rail access, short airport transfers*
Bad for *Skiing convenience, resort-level snow*

The home of racing champion Erika Hess is a town-sized and very traditional Swiss resort less than an hour south of Lucerne. It is splendidly set in a wide, steep-sided valley overlooked by the impressive dark walls and snowy peak of Titlis, which rises steeply to the west, keeping sun off the town centre for much of the day in midwinter. Its clientele consists of local skiers in very large numbers, and walkers and cross-country skiers attracted by the creature comforts and varied amenities of a typically well-equipped big Swiss resort and by the secluded beauty of the narrow, wooded head of the valley. It may also tempt a few demon skiers intrigued by the promise of some long, steep and beautiful runs (mostly off-piste) beneath the glaciers of Titlis. These exist, but they are not reliably open, and Engelberg's staple ski area is not very satisfactory: disjointed and limited by terrain fundamentally hostile to skiing.

The skiing Top 3020m bottom 1050m

Engelberg's two ski areas face each other across the wide valley and make a remarkable contrast. The smaller half (Brunni) is immediately accessible from the town: a wide, sunny and friendly area of woods and pastures between 1000m and 2000m, served by a simple chain of three lifts, not the height of efficiency but rarely oversubscribed. The bigger half (Titlis) is on the western side of the valley, its base station a short bus-ride from the town. Lifts climb over a series of cliffs and plateaux to a beautiful but awkward upland ski area of rocky slopes and glacier, much of it either too steep or too flat to be skiable.

An efficient two-stage gondola, duplicating a funicular and cable-car, has cut the previously long journey time to the cliff-top hotel and lift station at (or rather just above) Trübsee. This is where the main **Titlis** ski area starts. A cable-car to Stand and two chair-lifts serve a few fairly tough intermediate runs and the top chair gives access to Laub, a wide and mostly steep open wall of over 1000m vertical down to the Ritz restaurant near Gerschnialp, admirably viewed from the town centre. On its day this must be one of the great off-piste slopes in the Alps, but its days are not frequent. From Stand another cable-car spans some splendid ice falls on its way up to gentler glaciers on the peak of Titlis. Two drag-lifts now serve the glacier skiing, allowing Engelberg to extend its winter season through spring.

The only run down is a black, which ends with a narrow and awkward

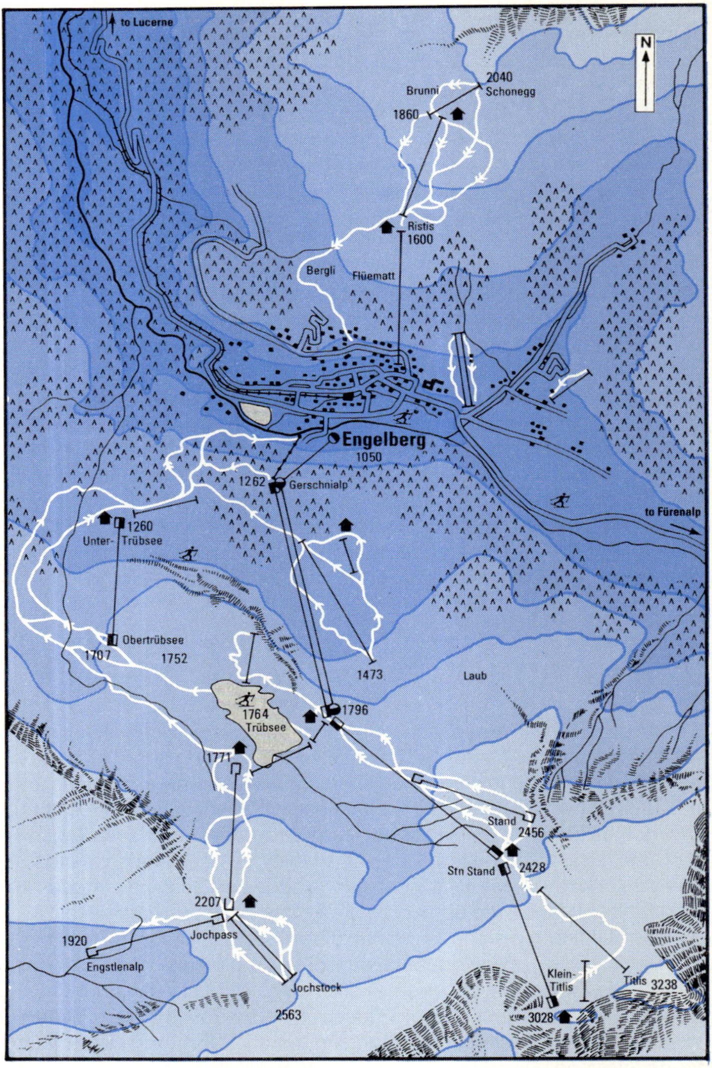

section above Stand. The views from the top are magnificent, and in fine weather the trip is well worthwhile even if you are not planning to ski down.

Inconveniently separated from the Trübsee top station by the lake itself (with flat drag-lifts beside it) is another area of intermediate runs, fairly straightforward on both sides of the Jochpass, more difficult and often bumpy beside the Jochstock drag-lifts.

After a long and tediously flat start, the single run down to the bottom station, accessible from both Trübsee and the bottom of the Jochpass runs, is an entertaining woodland trail, often spoilt by icy conditions and too many skiers, most of them racing each other down. In a couple of places there is a red variant to the main blue piste, but the run is nowhere very steep. The bottom section of the run can be reached from Gerschnialp (the mid-station below Trübsee) which has a small nursery and cross-country area.

The **Brunni** skiing starts, for practical purposes, from Ristis (1600m), reached directly from the town by cable-car. The runs served by the two drag-lifts above Ristis are straightforward intermediate pistes, open at the top and partly in woods lower down. The piste down to the village is varied and entertaining, but not a run to be skied repeatedly – it delivers you to a road on the edge of the village which is thoroughly gritted.

Mountain restaurants in the main ski area above Trübsee are fairly ordinary (we await reports on the recently enlarged Jochpasshütte), but there are two delightful ones lower down, at Gerschnialp (for off-piste skiers, beginners and walkers) and Untertrübsee (beside the main home piste). The new Titlis top station includes a big panoramic restaurant. There are two adequate restaurants on the Brunni side.

Queues are not the problem they once were – access to Trübsee is greatly improved by the gondola, and the bottleneck at Jochpass has been relieved by a four-seat chair-lift.

The resort

The impressive church of a large and very old monastery is still the prominent feature of Engelberg, and the monastic community adds an unusual element to the more colourful winter sports population. The centre has some attractive old buildings and a cheerful pedestrian shopping street in the middle, but there is also plenty of ugly modern building. Outside the central precinct, traffic nuisance is considerable, but to the south of town the valley remains quiet, peaceful and rural. A ski-bus does a 15-minute circuit around the town, taking in the main Trübsee lift departure.

Engelberg's visitors do not generate a very lively **après-ski** scene, but there are plenty of bars and restaurants around town and the casino stays open until 3am for dancing and boule, or so they say. Local youth crowds the pizzeria near the sports hall, for pool, ping pong and bowling, and the Angel Pub in the Hotel Engel.

It is a splendid resort for **non-skiers**, with long walks and sleigh rides along the quiet, increasingly narrow and wooded valley – a classically picturesque Alpine winter landscape, complete with benches and restaurants. There is also a path up to Gerschnialp and the piste-side Untertrübsee restaurant, and another across the lower slopes of the Brunni ski area. On a fine day the trip to Titlis top station is recommended. Engelberg also has a large new sports centre and a very good toboggan run down from Gerschnialp. **Cross-country** skiers can enjoy long runs in the same beautiful valley-floor setting and a few short runs at higher altitude. One is at Fürenalp, reached by a weekend cable-car reserved for non-skiers and langlaufers.

Accommodation consists mainly of solid and comfortable hotels old and new, widely spread round the town centre, with a few in a quieter, sunnier and more open position on the west-facing slopes immediately above the town, near the Brunni lift. The Engel (✆941182) claims to be the oldest hotel in town. It is conveniently placed (near the monastery), comfortable and attractively traditional, with a cosy café and sitting room. Near the station and within easy walking distance of the bus circuit, the Hess (✆941366) is large, comfortable and more expensive. It has its own sauna and fitness room.

There is a good sunny area of **nursery slopes** on the edge of town, beyond the monastery, not linked up with either of the main ski areas and not reliably snowy. The lifts at Gerschnialp are higher and more shadowy, secluded yet well placed for rendezvous with other skiers. Engelberg is not a very good resort for skiers just off the nursery slopes.

The **ski school** claims a maximum class size of eight pupils. The Neue Skischule has slightly shorter hours and higher prices than the Swiss Ski School, but an even lower maximum class size of five.

Engelberg facts

Lift payment

Passes General pass covers all lifts, available for any number of days, or for 4 out of 7 days and 7 out of 14. Limited area passes for Brunni and lower Trübsee lifts.
Cost 6-day pass SF162. 10% off for families and in low season (which includes late March).
Children Approx 35% off, under 15.
Beginners Pay by the ride.
Summer skiing Small area; 2 lifts.

Ski school

As well as the Swiss Ski School (for which we give details here) there is an alternative – the Neue Skischule.
Classes 9.45–3.15.
Cost 5 days SF247 including lift pass. Private lessons SF42/hr
Children Classes, ages 7–16, 9.45–3.15, 5 days SF199 including lift pass; lunch SF7/day. Ski kindergarten, ages 3–6, 10.00–3.00, 5 days SF194 including lift pass and lunch. Non-ski kindergarten: Age 3–6, 9.00–5.00, SF19/day with lunch.
Special courses Off-piste, touring.

Not skiing

Facilities 36km walks, sleigh rides, toboggan run, indoor and outdoor skating/curling, tennis, work-out room, sauna.

Cross-country skiing

Trails 15km (red), 10km (blue), 5km (green) on valley floor. 7km at Gerschnialp (intermediate), 4km at Trübsee, 4km itinerary at Brunni (intermediate), 2km at Fürenalp (intermediate).

Medical facilities

In resort Doctors, dentists, chemists.
Hospital Stans (23km).

Getting there

Air Zurich; transfer about 1½hr.
Railway Station in resort.
Road Via Basel, Lucerne; chains rarely needed.

Available holidays

Resort beds 2,300 in hotels, about 5,000 in apartments.
Package holidays Club Med (Ht), Made to Measure (Ht Sc), Ski Club of GB (Ht), SkiGower (Cl), Swiss Travel Service (Ht)
Package holidays Club Med (Ht), Made to Measure (Ht Sc), Ski Club of GB (Ht), SkiGower (Cl), Swiss Travel Service (Ht)

Further information

Tourist office ✆(41) 941161. Tx 866246.

Jungfrau undefiled

Wengen Switzerland 1270m

Good for *Beautiful scenery, nursery slopes, easy runs, big ski area, not skiing, family holidays, Alpine charm, rail access, chalet holidays, ski touring, freedom from cars*
Bad for *Tough runs, late holidays, skiing convenience*

Linked resort: Grindelwald

According to the authorised (British) version of skiing history, this is the cradle of the recreational and competitive sport of today. It was at Wengen that British skiers hit on the idea of using the mountain railway to turn skiing into a 'downhill only' pastime, and at Mürren (across the steep-sided Lauterbrunnen trench, and dealt with in the next chapter) that Arnold Lunn organised the first slalom race, in 1922. Wengen has changed less than most of the famous early resorts. It is still small, almost car-free and reached only by railway, and the atmosphere is still crusty and cliquey. Families return year after year to the same comfortable hotels, chalets and drinks parties, and treat the resort as a second home, which is what it is for many. There is a flourishing British racing club, and British skiers are still made to feel very welcome.

The regulars do not return purely out of nostalgia. The village is among the most picturesque of Alpine resorts, and the surrounding peaks are majestic, including the famous ascending trio of Eiger, Mönch and Jungfrau (4158m). The skiing, shared with neighbouring Grindelwald, is extensive and scenic, and mostly gentle; the lack of cars, the good sunny village nursery slopes and guaranteed English-speaking instruction make Wengen ideal for beginners and children.

Grindelwald, the original climbing resort, is overshadowed by the mountains (it gets one hour of sun a day in mid-winter) and by the special qualities of Wengen. It is larger, and the obvious access point to the skiing for motorists, local weekenders and commuters from cheap hotels in Interlaken. But a reporter points out that it enjoys superb views, is not full of British and has more to offer in the evening.

Taking a car to Wengen is not just pointless – you have to leave it at Lauterbrunnen – but seems at odds with the spirit of the place. Expeditions further afield than Mürren are unlikely.

The skiing top 2971m bottom 943m

The skiing shared by Wengen and Grindelwald falls into two areas. The main one, Kleine Scheidegg/Männlichen, is a rolling, partly wooded area of predominantly easy and intermediate pistes. The slopes above Wengen face west, those above Grindelwald mostly east. On the opposite side of Grindelwald is First, a smaller area of mainly easy south-facing runs, little used.

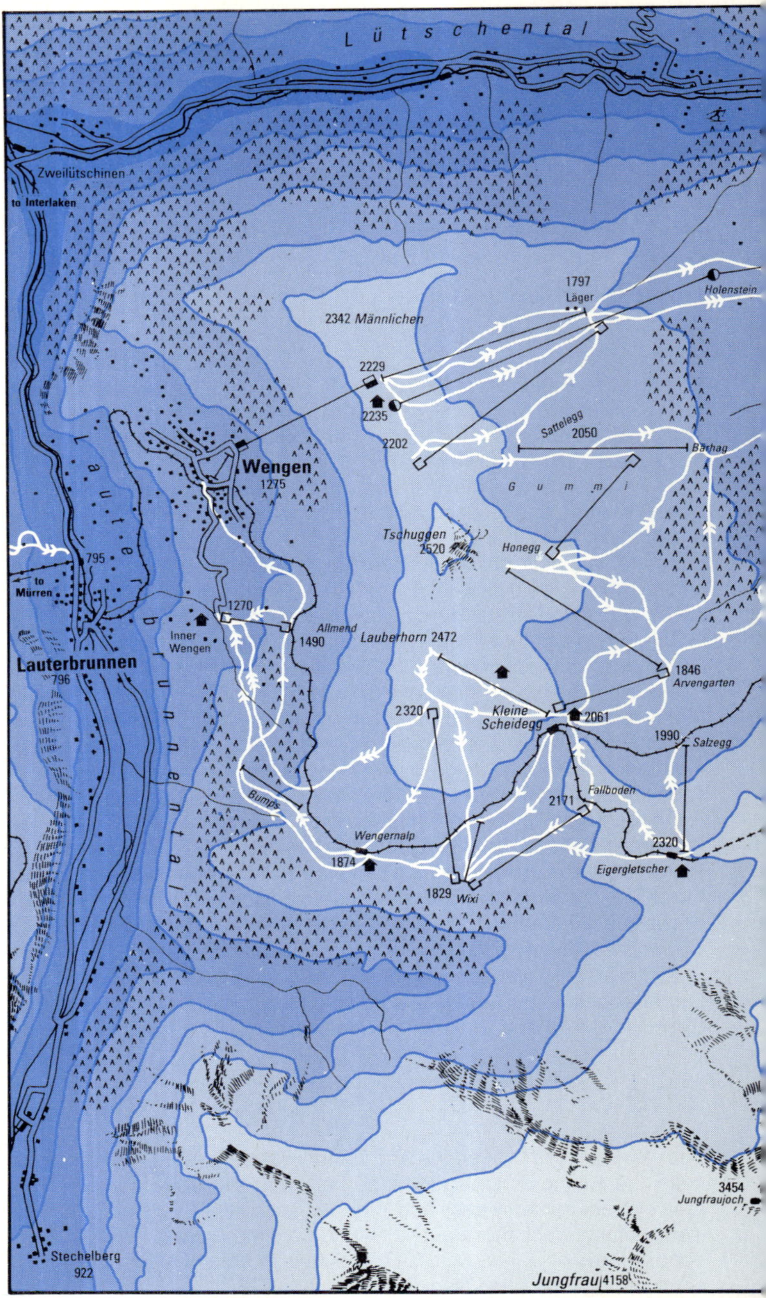

Lütschental
Zweilütschinen
to Interlaken
1797
Läger
Holenstein
2342 Männlichen
2229
2235
2202
Sattelegg
2050
Bärhag
Wengen
1275
Gummi
Tschuggen
2520
Honegg
795
to Mürren
Lauter
brunnental
1270
Inner Wengen
1490
Allmend
Lauterhorn 2472
Lauterbrunnen
796
1846
Arvengarten
2320
Kleine Scheidegg
2061
1990
Salzegg
Fallboden
2171
Bumps
Wengernalp
1874
2320
Eigergletscher
1829
Wixi
3454
Jungfraujoch
Stechelberg
922
Jungfrau 4158

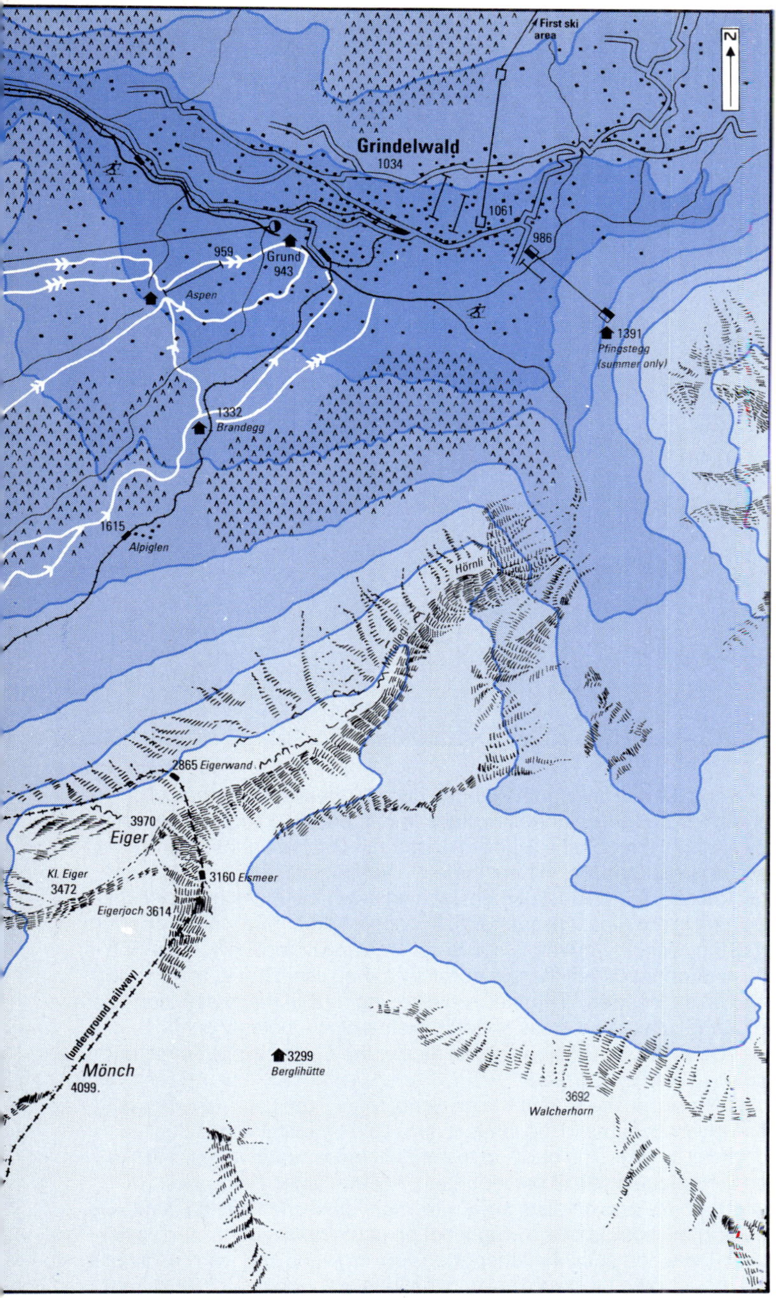
First ski area
N
Grindelwald
1034
1061
986
959
Grund
943
Aspen
1391
Pfingstegg
(summer only)
1332
Brandegg
1615
Alpiglen
Hörnli
Mittellegi
2865 Eigerwand
3970
Eiger
Kl. Eiger
3472
3160 Eismeer
Eigerjoch 3614
(underground railway)
Mönch
4099
3299
Berglihütte
3692
Walcherhorn

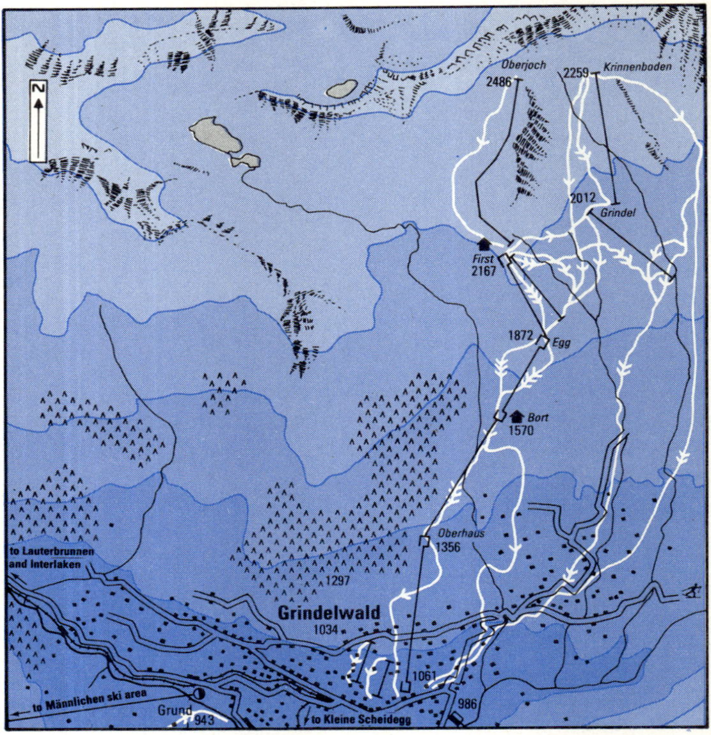

A cog railway links both Wengen and Grindelwald with the col of **Kleine Scheidegg**; another climbs from there to Eigergletscher and on, by a tunnel through the Eiger, to Jungfraujoch, the highest railway station in Europe. From here there are various off-piste and touring excursions, the easiest of them leading down the Aletsch glacier, the longest in the Alps, towards Brig. In good weather this makes a superb day trip, with a return train journey of amazing complexity; the skiing is easy throughout, but there is normally a hard climb out at the southern end (skins needed). There are challenging runs in many directions from Eigergletscher, and some good off-piste skiing – notably on the Grindelwald side under the north face of the Eiger ('White Hare') and down to Wixi by 'Oh God!'.

On the opposite side of Kleine Scheidegg is the Lauberhorn, which has given its name to the longest and most beautiful World Cup downhill course. The build-up to the race (in January) impedes skiing on the Wengen side of the mountain. At other times it is a good intermediate and off-piste area, with many possible variants of the run back to the bottom of the drag-lift or on down to Wengen – a mixture of open piste and path, the latter often very crowded and worn. Most of it can be avoided by skiing down to the Innerwengen chair. The Bumps drag, very popular with the ski school, serves an easy slope with steeper options at the finish.

On the Grindelwald side of Kleine Scheidegg a series of lifts link up with the **Männlichen**, which can also be reached by cable-car from Wengen and gondola from Grund. There are good intermediate pistes here, and some interesting off-piste skiing, particularly around the Gummi chair. The Arvengarten chair to Kleine Scheidegg and drag to Honegg give access to a lot of skiing but the chair suffers from being the only link back to Scheidegg. The Männlichen is mostly open and easy, with a few more challenging runs and open off-piste slopes below the summit, to the north of the lift station.

There are several routes down towards Grindelwald from both Männlichen and Kleine Scheidegg, with open pistes on top and wooded areas further down. The piste gradings overstate difficulty and, provided snow is good enough, these very long, beautiful and easy runs (including a blue of 8.5km) are a leisurely skier's paradise. The main disincentive is the lift ride back – the gondola is not much quicker than the train, and both are often crowded. Runs finish at Grund, a short train-ride below Grindelwald.

On the other side of Grindelwald, reached from the resort centre by bus or an entertaining cable-sleigh, the south-facing First area consists of a very slow (25-minute) chair-ride and a few drags below Oberjoch, with easy open skiing (and often good spring snow) on the upper slopes, and some touring possibilities for the adventurer. The black run down to Grindelwald is nowhere very steep, but snow conditions lower down are often difficult or muddy. There are easier indirect runs down.

Mountain restaurants are not very well distributed around the ski area, with lots by the railway and on the Grindelwald lower slopes, and few elsewhere. The Jungfrau at Wengernalp is highly recommended and Bodenwald (Haunted House) is the pick of the Grindelwald selection. Eigergletscher is reportedly the place to avoid weekend crowds.

Both the gondola and train at Grund can generate horrendous **queues** in high season and at weekends. Other serious bottlenecks are Arvengarten, the main link to Scheidegg, and the Männlichen drag-lift. Wixi has been relieved by the addition of two new lifts, though there may still be 15-minute queues at peak times. Several reporters have commented wearily on the amount of poling needed to get from lift to lift (and along the pistes), but routes can usually be planned to avoid awkward links. We understand that the trains are being replaced by new ones going at twice the speed and taking more people.

The resort

Set on an open shelf above the Lauterbrunnen valley and overlooked by the Jungfrau, Wengen is one of the most beautifully situated of Alpine resorts, surpassed for drama and views only by Mürren. Lots of chalets are dotted about the shelf, and the compact centre consists of large, comfortable, traditional hotels. The train from Lauterbrunnen to

Kleine Scheidegg runs through the resort and the station is the natural focus. All the activity is on or close to the main street, which is lined with hotels and shops (limited in range). There is an English church.

There is now a taxi service in the resort. The main access problem is the risk of missing the last train up from Lauterbrunnen to the resort (about 11pm).

Accommodation offered by UK tour operators consists mainly of hotels, with some staffed chalets; but there is also self-catering accommodation available locally. Although not a large resort, Wengen is quite spread out and hilly, and skiers not staying centrally can face walks of up to 15 minutes to the cable-car or station. Hotel standards are high. The newly rebuilt Eiger (✆551131), right beside the station, is a friendly family-run hotel. In the main street, the Victoria Lauberhorn (✆565151) and the Bernerhof (✆552721) are attractive, comfortable and traditional. Reporters have also recommended the central Silberhorn (✆565131), the Alpenrose (✆553216) – 'exceptional food, personal welcome' – the Schweizerheim (✆551112) – 'excellent value for money, comfortable rooms, good food in ample quantities' – the Regina (✆551512) – 'good atmosphere, friendly and efficient staff, sumptuous breakfast' – and the Bellevue (✆551121) – 'welcoming,

Wengen facts

Lift payment

Passes Jungfrau pass, available for 3 days and over, covers all lifts of Wengen, Mürren and Grindelwald, and trains between them. Local passes available (including day passes) and daily supplements to cover other areas.
Cost 6-day Jungfrau pass SF188. Trains between Eigergletscher and Jungfraujoch not covered by any pass; Kleine Scheidegg/Männlichen SF160.
Children 35% off, under 16.
Beginners Coupons.

Ski school

Classes 2hr morning and afternoon.
Cost 6 days SF156. Private lessons SF95/half day.
Children Ski kindergarten, ages 4–12, timetable and price as for adults, lunchtime care available from tourist office. Non-ski kindergarten, ages 3–7, 9.30–4.30, 6 days with lunch SF132.
Special courses Helicopter skiing.

Not skiing

Facilities Skating/curling (artificial and natural rinks), 20km cleared paths, swimming (in Park Hotel), sauna/solarium (in hotels), toboggan runs, ski-bobs, cinema (English films), sleigh rides, bowling.

Cross-country skiing

Trails None in Wengen, but 12km in Lauterbrunnen valley.

Medical facilities

In resort Doctor, chemist.
Dentist Lauterbrunnen.
Hospital Interlaken (12km from Lauterbrunnen).

Getting there

Airport Bern is the closest, but most operators use Zurich or Geneva; transfers 3hr–4hr.
Railway Station in resort.
Road Cars must be left at parks in Interlaken or Lauterbrunnen. Access via Basel; chains rarely needed.

Available holidays

Resort beds 2,200 in hotels; 3,000 in apartments.
Package holidays Club Med (Ht), Inghams (Ht Sc), John Morgan (Ht Ch), Kuoni (Ht Sc), Made to Measure (Ht Sc), Ski Club of GB (Ht), Ski Sutherland (Ht), Small World (Ch), Supertravel (Ht Ch), Swiss Travel Service (Ht), Thomson (Ht Sc)

Further information

Tourist office (36) 551414. Tx 923271.

family-run, excellent tea, beautiful views'.

Après-ski is fairly quiet and unsophisticated. The most popular meeting place, at least among the vociferous DHO (Down Hill Only) crowd, is the *stube* of the Hotel Eiger by the station, not to be confused with the smaller Eiger Bar on the main street – also popular and always packed after skiing. At night there is live music in a couple of bars. There are a few tea-rooms, evening skating once a week, a splendid toboggan run down to Lauterbrunnen, a night-club and a couple of discothèques. There are ice-hockey and curling matches, and occasional ski-jump and parallel slalom competitions. Evening meals at Kleine Scheidegg, followed by moonlit skiing, are often arranged.

Wengen is a splendid resort for **non-skiers**, and there are plenty of them, pottering around the delightful resort and having a go at curling. Long, beautiful mountain walks and the train make it possible to meet up with skiing companions; there's plenty of scope for longer excursions. It is no place for **cross-country** skiers.

Wengen is one of the best resorts in the Alps for beginners. The excellence of its **nursery slopes**, sunny and well-placed, is one of the reasons. Provided snow is good the transition to the large expanses of easy piste skiing accessible by train is not too traumatic, but one reporter found the path down to Wengen 'formidable' because of the crowds of other skiers.

Reports on **ski school** are mostly good, with English widely spoken and the timetable compensating for long train rides, but classes may be large. A good video system helps you select your class. Boy (and girl) racers can join the DHO club, which trains every Christmas and Easter. This is a good and popular area for ski touring and heli-skiing.

Grindelwald 1040m

Grindelwald is a large and busy year-round resort spread along the valley floor between the magnificent peaks of Wetterhorn and Eiger on the one side and the gentler wooded slopes of First on the other. The resort has lots of accommodation and leisure facilities including a good sports centre (skating, curling, swimming, sauna), long and beautiful walks high above the valley floor and (unlike the other Jungfrau resorts) long cross-country trails, totalling 45km. For skiers the place to stay is Grund, at the bottom of the main ski area, or near Grindelwald station, for easy access to Grund by train. Several reporters recommend the Hotel Derby (✆545461), right on the station – 'excellent value, good varied food, noise not a problem' – but one case of overbooking has been reported. The Bodenwald (✆531242) is also recommended – 'a comfortable small hotel with good food, and skiing to and from the door' – but it is very remote for après-ski purposes. Après-ski in Grindelwald itself is more varied than in the other local resorts, but even here there is not much going on into the small hours. There is a good daytime bus service linking Grund, Grindelwald centre and the First chair-lift (each stage is about 15 minutes on foot).

Tourist office ✆(36) 531212. Tx 923217. **Package holidays** Inghams (Ht), Kuoni (Ht), Made to Measure (Ht Sc), Small World (Ch), Swiss Travel Service (Ht), Thomson (Ht).

Towering inferno

Mürren Switzerland 1640m

Good for *Beautiful scenery, resort-level snow, family holidays, Alpine charm, freedom from cars, rail access*
Bad for *Easy runs, après-ski*

Like its neighbour and opposite number Wengen (see previous chapter), Mürren is one of the original and most fiercely traditional of ski resorts, with strong British connections based on a racing club for youngsters (the Kandahar) and the undying loyalty of many of its alumni, who include the Lunn family.

Genuinely traffic-free, Mürren has no serious rivals as a peaceful and idyllic winter hideaway: old chalets line snowy paths on a high cliff-top shelf (reached by funicular or cable-car) which is itself quite steep, so that most of the village shares the same glorious view across to the Eiger and Jungfrau.

The skiing is similarly spectacular, and the long run down from the famous revolving restaurant at the top of the Schilthorn is something no competent skier in the region should miss, weather permitting. There are a few other interesting runs on the slopes immediately above Mürren but not much of the skiing is easy and, for piste skiers at least, it is a bit of a one-run resort.

The skiing top 2970m bottom 1200m

The original lift in Mürren, opened in 1912, is the old funicular from the top of the village to the Allmendhubel. It still serves moderately easy runs down to the village and connections with the skiing on either side. Mürren's best gentle skiing is in the woods above Winteregg, where the middle station on the railway line provides Wengen-based skiers with a direct way into and out of the skiing. When snow is good it is possible to ski down to Lauterbrunnen via a long, tortuous and not particularly interesting path through the steep woods. This is the last leg of the famous Inferno course from the top of the Schilthorn (13km long, 2175m vertical). The race is run every January by over 1,000 skiers; the record time for the course is about 15 minutes, including some uphill skiing which holiday skiers can avoid by using the Maulerhubel drag. On the other side of the village, the steep Schiltgrat drag-lifts serve a serious black run of about 1.5km for 500m vertical, often huge moguls all the way, and some easier, sunny skiing down to Gimmeln.

The two-stage cable-car to Schilthorn climbs more than 1300m up the cliff face to Birg and onward over a deep bowl to the famous round (and revolving) restaurant which crowns Piz Gloria, as seen in the film *On Her Majesty's Secret Service.* The 360° views from the top are wonderful, and the run down is no less exciting. The first section is not

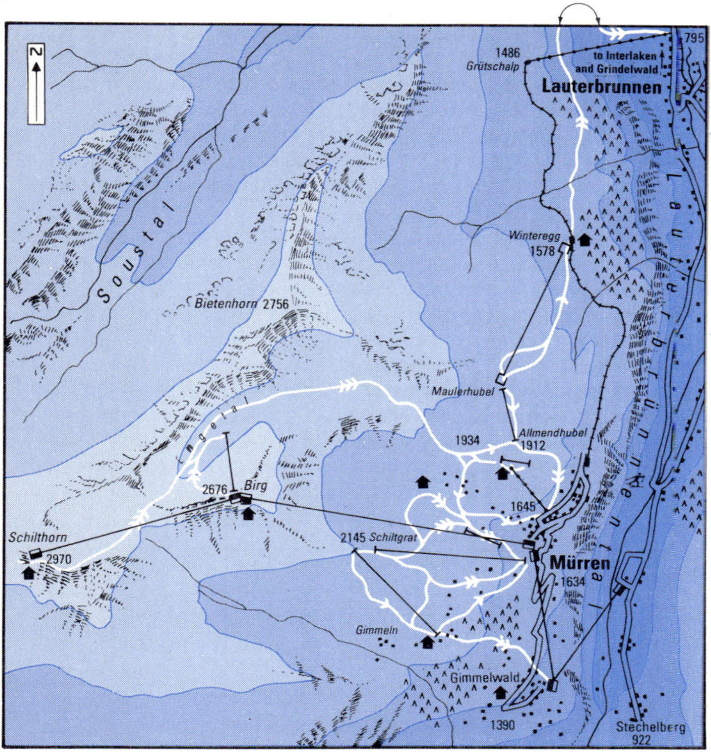

fearsomely steep, but usually very bumpy or wind-blown. The run opens out into a beautiful, gentle, open bowl (the Engetal), with a drag-lift up to Birg and open skiing on the steep slope beside it. Beneath the Engetal the run provides stunning views across to the Jungfrau massif before entering the Kanonenrohr (gunbarrel), an unnerving mixture of narrowness, rocks, moguls and a gaping precipice protected by nets before running out gently towards Allmendhubel. There are off-piste runs from Schilthorn and Schiltgrat, all of them difficult and often very dangerous. Descent by the cable-car is not covered by any lift pass.

Apart from their superlative views the **mountain restaurants** at Birg and Piz Gloria have little to commend them.

There are no serious lift **queues** except for the cable-car at peak times and when Wengen and Grindelwald are short of snow.

The resort

The train which winds along the mountain shelf from the top of the funicular up from Lauterbrunnen arrives at one end of the village, and at the other end is a station of the four-stage cable-car from Stechelberg to Piz Gloria. Between the two is the tightly-packed village.

Most of the **accommodation** is in hotels. There are a couple of large, expensive ones (the Mürren and the Eiger) and a smart new sports complex by the railway station – not well placed for skiing. Among the less expensive hotels, the Alpenruh (✆551055) is next door to the cable-car. The Bellevue (✆551401) near the Allmendhubel is recommended by a reporter for its tempting cakes and the view from its sunny rear terrace. About the cheapest accommodation is in the large, central Regina (✆551421).

Mürren's **après-ski** is very quiet indeed, with music in only one or two hotel bars. Evenings at Allmendhubel restaurant can be organised; they end perilously with a run down on skis or toboggan.

A village which is so small and quiet is difficult to recommend to **non-skiers**, despite the new and impressive sports facilities (it is hard to think of a more beautifully set ice rink), the very pretty walks and expensive sleigh rides. The local **cross-country** skiing trail is too short to be of much interest and the alternative is to face the indignity of taking a lift down to the valley trails.

The small **nursery slope** on the Allmendhubel is gentle, sunny and snow-sure. We lack recent reports on **ski school**.

Mürren facts

Lift payment

Passes Jungfrau pass, available for 3 days and over, covers all lifts of Wengen, Mürren and Grindelwald, and trains between them. Local passes available (including day passes) and daily supplements to cover other areas.
Cost 6-day Jungfrau pass SF188; Mürren 6-day pass SF140.
Children 35% off, under 16.
Beginners Coupons.

Ski school

Classes 2hr, mornings only.
Cost 6 half-days SF89. Private lessons SF90/hr am, SF80/hr pm.
Children Classes, 6 half-days SF76 under 12.
Special courses Ski-touring, heli-skiing.

Not skiing

Facilities Swimming, squash, sports hall (for tennis etc), skating (open-air artificial rink, tuition available), curling, toboggan run to Grindelwald, 15km walks, sleigh rides, sauna, solarium.

Cross-country skiing

Trails 1.5km loop, and 12km in Lauterbrunnen valley.

Medical facilities

In resort Doctor, chemist.
Dentist Lauterbrunnen.
Hospital Interlaken (12km from Lauterbrunnen).

Getting there

Airport Bern is the closest, but most operators use Zurich or Geneva; transfers 3hr–4hr.
Railway Station in resort.
Road Cars must be left at parks in Interlaken, Lauterbrunnen or Stechelberg. Access via Basel; chains rarely needed.

Available holidays

Resort beds About 700 in hotels and guest-houses, 1,100 in chalets and apartments.
Package holidays Kuoni (Ht), Made to Measure (Ht), Ski Sutherland (Ht), Supertravel (Ht Ch), Swiss Travel Service (Ht)

Further information

Tourist office ✆(36) 551616. Tx 923212.

Never on Sunday

Macugnaga Italy 1350m

Macugnaga is a small resort dramatically dominated by the towering rock and glacier of the eastern wall of Europe's second peak, the Monte Rosa (4638m) – a setting not unlike that of Saas Fee on the other side of the mountain. There are two villages (Staffa and Pecetto) about half a mile apart, both of them delightfully rustic and unspoilt by tourism. 'One of the most beautiful villages I have ever seen,' wrote one otherwise unimpressed reporter. Staffa is the busier of the two and more important for most skiers, being more convenient for the two-stage cable-car which climbs steeply from the resort nearly 1500m towards the Swiss border at the Passo di Monte Moro (2900m), where a statue of the Madonna surveys the deep and beautiful valley and the majestic array of peaks. There are a few nursery lifts at the bottom, two drags serving the top 500m of the slope, and a couple of lifts at the top where they once organised summer skiing, but the cable-car is what Macugnaga's skiing is all about, and when it is shut (as it often is), there is not much to be done. Variants of the descent to the middle station at Alpe Bill (1700m) include a 6km red and a direct black of only 3km for 1100m vertical. The only run to the village is an occasional black, and the bottom cable-car is very small. Queues at peak times, and especially on Sundays, can be very long indeed – uphill in the morning and downhill for lunch and in the afternoon. During the week queues are rarely a problem. Monte Moro is a good starting point for ski tourers, who can cross the mountains to Zermatt. In good conditions the run down from Monte Moro to Saas Grund is not difficult, but the return journey is very long. Heli-skiing is advertised, and the possibilities are enormous, including drops at over 4500m on Monte Rosa.

Above Pecetto and beneath the Monte Rosa glaciers, the smaller and less crowded Burky skiing is served by two chair-lifts from 1350m to 1900m. The east-facing skiing is gentle and wooded, much more suitable for timid skiers than Monte Moro, but very limited in extent.

The very necessary ski bus is reported to work well in the morning, but erratically after the driver has had lunch. Reporters agree that the people are as friendly as the resort is charming, and several hotels in Staffa are recommended, notably the well-placed Zumstein (✆65118): 'superb food and a friendly bar.' In Pecetto, the simple Cristallo (✆65139) and the very basic B&B Meublé Gnifetti (✆65055) are also recommended. Après-ski is mostly in Staffa and bar-oriented, quiet but cosy. There is very little for non-skiers, except skating and the pleasure of wandering around. One aspiring langlaufer was very disappointed.

Access is a by narrow, long and avalanche-prone road from Domodossola (39km) south of the Simplon tunnel. Transfers from Turin and Milan take about four hours.

Tourist office ✆(324) 65119. **Package holidays** Global (Ht).

Monterosa ski – Le Tre Valli

Gressoney, Champoluc, Alagna Italy 1400m–1650m

The very high but individually unspectacular little peaks making up the Monte Rosa stand between some of Europe's most famous ski resorts (Saas Fee and Zermatt) and some of its least well-known ones – the villages in the valleys on the Italian side of the massif, neglected by UK tour operators. By car these villages are many hours apart, but it is less than 15 miles as the chough flies from Cervinia to Macugnaga, and the heads of the three valleys between these two well-known resorts are even closer. The lift companies in these three valleys have got together under the Monterosa Ski banner, the main resorts being Champoluc in the Val d'Ayas, next door to Cervinia and Valtournenche; the two Gressoneys (St-Jean and La Trinité) in the central Val de Lys, like Champoluc reached from the Aosta valley; and Alagna in the Valsesia, which runs down towards Italy's lake district north of Milan. Lifts already link Champoluc and Gressoney and form the heart of the current Monterosa ski area. Getting from Gressoney to Alagna involves a half-hour walk from the top of the lifts and some off-piste skiing. This is not the only gap in the chain, and in general the Monterosa lift system has a lot of evolving to do. One thing greater efficiency is unlikely to change is the rather cramped nature of the skiing itself, confined by rocky terrain. Long runs extend over a large, beautiful and high area, but there are few wide open slopes and limited scope for varying the routes you take from A to B, mainly runs beside lifts and mainly of a similar blue to red standard of difficulty.

The resorts are also unusual, having grown out of villages colonised by tribes from the Valais in the Middle Ages, and still keeping their local traditions, costumes, Germanic dialects, and a traditional wood-and-stone chalet style of building. The Gressoneys, like Macugnaga, are among the most typically Alpine-looking and welcoming of Italian ski resorts. As their valley is the central one of the three it is the obvious choice for keen skiers. It sees little foreign tourism and is very quiet outside holiday periods and weekends. The long road up from Pont-St-Martin is narrow and takes over an hour.

The lower Gressoney (St-Jean, 1400m) has more villagey charm and a more open and sunny setting, but not much skiing except cross-country, for which it is an excellent base, with long trails along the valley floor and through the heart of the village where skiers have priority over cars. The Stambecco restaurant keeps Allsopps beer, and the Stadel (✆355264) is an attractive hotel, a modernised old chalet. Higher up the valley, Gressoney-La-Trinité (1650m) is the downhiller's resort, although the steep rocky slopes enclosing it are by no means ideal ski terrain. It is a quiet village with a few cheerful bars and restaurants and a couple of large hotels, including the comfortable Residence (✆366148), ideally placed for the lift on the eastern side of the village. The Scoiattolo (✆366313) is a smaller, newer chalet-style building in the middle.

Of the ski area's two flanks only the smaller eastern one is directly accessible from the resort itself. The departure for the larger western area going over to Champoluc is at Stafal 5km away at the head of the valley. There is a bus shuttle (free for lift pass holders) between Stafal and La Trinité, and less frequent buses between St-Jean and La Trinité. Stafal is not yet much of a resort, but there are a couple of hotels near the lift station, including the comfortable modern Adler (✆366159) and the simple old Peccoz (✆366201).

The main lift out of La Trinité is a single-seater chair which must generate queues at peak times. Three lift-rides take you to 2740m, about 150 metres below the Col d'Olen. There are intermediate runs back down to the resort, and some short lifts serving easy runs in the open sunny bowl at Gabiet (2350m).

For good skiers the great appeal of this sector is the trip to Alagna. From the Col d'Indren you ski off-piste down to the first mid-station of Alagna's three-stage cable-car and, snow permitting, to the resort (1200m) by red piste. The cable-car climbs more than 2000 metres to the glaciers at Punta Indren (3260m), a small summer ski area and a favourite starting point for ski-tours and climbs on Monte Rosa. The only run back down is a long black, which becomes red below the higher mid-station at 2400m. The off-piste return to Gabiet is downhill all the way from Punta Indren. Before setting off from Gressoney check that the Alagna lift is working.

The link between Stafal and Champoluc is relatively straightforward: a chain of lifts (up to 2861m) and intermediate runs straddling the Colle Bettaforca (2672m), with sun in the morning on the Gressoney side and in the afternoon at Champoluc, which has some attractive woodland skiing and sunny restaurants around the tree-line. The only access lift from Stafal is a chair, and queues are a problem here and at other key points on the circuit. At Champoluc congestion has recently been moved up the mountain by the installation of a six-seater gondola to Crest, a splendid sun-terrace and nursery area. The skiing is enjoyable and nowhere very difficult, and gives magnificent views of the Monte Rosa rising in a great wall of rock and glacier above Gressoney. From the Champoluc side of the pass a wider panorama embraces the Matterhorn and Gran Paradiso.

This is a popular area for heli-skiing. One hoist to the Col de Lys (4248m) opens up a huge day's skiing: off-piste down to Zermatt, lifts and pistes to Cime Bianche above Cervinia, off-piste down to the Val d'Ayas and Champoluc's lifts.

Tourist offices Gressoney ✆(0125) 366471; Champoluc ✆(0125) 307856.

Speed skiing for beginners

Cervinia Italy 2005m

Good for *Nursery slopes, easy runs, big ski area, sunny slopes, resort-level snow, late holidays, summer skiing*
Bad for *Alpine charm, not skiing, lift queues, tough runs, mountain restaurants, freedom from cars*

Cervinia is a styleless collection of ageing modern buildings set very high in a bleak, open setting on the sunny side of the Matterhorn (which was designed to be seen from Switzerland, and from Italy seems merely bulky). It was once the showpiece of Italian ski resort development. Half a century ago the old climbing base of Breuil became new Cervinia, with cable-cars spanning vast glacial wastelands up to the unprecedented height of 3500m, opening up enormously long, very sunny ski runs and bringing the smart set to Cervinia's new grand hotels. But times have changed. Despite some recent improvements, Cervinia's lifts are inefficient by modern standards, and its skiing lacks challenge as well as being notoriously windy. And the smart set has long since decamped.

Although a holiday in Cervinia represents a considerable act of faith in the weather, it is still a lively and popular international resort, with plenty of British visitors, who find it a friendly place. The skiing is still sunny and reliable for snow, and there is nowhere in the world where beginners and timid but enthusiastic skiers can cover so much ground in scenery of such grandeur with complete confidence. Several of our most enthusiastic reporters are elderly; 'Such marvellous geriatric skiing!' explained one. Cervinia's lifts link with Zermatt's, but on day-trips it is not possible to get more than a taste of Zermatt's skiing.

The skiing top 3490m bottom 1620m

The terrain is rocky and only a section of the horseshoe surrounding Cervinia is skiable, with slopes facing south and west. It is a remarkably open, sunny skiing area between 2000m and 3500m, shelving gently in steps, and broken up by clefts and lakes.

The main lifts from the resort are the cable-car and new gondola up to **Plan Maison,** and the Cretaz drag-lifts from the lower part of the village to much the same area – a vast nursery and sunbathing plateau. The chain of drag-lifts continues on up to the Theodulpass, where an awkward walk leads to the run down to Zermatt. On the Cervinia side there are long, easy motorways back down to Plan Maison, and from there a very gentle, roundabout green run goes back to the resort. On the lower slopes above Cervinia are more direct runs, but we have not seen the blacks below the cable-car and gondola being skied.

From Plan Maison a little cable-car with a big build-up of warnings

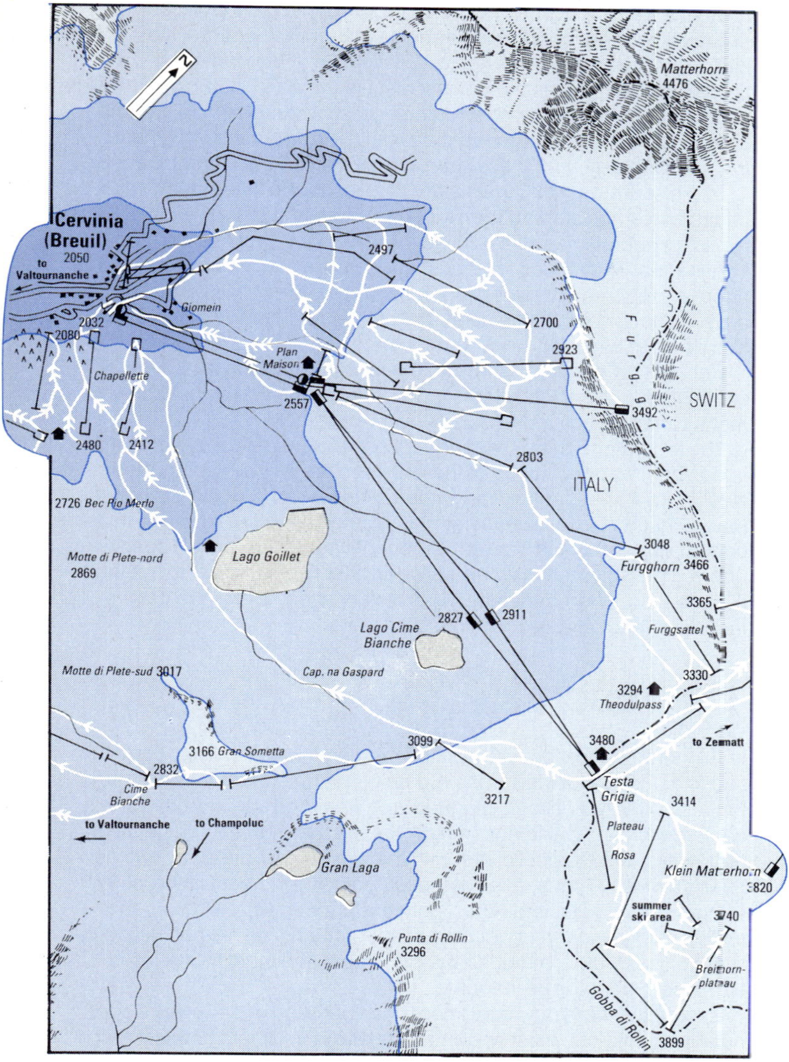

climbs nearly 1000m over an awesome cliff to Furggen at the shoulder of the Matterhorn. A tedious walk down an internal staircase of nearly 300 steps brings you to the broad ledge at the top of the cliff. It is a beautiful, isolated, long run, mainly easy but with a couple of short, moderately steep sections near the beginning. There are some adventurous off-piste variants, not obvious to the uninitiated.

The cable-cars up to Plateau Rosa give direct and easy skiing access to Zermatt. The main run back to Cervinia is the famous Ventina, an uninterrupted run of nearly 8km for 1500m vertical. There is no great difficulty involved, apart from keeping up your momentum on the flat bits. A short way down is a left fork for the run to Valtournenche, sometimes claimed as the longest piste in the Alps (starting at the Klein Matterhorn) but actually punctuated by a short drag-lift ride at Cime Bianche. The Gran Sommetta drag is at the head of the Val d'Ayas: tracks leading off from the bottom of the lift end up at Champoluc.

To the south-east of Cervinia are the **Carosello** lifts – little-used chairs and drags starting from the high part of the resort (each of the two luxury hotels has a lift outside the front door), accessible from the Ventina run. The slopes face west and north-west, are fairly steep and often unprepared, with scope for exploring between the pistes. There are runs back down to the cable-car station and, near the bob-sleigh run, down to Lago Blu below the resort.

Cervinia's **mountain restaurants** are inadequate in number, expensive by Italian standards, and insanitary. We hear that some new restaurants are being built.

The lift system, heavily dependent on small cable-cars, is not at all good. Despite doubling up of the lifts there are still very long **queues** at weekends and at peak holiday times, when it can take over two hours to reach Plateau Rosa; queues at Plan Maison are often worse than at the bottom. At quiet times lifts run infrequently and there are still long waits. There are also irritating walks between lifts. The cable-cars (notably Furggen) are often closed by wind, at very short notice. We have reports of long queues for lift passes.

The resort

In the centre at the foot of the slopes is a small area of lively bars and shops at the foot of the slopes. Some of it is reserved for pedestrians, the rest a one-way circuit, plagued with weekend traffic. Above the cable-car station, buildings (mostly the smarter hotels) stretch on up the hill towards the Carosello lifts, with the two luxury hotels and two new apartment-hotel complexes at the top enjoying the best views of the Matterhorn and glaciers. Apart from this upper part, it is a compact resort, easily enough negotiated on foot (there is no ski-bus, and a car is not of much use), although the climb up to the main lift station is tiresome. Shopping is adequate.

Except for some new apartment development on the lower slopes near the cable-car, most **accommodation** is in simple hotels. Most of the hotels used by UK operators are in the main centre of the village, within walking distance of the Cretaz drag-lifts. We have had few enthusiastic reports and several very unenthusiastic ones. The more comfortable hotels are more spaciously set above the cable-car station, beneath the Carosello lifts. Only the smartly modernised, expensive Grand Cristallo (✆948125) is at all luxurious and cosmopolitan. One regular visitor to the resort recommends the Fosson (✆949125) – 'simple, friendly, popular with Italians' – and well placed for the drag-lifts. We also have good reports of the Rosa (✆949022) and particularly

Cervinia facts

Lift payment

Passes Cervinia general pass covers all lifts on the Italian side of the border, except Valtournenche gondola before 11.30. Passes of over 5 days valid for one day a week in Courmayeur. For Zermatt, international day pass available, or daily supplement covering Klein Matterhorn and Schwarzsee lifts.
Cost Cervinia 6-day pass L130,000. International supplement about L20,000, depending on exchange rates.
Beginners Coupons or payment by the ride.
Summer skiing Extensive; 8 lifts, 2935m to 3899m, all on Swiss territory.

Ski school

Classes 3hr, mornings only.
Cost 6 days L103,000. Private lessons L24,000/hr.
Children No ski kindergarten facilities. Baby-sitting can be arranged by Mariani Tours, near church.
Special courses Heli-skiing, touring.

Not skiing

Facilities Natural ice rink (until March), hotel pools/sauna, bowling.

Cross-country skiing

Trails Two 5km trails (graded medium), one of them near the resort, one a mile or two out on the way to Valtournenche, at Perreres.

Medical facilities

In resort Fracture clinic, doctor, chemist.
Hospital Aosta (52km).

Getting there

Airport Turin; transfer about 2½hr.
Railway Châtillon (27km); several buses daily.
Road Via Lyon/Annecy or Geneva, Mont Blanc Tunnel; chains may be needed.

Available holidays

Resort beds 2,150 in hotels, 3,000 in apartments.
Package holidays Blue Sky (Ht), Enterprise (Ht), Horizon (Ht), Intasun (Ht Sc), Neilson (Ht Sc), Pegasus (Ht), Ski Club of GB (Ht), Thomson (Ht)

Further information

Tourist office ✆(166) 949136. Tx 211822.

the Bucaneve (✆949119). The well-placed Al Piolet (✆949161) and the Edelweiss (✆949078) are relatively attractive and cheerful – though the latter is 'not up to Austrian standards'. The Hermitage (✆948918) is a quiet, comfortable and fairly expensive hotel beside the road up to the Cristallo.

Après-ski is not very varied, consisting of hotel bars without much character, except for the Dragon Pub in the Hotel Pelissier, a favourite British haunt with British beer ('worth missing,' according to a recent reporter. There are several discos (which may be lifeless except at weekends) and occasionally evening bob-sleigh. Eating out is not generally very cheap, but the Matterhorn is 'excellent value' and we have good reports of the Copa Pan, which describes itself as 'naif-elegante'. Cervinia is not recommended for **cross-country** skiers or **non-skiers**.

The **nursery slopes** on the edge of the village get very crowded, but there are better ones at Plan Maison. Sporty beginners can be roaring down very long nursery-ish runs at the end of a week.

We still hear mixed views on the **ski school**, but our most recent reporter found no language problems and general satisfaction with standards of instruction.

The tills are alive....

Zermatt Switzerland 1620m

Good for *Tough runs, off-piste skiing, ski touring, beautiful scenery, mountain restaurants, big ski area, rail access, Alpine charm, après-ski, late holidays, chalet holidays, resort-level snow, summer skiing, not skiing*
Bad for *Skiing convenience, easy road access, short airport transfers, nursery slopes*

Few resorts can rival Zermatt for picturesque village charm, exciting skiing or beautiful scenery. For a combination of the three it is way out in front, and it can also boast plenty of nightlife, the best mountain restaurants in the Alps, luxury hotels and history. Zermatt regulars fail to understand how anyone can want to go anywhere else, and it is hard to deny that on any objective assessment this is quite simply the best resort there is – particularly now that a formidable campaign of modernisation has made the resort and its lift system run more smoothly. Yet a number of reports sent to us confirm that it is possible to visit Zermatt and come away uncaptivated.

Zermatt is a large, close-knit village which has grown to fill the limited space available at the foot of a steep ring of very high mountains, the Matterhorn outstandingly beautiful among them. It is a world of its own, naturally cut off from Täsch and the valley below by a narrow, steep-sided pass which is prone to avalanche blockage. There is a vast car park by the station at Täsch, where someone makes a living resurrecting dead car batteries; trains run frequently to the centre of Zermatt, where the only transport is electric and horse-drawn taxis and a new electric bus.

The village became a busy climbing resort in the 19th century. Like Chamonix, it does as much summer as winter business and is a fascinating place for anyone with an interest in Alpine history (a visit to the graveyard is a must). In the early days, the British were prominent, and there is still a sizeable contingent of traditionalists to attend the English church, and a new generation of keen young skiers and après-skiers. But there are more American visitors than British, and more Germans than Americans. The style of the village is increasingly plush and expensive, and the American influence is more obvious than anywhere else in the Alps except St Moritz.

So do not expect a small unspoilt Alpine village full of friendly rustic folk. Zermatt is big business. The village is large and has areas (including the main shopping streets) of fairly anonymous modern buildings, albeit traditional in style. Although car-free it is by no means traffic-free: electric taxis, rushing around at hazardous speed, detract significantly from Zermatt's appeal as a remote mountain hideaway. It is easy to get the impression (which the locals do not try very hard to dispel) that Zermatt is a very artfully laid, very beautiful trap. A particularly black mark concerns ski school, about which reports (including the most recent) are almost unanimously unfavourable.

The skiing is beautiful and enormous in both extent and variety, but can be awkward for inexperienced skiers: for good cover the rocky slopes need heavy snowfalls and often do not get them. Zermatt will never be a convenient resort. The ski areas are not well connected, and in town long and icy walks are avoidable only by paying for a ride. 'Many a boot blister resulted,' reports one sore skier. So has many a bruised coccyx. The skiing links with that of Cervinia, though the attractions of crossing the border are limited.

Zermatt is one terminus of the spectacular Glacier Express, which runs to St Moritz via Andermatt. It is one of the few resorts which from Britain is still most conveniently reached by train.

The skiing top 3820m bottom 1620m

Zermatt's skiing divides naturally into three sectors. On the eastern side of the deep horseshoe of mountains surrounding the village are the two linked sectors of Blauherd and Gornergrat, both providing a mix of easy intermediate and steep skiing, much of it north-facing. To the south of the resort the Schwarzsee and Trockener Steg lifts climb over steep north-facing slopes (valuable to good skiers when the weather is bad higher up) to glaciers, where Europe's highest lifts provide a huge area of easy skiing.

The **Gornergrat/Stockhorn** skiing starts with a 40-minute train ride to Gornergrat, passing an area of excellent, very easy runs above Riffelberg – Zermatt's best nursery area, with plenty of sun and beautiful views of the Matterhorn. The run down to Zermatt has some steep sections but in good conditions is not difficult. There is a tough intermediate run towards Gant and Findeln, and some steep off-piste slopes. Beyond Gornergrat a two-stage cable-car to Stockhorn via Hohtälli stretches along a narrow, rocky crest, not climbing much but serving the wide, north-facing slopes above the Findeln glacier. This area, rarely open before February, is one of the premier tough skiing areas in the Alps, with huge mogul fields and late powder (beware crevasse and rock danger off-piste). A short cable-car has replaced what used to be an unpleasant ridge walk between Rote Nase and Hohtälli, for access from Triftji to Gornergrat and Stockhorn.

The **Blauherd** sector is now served by the three-minute Sunegga Express underground railway. There are easy, very sunny slopes between Blauherd and Sunegga and down to Findeln, and easy runs winding around the steep, wooded mountainside to the resort. There are also much steeper descents, notably the famous National downhill course, often crowded and bumpy. The **Unterrothorn** cable-car gives access to an excellent, long, steep, open face with an easier, sheltered intermediate run behind the ridge.

The **Trockener Steg/Schwarzsee** lifts start a brisk 15-minute walk from the centre. A cable-car and a gondola climb gently over the often rocky lower slopes to Furri, where three cable-cars fan out. One climbs

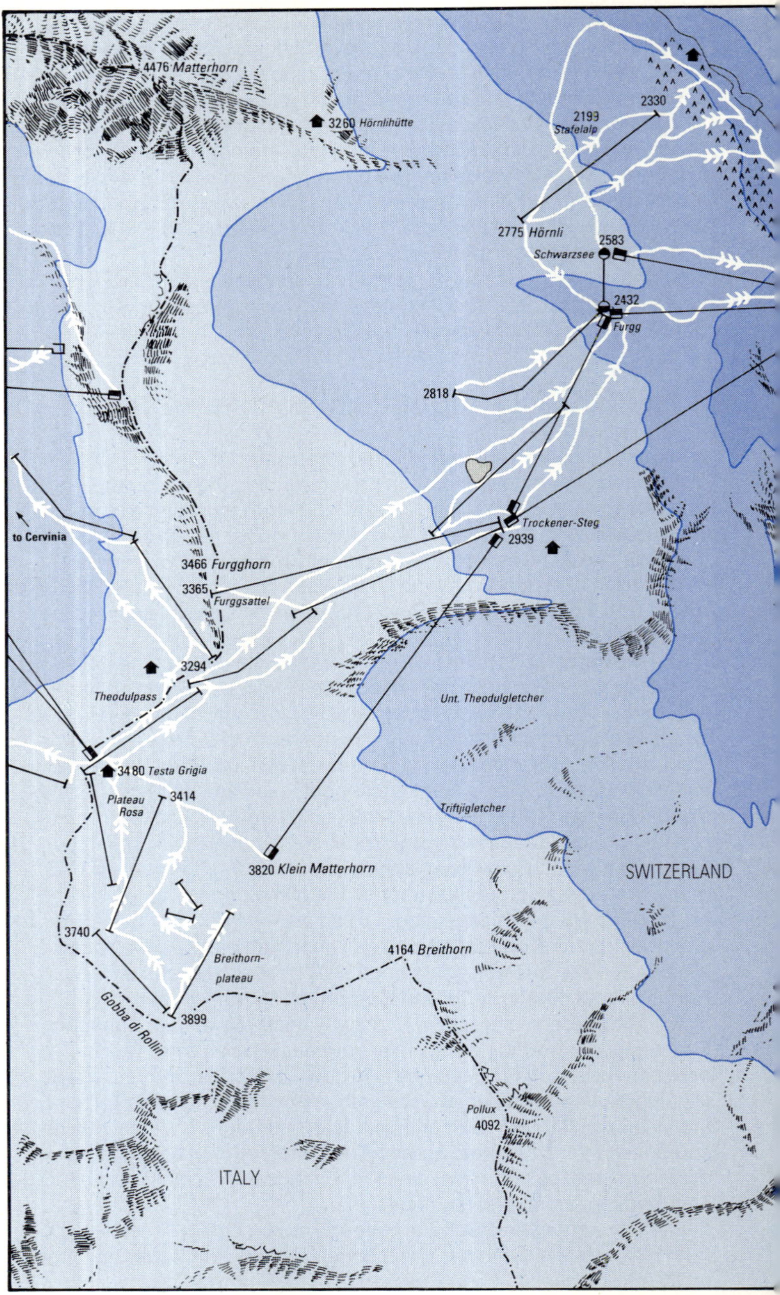
4476 Matterhorn
3260 Hörnlihütte
2330
2193
Stafelalp
2775 Hörnli
2583
Schwarzsee
2432
Furgg
2818
Trockener-Steg
2939
to Cervinia
3466 Furgghorn
3365
Furggsattel
3294
Theodulpass
Unt. Theodulgletcher
3480 Testa Grigia
Plateau
Rosa
3414
Triftjigletcher
3820 Klein Matterhorn
SWITZERLAND
3740
Breithorn-
plateau
4164 Breithorn
Gobba di Rollin
3899
Pollux
4092
ITALY

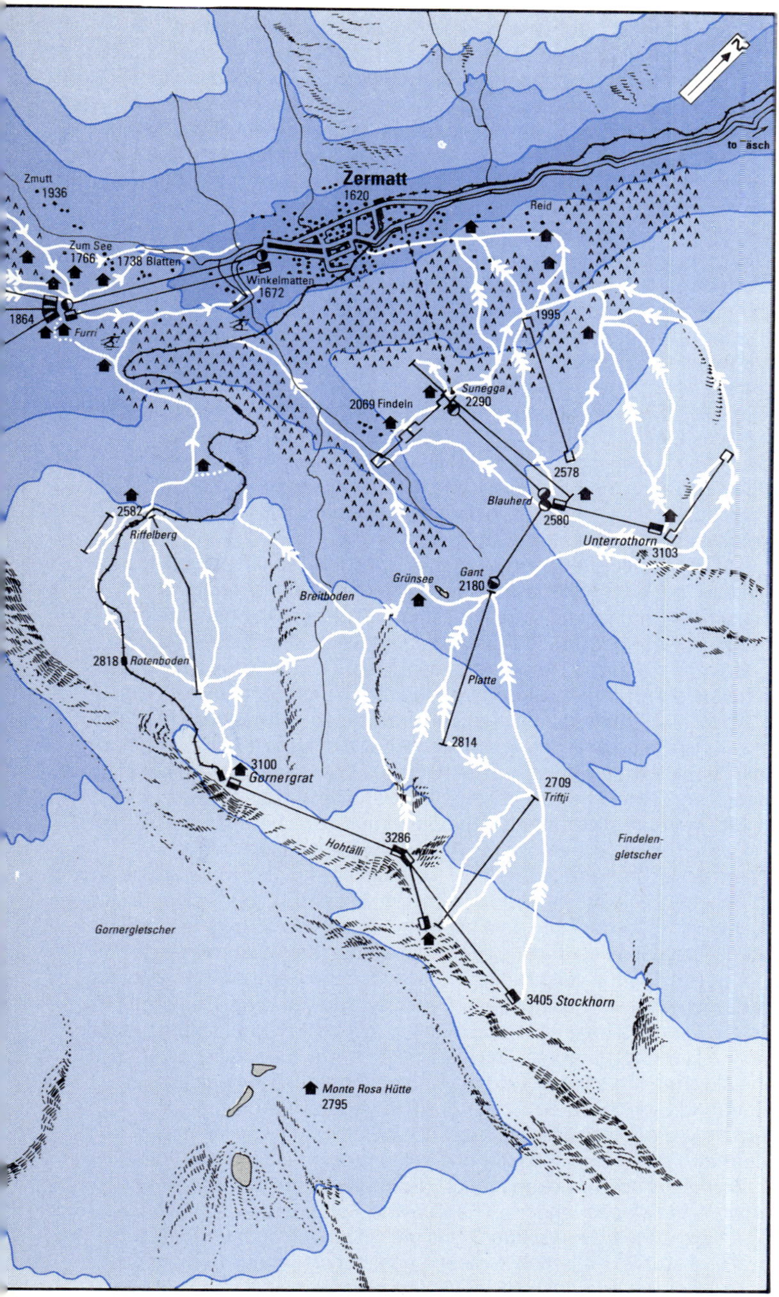
N
to Täsch
Zermatt
1620
Zmutt
1936
Zum See
1766
1738 Blatten
Winkelmatten
1672
1864
Furri
Reid
1995
2069 Findeln
Sunegga
2290
2578
Blauherd
2580
Unterrothorn
3103
2582
Riffelberg
Grünsee
Gant
2180
Breitboden
2818 Rotenboden
Platte
2814
3100
Gornergrat
2709
Triftji
3286
Hohtälli
Findelengletscher
Gornergletscher
3405 Stockhorn
Monte Rosa Hütte
2795

to Trockener Steg, above which the Klein Matterhorn cable-car, Zermatt's flagship, spans ice falls and an almost vertical face to reach the highest cable-car station in Europe. A long tunnel leads to easy glacier slopes with just one moderately steep pitch in the long run down to Trockener Steg via Testa Grigia on the Italian border, where the Zermatt and Cervinia lift systems meet. Several long drag-lifts serve an enormous area of uncomplicated easy skiing here, on top of the world. Unfortunately the lifts are often closed or very unpleasant in bad weather. A very beautiful run in this sector heads gently west across a crevassed glacier from just below the Furggsattel towards the Matterhorn and from there either sharply round and back to Furgg or up to the top of the Hörnli lift, which involves a short climb.

Intermediates can ski down to Furgg, to the top of the second cable-car from Furri. There are some more difficult pistes and hazardous off-piste runs served by the bent Garten drag-lift, and the run down from Furgg to Furri is an awkward reddish-black. In general, good skiers find the runs down from Schwarzsee more satisfying. There are several black ones plunging down towards the woods and through them to Furri, including the tough and narrow Tiefbach, and a couple of beautiful easier and longer ways down past the Hörnli drag-lift, which itself serves interesting north-facing gullies.

We have not visited Zermatt in the right conditions to sample the off-piste skiing. Although there are few wide open slopes (apart from Stockhorn) and limited slope for casual off-piste skiing near the pistes, there are enormous possibilities, both above and below the tree-line, for good skiers with local knowledge or guides. The rocky terrain makes off-piste skiing very hazardous when snow is not plentiful. Beneath the 29 local 4000-metre peaks there are vast areas of skiable glacier, and thanks to the new heights reached by the lift system (Klein Matterhorn and Stockhorn) day tours do not have to be very arduous. Plenty of people in Zermatt can afford to heli-ski, and drops need to be booked.

Mountain restaurants are greater in number, charm and privileged view than anywhere else in the Alps. As well as the smart, characterless new restaurants at the main lift stations, there are dozens of delightful little huts spread around the wooded slopes – skiing home at the end of the day can be a protracted business. Enzo's at Findeln, Otmar's above Ried and the Aroleid at Blatten are outstanding.

Considering the constraints of the landscape Zermatt's lift system is impressive, despite its antiquated railway. The very swift Sunegga underground railway has done much to relieve the awful scrums for and on the Gornergrat railway, but it still takes a long time to travel around the ski area and especially to reach Stockhorn (usually quicker via Sunegga/Blauherd than Gornergrat). In general it is difficult for separate groups of skiers to meet up, and the best way to enjoy Zermatt's skiing is to settle for one sector and spend the day there.

Zermatt is not a weekend resort (Saturday is one of the least busy days on the slopes) and from February to April **queues** do not vary greatly, except when weather limits the skiing. A March visitor reports 'waits of about 15 minutes in most areas, but no serious bottlenecks'. Lift passes are scrupulously inspected, and plain-clothes policemen patrol the pistes to keep order. There are snow-machines on the slopes between Findeln, Sunegga and Unterrothorn, and from Trockener Steg down to Furri. At the black end of the ski area (Triftji), the new Rote Nase cable-car is a distinct improvement, as the new National chair-lift will be.

The link with Cervinia involves no difficult skiing, but is very high: closure because of bad weather is frequent and unpredictable. Information is available at the bottom station, but it cannot be relied upon for the whole day. A lot of time is needed for the return journey, but from Zermatt it is possible to do most of Cervinia's skiing in a day (in low season). Cervinia is widely advertised as a delightful place for a cheap lunch. It isn't. Take loo paper, a passport and money (in case you get stranded for the night). The run down to Cervinia and back from it is more enjoyable via Testa Grigia than Theodulpass.

The resort

The village is a delightful maze of snowy paths, and all the buildings are in traditional chalet style except for the large luxury hotels, old and new, in the centre. The very picturesque old quarter above the church is a neglected backwater, and most of the resort is new. The busy main street is lined with new hotels, expensive shops and banks. The centre is flat, and walking around is not difficult, apart from the considerable hazards of taxis and icy paths. The bus from the station to the bottom of the Matterhorn lifts cost SF2 a ride, and is not covered by the lift pass; the walk takes about 15 minutes. When there's enough snow, people ski along the village streets, although they're not supposed to.

Accommodation is mostly in hotels, new, luxurious and very expensive or simple and slightly less expensive. A few companies offer staffed chalet holidays and self-catering in chalet apartments which tend to be less cramped than flats in modern French resorts. The least inconvenient location is probably in the middle near the river, the most inconvenient up in the old village. For up-to-the-minute facilities the luxury hotels to choose are the Zermatterhof, the Schweizerhof, the Alex or the Mont Cervin, but for style there is no beating the elegantly modernised Monte Rosa (✆661131), the original Zermatt hotel, with its Alpine club mementoes and its Whymperstube bar. Most of the simpler hotels are clean and comfortable in a typically Swiss way: reporters were well pleased with the Gornergrat (✆671027), near the stations. The Sport is a popular British haunt, but inconvenient. The Mischabel (✆671131) is cheapish, very simple and central.

Après-ski is very varied, with bars, restaurants and dance spots to cater for most tastes and full pockets. Youth gathers in the Papperla Pub and the plastic neo-ranch-style Broken Bar/Brown Cow for drinking, pasta and disco (in separate rooms). For a more civilised atmosphere, there is Elsie's bar for snails and hock, the Alex for cocktails, or the Whymperstube, recommended by one reporter for cheaper Swiss food. The Stockhorn is recommended for meat fondue, the Tenne for 'haute cuisine at London prices'. There is a tea-dance at the Hotel Bristol. The cheapest place to dance is the Walliserkanne – 'a bit grubby and jammed full'. Curling evenings are organised by tour operators, and very popular.

Summer is probably the best time for a **non-skiing** visit to Zermatt, but there are beautiful winter walks around the village and the lower reaches of the ski area (to Zmutt, Riffelalp and Findeln restaurants), and various sports facilities in the village. Zermatt's own **cross-country** skiing is very limited, but there are long trails around Täsch.

There is no village nursery area and the main ski school **nursery slope** is at Sunegga, set apart but small. Riffelberg also has a nursery lift and a much larger area of easy skiing beside the railway. Both these areas are sunny and panoramic. Zermatt's unsuitability for inexperienced skiers has a lot to do with the shortcomings of the **ski school**. A 1988 report underlines those we have received over recent years, telling of large class sizes, frequent changes and occasional non-appearance of instructor, anti-social hours and an unhelpful attitude. See the Introduction to the *Guide*.

Zermatt facts

Lift payment

Passes Zermatt pass covers all lifts on the Swiss side of the border. Various partial coverage passes for different sectors. International day pass or daily supplement available for Cervinia; supplement not valid on all Cervinia lifts.
Cost Zermatt 6-day pass SF212. 25% reduction for men over 62, women over 65. International day pass SF46, supplement SF23.
Children 50% off under 16.
Beginners Coupons or payment by the ride.
Summer skiing Extensive; 8 lifts, 2935m to 3899m.

Ski school

Classes 2hr morning and afternoon.
Cost 6 days SF155. Private lessons SF110/half day (1 or 2 people).
Children Classes, ages 6–12, times as adults, 6 days SF120. Ski kindergarten, ages 4–8, 9.00–5.00, 6 days with meals SF250. Non-skiing kindergarten, ages 2–8, 9.00–5.00, 5 days with meals SF200.
Special courses Powder, wedel, racing, monoski, touring.

Not skiing

Facilities Curling, sauna, tennis, skating, swimming, museum, squash, billiards, riding, 30km cleared walks.

Cross-country

Trails Winkelmatten to Tuftra (3km), Furri to Schweigmatten (4km). More extensive trails (up to 15km) at Täsch. 'Ski walking' trails at altitude (60km).

Medical facilities

In resort Fracture clinic, dentist, doctor, chemist.
Hospital Visp

Getting there

Airport Geneva; transfer about 4½hr (3½hr by train).
Railway Station in resort.
Road Access only to Täsch (5km). Via Lausanne; chains may be needed.

Available holidays

Resort beds 6,000 in hotels, 12,000 in apartments.
Package holidays Bladon Lines (Ht Ch Sc), Inghams (Ht Sc), John Morgan (Ht Ch), Kuoni (Ht), Made to Measure (Ht), Mark Warner (Ch), Ski Club of GB (Ht), Ski MacG (Ht Ch), SkiGower (Cl), Supertravel (Ht Ch), Swiss Travel Service (Ht), Thomson (Ht Sc)

Further information

Tourist office ✆(28) 661181. Tx 472130.

On the shelf

Grächen Switzerland 1600m

Grächen is a small resort, not widely known in Britain, on a sunny shelf reached by a precarious road winding up the very steep, wooded side of the valley leading to Zermatt; immediately above it is another broad band of rough, steep, wooded mountainside. The skiing is higher still in three distinct areas linked by long traverses, only one of which has a run to the village.

Two gondolas go up from separate stations on the upper fringes of the resort to points almost at the two ends of the system. The right-hand lift goes up over the unskiable face of the mountain to **Seetalhorn** (2870m). A network of intermediate pistes served by a chair-lift goes off southwards from here, down an undulating, rocky, open slope – prone to ice in the mornings – to the foot of another chair-lift at Riedberg (about 2500m) serving genuinely steep black runs of 500m vertical.

A long red piste northwards across the mountainside from Seetalhorn links this area with the foot of a drag-lift to **Wannihorn**; the piste map also shows a black link at higher altitude, not open when we visited. There is no link in the opposite direction. The direct runs down the Wannihorn lift are all marked black, but are not severe; a red loops around to the south, joining the link from Seetalhorn.

There are blue links to and from the third area. **Hannigalp** (2114m) – a large, open congregation area where most of Grächen's family visitors spend their time. Drag-lifts up to Furggen (2272m) serve easy red runs down lightly wooded slopes, and a very easy blue piste goes a little way down the mountain. A good, broad forest trail goes further down, dropping almost 500m to the return drag-lift at Bärgji; its barely justified black grading keeps most skiers away. The one piste down to Grächen is a fine red run through the woods – south-facing, and possibly unpleasant at either end of the day.

The heart of the village, between and below the two lift stations, has everyday shops and traditional chalet-style hotels, among them the central, jolly Walliserhof (✆561122). There is a lot of new development along the road which loops into the village on the northern side. In sharp contrast, the mountainside south of the centre is an open area of snowy fields and car-free lanes dotted with chalets and family hotels, including the Hannigalp (✆562555), which has a fair-sized swimming pool (open to the public). Most of the accommodation is in self-catering apartments and chalets. There is a good, spacious, sunny nursery slope just below the northern end of the village.

The sports centre at the top of the resort has a natural skating rink and two curling rinks, two tennis courts and a fitness room. There are 16km of cross-country trails, of all grades, including 6km up at Hannigalp. There is a toboggan run from there too.

Tourist office ✆(28) 561300. Tx 38582.
Package holidays Kuoni (Ht), Ski Sutherland (Ht).

Pearl or plain?

Saas-Fee Switzerland 1800m

Good for *Alpine charm, late holidays, family holidays, nursery slopes, beautiful scenery, freedom from cars, resort-level snow, ski-touring, summer skiing*
Bad for *Short airport transfers, skiing convenience, lift queues, easy road access*

Saas Fee calls itself the pearl of the Alps. It certainly has a pearl-like setting, in the pit of a tight, deep horseshoe of mountains; and in some eyes at least it is what might be called a pearl of a ski resort. Like neighbouring Zermatt, it is one of the very few resorts to be both long-established and car-free – but unlike Zermatt it has not developed into a noisy international resort; relatively few electric carts whirr along between its beautiful old log cabins. The setting is dramatic and beautiful, though oppressive in mid-winter when little sunshine reaches the village. The skiing has in the past disappointed some visitors, and the considerable extra skiing opened up by the new Metro Alpin underground railway only partly answers the critics. Although there are excellent nursery slopes beside the resort, and splendid, open, easy slopes up the mountain, much of the skiing is on the steep side – but there is not enough of it to keep eager piste-bashers happy for long, and experts are frustrated by the lack of off-piste skiing (limited by glacier danger). On the other hand, it is a major point of departure for ski-tours. The resort is inconvenient for weekenders, but the skiing reached via the main cable-car is now sufficiently attractive to generate very long queues, especially late in the season.

Cars must be left in car parks at the edge of the village, but are handy for exploring Saas Grund and for day trips around the mountain to Zermatt. Crans-Montana is also within reach.

The skiing top 3600m bottom 1800m

Saas Fee has skiing all year round thanks to the Feegletscher, hanging impressively on the mountainside south of the village. But at lower altitudes the glacier is a nuisance, dividing the north-facing skiing into two areas. Most obvious from the terraces of the village hotels are the mogul-fields of the Längfluh, embraced by two arms of the glacier. There are links (just) at the top of this area to the major Felskinn sector. The Plattjen area is a north-east facing slope, closer to the village and much used by the ski-school. Last, and distinctly least, is the Hannig on the opposite side of the village – low, little and south-facing.

The **Längfluh** area is consistently fairly steep, and well suited to intermediate skiers wanting a bit of a challenge. The gondola from the extreme edge of the village to Spielboden is surmounted not only by a

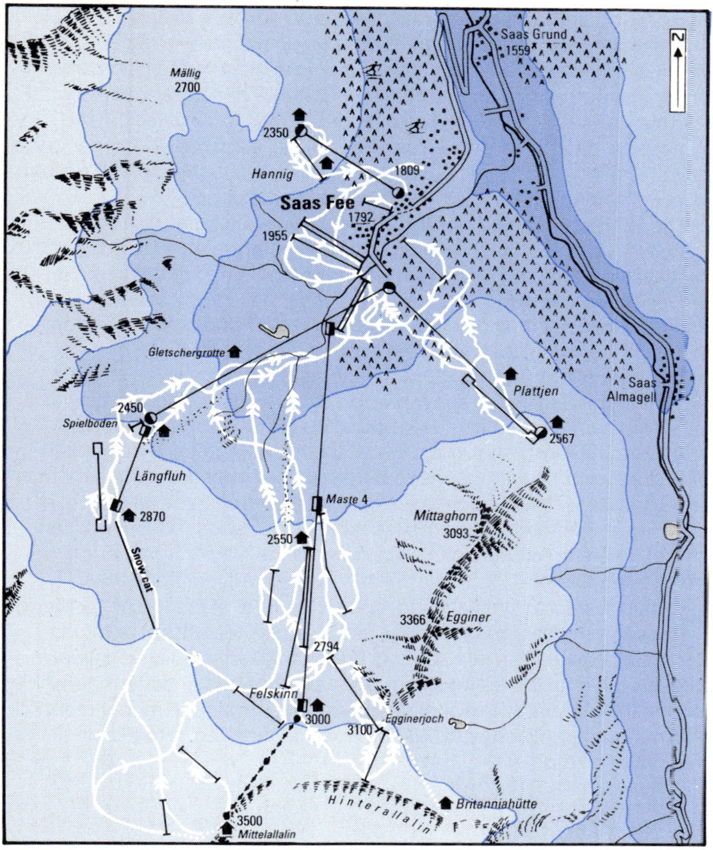

cable-car (to 2870m) but also by a curious drag serving the shortest genuine black run we have encountered. Instead of going back down the reds and blacks from here, or playing on the middle-of-the-road reds served by the top chair-lift, you can take the 'snow-cat', which serves a very gentle run back to Längfluh and connects with the Felskinn area.

The **Felskinn** skiing, normally reached by a cable-car which starts an annoying drag-lift-ride away from the edge of the resort, is more extensive. There is some very easy skiing on the top half (between 3000m and 2500m) served by drag-lifts; lower down it becomes steeper and bumpier, and inexperienced skiers can join the cable-car in mid-air at Maste 4 – though the easiest runs down are not intimidating. The Metro to Mittelallalin (3500m) has opened up more glorious open skiing, and makes it possible to ski across to Längfluh. At the top of the Metro, those up to a few metres of steep black run can put on their skis almost immediately, but the red starts an exhausting hike up the mountain and the blue starts higher still, involving a 15-minute trudge.

Two new drag-lifts have been installed to serve these pistes, so that to ski them (or parts of them) repeatedly you do not have to use the Metro, which is regained via a short drag to a hole in the mountainside or via the drags to Egginerjoch and Kamel (3250m). These drags serve what was the pre-Metro summer skiing, and are often closed early in the winter season; the lower drag serves a broad, easy red, the upper one a pair of short but worthwhile blacks. The black run to the top of the Metro involves a tiring walk but is nowhere steep.

The **Plattjen** gondola runs (from the same building as that for Längfluh) up to 2567m. Its skiing is of easy-intermediate difficulty, with a slightly awkward start at the top. The main slope, above the trees, is served by a chair where moderate queues tend to form; there are easy and more difficult runs down from there through woods to the village – the black justifying its grading because of lumpy terrain.

The gondola to **Hannig** (2350m) serves short runs which are little skied except early in the season when other areas are cold or closed.

All the main lift stations have **mountain restaurants** which are adequate but rarely charming; that at the top of Plattjen is particularly dire, but there is an atmospheric Berghaus half-way down the hill which compensates. The Gletschergrotte, hidden among trees off the piste down from Spielboden, is worth seeking out for good food as well as charm. There are superb close-up views of the glacier from Längfluh – worth a trip for non-skiers. We still have no reports on the highest revolving restaurant in the world, opened in 1986 at the top of the Metro.

Recent reports suggest that the skiing is now too attractive for the access lifts, at least in late season: huge (and very nastily behaved) **queues** build up for the Felskinn cable-car, morning and afternoon, forcing the ski school to adopt staggered class timing. A recent report tells of hour-long queues at 8.30 on a March morning. Once up the mountain, no problem.

The resort

Although a small resort in a confined setting, Saas Fee is by no means compact enough to suit idle or weary ski-booted pedestrians: it spreads for over half a mile along a couple of narrow, car-free, occasionally hilly streets, through something like a resort centre where streets converge, along over a river to the bottom of the north-facing ski slopes, where skiers' hotels have grown up. There are depots here where you can leave your skis and boots at not exhorbitant cost. Shopping facilities are adequate, with food shops at both ends of the village. Within the village there are pricey electric carts and taxis to help you get around.

Accommodation is mostly in traditional-looking hotels, comfortable but not luxurious, and self-catering chalets. The bulk of the resort is near the entrance car parks. Hotels over the river at the far end are much more convenient for skiers, and this is the main consideration – there are no outstandingly attractive or unpleasant hotels. Two typical chalet-style hotels which are ideally placed for the lifts are the Waldesruh (✆572295) and the Derby (✆572345) – both medium-sized, comfortable but slightly dull. The central Dom (✆591101) is friendly, with a jolly restaurant.

Après-ski is limited; there are live bands in a couple of hotels, and one or two discos. No restaurants or bars linger on the palate or in the memory. There is floodlit night skiing once a week on the Hannig.

Saas Fee is not a particularly good resort for **cross-country** skiers, though there are local trails and it is not far by bus down to the extensive trails along the valley between Saas Almagell and Saas Grund, and beyond. **Non-skiers** should enjoy the attractive walks, and the village itself, but it is a bit claustrophobic. The leisure/sports centre is a great asset – very well equipped and civilised. On our several visits we have never seen the skating rink in operation.

The **nursery slopes** are excellent – broad, gentle and well-placed for lunches and meeting up with other skiers; but the bottom, flat parts are not very sunny in mid-winter.

The **ski school** touring weeks involve several nights spent in refuges and a trip to Zermatt. Monte Rosa, Europe's second-highest peak (4634m), is nearby, and a ski-touring proposition.

Saas Fee facts

Lift payment

Passes One pass covers all lifts but not the Längfluh snow-cat (SF4). Day, afternoon and local passes available.
Cost 6-day pass SF190
Beginners Coupons for nursery lifts.
Children 30% reduction, up to 16.
Summer skiing Extensive runs from 3600m (Mitelallalin) and 3250m (Kamel) to Felskinn mid-station (2550m). 20km of piste.

Ski school

Classes 2hr morning and afternoon.
Cost 6 days SF145. Private lesson SF35/hr.
Children Ski kindergarten, ages 5–12, adult hours, 6 days SF110, lunch available. Hotel Beau Site non-ski kindergarten, ages 3–6, 9.00–4.30, 6 days with lunch SF113.
Special courses Touring weeks (March, April, May and June).

Not skiing

Facilities 20km cleared walks, swimming, natural ice rinks for skating, curling, tennis, fitness centre (sauna, solarium, massage), ski-bob runs, cinema, museum.

Cross-country skiing

Trails 7½km loop, starts near entrance to village. Instruction available.

Medical facilities

In resort doctor, chemist, dentist.
Hospital Visp (26km);

Getting there

Airport Geneva; transfer 3½hr.
Railway Brig; frequent buses.
Road Via Geneva or Basel/Bern. The 26km drive from the main road near Visp is slow and may require chains.

Available holidays

Resort beds 2,300 in hotels, 5,700 in apartments.
Package holidays Best Skiing (Ht Ch Sc), Bladon Lines (Ht Ch Sc), Horizon (Ht), Inghams (Ht Sc), Inghams (Ht Sc) John Morgan (Ht Ch), Kuoni (Ht), Made to Measure (Ht Sc), Neilson (Ht Sc), Ski Club of GB (Ht), Ski Sutherland (Ht), SkiGower (Cl), Small World (Ch), Swiss Travel Service (Ht), Thomson (Ht Sc)

Further information

Tourist office ✆(28) 571457. Tx 472230.

No grounds for dismissal

Saas Grund Switzerland 1560m

It is not surprising that Saas Grund is overshadowed by the growing international reputation of Saas Fee, 250m and a ten-minute drive above it. Grund does not have nearly such an extensive ski area; more importantly, it has none of the appeal of Saas Fee as a village. Far from being traffic-free, it is strung out along the approach road to the higher and bigger resort, which means that Grund is never a peaceful place and at weekends is plagued by traffic. But this poor relation of a resort should not be written off: its skiing is high and sunny, and not without interest for intermediate and off-piste skiers. Although it is difficult to recommend for a whole holiday, Saas Grund may make an interesting change of scene for skiers based in Saas Fee who have not committed themselves to a week's lift pass – perhaps with the idea of taking a trip or two around the mountain to Zermatt.

A gondola goes up from a point not far from the village centre to Kreuzboden (2400m), a sunny shelf which is the heart of the skiing. The only ways back to the valley (apart from the lift) are an off-piste itinerary, starting with a long traverse to a gully above the village, and a long narrow path with unpleasantly exposed drops at the side – so it is not surprising that the gondola is queue-free for much of the day. A popular and harmless red run which goes part-way down from the top of the gondola is served by a chair-lift, while above Kreuzboden a pair of longish drag-lifts serve broad, open pistes which are graded blue and red but are both gentle. The real interest of the skiing is the runs opened up by the further section of the gondola going up to Hohsaas (3098m), beneath the Laquinjoch. (The name spells danger, and it was on the slopes below here that an April avalanche a few years ago engulfed a party of skiers.) There is basically only one piste from Hohsaas, graded red, but it is long and varied, and on the occasion of our March visit both piste and lift were blissfully uncrowded – in marked contrast to the major lifts at Saas Fee. There is also plenty of opportunity to venture off-piste – another difference from Saas Fee. There is a big restaurant at Kreuzboden, and a little hut at Hohsaas of no particular charm but with a glorious view from its sun-terrace across to the mountains ringing Saas Fee.

Saas Grund has adequate nursery slopes on the fringes of the village as well as the gentle runs at Kreuzboden, a natural ice rink which is floodlit in the evenings, and long cross-country trails along the valley, climbing gently towards Saas Almagell and descending equally gently towards Saas Balen. There are a great many chalets and apartments to rent, and a wide choice of modest hotels, two or three of which have swimming pools.

Tourist office ✆(28)572403. **Package holidays** Ski Sutherland (Ht).

Bonvin chaud

Crans-Montana Switzerland 1500m

Good for *Sunny slopes, beautiful scenery, big ski area, easy runs, not skiing, cross-country skiing, rail access, easy road access*
Bad for *Tough runs, Alpine charm, skiing convenience, late holidays, freedom from cars*

Crans and Montana, once separate, have now merged to form the largest resort in Switzerland – a vast suburban sprawl whose main quality is a splendid south-facing balcony setting, high above the Rhône valley on a wooded ledge broad enough to accommodate two golf courses, one of which hosts the Swiss Open. Arnold Lunn, who had seen a few, rated the view across the valley as one of the seven finest panoramas in the Alps. On a fine day in December the resort gets eight hours of sun, when Grindelwald gets one.

As they have grown together the distinction between simple Montana for skiers and smart Crans for furs, bridge and golf has become less and less noticeable. Both parts of the resort lack village atmosphere, with residential outskirts, traffic jams and one-way systems, parking meters, and concrete shopping precincts not obviously geared to winter sports. The building style is mostly urban and undistinguished. The resort has the characterless comfort and multiple amenities of a conference town, with all the dullness of Switzerland at its worst and none of the charm of Switzerland at its best. Despite the many smart shops in Crans (Cartier, Gucci, caviar, furs), the resort as a whole is more expensive than stylish, and its skiing more extensive than interesting.

Yet we have reports from satisfied customers. What they tell us is that the comfortable hotels and the outstanding range of off-slope facilities (including beautiful walks and cross-country trails) count for less than a broad area of sunny, panoramic, intermediate runs which offer lots of thoroughly enjoyable skiing when the sun is out – at least until it spoils the snow.

Day trips to several major resorts on the south side of the Valais trench are possible for skiers with a car – Zermatt and Saas Fee to the east, Verbier (via Super Nendaz) to the west.

The skiing top 2950m bottom 1500m

There are three well-linked areas accessible from four base stations along the broad south-facing mountainside. There are one or two difficult runs and plenty of space, especially at the Aminona end, for off-piste skiing; but in general the skiing is much more suitable for leisurely skiers than adventurous ones. Virtually all of the skiing is between

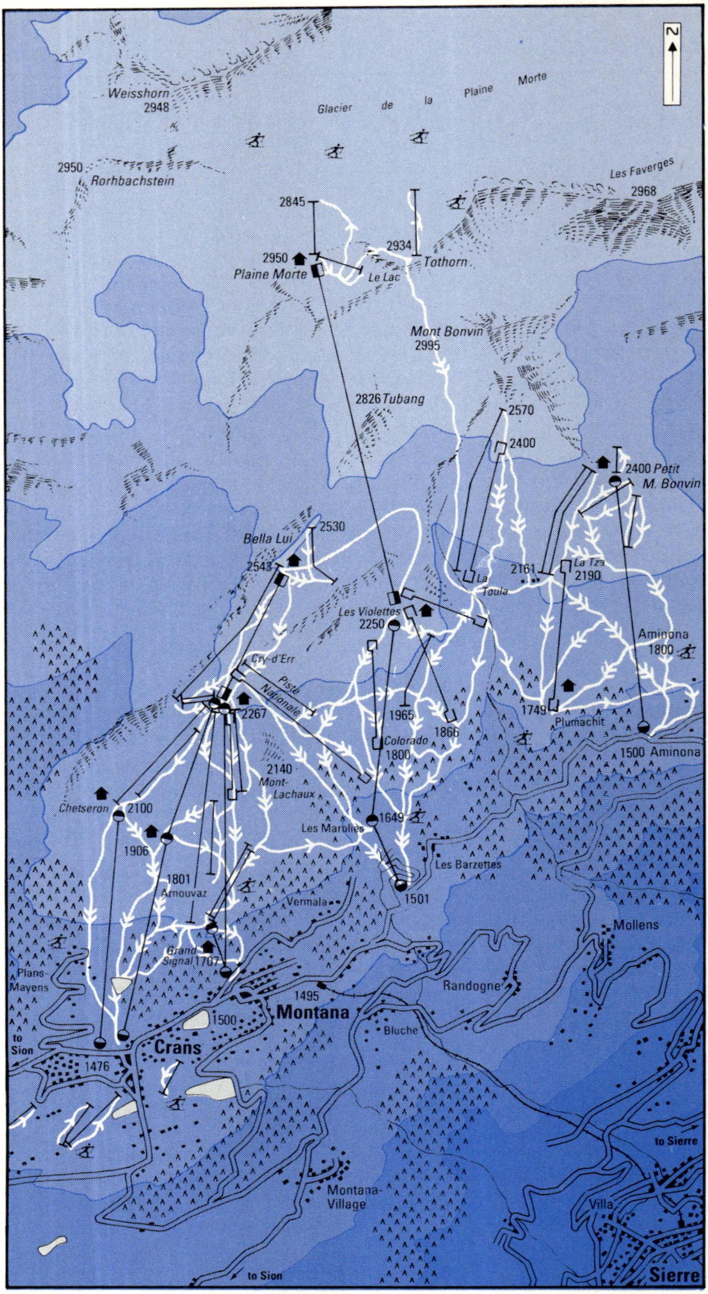
N
Weisshorn
2948
Glacier de la Plaine Morte
2950
Rorhbachstein
Les Faverges
2968
2845
2934
2950
Plaine Morte
Le Lac
Tothorn
Mont Bonvin
2995
2826 Tubang
2570
2400
2400 Petit M. Bonvin
2530
Bella Lui
2543
2161
La Toula
La Tza
2190
Les Violettes
2250
Aminona
1800
Cry-d'Err
Piste Nationale
2267
1965
1866
1749
Plumachit
Colorado
1800
1500 Aminona
2140
Mont-Lachaux
Chetseron
2100
1649
Les Marolires
1906
1801
Arnouvaz
Les Barzettes
Vermala
1501
Mollens
Grand Signal
1707
Plans-Mayens
1495
Randogne
Montana
1500
Bluche
to Sion
Crans
1476
to Sierre
Montana-Village
Villa
to Sion
Sierre

1500m and 2500m and is evenly split between open and wooded terrain; the exception is the Plaine Morte glacier and the single intermediate run down from it.

The main lifts out of Crans and Montana meet up at **Cry d'Err**, at the heart of the western sector of the ski area – the one most used by holiday skiers and the most suitable for the timid. Most of the skiing nearby is easy, and the run to Chetseron is flat enough for near-beginners. The area above Grand Signal, reached by short gondola from Montana, is a crowded junction of lifts and pistes which serves as the nursery area. Runs down to Crans and Montana are paths, not always easy to distinguish from roads, footpaths and cross-country trails, and often crowded and in poor condition. The woods below Chetseron sometimes provide some good off-piste skiing. There is tougher skiing on the eastern side of Cry d'Err, notably the excellent racing slopes beside the Nationale lift and below it, past Vermala, to Les Barzettes. The marked off-piste run from Bella Lui to Les Violettes is useful for access to Aminona but is largely a traverse.

The **Les Violettes** sector, also accessible by an easy path from Les Verdets, consists of a web of criss-crossing red runs, with mogul-fields and some scope for exploring between the pistes. The great attraction is the **Plaine Morte** cable-car, which adds a spectacular new dimension to the skiing area, climbing to the rim of an oceanic expanse of flat glacier (used in summer for cross-country) with a breathtaking view of famous peaks to the south. The glacier is a famous and excellent starting point for ski tours (short climbs to Wildhorn and Wildstrubel and long descents over the other side towards Gstaad, Lenk and Adelboden) but the terrain is such that skiing possibilities down from Plaine Morte are strictly limited. Apart from the occasional, hazardous off-piste route beneath Les Faverges to Aminona, there is only one run down from the glacier to the resort – a red piste that is wide and nowhere steep. It drops into a steep-sided valley which has some off-piste skiing and the resort's only black run, served by the Toula chair and drag. This is neither long nor steep, but the lifts offer an alternative way into the pleasantly uncrowded **Aminona** sector of the ski area, otherwise reached by a long, pretty path through the woods to Plumachit. There is lots of easy, wide-open skiing on the slopes below Petit Bonvin, and some more challenging runs (including good off-piste skiing) below the tree-line. The run down to Aminona itself is mostly an easy path.

Mountain restaurants are in all the obvious places, but there are few in the Violettes and Aminona sectors. There is an excellent restaurant at the mid-station of the Crans gondola, but the majority are convenient and efficient rather than captivating.

In so large a resort it is not surprising that there are high-season **queues** for the main access lifts in the mornings. Our latest information comes from the tourist office but may be worth passing on: 'no queues for Grand Signal or Les Violettes; some queues for Chetseron and Cry d'Err, and at Aminona'. Higher up, the problems are queues for the cable-car to Plaine Morte and for the chair-lifts up to Les Violettes in late afternoon. There is a ski-bob run on Chetseron.

The resort

Crans stretches up through the woods to Plans Mayens (1620m). Montana's upper suburb is Vermala (1600m), a string of residential chalets and a couple of tall hotel blocks. East of Montana the road along the mountainside is built up as far as Les Barzettes, a convenient skiing access point with some hotels but no resort life. Aminona is a self-contained satellite, well away from the rest of the resort, consisting of no more than a large car park for local skiing day-trippers, a cluster of tall modern apartment blocks and some chalets.

The free ski-bus is an invaluable complement to the lift system, running regularly to a timetable between Crans and Aminona, serving all the main lift departures. There is no evening service. The resort is easy to reach by car, and having a car is a considerable asset given the extent of the resort and skiing; but parking anywhere in the centre of the resort is difficult and restricted.

Accommodation is mostly in apartments and comfortable hotels, some of them modern and very expensive, others long-established and old-fashioned. Staffed chalet holidays are also available. The resort is large and the lift departures are a long walk from some hotels in the centre of Crans and at the eastern end of Montana near the Sierre funicular station. Among the expensive hotels, the Parc (✆414101), opened in 1892 and set beside the water in Montana, is handsomely traditional. The Hauts de Crans (✆415553) is brand new, a luxury chalet-style development in the woods above Montana, well placed for skiers and walkers. The Etoile (✆411671), National (✆412681) and Robinson (✆411353) are simple hotels within easy walking distance of the Crans lifts; the Robinson is friendly and has a good restaurant. The very friendly old Mont Blanc (✆412343) is particularly beautifully set above Plans Mayens, a long way from the resort but beside the pistes down from Chetseron and excellent for walks and cross-country. Despite its inconvenient location near the funicular station in Montana, the Curling (✆473282) is recommended by a recent visitor ('quiet, friendly, excellent food').

Après-ski includes discos, lots of bars and tea-rooms, a cinema and a casino in Crans. There is no shortage of expensive restaurants, with much more variety than in most Swiss resorts. Montana has a wider range of inexpensive places to eat and drink, including a pizzeria and a noisy, crowded pub.

Crans-Montana is an excellent resort for **cross-country** ('especially for those who like to explore and do not want to go round and round the same loop every day') and **non-skiers**. There are long, sunny and beautiful walks, many of them beside the cross-country tracks, punctuated by restaurants with sun terraces on the lower slopes of the Alpine skiing area. The Hotel Aïda Castel in Montana has weekly bridge tournaments, there are frequent curling tournaments, and golf on snow at New Year and in mid-February.

Nursery slopes are excellent at Crans. There is flat skiing, with baby lifts, on the golf course, and easy runs around Cry d'Err. Montana's

Crans-Montana facts

Lift payment

Passes General pass covers all lifts and ski-bus. Available for all periods including 'hourly' passes giving a refund when handed in early.
Beginners Coupons.
Cost 6-day pass SF164. 10% off for families of four plus.
Children 40% off, under 16.
Summer skiing Small area from 2800m to 2950m. 2 lifts.

Ski school

Classes 2hr mornings or afternoons.
Cost 7 half days SF90. Private lessons SF40/hr.
Children 20% off, up to 12. Ski kindergarten, ages 3–6, 8.30–4.30, with lunch SF40 a day, SF140 a week. Non-ski kindergarten, ages up to 12.

Cross-country skiing

Trails 40km in three areas. 15km (easy) around Crans; 10km (more difficult) across the mountain between Plan Mayens and Aminona via Grand Signal; 15km trail at Plaine Morte, open in summer.

Medical facilities

In resort Fracture clinic, doctor, dentist, chemist.
Hospital Sierre (15km).

Not skiing

Facilities Skating, curling, swimming (hotel pools), tennis, toboggan run, ski bob, fitness centre, bowling, 50km walks, indoor golf, bridge, hot-air balloon rides, husky-drawn sled rides, squash, riding, concerts.

Getting there

Airport Geneva; transfer about 3hr.
Railway Sierre (15km); funicular or bus to resort.
Road Via Pontarlier, Lausanne; chains may be needed.

Available holidays

Resort beds 5,000 in hotels, 25,000 in apartments.
Package holidays Best Skiing (Ht Ch), Bladon Lines (Ht Ch Sc), Inghams (Ht), Kuoni (Ht), Made to Measure (Ht Sc), Schoolplan (Ht Sc), Ski Club of GB (Ht), SkiGower (Cl), Swiss Travel Service (Ht)

Further information

Tourist office Crans ✆(27) 412132. Tx 473173. Montana ✆(27) 413041. Tx 473203.

Grand Signal area is crowded and a bit steep, but has the advantage of being part of the main ski area.

Crans and Montana have separate **ski schools**, with various meeting places around the slopes for different classes. A pupil reports an uneven style and standard of instruction, but was glad to be able to buy a ticket for three non-consecutive days. The ski schools have mountain guides.

Balanced view

Anzère Switzerland 1430m

Anzère is a small, modern resort just along the hill from Crans-Montana but with a quite separate, equally beautiful ski area. It is not the ultimate convenience resort, but neither is it the soulless monstrosity that many such resorts are. It consists mainly of apartment buildings, cleverly disguised as giant chalets, with a car-free commercial precinct in the centre, where there are a couple of hotels. In general the self-catering accommodation is of a very high standard, and it includes some individual chalets on the edges of the main complex. The village is built on a slope (1430m to 1550m) and extends a long way across the mountainside, but there are ski-lift departures from each end, so location of apartment is not critical – except in mid-winter, when the westerly gondola is naturally to be preferred to the easterly chair-lift. A recent visitor found Anzère 'a friendly place where everyone got on easily. Despite its being new, you feel you're in a village.'

The ski area (up to 2420m) is small and very sunny, with magnificent views across the Rhone valley. It consists mostly of easy and intermediate skiing above the tree-line, including a good nursery area at the top of the mountain, with restaurant to hand. The piste map shows no blue runs, and indeed the terrain does not provide runs that are ideal for the near-beginner to progress to. There are longer runs through the woods to the village offering more variety and challenge – but changing snow conditions through the day can create treacherously icy mogul-fields which may prompt even the most accomplished skiers to go down by lift. At the bottom of the long, gentle, east-facing Combe de Serin run down to Les Rousses (1780m) you can grill your own lunch at the restaurant. Anzère is small (about 6,500 beds) and the lifts hardly ever suffer from serious crowds ('maximum wait 15 minutes on Good Friday morning').

The resort is quiet after dark, but there are a couple of discos and some good restaurants. There are two cross-country skiing trails (total 18km), a toboggan run, and marked walking paths through the woods at resort level. Other facilities include an artificial skating and curling rink, a fitness room, a swimming pool and several saunas. The valley town of Sion is easily reached by car or bus, for a change of scene. The ski school is reported to be 'cheerful and well run', and there are skiing and non-skiing kindergartens. A lift pass for seven non-consecutive days is available – attractive for car-borne visitors staying for a fortnight and wanting to branch out to places such as Verbier and Zermatt, though it costs more than an ordinary pass for nine days.

Tourist office ✆(27) 382519.
Package holidays Made to Measure (Ht Sc), Ski Sutherland (Ht).

Skiing for achievers

Verbier Switzerland 1500m

Good for *Off-piste skiing, tough runs, big ski area, ski touring, après-ski, easy road access, beautiful scenery, sunny slopes, chalet holidays, rail access*
Bad for *Skiing convenience, lift queues, easy runs, not skiing*

Linked resorts: Haute Nendaz, Thyon 2000, Veysonnaz

Lots of smart young Britons go to Verbier for social reasons. It offers an unmatched range of chalet accommodation, which means lots of winter job opportunities and a good social life for the seasonal immigrants and, up to a point, their house guests. It has become the prime target for the yuppy generation of British weekend skiers.

Lots of keen skiers choose Verbier for the skiing – a big, beautiful and mostly challenging ski area with some formidable black runs and tremendous off-piste skiing. But it also has important drawbacks. There are lift bottlenecks, where big queues are common; the main ski area around Les Attelas is too congested for the good of the pistes or skiers; the only run out of this area is steep and officially off-piste; and the lift pass is the most expensive in Europe. The building of a big new cable-car has provided some relief for the first three problems, and helps to explain the fourth.

The resort is a vast sprawl of chalets and chalet-style hotels, spacious to a fault and devoid of character. Although fashionable in its way, it is loud rather than stylish, with none of the glitter of traditionally grand resorts. The après-ski is lively but casual, and there are no sumptuous hotels and few inviting shop windows.

Haute Nendaz is a large and amorphous apartment resort, better placed than Verbier for skiers who want to explore the whole region. Its queues and layout make it best suited to skiers with a car. Veysonnaz and Thyon 2000 are much smaller, modern self-catering resorts at the eastern end of the ski area. Thyon is high, open and convenience-oriented, and well suited to families. Veysonnaz is below it, at the bottom of some splendid woodland runs.

Verbier is not far from the Alpine crossroads of Martigny, from which point there are other resorts within day-trip range in all directions – including the Chamonix valley in France, over the Col des Montets.

The skiing top 3328m bottom 821m

Verbier's local skiing takes place in two separate areas, with lift departures at opposite ends of the resort. The two are linked by gentle off-piste runs which are often skied into a piste-like state.

The smaller area is **Savoleyres**, nearly always pleasantly quiet, and reached by lifts starting high above the centre. The runs down on the

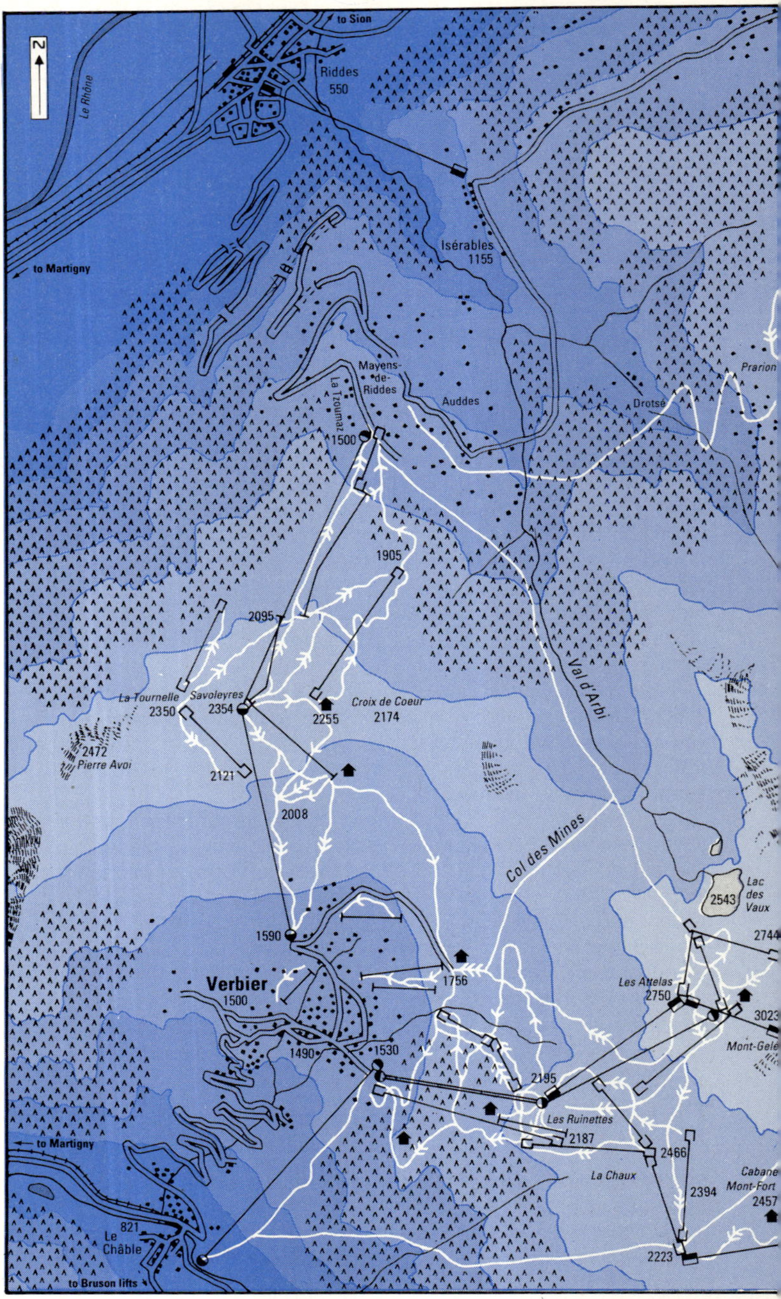

N
to Sion
Riddes
550
Le Rhône
to Martigny
Isérables
1155
Mayens-de-Riddes
La Tzoumaz
Auddes
Prarion
Drotsé
1500
1905
2095
La Tournelle
2350
Savoleyres
2354
2255
Croix de Coeur
2174
2472
Pierre Avoi
2121
2008
Val d'Arbi
Col des Mines
Lac des Vaux
2543
2744
1590
Verbier
1500
1756
Les Attelas
2750
3023
Mont-Gelé
1490
1530
2195
Les Ruinettes
2187
2466
La Chaux
2394
Cabane Mont-Fort
2457
to Martigny
821
Le Châble
2223
to Bruson lifts

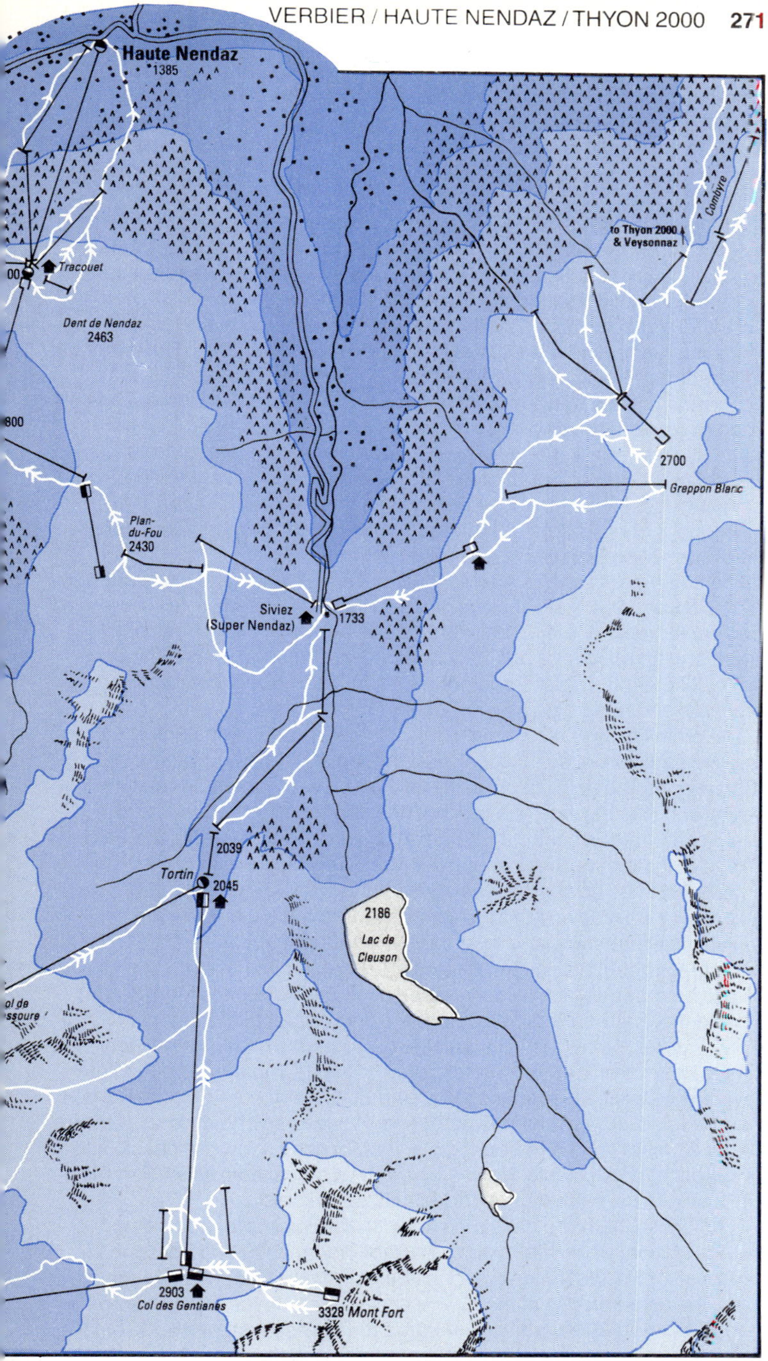
Haute Nendaz
1385
Tracouet
Dent de Nendaz
2463
to Thyon 2000
& Veysonnaz
Combyre
2700
Greppon Blanc
Plan-
du-Fou
2430
Siviez
(Super Nendaz)
1733
2039
Tortin
2045
2186
Lac de
Cleuson
2903
Col des Gentianes
3328 Mont Fort

sunny Verbier side of the mountain are mostly open and intermediate, and there can be good spring snow skiing off-piste. Snow on the lower slopes is unreliable and conditions often difficult. On the north-facing side there are long trails, none of them very difficult, through the woods to La Tzoumaz – little skied and usually with good snow.

At the other end of the village various alternative lifts go up to the heart of Verbier's skiing on the slopes beneath the ridge of **Les Attelas**. The skiing in the sheltered Lac des Vaux bowl covers a wide range of intermediate difficulty, and the area is popular with ski school classes just off the nursery slopes. Skiing down towards Ruinettes is tougher, with a mogul-field near the top and no easy way down. From Ruinettes to Verbier there is a good variety of runs, with a blue path as well as tough runs directly down through the trees for keen mogul skiers. These wooded slopes are very useful in bad weather. A much-used way home from Lac des Vaux is the attractive Col des Mines off-piste route which runs round from the bottom of the lifts before crossing over the ridge to the south-facing slopes above the nursery lifts. Although not difficult, this slope is often unsafe. An alternative off-piste run is the Val d'Arbi, prettily down through the woods to La Tzoumaz.

The cable-car from Les Attelas to Mont Gelé is small and short but serves some of Verbier's most famous skiing – all of it off-piste. There are very extreme couloirs down to Les Attelas which are occasionally skied, but the main runs are the longer steep and open ones behind Mont Gelé, ending up at Tortin or La Chaux. The slopes are rocky and exposed, and require good snow cover for safety.

The main link with the eastern half of the skiing is the chair-lift from Lac des Vaux to Col de Chassoure at the top of a dauntingly long, wide and steep mogul-field which is officially off-piste – a splendid run for skiers who like that kind of thing, but often congested by skiers who don't. The run (or a gondola-ride down) ends at Tortin plateau, the base station of the original lifts serving the Mont-Fort glacier skiing.

Mont-Fort has added enormously to the available skiing but, unusually for a glacier, not much of its skiing is easy. From the top (which gives spectacular views) there is a roundabout alternative to the very steep (about 35°) direct run under the cable-car, but even this should be graded black (which it was not on the 1988 piste map). Around the Col des Gentianes there are some splendid, open, very easy runs served by drag-lifts, but the only run down to Tortin is a long, not too tough black, with some excellent off-piste variants. The long run down from Col des Gentianes to La Chaux, under the new cable-car, is much less difficult (a lot of it is path) and provides splendid views of the Grand Combin and neighbouring glaciers. In good snow it is possible to ski off-piste to Le Châble, across vineyard terraces; from Mont-Fort the run is said to be 18km for the enormous 2500m drop.

From Tortin there are easy runs down to the Super-Nendaz skiing service station, where lifts branch east for Thyon 2000 and Veysonnaz, and west for Haute-Nendaz. A long chain of short lifts and easy runs along the upper slopes of the mountainside leads to the high modern resort of **Thyon 2000**, where there are broad nursery slopes and some excellent long runs down through the woods to Veysonnaz and

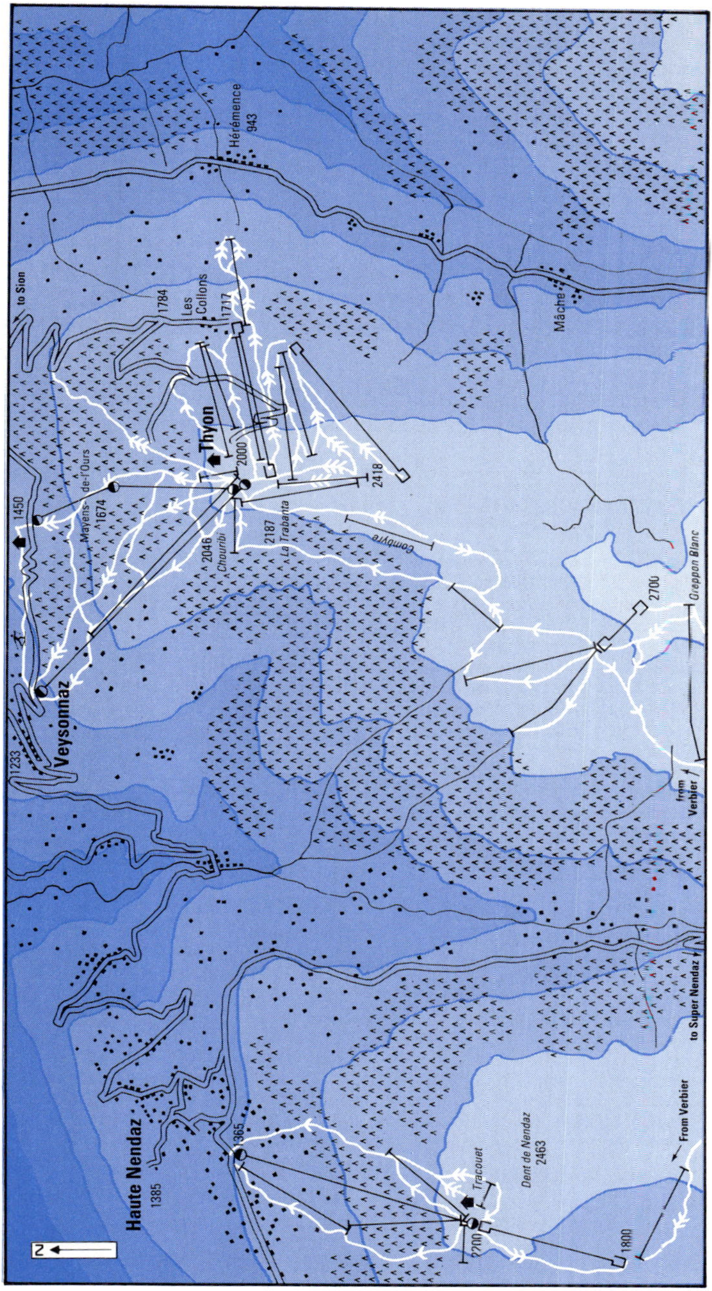
Hérémence
943
to Sion
1784
Les Collons
1717
Thyon
2000
2418
1450
Mayens-de-l'Ours
1674
2046
Chouribi
2187
La Trabanta
Combyre
Mâche
2700
Greppon Blanc
Veysonnaz
1233
from Verbier
to Super Nendaz
Haute Nendaz
1385
1365
Tracouet
2200
Dent de Nendaz
2463
From Verbier
1800
N

Mayens-de-l'Ours. On the other side of Super Nendaz two steep drag-lifts to **Plan-du-Fou** give access to an off-piste run (not difficult) to Prarion and on down through woods past Drotsé to Auddes, where a special bus links up with La Tzoumaz/Savoleyres lifts.

Haute Nendaz skiing is a simple arrangement of long intermediate north-facing runs above the resort, served by the long Tracouet gondola or alternative drags, and shorter south-facing slopes behind Tracouet down to Prarion. The new Plan-du-Fou cable-car makes it possible to get to Super-Nendaz and Tortin on skis.

Above Le Châble at **Bruson** there is a quiet skiing area, between 1000m and 2300m, described by a reporter as surprisingly interesting and extensive, and very pleasantly uncrowded. The lift pass also encourages excursions to other nearby resorts, notably **Champex** and **La Fouly** in the beautifully secluded Val Ferret, which is very well suited to cross-country skiing as well as having some small but far from boring Alpine ski areas. There is also some excellent high skiing, on piste and off it, above the entrance to the **St Bernard** tunnel, around the pass

Verbier facts

Lift payment

Passes Four Valley pass covers all the lifts and ski buses in this area and lifts in several other nearby ski areas (Bruson, Val Ferret). Day and half-day passes, 10 days non-consecutive, and passes excluding Mont-Fort available.
Cost 6-day pass SF240 inc Mont-Fort, SF208 exc Mont-Fort. Mont-Fort supplement SF12/day. Super-St-Bernard supplement SF10/day. Reductions for families and over-60s.
Children 50% off, up to 16.
Beginners Day and half-day passes for nursery lifts.
Summer skiing Small area at Mont-Fort, 2700m to 3300m.

Ski school

Classes 2¼hr mornings.
Cost 6 consecutive half days SF87. Private lessons SF40/hr.
Children Classes, ages 3 up, mornings, 6 half-days SF64. Ski kindergarten, ages 3–10, 9.00–4.30, 6 days with lunch SF195. Non-ski kindergarten, ages 18mth up, 8.30–5.30, 6 days with lunch SF192.
Special courses Cours de Godille (wedel courses), ski tours, heli-skiing.

Cross-country skiing

Trails 4km trail at Verbier, 30km at Le Châble, 4km at Bruson.

Not skiing

Facilities Indoor skating and curling, swimming, sauna, solarium, squash, tennis fitness centre, cinema, ski-bob, 15km cleared paths.

Medical facilities

In resort Clinic, doctor, dentist, chemist.
Hospital Martigny (20km).

Getting there

Airport Geneva; transfer 2½hr.
Railway Le Châble (10km); bus or gondola to resort.
Road Via Pontarlier, Lausanne; chains may be needed.

Available holidays

Resort beds 1,500 in hotels, 22,000 in chalets and apartments.
Package holidays Activity Travel (Ht Ch), Beach Villas (Ht Ch Sc), Best Skiing (Ht Ch Sc), Bladon Lines (Ht Ch Sc), Crystal (Ht), John Morgan (Ht Ch), Made to Measure (Ht Sc), Mark Warner (Ch Cl), Ski Club of GB (Ht Ch), Ski Esprit (Ch), Ski MacG (Ht Ch Sc), Ski West (Ht Ch Sc), Ski Whizz (Ch Cl), Small World (Ch), Supertravel (Ht Ch Cl Sc), Thomson (Ch Sc)

Further information

Tourist office ✆(26) 76222. Tx 473247.

(between 1900m and 2800m) and over into the Italian sun.

Mountain restaurants are not very plentiful, and the one at Tortin is very inadequate and expensive. The Carrefour at the top of the nursery slopes and the bottom of the pistes down to the resort is friendly and popular throughout the day and evening. Attractive, out-of-the-way restaurants are at Clambin (on one of the indirect runs from Ruinettes), the Cabane de Mont-Fort and Les Marmottes, at the bottom of Savoleyres Sud drag-lift. The Violon d'Ingres at Ruinettes is excellent.

Verbier has an unenviable reputation for **queues**. New lifts over the last few years have improved the flow from the resort by increasing capacity and providing alternative ways into the ski area, at the cost of ever-increasing piste congestion. Queues for the four-seater Medran gondola are so bad at times that skiers still ride down to Le Châble for a seat back up to Les Attelas, and there are still long queues for the lifts on both sides of the Col de Chassoure and on Mont-Fort. The new 150-person cable-car from La Chaux to the Col des Gentianes makes travelling from Verbier to Mont-Fort much quicker and easier (which is bad news for skiers based in Nendaz). The lift is not open to skiers without the Mont-Fort lift pass/supplement. Tortin and La Chaux lifts usually stay open after closing time to clear any backlog of skiers returning to Verbier. There are spot checks on lift passes (up on the mountain, not at the bottom lift stations), and fines of up to SF200 for cheating. High-season queues for lifts and buses at Nendaz are reported to be 'horrific'. Four Valleys lift passes do not cover lifts on the slopes beyond Thyon 2000 village (above Les Collons), where snow cannons cover a run of nearly 700m vertical.

The resort

Verbier is splendidly set on a wide, sloping, sunny ledge high above Le Châble, with beautiful views of the mountains that separate Switzerland, Italy and France. A central square is the focal point of the resort, surrounded by a complicated one-way system of busy streets, often congested at weekends, when all the second-home owners pour into town. Most of the shops, bars and hotels are on, or close to, the square and the street up to the Medran lifts. Below it there is still a bit of an old village backwater, but most of Verbier's continuing expansion has taken place across the broad slopes between Ruinettes and Savoleyres, where it is very easy to get lost among so many identical chalets. Shopping is good but not spread widely around the resort.

Regular but not very frequent buses link Savoleyres and Medran lifts with the Place Centrale from about 8.30am to 7.30pm. They are free to lift pass holders and get very crowded at peak times. Parking centrally is difficult and vigorously policed. There's a multi-storey car park at the entrance to the resort. A car is useful for getting around in the evening, and for exploring fringe areas covered by the lift pass.

Verbier is not generally suitable for **cross-country** or **non-skiers**, but several reporters enjoyed the facilities at the smart new sports centre (squash, swimming, artificial ice rink). Ski-bobbing is popular on

Savoleyres (instruction is available), and once again permitted on pistes and some lifts between Verbier and Attelas.

Accommodation offered by British operators is mostly in chalets, of which there is a huge variety. Location matters: the top of the resort is good for skiing but very tiring for après-ski and especially inconvenient for self-caterers, who face long walks to and from shops. Most of the hotel accommodation is central: we have had good reports of the small Les Chamois (✆76402): 'comfortable, good food, convenient for Medran.' Other central, comfortable hotels include the large, friendly Hotel de la Poste (✆75681) and its less expensive modern annexe L'Auberge (✆75272). There is some budget accommodation in Le Châble for skiers with no taste for the bright lights and British voices.

Après-ski is livelier than in many chalet resorts. As well as all the chalet-party parties there are loud and popular bars, notably the teeming Pub Montfort and the Nelson, a typical plush Continental pub with draught bitter. Of the discos, the Farm Club is the smartest and very expensive, the Scotch cheapest and very crowded. There is a wide range of restaurants, from very expensive (the Hotel Rosalp is the best) to simple pizzas at the crowded Fer à Cheval. Booking is prudent at weekends. Reporters recommend Robinsons and Le Caveau (fondue and raclette).

Verbier's **nursery slopes**, between Ruinettes and Savoleyres, are sunny and gentle, but they have been encroached upon by the growth of the resort, are not very reliable for snow, and suffer from skiers in transit at the beginning and end of the day. The ski area is not suitable for skiers progressing from nursery to piste.

The main **ski school** meeting places are by the post office and at Ruinettes. A recent report speaks of 'small and good' classes, and 'excellent' private lessons. A second ski school, L'Ecole du Ski Fantastique, specialises in off-piste skiing, adventure skiing, heli-skiing, and tours. Verbier is on the Haute Route, so tourers can find plenty to do.

Haute Nendaz 1350m

High up on the steep southern wall of the Rhône Valley, Nendaz Station and Haute Nendaz have merged to form a long, hilly hairpin resort without much village atmosphere, with most of its self-catering a 15-minute walk below the lifts. Unfortunately its lift system is inadequate and inconvenient, and for many skiers the day starts with a queue for the bus up to **Super-Nendaz** (now officially Siviez), no more than a cluster of service buildings at the foot of lifts up to Tortin, but genuinely convenient, at the centre of the linked ski area and ideal for early access to Mont-Fort – keen skiers who don't mind evening isolation should consider the hotel Siviez (✆882458). There are a few hotels in the main resort; Le Déserteur (✆882455) is friendly, simple and lively, and not too inconveniently placed (there is a bus stop outside). There are 20km of cross-country trails, an artificial ice rink, swimming, squash, long walks and an all-day kindergarten.

Tourist office ✆(27) 881444. Tx 38643. **Package holidays** Bladon Lines (Ch Sc), Snow World (Ht Sc).

A house divided

Adelboden Switzerland 1400m

Good for *Sunny slopes, cross-country skiing, Alpine charm*
Bad for *Skiing convenience*

Linked resort: Lenk

Adelboden and Lenk are widely differing but connected resorts a couple of valleys to the west of the famous Jungfrau region.

Adelboden is a charming old village, its long main street lined with overhanging wooden buildings. It has around it a considerable quantity and variety of skiing, but – and it's a big but – that skiing is split into no less than five widely separated areas, of which only one is at present directly accessible from the village. The resort literature lists the linking buses as just another form of ski-lift (eg No 5 – height gain 357m, length 7500m), and for some time there have been ambitious plans for new lifts to improve matters. But for the moment the resort continues to appeal to those who put a welcoming Alpine atmosphere ahead of the more recently promoted virtue of skiing convenience.

Lenk is less appealing as a village than Adelboden – it has been more vigorously developed in recent years. Its skiing is not quite as spread out, but it still relies on 50-seat ski-lifts with four wheels.

The skiing top 2330m bottom 1330m

Adelboden's main ski areas are the Schwandfeldspitz, immediately above the village on the west side; Fleckli, across the valley on the east; Hochsthorn, to the south; Engstligenalp, 6km away to the south; and Geils, slightly further away to the south-west, which links with Lenk.

The skiing on Schwandfeldspitz starts from a chair-lift close to the main street, going up to 1938m; there is a justifiably black run back to the village, but most of the skiing is open intermediate runs on the wide flank of the mountain facing north-east – shortish pistes served by a drag, and a fine long red to Möser with a chair-lift return. Those not up to the black to the village can take a long roundabout blue run ending up on the northern fringes of the resort.

In the rural suburb of Boden, there are nursery lifts and a drag-lift above them going up to Kuonisbergli (1730m) and on to **Höchsthorn** (1903m); the spectrum of gradings of the runs on the lower part of the mountain exaggerates the variety of pistes – all the skiing is of easy to moderate difficulty. The main hazard is the risk of losing your way in poor visibility, because of non-existent piste marking. Across the valley, the drag-lift to **Fleckli** (1862m) serves runs which are marked red and black but which again hold no terrors other than poor marking – leading to unpleasant encounters with buried farm fences.

A minibus takes you to the cable-car which climbs steeply over 500m

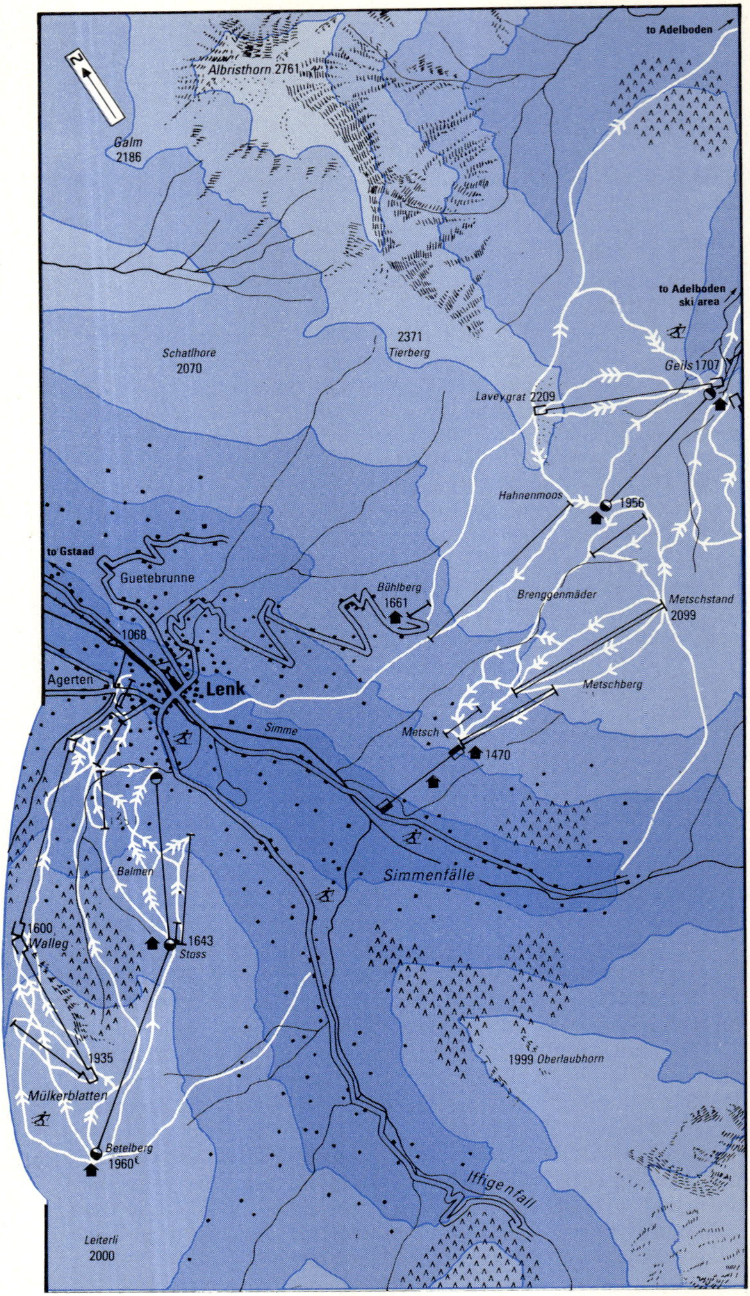
to Adelboden
Albristhorn 2761
Galm
2186
to Adelboden
ski area
Schatlhore
2070
2371
Tierberg
Geils 1707
Laveygrat 2209
Hahnenmoos
1956
to Gstaad
Guetebrunne
Bühlberg
1661
Brenggenmäder
Metschstand
2099
1068
Agerten
Lenk
Metschberg
Simme
Metsch
1470
Balmen
Simmenfälle
1600
Walleg
1643
Stoss
1935
1999 Oberlaubhorn
Mülkerblatten
Betelberg
1960
Iffigenfall
Leiterli
2000

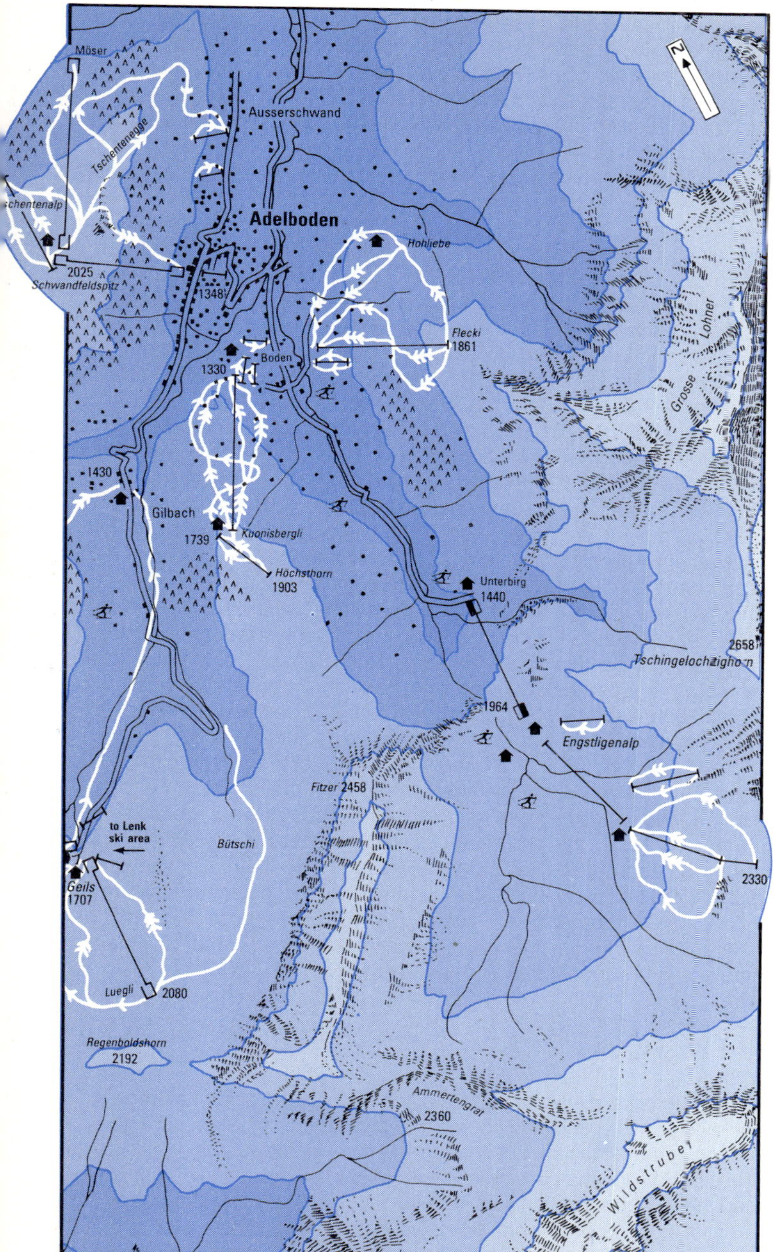

N
Möser
Ausserschwand
Tschentenegge
Tschentenalp
Adelboden
2025
Schwandfeldspitz
1348
Hohliebe
Flecki
1861
Boden
1330
Grosse Lohner
1430
Gilbach
1739
Kuonisbergli
Höchsthorn
1903
Unterbirg
1440
2658
Tschingelochtighorn
1964
Engstligenalp
Fitzer 2458
to Lenk
ski area
Bütschi
Geils
1707
2330
Luegli
2080
Regenboldshorn
2192
Ammertengrat
2360
Wildstrubel

to the extraordinary **Engstligenalp** (1964m). Beyond the cluster of hotels and houses is a flat-bottomed bowl of mountains; it has only one lift of any significance, on the far side, which serves pistes of moderate length and steepness and is a launching point for off-piste skiing in the bowl and for ski-tours outside it. There's a flat tow-drag across, but still a lot of plodding.

Even without the Lenk link, **Geils** would be worth the journey for the extent and variety of skiing it offers. Chairs up each side of a wide, open bowl to Luegli (2080m) and Laveygrat (2200m) serve intermediate and genuinely black runs back to Geils, but there are also links to the easier runs towards the centre. The run from Luegli marked black on the map was more accurately marked red on the mountain when we visited – though it is certainly more difficult than most other reds in the area, with modest moguls. The chair to Laveygrat (the high point of the area) is of particular interest to good skiers; not only does it offer challenging, genuinely steep runs back to Geils of almost 500m vertical (with big moguls at the top), but it also gives access to long intermediate runs back towards Adelboden (ending in a long walk or a short bus-ride to the village) and to an off-piste descent off the back of the hill to Lenk.

The normal access to Lenk is via the gondola to Hahnenmoos, a broad col only 250m higher than Geils. The blue run underneath the lift is easy and attractive, and very popular with near-beginners. In the **Lenk** direction, an easy piste goes down only as far as Bühlberg – though there are off-piste ways down when snow permits.

The more interesting skiing on this side of Lenk is the broad, open expanse of mountain above Metsch, served by two double drag-lifts up to Metschstand (2098m) giving long, easy and intermediate west-facing runs of 600m vertical. Metsch is reached from Lenk by bus and cable-car, and again there are only off-piste ways back to the valley.

The Betelberg area, on the far side of Lenk, starts closer to the village than the other areas, but for most skiers it still entails a bus-ride. The main gondola gives access to all the skiing, though there are supplementary drags and chair-lifts as alternatives. The runs are broad, partly above the trees and partly cut through them, and almost entirely gentle. The blues can be schussed by anyone but beginners (and are often used by cross-country skiers), the reds are in general too gentle to form moguls. The one black run, down the lower half of the gondola, has a fairly steep mogul-field at the bottom.

The resort

Adelboden sits in a slightly elevated position to one side of a broad valley which is split by the course of the swift-flowing Allebach. The village spreads down to the river from the main street running across the hillside, with the nursery slopes and sports centre between the two and the lift departure for Schwanfeldspitz on the other, uphill side.

Most of the **accommodation** is in chalets and apartments, but there are numerous hotels and guest-houses. Among the most welcoming is the modest Kreuz (✆732121), on the main street directly below the

Adelboden facts

Lift payment

Passes Single pass covers all Adelboden and Lenk lifts, and buses during the skiing day. Also gives reduction on Lenk swimming pool entrance. Day pass available, and local area passes for half-day and 1, 2 or 3 days. Passes for 6 or more days give a reduction on day passes for the Weisse Hochland area (Gstaad etc).
Cost 6-day pass SF162.
Beginners Coupons or electronic points card.
Children 40% off, under 16.

Ski school

Classes 2hr morning and afternoon.
Cost 6 days including lift pass SF256. Private lessons SF38/hr.
Children Classes, 6 days including lift pass SF207. Ski kindergarten, ages 4–6, 6 days with lunch SF196.
Special courses Racing.

Cross-country skiing

Trails Total 40km easy trails at Ausserschwand and Engstligenalp (at almost 2000m), easy and intermediate ones at Boden, Stiegelschwand and Geils.

Not skiing

Facilities Skating (artificial rink), curling (indoor and outdoor), swimming (hotels), museum, 40km cleared paths, hang-gliding, sleigh rides, riding, ski-bobs, skittles.

Medical facilities

In resort Doctors, chemist.
Dentist Frutigen (16km).
Hospital Frutigen (16km).

Getting there

Airport Basel, transfer about 3hr; also Bern, Zurich, Geneva.
Railway Frutigen (16km); regular buses.
Road Via Basel and Bern; chains may be needed.

Available holidays

Resort beds Over 1,000 in hotels and pensions, 7,000 in chalets and apartments.
Package holidays Made to Measure (Ht), Swiss Travel Service (Ht)

Further information

Tourist office ✆(33) 732252. Tx 922121.

chair-lift, and quite close to the bus station. At the southern end of the main street (but close to a stop for the Geils bus) is the more expensive Huldi (✆731531), with good views and a highly regarded restaurant.

Adelboden has extensive **cross-country** skiing trails of easy and medium grades at Boden, Geils and Engstligenalp, and is an attractive resort for that purpose. It has considerable appeal for **non-skiers**, too – quite good sports facilities as well as the charming atmosphere of a traditional Alpine village, and good excursion prospects.

There are good **nursery slopes** in the heart of the village (admirably gentle), on the northern fringes, and at Boden (at the foot of the Hochsthorn). We lack recent reports on **ski school**; it meets both at the village slopes and at Boden.

Lenk 1070m

Lenk has been greatly expanded in recent years, mainly in chalet style. It is spacious and not unpleasant, but does not add up to a particularly appealing whole. It attracts many middle-aged German cross-country skiers and walkers (for both of whom there are abundant opportunities), offering spa treatments as well as good non-skiing sports facilities including swimming, skating and curling (natural rinks).

Tourist office ✆(33) 732252. Tx 922121. **Package holidays** Made to Measure (Ht), Swiss Travel Service (Ht).

Catch a falling star

Gstaad Switzerland 1100m

Good for *Big ski area, easy runs, cross-country skiing, mountain restaurants, not skiing, Alpine charm, rail access, easy road access*
Bad for *Tough runs, skiing convenience, late holidays, resort-level snow*

Linked resorts: Rougemont, Schönried, Saanenmöser, Zweisimmen, St Stephan
Separate resort: Château d'Oex

The Gstaad area – Das Weisse Hochland or Le Blanc Pays d'en Haut, depending which side of the German/French language barrier you're on – could hardly be less appropriately named. The valleys between the Bernese Oberland and Lake Geneva have many attractions, but exceptional height and complete winter whiteness are not among them. This is a pretty, medium-high region of charming villages dotted around wide, wooded valleys, with lots of little skiing areas between 1000m and 2000m which are linked fully by lift pass, post bus and the little Montreux-Oberland-Bernois railway (MOB), and rather less completely by ski-lift and piste.

Gstaad is a picturesque, expensive village with an impressive list of famous visitors and part-time residents. This does not mean that it is a tremendously exciting place; it is genuinely exclusive, in the sense that celebrities go there to escape the consequences of celebrity – to live and party behind the closed doors of private chalets. Gstaad is also one of the few fashionable resorts where it really is more-or-less impossible to live economically; there are no inexpensive hotels. Although not an old village, it is traditional in style. The few old buildings have been carefully maintained and form a charming nucleus, and the rest of the village is also attractive in a neat, solid way. It is traditional, too, in the style of affluent Alpine holiday it offers. Lots of people go there not to ski, and there is plenty for them to do.

Not far to the north-east of Gstaad is a large area of friendly skiing shared by the more ordinary villages of Schönried, Saanenmöser, Zweisimmen and St Stephan. On the other side of the resort, Gstaad's skiing is linked to that above the unspoilt French-speaking village of Rougemont. And away at the western extremity of the region is the self-contained towny resort of Château d'Oex. The skiing is extended vertically by the glacier des Diablerets, to the south, which is shared with the resort of Les Diablerets (see Villars chapter).

There are no very attractive major resorts within day-trip range, but having a car is handy for exploring the Weisse Hochland, and for après-ski purposes. Parking can be a problem in Gstaad itself but not usually elsewhere. Access roads are often congested at weekends (especially the Spiez road), but otherwise not difficult. The Col du Pillon (for Les Diablerets) is occasionally closed.

The skiing top 2275m bottom 975m

The White Highlands skiing is scattered widely around the mostly north-facing aspects of the Saane/Sarine Valley, and of the saddle which separates this from the Simmental. Gstaad, the main resort, has three small separate areas, all of them starting a rather inconvenient distance from the resort centre and railway station. The large ski area on the broad flank of the mountains between Schönried and St Stephan is not connected by piste. In the other direction, Gstaad's Eggli ski area links up with the Videmanette area above Rougemont. (The outlying parts of the skiing can be reached by bus or by the little MOB railway which runs through Gstaad.) The Glacier des Diablerets, to the south, is useful for late-season skiing – see the chapter on Villars.

Gstaad: Wasserngrat A two-stage mixture of open and closed chair-lifts serves an interesting and challenging range of slopes. The middle station is low down, giving fairly long runs down the top half of the mountain – useful in poor snow conditions. The blue/red/black gradings reflect real differences in steepness, with moguls under the top chair, open intermediate slopes served by a long drag-lift to one side, and gentle easy runs down to the bottom station.

Gstaad: Wispile A similar area to the Wasserngrat, served by a two-stage gondola. Runs on the top half are challenging, those down to the valley rather less so but still interesting. Pistes on both the Wasserngrat and Wispile cover only a small part of the round, steeply-sided wooded mountains. From both top stations there is scope for off-piste descents through the woods, steeply into the side valleys.

Gstaad: Eggli The Eggli plateau is a popular sunny rendezvous, good for beginners if snow is sparse lower down. There are some good, easy slopes served by short drags and chair-lifts above and below it, going down to Saanen. The direct black run underneath the gondola is not very steep but it often presents challenging off-piste or half-piste conditions. There is an easier way back to Gstaad from the mid-station of the lifts up from Saanen. Wide trails through woods go down into the very attractive and peaceful Chalberhöni valley with a connecting lift to the Rougemont skiing up the far side.

Rougemont: Videmanette The two-stage gondola from Rougemont starts quite a walk below the village centre and station. One regular visitor reports that this lift is frequently closed in bad weather or windy conditions, when skiers who go via Eggli can enjoy marvellously empty slopes. The top of Videmanette is impressively hostile; the run down the front is steep and very narrow in parts, and skiable only infrequently. The main runs are behind the rock, with a wide, very gentle bowl served by chair-lift, reached from the top by a steep mogul field or an exposed path skirting it or by taking a short shuttle lift down. Below the chair-lift, a good, long varied red run goes back to Rougemont. Towards Eggli there are several variants of the descent down a wide, wooded but spacious slope under the long chair-lift up from the Chalberhöni. The black run is not a severe one.

Schönried Schönried's skiing is on both flanks of the gentle saddle on

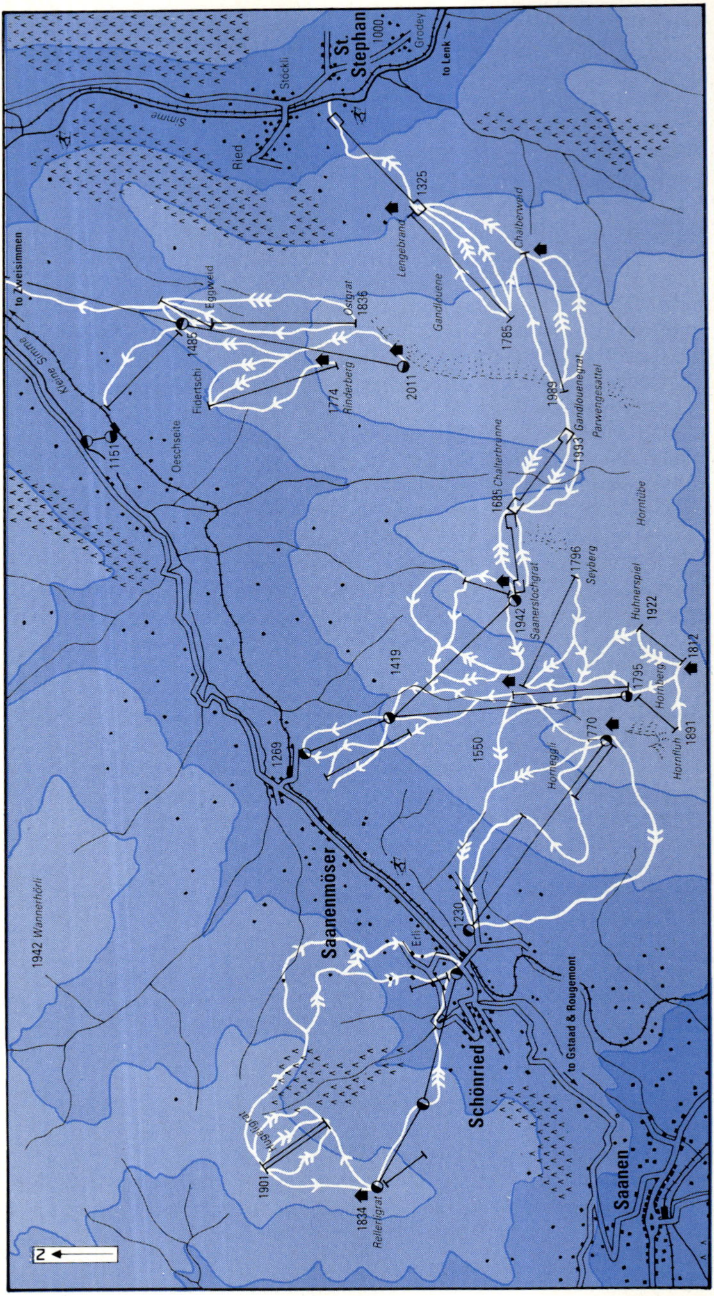
St. Stephan
to Lenk
Grodey
1000
Stöckli
Simme
Ried
1325
Lengebrand
Chalberweid
Gandlouene
1785
to Zweisimmen
Eggweid
Ostgrat
1836
1485
2011
Fidertschi
1774
Rinderberg
Kleine Simme
1151
Oeschseite
1989
Gandlouenegrat
Parwengesattel
1993
1685 Chalterbrunne
Horntübe
1796
Seyberg
1942
Saanerslochgrat
Hühnerspiel
1922
1812
1419
1795
Hornberg
1891
Hornfluh
1770
Horneggli
1550
1269
Saanenmöser
1942 Wannerhörli
1230
Erli
to Gstaad & Rougemont
Schönried
Saanen
1901
1834
Rellerligrat
N

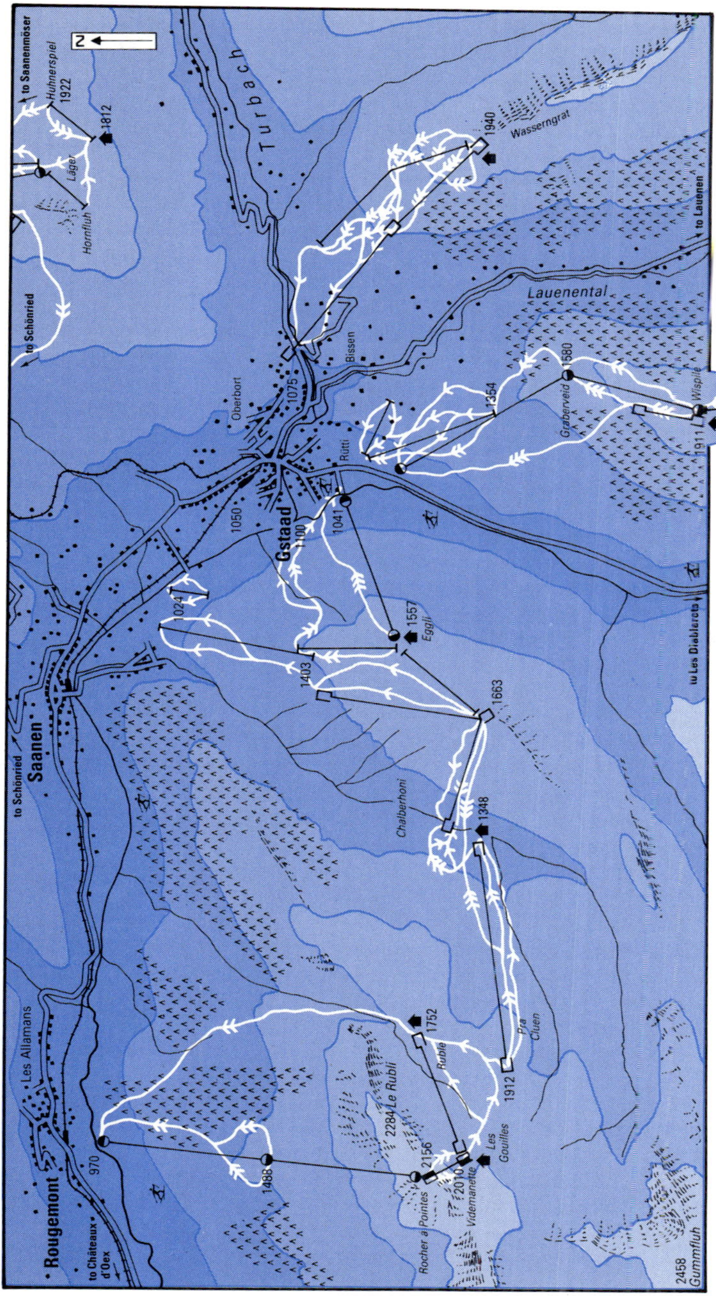
N
to Saanenmöser
Huhnerspiel
1922
1812
Läger
Hornfluh
to Schönried
Turbach
1940
Wasserngrat
to Lauenen
Lauenental
Bissen
Oberbort
1075
1580
Graberveid
1354
Wispile
1950
1911
Stand
Rütti
1050
Gstaad
1100
1041
1024
1557
Eggli
1403
to Les Diablerets
1663
to Schönried
Saanen
Chalberhöni
1348
Les Allamans
1752
Rubli
Pra
Cluen
1912
2284 Le Rubli
970
1488
2156
2010
Les
Gouilles
Rougemont
to Châteaux d'Oex
Rocher à Pointes
Videmanette
2458
Gummfluh

which the village (1231m) sits. A gondola from close to the road goes up to the top of the south-facing skiing at Rellerligrat (1834m). The most direct run, almost following the gondola, is graded black but is a straightforward intermediate run. A pair of short drags below the top serve worthwhile red slopes and give access to pleasant, long, easy blue and red runs to the village from Hugeligrat (1901m). Across the main road, from a point below and well away from it, a three-seat enclosed chair-lift has replaced the drag-lift up to Horneggli, from where indistinguishable black, red and blue pistes descend through another amiable wooded landscape. Better snow on the black can make it the easiest run on the mountain.

Saanenmöser/St Stephan Although Saanenmöser is only a mile or two along the road from Schönried and the resorts have lifts converging on the Hornfluh, their ski areas are for practical purposes separate. Saanenmöser's skiing is however shared with St Stephan, over the mountain in the Simmental, leading to Lenk. The skiing covers two valleys and the flank of the Simmental. From Saanenmöser a gondola goes up to Saanerslochgrat, and now also to Hornberg, previously served by a funicular. The valley between the two branches of the gondola is a network of pleasant easy and intermediate pistes, partly open and partly wooded, served by two drags starting from Lochstafel. Hornberg links by drag and piste with a short run on the Hühnerspiel, facing south-west, which is the steepest bit of skiing in this area, but barely black. From Saanerslochgrat, pistes descend into the open bowl of the Chaltebrunne valley; except in poor snow conditions (which are not uncommon on these sunny pistes) the red and black runs hold no terrors. On both flanks of the valley there is scope for gentle off-piste exploration. Beyond the valley are the open slopes above St Stephan; this is an extensive area with the standard tri-colour set of runs on each of the top lifts providing good, fast intermediate skiing of no great difficulty. The west-facing descent from Gandlouenegrat, encountered on the return, often provides well developed and challenging moguls.

Zweisimmen Although surrounded by the linked skiing of Saanenmöser and St Stephan, the ski area of Zweisimmen is not connected to it by piste or lift; there are reputedly off-piste routes between the two areas. The long gondola from the village to the Rinderberg serves a glorious, gentle, north-facing slope with motorway blue runs on most of its length and fast intermediate pistes at the top and down the supplementary drag-lifts. The skiing is largely open, but with patches of forest around.

Mountain restaurants are to be found in most of the obvious places; they are generally attractive, but expensive. There are particularly attractive restaurants on the way down from the Videmanette to the Chalberhöni, in the valley itself and around the Eggli.

The lift system is a bit old-fashioned, but **queues** are not usually a problem except during Swiss holidays in February and at weekends. Around Gstaad the main complaint is the annoying distance of lifts from the resort centre. Zweisimmen's skiing is still not linked to the surrounding lift network. Helicopter lifts can be had to various peaks.

The resort

Gstaad amounted to very little until the railway came in the first decade of this century. The village centre is spacious but not awkwardly spread out, and is set in and around a wide U-bend in the railway line, mostly along a single, winding main street which is a busy through-route. There are dozens of luxury shops for furs, food, jewellery and clothes (Dior, Hermès, Piaget), and watchmakers by appointment to sheikhs, who have winter branches in Gstaad.

Nearly all the **accommodation** is in hotels, nearly all expensive, especially in Gstaad itself. The famous and fantastic Palace dominates the resort from its hillside. It costs about £100 a head for half board unless you are someone's servant (in which case you cost a mere £30) or a dog (£10 with food). For this, needless to say, there are plenty of facilities – fitness centre, pool, ice rink, nightclub and squash courts. Other large, very comfortable hotels around the town are quieter and, at about half the price of the Palace, still expensive. In the village centre, most of the hotels are along the main street. By far the most attractive are the Rössli (✆43412) and the Olden (✆43444), beautiful old chalets right in the middle of town, both comfortably modernised without losing

Gstaad facts

Lift payment

Passes Area pass covers all lifts in Gstaad, villages east to St Stephan and west to Château d'Oex, and the Glacier des Diablerets; also train, local buses and swimming pool. Passes available for day and half day; also any six days in the season.
Cost 6-day pass SF180.
Children 40% off, under 16.
Beginners Coupons or lift pass.
Summer skiing Diablerets glacier; 3 lifts.

Ski school

Classes 10.00–2.45 with 60min for lunch.
Cost 6 days SF137. Private lessons SF40/hr.
Children Ski kindergarten, age 4 up, 10.00–2.45, 6 days SF137. Non-ski kindergarten, ages 3–7, 9.30–5.00, 6 days SF125.
Special courses

Cross-country skiing

Trails Gstaad to Château d'Oex 15km, Gstaad to Gsteig 11km, 6km of loops in Launen Valley.

Not skiing

Facilities Swimming (free with lift pass), sauna, tennis, squash, skating (natural and artificial rinks), curling, fitness centre, 50km cleared paths, hot-air balloons, horse-riding, bowling, cinema, sleigh rides.

Medical facilities

In resort Doctor, dentist, chemist.
Hospital Saanen (3km).

Getting there

Airport Geneva; transfer about 3hr.
Railway Station in resort.
Road Via Lausanne or Bern; chains may be needed.

Available holidays

Resort beds 1,000 in hotels, 3,500 in apartments.
Package holidays Kuoni (Ht), Made to Measure (Ht), Ski Club of GB (Ht), Ski Sutherland (Ht), Swiss Travel Service (Ht)

Further information

Tourist office ✆(30) 41055. Tx 922211.

their character. They are very popular places to eat and drink, with a lively atmosphere and a variety of bars and restaurants, as well as being comfortable and very friendly places to stay. The Olden is slightly smarter, has more comfortable bedrooms and is more expensive, especially its restaurant.

There is plenty of **après-ski** entertainment, traditional and modern. Tea-rooms (Chez Esther), simple woody bars where locals gather for beer and cards (the Olden), smart restaurants with musical entertainment (the Chesery), discothèques (the Palace hotel's Green-Go), fondue evenings in various mountain restaurants. Among Gstaad restaurants the Olden is good, fashionable and expensive; the Curling-Restaurant and the Rössli are popular, friendly and less expensive. The Chlösterli is a magnificent 17th-century barn of a chalet about 3km towards Gsteig; dancing to a live band in the central open-plan area and small dining rooms adjoining; expensive. Local youth fills the rather kitsch Harvey's Pub in Saanen. Much more commendable is the Reusch in Gsteig. Up-to-date films, many in English.

Gstaad is a very attractive and popular place for a **non-skiing** holiday. Apart from good resort facilities, there are plenty of interesting excursion possibilities. **Cross-country** runs are long and attractive, but all at low altitude along the valleys except at the recently developed Sparenmoos area above Zweisimmen. The tourist offices provide maps indicating the trail gradients. Cross-country skiers can catch buses back to Gstaad from Chlösterli (half way to Gsteig), and trains back from Château d'Oex and Rougemont. There are trails illuminated in the evening.

Provided snow cover is adequate, the **nursery slopes** at the bottom of the Wispile (Gstaad), Saanen, Schönried and Saanenmöser are all adequate, and there is plenty of scope for progression to longer runs.

We have no recent reports on **ski school**. Although this is mainly a medium-altitude skiing area, there are high mountains to the south and plenty of ski touring excursions are possible, notably to the Wildhorn, reached via Lenk. Guides can be hired.

Minor resorts

Rougemont 870m
Only a few miles from Gstaad, this French-speaking village is in another, more picturesque, world of old wooden chalets and barns. The Valrose (✆48146) is adequately placed for the station and the Videmanette gondola, and one of the cheapest places to stay in the whole area. Among the attractions of the village is the warm, rustic and inexpensive Cerf restaurant (excellent fondues to the accompaniment of saw-playing). There is a floodlit slalom course with artificial snow. Cross-country trails stretch for miles in both directions along the valley.

Tourist office ✆(29) 48333.

Schönried 1230m
Schönried is a roadside straggle of a village, with no particular appeal

except that it is fairly centrally placed for the Weisse Hochland skiing, and has some of it on its doorstep – or nearly so. It is also slightly higher than neighbouring resorts, presumably to the benefit of its nursery slopes. Hotels along the road include some fairly sumptuous ones with swimming pools open to the public, and simpler places. There is squash, a natural ice rink and a cross-country trail to Saanenmöser.
Tourist office ✆(30) 41919.

Saanenmöser 1270m

Saanenmöser barely amounts to a village, but has a couple of hotels well placed for access to the skiing – the Hornberg (✆44440) and the less expensive Bahnhof (✆41506) – about the cheapest hotel in this whole area. There is a natural ice rink.
Tourist office ✆(30) 42222.

Zweisimmen 950m

Zweisimmen is an unexceptional village of no great charm, but with abundant inexpensive accommodation well-placed for the ski-lifts and the station (for connections to other resorts). The very simple Derby (✆21438) is right beside the Rinderberg lift. Two larger and more comfortable hotels are the Rawyl zum Sternen (✆21251) by the station, and the Krone (✆22626) in the centre. Cross-country skiing is good, with very extensive trails along the Simmental to Lenk, and a recently developed domain up on the Sparenmoos (1640m–1790m). There are long cleared walks, a 7km toboggan run down from Sparenmoos, snowshoe outings, badminton and tennis, a kindergarten (in high season), natural ice rink, and some fairly unsophisticated nightlife, including evening fondue parties in mountain restaurants. **St Stephan** is a small, peaceful village a few miles up the valley towards Lenk, with some attractive old hotels. Although it has the attraction of skiing links with Saanenmöser, getting around by train to take advantage of the lift pass is less easy than it is from Zweisimmen.
Tourist office ✆(30) 21133. Tx 922284.

Château d'Oex 1000m

Château d'Oex is a small established resort, pleasant enough but without much Alpine atmosphere. It has plenty of cross-country skiing on hand, and an artificial rink, but no pool. A cable-car from the centre climbs steeply to the base of the ski area (1225m), where a gondola goes up to La Braye (1630m). Supported by three drag-lifts, the gondola serves a friendly, wooded area of imprecisely defined easy and intermediate pistes facing roughly north-east – pleasant, but rather limited. Easy and intermediate pistes go on down to the valley in much the same vein, but arrive some way from the resort, at the foot of a chair-lift which will take you back into the skiing. Buses run to the resort. Cross-country trails run along the valley to Rougemont and beyond. There is an artificial rink for skating and curling, and indoor riding. A six-day local lift pass costs much less than the area pass.
Tourist office ✆(29) 47788. Tx 940022. **Package holidays** Global (Ht), Intasun (Ht), Made to Measure (Ht Sc), Neilson (Ht), Ski NAT (Ht), Ski Sutherland (Ht), Ski Travelaway (Ht), Swiss Travel Service (Ht).

Sanatorium rejuvenated

Leysin Switzerland 1300m

Leysin is a large and decidedly institutional-looking old health resort spread widely across a steep and very sunny mountainside, high above the dark Rhône valley near Lake Geneva. Its annual 1,900 hours of intense sunshine are nearly double the London average, so they say.

Several of the largest residential establishments, including the former Grand Hotel at the top of the resort, are now colleges – two of them American – and the resort attracts many school parties, not least from Britain. As a result Leysin has a much less aged population and a much less staid atmosphere than its looks suggest, and denim and cowboy hats are an incongruous feature of both resort and the slopes. Equally unexpected is Leysin's appeal to serious climbers, who are attracted by the two impressive dolomitic towers – the Tour d'Aï (2331m) and Tour Mayen (2326m) – that dominate the resort.

A train climbs directly from the valley town of Aigle to Leysin, stopping at various points on its way up through the resort, between 1250m and 1450m. Roads zig-zag up the hill from the old village, with the main lift station on a hairpin about half-way up. It is an awkward place to negotiate, whether on foot or in a car (parking is difficult), but a bus service (not free) does a regular circuit. Below the village is a large flat area of open fields with good nursery slopes and paths for walkers and riders.

Leysin's main area of skiing starts with a gondola ride to Mayen (1940m) and extends eastwards across the mountainside, lightly wooded and dotted with chalets, in a chain of short runs and lifts, nowhere very taxing on the legs – all the runs are blue and all the lifts are chairs. The scenery is very pretty and the skiing agreeable. Most of the runs get a lot of sun (the mountain faces south-east), and snow cover is presumably not ultra-reliable. It will not be long before the far end of Leysin's lift chain links up with the skiing of the small resort of Les Mosses. The longest runs are back down to the resort, a fast trail through the woods with some off-piste variations cutting the corners. A recently added T-bar makes it possible to get back up to Mayen without traversing back past some nursery lifts to the base station.

The alternative access lift, another gondola from the same main lift station, climbs more steeply to the peak of Berneuse (2048m) over a very tempting open slope to which skiers are denied access in the interests of young trees and perhaps their own safety: it was here that Dougal Haston, conqueror of so many infinitely more fearsome mountains, died in an avalanche. The view from the top station, which sweeps round in an arc from Mont Blanc to the Eiger, may by now be enjoyable from a new revolving panoramic restaurant. From Berneuse an easy path leads across to just above Mayen, but the main runs are back down to the bottom, soon joining up with the runs down from Mayen. One is black, starting with an awkward walk along a ridge from the top station. Skiing of a different kind from the Leysin norm is provided by a single drag-lift in the wide bowl behind Berneuse and beneath the cliffs of the Tour d'Aï. There is (or at least was, when we visited) no piste in this bowl: you just go up and pick a way down. The vertical range is not great, but there is plenty of space and one side is fairly steep.

Out of the way on the western side of the resort, a separate ski area consisting of a chair and a couple of short drags is little used except by ski-bobbers and residents of this extremity of the diffuse resort.

The main lift pass covers all lifts but not the resort bus. Adventurous skiers may prefer the Alpes Vaudoises lift pass, about 50 per cent more expensive, but also valid at Villars and Les Diablerets (including the glacier lifts) and a few smaller nearby resorts, and on the bus services between the resorts.

Like other resorts of its kind, Leysin caters for a wide range of activities – squash, riding, tennis, skating, curling, walks, sleigh rides, 15km of cross-country trails – and there is the usual assortment of clinics, gyms, saunas and beauty parlours.

The Hotel La Paix (✆341375) is a delightful old chalet beside the railway just above the centre of the resort. It is proud of its subtitle, Au Vieux Pays: do not expect up-to-the-minute Swiss comfort. At the other end of the range of style and price, the Hotel Central Residence (✆341211) is a large modern block with conference rooms, an indoor pool and gym. Between the two extremes, the Colina (✆341012) is a three-star hotel close to the lift station. Club Med occupies two hotels in the middle of the resort, and its ski school is very prominent on the slopes.

Tourist office ✆(025) 342244. Tx 456166. **Package holidays** Club Med (Ht) Kuoni (Ht), Schools Abroad (Ht), Ski Sutherland (Ht), Skiscope (Ht), SkiSet (Ht).

Missing link

Villars Switzerland 1300m

Good for *Easy runs, beautiful scenery, sunny slopes, cross-country skiing, not skiing, short airport transfers, easy road access, rail access*
Bad for *Tough runs, freedom from cars*

Linked resort: Les Diablerets

Villars is a long-established all-round resort (complete with mountain railway from the valley and up into the skiing) in a beautiful, sunny balcony setting, facing south-west across the Rhône valley. A former British favourite, it has been rather neglected by tour operators in recent years but is now enjoying something of a revival of interest – perhaps triggered by the opening of a skiing link with Les Diablerets (though, as we explain below, that link does not seem to be operated with any great conviction).

The resort does not have the charm of some of its traditional Swiss competitors – in particular, it suffers from traffic in the main street close to the station – but most of the buildings are in chalet style, and the fringes of the village are pleasantly rustic. It is in the French-speaking part of Switzerland. There are several boarding schools in the locality, Aiglon College most prominent among them.

Villars' ski area is not large, does not reach very high, and contains little to challenge the expert; but it is attractive and varied – well suited to intermediate skiers who have not been spoilt by the vast networks of French mega-resorts. The link with Les Diablerets – another friendly, intermediate's resort with the additional feature of glacier skiing on the mountain of the same name – is rather awkward, but certainly adds to the appeal of the place for adventurous skiers.

The skiing top 2970m bottom 800m

The mountain railway from the west side of the resort centre goes up to **Bretaye** (1800m) – a col with a couple of hotel-restaurants at the heart of the main ski area, with drags and chair-lifts going up the slopes on either side. The east-facing runs from Grand and Petit Chamossaire are open red slopes, very exposed at the top, steep enough to be satisfying, but not long. Roc d'Orsay, on the flank of Grand Chamossaire, can be reached by a gondola from the northern fringes of the resort as well as a drag from Bretaye, and has a couple of entertaining runs served by a short drag on the back of the hill. The west-facing runs from Chaux Ronde to Bretaye cover an open slope which is steep enough to provide a slalom course directly above the col, with easier blue routes available. The black run from Chaux Ronde served by a chair-lift is pretty and uncrowded, but of nothing like black steepness and easily skied by intermediates (though it is unprepared,

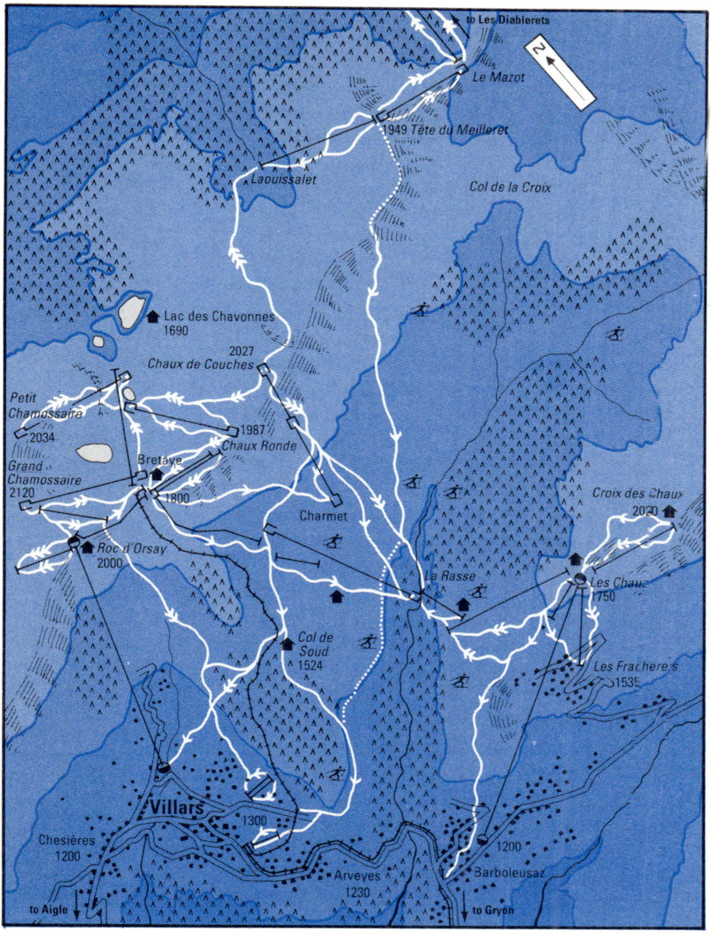

and takes some time to become skied into a piste-like state).

There are pistes from Roc d'Orsay and Bretaye to the village, the latter linking with extensive, open, easy, sunny slopes going down to La Rasse. The chair-lift to Chaux de Conches from this area serves a range of amiable blue and red runs across the mountainside from its middle station, and below the top section is a bumpy black run which is reportedly 'very steep, very worthwhile'.

Drag-lifts from La Rasse link with the otherwise separate skiing on the open flanks of **Les Chaux** – further easy-intermediate skiing of modest extent. The run to the hamlet of Les Fracherets gets a lot of sun and suffers accordingly. A long gondola from Barboleusaz (where there are big car parks) offers an alternative way into the skiing. The run down the gondola poses no difficulties except that it gets an unhealthy amount of afternoon sun.

The Chaux de Conches chair-lift also gives access to Les Diablerets. The link is not organised as well as we or our reporters would wish. When we skied it in 1986, it was only at the point of departure from the Villars lifts that we encountered a sign announcing that the run was effectively off-piste. A reporter who visited in high-season 1987 was told the link was open, but found it closed. The run is rightly graded black because of an unprepared and steep mogul-field near the top. It is a pity that it is thus, because the run thereafter is lovely motorway cruising, and the skiing of Les Diablerets at the end of the journey is not difficult. The Laouissalet drag delivers you to the Tête du Meilleret, the top of Les Diablerets' skiing (excluding the glacier). On your return you are delivered to this same point by a chair-lift, and then face a long, tedious plod along the ridge before embarking on the splendid easy run, across an open mountainside dotted with chalets, back to La Rasse and from there up to Bretaye or down to Villars.

The skiing on the Villars side of **Les Diablerets** is nicely varied easy-intermediate stuff, on north-facing trails cut through the forest, down to the resort and to the slightly lower village of Vers l'Eglise. The runs are not graded on the piste map, but are in practice all easy reds or interesting blues. On the far side of the village, a gondola goes up to the sunny, open slopes of Isenau – a consistently gentle area apart from one moderately steep drag at the top.

On our winter visits we have not found the **Glacier des Diablerets** open, so we have not experienced the apparently very worthwhile runs round the back of the Oldenhorn from the top station. Nor have we been able to sample the runs to the bottom stations. We can report that the remaining run from Cabane des Diablerets to Oldenegg (although scenically impressive and a distinctive high-mountain run) is hardly worth the effort involved in getting to it.

There is no shortage of **mountain restaurants**, several of them accessible to non-skiers; the main one at Bretaye is an 'awful cafeteria', but there are more attractive chalets beyond the col.

Lift **queues** are rarely serious, even in high season; congestion on the pistes, particularly the gentle run behind Bretaye down towards Lac des Chavonnes, can be more of a problem. The piste map looks clear but misrepresents some runs and invents others.

The resort

The resort is a slightly diffuse affair, spread along a road which descends to the valley in both directions; there is one village focus at the junction of the road up to the Col de la Croix (closed in winter) and another along the hillside at the station where the railways up and down the mountain terminate. The road in one direction passes through the satellite village of Chesières; in the other, through the spread-out community of Arveyes.

Most of the **accommodation** is in apartments and private chalets, but there are also numerous hotels, many of them above the centre of the village in quiet wooded suburbs leading to the Roc d'Orsay gondola

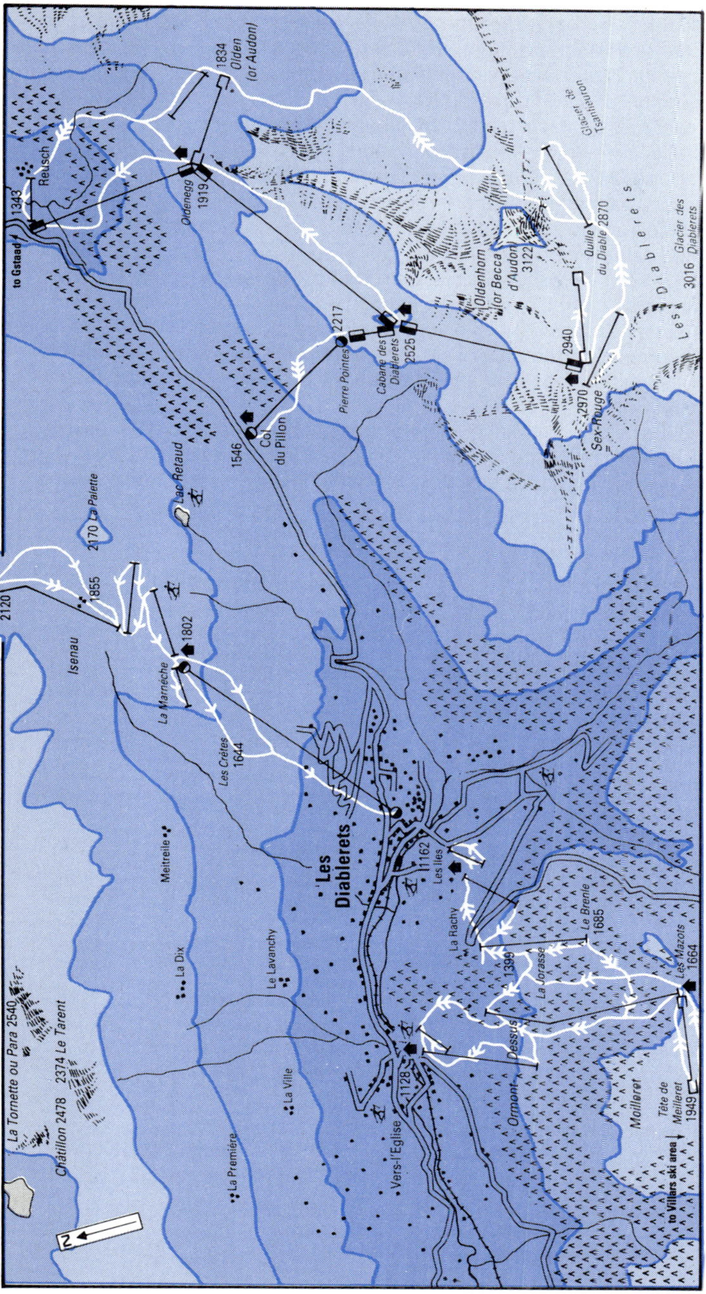

to Gstaad
1343
Reusch
Oldenegg
1919
1834
Olden
(or Audon)
Glacier de
Tsanfleuron
Quille
du Diable 2870
Oldenhorn
(or Becca
d'Audon)
3122
Les Diablerets
Glacier des
Diablerets
3016
2940
2970
Sex-Rouge
2217
Pierre Pointes
Cabane des
Diablerets
2525
1546
Col
du Pilon
Lac Retaud
2170 La Palette
Florietaz
2120
1855
Isenau
1802
La Marnèche
Les Crêtes
1644
Les Diablerets
1162
Les Iles
La Rachy
Le Brenle
1685
1399
La Jorasse
Les Mazots
1664
Meitreile
La Dix
Le Lavanchy
La Tornette ou Para 2540
2374 Le Tarent
Châtillon 2478
La Ville
1128
Vers-l'Eglise
La Première
Ormont-Dessus
Meilleret
Tête de
Meilleret
1949
to Villars ski area
N

and accessible on skis from Bretaye when snow conditions are good. One such is the pleasant Renardière (✆352592), occupying three large chalets. Reporters are unanimous in speaking highly of the big, modern Eurotel (✆353131), in a similar position – 'good food, good service, quiet rooms'. It has a pool and other facilities. Directly opposite the station is the chalet-style Alpe-Fleurie (✆352494) – friendly, but reported to have small rooms. The Montesano (✆352551), out of the resort at Arveyes, is reportedly very jolly. The monstrous Palace hotel, which dominates the resort when seen from a distance, is now a Club Med establishment.

On our own January visits we have not been surprised to find the **après-ski** scene quiet. But a February visitor reports that 'the town seemed to stop in the evenings. Everyone disappeared – the streets became deserted'. There are tea-rooms, bars, one or two discos and a reasonable range of restaurants, from a pizzeria to the determinedly rustic Vieux Villars.

Villars is an excellent resort for **non-skiers**. The mountain railway gives dignified access to Bretaye for meeting up with skiers, the village is an attractive place to while away time, the sports facilities are good

Villars facts

Lift payment

Passes Single pass covers Villars and Les Diablerets lifts (but not the glacier). Regional passes also available covering Leysin and other resorts. Day, morning and afternoon passes available.
Cost 6-day pass SF155.
Beginners Limited lift pass included in ski school rates.
Children 20% off, under 16.

Ski school

As well as the main Swiss Ski School (of which we give details here) there is an Ecole de Ski Moderne, which employs *ski évolutif* for beginners.
Classes 1¾hr, mornings only.
Cost 6½ days SF90. Private lessons SF40/hr.
Children Classes, 6 days SF75. All-day skiing, including meals and lift pass, 6 days SF360. Ski kindergarten, ages 3–10, 9.00–4.30, 6 days with meals SF230. Several non-ski kindergartens.
Special courses Monoski, surf, racing, off-piste, touring.

Medical facilities

In resort Doctors, dentist, physiotherapist, chemists.
Hospital Aigle (13km).

Cross-country skiing

Trails 30km in total, mainly up the valley which splits the Alpine ski area, towards the Col de la Croix; shorter loops at Bretaye.

Not skiing

Facilities Tennis (6 courts), skating (indoor artificial rink), curling, swimming, bowling, riding, fitness centre, ski-bob runs, 25km signposted walks.

Getting there

Airport Geneva; transfer about 2hr.
Railway Mountain railway in village, connects with main line at Aigle or Bex.
Road Via Lausanne or Bern (longer but simpler); chains may be needed.

Available holidays

Resort beds About 1,700 in hotels, 5,000 in chalets and apartments.
Package holidays Club Med (Ht), Crystal (Ht), Inghams (Ht Sc), Intasun (Ht), Made to Measure (Ht), Neilson (Ht Sc), Ski Club of GB (Ht), Ski Esprit (Ch Ap), Swiss Travel Service (Ht)

Further information

Tourist office ✆(25) 353232. Tx 456200.

(though the smart tennis/squash centre is extremely expensive), and excursions to Montreux, Lausanne or even Geneva are possible. The **cross-country** skiing trails are attractive.

The **nursery slopes** immediately above the railway station are gentle, open and sunny and there are very easy (though sometimes crowded) pistes up the mountain at Bretaye.

Most **ski school** classes meet at Bretaye, though the beginners classes meet at the Palace nursery lift above the village. Our most recent reporter found his instructor 'very, very helpful, with perfectly good English'. Earlier reports are less strongly expressed, but still favourable. There are guides available for ski tours, including the Haute Route, a few miles away to the south.

Les Diablerets 1160m

Les Diablerets (the village) is a relaxed, spacious sprawl of chalets at the bottom of a broad U-shaped valley with the craggy crest of Les Diablerets (the mountain) at its head. There are adequate non-skiing amusements – swimming, 20km of cross-country trails, indoor and outdoor skating and curling, toboggan descents from the Col de la Croix, and riding. There are only a few hotels, mostly modern and anonymous, and a couple of them conspicuously at odds with the general chalet style of the resort. The modest old Auberge de la Poste (✆531124) is a cheap and cheerful exception, in a good central position slightly closer to the Isenau lift than to the Meilleret ones. Après-ski is not riotous, but the resort works hard to lay on musical and other events. As well as a branch of the Swiss Ski School, there is a group of mountain guides operating under the name Ski Total, specialising in off-piste excursions. There is an kindergarten offering all-day care with lunch.

Tourist office ✆(25) 531358. Tx 456175. **Package holidays** Bladon Lines (Ht Ch), Crystal (Ht), Made to Measure (Ht), Ski Sutherland (Ht).

Portes du Soleil: open invitation

Avoriaz France 1800m

Good for *Big ski area, nursery slopes, skiing convenience, family holidays, freedom from cars, short airport transfers, resort-level snow*
Bad for *Not skiing, Alpine charm, après-ski, mountain restaurants*

Linked resorts: Châtel, Champéry, Les Crosets, Champoussin, Morgins

If 'Portes du Soleil' doesn't tempt you, the promoters of this huge Franco-Swiss ski area have a ready supply of other slogans. How about 'Ski sans frontière'? Or 'Le plus grand domaine skiable du monde'? This last may sound familiar, because the rival French ski area of the Trois Vallées has for years been awarding itself the very same distinction. The fact that neither area has established its superiority over the other should not be taken to mean that they are indistinguishable. Whereas the Trois Vallées is four adjacent, densely mechanised ski areas efficiently linked together, the Portes du Soleil is a looser network of skiing in as many as 15 resorts, some of them linked up in only twos and threes. There is a core circuit of skiing linking the resorts of Avoriaz and Châtel in France with Morgins and Champéry in Switzerland – and it is the linked skiing of these resorts (and one or two smaller Swiss ones) which draws people back. The skiing in Avoriaz caters well for most standards of skier, and the circuit can be done by early intermediates with a sense of adventure. There is now also a linear link between Avoriaz and the extensive Morzine/Les Gets area (see separate chapter).

Avoriaz is much the most popular resort with British skiers. It is one of the most individual of French purpose-built resorts, built on a steep slope, in a bold architectural style which fits in with the high, craggy surroundings better than most such developments. It has adopted neither the monolith approach nor the multiple hamlet approach, but is basically a village made up of apartment blocks. There is skiing below it, above it, beside it, through it; but it is not quite as convenient as it sounds, because most of the skiing ends up at the foot of the village and you often need to take a lift to get home. It is predominantly a family self-catering resort, and is not fashionable or smart, but has more après-ski life than many other such places. The apartments in which you cater for yourself are unlikely to be the high point of your holiday.

The main alternatives for British skiers are Châtel and Morgins, both of them on the main skiing circuit. Châtel is a much-developed old French village with a lot of modest hotel accommodation, now with an established place on the British market. Morgins in Switzerland is a pleasant, spacious, chalet-style resort, mainly of recent development. The other main resort is Champéry, an atmospheric old Swiss mountain village, its long main street lined by wooden chalets; it is not ideally placed for skiing, whether on the circuit or off it.

You are unlikely to make any use of a car while in Avoriaz, and you may spend your time wondering whether it will start on departure day after sitting on an exposed col at 1800m for a week or two. The road up to the resort is long, tortuous and snowy, and expeditions are better organised around the cable-car to the valley. Bus connections into Morzine, however, are reported to be infrequent and erratic.

The skiing top2275m bottom 1100m

The skiing covered by the Portes du Soleil lift pass embraces hundreds of miles of piste. We are limiting ourselves here to the main circuit, where most British visitors spend their time. Reporters are unanimous in finding the Portes du Soleil piste maps unhelpful. Piste marking and direction signing on the Swiss side of the circuit, dangerously casual in our experience, have been improved according to a recent reporter who had no problem with the complete circuit; but another still found the route marking confusing. You may be well advised to allow time for retracing steps. The skiing of Morzine and Les Gets, covered by the pass, is described in a separate chapter.

Avoriaz The skiing around Avoriaz itself can be divided into four areas. Above the village is an upward extension of the main nursery slopes, Le Plateau, with a variety of drags serving runs from green to very green – a splendid though rather exposed area for confidence-building. At the bottom of the village there are essentially three alternative directions.

Directly south of the village is the main Hauts Forts sector, which from Avoriaz looks steeper than it is. There are some trees towards the bottom, but the skiing is mainly above the tree-line; there are several marked pistes, but the whole bowl becomes a piste as skiers stray all over it. The runs are all easy, getting a little more difficult towards the bottom. Unfortunately, they get very crowded; the ski school comes up here and so do the fledgling racers, who occasionally close off part of the piste for practice.

A long chair starting on the left but veering right from the same area at the bottom of the village takes you to the most challenging skiing in Avoriaz. There are several routes descending all or part of the way towards Prodain, 650m below Avoriaz and over 1300m below Les Hauts Forts. The mogulled pistes become narrower as you descend into the trees, with an easier variant via the Le Crot chair-lift. The runs are crowded in the late afternoon, and dodgy for snow, but very valuable in bad weather.

The third direction is by chair and drag to the north-west-facing bowl between Pas de Chavanette and Col du Fornet. Here there are several marked runs but it is another area of wide open, intermediate skiing above the tree-line where you can ski virtually wherever you want; there is an easy trail back to the bottom of the village. An alternative way back from Chavanette for adventurous intermediates is over into the next valley – a lovely, easy run after the top mogul-field – down to Les Marmottes and now on down to Ardent, from where a ten-person gondola now goes back up to Les Marmottes.

Champéry/Les Crosets/Champoussin Chavanette is where the skiing of Avoriaz meets the big, open ski-fields of these three Swiss resorts. It starts with the notorious 'Swiss Wall' – a long, steep mogul slope of about 300m vertical, easily covered in a single fall when the snow is hard. The severity and danger depend critically on the very variable snow conditions – the slope gets a lot of sun. There is reportedly an alternative, easier black to the left side, or you can take the chair-lift down instead. There is acres of open easy skiing served by the drags either side of the Chavanette chair, connecting with the Planachaux slopes above Champéry, and with the adjacent bowl of Les Crosets. Planachaux is now reached from Champéry by a big cable-car, or by chair-lift from Grand Paradis. The pistes down to the valley end at this point, having wound their way through hamlets and across the river

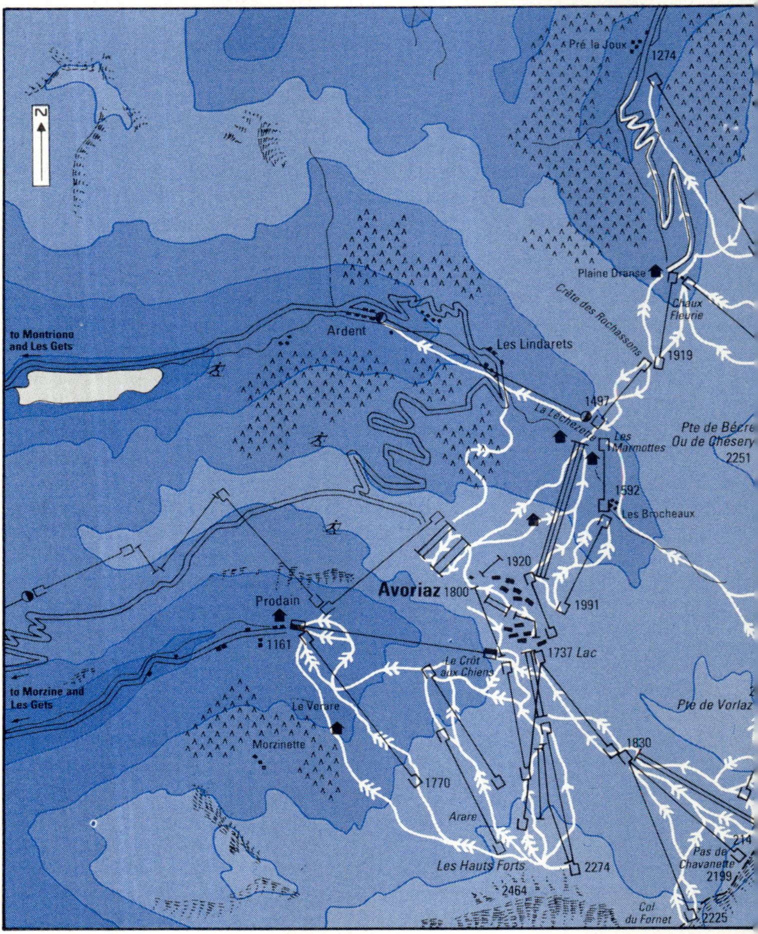

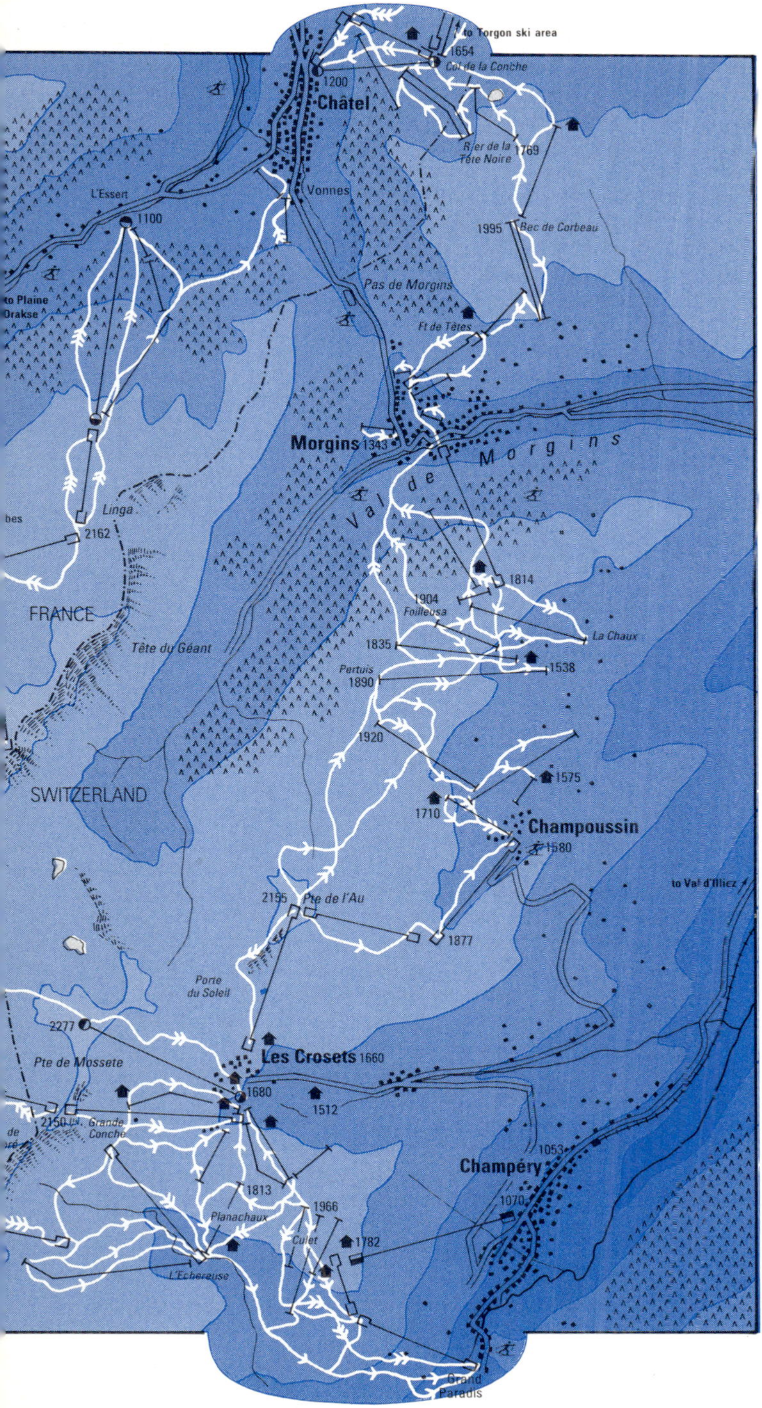
to Torgon ski area
1654
Col de la Conche
1200
Châtel
Rier de la Tête Noire
1769
L'Essert
1100
Vonnes
1995
Bec de Corbeau
to Plaine Drakse
Pas de Morgins
Ft de Têtes
Morgins
1343
Val de Morgins
Linga
2162
1814
1904
Foilleusa
La Chaux
FRANCE
1835
Tête du Géant
Pertuis
1890
1538
1920
1575
SWITZERLAND
1710
Champoussin
1580
to Val d'Illiez
2155
Pte de l'Au
1877
Porte du Soleil
2277
Les Crosets
1660
Pte de Mossete
1680
1512
2150
Grande Conche
1053
Champéry
1813
1966
Planachaux
1070
Culet
1782
L'Echereuse
Grand Paradis

– an interesting route, and not difficult, but hard work. There are minibuses between Grand Paradis and Champéry.

Les Crosets sits above the tree-line surrounded by abundant, wide open pistes – good, easy to intermediate skiing, some of it north-facing but most of it sunny. There are lifts up to points on the French border, that to Cubore serving a steep unprepared (and often uncovered) black slope at the top which mellows as it descends. Via the Pointe de l'Au, a series of linked drags and easy-intermediate pistes makes the connection first with Champoussin and then with Morgins. The mountainside above Champoussin is broad and sunny, with little variety of terrain. This whole area is ideally suited to the beginner to intermediate skier; for good skiers the main interest will be in the extensive opportunity to venture off-piste.

Morgins/Châtel Morgins does not have much skiing on the side reached from Champoussin, but it includes a splendid north-facing intermediate trail through tall pine forests to the village. Skiers bent on the Soleil circuit then face a tedious uphill walk across the village to the nursery slopes and the lifts for Châtel. The area between Morgins and Châtel is a pleasant contrast to the bleak ski-fields of Avoriaz and Planachaux – a series of short drags and winding pistes, largely among thin woods, eventually takes you over the border to the open slopes of Super-Châtel, in France. The Morclan chair-lift from Super-Châtel up to 1970m serves the most challenging slope – basically a moderate red mogul-field. The map also shows a black piste down towards the village, which proved elusive when we visited. The top of this chair is the point of departure for Torgon, one of the furthest outposts of the Portes du Soleil empire. The rest of Super-Châtel's skiing is mostly easy-intermediate stuff, on wide areas above and below the big restaurant and lift station; the runs to the valley can be tricky in poor snow, which is not infrequent (they get the afternoon sun).

Châtel/Avoriaz It is at Châtel that the Soleil circuit breaks down. Whichever way you are travelling, the link cannot be made on skis; if going clockwise, a green traverse from the Linga lifts delivers you to the nursery slopes of Châtel, leaving a walk across the village to the ten-person gondola for Super-Châtel; if going anti-clockwise, a substantial bus-ride is needed from downtown Châtel to the gondola up to Linga, the first of a long chain of lifts and pistes towards Avoriaz. The skiing in this sector offers more variety than other major legs of the circuit, and includes a long, challenging but not severe black beside the Linga gondola (for skiers going clockwise or with the time to play about en route). The steepish slope above the gondola, served by a chair-lift, apparently now has a blue traverse built in to it as well as the red and black routes shown on the piste map. The run down the Combes chair-lift towards Avoriaz is a satisfying and attractive red, and the recently built Cornebois chair-lift which goes up from the same point should by now have some pistes of its own as well as connecting with the top of the Chaux des Rosées chair up from Plaine Dranse. The runs down this latter chair are quite challenging, the black offering a choice of routes down its wide mogul-field, with the steepest approaching 35° over a short pitch. One more lift and an easy run down brings you to Les

Marmottes, along with a lot of other skiers wanting a lift up to Avoriaz.

Mountain restaurants are not a strong point of the area as a whole. You need to plan your breaks, rather than hoping to find yourself happening on a suitable hut at just the right time. There is a charming little refuge on the way down to Grand Paradis from Planachaux, and Plaine Dranse between Avoriaz and Châtel has a couple of pleasant chalets, but most restaurants are purpose-built and not particularly pleasant.

At the end of the day, skiers returning to Avoriaz from Hauts Forts and Champéry form big **queues** at the bottom of the village for lifts up to their accommodation. Skiers returning from Châtel now do not meet quite such big queues as they once did at Les Marmottes, because of a recently added chair-lift up the valley to Les Brocheaux, where another chair, previously under-used, gives alternative access to Avoriaz. Geneva is close; and weekend skiers add to the crowds.

The resort

Avoriaz is reached from the valley either by a narrow, winding road or cable-car from Prodain, near Morzine. It is set on a long south-facing slope which steepens towards the bottom. Cars must be left in parks at the top of the slope; you have to take a horse-drawn sleigh or ratrac to get you and your luggage to your accommodation. The combined cost of parking and carriage (twice) came to £28 in 1988. There are also public lifts within buildings to help you get about when you're not on skis. The busiest part of the resort is the middle section, around the foot of the nursery slopes; there are lots of bars and restaurants lining the slopes, and shops for ski gear, clothes and food. The shopping is more varied than in some modern resorts; we have reports of reasonable prices in the Codec supermarket. What used to be an entirely open area beside the nursery slopes has now had an extravagant Maison du Tourisme placed in the middle of it, rather spoiling the view from the chairs which appear outside the cafés on a sunny day. The lack of cars and the specially enclosed nursery area suits children well, but with skiers and sleighs cutting through the resort it is hardly hazard-free.

Nearly all **accommodation** is in apartments; there are a couple of hotels, too, but they're indistinguishable from the apartment blocks. Some of the apartments are now getting tatty, and reports suggest that newer buildings are the best bet. Saskia 3, for example, is 'well equipped and comfortable', provided you halve the advertised number of bed spaces. Apartments in Alpages II are described by one reporter as 'quite disgracefully cramped'; another reporter went without hot water for a week. The Residence du Portes du Soleil is reportedly well maintained and has 'reasonable space'. Location in the resort is not very important for skiing purposes, but if you stay right at the top it can be rather a hike back after a night out.

Après-ski is fairly lively and varied by the standards of purpose-built resorts. There are lots of bars and all are fairly crowded in the evening; reporters felt they were generally expensive. There are more relaxed

Avoriaz facts

Lift payment

Passes Portes du Soleil pass covers all lifts. Local, day and half-days passes available.
Cost 6-day Portes du Soleil pass FF660. 6-day Avoriaz pass FF475.
Children 25% off Portes du Soleil pass, 21% off Avoriaz pass.
Beginners Special passes.

Ski school

Classes 2hr morning, 3hr afternoon.
Cost 6 full days FF625. Private lessons FF120/hr.
Children Ski school classes, ages 5–12, 6 days FF450. Ski kindergarten, ages 3–16, 9.00–5.30, 6 days with lunch FF820.
Special courses Touring, racing.

Cross-country skiing

Trails There are four circuits totalling 30km, on the way into the resort, of which 1km is for beginners.

Not skiing

Facilities Sauna, squash, aerobics, cinema, hang-gliding, snow motorcyles.

Medical facilities

In resort Medical centre, dentist, chemist.
Hospital Thonon (45km).

Getting there

Airport Geneva; transfer 2hr.
Railway Cluses (40km); bus and cable-car to resort. Thonon (45km); bus and cable-car to resort.
Road Via Geneva; chains may be needed. Cars must be left in open or covered parks away from the resort.

Available holidays

Resort beds 120 in hotels, 12,000 in apartments.
Package holidays Bladon Lines (Ht Sc), Blue Sky (Ht), Club Med (Ht), Enterprise (Sc), Horizon (Ht Sc), Inghams (Ht Sc), Made to Measure (Ht Sc), Neilson (Ht Sc), Ski West (Ht Sc), Supertravel (Ch), Thomson (Ht Sc), Vacations (Ht Sc)

Further information

Tourist office ✆50740211. Tx 385578.

cocktail and piano bars with even higher prices, and three discos. There are lots of restaurants, including pizzerias and several Asian/Oriental ones as well those doing serious French food, and reporters generally enjoyed their eating out.

We lack informed reports on the rewards of the **cross-country** trails, but they are quite lengthy and at high altitude. The resort cannot be recommended for **non-skiers**, although the cable-car (and then bus) offers a way of escape to less hostile surroundings in Morzine, and thence further afield. There is very little to do apart from skiing.

At Avoriaz the **nursery slopes** run alongside the top half of the village to Le Plateau; it is an excellent area, convenient for the bars and restaurants of the village, high and sunny.

Reports on the **ski school** are divided, with some highly complimentary comments and some quite scathing; one reporter had to change classes twice in search of the right standard and a caring instructor; another reporter found a 3½hr private person 'well worthwhile'. Opinions are divided, too, about the children's village; in principle, it seems a splendid facility, with games rooms as well as specially contrived slopes – and we have one recent favourable report. But other reports suggest that there is a lack of sympathy towards children who don't like wearing ski boots all day, and perhaps towards non-French children.

Minor resorts

Châtel France 1200m

Châtel is an old village which has been thoroughly overwhelmed by its recent development as a ski resort. It now sprawls along the road running through towards Morgins, down the hillside and along the valley towards the Linga lift which is its connection with the skiing of Avoriaz. In the opposite direction, taking the Portes du Soleil clockwise, is Morgins, reached via Super-Châtel (1650m). This skiing service station is the heart of Châtel's own skiing, directly above the village. The valley lift departures are linked by free *navettes*, which have to fight their way through a village centre which is choked with cars and buses – particularly at weekends. There are lots of hotels – the great majority modest chalets offering good value – and hundreds of private chalets and apartments to rent; there are 20 ski shops and a dozen restaurants – all buzzing when the French are in town. Long cross-country trails go up and down the valley, and there is a short loop at Super-Châtel. Châtel has large nursery slopes inconveniently located outside the village, and big open areas up the mountain at Super-Châtel.

Tourist office ✆50732244. Tx 385856. **Package holidays** Bladon Lines (Ht Ch Sc), Enterprise (Ht Sc), Freedom (Ht), Global (Ht), Horizon (Ht), Hourmont (Ht), Ski Club of GB (Ht), Ski Total (Ht Sc), Ski West (Ht Ch Cl Sc), Thomson (Ht Sc), VFB (Ht Sc).

Morgins Switzerland 1350m

Morgins is a spacious residential resort spreading across its valley just below the pass separating it from French Châtel. Almost all the accommodation is in chalets and apartments, and the resort is fairly quiet and relaxed. The broad, sunny nursery slopes, of which there are two, are 'excellent, but prone to invasion by other skiers.' There are a handful of hotels; most reporters have stayed in the big, token-chalet-style Bellevue (✆772771) which looks over the resort from its hillside, and have generally approved. Reporters say that La Forêt is 'a glorified youth hostel' and the Bellavista is largely given over to school groups. There is a reasonable range of shops, two discos and a few bar-restaurants, but it is not a resort for keen après-skiers. There is indoor tennis and a natural ice-rink which is not reliably available; the small pool at the Bellevue is open to the public. The three cross-country loops amount to 15km, and there is a long marked but not prepared route to Champoussin. The one report we have on ski school is favourable.

Tourist office ✆(25) 772361. Tx 456261. **Package holidays** Kuoni (Ht), Schools Abroad (Ht), Ski Esprit (Ch), Skiscope (Ht), SkiSet (Ht).

Champéry Switzerland 1050m

Champéry is a pretty and rather sleepy traditional Alpine village set in attractive surroundings on the side of a valley facing the savage peaks of the Dents du Midi. The main street, mainly closed to traffic, runs the length of the village, climbing gently from the station to the ski-lifts at the opposite end. Most of the hotels, restaurants and shops are to be found along its length, although there is some new development down the hill on the valley road which skirts the village. The sports centre is also in the valley bottom, with good facilities for skating, curling, swimming and bowling. There are cleared walks, and a short cross-country course up the valley at Grand Paradis. Champéry's nursery slopes, at Planachaux, are a bit on the steep side. Food shopping is good – in addition to the supermarkets there are small specialist shops; there are also shops selling clothes and souvenirs as well as ski equipment (a clue to the village's summer popularity). There is not much après-ski – a couple of discos and some live music, and several bars and restaurants. Le Farinet is the most lively and sophisticated venue for both dining and dancing. Most of the other restaurants are rather anonymous Swiss neo-Alpine in style. Hotels range from the fairly simple to the moderately plush. The cable-car is a stiff climb above the end of the main street, so a long walk as well is to be avoided (though there is a ski-bus). The Beau-Séjour (✆791701) is ideally placed, and has been comfortably refurbished. The Hotel de la Paix (✆791551) is a friendly, cheaper alternative.

Tourist office ✆(25) 791141. Tx 456263. **Package holidays** Kuoni (Ht), Made to Measure (Ht), Ski Club of GB (Ht), Ski Sutherland (Ht), Ski Whizz (Ch).

Les Crosets Switzerland 1660m

Les Crosets is a ski station in the heart of the open slopes on the Swiss side of the Portes du Soleil circuit. It is a tiny place, with a couple of hotels and a handful of restaurants, all fairly functional and with no obvious appeal – though one recent visitor found it 'blissful – absolutely *no* nightlife'. For sporting facilities or a bit more life, it's a two-hour walk into Champéry according to another reporter, who 'didn't see a bus all week'.

Tourist office ✆(25) 791423. **Package holidays** Hourmont (Ht).

Champoussin Switzerland 1580m

Champoussin represents more of an attempt to create a mini-resort than Les Crosets. Its new buildings, in rustic style, are almost all apartments under the skin, but most of our reporters have stayed in the main hotel, the Alpage (✆772711), and have been impressed by everything except the inadequately heated pool. It also has a sauna, and a disco – but the resort is 'death to après-skiers'. There is a skating rink, and a para-gliding school.

Tourist office ✆(25) 772727. **Package holidays** Global (Ht Sc), Made to Measure (Ht).

Height anxiety

Morzine France 1000m

Good for *Beautiful scenery, big ski area, easy runs, short airport transfers, easy road access, cross-country skiing, not skiing, mountain restaurants*
Bad for *Tough runs, late holidays, resort-level snow, skiing convenience, freedom from cars*

Linked resort: Les Gets

Morzine is a long-established resort at the foot of the final ascent to Avoriaz – the high, purpose-built village which (on the British market at least) dominates the sprawling Portes du Soleil ski area. Readers who have enjoyed holidays in Morzine have written to suggest that it deserves fuller treatment than we have given it in earlier editions, and having revisited the place under ideal conditions we are happy to comply. Like La Clusaz and Megève, distant neighbours in Haute Savoie, Morzine combines the traditional all-round charm of an old chalet-style resort, a prettily wooded Alpine landscape, a very French atmosphere, family hotels in the best gallic tradition, and a large and attractive ski area. What more could you ask for?

In a word, altitude. This is skiing as you find it in the lower resorts of Austria, nearly all below the tree-line and with only two lifts reaching 2000m. As any Kitzbühel regular will tell you, at this height you take the rough (or rather the ice and slush) with the smooth – snow guns or no snow guns. It is when snow is in short supply, as several of our reporters have found, that nearby Avoriaz (now linked by lift to Morzine) can prove invaluable.

The linked resort of Les Gets is smaller, slightly higher, similarly long-established. The village is sunny, spacious and architecturally unobjectionable, but has no great character and suffers from through traffic.

If you have a car you do not have to start your exploration of the main Portes du Soleil at Avoriaz: it is a beautiful hour's drive to Châtel, and the low pass from there to Morgins in Switzerland is kept open. Flaine and the resorts of the Chamonix valley are within reach.

The skiing top 2000m bottom 975m

A gondola and a cable-car climb steeply from the edge of the village to **Le Plénay** (1500m), less of a peak than a sunny ridge, with a path/cross-country trail along it. From the lifts you look down on the less enticing sections of the direct black run down from Le Plénay, fairly steep and often scraped. There is easy skiing on the north-west side of the hill, including a long blue down to the resort with snow machines near the bottom; and on the eastern side is an attractive area of intermediate runs, mostly red and complicated only by piste cross-roads. From the eastern extremity of this area (Les Fys, 1150m) a new four-seater chair gives direct access to Plateau de Nyon; the Fys chair climbs back to the top of the ridge (Belvedere), from where easy link runs go down both wooded flanks of the ridge – south-west to the village of Les Gets, and south-east to the junction of Le Grand Pré, where a chair-lift and a drag link with Nyon and a long chair (Charniaz) climbing gently and very prettily to the Tête des Crêts. This lift is the usual access route to the Les Gets ski area, and the runs beneath it – a red which is mostly a schuss, then a green along a road – are the only ways back to Morzine.

Plateau de Nyon can be reached by cable-car from outside Morzine. Its main appeal is to good skiers: the Pointe and Chamossière chair-lifts reach the high points of the system and serve its most challenging skiing: shadowy north-facing coombs beneath the beautiful sharp peaks which dominate Morzine's ski area and keep the early sun off much of it. Of the two black runs, Aigle (from the Pointe) is narrower and steeper. The wide bowl below the Chamossière lift offers more space for skiing off-piste; extremists sometimes tackle the steep slopes between the two lifts (Nant Golon). Behind Chamossière, a splendid sunny red also has some good off-piste variations before following a summer road through the woods to Le Grand Pré. From the Plateau de Nyon you can ski down either to the bottom of the cable-car or, via a flimsy-looking but well protected bridge over a gaping river gorge, directly back to Morzine – apparently 11.5km from Chamossière.

The Tête des Crêts (1660m) is near the top of the north-facing half of Les Gets' skiing. This is gentle and pleasantly pastoral, with long easy runs over lightly wooded slopes to the resort, passing through **Les Chavannes** – a cluster of restaurant and hotel buildings with an area of nursery slopes, paths and cross-country trails (linking up with Le Plénay), accessible by road as well as by lift from Les Gets. Only one of the Les Chavannes drags climbs to Tête des Crêts, for access not only to Morzine but also to a broad upper bowl where a fan of six lifts offers a variety of short intermediate runs and one moderate black. The direct blue run to Les Gets from here is not obvious; the piste down the La Turche drag to the edge of the village is an equally gentle alternative.

The south-facing skiing of Les Gets is on **Mont Chéry**, reached by a six-seater gondola, its bottom station a short walk across road and resort from the Les Chavannes lifts and runs. Good snow on the lower runs (red and black) must be short-lived. The black has some steep moguls just below the mid-station, distinctly tricky on a cold morning. The top half of the mountain has easier open skiing (the black is not all difficult above mid-station), with magnificent views of the Mont Blanc massif to the south. The fairly steep open slope behind Mont Chéry has good black and red runs of about 400m vertical down to the Col de l'Encrenaz, quite deserted when we came upon them, and well worth the journey from Morzine. Alone on the dark north side of the mountain, Bouquetin is a short sharp run which tempts even fewer skiers. The bowl at the top is genuinely steep.

Mountain restaurants are in most of the obvious places, mostly

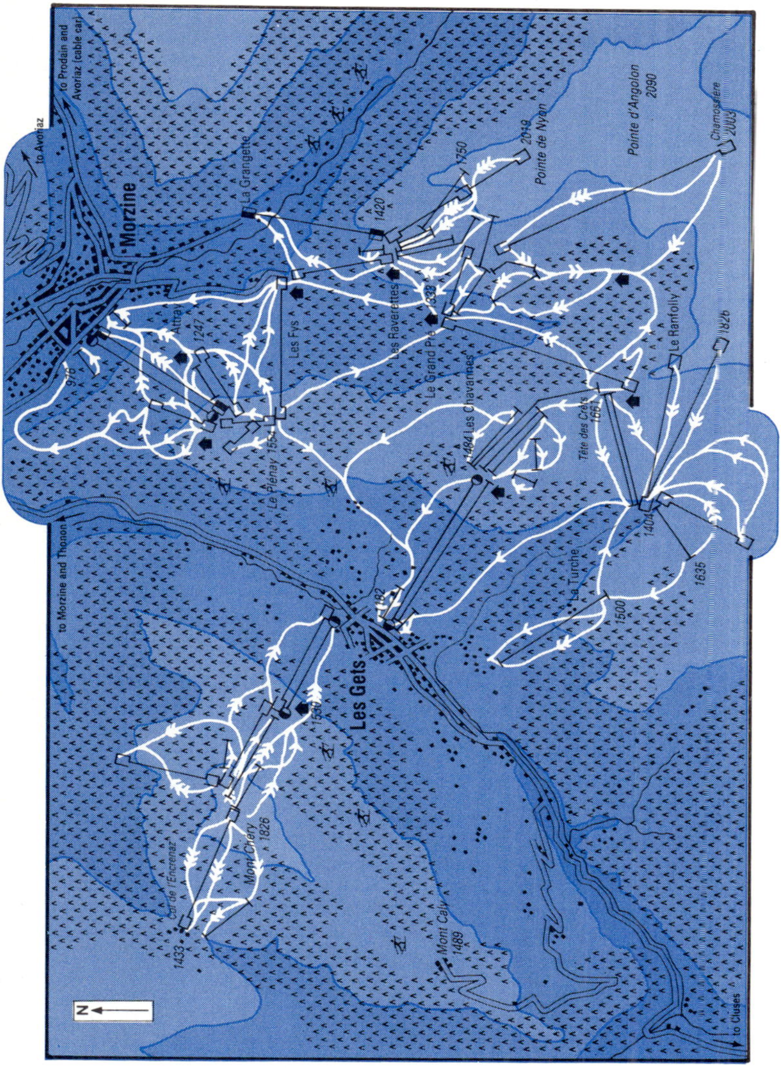

reasonably attractive and reasonably priced. The little restaurant at the foot of the Attray chair-lift is particularly welcoming and well adapted for all conditions, with a warming stove inside and a sun terrace.

We have neither high-season nor weekend experience of Morzine's skiing, but its size and location suggest that **queues** must be a problem. We have found queues for the Avoriaz cable-car at Les Prodains, and await reports on the new direct link – a long series of lifts starting at the bottom of Morzine near the sports centre.

The resort

Morzine is a confusing town covering a large area on both sides of a river gorge and on several levels. It is a thoroughfare with a significant traffic problem, but a high foot-bridge over the river makes getting around less tortuous for pedestrians than motorists. A single congested shopping street climbs from the old village centre beside the river to the more open ground where the resort has developed, with hotels and shops around the tourist office at the foot of Le Plénay. There is a bus service around the western side of the resort, and also several buses a day to Les Gets, Avoriaz and the Avoriaz cable-car at Les Prodains (where the fight for a place on returning buses can be nightmarish).

Accommodation consists of chalets and some 70 hotels, widely scattered around the resort and varying in convenience from very to not at all. Most of the hotels are chalet-style buildings, none is luxurious and many are simple and inexpensive. In the central area around the tourist office, the big Airelles (✆50791524) is one of the more comfortable (pool and sauna) though less personal hotels. The Tremplin (✆50791231) is also comfortable, and right at the foot of the

Morzine facts

Lift payment

Passes Half-day and day passes for Nyon or Plénay; passes of any duration for Nyon and Plénay. To ski both Les Gets and Morzine you need the Portes du Soleil pass (see Avoriaz chapter).
Cost 6 days Portes du Soleil FF660, Nyon/Plénay FF500.
Beginners Coupons for Plénay.
Children 30% off under 12.

Ski school

Classes 9.30–noon, 2.30–5.00, except Saturday pm.
Cost 6 days (11 lessons) FF500. Private lessons FF110/hr.
Children Timetable as for adults. 6 days FF400 (under 12 yr). Non-ski kindergarten ages 2mth–6yr, 8.30–6.00, 6 days FF600, meals extra (FF30). Older tots taken to and from ski school.

Cross-country skiing

Trails 6km beside river in resort centre, easy; 48km in Vallée de la Manche, all grades; 9km Super-Morzine/Avoriaz, all grades; 6km around Lac de Montriond, easy; 7.5km Le Plénay/Les Chavannes, easy/moderate.

Not skiing

Facilities Riding, skating/curling (indoors), bowling, cinemas, sleigh rides, sauna, massage, gym, table tennis.

Getting there

Airport Geneva (63km); transfer 1½hr. Several daily buses to resort.
Railway Cluses or Thonon (30km). Bus connections to resort.
Road Via Geneva, Cluses; chains may be needed.

Medical facilities

In resort Doctor, dentist, chemist.
Hospital Cluses and Thonon (30km).

Available holidays

Resort beds 4,000 in hotels, 11,000 in apartments and chalets.
Package holidays Beach Villas (Ht Ch Cl Ap Sc), Enterprise (Ht), Global (Ht Sc), Made to Measure (Ht Sc), Neilson (Ht), Ski Esprit (Cl)

Further information

Tourist office ✆50790345. Tx 385620.

slopes. The very attractive Chamois d'Or (✆50791378), also well placed, is smaller, less expensive and very friendly. The Dahu (✆50791112) is out of the way, but highly recommended: comfortable, quiet, welcoming, sunny and panoramic, with good food – 'the best hotel we have ever stayed at', says our latest report.

There is plenty for **non-skiers**: a good sports centre with ice rinks, enormous scope for walking and riding in beautiful surroundings (both in the ski area and away from it in quiet valleys), and sleigh rides.

There are very extensive **cross-country** trails in several different sectors served by morning and afternoon buses. The beautiful Vallée de la Manche has varied runs along the valley floor and long itineraries for experts. The Supermorzine trails are higher and sunnier than others. Access to the trails between Le Plénay and Les Chavannes (above Les Gets) is by cable-car; there is a 7km itinerary for the return via the old hamlet of Les Nants, where a farm offers tastings of Savoyard produce.

The resort's **après-ski** lacks the glitter of Megève, its most direct competitor, but there is no shortage of bars, tea-rooms, restaurants or discos, or of British companions. The young crowd into the Wallington – bowling alley, pool hall, bar and video disco.

The village **nursery slopes** are at the foot of Le Plénay, with plenty of bars and restaurants close at hand, and a slalom practice slope for precocious beginners. Although wide and gentle, the area suffers from through-traffic. There are snow machines, but they don't work miracles in mild weather. Nyon has a higher nursery area accessible by cable-car, and in good conditions there is no shortage of runs suitable for those just out of skiing rompers.

Ski school usually meets at the foot of Le Plénay. Recent reports are mixed: children may or may not find an English-speaking instructor, high-season classes may or may not be kept to a reasonable size.

Les Gets 1175m

Les Gets is strung out along a low pass 6km from Morzine, with lifts and pistes on both sides, and good nursery slopes on the edge of the village and at Les Chavannes (1490m), reached by road or gondola.

Large parts of the ski area, and many of the restaurants within it, are accessible on foot: there are 50km of walks on minor roads and cleared paths, and 25km of cross-country trails around the half-way stations on both sides of the resort. Les Gets has two ski schools, various kindergartens for children and babies from three months old, a pool in the hotel Marmottes, a circuit for motor tricycles, two cinemas, three discos, and bars and restaurants in most of the hotels. There are about 20 of these, mostly simple and nearly all attractive-looking chalet buildings. The Régina (✆50797476) is in the middle of the price range, and well placed on the quieter of the main streets. We have good reports of the restaurant at the small Boule de Neige (✆50797508) quietly set near the bottom of the La Turche drag.

Tourist office ✆50797555. Tx 385026. **Package holidays** Made to Measure (Ht), Ski Total (Ht Ch Sc), Ski West (Ht Ch Sc).

Happy families on the moon

Flaine France 1600m

Good for *Family holidays, nursery slopes, big ski area, skiing convenience, short airport transfers, freedom from cars, late holidays, easy runs, resort-level snow*
Bad for *Alpine charm, not skiing, mountain restaurants, après-ski, tough runs*

Linked resort: Les Carroz

Le Grand Massif is a loosely linked ski area spread over what is indeed a large, although not outstandingly high, group of mountains. At its heart is Flaine, the modern French ski resort without a difference. It is all new, and grey. It is also ideal for what the tourist office calls careless skiing: hardly any footslogging, hardly any cars, excellent nursery slopes and facilities, a wide range of intermediate runs, reliable snow, not much queuing. Add very short transfers from Geneva, and its popularity with British families is explained. For a purpose-built resort it has until recently been under-endowed with lifts out of the village. A gondola/cable-car hybrid (of the kind springing up all over the French Alps) put paid to that complaint a couple of seasons ago.

One of Flaine's attractions is that it is close to Geneva and relatively close to the Channel. But the climb up from the valley is a slow, tortuous 30km, and often snowy beyond Les Carroz. Cars are banished to become snow-drifts in peripheral car parks and useful only for day-trips to other resorts (Morzine/Avoriaz and Chamonix/Argentière are the obvious candidates).

The link with Samoëns, Morillon and Les Carroz extends Flaine's skiing greatly and adds missing ingredients – long runs through a wooded, inhabited landscape. Unfortunately, the exposed link lifts are often closed in bad weather, when these sheltered slopes are most appealing. Les Carroz is the most attractive as a base for skiers. It is a sharp contrast to Flaine – inconveniently arranged on the road up, in a beautiful setting with good cross-country trails.

The skiing top 2480m bottom 690m

The Grand Massif skiing divides into several sectors, each linked to the next at only one or two points. Most of **Flaine's** skiing is spread around the north-facing half of the basin in which the resort lies, with several lifts climbing to different points around the rim at nearly 2500m, giving a vertical range of some 900m. Most of the skiing is above the tree-line. The main lift is the new gondola-cum-cable-car to Grandes Platières, a broad, high plateau, flat enough for walking and cross-country, with a panoramic view including the magnificent spikes, glaciers and domes of Mont Blanc. From here a large number of intersecting runs go down to the resort, most of them easy red or stiff blue. For timid skiers there are less direct, open blue runs. The most difficult descents are in the middle of the ski area, where the terrain is very fragmented. This means tricky sections in the middle of otherwise uncomplicated runs – the black run under the cable-car would otherwise be red.

The off-piste routes in the main bowl are very often skied into a piste-like state, and exploration in search of virgin snow is likely to end abruptly at the brink of a cliff or a pot-hole. But there is good off-piste skiing recently opened up by the long Gers drag-lift – reached with some difficulty from Grandes Platières. It is a steep, deep coomb, prone to avalanche; the lift opens late in the season, and closes early in the afternoon. The much shorter Véret lift serves a similar, fairly steep, often dangerous bowl, mainly of interest to off-piste skiers.

The rest of the Grand Massif skiing is reached via the valley of the Lac de Vernant, which is often very crowded with commuting skiers. The Tête du Pré des Saix on the far side is the central point of the whole system. North-facing runs descend steeply down towards **Samoëns** far below. The top section offers some of the best, albeit short, tough runs in the area (bumpy piste and off-piste). The skiing is interrupted by a short chair-lift at the Plateau des Saix, then there's a further 800m vertical down to the outskirts of Samoëns; the steeper black option is a splendid sweeping course through the woods, but is soon scraped bare. On the other side of a wide valley, the parallel **Morillon** runs are long, gentle, woodland trails – less varied than the piste map suggests – punctuated by clearings with restaurants. The runs down to **Les Carroz** are shorter but offer a broader network and greater variety of trails (all below the tree-line), with distinctly blackish sections at the top of some of the red runs, and some good off-piste slopes. There are some very gentle runs around the top of the gondola, but the blue run to the village is often in poor condition and crowded.

There are three **mountain restaurants** above Flaine; they have sunny terraces and the one at the top of the cable-car serves as one of the most spectacular sun-bathing and picnic spots in the Alps.

The new Grandes Platières lift has 30 cabins each holding 23 people; the result is that it can move people at four times the rate of the old conventional cable-car, apparently solving the problem of **queues** to get out of the village. The nursery slopes and lifts are often crowded, and commuter traffic leads to queues for the lifts at Lac de Vernant. Piste signing is inadequate, considering the number of intersections, but at last there is a good map.

The resort

Flaine is a tiny place, 200m below the point at which the access road breaches the rim of a wide, desolate basin. It has been built in two parts – Flaine Forêt (mostly apartment buildings) is on a shelf above Flaine Forum, which is a square at the heart of the resort, with most of the bars, restaurants, shops and hotels. There is a free lift shuttle between the two, day and night. Front de Neige is simply a piste-side extension

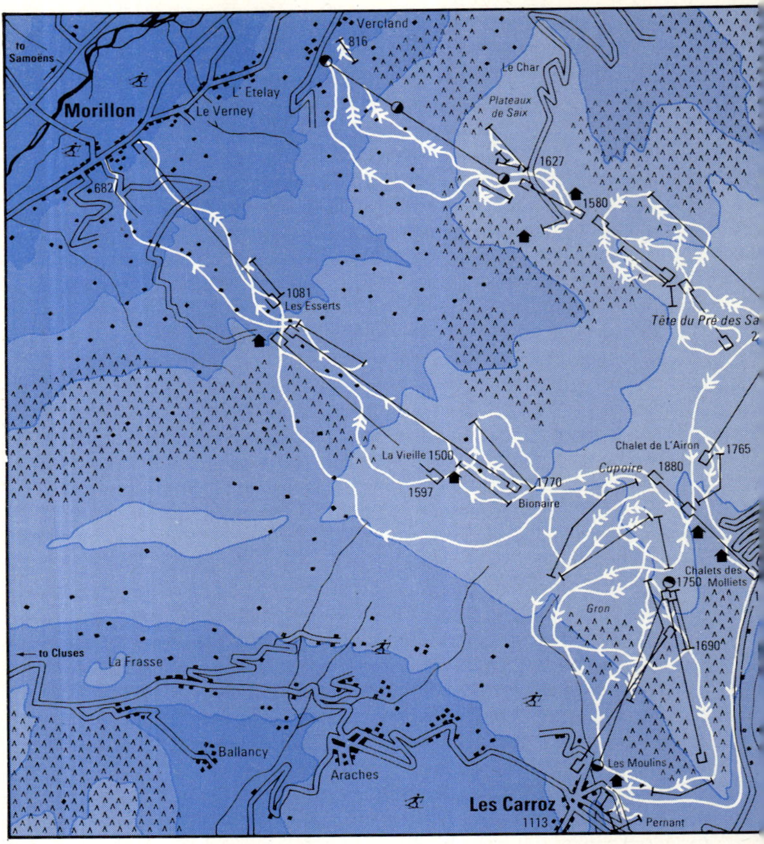

Most of the hotel **accommodation** is in Forum, with self-catering flats – at least as far as UK packages are concerned – mostly in Forêt. Reporters express frustration at having to queue for a lift down to the cable-car in the morning. The hotels are very similar – bright, modern, and adequately comfortable, with small bedrooms and spacious public rooms. Reports are generally favourable, especially of Le Totem (✆50908064) – 'better than ever: more like a country club than an impersonal hotel' and Les Lindars (✆50908166), which is outstandingly caring for young families. Apartments in Front de Neige are well placed for skiing from and to your door.

Après-ski is very muted; few people bother to use the two discothèques, and confine themselves instead to various restaurants and bars. They are expensive – even the lively White Grouse Pub, with its darts and bitter and happy hour. There are organised outings.

Flaine cannot be recommended for **non-skiers**. For **cross-country** skiing you have to be prepared to take buses or lifts to the trails, which

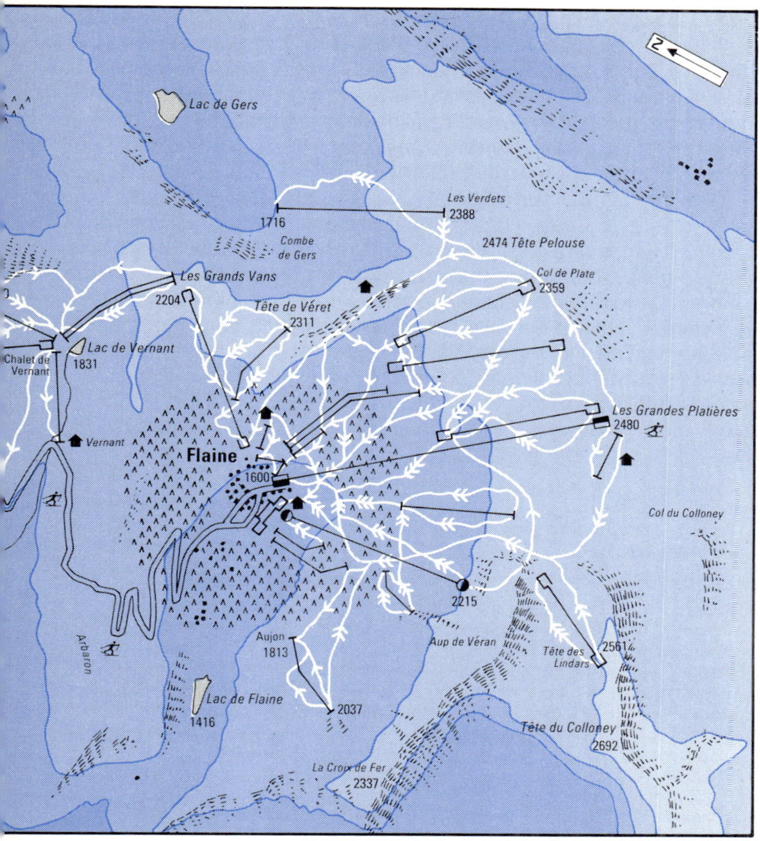

is hardly ideal; Les Carroz is much more suitable.

The **nursery slopes** are excellent – spacious and absolutely central, and ranging from the gentle to the flat, but the slopes and lifts are used by lots of other skiers on their way to and from the main runs.

The differences between the two main **ski schools** are not great. Flaine is where the Ski Ecole International was started 15 years ago to shake up the Ecole du Ski Français. It is reputedly stronger on languages, and has many more English than French pupils, but the ESF can provide English-speaking instructors. Reports are generally favourable, but include observations of large classes, slow learners being left behind by instructors, and changes of instructor during the week. A third school, Flaine Super Ski, is for advanced skiers only (off-piste and racing).

Les Carroz 1160m

Last outpost of civilisation on the road to Flaine, Les Carroz is an attractive, spacious village, spread broadly across a sunny, sloping shelf. It attracts lots of families and weekend day-trippers whose cars strangle the resort. The gondola and chair-lift are a steep walk above the centre of the village, but within easy reach of some attractive, simple old hotels – Airelles (✆50900102), Belles Pistes (✆50900017) and the charming Croix de Savoie (✆50900026). Most of the self-catering accommodation is much less conveniently placed. Cross-country skiing is very good; the trails (64km) are not immediately by the village – the ski-bus serves them as well as the lift station. Les Carroz is quiet in the evenings except during school holidays. There is a single discothèque, outside the village, and several friendly bars and restaurants. The chance to go riding in the snow is apparently '*une des dernières expériences inoubliables*'. There are good babysitting and kindergarten facilities.

Tourist office ✆50900004. Tx 385281. **Package holidays** Enterprise (Ht Sc), Neilson (Ht Sc), Schoolplan (Ht Sc).

Flaine facts

Lift payment

Passes Grand Massif pass covers all lifts and a day in La Clusaz, Argentière or Avoriaz. Local pass also available – can be extended once only to Grand Massif; available for day and half-day.
Cost 6-day Grand Massif pass FF600. Flaine pass FF510. 20% low-season reduction only on Flaine pass.
Children About 20% off, under 12.
Beginners Several free lifts, limited day pass FF50.

Ski school

Two main schools – Ecole du Ski Français and Ski Ecole International.
Classes 2hr morning and afternoon.
Cost 6 days ESF FF490, SEI FF480. Private lessons FF125/hr.
Special courses Competition, off-piste, touring, excursions, freestyle private lessons, monoski, ski surf.
Beginners *Ski évolutif* on request.
Children 25% off adult class prices, under 13. Ski kindergartens, ages 3–12, 6 days with lunch ESF FF810. Non-ski kindergarten, ages 3–7, at Hotel Les Lindars, 9.00–6.00, 6 days FF525.

Not skiing

Facilities Swimming, sauna, natural ice rink, snow-shoe excursions, hang-gliding, ice driving, art/crafts gallery.

Cross-country skiing

Trails 700m loop at Flaine; 8km off-piste trail at Grandes Platières (cable-car from Flaine), 8 km of trails at Vernant and Col de Pierre Carrée (bus from Flaine). Longer trails near Les Carroz.

Medical facilities

In resort Doctor, chemist.
Hospital Sallanches (45km).
Dentist Cluses (30km).

Getting there

Airport Geneva; transfer about 1½hr.
Railway Cluses (30km); several buses daily.
Road Via Geneva or Lyon/Annecy; chains often needed.

Available holidays

Resort beds About 8,000, mostly apartments.
Package holidays Bladon Lines (Ht Sc), Blue Sky (Ht Sc), Enterprise (Ht Sc), Horizon (Ht Sc), Inghams (Ht Sc), Made to Measure (Ht Sc), Neilson (Sc), Ski Club of GB (Ht), Ski West (Ht Sc), Supertravel (Ht Ch Sc)

Further information

Tourist office ✆50908001. Tx 385662.

Cuisine classique

La Clusaz France 1100m

Good for *Cross-country skiing, easy road access, short airport transfers, beautiful scenery, mountain restaurants*
Bad for *Skiing convenience, late holidays, freedom from cars*

Separate resort: Le Grand-Bornand

La Clusaz is a large, long-established summer and winter resort just up the road from Annecy – in style, as in location, mid-way between the small, old-fashioned family resorts of the Mont Blanc area and the big, modern sporty ones of the Tarentaise. The layout of the resort is messy and inconvenient, but its atmosphere is very French and unfussy and, for a resort that only recently attracted the attention of the international package industry, it has a lot of skiing. Much of the skiing is below 2000m and consists of broad runs through woodland, but there is also some high, open skiing with good off-piste runs – making it a flexible resort, capable of amusing most categories of skier in most weather conditions. Its all-round appeal is like that of nearby Megève, but with a difference of emphasis: La Clusaz is less self-consciously fashionable and its skiing is less extensive but more challenging, more varied and slightly less inconveniently arranged. The village fills up with local youth at weekends and holiday times, when it is very lively; out of season it is almost too quiet, as old couples and young families on tight budgets while away their evenings playing cards in simple hotels.

The only resort within practical reach for day trips is Le Grand-Bornand, to which the ski pass gives limited access – a handsome village at one extremity of a modest ski area based on the higher but less handsome ski station of Le Chinaillon. There is an adequate bus service, so a car does not offer much advantage, though it would allow determined explorers to venture further afield – over the snowy Col des Aravis to Megève. Having a car in the resort is handy but not really necessary. Parking can be a problem at weekends, when the centre becomes jammed. There is an underground car park.

The skiing top 2490m bottom 1100m

With the recent addition to the lift pass of the skiing at Col de la Croix-Fry and Merdassier, La Clusaz now gives access to five more-or-less distinct ski areas, spread round the sides of several valleys and facing north, east and west. Two – Beauregard and L'Aiguille – are reached by lifts from the resort centre, the other three from points along the valleys. Despite roads and rivers, all five areas are linked by lift or piste – though some of the links are long green pistes involving some walking, and another is a cross-valley cable-car shuttle.

Beauregard, served by a single cable-car from the bottom of the

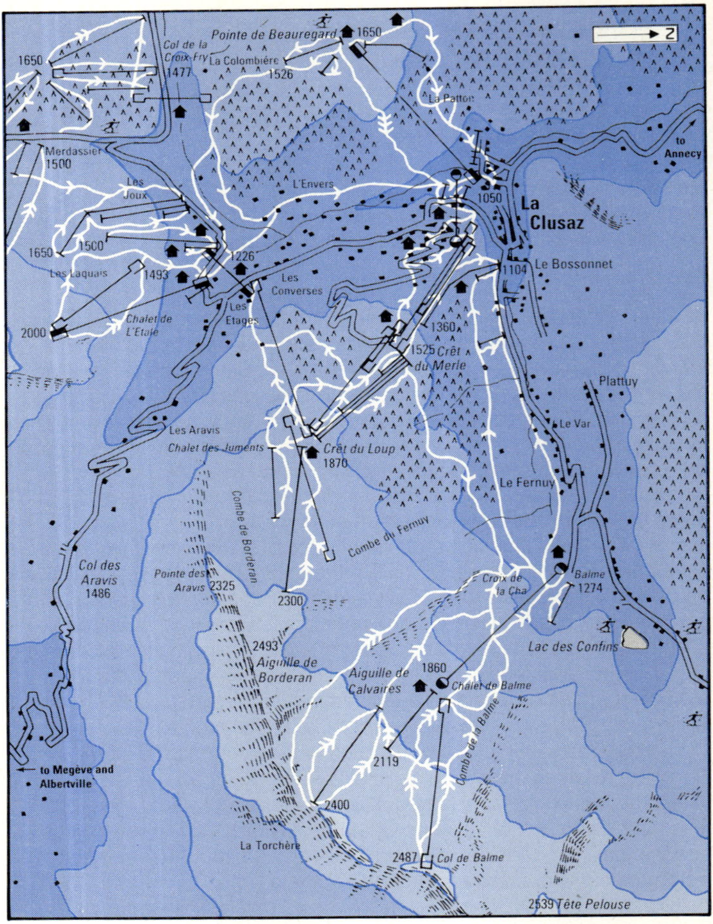

resort, is a flat-topped wooded mountain with very attractive easy skiing in pastoral surroundings at the top (1650m) – good for beginners, walkers and cross-country skiers – and a couple of longer runs back down to the resort. The black starts gently but becomes genuinely steep, with an awkward link between two pitches, the first a short but impressive mogul-field of nearly 35°. The blue on the other side of the cable-car is a splendid varied run, not all of it easy. The green run round the mountain is very gentle for most of its length.

A chair-lift beside the run down from Beauregard to L'Etale has created a one-way link with the enjoyable area of short, gentle woodland runs spread over a knoll between the cols of **La Croix-Fry** and **Merdassier**. There are some steeper and more open runs on the other side of Merdassier, and a very gentle run across to L'Etale providing the return link. Apart from the attraction of the extra skiing, the new area is well provided with restaurants beside the two cols.

L'Etale, like Beauregard, is mainly served by a single cable-car from bottom (1250m) to top (1960m). Skiing is limited to one flank of the mountain (facing north-west), open and fairly steep at the top, with several drag-lifts serving the gentler and more spacious slopes at the bottom. From the bottom station, the Transval cable-car shuttles skiers to and from the Aiguille area.

L'Aiguille is the largest area, directly accessible from the village by gondola, an efficient chair and a drag-lift. There are several sections. The Crêt du Merle is a half-way station with a small nursery area, ski school assembly point and restaurants. None of the several ways back down to the village is particularly difficult. Above Crêt du Merle there are some fairly stiff red runs from Crêt du Loup, with plenty of room for a gentler course to be taken. The west-facing run from Crêt du Loup to the valley is marked blue, but is long (over 600m vertical) and in places fairly steep. In deep snow, off-piste skiers can have fun under the chairs. The bowl above Crêt du Loup is mostly fairly gentle, but the lifts give access to some interesting off-piste skiing – the Combe de Borderan and the Combe du Fernuy, the first of about a dozen long, steep gullies in the wall of the Chaîne des Aravis.

The north-west-facing **Balme** and Torchère slopes provide La Clusaz's highest and most challenging pistes, with fine, long runs down two more of the Aravis coombs giving skiing of over 1200m vertical. The main black run is steep enough to serve as a speed-skiing course. There are moderate reds from both top stations (one is very poorly marked) and a long blue down from the top of the Bergerie drag.

Except in the Balme area, **mountain restaurants** are plentiful, attractively old-fashioned and inexpensive (especially at Croix-Fry/ Merdassier). The Vieux Chalet beside the piste and road at the top of the Patinoire gondola is expensive and very good.

Queues are long for the Beauregard cable-car at peak times, but not too bad elsewhere. Access to Balme has been much improved by the new stand-up gondola. Piste marking is somewhat indeterminate, especially on Beauregard.

The resort

The setting of La Clusaz is a rather enclosed one beside a river at the meeting point of several steep-sided wooded valleys. The village has grown and no longer fits comfortably into its narrow slot, and the sprawl of buildings along the valley and up its sides is complicated by a series of road junctions and roundabouts; it is a somewhat confusing and traffic-ridden place. Downtown La Clusaz, or La Clusaz Sud as it is signposted, is pleasantly traditional, built around a large bulbous-towered church, with a stylish modern shopping precinct beside it and a fast-flowing stream below. Shopping is attractively varied, and there are the very ordinary cafés you find in every French village but in few French ski resorts. A daytime bus shuttle service runs along two routes, linking the various ski areas with the resort centre.

La Clusaz is very much a weekend resort for inhabitants of Annecy and Geneva, and most of the **accommodation** is in private chalets dotted around the hillsides, many of which are available for rent. In the centre of the resort there are lots of simple, reasonably priced hotels. The Christiania (✆50026060), the Aravis-Village (✆50026031) and the Montagne (✆50026161) are all centrally placed, quiet family hotels. The very welcoming Lac des Confins (✆50024171) is in a remote and beautiful but not particularly inconvenient setting, ideal for cross-country skiers and escapists. We have good reports of the Vieux Chalet (✆50024153), a smart restaurant with a few bedrooms, beside the piste and road below Crêt du Merle.

Après-ski is lively at weekends and peak holiday period, otherwise quiet. The small rink is open every evening, snow-shoe excursions to mountain restaurants for a fondue are organised once a week and there are four discothèques. There are lots of restaurants, both in the resort centre and dotted around the valleys. Le Foly is a particularly attractive (but expensive) log cabin up in the Les Confins valley.

Cross-country trails are varied and beautiful although not immediately accessible from the resort. For access to Beauregard, there is no alternative to paying for the cable-car trip by trip. For **non-**

La Clusaz facts

Lift payment

Passes Area pass covers all La Clusaz and Croix-Fry/ Merdassier lifts; available for day, half-day, four days and longer; longer ones cover ski-bus; weekly pass valid one day at Le Grand-Bornand (free bus service).
Cost 6-day pass FF545. Small reduction with la Carte Neige.
Children About 20% off, under 12.
Beginners Cash or lift pass.

Ski school

Classes 2½hr morning and afternoon.
Cost 6 days FF550. Private lesson FF120/hr (1–3 people).
Children 20% off, under 12. Ski kindergarten, ages 3½–6, 8.30–6.00, 6 days with lunch FF678. Non-ski kindergarten, ages up to 4½, 8.30–6.00, 6 days with lunch, FF678.
Special courses Off-piste, ski touring by the week or day, mono ski, surfing.

Not skiing

Facilities Walks and snowmobile rides in cross-country areas, artificial outdoor ice rink, hang-gliding, para-gliding, fitness centres, motor bike circuit.

Cross-country

Trails 4km green, 8km blue, 9km red, 20km black in Les Confins valley; 4km green, 3km blue, 6km red, 13km black at Beauregard. Ski school in each sector.

Medical facilities

In resort Doctors, dentist, chemist.
Hospital Annecy (32km).

Getting there

Airport Geneva; transfer 2hr.
Railway Annecy (32km); frequent buses.
Road Via Lyon/Annecy; chains rarely needed.

Available holidays

Resort beds 2,200 in hotels, about 7,200 in apartments
Package holidays Activity Travel (Ht Ch Sc), Enterprise (Ht Sc), Made to Measure (Sc), Neilson (Ht Sc), Schools Abroad (Ht), Ski Club of GB (Ht), Ski Total (Ht Ch Sc), Ski Whizz (Ch Cl), Skiscope (Ht), SkiSet (Ht), Sunmed (Ht Sc), Vacations (Ch Sc), VFB (Ht Sc), Waymark (Ht)

Further information

Tourist office ✆50026092. Tx 385125.

skiers there are good walks, and excursions for sightseeing and shopping to Thônes and Annecy are easy and worthwhile.

There are small **nursery slopes** beside the resort and at the bottom of each sector. The best nursery areas are at the Crêt du Merle and on the top of Beauregard, which is delightful. There is plenty of skiing for timid intermediates as long as the snow on the lower slopes is good.

Le Grand-Bornand 1000m

Le Grand-Bornand is a real village, its chalets harmoniously gathered around the solid old church; its central square is as animated on summer market days as it is on winter Saturdays when the French skiers who fill it are arriving and departing. The sense it gives of being a mountain community under snow, rather than a ski resort, is reinforced by the fact that its lifts and pistes touch only one extremity of the village. A gondola of modest capacity goes up over a partly wooded hillside to the open, sunny, gentle ski-fields of La Joyère (1450m), where a chair-lift and several drags serve a broad area of pistes graded green to red – though the latter barely deserves its distinction. A new 12-person gondola now connects the village directly with La Côte, a shelf from where lifts fan out in four directions. The most important are those to the high point of the system, Le Lachat (2100m) and the lower shoulder of La Floria (1800m), from where mogulled pistes of justifiably black grading go directly down the north-west-facing slope to Le Chinaillon (1300m), a satellite village developed specifically for skiing. Red runs go down the flanks of the mountains to left and right of the black, and the whole wide mountainside is covered by chair-lifts and drags, and pistes of all colours – the greens crossing diagonally from one side to the other. Further up the valley, beyond Le Chinaillon, there are further expanses of undulating open mountain with red and blue pistes served by another row of lifts, and over on the south-east side of the Lachat ridge is more easy skiing, including a glorious long blue dropping less than 400m in its 4km length. The range and value of the bars and restaurants impressed one reporter.

There are a few good-value family hotels in both the village of Le Grand-Bornand and in Le Chinaillon, and many apartments to rent in the latter. There are extensive cross-country trails along the valley, and a short floodlit loop. The ski school is reportedly chaotic. Both parts of the resort have ski and non-ski kindergartens. Après-ski and non-skiing activities are limited. Skiers wanting equally efficient access to La Clusaz and Le Grand-Bornand could consider staying in St-Jean-de-Sixt (960m), a collection of chalets and small hotels around a road junction between the two.

Tourist office ✆50022033. Tx 385907. **Package holidays** SkiBound (Ht, Ch, Cl).

French skiing with a human face

Megève France 1100m

Good for *Easy runs, big ski area, mountain restaurants, beautiful scenery, cross-country skiing, not skiing, après-ski, short airport transfers, easy road access, sunny slopes*
Bad for *Tough runs, skiing convenience, late holidays, resort-level snow, freedom from cars*

Linked resorts: St-Gervais, St-Nicolas-de-Véroce, Combloux

Megève, an old village in a beautiful, sunny setting at medium altitude, became France's fashionable ski resort in the early days of the sport. Many keen skiers have come to demand more of a challenge than the gentle surroundings of Megève can supply, but the resort has not lost its popularity. It has the traditional charm of a village where, in the words of the tourist office, wood has not given way to concrete, and where the variety of wintersports has been maintained. Horses and (wheeled) sleighs wait in the square, before a fine old church; carefully restored old buildings and an open-air ice rink add to the scene. The narrow central streets are car-free most of the time, and lined by attractive and expensive shop windows. Unfortunately there is a lot of Megève between the centre and the ski areas; the inconvenience and the often heavy traffic around town do a lot to mar the general effect.

Megève's skiing is not enormously varied, but there is a lot of it. It is friendly skiing, mostly below the tree-line but with open pastures giving long, gentle runs for near-beginners and intermediate skiers, lots of sun and superb views. Old restaurants and even hotels are spread round the ridges at the top of the lifts, and much of the area is as easily enjoyed by walkers and cross-country skiers as by downhillers. It is not super-reliable for snow, and queues can be a problem; but Megève has recently spent heavily to add height to its ski area and improve the capacity and co-ordination of its lift system, which no longer seems hopelessly old-fashioned. Cross-country and downhill runs link up with St-Gervais, a 19th-century spa town which also has a funicular link with Les Houches in the Chamonix valley.

The skiing top 2350m bottom 900m

The skiing is in three widely separated areas. The least busy is reached by gondola starting some way north of the town and going over open slopes to the sunny, wooded knoll of **Le Jaillet**. To the west, beyond a dip, is the bald high-point of Le Christomet. To the north, drags take you into the skiing above Combloux. The skiing in this area is as a whole friendly and easy, though there are more challenging runs under both the gondola and the Christomet chair. On the other side of the resort there is much more skiing, mostly facing west and north, on the two sides of the wide horseshoe of mountain slopes curving round beneath the elegant peak of Mont Joly.

Megève's original cable-car, to the plateau of **Rochebrune**, starts a long way from the centre, but is now duplicated by a gondola from the centre of town followed by a chair-lift. There are then a couple of short lifts up to the Alpette, the top of the sector and of Megève's famous downhill course, still marked as a piste on many maps but rarely used as one. None of the other runs is particularly difficult, and intermediate and inexperienced skiers will particularly enjoy the length of them (up to 760m vertical). The chair-lift back up to Rochebrune makes it possible to avoid the flat nursery fields at the bottom of the cable-car, and a new cable-car across the valley links up with the Mont d'Arbois skiing. Three long drag-lifts now make a link (not without some poling) across the wide mountainside between Rochebrune and the **Côte 2000** lifts, where two drags serve fairly challenging skiing, including the women's downhill course and some good off-piste slopes. The area is sheltered from the sun, and usually holds its snow well. The linking lifts themselves serve enjoyable woodland runs.

Megève's most famous skiing mountain is the rounded end of the easterly arm of the horseshoe. The new gondola and drag-lift to the **Mont d'Arbois** depart from high above the resort. Princesse is the north-facing side of the mountain, served by a long, two-stage gondola starting way out of town at Demi-Lune. On the crest where these lifts meet the cable-car and gondola from Le Bettex (an outpost of St-Gervais), there are lots of little link runs, a few hotels and restaurants, and panoramic walking paths. The runs down to Megève are mostly open and easy, and include a long green. There is some more challenging skiing around Mont Joux, the next peak along from Mont d'Arbois on the ridge which climbs towards Mont Joly, with increasingly steep slopes around the bowl. The scope here has been greatly increased by the opening of a new chair-lift going up to the top altitude in the area over an impressive open slope of about 33° in places. The nearby Epaule also serves short, challenging pistes and gives access to some splendid gentler runs and wide, little-used off-piste slopes above St-Nicolas-de-Véroce (1200m). For good skiers this is some of the best terrain in the whole area. From Mont Joux there are also long easy runs, mixed open and woodland terrain, down to Les Communailles near Le Bettex, with drag-lifts back up to the ridge. The route back from Croix du Christ is extremely laborious.

The slopes on the north-facing Princesse side of the mountain are wooded and more challenging than the runs down to Megève from Mont d'Arbois, but the black labels overstate the difficulty. There is often some good off-piste skiing among the trees underneath the top half of the gondola. The lower slopes of the Princesse are gentle and often lack snow.

Mountain restaurants are one of the great attractions of skiing in Megève: numerous, mostly attractive and panoramic, but expensive. Old restaurants and hotels easily accessible to skiers and non-skiers alike stand at the top of the Mont d'Arbois. The shoddy restaurant at the top of the Rochebrune cable-car is a marked exception to the general

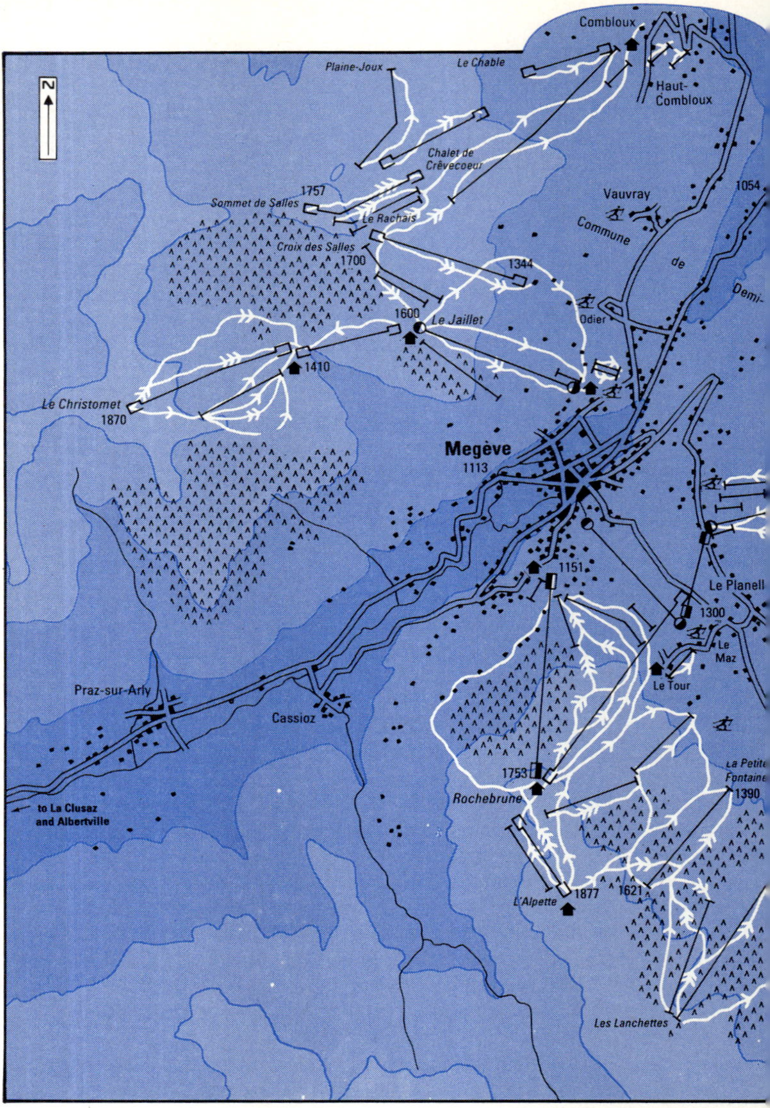

rule. The Côte 2000 is a smart and civilised chalet restaurant; the Le Rosay self-service cafeteria offers good value by exalted local standards.

Queues have diminished thanks to new lifts, especially the efficient new gondola and three- and four-seater chairs in the Mont d'Arbois/Mont Joly sector; but they can still be a problem in French holiday periods and at weekends. The new Rocharbois shuttle cable-car makes

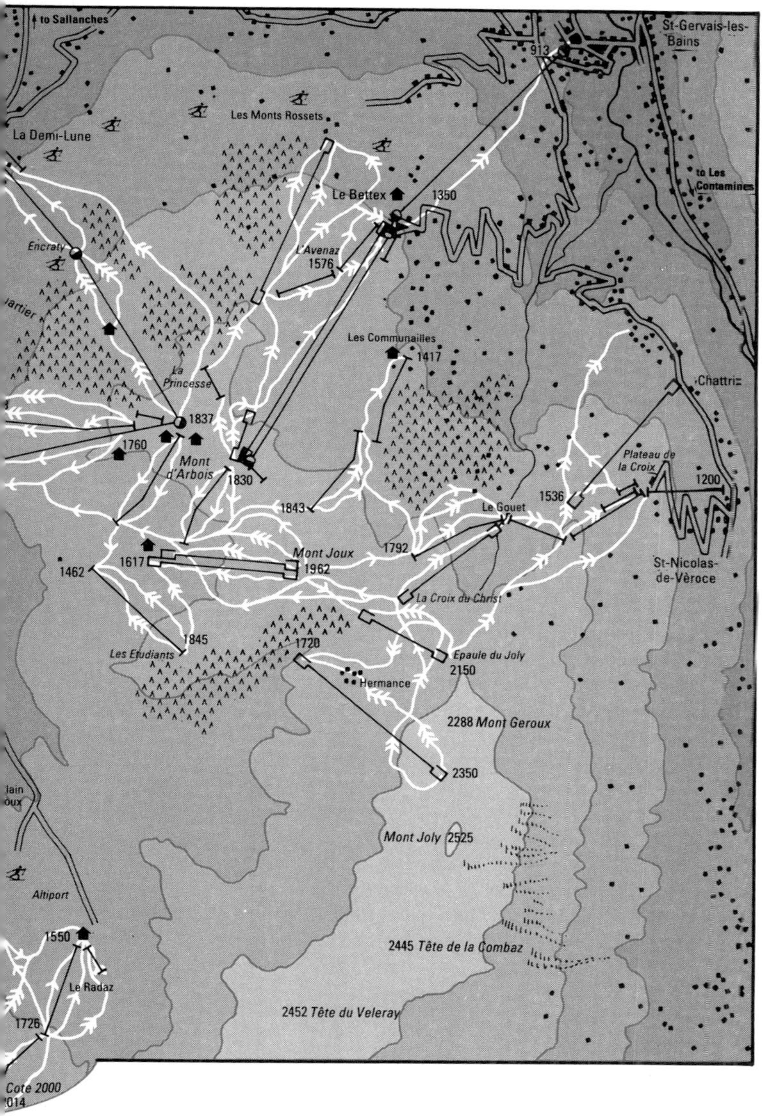

a welcome link between the Rochebrune and Mont d'Arbois, but the ski areas are inherently fragmented, and getting around involves riding a lot of lifts with short linking runs and a frustrating amount of poling (especially at Alpette). The run down to St-Gervais is often unskiable (and always awkward, with road crossings), generating long queues for the lift down from Le Bettex, especially at weekends.

The resort

As Megève has grown to become one of the largest resorts in France, it has spread far in all directions from the centre, with a complicated system of roads radiating from the hub of the resort centre. A main road runs through the resort but by-passes the centre. Megève is not easy to negotiate by car and often has more traffic than it can cope with – no doubt because a car is very handy, and more or less essential for skiers with a Mont Blanc lift pass and a sense of adventure. There are indoor car parks. Daytime buses link the centre with Rochebrune and Mont d'Arbois access lifts. Sleigh rides are so organised that they form an effective (and expensive) transport system.

Accommodation is in a wide range of hotels and private chalets let out for self-catering holidays. For those without a car, the resort centre is the best compromise location. Outstanding luxury hotels are the central Mont Blanc (✆ 50212002), murals by Jean Cocteau, and the Chalet Mont d'Arbois (✆50212503) near the cable-car. The comfortable Ferme-Hotel Duvillard (✆ 50211462) is very convenient for the Mont d'Arbois lift. The Castel Champlat (✆50212549) is central and comfortable; it has no restaurant. The simpler Mont Idéal (✆50212416) is next door to the Mont Blanc.

Après-ski is lively and smart, at least until the end of February. There are scores of restaurants in a great variety of styles, some smart nightlife in the disco/cabaret/casino and the Club des Cinque Rues (a jazz club), but not much cheap, informal après-ski apart from a bowling alley and ice hockey matches in the Palais des Sports. The Megève/St-Gervais team are the French champions.

The resort is very large, and no tranquil Alpine backwater, but **cross-country** trails are in varied and attractive surroundings. The Mont d'Arbois/Princesse trails link up with the St-Gervais ones. There is plenty for **non-skiers** to do, with a big sports/conference centre and particularly good walks in the ski areas, all of which give marvellous views. Walks are graded from easy to off-piste (there are no black walks). Annecy makes an attractive excursion.

Nursery slopes at the bottom of the major lifts are good but not very reliable for snow. In good conditions most first-year skiers will soon be able to handle Le Jaillet. We have no reports on **ski school**, which has offices at the foot of all the main ski areas.

St-Gervais 850m

St-Gervais is a large and old-fashioned spa on the western flanks of the Mont Blanc massif, boasting the largest vertical range of any commune in France – 4222 metres from the summit of Mont Blanc to Le Fayet. In winter its main attraction is as a base for exploring a large number of other resorts with interesting skiing. There is a large indoor ice rink and a kindergarten.

The resort is inconveniently arranged in a cramped setting on both sides of an impressive river gorge; the main street is a busy road. The main ski area is on the Megève side, reached by a fast 20-person gondola from the edge of the resort to Le Bettex, which has some accommodation, including the comfortable Hotel Arbois/Bettex (✆50931222). The second stage of the lift goes up to Mont d'Arbois, known on this side of the hill as St-Gervais 1850. This is a popular way into the Megève ski area for day-trippers (you can be at the top of the Mont Joly lift in an hour from St-Gervais), and often crowded, especially at the end of the day if the run down is unskiable. Le Bettex is accessible by car and has good cross-country trails and walks around the mountain in both directions (Megève and Le Bettex trails link up). A good hotel at the foot of the Le Bettex lift is the Carlina (✆50934110).

Skiing on the Mont Blanc side of St-Gervais is served by the Tramway – a funicular which climbs occasionally and very slowly to the Col de Voza (1653m) where it links up the skiing above Les Houches. There are a few short runs and lifts on the St-Gervais side of the col, but the only run down back to St-Gervais (to a point near the station) is off-piste and often unskiable. A daytime bus service runs between the lift stations, via the resort centre.

Tourist office ✆50782243. Tx 385607. **Package holidays** Snowbird (Cl).

Megève facts

Lift payment

Passes Mont-Blanc lift pass (4 or 6 days) covers all the lifts and resort buses, as well as those of St-Gervais, the Chamonix valley and several other resorts. Various other passes are available for any number of days. All lifts can be paid for individually.
Cost 6-day Mont Blanc pass FF670. Megève/St-Gervais pass FF650.
Beginners Local pass or cash.
Children 10% off local pass, under 10, 8% off Mont Blanc under 13.

Ski school

Classes 2hr morning and afternoon (3½hr lunch-break).
Cost 6 days FF375. Private lessons FF130/hr (1 or 2 people).
Children 20% off under 13. Several kindergartens, ages 1–6, 6 days with lunch FF720–1470.
Special courses Competition classes in school holidays. Guides available for off-piste excursions.

Not skiing

Facilities 50km cleared paths, skating (outdoor and indoor), curling, swimming, riding, sleigh rides, judo, dance classes, bridge, plane trips, tennis, body-building, yoga, gym, archery, pottery.

Cross-country skiing

Trails Three areas, each with green, blue and red loops: bottom of Jaillet (total 17 km); bottom of the Mont d'Arbois cable-car to Princesse mid-station (total 8km); beyond Le Mas in valley between bottom of Rochebrune and Côte 2000 lifts (total 33km).

Medical facilities

In resort Doctors, dentists, chemists.
Hospital Sallanches (13km).

Getting there

Airport Geneva; transfer about 1½hr.
Railway Sallanches (13km); frequent buses.
Road Via Geneva or Lyon/Annecy; chains rarely needed

Available holidays

Resort beds 3,000 in hotels, 28,700 in apartments.
Package holidays John Morgan (Ch), Made to Measure (Sc), Ramblers (Ht), Ski Club of GB (Ht), Ski West (Ht Ch), Ski Whizz (Ch Cl), Snow World (Ht Ch), Sunmed (Ht Sc)

Further information

Tourist office ✆50212728. Tx 385532.

Savoie uncontaminated

Les Contamines France 1164m

This small village near the head of the quiet, narrow Montjoie valley, a few miles from stodgy St-Gervais, is best known as a stage on the walking tour of Mont Blanc and could serve as a model of poor ski resort planning. The long village is on one side of the river and the ski area on the other, its bottom station a long uphill walk from the centre. Two access lifts (both now efficient gondolas) converge on a narrow plateau (1500m) where queues form for the next lift stage, to Le Signal (1900m), where the real skiing starts. Runs back from Le Signal to the plateau are few, and thus often crowded, and there is only an unpisted route down to the valley. Apart from the bottom of this awkward run there is little challenging skiing, and little that is very easy.

But not a few people like Les Contamines. They like it mainly because it is just a quiet, unspoilt Savoyard village with simple, inexpensive accommodation; and because once you get to the ski area it gives splendid views, reliable snow, and a fair amount of open intermediate skiing. A large number of short runs are spread around a vast bowl (mainly north-east facing) behind Le Signal, between 2450m and about 1700m, with plenty of space for off-piste skiing between the pistes in good conditions. There is no piste down from the pit of the bowl to the valley: you take a chair up a short, steep slope to Signal for the run back to the plateau. The Col du Joly (2000m) separates Haute Savoie from Savoie and the main bowl from a smaller but equally open area of south-west-facing intermediate runs, and has a splendid restaurant. The Savoie side of the ski area is little used; the bottom station, with a piste down to it, is a restaurant at 1160m about five miles from the small village of Hauteluce, above cheesy Beaufort.

The village runs along a single long street (no longer carrying traffic up the valley to the ski-lifts), with an old church, a row of similar old-fashioned family hotels, a few shops and cafés, and sleighs outside the tourist office. Some new development has taken place on the other side of the river near the main access gondola: Le Chemenaz (✆50470244) is an ideally-placed, attractive and comfortable modern hotel. The resort has very limited nightlife and not much to offer non-skiers apart from a natural ice rink and weekly excursions to Aosta. Cross-country trails are reasonably extensive and the ski school advertises off-piste excursions into Italy for advanced *fondeurs* (as well as ski touring and off-piste for Alpine skiers). There are ski and non-ski kindergartens, and small nursery areas on both sides of the valley at the top end of the village. There is a ski bus, but having a car is useful, especially now that Les Contamines has rejoined the Mont Blanc lift pass area.

Tourist office ✆50470158. Tx 385730.
Package holidays Enterprise (Sc), Hourmont (Groups) (AP).

Macho Mecca

Chamonix

Good for *Beautiful scenery, tough runs, ski touring, off-piste skiing, après-ski, cross-country skiing, late holidays, rail access, easy road access, short transfers*
Bad for *Skiing convenience, nursery slopes, resort-level snow, lift queues, easy runs, mountain restaurants, freedom from cars*

Separate resorts Argentière, Les Houches, Le Tour

Chamonix grew up with the fashion for climbing and mountain sightseeing in the 19th century, and remains a town of mountain guides and hoteliers. Although not pretty, it has great character and a history that dominates the town in the form of the mountains and glaciers of Mont Blanc. Its population is diverse and colourful, and to its resident colony of Real Mountain Men from all over the world is added a large winter influx of young adventurers and groupies, mostly from North America and Sweden. After going through its dark age as a winter resort, the home of the first Winter Olympics is now in full renaissance as more skiers develop a taste for the excitement these mountains can offer. The number of British visitors is growing, though many of them find the local skiing not greatly to their liking, and are equally put off by the macho-chic atmosphere.

The drawbacks of the skiing are clear: the areas are not linked and only one is immediately accessible from the centre of Chamonix; there is not much gentle skiing; runs down to the valley on the south-facing side are difficult and often closed; and queues are often long – though the conservationist grip on the valley has at last been prized open a little, and new lifts already installed at Argentière are to be followed by others elsewhere. But, for skiers fit enough for long challenging runs and with an eye for the grandest of all Alpine scenery, it is intensely enjoyable, and makes skiing in most other resorts seem a bit predictable. To make the most of it you need luck (with the conditions) and the services of a mountain guide. 'Packaged adventure' may seem a contradiction in terms, but that is what the Chamonix valley has to offer, and its high tourist mortality rate is a reminder that these mountains have not been tamed.

The main alternative to Chamonix for skiing or accommodation is the old village of Argentière, five miles up the valley at the foot of the Grands Montets, perhaps the most impressive ski hill of them all. At the head of the valley, little Le Tour claims to be the snowiest village in France; it is old, picturesquely set at the foot of its glacier, and has some open, easy skiing. Below Chamonix is Les Houches, an old farming village that has become a sprawling resort suburb with an old-fashioned, low skiing area, useful in bad weather.

Despite the frequency of rain in the valley, Chamonix is usually at its best late in the season when the high glacier runs are accessible to

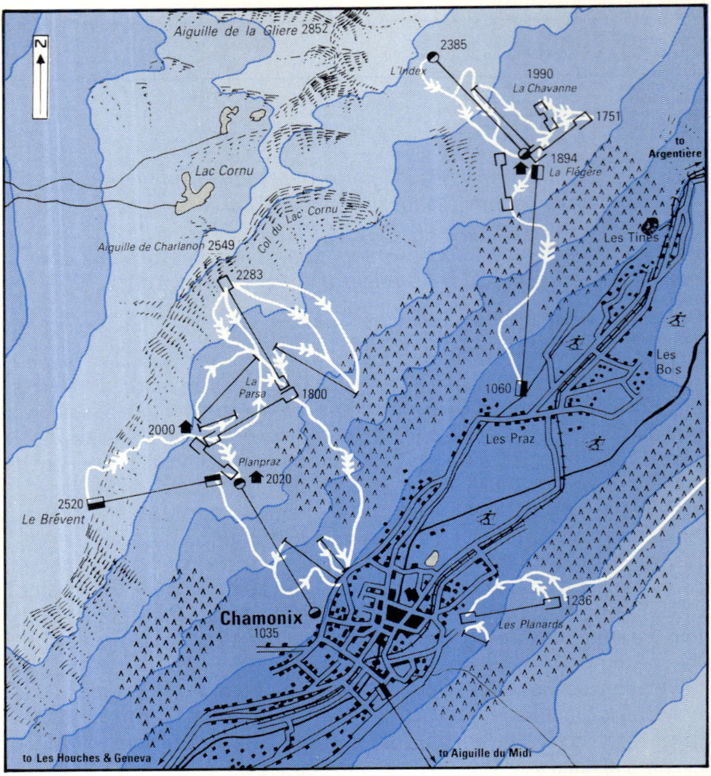

skiers and ski tourers. A car is useful both in the valley and for excursions outside it. Courmayeur and Megève are within easy reach and offer good skiing in bad weather, and it is now usually possible to drive to Verbier even when the Col des Montets is closed – the rail tunnel is opened to alternating one-way road traffic.

The skiing top 3790m bottom 1035m

The Chamonix valley skiing is split up into six separate areas. The best of the scenery and skiing is on the enormous, steep, mostly north-facing slopes of the mountains at the shoulder of Mont Blanc, served by cable-cars from Argentière to the Grands Montets and from Chamonix to the Aiguille du Midi – still Europe's most spectacular cable-car, and giving access to the famous Vallée Blanche run.

Chamonix's original skiing fame was based on **Brévent**, now served by a six-seater gondola starting a steep walk from the centre (also reachable on skis from the nursery slopes) followed by an exciting cable-car over an abyss to the top station, which gives marvellous views of Mont Blanc. Apart from a few short lifts serving easy runs near

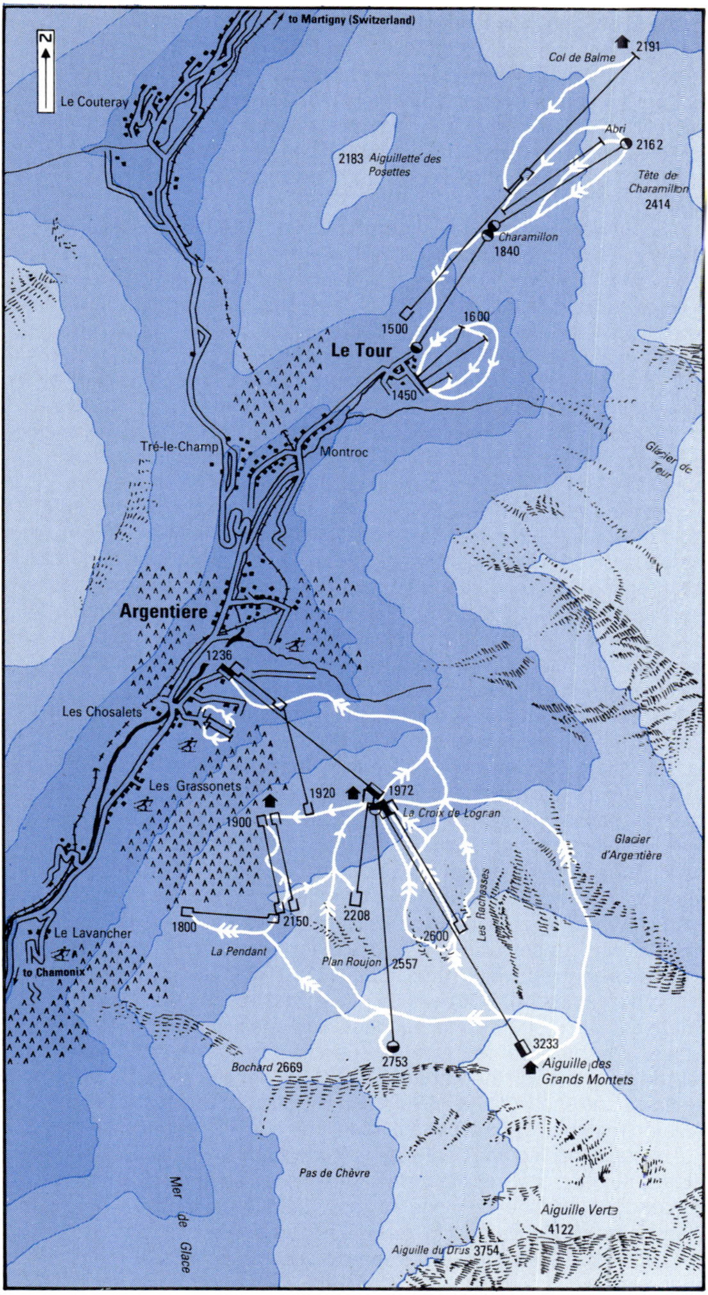
to Martigny (Switzerland)
N
Le Couteray
Col de Balme
2191
Abri
2162
2183 Aiguillette des Posettes
Tête de Charamillon
2414
Charamillon
1840
1600
1500
Le Tour
1450
Tré-le-Champ
Montroc
Glacier de Tour
Argentiere
1236
Les Chosalets
Les Grassonets
1920
1972
1900
La Croix de Logran
Glacier d'Argentière
Les Rachasses
2208
1800
2150
2600
Le Lavancher
La Pendant
Plan Roujon
2557
to Chamonix
3233
Bochard 2669
2753
Aiguille des Grands Montets
Pas de Chèvre
Mer de Glace
Aiguille Verte
4122
Aiguille du Drus 3754

mid-station, and a new chair-lift up to the Col Cornu, Brévent has basically one run. It is quite a run: the top section to Planpraz is an impressive descent with an exposed, bumpy wall, the much longer bottom section (no longer a piste) even more demanding – a long, narrow gully is followed by a wider, bumpy section, which seems to go on for ever. All in all, a relentless 1500m vertical. A new black run has been cleared through the woods, from the bottom of the Combe de Vioz chair-lift.

The **Flégère** skiing, a few ridges along from Brévent, is similar in many ways. The top section, served by an enclosed chair-lift, is less awesome but has a greater variety of runs, mostly tough blue to tough red. As at Brévent, there is only one run to the valley, and that is difficult and often closed. Snow permitting, La Flégère has better off-piste possibilities; it is especially good for spring snow.

The notorious cable-car at **Argentière** has at last been relieved by a parallel lift up to the tree-line, which is the bottom of the main skiing – there is only one run down the steep, wooded slope to the valley, a long and tiring red, not in itself particularly difficult, but often in poor condition, and very crowded in the late afternoon. The area above Lognan may seem limited, but, with the right conditions and the right guidance, good skiers can find more satisfaction and even more variety here than in far more extensive ski areas – and it attracts an unrivalled congregation of rubber-legged experts and bone-headed maniacs putting on a constant display of the state of the art. Crevasse and avalanche danger is considerable. Last season, the gradings of ski runs was in a state of flux, with maps showing as red several runs which have quite properly been regraded black.

Most of the main face of the mountain between about 2000m and 2600m is a wide open area of ridges and bowls, mogul-fields and gullies where the distinction between piste and off-piste means little more than a line of poles to follow in bad visibility. The chair-lift under the top section of the cable-car alone offers at least half a dozen different descents, including a stiff mogul-field of nearly 30°, but no easy piste. The new development has added some good new runs and a very welcome new restaurant, but there are still few bashed runs. One of the few is a long and often crowded red served by a hybrid gondola/chair-lift which also gives access to a magnificent wide bowl and steep wooded slopes above the hamlet of Le Lavancher. Although the bowl (served by a new chair-lift) has now been staked out with a long unbashed run (1000m vertical), there is still masses of room off-piste. The shorter run (Arolles) under this new lift has a serious 30° wall. The off-piste run through the woods to Le Lavancher has several steep sections and snow conditions are usually difficult. There is a delightful bar and restaurant at the bottom and a free bus back to Argentière.

The top section of the cable-car is followed by an exposed 200-step metal staircase down to the pistes. The views from here are stupendous, and the runs long and consistently challenging – 4km and 5km for the 1260m vertical to the mid-station. Of the two runs, the longer is more scenic and gives some awesome views of some of the choppiest sections of the Argentière glacier. The various off-piste descents offer a choice of grandiose glacier scenery or steep, open slopes. The most notorious of all Argentière's runs is the Pas de Chèvre (Goat's Hop), down an often dangerous west-facing slope, all the way from the top of the Grands Montets to join the Vallée Blanche run to Chamonix.

Le Tour's skiing is open, gentle, sunny and uncomplicated. As well as the long, easy intermediate runs (easier above the gondola mid-station), there are a couple of drag-lifts at the bottom, with the valley's best nursery slopes. There is also scope for interesting off-piste skiing to stations on the railway line from Switzerland.

Les Houches' skiing would seem a perfectly agreeable little area were it not overshadowed by the rest of the Chamonix valley. It is served by a small cable-car and a gondola from either end of the village over steep, wooded slopes to either side of the Col de Voza (1653m) – also accessible, two or three times a day, by railway from Le Fayet and St-Gervais. From both these points (Bellevue, 1812m, and Prarion, 1966m) there are splendid long, wide trails through the woods to Les Houches. The run down from Prarion is the official downhill course and is categorised black. There is a small network of drag-lifts between the Col de Voza and Prarion, serving an open slope of about 300m vertical, and some small drag-lifts with slopes suitable for beginners. There is also a wide blue run down to Les Houches. Behind the Col de Voza a good, wide red piste beside the Plancerts drag turns into an off-piste run down to the edge of St-Gervais, not far from the station. After a deceptively pleasant start, the run becomes obscure, and there are only two or three trains a day (not covered by day passes) back up to the col.

Chamonix is a place for off-piste picnics rather than leisurely lunches, and **mountain restaurants** are few, uninteresting and expensive, except at Les Houches. The new one at the bottom of Argentière's Plan Roujon chair-lift is an attractive exception.

The new lifts at Argentière are an enormous improvement. There are still long **queues** for the top cable-car despite the hefty supplement (payable before you join the queue) and the bottom run is now even more crowded at the end of the day, but at least it is possible to get up the mountain and ski. Other queues remain, notably for the Aiguille du Midi (if you hire a guide he'll queue for you), to get down from Flégère when the valley run is closed, and in bad weather at Les Houches (although a new chair-lift has improved matters). Because of the risk of lift closures in bad weather, many skiers prefer the coupon-for-day-pass formula, although the new arrangement with Courmayeur adds to the attraction of the area pass.

The resort

Traditional and old-fashioned though its centre is, Chamonix is no longer pretty. The centre is crowded, noisy and full of traffic. Modern blocks stand around the edge of town, and Chamonix merges with neighbouring hamlets and villages. Bus services (covered by the area lift pass but otherwise expensive) link the town centre with Argentière,

Le Tour and Les Houches. They are just about adequate for skiing purposes but stop at about 7pm. There is also a small railway from Le Fayet (below St-Gervais) to Martigny in Switzerland via Chamonix and Argentière, and linking up with main-line services at both ends.

Most of the **accommodation** offered by British operators is in or near Chamonix. There are a few expensive comfortable hotels, many simple old cheap ones, a few hostels with beds for less than £5 a night, and plenty of self-catering accommodation in new complexes (the main one is Chamonix Sud, near the Aiguille du Midi cable-car) and chalets around the valley. There is no ideal location, except perhaps near the bus terminal. Unless taking a car, avoid accommodation downstream of Chamonix, which means a change of buses to reach Flégère and Argentière. The Bois Prin (✆50533351) is the most expensive and desirable hotel in town, a luxury chalet in a magnificent but very inconvenient position not far from the Brévent lift. The Mont Blanc (✆50530564) is large and absolutely central, has a heated outdoor pool

Chamonix facts

Lift payment

Passes Mont Blanc area pass (4 or 6 days) covers lifts and buses in vicinity of Chamonix and Megéve. Passes for 6 or more days valid for one day in Courmayeur. Local day and part-day passes and coupons (valid all season) exchangeable for passes. No pass covers Grands Montets cable-car.
Cost 6-day Mont Blanc pass FF670.
Children 8% off, under 13.
Beginners Day passes or cash for nursery lifts. Limited passes at Argentière and Le Tour.

Ski school

Classes 2hr morning and afternoon or 4hr morning (good skiers).
Cost 6 days FF450. Private lessons FF120/hr. Mountain guide about FF900/day.
Children Ski kindergarten ages 4–12, 9.00–5.00, 6 days with lunch FF800. Lessons only, 20% off adult school prices for ages 6–12, 5% added to adult prices for ages 4–6. Three non-ski kindergartens, for ages up to 8.
Special courses Guided ski tours, off-piste courses, monoski courses and lessons, race training.

Medical facilities

In resort Hospital, chemists, doctors and dentists.

Cross-country skiing

Trails At Chamonix and Argentière with 2km (black) trail linking the two networks. Chamonix (from Les Praz): 10km green, 6km blue, 4km red. Argentière: 3km green, 3km blue, 4km red. Also 14km trails at Les Houches.

Not skiing

Facilities Artificial indoor and outdoor ice rinks, tennis, swimming, fitness centre, saunas, Alpine museum (school holidays), coach and aeroplane excursions, snowshoe outings, ice driving, squash, archery.

Getting there

Airport Geneva (83km); transfer 1½hr.
Railway Station in resort.
Road Via Lyon/Annecy or Geneva; chains rarely necessary, except higher up the valley.

Available holidays

Resort beds 4,900 in hotels, 9,200 in apartments and chalets.
Package holidays Brittany Ferries (Sc), Club Med (Ht), Inghams (Ht Sc), Made to Measure (Ht), Sally Tours (Sc), Ski Esprit (Ch), Ski Whizz (Ch), Skiscope (Ap)

Further information

Tourist office ✆50530024. Tx 385022.
Weather ✆50530340.

and is also expensive. The Albert Premier (✆50530509) is large, comfortable and fairly convenient, with a bus stop nearby. All these hotels have excellent restaurants. The Sapinière (✆50530763) is one of Chamonix's most handsomely traditional large hotels, in a beautiful, peaceful but not inconvenient position near the nursery slopes. A town-centre hotel without a restaurant is an attractive formula; we have good reports of the inexpensive Vallée Blanche (✆50530450).

The valley is too built-up near Chamonix for **cross-country** skiing, but interlinked woodland loops of different grades further up the valley, between Les Praz and Argentière, offer lots of scope. Accomplished *fondeurs* may be tempted to join the small but growing community of telemark skiers. Instruction can be arranged (✆50540125).

In winter, the valley is no place for mountain walkers, but there is plenty for **non-skiers** to do: beautiful cable-car excursions, an excellent sports centre, an Alpine museum (fascinating provided you can read French) and plenty of organised coach trips.

Après-ski is varied and very lively, at least so far as bars (with and without music and videos) and restaurants go. The most popular places to hang out and pick up something young and virulent are Chambre 9, Choucas, Jean's Bar and the Brévent. All these are usually full far past the gunwhales, unlike the National, a good quiet place for everyday (in other words, good) French food and drink. There are dozens of restaurants, including a number of cheap pizzerias and crêperies. The Bartavel, a wine bar and restaurant with Gascon specialities, is recommended. Chamonix also has a casino and a few discos.

Chamonix is hardly the place for beginners but there are **nursery slopes** at various points along the valley, the best of them at Le Tour – open, sunny and reliable for snow. Chamonix has a sunny nursery area near the bottom of the Brévent lift, and the gentle slopes of Les Planards (at the bottom of the Vallée Blanche run) now have snow-making machines. There are small areas of sunny easy skiing around the half-way stations of Brévent and Flégère.

Chamonix is the HQ of French ski teaching. The local branches of **ski school** have tried hard to keep up with the times, and offer a variety of inclusive courses designed to appeal to the skiing adventurer. We have no reports on these or the quality of instruction in basic ski school. The valley is one of the most famous ski touring areas in the Alps, and Chamonix has two associations of mountain guides. You can hire a guide individually or join an organised tour: there are daily excursions (including the Vallée Blanche) and weekly departures in April and May for the famous Haute Route from Argentière to Saas Fee.

Argentière 1240m

Argentière is a small but strung-out village, beautifully set beneath the local glacier, its church's bulbous belfry outlined against the ice-falls and jagged peaks in a natural postcard scene. Chalet development and some ugly modern blocks are spread up and down the valley on either side of the old village centre. The main street is the Chamonix to Martigny road; although no major route, this sees quite a lot of traffic. A further hazard to pedestrians is the large and unruly dog population.

In the evening you can eat and drink in congenial surroundings, and occasionally dance; during high season the few establishments are very crowded. To sample the much brighter lights of Chamonix, a car is more or less essential; taxis are reportedly hard to come by late at night. Hotels are mostly simple. The Grands Montets (✆50540666) is best placed for the cable-car; it has no restaurant and is more expensive than most. The Savoie (✆50540013) is cheap, cheerful, and a perfectly manageable walk from the cable-car. Argentière has a small playgound/nursery area near the bottom of the cable-car, a kindergarten and ski school, its guides and off-piste skiing tuition (aimed at very strong skiers) run by a celebrated precipice-skier.
Tourist office ✆50540214.
Package holidays Ski Club of GB (Ht).

The Vallée Blanche

The Vallée Blanche is no longer the most famous ski run in the world, but it remains one of the most alluring. Estimates of its length range up to 24km, with a vertical drop of 2770m – impressive statistics which immediately suggest one of its characteristics: that it is not at all steep. Many good skiers expect a technical challenge, and are disappointed – all you need is control over your speed and direction on a moderate slope. The run gives intermediate skiers the chance to enjoy grandiose glacier scenery normally reserved for a hardy minority of adventurous off-piste skiers and ski tourers. It is a sightseeing excursion on skis, to be done on a good day and at a gentle pace. Naturally, the run is extremely popular, and on a fine day at Easter there are enormous queues for the lift and at bottlenecks on the way down. Although usually easy to follow, the Vallée Blanche is not a piste, and it makes sense to ski it in a group with a guide.

Not the least spectacular part of the experience is the astonishingly engineered two-stage cable-car to the Aiguille du Midi from the edge of town. At the top, a tunnel cut in the ice leads to a long, steep, narrow ridge with terminal drops on either side; you have to clamber down this ridge, usually with the help of makeshift steps and a rope, before putting on skis, and for most non-mountaineers it is an uncomfortable few minutes. A guide can provide useful advice and help carry skis.

From the bottom of the ridge, the long run cruises off through a white wilderness of ice, snow and rock, with long stretches where speed has to be kept up, not down. The most awkward section is a junction of glaciers known as the Salle à Manger, where steeper terrain breaks up the ice with huge crevasses gaping beside the narrow path where queues of skiers build up. Even here the skiing is not technically difficult. The glacier section of the run ends with a walk uphill off the Mer de Glace on to terra firma; again queues can be a problem. From here, it is a long ski down around the mountain to Chamonix, mostly a path across the steep hillside, very messy when short of snow.

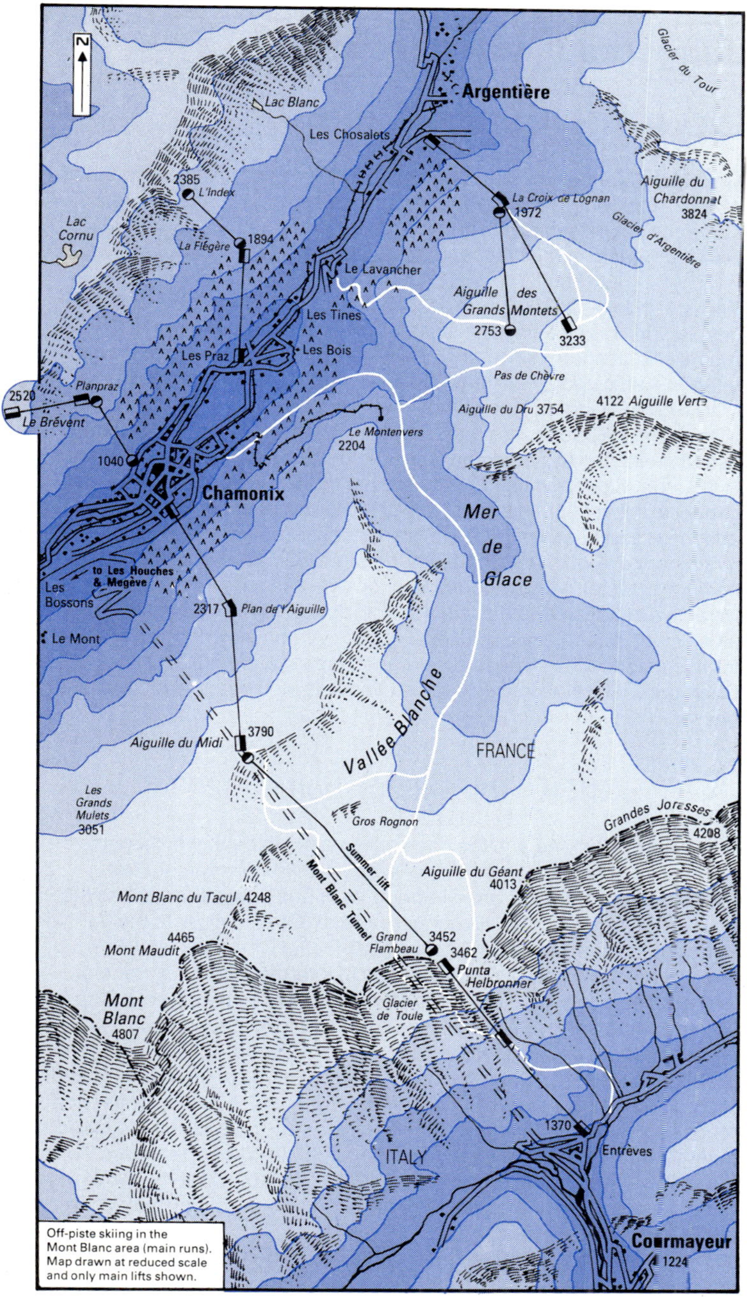

Off-piste skiing in the Mont Blanc area (main runs). Map drawn at reduced scale and only main lifts shown.

Juggernaut withstanding

Courmayeur Italy 1230m

Good for *Mountain restaurants, beautiful scenery, après-ski, off-piste skiing, ski touring, easy road access, short airport transfers, cross-country skiing, Alpine charm*
Bad for *Skiing convenience, nursery slopes, tough runs, easy runs*

The British love Courmayeur, despite its highly inconvenient layout and despite the complete loss of its seclusion and the partial loss of its Alpine village charm since the Mont Blanc road tunnel forced heavy through-traffic upon it. Its main ski area is not very big; there is no very challenging skiing, not much that is very gentle, few very long runs and normally none back to the resort. But it is an attractive and remarkably varied area, with lots of restaurants and beautiful changing views, and with some wilder and higher runs served (not very reliably) by the top cable-cars. Lift queues are not now the problem that they used to be, and the resort has invested in a very extensive network of snow-making machinery on both flanks of the mountain. The village is stylish without being exclusive, lively without being rowdy – still one of the most attractive of Italian resorts. It is also the closest to the Channel. Having a car is not particularly useful (the village is vigorously policed) except for excursions. The lift pass encourages trips to Cervinia and Chamonix, which is much closer. La Thuile is also nearby, and worth a day trip.

The skiing top 3452m bottom 1293m

Most skiers start and end the day on the vast cable-car which spans the river valley, linking the edge of the village with the plateau of **Plan Checrouit**. Alternatives are a short drive or bus ride, either across the valley to Dolonne for the old gondola to Plan Checrouit, or to the Val Veny cable-car, near Entrèves. The east-facing Checrouit bowl has a large number but hardly a great variety of intermediate runs, none of which is very long. The pistes are often crowded, especially near the bottom where they meet. There are surprisingly steep, narrow passages even on some of the variants graded blue.

The wooded north-west-facing **Val Veny** side of the mountain, linked in a couple of places with the Checrouit bowl, has beautiful, longer and more varied runs, with some challenging bumpy trails taking the hillside fairly directly and an easy, wide, winding path. In places, there are dangerously steep slopes beside the pistes (notably piste 19). The run back to the bottom of the cable-car is easy, but crosses an avalanche slope and is often closed.

The very inefficient Youla cable-car above Lago Checrouit opens up a deep and sheltered bowl, usually keeping good snow, and a single

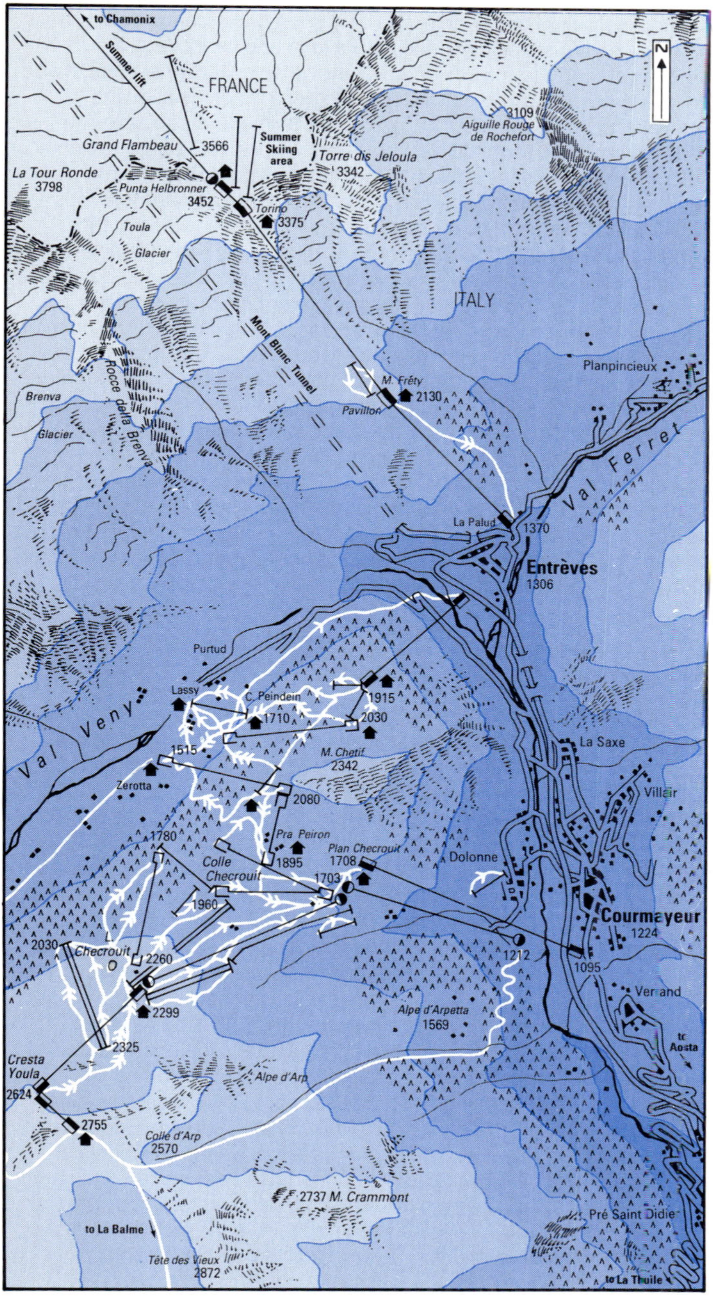
to Chamonix
Summer lift
FRANCE
Summer Skiing area
Grand Flambeau
3566
La Tour Ronde
3798
Punta Helbronner
3452
Torre dis Jeloula
3342
Torino
3375
3109
Aiguille Rouge de Rochefort
Toula
Glacier
ITALY
Mont Blanc Tunnel
Rocce della Brenva
Brenva
Glacier
M. Fréty
2130
Pavillon
Planpincieux
Val Ferret
La Palud
1370
Entrèves
1306
Purtud
Lassy
C. Peindein
1710
1915
2030
M. Chetif
2342
Val Veny
1515
Zerotta
2080
Pra Peiron
1780
1895
Plan Checrouit
1708
Dolonne
Colle Checrouit
1703
1960
Courmayeur
1224
2030
Checrouit
2260
1212
1095
Verrand
2299
Alpe d'Arpetta
1569
2325
to Aosta
Cresta Youla
2624
Alpe d'Arp
2755
Colle d'Arp
2570
2737 M. Crammont
Pré Saint Didier
to La Balme
Tête des Vieux
2872
to La Thuile

uncomplicated run back down. A further short cable-car gives access to the serious off-piste skiing, principally a long and very beautiful run (1500m vertical) down a secluded valley, via an awkward and not at all obvious path through steep woods to Dolonne. There is also an excellent run to Zerotta, and another to La Balme and La Thuile.

The three-stage **Mont Blanc** cable-car climbs over 2000m to Punta Helbronner, giving easy access to the famous Vallée Blanche run – see the Chamonix chapter preceding this one. There is an afternoon bus back from Chamonix. The off-piste run down the Italian side of the Massif is very steep at the top (a rope is followed by a long exposed staircase) and often dangerous. By contrast the run down the bottom stage of the cable-car is a long, straightforward, and rarely skied piste.

Mountain restaurants are, to quote one satisfied reporter, 'a point of special commendation', and remarkably numerous, with lots of mostly very welcoming chalets and converted cow-sheds dotted around. Plan Checrouit is a proper little Hochcourmayeur, with accommodation and ski shops as well as a number of bars and restaurants. There is an excellent restaurant and sun terrace at Pavillon.

The Checrouit cable-car is a long walk from the centre, but fairly free of **queues** except at weekends, when the black spots are Zerotta and the Youla cable-car, both due to be relieved soon by new lifts. The top cable-cars are very often closed. Ski and boot depots at Plan Checrouit take a lot of the unpleasantness out of getting to and from skiing.

The resort

Courmayeur is a long village which now merges with its neighbouring hamlets Verrand, Villair and La Saxe, all of them quiet and prosperous second-home areas with some beautiful old rough-stone buildings. Some haphazard and unbecoming expansion has taken place along the Verrand road near the cable-car, about half a mile from the old centre – now just an open space beside the main busy road. On Wednesdays the vacuum is filled by a large and lively market. The heart of the old village is a delightful maze of cobbled alleys partly reserved for pedestrians, full of a very attractive variety of shops and bars, from typical Italian cafés to pubs and fast-food counters. The main resort bus service, serving cable-cars and cross-country area, runs about every 15 minutes. There are less frequent buses to Dolonne.

There is a great variety of **accommodation**. Few hotels are well situated for the main lift. The Pavillon (✆842420) is the best situated of all Courmayeur's hotels, and one of the most comfortable and expensive; it has a very good pool and sauna. In the old village, the Cristallo (✆ 842015) is very attractive and comfortable; the Edelweiss (✆841590) is friendly, cosy, and less expensive. Near the gondola station, the Dolonne (✆841260) is a comfortable B&B place.

Après-ski resides mainly in the many bars and restaurants. The Bar Roma with its comfortable sofas and armchairs is the most popular and lively place in the early evening. There are a few discos and lots of restaurants, including cheap places to fill up with pizza or pasta,

Courmayeur facts

Lift payment

Passes All Checrouit/Val Veny lifts covered by a single pass. Passes for 3 or more days cover Monte Bianco cable-cars. Passes for 6 or more days valid for one day in Cervinia and one of the Mont Blanc lift pass resorts (Chamonix, Megève and neighbours).
Cost 6-day pass L152,000. 20% off in low season.
Children No reduction.
Beginners Free nursery lifts at Plan Checrouit and top of Val Veny cable-car (which can be paid for by the ride). Otherwise general pass needed.
Summer skiing Small area at top of Mont Blanc cable-car. 3 lifts.

Ski school

Classes 3hr mornings only.
Cost 6 days L103,000. Private lessons L24,000/hr.
Children Ski kindergarten, ages 5–10, 9.00–4.00, 6 days with lunch about L200,000.

Cross-country skiing

Trails Several, 3km to 20km, in Val Ferret. 5km difficult and 3km easy at Dolonne. 4km at Entrèves.

Not skiing

Facilities Swimming/sauna in Hotel Royal and at Pré-St-Didier (5km), artificial ice rink, Alpine museum, tennis, cinema, bridge, walking paths in Val Ferret and Dolonne.

Medical facilities

In resort Doctors, dentists, chemists.
Hospital Aosta (36km).

Getting there

Airport Geneva; transfer about 2hr. Turin almost as convenient.
Railway Pré-St-Didier (5km); frequent buses.
Road Via Geneva or Lyon, and Mont Blanc Tunnel; chains rarely needed.

Available holidays

Resort beds 2,600 in hotels, 17,400 in chalets/apartments.
Package holidays Bladon Lines (Ht Ch), Horizon (Ht), Mark Warner (Cl), Pegasus (Ht), Ski Club of GB (Ht), Ski Falcon (Ht), Ski West (Ht Ch Sc), SkiBound (Ht), SkiSet (Ht), Thomson (Ht Sc)

Further information

Tourist office ✆(165) 842060. Tx 215871. Fax (165) 84272.

nowhere cheaper or heartier than the Turistica. Of the more ambitious restaurants the most famous are the Maison de Filippo in Entrèves, a splendid place for an empty stomach and an unfussy palate, and K2 in Villair. In the village centre, Leone Rosso is recommended. There are also some restaurants and discos at Dolonne and Verrand. The ice rink is open every evening until midnight, with disco music and lights.

The main **cross-country** trails involve a bus ride but are excellent – long, varied and beautiful. For **non-skiers** there are plenty of interesting excursions (Aosta is recommended for sightseeing and cheap shopping) and good walks. In fine weather the cable-car ride to Punta Helbronner is spectacular.

Nursery slopes at Plan Checrouit are cramped by all the buildings and milling skiers. The progression to the rest of Courmayeur's skiing is also not an easy one. There are quieter nursery areas at the top of the Val Veny cable-car and at Dolonne.

The **ski school** and the local mountain guides run programmes of off-piste skiing and helicopter skiing. Courmayeur is a famous mountaineering centre, and the scope for ski touring is vast.

Follow the herd

La Thuile Italy 1450m

Good for *Big ski area, beautiful scenery, easy runs, skiing convenience, short airport transfers, lift queues*
Bad for *Tough runs, après-ski, not skiing, Alpine charm*

Linked resort: La Rosière (France)

Of all the Alpine passes over which Hannibal may have driven his elephants, the Little St Bernard is the most likely candidate. Nowadays the pass is closed in winter, but lifts across the open slopes above it enable skiers to follow in Carthaginian footsteps while exploring the long and interesting ski area shared by La Thuile in the Italian Val d'Aosta and La Rosière in the French Tarentaise.

If you equate the Tarentaise with all that is biggest and best in skiing, it may come as a surprise to learn that La Rosière is very much the minority shareholder in this international joint venture. Italy has most of the skiing and the best of it, with very long and beautiful intermediate runs, a few good blacks in the woods and a reputation for extreme cold. La Thuile itself is less appealing than its skiing: an odd combination of a depressingly run-down old mining village and an ambitiously large and fairly stylish new hotel and apartment complex, complete with conference halls, cavernous car parks and long echoing corridors. Someone has invested a lot of money in the belief that La Thuile is going to catch on in a big way. So far, it hasn't.

La Rosière is a small, very sunny resort with a small, very sunny ski area high above Bourg-St-Maurice. Apart from the sunshine, its main attraction as a base is the chance to make day-trips to Les Arcs and Val d'Isère/Tignes. Motorists in La Thuile are well placed for excursions to Courmayeur and Chamonix.

The skiing top 2642m bottom 1450m

La Thuile's ski area consists of steep wooded slopes above the resort, a wide and gentle east-facing mountainside above the trees and steeper north-facing slopes from the top lifts down towards the Little St Bernard road. On both sides of the mountain the steeper slopes are skirted by very long intermediate pistes, giving a good variety of runs of different grades back down to the resort, although the gentler ones are graded red because of their great length. La Rosière's area is a wide, mainly south-facing mountainside criss-crossed by intermediate runs and giving a vertical range of little over 500 metres. The mountain crests at the top of each resort's ski slopes are separated by a wide, pylon-scarred no-man's-land above the pass, where lifts have recently been installed to bridge the gap.

A fast new gondola and a chair-lift climb steeply from the edge of La

Thuile to **Les Suches** (2200m), a cluster of buildings above the woods where the mountain flattens out. Two blacks plunge back down through the woods, splendid runs when snow cover is good. Red 4 provides an easier option. Above Les Suches a narrow area of very easy runs opens out into a wider bowl of intermediate skiing beneath the rocky peaks of **Belvedere** and **Chaz Dura**, the two high points of the ski area. Most of the runs are wide and easy, very gentle under the long Belvedere and Cerellaz chair-lifts, slightly steeper on the slopes of Chaz Dura. From the higher slopes there are magnificent views: a vast wave of glacier on the Rutor to the south (much used for heli-skiing); the Matterhorn poking up through a chink in the mountains to the east; and a marvellous view of the south side of Mont Blanc, with a series of empty valleys reserved for ski touring explorers.

Some of La Thuile's best skiing is on the rocky north-facing slopes above the St Bernard road, served by a chair-lift and accessible from both Chaz Dura and, by a less than terrifying black, from Belvedere. There is good off-piste skiing as well as the red and black pistes, and the slope offers a worthwhile drop of some 600m. The least direct route is a run of 11km for 1100m vertical: wide, easy and panoramic, cruising on past the chair-lift station and following the road gently around the mountain to La Thuile, joined by the steeper and more direct descents from Les Suches as it approaches the resort. The return from La Rosière joins this run near the top, and it makes a splendid end to the day. On the opposite, easterly side of the ski area the run down through the woods is also very long and perhaps even more satisfying: less flat, little skied and very beautiful, with views of sunset on the Grandes Jorasses framed by the trees.

The top of the Belvedere chair is the point of departure for excursions to La Rosière, a long schuss down to a short steep chair-lift that hoists you to the **Col de la Traversette** (2383m), a gap in the rocky crest crowning La Rosière's ski-fields, complete with dilapidated fortifications commanding the pass. From the col and all over the ski area there are fine views across the deep Isère valley to Les Arcs and the Aiguille Rouge. A long blue run traverses the mountainside and leads directly to La Rosière village; tedium is relieved by numerous piste crossroads. Alternatively you can zig-zag up and down the various lifts beneath the crest, exploring the red runs and a single moderate black beside them. This is a wide and uncomplicated area of open, very sunny intermediate skiing, with short easy runs and nursery lifts near the village. There must often be excellent spring-snow skiing all over the mountainside. We have no knowledge of the runs, graded red and black, that skirt the resort and end up below it at the bottom of a chair-lift at 1500m. Only two chair-lifts are necessary for the return from La Rosière to the Col de la Traversette. The black run down behind the col is a hairpin track, only moderately steep and not particularly intimidating. From the bottom of it a long and very cold drag-lift tows you across a white wilderness to a point from where it is gently downhill all the way to La Thuile. You look down on pylons and the battle-scarred hospice buildings round the pass, a World War II memorial that has not had to be erected.

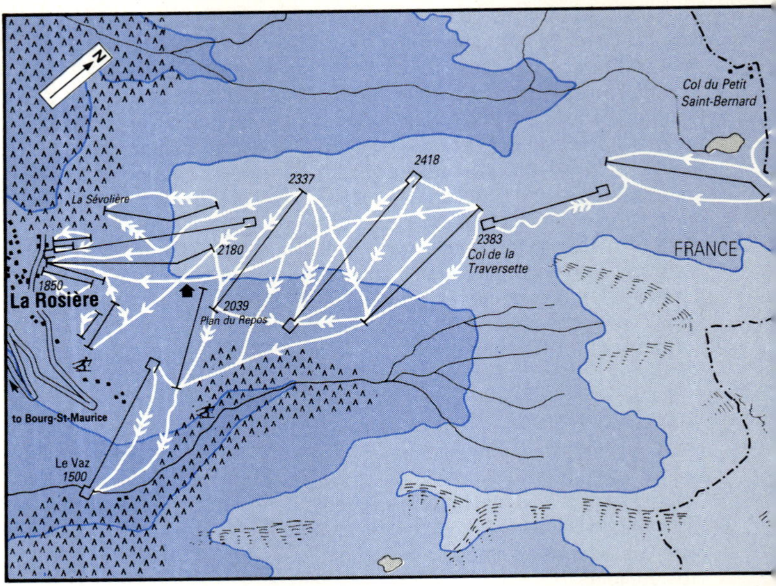

Mountain restaurants are few, and unmarked on the piste map. The main one is the excellent Le Foyer in the middle of the upper La Thuile bowl, with a sunbathing terrace and a good restaurant beneath a large bar with an open fire. There are several sunny places to eat and drink at the foot of La Rosière's pistes.

Queues for access to Les Suches should no longer be a problem, thanks to the new high-speed gondola from the resort. The Fourclaz chair up to Chaz Dura is often a bottleneck, but will be relieved if (as is rumoured) La Rosière builds a lift up to Belvedere. La Rosière is small and probably queue-free.

The resort

La Thuile stands in a rather austere and enclosed setting a few miles from Pré-St-Didier beside the Little St Bernard road, which climbs no further than the resort in winter. Strung out beside road and river, the old village now has a very neglected look, with a few basic shops and old hotels standing peeling and abandoned. The disused mining buildings are to be turned into a national sports academy, and the process of renewal has already started with the creation of a new La Thuile above the old village at the foot of the ski slopes. It is a handsome and harmonious complex of modern buildings with a vast hotel, a huge area of underground parking, a shopping precinct with some fashionable boutiques, and apartment buildings with good indoor sports facilities. All it lacks is the breath of life.

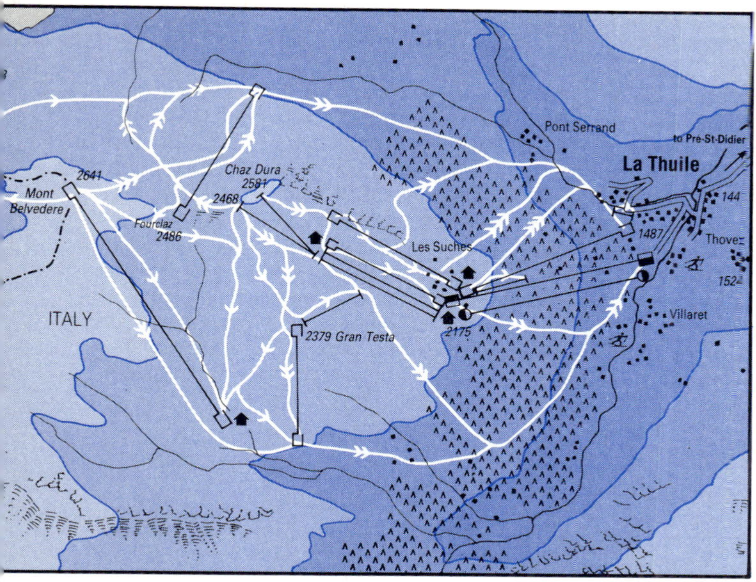

For the purposes of British package holidaymakers, who now account for 20% of La Thuile's winter custom, **accommodation** is mainly in the modern apartments, which are convenient for skiing, shopping, swimming and skating. The modern Planibel (✆884541) is a vast, comfortable, expensive business-style hotel of nearly 300 rooms; there are often large conference groups. The hotel serves good buffet breakfasts and has a piano-bar, a disco and its own pool. Among the old hotels, the simple Edelweiss (✆884144) is a good choice, well placed at the top of the village beside the runs down from the pass.

The sports centre is open to allcomers but does not in itself make La Thuile a good resort for **non-skiers**. It is useful as a substitute for **après-ski** of which there is not much, with the notable exception of La Bricole, a beautifully converted old building between old and new parts of the resort. It has a bar, a crypt disco and a smartly rustic restaurant.

Cross-country trails are not enormously extensive but attractively set in the wooded valley that runs down from the Rutor to La Thuile. The trails are directly accessible from the Planibel complex and link up with an open area of sunny loops on the other side of the river, which is where the main cross-country centre and the resort's one instructor are to be found.

There is a small area of **nursery slopes** near the main lift station on the edge of the new part of the resort, which is also the **ski school** meeting place. Above Les Suches is a large sunny area of very easy runs suitable for near-beginners.

La Rosière France 1850m

La Rosière is little more than a gathering of mostly traditional-looking buildings around the hairpin bends of the road up to the Little St Bernard. It is not particularly villagey, but there are several old hamlets dotted around the sunny slopes nearby, and the style of the place is generally attractive. In winter the road ends with a snow bank at the top of the village beside a pen containing a few sunbathing St Bernard dogs (and a husky) which line up obligingly at the sight of a camera. Access to the skiing area is from the roadside at the top of the village, and there are several simple, convenient hotels, including the Relais du Petit St Bernard (✆79068048). There are a few bars, restaurants and a couple of discothèques, some sunny walks, a straightforward cross-country trail and a kindergarten. Unlike La Thuile, La Rosière offers a lift pass covering only its share of the lift system, about 30% cheaper than the overall area pass and possibly worthwhile for inexperienced skiers. Road access to the resort is via Moûtiers, notoriously congested on Saturdays.

Tourist office ✆79068051.

La Thuile facts

Lift payment

Passes One pass covers all La Thuile/La Rosière lifts. Available for afternoon and any number of days.
Cost 6 days L110,000 (L129,000 at New Year and Easter). Pass for 6 non-consecutive days available.
Beginners Day pass for nursery lifts.
Children No reduction.

Ski school

Classes 2½hr mornings only, Monday to Saturday (2hr only, if class size smaller than 5).
Cost 6 days L86,000 high season, 80,000 low season. Private lesson L24,000/hr high season, L20,000/hr low season.
Children No kindergarten facilities.

Medical facilities

In resort Fracture clinic, doctor, chemist.

Cross-country skiing

Trails Loops of 1km (easy), 3km (medium), 5km (medium) and 7½km (difficult).

Not skiing

Facilities Squash, indoor skating, swimming, bowling, sauna, gym, jacuzzi, massage.

Available holidays

Resort beds 1,600 in hotels, 1,800 in apartments.
Package holidays Schools Abroad (Ap), Ski Falcon (Ht Sc), Skiscope (Ap), SkiSet (Ht), Snowbird Holidays (Ap)

Further information

Tourist office ✆(0165) 884179.

Le ski rules, OK?

Val d'Isère France 1850m

Good for *Big ski area, easy runs, tough runs, off-piste skiing, late holidays, resort-level snow, après-ski, lift queues, sunny slopes, summer skiing, chalet holidays*
Bad for *Alpine charm, mountain restaurants, short airport transfers, easy road access, not skiing, skiing convenience*

Tignes France 2000m

Good for *Big ski area, off-piste skiing, tough runs, late holidays, resort-level snow, lift queues, skiing convenience, summer skiing*
Bad for *Alpine charm, après-ski, not skiing, easy road access, short airport transfers, mountain restaurants*

These two very different resorts share only a lack of charm and an almost inexhaustible, high-altitude ski area which has established itself as one of the world's premier destinations for keen skiers. Opinions about the relative merits of the two resorts vary, but our scores of reporters are almost unanimous in their approval of the skiing and in their desire to return for further exploration of its enormous off-piste potential, some of the easiest slopes any skier could ask for (on top of the world at over 3000m), and mile upon mile of motorway ideally suited to the Great British piste-basher. Crowds are rarely a problem except in bad weather (when there is very little skiing to be done, especially at Tignes) and snow conditions are reliable until late April.

Both are skiers' ski resorts; you don't have to be an expert, but you do have be keen. Anyone who wants to do more on a winter holiday than ski, drink, eat, dance and sleep should not be tempted. Tignes is the very model of a modern French resort, built up rapidly and not at all prettily from nothing in the pit of a huge treeless horseshoe of mountains, beneath the glaciers of the Grande Motte, one of Savoie's highest and most shapely peaks. It is a large, mostly self-catering resort split into three parts around a small lake – Tignes-le-Lac and La Lavachet north of the lake, and Val Clavet to the south. It now has a range of sports facilities, but is quiet after dark. Most of the resort is ideal for convenience skiing. There is more to find fault with in Val d'Isère; the resort is a styleless straggle, the lifts aren't central, and the runs down to the valley are difficult. But at least it feels like a village, and is increasingly lively in the evenings. Young enthusiasts from all over the world fill the resort. The large British presence is particularly obvious in low season.

The resorts are not easy to reach by car, but having one facilitates day trips to Les Arcs or La Plagne, and makes it possible for skiers based in Tignes to have a bit of fun in Val d'Isère.

The skiing top 3488m bottom 1550m

Val d'Isère/Tignes divides naturally into at least six separate sectors. On the Val d'Isère side, the Le Fornet/Iseran, Solaise and Bellevarde/ La Daille sectors are strung in a row along the curving road up from Bourg-St-Maurice to Le Fornet, served by efficient ski-buses through the resort (Train Rouge). The first two sectors are linked by lift at altitude; Solaise and Bellevarde only at valley level, just beside Val d'Isère. Bellevarde/La Daille links up over the Tovière ridge with Tignes, which has skiing around all sides of a horseshoe, in three main sectors – Tovière, Grande Motte (going up to the glacier), and Palet/ Palafour/ Aiguille Percée. Behind the Aiguille Percée there is still more skiing down to the hamlets of Les Brévières and Les Boisses.

The **Solaise** cable-car was Val d'Isère's first lift, installed in 1943. Under it and the parallel chair-lift there are some steep, awkward and often bare runs through the trees. Above the tree-line, underneath the top half of the cable-car, and served by its own drag-lift is Val d'Isère's most famous run: the Plan, or simply the Bumps – a wide mogul-field, not particularly long or steep (patches of over 30° are few, and short), but a cult. Bumps are left to grow to very impressive dimensions. Descending to the left of the cable-car, missing out most of the bumps run, Piste S is one of the most difficult in the area, very often just as bumpy as the Plan but longer, steeper and narrower: a run to sort out real skiers from Solaise swanks. Beyond the Tête de Solaise, a high, long, gentle bowl provides a lot of long, easy runs (green and blue) complicated only by piste crossroads. Around the steep rims of the bowl there is a lot of off-piste skiing, often dangerous. The long Cugnaï chair-lift gives access to runs down a beautiful off-piste back bowl – often skied into a piste-like state – leading to lifts back up from Le Manchet. The pistes down from Cugnaï join up with the Arcelle/Manchet area – open slopes with good intermediate skiing beside the lifts.

From behind Tête de Solaise there is some particularly beautiful, uncrowded skiing down to Le Laisinant, between Le Fornet and Val d'Isère, where you pick up the bus. The runs are marked red and blue, but the blue is not as easy as the blues higher up, and long. This is another area for excellent off-piste skiing of varying difficulty.

At the top of the bowl behind Solaise there is a short, steep drag-lift with a run beside it, and a tunnel near the top through to the Le Fornet ski area. The run down the other side to the gentle pistes around the Col de l'Iseran is awkward at the best of times, and most skiers opt for the dramatic chair-lift ride over the ridge and down the other side.

The **Le Fornet** skiing starts with a cable-car (often the least crowded way of getting out of the valley) up over steep, wooded slopes – in this case only 400m vertical – above which the ground flattens out, giving a lot of very easy motorway skiing. From the Col de l'Iseran lifts continue round the corner, up on to the Pissaillas Glacier which offers open, extensive, easy skiing, winter and summer. For good skiers the attraction of Le Fornet is the off-piste skiing among the trees, and above all the off-piste runs from the glacier. The so-called Col Pers run from

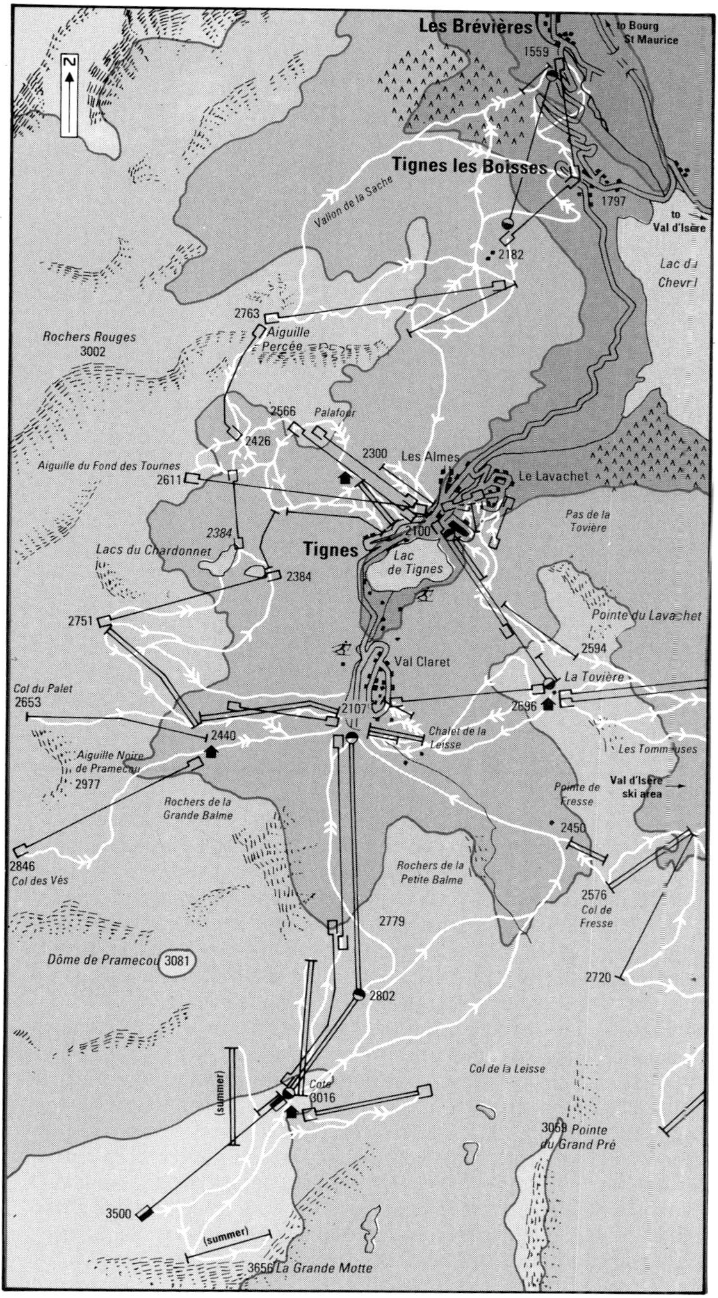
N
Les Brévières
to Bourg St Maurice
1559
Tignes les Boisses
1797
to Val d'Isère
Vallon de la Sache
2182
Lac du Chevril
2763
Aiguille Percée
Rochers Rouges
3002
2566
Palafour
2426
2300
Les Almes
Le Lavachet
Aiguille du Fond des Tournes
2611
Pas de la Tovière
2100
2384
Tignes
Lacs du Chardonnet
Lac de Tignes
2384
2751
Pointe du Lavachet
2594
Val Claret
La Tovière
Col du Palet
2653
2107
2696
2440
Chalet de la Leisse
Aiguille Noire de Pramecou
Les Tommeuses
2977
Pointe de Fresse
Val d'Isère ski area
Rochers de la Grande Balme
2450
2846
Col des Vés
Rochers de la Petite Balme
2576
Col de Fresse
2779
Dôme de Pramecou
3081
2720
2802
Col de la Leisse
(summer)
Cote 3016
3059 Pointe du Grand Pré
3500
(summer)
3656 La Grande Motte

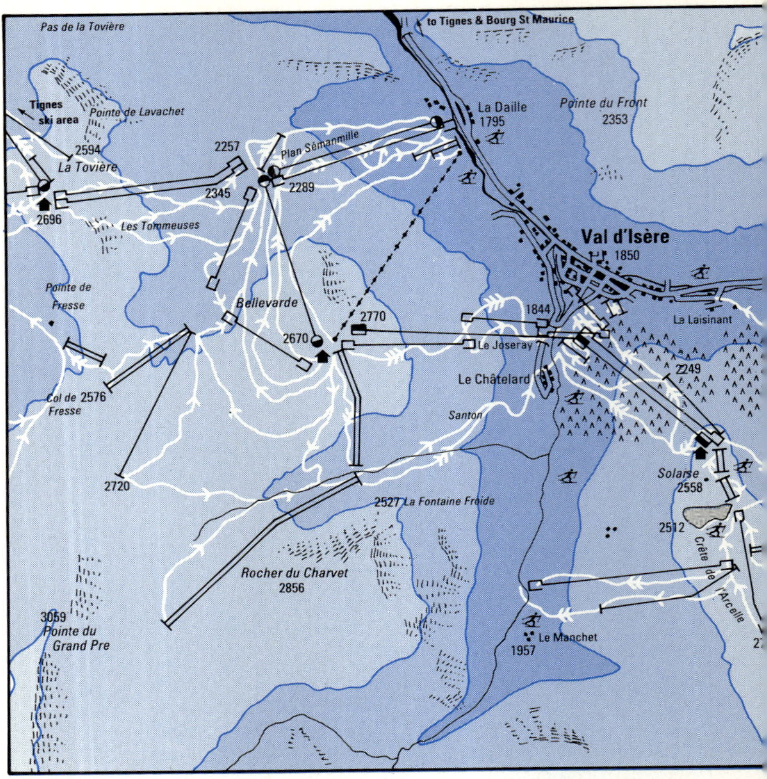

the glacier is long and beautiful but not difficult, though guidance is needed. The off-piste skiing behind the Signal drag-lift is much more open, and much steeper. There is a blue run marked down under the Le Fornet cable-car – mostly traversing, with some awkward passages.

The Rocher de **Bellevarde** rises steeply and impressively on the western side of Val d'Isère, and a long cable-car climbs quickly from the same station as the Solaise lift on the edge of town to near the peak, over 900m above the resort. As in so many parts of the area, an alternative chair-lift route makes it possible to get up without too much of a queue. The runs directly down from Bellevarde to Val d'Isère, under the cable-car, are long, steep and demanding – about the most difficult piste skiing in the area. There is also some very good off-piste skiing. Bellevarde gets a lot of sun, and snow tends to deteriorate quickly. There are easier ways to the village, but a narrow gunbarrel on the blue Santon run makes it more difficult than most people expect. Near the Santon is a black run (the Epaule) which is more open, and has fewer people on it. Though no match for the face of Bellevarde in terms of sustained challenge, it certainly deserves its grading. The long twin drag-lift round the back of the Rocher du Charvet gives access to an off-

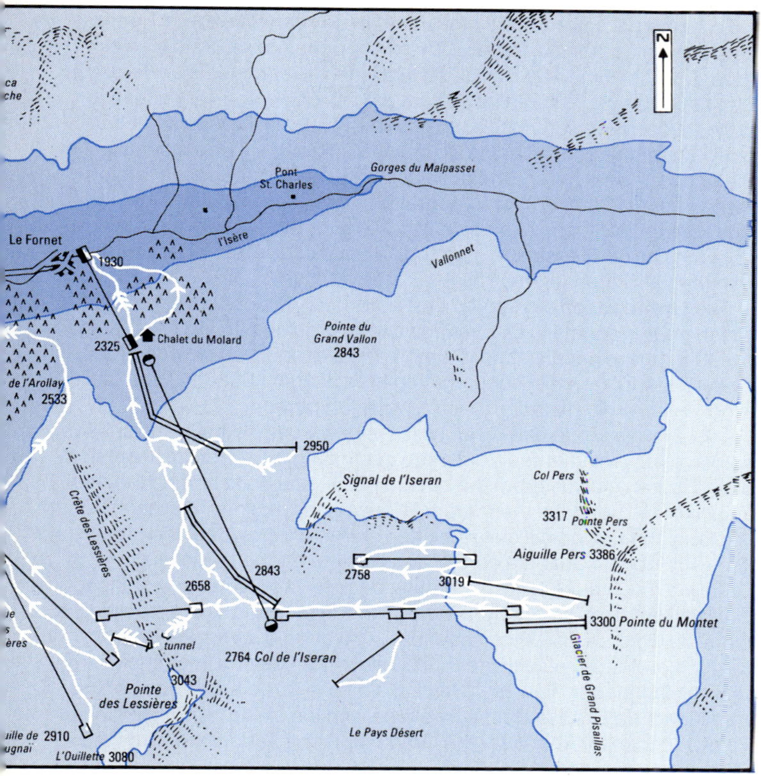

piste run called the Tour du Charvet, similar in appeal to the Col Pers – beautiful and not too difficult although often dangerous.

From La Daille the other, more gentle side of the mountain has long been served by a long two-stage dog-leg gondola to a sunny plateau below the top cable-car station. This is now joined by an underground funicular of formidable speed and capacity, going directly to Bellevarde; the walk across to the base station from the ski-bus stop is a short but annoying plod which becomes a scurrying scramble at peak times. The many runs from the top of Bellevarde down to the middle station above La Daille are spread around a wide area, and nearly all very easy except for the splendid downhill race course (the OK run) underneath the gondolas hugging the Bellevarde rock. It is quite often closed, either for races or because of avalanche danger. The bottom half of this area mostly consists of pistes and off-piste runs through trees, which are the main characteristic and attraction of the area, along with splendid views northwards to Mont Blanc. The runs to La Daille are the easiest ways down to the valley but often unpleasantly crowded and icy. An interesting off-piste excursion is the so-called Piste Perdue, more or less following the course of a river, down a gully.

From the La Daille middle station the main connection with Tignes is a pair of triple chairs to **Tovière**. There is a good open off-piste area down from Tovière to La Daille, left of all the lifts and the Piste Perdue. The main lift out of Tignes for Tovière, is now one of the very effective gondola/cable-car hybrids (from Tignes-le-Lac). The run straight back down under the lift is a very good one – black with a steep mogul field at the bottom – and there is the possibility of an even steeper variant on the top section (the Mur de Paquerettes). Less severe runs (blue and red) lead to Val Claret, joining up with the fairly straightforward run down from the Col de Fresse and merging, to the discomfiture of beginners, with the Val Claret nursery lifts.

The **Grande Motte** is served by a notorious old double gondola lift, which always seems to be overcrowded or breaking down. A two-stage chair-lift runs in parallel, and is a more reliable and less crowded (but colder) way to the main congregation area at about 3000m. Here there is now a splendid restaurant with a wide sun terrace.

The Grande Motte cable-car, which is rarely open early in the season, serves a run which is easy, but more interesting than most of the pistes on the Iseran glacier. From the bottom of the glacier, at around the mid-station of the gondola, there are two long pistes down to Val Claret. One is a long and not too difficult red, often extremely crowded; the other is a fairly straightforward blue connecting with the Col de Fresse lifts – usually a much quicker way of getting back to Val d'Isère than going to down to Val Claret and up to Tovière. The run for good skiers to tick off is the Wall, which is just what it sounds like: a short but very steep drop over the end of the glacier, near the piste. A particularly fine off-piste run crosses the glacier high up, involving a bit of a climb and drops behind the Rocher de Grande Balme to join up with the skiing below the Col du Palet. A cable-car from near the Grand Motte mid-station towards the Dôme de Pramécou is planned.

The **Col du Palet/Aiguille Percée** area above Val Claret and Tignes-le-Lac is probably the least exciting skiing in Tignes, but there is a lot of it. It is very sunny and rarely crowded, with lots of runs which do not differ greatly – nearly all in the blue or easy red category, with a few steeper pitches. There is a superb, very long and beautiful piste (La Sache, now graded black but not difficult) and an off-piste alternative down from Aiguille Percée to Tignes-les-Brévières. There is also a blue via Tignes-les-Boisses, which at the bottom may be icy and so not as easy as a blue run should be. This area is attractive, and Les Brévières itself is a pleasant place for lunch. The Col du Palet is the starting point of long off-piste runs down to Champagny and Plan Peisey, not difficult on firm late-season snow, according to one report.

Despite continued and long overdue improvements in the provision of inviting **mountain restaurants** and working loos ('great progress,' says the tourist office), Val and Tignes still have a long way to go before they can claim to be properly equipped in this respect. The chalet at the top of Tovière and the new Panoramique on the Grande Motte are exceptions, and the rebuilt La Datcha in the middle of Solaise is much improved. Not surprisingly, many skiers go down to the valley for lunch.

The lift system is well conceived and energetically improved every year, so that when everything is working **queues** should not be a problem. But we nevertheless receive repeated complaints about queues, queue behaviour, lift breakdowns and lunch-time closures. The main recent black-spots have been the return to Tignes via Tovière in the afternoon and all the lifts out of Val Claret. There are often queues for the Grande Motte cable-car. A greater problem is piste congestion, especially on the Grande Motte, Solaise and runs to La Daille. Piste grading is unreliable, often representing quite difficult runs as easy – a problem compounded by lax piste maintenance (even green runs may be mogulled). Marking also is erratic.

Among off-piste skiers this is a pilgrimage resort thanks to the sheer extent of the skiable region and the number of open slopes you can reach by lift, many of them skiable (with guidance) by non-experts. The area has a reputation for avalanches, but this may have a lot to do with the numbers of people who go off-piste skiing. In our experience the authorities take the dangers seriously and work very hard, not only to make the mountains secure, but also to inform skiers about off-piste as well as piste conditions. But at least one visitor last season felt that the dangers of going off-piste were not made sufficiently clear.

Val d'Isère

Val d'Isère is set in a remote steep-sided valley, beyond the reservoir which drowned the old village of Tignes some 30 years ago. The road emerges from a series of tunnels into the valley at La Daille, little more than a cluster of modern apartment buildings at the foot of the pistes. Val d'Isère proper starts half a mile or so up the road, a gathering density of mostly ugly blocks and a few chalets. The road becomes a long, wide main street, with shops, bars, and hotels on either side and parking in the middle where once was the river. A fine old 11th-century Savoyard church and some rough old buildings huddled around it are all there is to old Val d'Isère. The resort is long and strung-out, but it is not huge, and nowhere is far from the main-road bus route; it is also flat, so walking is no great hardship. Although the road goes only to Le Fornet (the Col de l'Iseran, Europe's highest road, is closed in winter), there are always lots of cars and buses around. The shopping isn't very exciting, but there are a few excellent shops for gourmet self-caterers.

There is a free and frequent ski-bus service along the valley which is invaluable, although a terrible crush at peak times (skis have to be taken inside). There is a less frequent evening service to La Daille Buses to Tignes are occasional and expensive.

There is a much wider choice of **accommodation**, and many more hotels, than in most purpose-built resorts. Central hotels and residences are within easy walking range of the main cable-car station and nursery slopes; from other places you either face longer walks or the bus. There are no really luxurious hotels and plenty of small, simple ones offering good value. At the top end of the range the rather soulless Sofitel (✆79060830) is central and the Grand Paradis (✆79061173) is even better placed for the main lifts. Of the other hotels, we have favourable reports of the Aiglon (✆79060405) – good food, French atmosphere but not a very convenient location; and of the central Squaw Valley (✆79060272). The Bellier (✆79060377) is another welcoming, traditional French family hotel with good food; it is quietly but not inconveniently located and the views are splendid. The Savoyarde (✆79060155) has been revamped after a fire; we await confirmation that the food is still excellent. Of the several well-placed, adequately comfortable B&B hotels the Henri Oreiller (✆79060845) is more attractive than most.

The new funicular confirms La Daille as the most convenient place to stay from the skiing point of view; as well as direct access to Bellevarde, there is fairly quick access to Tignes. But après-skiers without cars will find La Daille dull. There is an 'excellent' supermarket.

Après-ski is plentiful and varied, with more excellent restaurants than you are likely to need, even for a holiday of great indulgence. Several are more distinguished than the Bar Jacques, which stays open until 4am, but none is friendlier. The Crech 'Ouna, just above the bottom station of the La Daille lifts, is an atmospheric and popular restaurant. Hotels offer excellent fixed-price meals, and you can get very good traditional Savoyard meals in La Daille and Le Fornet. The variety and entertainment value of bars is as good, some totally British, others hardly at all (and more expensive). Dick's Tea-Bar (a joke) is reportedly less of a forum for piste-chat and more of a stick disco. Jasper's piano bar is British-run, and said to be cheaper than its competitors. Play Bach/Feedback (another joke) is recommended for music and meals.

Despite the various provisions for **cross-country** and **non-skiing** activity, serious practitioners of either should look elsewhere.

Val d'Isère's main **nursery slopes** are conveniently located (between the old village and the Solaise cable-car station), and quite gentle, with plenty of bars and restaurants nearby. La Daille has a smaller area. There is enormous scope for near-beginners way up on the Iseran glacier, on the slopes above La Daille and on Solaise.

We have favourable recent reports on both **ski schools**, but particularly on Snow Fun's off-piste guiding. There is huge potential for day-trip ski-tours – some into the nearby National Park, and many skiable by non-experts. Val d'Isère is full of freelance instructors, including off-piste specialist teams. Heli-skiing on nearby Italian mountains can be arranged.

Tignes

The setting of Tignes is austere, with no woodland to relieve the bare mountain scenery. Its high and open situation makes it a good place to ski late in the season, but not a good place in bad weather. The centre is Tignes-le-Lac, beside the lake, already rather shoddy but at least with some variety of building style and the usual selection of bars, restaurants and shops. There are some sunny restaurant terraces. Le Lavachet is a nearby but inconvenient satellite which is linked by ski-lift shuttle. Val Claret is cluster of tall, modern blocks at the foot of the

Grande Motte lifts. From here there is easy access to all skiing areas, and reporters found they were able to satisfy all their material requirements within the one building where they were staying.

There is a free shuttle bus around the resort until midnight ('very, very crowded at peak times'). There is also a bus service from Les Boisses and Les Brévières to Tignes, which is much less reliable. There are few buses to Val d'Isère.

Accommodation, at least that offered by UK operators, is largely self-catering or staffed apartments. Most of the hotels are in Tignes-le-Lac and are neither attractive nor luxurious. One exception in all respects is Le Ski d'Or (✆79065160), an expensive, very comfortable modern chalet hotel in Val Claret. Most of the self-catering accommodation is in Val Claret and Le Lavachet. We have a comprehensively negative report on the tiny studios in Chalet Club. Les Brévières is attractive, but best enjoyed on excursions from Tignes. Val Claret's one supermarket is 'good but pricey'.

Après-ski is generally quiet – 'dead' in the view of one recent visitor – but there are plenty of restaurants and a few nightclubs in all sectors. Of the restaurants, Le Ski d'Or is outstanding in cost and quality. One report recommends the Boeuf Mich, at least on weekdays, another the Chamois and the Arbina – 'the closest thing to après-ski you'll find'. Harry's Bar in Le Lavachet is a pale imitation of the originals, but nevertheless a fairly cheap place to drink, with musical accompaniment; it rarely merits the term discothèque. There are a couple of discothèques in both Tignes-le-Lac and Val Claret. Le Palaf (Lac) is usually the most lively of them.

We have reports of reports of weekly duplicate bridge. Even more emphatically than Val d'Isère, this is no place for **cross-country** skiers or **non-skiers**, despite the construction of a new sports centre providing tennis and many other activities. The ice rink is reportedly 'appallingly maintained'.

Tignes' **nursery slopes** are very reliable for snow, but tend to be crowded – especially at Val Claret – and bumpy.

Recent reports praise the **ski school** both for classes ('good instruction in English') and private lessons, although one reporter complained of mixed teaching methods. The school can provide guides for the very attractive excursion to Champagny or Plan Peisey via the Col du Palet, and will arrange transport back.

Val d'Isere/Tignes facts

Lift payment

Passes Area pass covers all lifts, swimming pool (Val d'Isere only) and resort buses, and gives one day a week in La Plagne or Les Arcs. Day passes available.
Cost 6-day pass FF680; 30% off over 60.
Children 30% off, under 13.
Beginners Free lifts on all main nursery slopes.
Summer skiing Very extensive, both at Tignes (2700m to 3500m, open all year) and at Val d'Isère (2700m to 3300m, open July to mid-Aug).

Val d'Isère facts

Ski school

ESF (centre and La Daille), and Snow-Fun (English section at Hotel Solaise).
Classes (Both schools) 2½ or 3hr morning or afternoon, or both.
Cost ESF 6 days FF635 (FF570 if early afternoon session taken). Private lessons FF125/hr. Snow-Fun 6 days FF640. Private lessons FF170/1½hr.
Children 30% off ESF prices, 35% off Snow-Fun. ESF ski kindergartens (centre and La Daille); cost as for classes. Non-ski kindergartens in centre.
Special courses ESF: monoski, race training, off-piste, tests. Snow-Fun: off-piste, *ski extrême*, Inner Skiing.

Cross-country skiing

Trails 17km of easy trail around the resort and towards La Daille.

Not skiing

Facilities Walks in Le Manchet valley. Swimming (free with lift pass for 7 days plus), natural ice rink (free), curling, dance/aerobics, hang-gliding, sauna/massage, solarium, gym, bridge, motor-trikes.

Medical facilities

In resort Fracture clinic, doctor, dentist, chemist.
Hospital Bourg-St-Maurice (33km)

Available holidays

Resort beds 2,500 in hotels, 22,000 in apartments.
Package holidays Air France (Ht Sc), Bladon Lines (Ht Ch Cl Sc), Crystal (Ht Sc), Horizon (Ht Sc), Inghams (Ht Sc), Intasun (Ht Sc), John Morgan (Ch), Made to Measure (Ht Sc), Mark Warner (Ch Cl), Neilson (Ht Sc), Ski Lovers (Ap Sc), Ski MacG (Ht Ch Sc), Ski West (Ht Ch Cl Sc), Ski-Val (Ht Ch Cl Sc), Skiworld (Sc), Supertravel (Ht Ch Cl Sc), Thomson (Ht Sc), Tourarc (Ht), Vacations (Ht Sc)

Further information

Tourist office ✆79061083. Tx 980077.

Tignes facts

Ski school

ESF (Lac de Tignes, Val Claret).
Classes 3hr morning and/or afternoon.
Cost ESF: 5 days FF745. Private lessons FF125/hr.
Children 25% off classes. Also separate children's branches of both ski schools, and kindergartens in Lac and Val Claret offering all-day care with skiing available; 6 days all inclusive FF925.
Special courses Freestyle, tests, racing, off-piste, monoski, slalom, powder.

Cross-country skiing

Trails 9km of easy trails around Lac de Tignes and at Les Boisses. Summer trail on the glacier.

Not skiing

Facilities Natural ice rink; 'Tignespace' centre has sauna, solarium, gym, aerobics, dance, squash, tennis, golf; also hang-gliding, scuba diving, bowling.

Medical facilities

In resort Doctor, fracture clinic, dentist, chemist.
Hospital Bourg-St-Maurice (25km).

Available holidays

Resort beds 1,200 in hotels, 20,100 in apartments.
Package holidays Alpine Activity Club (Cl Sc), Bladon Lines (Ht Ch Sc), Blue Sky (Sc), Brittany Ferries (Sc), Club Med (Ht), Crystal (Cl Sc), Enterprise (Ht Sc), Horizon (Ht Sc), Inghams (Ht Sc), Intasun (Sc), Made to Measure (Ht Sc), Ski Club of GB (Ht Cl), Ski Falcon (Ap Sc), Ski Lovers (Ch Ap Sc), Ski West (Ht Sc), Ski-plan (Ht), Ski-Val (Cl Sc), Skiworld (Ht Sc), Supertravel (Ht Ch), Thomson (Sc), Tracer (Sc)

Further information

Tourist office ✆79061555. Tx 980030.

Getting there

Airport Geneva; transfer 4hr plus.
Railway Bourg-St-Maurice (33km); four buses daily.

Road Via Lyon/Chambéry; chains often needed. Horrific peak weekend traffic jams.

Learn to ski fast – 200km/hr

Les Arcs France 1600–2000m

Good for *Ski évolutif, tough runs, big ski area, off-piste skiing, skiing convenience, lift queues, beautiful scenery, family holidays, freedom from cars, late holidays, resort-level snow, sunny slopes, rail access*
Bad for *Alpine charm, mountain restaurants, après-ski, not skiing, short airport transfers, easy road access*

Les Arcs is a modern, predominantly self-catering resort in three parts: Arc 1600 (or Arc Pierre Blanche) and Arc 1800 are close neighbours on the broad flank of the main Isère valley above Bourg-St-Maurice; Arc 2000 is in a secluded high bowl of its own at the heart of the skiing.

Thanks to new lifts at the top and bottom, the skiing is extensive, interesting and suitable for all grades of skier, with plenty of easy runs above Arc 1800 and Arc 2000, and more than enough challenge on the slopes of the Aiguille Rouge for most skiers. The lift system is well thought-out, and queues are rarely bad; and accommodation is nearly all conveniently placed for skiing. But for après-ski and non-skiing facilities the resort scores very low marks – a view which only those with an interest in the matter dispute. One of Les Arcs' greatest selling points is the *ski évolutif* method of tuition (see 'A Skiing Primer') which was introduced to Europe here. Opinions on it vary widely; it suits many people, but it should not dominate your choice of resort.

In holiday periods, when the French are in residence *en masse*, Les Arcs may be smart, but off-season it isn't – the noisy, young British presence is very obvious. The resort has hit a vein of demand in Britain for self-catering holidays among budget-conscious skiers, many of whom are surprised by the high cost of everything in Les Arcs.

Les Arcs has a cable-car link with Bourg-St-Maurice, a real town with a good Saturday market, real locals and reasonable prices. There are also plenty of good-value restaurants and hotels.

Cars have to be parked at the edge of each complex, but having one is handy for exploring the three resort centres and for making use of the pass-swapping arrangement with other resorts.

The skiing top 3226m bottom 1100m

The broad north-west facing mountain flank above Arc 1600 and Arc 1800 is well served by chairs and drag-lifts to a ridge of rocky peaks with skiing up to about 2400m. On the other side of this ridge is a wide bowl with Arc 2000 in the pit, lifts up from it to over 3000m, and ski runs on down below the resort to Villaroger, a hamlet beside the road to Val d'Isère (and lifts back up – handy for Val-based excursionists).

The runs above **Arc 1800** are open and relatively easy, even those marked red. These slopes, on which many inexperienced skiers rely, get a lot of afternoon sun, and late in the season tend to be icy in the morning and slushy in the afternoon. The skiing connects with lifts up from Vallandry, Plan Peisey and Nancroix, between Les Arcs and La Plagne. This is an excellent area for skiing in bad weather, with plenty of good runs on and off the piste in woodland.

The skiing above **Arc 1600** is steeper and more wooded. There are some excellent broad, fairly steep trails, and there is some good off-piste skiing between them. Timid intermediate skiers can take a blue run down from top (Les Deux Têtes) to bottom or over to Arc 1800, but even this run has a few awkward passages. In good conditions it is possible to ski down towards Bourg-St-Maurice.

The bowl above **Arc 2000** has easy runs down into it from several points along the ridge reached from Arc 1600 and Arc 1800. It is a splendid area for inexperienced skiers to enjoy a lot of space and beautiful scenery. The far side of the bowl is dominated by the Aiguille Rouge, served by a number of lifts and Les Arcs' only cable-car. The Aiguille Rouge is what makes Les Arcs special. It is one of the few lift-served mountains in the Alps which is entirely of black steepness. Unfortunately it is often closed when conditions are not good. From the exposed open peak there are magnificent views across to the glaciers of the Mont Pourri (3782m). Off-piste slopes are in many places so steep and rocky that they are skiable only by very expert skiers; pistes are long and challenging. The Villaroger run, giving the world's greatest vertical drop for a marked run – over 2100m – has an enormous variety of terrain, and for much of its course is dark red to black.

The face of the Aiguille Rouge above Arc 2000 is the setting of the fastest European speed-skiing run. This track starts off extremely steeply (about 45 degrees) and then levels out gradually into a huge open runout down to Arc 2000, which is just what the competitors need, along with high altitude for low air resistance. When the speed-skiers are at it, in their rubber suits, streamlined helmets and 240cm skis, the spectacle is very impressive; 200km/hr is the going rate these days. There are plenty of challenging runs not served by the cable-car. Underneath the chair-lift to the bottom cable-car station there are usually some formidable bumps. Exciting off-piste runs start from the top of the drag-lifts at the Grand Col, (behind the Aiguille Rouge to Villaroger), and beside the Aiguille Grive in the other direction to Nancroix and Plan Peisey. These runs are a long way from pistes and should not be attempted without guidance.

Mountain restaurants are of varying quality but generally inadequate; a recent report picked out the Chez Felix at Plan Peisey as 'very good'. Most people return to the resort complexes. In the Arc 2000 valley there is a very attractive old chalet beside the river near the bottom of the Comborcière lift. There is an attractive rustic restaurant at the bottom of the pistes down to Villaroger.

For a new French ski resort Les Arcs' lift system is surprising: it is all chairs and drags except for the single cable-car at the top. The lifts work well, with few **queues** – there are multiple routes out of the main resorts and lots of triple chairs up to the dividing ridge. Getting back from Arc 2000 in the afternoon can involve longer waits for the two main linking

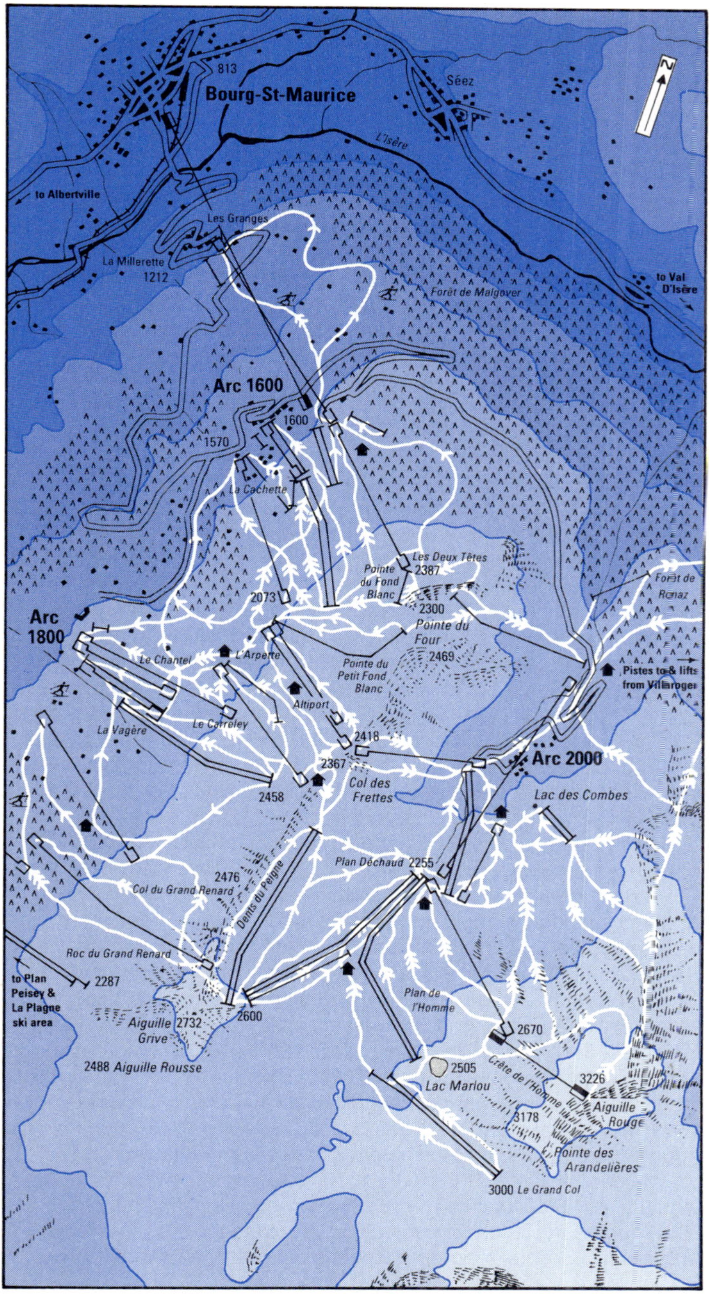
N
Bourg-St-Maurice
813
Séez
L'Isère
to Albertville
Les Granges
La Millerette
1212
Forêt de Malgover
to Val D'Isère
Arc 1600
1600
1570
La Cachette
Les Deux Têtes
2387
Pointe du Fond Blanc
2073
2300
Forêt de Renaz
Arc 1800
Pointe du Four
2469
Le Chantel
L'Arpette
Pointe du Petit Fond Blanc
Pistes to & lifts from Villaroger
Altiport
La Vagère
Le Carreley
2418
2367
Arc 2000
Col des Frettes
2458
Lac des Combes
Plan Déchaud 2255
2476
Col du Grand Renard
Dents du Peigne
Roc du Grand Renard
to Plan Peisey & La Plagne ski area
2287
Plan de l'Homme
Aiguille 2732 Grive
2600
2670
2488 Aiguille Rousse
2505
Lac Marlou
3226
Crête de l'Homme
Aiguille Rouge
3178
Pointe des Arandelières
3000 Le Grand Col

lifts. There are often queues for the Aiguille Rouge cable-car. Queues in 1800 to buy lift passes at weekends can be serious; if driving, buy lift passes at the Bourg-St-Maurice cable-car station.

The resort

The two important parts of Les Arcs are Arc 1600 and Arc 1800. Both command magnificent views north-west across to Mont Blanc, and west along the valley into the setting sun. They are both compact clusters, with curving forms hugging the mountain, designed to make sure that many of the apartments and hotels have sunny terraces and balconies. Wood has been widely used, but the original buildings were poorly finished and are now beginning to look distinctly tatty.

Frequent daytime buses run between Arc 1600 and Arc 1800 until 8pm, and occasionally to Arc 2000 until 6pm. The cable-car to and from Bourg-St-Maurice runs until about 6.30pm.

Of the two main units, Arc 1800 is bigger and has most of the bars and shops, restaurants and apartment blocks. It is itself split into two sectors – Le Charvet and Les Villards – each with a supermarket in easy reach of all the apartments. We have mouth-watering reports of good take-away cooked dishes taking the sweat out of self-catering. Arrangements for getting luggage across the resort from the car parks to the more remote apartments are imperfect. Arc 1600 is smaller and quieter, and although the standard brochure term 'villagey' is misleading, the bars and restaurants are smaller and more personal. Most of 1600 consists of a horseshoe of buildings around the Hotel La Cachette with sunny terraces in front of the shops and restaurants. Arc 2000 is for the moment little more than a couple of large, squarish dull blocks (including the Club Méditerranée) and a very limiting place to stay – though there are ambitious plans for its development into the major Arc. A new hotel, the Eldorador, opened last season.

Most reporters took self-catering **accommodation** in Arc 1800 and one or two were disappointed at having to walk up from the lower blocks to the slopes. The standard of apartments varies little – most are tight on space and unluxurious, and cooking facilities are limited. There is a widespread use of bunk beds and the usual sofa beds in living areas. Plenty of apartments get a lot of afternoon sun, but promises of day-long balcony sunbathing should be treated sceptically. Les Arcs' smartest existing hotel is in Le Charvet (1800) – the Golf (✆79072517) – as is the most modern – the Latitudes (✆79074979). Neither is cheap. People not wanting a self-catering holiday should consider Bourg-St-Maurice. There are a number of small hotels near the cable-car to Arc 1600 offering cheap rooms or half-board.

Après-ski is very limited. There are bars, restaurants and discothèques in Arc 1600 and Arc 1800, none of them with much atmosphere. The Hotel du Golf is probably the best nightspot.

Les Arcs is not recommended either for **cross-country** skiers or **non-skiers**. Several reporters regretted the lack of a swimming pool. Availability of skating is unreliable.

For adult beginners (but not children), **ski school** means *ski évolutif*. Though there is a theoretical class size limit of 10 people, reporters say that this is disregarded ('regularly 14 or 15 pupils'). But a recent reporter found movements between classes were well handled. If you want to have a go at speed-skiing, apply at Arc 2000.

It is perhaps just as well that *ski évolutif* does not involve long days spent on **nursery slopes**, as Les Arcs is not ideally provided with these. Areas are roped off near the resort for the first stages of *ski évolutif* and for children's ski playgrounds. Arc 1800, in particular, does cater well for near-beginners, with a long, wide, easy but varied slope just above the resort.

Les Arcs facts

Lift payment

Passes Area pass covers all lifts of Les Arcs and Plan Peisey, including Bourg-St-Maurice cable-car, but no bus services. Weekly passes valid for one day in La Plagne and Val d'Isère/ Tignes. Pass also available to cover La Rosière/ La Thuile. Coupons available for some lifts (notably Bourg-St-Maurice cable-car).
Cost 6-day pass FF640.
Children Free under 7 if parent buying pass.
Beginners Limited day pass for lower lifts of each resort centre.

Ski school

Classes 2hr, morning and afternoon.
Cost 6 days FF1,175 including lifts and *évolutif* equipment. 6 days for non-beginners FF500. Private lessons FF130/hr.
Children Ski kindergartens, ages 4–8, 6 days with lunch and equipment hire FF1,105. Non-ski kindergartens, ages 1–6, 8.30–6.00, 6 days with lunch FF795.
Special courses Intensive race training, powder skiing weeks or guided day excursions, *ski extrême* weeks, monoski lessons or courses, speed-skiing.

Cross-country skiing

Trails 4 and 7km trails, accessible from 1600 and 1800.

Medical facilities

In resort Doctor, dentist, chemist.
Hospital Bourg-St-Maurice.

Not skiing

Facilities (Not all present in all resort units – check). Natural ice rink, saunas in hotels, organised snow-shoe outings, 10km cleared walks, squash, solarium, chinese gymnastics, keep-fit sessions, bridge, hang-gliding, cinemas, fencing, karate.

Getting there

Airport Geneva, transfer 4hr plus. Horrific peak weekend traffic jams. (Several tour operators now use Lyon, and at least one uses Chambéry.)
Railway Bourg-St-Maurice; frequent buses and direct cable-car to resort.
Road Via Lyon/Chambéry; chains often needed from Bourg-St-Maurice.

Available holidays

Resort beds 960 in hotels, 8,830 in apartments.
Package holidays Air France (Ht Sc), Brittany Ferries (Sc), Club Med (Ht) Enterprise (Ht Sc), Horizon (Ht Sc), Made to Measure (Ht Sc), Neilson (Ht Sc), Sally Tours (Sc), Ski Lovers (Ch Sc), Ski-Val (Ht Cl Sc), SkiBound (Sc), SkiSet (Ht), Thomson (Ht Sc), Tourarc (Ht, Sc), Tracer (Sc)

Further information

Tourist office 1600 ✆79077050. 1800 ✆79074800. 2000 ✆79073255. Tx 980347. The resort is represented in Britain by the specialist tour operator Tourarc ✆01-589 1918. Tx 269710.

Ski yourself to sleep

La Plagne France 1800–2100m

Good for *Nursery slopes, easy runs, big ski area, skiing convenience, family holidays, late holidays, off-piste skiing, resort-level snow, freedom from cars, beautiful scenery, sunny slopes*
Bad for *Après-ski, not skiing, Alpine charm, short airport transfers, easy road access, mountain restaurants*

Linked resorts: Montchavin, Les Coches, Champagny, Montalbert

La Plagne, which celebrated its quarter centenary in 1986, represents the state of the art of resort-building. It is a large and very fragmented place, confusing at first, but very straightforward in its appeal. The skiing is enormous in extent and vertical range; few of the pistes are challenging, but the off-piste skiing is excellent. Snow conditions are reliable except at the lower extremes of the network. Nursery slopes are abundant and immediately accessible, and child-care facilities are excellent. Nearly all accommodation is in modern apartments, conveniently placed for getting to and from skiing. And there you have it – apart from some lift bottlenecks which manifest themselves in the peak holiday season, a perfect recipe for a rather limited winter holiday that suits many skiers very well indeed.

There are bits of La Plagne on the gentle slopes above the tree-line dominated by the huge monolith of Aime la Plagne, where thousands of skiers can be pigeon-holed and processed under one roof. In the more modern of these centres the designers have tried, with some success, to reproduce some village atmosphere. There are also smaller resort components much lower down, some of them modified old villages, others new developments. These low resorts are not directly below the main parts of La Plagne, but are reached by taking lifts up to the rim of the wide bowl around the resort centre. This makes the low skiing less valuable in bad weather. Champagny-en-Vanoise, a peaceful collection of hamlets, on the south side of the area (not far from Courchevel), is set to become an important access point since the construction of its big new gondola.

The lift pass is wide-ranging, and a car is helpful in making full use of it on excursions to Les Arcs and Val d'Isère (though for little else).

The skiing top 3250 bottom 1250

The core of La Plagne's skiing is a central area above Plagne Centre and its close neighbours Plagne Villages, Bellecôte and Belle Plagne, all of them set between 1900m and 2050m. The western side of this basin is dominated by the single building of Aime la Plagne (at 2100m), from which it is easy to ski down to Centre. Below it is Plagne 1800, or Plagne Lauze, the newest of the resort units. There are three other facets to the skiing: through woods behind Aime la Plagne as far as Montalbert; south-facing slopes above Champagny, on the side of an entirely different valley; and, at the eastern end of the skiing area, a high area of glacier skiing and a low area of woodland runs towards Montchavin and Les Coches. From the glacier to Montchavin gives an enormous descent of 15km and 2000m vertical, but there are no prepared pistes down, and (as yet) no lifts directly back up.

The central basin above the five residential units provides timid skiers with a very extensive range of not very long, not at all steep runs with a vertical range of about 500m. There are slightly longer descents from Roche de Mio, and a greater scope for challenge (bumps under the chair and open off-piste areas). The basin is split up by broken ground, and you have to be constantly on your guard against losing your way. One neglected and exceptional feature of this area is the long runs directly down from Aime la Plagne, through woods past Plagne 1800 – far enough (to 1400m) to give a long and challenging run (the black Emile Allais).

Behind the Le Biolley lifts above Aime la Plagne there are stiff runs with pitches of over 30°, initially west-facing and liable to be icy and very difficult in the mornings. After this steep open slope a gentle trail through woods links with the Emile Allais run or with the Les Adrets lift for a gentle run through the woods to **Montalbert**.

The south-facing slopes above **Champagny** can be reached from several points above the central resort units without any great difficulty. For good skiers the toughest skiing and usually the best snow is in the area beside the long, steep Verdons lifts (a four-seater chair now duplicates the drag); from here a splendid red run goes all the way down to Champagny. The rest of Champagny's skiing is easy, sunny and not very extensive.

The Bellecôte glacier is the ace in La Plagne's hand. Unlike many glacier skiing areas it opens up plenty of challenging skiing, with long and wide black runs of nearly 1000m vertical and even longer off-piste runs down to Les Bauches, where there are lifts back towards Plagne Bellecôte and an easy piste on down to Montchavin. There are more adventurous things to be done from the glacier with a guide, including very long runs down towards Peisey and the Champagny valley, and there is also a moderately easy red run back from the glacier to the Col de la Chiaupe. Unfortunately the lifts are often closed, particularly early in the season.

The **Montchavin/Les Coches** runs are reached by an improved chair-lift from Plagne Bellecôte as well as by off-piste run down from the glacier, by a good open red from Roche de Mio (now served by a new chair-lift) or by off-piste run down from the glacier. They provide plenty of variety of woodland skiing, most of it intermediate, with a drop of over 1000m vertical from the Arpette chair-lift to Montchavin. One reporter recommends the off-piste skiing among the trees between the pistes in this sector. Getting back to the Arpette has been a slow business, involving a chair and three drag-lifts, and although the new Crozat four-seat chair-lift will open up quite a lot more skiing it does not seem likely to solve the problem. From Montchavin there are buses down to Peisey-

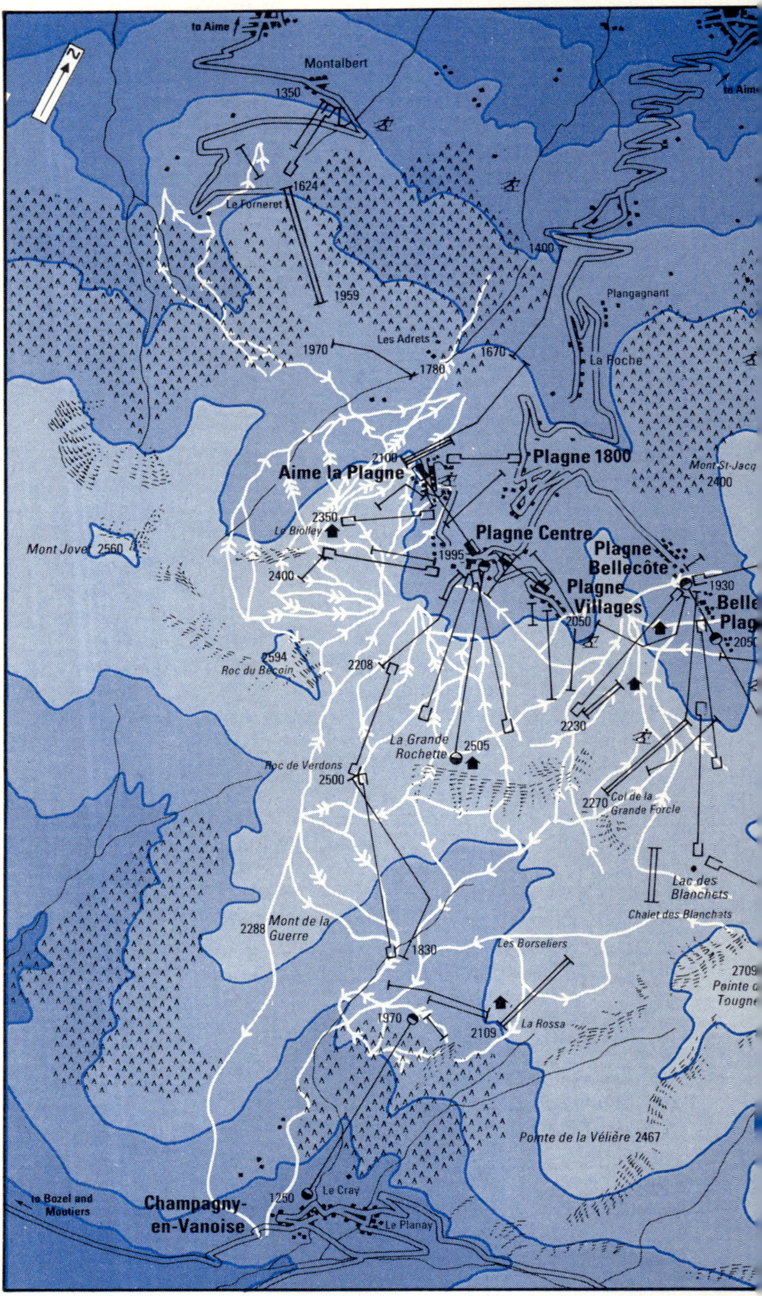
to Aime
N
Montalbert
1350
1624
Le Forneret
1959
1970
Les Adrets
1780
1670
1400
Plangagnant
La Roche
to Aime
2100
Aime la Plagne
Plagne 1800
Mont St-Jacq
2400
2350
Le Biolley
Mont Jovet 2560
2400
1995
Plagne Centre
Plagne Bellecôte
Plagne Villages
1930
2050
2594
Roc du Becoin
2208
2230
La Grande Rochette
2505
Roc de Verdons
2500
2270
Col de la Grande Forcle
Lac des Blanchets
Chalet des Blanchets
2288
Mont de la Guerre
1830
Les Borseliers
1970
2109
La Rossa
Pointe de la Vélière 2467
to Bozel and Moutiers
Champagny-en-Vanoise
1250
Le Cray
Le Planay

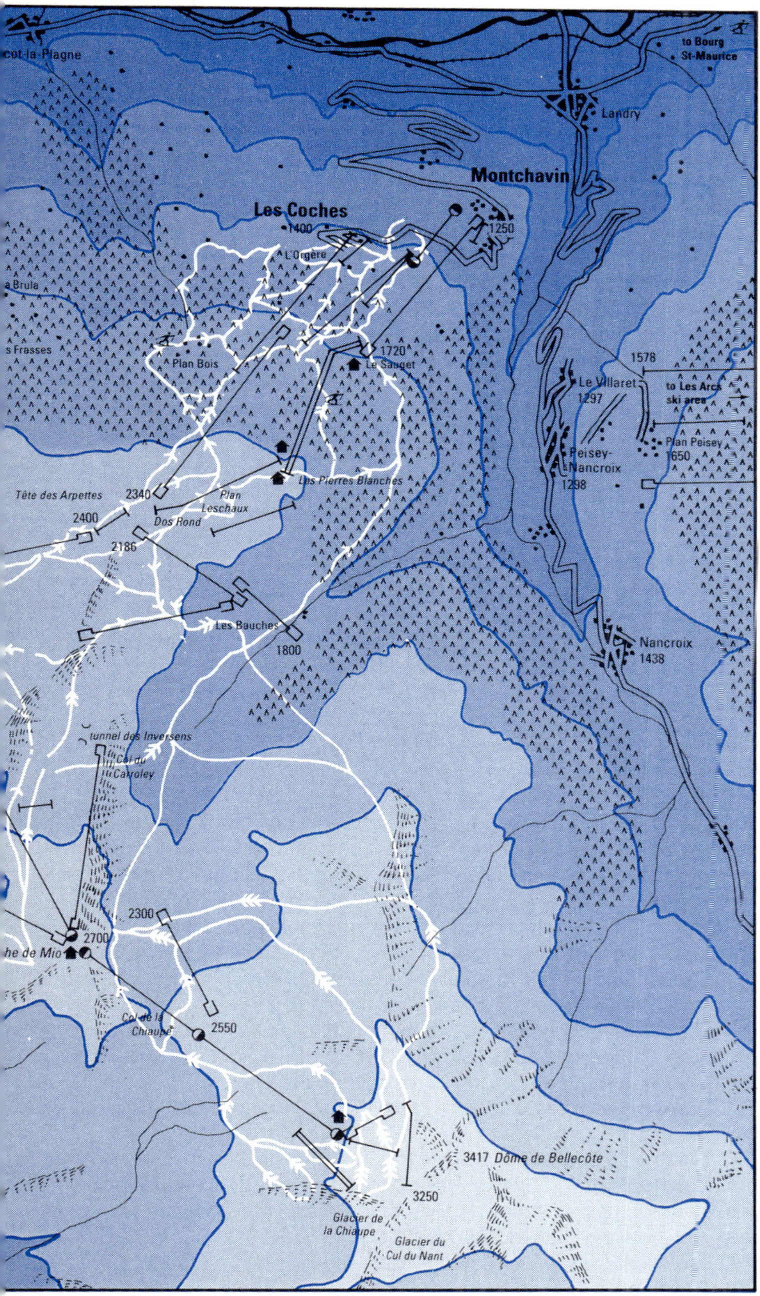
to Bourg St-Maurice
Landry
Montchavin
1250
Les Coches
1400
L'Orgère
a Brula
s Frasses
1720
Le Sauget
Plan Bois
1578
Le Villaret
1297
to Les Arcs ski area
Plan Peisey
1650
Peisey-Nancroix
1298
Les Pierres Blanches
Tête des Arpettes
2340
Plan Leschaux
2400
Dos Rond
2186
Les Bauches
1800
Nancroix
1438
tunnel des Inversens
Col du Carroley
2300
2700
Col de la Chiaupe
2550
3417 Dôme de Bellecôte
3250
Glacier de la Chiaupe
Glacier du Cul du Nant

Nancroix for access to Les Arcs.

Mountain restaurants are not very many and not very special, but there is easy access to restaurants in the many bits of resort dotted around the ski area. Several reporters mention the boisterous warmth of the lunchtime atmosphere and excellent value for money at Chez Thérèse in the Hotel Bouquetin at Champagny.

In general the system runs smoothly, even if you do spend a very long time on lifts getting around the large and not at all steep ski area. But during the February holidays, **queuing** can be a serious problem. About 80 per cent of the resort's beds are in the central area, which means lots of skiers leaving it in the morning and crowding the lifts back in the afternoon. The main bottleneck is Plagne Bellecôte; queues of at least half an hour for the Roche de Mio lift are common. Similar queues for the Grande Rochette lift out of Centre should be partly relieved by the addition of an efficient new chair-lift to Verdons, giving an alternative access to Champagny. Another capacious four-seat chair has replaced the drags climbing steeply to the east of Centre. Links to and from Les Coches and Montchavin have been similarly improved.

The resort

The original 1960s development is Plagne Centre, still the main centre for shopping, entertainment and après-ski. The buildings are big, square blocks, many of them linked by covered walkways. The hub is a dark and dank underground commercial precinct with lots of shops, bars and restaurants in little cubicles. The other units are all largely colonies of self-catering **accommodation**. Aime la Plagne and Bellecôte consist of large blocks; Bellecôte is recommended by several reporters, and convenient for skiing. Belle Plagne, Plagne Villages and Plagne 1800 (Plagne Lauze) all have smaller buildings less densely concentrated; they have less shopping and entertainment, but are linked to Bellecôte and Centre. The most popular unit with British skiers (including our reporters) is Belle Plagne, which has a more colourful and fanciful design than the others; it is convenient for skiing, especially for Roche de Mio, and has adequately comfortable and quiet apartments. Although rather out of the way, Plagne 1800 is the newest development and the standard of the apartments is reported to be high. We deal separately with the lower satellite villages.

There is some staffed chalet accommodation in Centre, as well as a few functional hotels. The Graciosa (✆79090018), on the edge of the resort, is small and friendly, and its restaurant, the Etoile d'Or, highly reputed. A recent visitor was happy with the big France ✆79092815 – 'spacious rooms, excellent dinners, outrageously expensive wine.'

All five main bits of La Plagne are linked by bus or lift from 8am until 1am, but the Plagne 1800–Centre bus operates only until early evening. Buses have to be paid for by all. Buses from Bellecôte to Centre are often crowded late in the afternoon.

Après-ski activity is very limited. There are bars and restaurants in all the residential units and a few discothèques, the greatest selection

La Plagne facts

Lift payment

Passes Single pass covers lifts of La Plagne, and is valid one day a week in Les Arcs, Val d'Isère or Tignes. Half-day and day passes available. A few main lifts can be paid for by the ride.
Children Under 6 free. 25% off 6–13.
Cost 6-day pass FF680. 25% off over 60.
Beginners Limited passes in each of the four main areas (Central La Plagne, Champagny, Montchavin and Montalbert) available by the day. Also combined pass/ski school deals in low season.
Summer skiing Small area on the Bellecôte glacier (3000m to 3250m) served by 4 lifts.

Ski school

Classes 4hr to 5hr depending on location, with extra classes over lunchtime in holiday periods.
Cost 6 days (5hr daily) FF590–900. Private lessons FF130/hr (1–4 people).
Beginners
Children Classes, ages 6–13, 6 days FF490. Ski kindergarten, ages 3–5, 9.00–5.00, 6 days with lunch FF800. Non-ski kindergarten, ages 2–6, at all main centres, 6 days with lunch FF900.
Special courses Slalom, sprint, mono ski, off-piste, powder, surf skiing, artistic skiing.

Not skiing

Facilities Swimming (Bellecôte), skating (Bellecôte), 20km marked walks, squash (Plagne 1800, Aime la Plagne), tennis (Aime la Plagne), sauna/solarium (Centre, Plagne 1800).

Cross-country skiing

Trails 26km trail from Montalbert to Peisey Nancroix. Short trail at Plagne Villages. Extensive trails (15km, 10km, 8km, 5km and 4km) and off-piste itineraries in the valley above Champagny.

Medical facilities

In resort Doctor, chemist.
Hospital Bourg-St-Maurice (35km).
Dentist Aime (18km).

Getting there

Airport Geneva; transfer 4hr plus.
Railway Aime (18km); frequent buses.
Road Via Lyon or Geneva; chains often necessary. Horrific peak weekend jams.

Available holidays

Resort beds 2,000 in hotels, 25,000 in apartments.
Package holidays Air France (Sc), Brittany Ferries (Sc), Crystal (Sc), Enterprise (Ht Sc), Horizon (Sc), Inghams (Ht Sc), John Morgan (Ch), Made to Measure (Ht Sc), Neilson (Ht Sc), Sally Tours (Sc), Schools Abroad (Ht), Ski West (Ht Sc), SkiBound (Sc), SkiSet (Ht), Skiworld (Ch Sc), Snow World (Ht Sc), Sunmed (Ht Ch Sc), Supertravel (Ch Sc), Thomson (Ht Sc), Tourarc (Ht), Tracer (Ch Sc), Vacations (Ht Sc)

Further information

Tourist office ✆79097979. Tx 980973.

being in Centre, but not many places with any character or animated atmosphere. A reporter has been impressed by 'surprisingly reasonable prices but unremarkable quality' in most places. The Grande Rochette gondola is sometimes open in the evening, with fondues and *braserades* served at the mountain restaurant at the top.

In general, the high units of La Plagne are suitable only for downhill skiers. Montalbert and Champagny are better for **cross-country** skiing. **Non-skiing** facilities have been improved, but La Plagne remains a skiers' resort.

Nursery slopes are generally very good, with playgrounds for children on the doorsteps of most of the resort units. Plagne Centre, Plagne Villages, Belle Plagne and Bellecôte are the most suitable of all, with gentle surrounding slopes, very reliable for snow.

We have few reports on **ski school**, but they are unenthusiastic – English is spoken with reluctance. Facilities for children are generally excellent, with nurseries and kindergarten playgrounds in all the main resort units.

Champagny 1250m

A peaceful collection of hamlets, some of them old, in a secluded valley. The main community (Champagny le Bas) is linked to the La Plagne ski area by a chain of lifts starting a stiff walk above the village centre. The simple Les Glières (✆79220446) is the larger of Champagny's two hotels, and convenient for the chair-lift. Beyond the village the mountains form a narrow gateway into a beautiful lonely upper valley (Champagny le Haut, 1450m) – an excellent place for cross-country skiing.

Tourist office ✆79220953.

Montchavin 1250m

Montchavin is a little old village which had most of its rustic wrinkles ironed out when it was transformed into a miniature ski resort in the early 1970s; but it is still undeniably attractive, with the pistes down from the main bowl of La Plagne ending in an orchard in front of jolly restaurant terraces. And it has some village atmosphere in its bars and restaurants in the evening. Practically all the accommodation is in apartments, but the Bellecôte (✆79078330) is a small, simple hotel close to the centre. There is a ski kindergarten (Le Chat Bleu).

Tourist office ✆79078282. **Package holidays** Made to Measure (Sc), Ski Esprit (Ch).

Montalbert 1350m

Montalbert is a tiny (1,650-bed) purpose-built satellite below Aime la Plagne, on the western extremity of the ski area. Its position is a key factor: the skiing immediately above the resort is limited (and exposed to the afternoon sun), and connections with the more extensive areas beyond Plagne Centre are time-consuming. All the accommodation is in apartments. A long cross-country trail climbs through woods along the mountainside past Les Coches to Peisey-Nancroix. There is a ski kindergarten (Le Gros Calin).

Tourist office ✆79097733.

Les Coches 1450m

One of the newest components of La Plagne, Les Coches was purpose-built in the early 1980s, in a sympathetic style and on a human scale – not unlike Belle Plagne. Small though it is, the village is broken into three 'hamlets'; the main one is Hameau du Carreau, at the foot of the main lift, with a sunny restaurant terrace facing up the wooded slopes. All the accommodation is in apartments. There is a ski kindergarten (the Pirouette).

Tourist office ✆79078282. **Package holidays** Inghams (Sc), Made to Measure (Sc), Ski Esprit (Ch), Vacations (Sc).

Les Trois Vallées: big is beautiful

Courchevel France 1300–1850m

Good for *Nursery slopes, easy runs, big ski area, skiing convenience, après-ski, resort-level snow, chalet holidays, family holidays, lift queues*
Bad for *Alpine charm, short airport transfers, easy road access, not skiing*

Méribel France 1450–1700m

Good for *Big ski area, lift queues, sunny slopes, chalet holidays, resort-level snow*
Bad for *Après-ski, short airport transfers, nursery slopes, easy road access, not skiing*

Val Thorens France 2300m

Good for-*Big ski area, tough runs, off-piste skiing, late holidays, nusery slopes, skiing convenience, summer skiing, resort-level snow*
Bad for *Mountain restaurants, not skiing, Alpine charm, après-ski, short airport transfers, easy road access*

Linked resort: Les Menuires

'Le plus grand domaine skiable du monde' is the rather nebulous catchphrase of one of the skiing industry's biggest conglomerates. Four important resorts share an enormous linked ski area (at the latest count, some 190 lifts and 500km of piste) which in one holiday many skiers can barely come to terms with, never mind exhaust. The *domaine skiable* may or may not be the biggest in the world, or even in the Alps – the Portes du Soleil area makes the same claim – but it is certainly one of the most impressive and dynamic.

Parisians who can afford it fly with their poodles to Courchevel, stay in comfortable hotels, and dine and dance without counting the *centimes*. For them, Courchevel is one of the best equipped of all French resorts; and for skiing gourmets it is without doubt the best resort in the world (which is not saying much). Its slopes offer enormous scope for beginners and timid skiers, and enough variety of difficulty and terrain to satisfy experts. The major drawback of staying here is the difficulty of making much use of the high-altitude skiing in Val Thorens, at the opposite end of the ski area. Courchevel is split into several parts, usually referred to by numbers approximating to altitude. The resort centre is at 1850, the highest part.

Méribel is a British favourite. Its attractions are that it occupies the central valley, from which you can make the most of the enormous skiing, and that it is the prettiest of the resorts; it does not face much

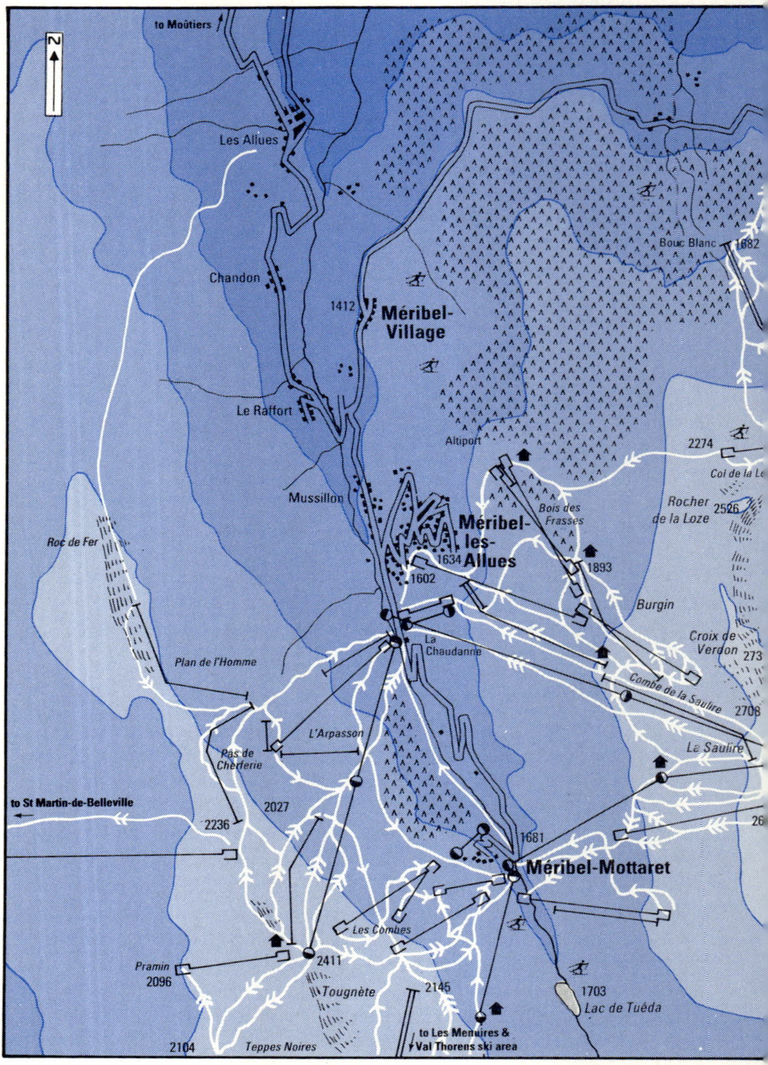

competition. There are two separate resort villages: Méribel-les-Allues (which we're calling Méribel) resembles a real village, and sprawls widely across a steep hillside as a real village might; parts of it are very convenient for skiers, but most parts are not. Méribel-Mottaret (Mottaret), higher up the valley, has been built (more recently) very much for skiing convenience. Neither has much après-ski. The local skiing of these central resorts has never compared very favourably with

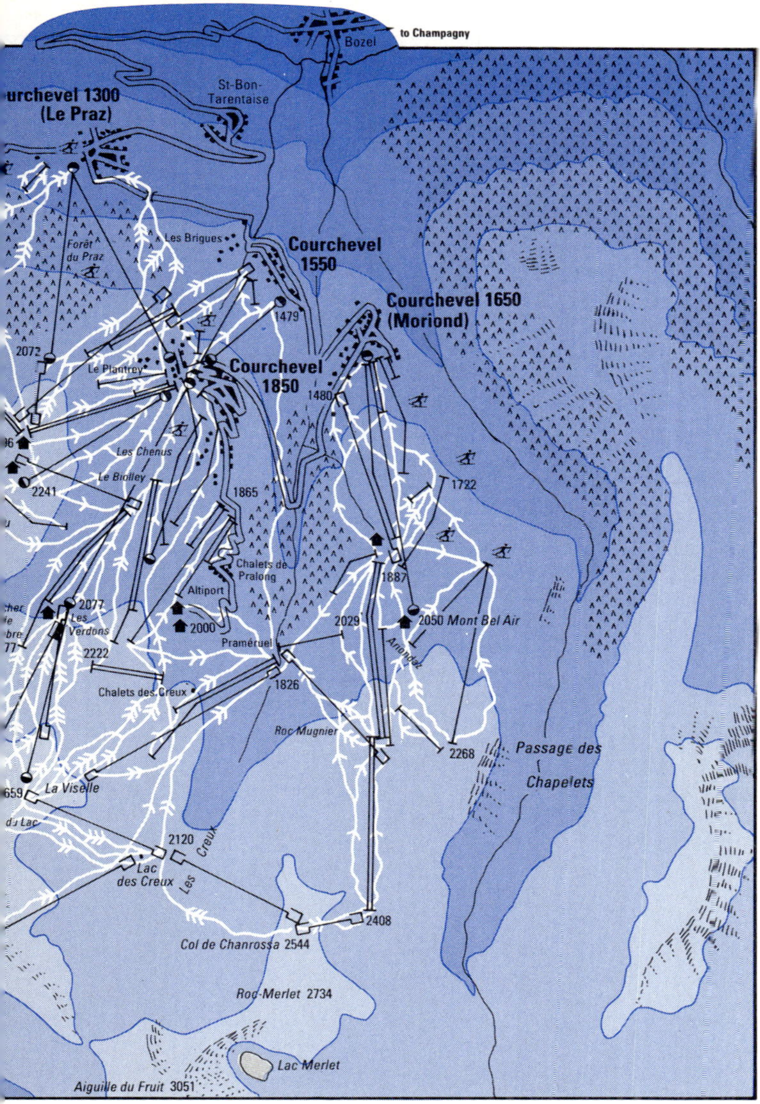

that of their neighbours, but that was to some extent remedied in 1987–88 with the opening up of the Mont du Vallon.

The appeal of Val Thorens is simple: snow. It is the highest resort in Europe, and its moderately steep slopes face mainly away from the sun. They do not reach spectacular heights, but they offer reliable snow down to resort level (on runs of interest to all grades of skier) at times when the sunnier, lower slopes of Les Menuires and Méribel, in

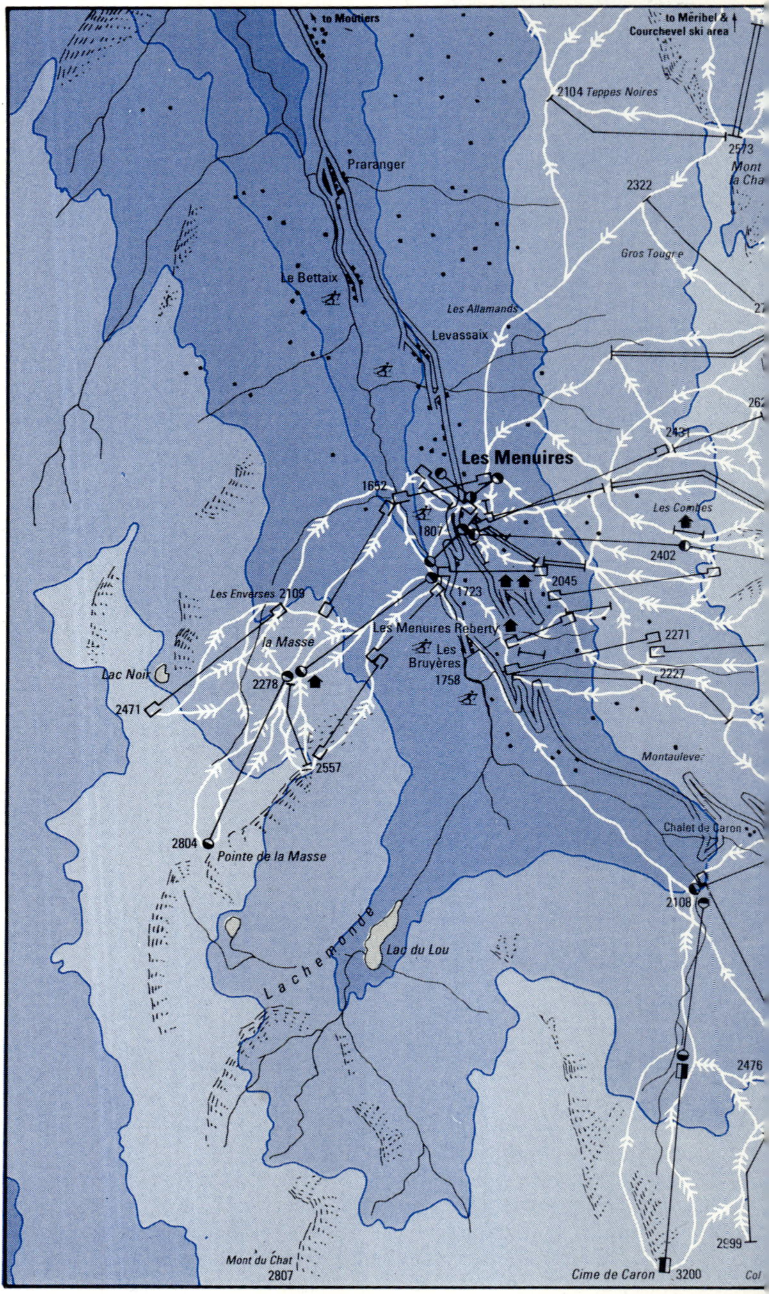
to Moutiers
to Méribel & Courchevel ski area
2104 Teppes Noires
2573
2322
Gros Tougne
Praranger
Le Bettaix
Les Allamands
Levassaix
Les Menuires
1652
1807
2402
Les Combes
2045
1723
Les Enverses 2109
la Masse
Les Menuires Reberty
Les Bruyères
1758
2271
2227
Lac Noir
2278
2471
2557
Montaulever
Chalet de Caron
2804
Pointe de la Masse
2108
Lachemonde
Lac du Lou
2476
2999
Mont du Chat
2807
Cime de Caron
3200

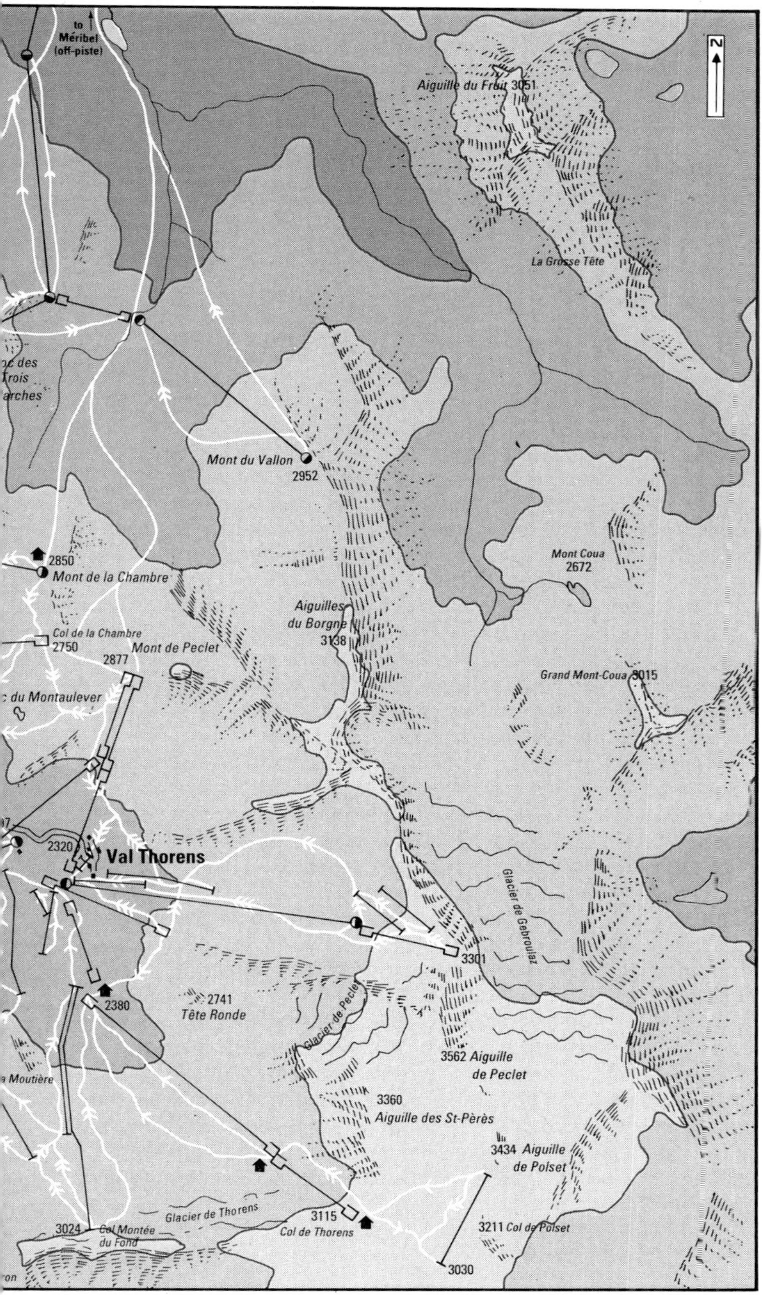
to Méribel (off-piste)
N
Aiguille du Fruit 3051
La Grosse Tête
Mont du Vallon
2952
Mont Coua
2672
2850
Mont de la Chambre
Aiguilles du Borgne
3138
Col de la Chambre
2750
Mont de Peclet
2877
Grand Mont-Coua 3015
2320
Val Thorens
Glacier de Gebroulaz
3301
2380
2741
Tête Ronde
Glacier de Peclet
3562 Aiguille de Peclet
3360
Aiguille des St-Pères
3434 Aiguille de Polset
Glacier de Thorens
3115
Col de Thorens
3024
Col Montée du Fond
3211 Col de Polset
3030

particular, are alternating between slush and ice. The setting is remote and bleak, and the buildings are no more than functional, but Val Thorens is less of an eyesore than many purpose-built resorts, and aims to sell not just on price but on quality of facilities.

Les Menuires is one of the ugliest blots on the Alpine landscape – a cheerless, functional scattering of apartment blocks, shopping blocks and lift pylons. But it serves a purpose, providing many ordinary French (and not a few British) families with economical apartment accommodation conveniently placed for access to a lot of good skiing.

The skiing top 3200m bottom 1270m

The Méribel and Courchevel valleys are well linked by a simple arrangement of lifts up to a single point on the mountain dividing the two. Les Menuires and Val Thorens are not quite so well connected to Méribel, because they are much further up their valley.

The **Courchevel** skiing is spread widely across the mountainside with a great variety of terrain and orientation. The shape of the mountains is concave, with the steeper runs around the rocky rim dividing Courchevel from Méribel, and a huge area of gentle slopes just above the resort which gives rise to the idea that the skiing consists entirely of nursery slopes. This is far from the truth.

From the big central station in Courchevel 1850 the left-hand gondola goes up to Verdons, where a vast new cable-car climbs to the top of the skiing at Saulire. This is the only lift from Courchevel which gives access to the three notorious couloirs dropping from the mountain crest – scoffed at by connoisseurs as being neither long nor steep nor narrow, but as graded pistes indisputably severe.

All the other runs served by the cable-car can also be reached from the alternative gondola from Verdons. There are several steepish red and genuinely black alternative ways back to Verdons; other pistes lead over to Méribel; more still around and down into the beautiful wide Vallée des Creux and from there either down to 1550 (a tediously flat trail) or, via linking lifts, back to 1850 or over to 1650. These are long runs with plenty of opportunity for exploration (by no means always safe) near the pistes on the top half.

Each of the three chair-lifts from Lac des Creux serves interesting, challenging skiing. The new Creux Noirs lift opens up an off-piste run to Mottaret. The Chanrossa lift serves an impressive, wide slope of about 500m vertical; the black piste is only moderately steep but the heavily skied off-piste area is steeper. Chanrossa gets a lot of afternoon sun and the snow deteriorates. Behind Chanrossa harmless red runs lead into the extensive Courchevel 1650 skiing – wide, open and easy.

The right-hand gondola from 1850, and several drag-lifts nearby, serve the skiing below the Col de la Loze. Long black trails, not steep but consistently challenging, go down through thick woods to Le Praz, giving 900m vertical. There is plenty of off-piste scope. There is some less demanding skiing in this sector – easy runs in the morning sun down to 1850 and 1550. From the Col de la Loze itself, an attractive piste – not difficult but often with poor snow – leads to Méribel Altiport.

For many years the skiing of the **Méribel** valley was largely confined to the two flanks, facing roughly east and west, between Méribel and Mottaret – ideal for sunny skiing morning and afternoon. In this area there is no difficulty in getting across from one side to the other or making the links along the mountainsides above the two resorts. The slopes are open, and wooded only above Méribel. Most of the runs are intermediate, with blue runs that are often unpleasantly difficult, and black runs which are mostly not. Mottaret and Méribel are linked directly by a very easy, wide green run. Both villages now have ranks of snow-cannons on their major low-altitude pistes.

Above Mottaret there are many variants of the open runs directly down from La Saulire, mostly stiff red but with some winding routes which are just about blue. The slopes face south-west and snow conditions are often treacherous. In good conditions, the little-used Grande Rosière run is a splendid sustained black. The excellent black race-course down to Méribel is rarely open to holiday skiers.

The runs in the Burgin sector immediately above Méribel are mostly shorter and easier, and have more reliable snow. Above the Altiport is a particularly fine green run for near-beginners. From Rond-Point, at the top of the village, a piste runs down beside the resort.

The east-facing slopes are more varied and fragmented, with little bowls and ridges out of the way of the piste network. Above Méribel the long two-stage gondola to Tougnète serves a long black run back down to the base station – a short steep mogul-field at the top, an easy middle section with connections to Mottaret, and a steeper run down through the woods under the bottom section of the lift, often short of snow. There is a large, uncrowded area of easy and intermediate runs in the Roc de Fer/Pas de Cherferie sector, which is now linked to a couple of lifts and runs over the ridge, above St-Martin-de-Belleville. The easy black and enjoyable red runs served by the Mont de la Challe drags often provide good snow when it's in short supply.

Only in the last few years have lifts been installed to open up the head of the valley, beyond Mottaret – first the Plattières gondola to Roc des Trois Marches above Les Menuires, and last season a big new gondola/ cable-car hybrid on the opposite side of the valley, going up to over 2900m on the virgin Mont du Vallon.

The Plattières gondola has a wide, easy blue trail beneath the first two sections, and a short, unprepared black pitch under the top one. From the Roc de Tougnes and Roc des Trois Marches there is plenty of scope for finding off-piste ways down between the runs; some of these slopes can be dangerous. The base of the Mont du Vallon gondola can be reached from the top or the second station of the Plattières gondola, or from the top lifts of Val Thorens and Les Menuires. The piste map shows two runs from the top of the very effective new lift, but our reporters found only one – a long, relentless piste ('moguls from top to bottom') graded red but of black steepness – which rejoins the old *itinéraire* about half-way to Mottaret.

The skiing of **Les Menuires**, like that of Méribel, is spread over two sides of a valley, but here connections from one side to the other are awkward. Above the resort are various long runs, facing south-west, of about 1000m vertical from Roc des Trois Marches and Mont de la Chambre (the main links with Méribel). The many variants are stiff intermediate runs, often made more difficult and unpleasant by poor snow and crowds of skiers in transit. There are much-skied off-piste itineraries, only occasionally steep, to Mottaret behind Mont de la Chambre – down a wide and beautiful valley to the foot of the new lift serving Mont du Vallon and of the Plan Mains chair-lift.

Opposite Les Menuires, La Masse is a much more tempting mountain for good skiers. Its slopes face north-east and usually have much better snow; the runs are long (again about 1000m vertical) and tough, including some genuine blacks, and are not busy with transit crowds. The main off-piste run to La Châtelard and St-Martin-de-Belleville runs high along the crest of the mountains. Another run drops down into the valley between La Masse and the Cime de Caron.

Val Thorens is set at the head of the Belleville valley and is tightly enclosed by a horseshoe of mountains with slopes facing south, west and north. Most of the lift departures are below the resort, and the lower slopes are gentle; streams (and associated ice) are a hazard.

The big Cime de Caron cable-car climbs swiftly to the highest point in the Trois Vallées winter skiing, and opens up some magnificent runs. An easy track runs round the back of the peak with a long off-piste run down into the valley between Caron and La Masse. The black north-facing piste is a long, wide, open, steep slope – couloirs apart, the most challenging piste in the Trois Vallées. The red runs on the shoulder of the mountain are often closed.

The rest of Val Thorens skiing seems rather ordinary after Caron, though the drags to the east of it serve north-facing slopes which are enjoyable for their reliably good snow. Runs on the glacier from the Col de Thorens are wide and easy. Those on the other side of the rocky Aiguille de Péclet are slightly more challenging, and this area is reported to be good for off-piste.

Mountain restaurants are more numerous in the Trois Vallées than in many modern resorts, though few are particularly attractive. There are good and easily accessible restaurants in the resorts.

The Trois Vallées lift system copes with the enormous numbers of

Three Valleys lift payment

Passes Three Valleys lift pass covers all lifts of Courchevel, Méribel, Les Menuires and Val Thorens, but not bus services. Each valley has a variety of local passes, of which the more extensive ones can be extended to cover the Three Valleys by the day. Main pass available by the day, six days or longer including ten non-consecutive days, valid all season.

Cost 6-day Three Valleys pass FF750. 15% off, adults over 60. 10% off in low season.

Children 10% off, under 13 – more on most local passes.

Beginners Coupons valid for limited areas of lifts in Courchevel, Méribel and Les Menuires. One free lift in Mottaret; 2 free lifts in Val Thorens, and limited-area lift pass.

Summer skiing Extensive at Val Thorens, 2800 to 3300m.

skiers remarkably well. The main **queue** black spots are the major lifts out of Courchevel and Les Menuires at peak periods. Mottaret also gets crowded by skiers returning to Courchevel, though the improved alternative route via Méribel has helped.

Courchevel

Courchevel consists of a string of communities along the road which winds up one flank of the wide Bozel valley. 1300, 1550, and 1850 are stacked up the same hillside, with lift and piste connections between each other; 1650 is out of the way on the other side of a river gorge.

1300 (Le Praz) is an attractive hamlet with a few hotels and a couple of restaurants at the bottom of the skiing, handy for the cross-country trails. 1550 is more of a resort, but a characterless one – a dormitory suburb, by-passed by the road, by most skiers and by all serious après-skiers. It has some inexpensive hotels and restaurants. 1650 (Moriond) is a straggle of roadside apartment blocks and hotels.

The main focus is 1850; it was built without much style in the early days of French purpose-building (the late 1940s) and much added to since with no advance in aesthetic achievement – though a campaign of 'embellishment' embarked upon four years ago has had some effect in softening buildings and taming traffic. It is now a large resort spread between 1700m and 1900m, above and below the original site on a wide shelf about on the tree-line. The hub is a huge lift-station complex

Courchevel facts

Ski school

Classes 2½hr morning, 2hr afternoon.
Cost 6 days FF588. Private lessons FF130/hr (1 to 4 people).
Children About 25% off, under 12. Ski kindergarten (1850), ages 4 up, 9.00–5.00, 6 days with lunch FF972. Non-ski kindergarten (1850 and 1650), ages 2–5, 6 days with lunch, FF900.

Cross-country skiing

Trails Ten, totalling 50km; mostly easy, in woods above Le Praz and at each major resort centre.

Not skiing

Facilities Artificial skating rink, hang-gliding, bridge, chess, scrabble, plane joy rides, ski-jumping, parachuting, 35km cleared paths.

Medical facilities

In resort Doctors, chemists, dentist.
Hospital Moûtiers (25km).

Getting there

Airport Geneva; transfer 3½hr plus. Direct flights from Paris twice daily, and from Lyon and Geneva on Saturdays
Railway Moûtiers (25km); frequent buses.
Road Via Lyon/Chambéry; chains may be needed. Horrific peak weekend jams.

Available holidays

Resort beds 5,400 in hotels, 26,400 in apartment/chalets.
Package holidays Activity Travel (Ht Ch Sc), Air France (Ht), Bladon Lines (Ht Ch), Inghams (Ht), John Morgan (Ht Ch), Made to Measure (Ht Sc), Ski West (Ht Ch Cl Sc), Ski Whizz (Ch) SkiSet (Ht), Snowbird Holidays (Ht), Supertravel (Ht Ch Cl Sc)

Further information

Tourist office ✆79080029. Tx 980083.

known as La Croisette. Either side of it there are lively and very smart shopping streets. The centre is reasonably compact, but chalets and hotels are spread far and wide across the hillsides, mostly on or near an easy piste.

A bus shuttle service (not covered by the lift pass) links the different parts of the resort. There is an hourly service until about 10pm. If you go up to Courchevel 1850 from the lower stations you can always toboggan, slide or ski back down the pistes if the moon is out. For après-ski excursions a car is of value.

Accommodation is in staffed chalets, apartments in chalets, and lots of hotels. Most chalets used by UK operators are on the east side, if not in the centre. In general, standards of accommodation are high, and hotel prices are high too. No less than four of the better hotels have restaurants with Michelin rosettes. Of the less expensive hotels, the Dahu (✆79080118) is quiet and central. In 1550, the Chanrossa (✆79080658) is friendly and well-placed for lifts. There are good food shops, at least in 1850.

When the French are on holiday there is a lot of expensive, chic, late

Méribel facts

Ski school

ESF and international school.
Classes ESF 2½hr morning, 2hr afternoon. International school morning or afternoon.
Cost 6 days FF500 (25½hr) ESF. International school (15hr) FF550. Private lessons FF120/hr.
Children About 33% off (ESF), under 12. Ski/non-ski kindergarten at Méribel, ages 2–8, 9.00–5.30, 6 days with meals FF800; at Le Hameau (Mottaret), ages 3–8, 9.00–5.00, 6 days with meals FF810/930.
Special courses Competition, free-style, monoski.

Cross-country skiing

Trails 4.5km blue track and 2km green track at Mottaret; 10km red, 5km blue, 1.5km green track near Altiport, above Méribel and itinerary from Altiport to Courchevel.

Not-skiing

Facilities Artificial ice rink, swimming, flying lessons and joy rides, hang-gliding, about 10km cleared paths, bridge, motor trikes, fitness centres, sauna, jacuzzi, planetarium, indoor golf.

Medical facilities

In resort Doctors, chemists, dentist.
Doctors and chemists Mottaret.
Hospital Môutiers (18km).

Getting there

Airport Geneva; transfer 3½hr plus.
Railway Moûtiers (18km); 5 buses a day.
Road Via Lyon, Chambéry; chains may be needed. Horrific peak weekend jams.

Available holidays

Resort beds 1,700 in hotels, 22,000 in apartments and chalets.
Package holidays Activity Travel (Ht Ch Sc), Beach Villas (Ht Ch Sc), Bladon Lines (Ht Ch Sc), Enterprise (Ht Sc), Global (Sc), Horizon (Ht Sc), Inghams (Ht Sc), John Morgan (Ht Ch), Made to Measure (Ht Sc), Mark Warner (Ch Cl), Neilson (Ht Sc), Sally Tours (Sc), Ski Club of GB (Ch), Ski Lovers (Ap Sc), Ski MacG (Ht Ch Sc), Ski West (Ht Ch Cl Sc), Ski Whizz (Ch), Ski-Val (Ht Ch Cl Sc), Skiworld (Ht Ch Sc), Small World (Ch), Snowbird Holidays (Ht), Snowtime (Ht Ch Sc), Supertravel (Ht Ch Cl Sc), Thomson (Ht Sc), Tourarc (Sc), Vacations (Ht Ch Sc)

Further information

Tourist office ✆79086001. Tx 980001.

après-ski. One reporter summed up the discos as 'the best I've ever encountered – expensive, stylish and yobbo-free'. There are places with a more Alpine atmosphere, relaxing piano bars, and many good restaurants, including the two down in Le Praz. The resort is quieter when the après-ski depends more on the British.

Courchevel is not a very attractive resort for **non-skiers** (except full-time après-skiers). Interesting excursion possibilities are few. The resort is not really a natural choice for **cross-country** skiers, either.

There are very good **nursery slopes** – both 1850 and 1650 have huge areas of very green skiing immediately above the resort.

Reports on **ski school** indicate rather undesirably frequent changes of instructor, but are generally favourable. One recent reporter was very unhappy with the kindergarten and children's classes.

Méribel

Méribel-les-Allues (Méribel) spreads steeply from about 1400m, beside the river, up the west-facing side of the valley to about 1700m, with large chalet-style buildings all along the road which winds up the hillside and continues past the top of the resort (Rond-Point, where the ski school meets) on through the woods to the Altiport. Life revolves around the hectic little square at the bottom of the village.

Having a car is a considerable advantage, especially for those who want to go out in the evening to eat, drink or dance. There is a daytime bus service between Mottaret and Altiport via Méribel.

Accommodation in Méribel is mostly in apartments and staffed chalets, of which there is an enormous choice. There can be long walks to and from skiing unless you are based close to the village piste. Of the hotels, the Orée du Bois (✆79005030) is conveniently placed at Rond-Point, and is straightforwardly comfortable. The Adray (✆79086026) is isolated but very conveniently on-piste. The Altiport (✆79005232) is comfortable, expensive and isolated.

Après-ski is quiet, though there are now three disco-nightclubs. Central bars and restaurants are few, and unappealing. There are smarter restaurants up the hillside, of no great culinary distinction. The tiny Galette (must book) is said to have 'good atmosphere, excellent food and reasonably priced wine'.

The **cross-country** trails in the woods around the Altiport are in beautiful surroundings and suit not very ambitious practitioners well. Méribel does not have a lot to offer **non-skiers**, Mottaret even less.

The **nursery slopes** of both Méribel and (particularly) Mottaret are too steep and busy for comfort. The international section of the **ski school** guarantees instruction in perfect English except during the February holidays. The price is high. We have favourable reports of the Pingouins kindergarten at Le Hameau; there is now an equivalent facility (Club Saturnin) in Méribel.

Mottaret is better placed for skiing links with Courchevel and (especially) Les Menuires. Like Méribel it climbs high up the side of the valley – in this case the east-facing side, up to 1850m – and again there is a piste down the southern side of the centre (access to which is easy); further hotel and apartment building is going on 200m south, up the valley, this time on the west-facing side, and this section also has easy ski links with the centre. Accommodation is nearly all in apartments (though there are several hotels), generally favourably reported upon. Most reporters stayed at the top of the resort (Le Hameau) where many of the apartments have balconies with splendid views. There is not much aprés-ski here – just a few restaurants and a big, anonymous congregation area and expensive bar. There are more stylish restaurants and bars in the centre of Mottaret, and although it's a steep 20-minute walk back, the village lift now runs from 8.45am to 11.50pm (covered by the lift pass until 8pm, FF6 thereafter). The best compromise is to eat at the hotel Les Arolles, a little way down – 'excellent food and service'. The new Pierre et Vacances apartments on the Courchevel side of the resort are 'excellent – good-sized', and this development includes several new shops.

Val Thorens 2300m

Val Thorens is all-new, and built with at least some concern for appearance. It is not very large – two loosely-grouped clusters of tall, white-and-wood blocks built along a winding spine of road, with pistes on all sides (and through the middle), most of them broad and easy; skiing to and from most residences is possible, and for skiing purposes location is unimportant. In the lower part of the resort is the very smart

Val Thorens facts

Ski school

Classes 3hr or 5hr per day.
Cost 6 full days FF620. Private lessons FF135/hr.
Children About 20% off classes. Ski kindergarten, ages 3–8. 6 full days with meals FF1,050.
Special courses Monoski, ballet, powder and others.

Cross-country skiing

Trails Several km, down the valley.

Not-skiing

Facilities Tennis (6 courts), squash, swimming pool, fitness room, saunas, spa baths, solarium, golf-simulator, snow-scooters, hang-gliding, cinema.

Medical facilities

In resort Doctors, dentist, chemist.
Hospital Moûtiers (37km).

Getting there

Airport Geneva; transfer 3½ plus.
Railway Moûtiers (37km).
Road Via Lyon, Chambéry; chains may be needed. Horrific peak weekend jams. Covered parking available.

Available holidays

Resort beds 600 in hotels, several thousand in apartments.
Package holidays Blue Sky (Ht Sc), Brittany Ferries (Sc), Crystal (Ht Sc), Enterprise (Ht Sc), Global (Sc), Horizon (Ht Sc), Inghams (Ht Sc), Made to Measure (Ht Sc), Neilson (Ht Sc), Sally Tours (Sc), Schools Abroad (Ap), Ski Lovers (Sc), Ski Sutherland (Ht), Skiscope (Ap), Thomson (Ht Sc), Tourarc (Sc), Tracer (Sc), Vacations (Ht Sc)

Further information

Tourist office ✆79000808. Tx 980572.

sports complex, and lower still, in a rather isolated position, is another smart new development, the imaginative Temples du Soleil residential complex. It is not actually a traffic-free resort, but in practice cars tend to remain immobile during the week and traffic is insignificant.

All the **accommodation** is convenient for skiing and shopping. We have had very mixed reports about the quality of apartments and the service provided by the rental agencies. Few reporters have stayed in hotels, but two have recommended the well-placed and comfortable Val Chavière (✆79000033). An expensive new hotel has been built near the sports club, the Val Thorens (✆79000433) which has been highly praised by a recent reporter ('excellent food, manager remembered us and came to welcome us'). There are a few enticing food shops, and new supermarkets have improved the outlook for self-caterers.

Après-ski is limited, though there are more bars and restaurants (several with music) than in many resorts of this kind, and a couple of discos. Despite the impressive sports facilities, the resort cannot be recommended for **non-skiers**. There is **cross-country** skiing down the valley to Les Menuires and beyond.

The **nursery slopes** are spacious and gentle, and have reliably good snow; but they are much used by non-nursery skiers. Reports on the main **ski school** are mixed. There are also several independent sources of instruction.

Les Menuires 1850m

Les Menuires has five major components (though more can be distinguished), all of them ranged along the east side of the valley. The centre is La Croisette, a crescent of linked blocks with cars and road outside and an open, snowy plaza of lifts, pistes and café sun-terraces inside. Nearly all the entertainment (numerous bars and restaurants, and three discos) and shopping facilities are here. Reberty, about 1km south, is the satellite most often offered by British operators. It gives easier and less crowded access to Val Thorens, but we have reports of very cramped accommodation, crowds in the supermarket, and annoyance at having to walk to La Croisette for evening entertainment. (The free shuttle bus stops about 7.30. The gondola up from the lower satellite of Preyerand runs until midnight.)

The nursery slopes are broad, gentle and sunny, and right in the heart of the resort, but they are often hideously crowded and in the past have been prone to ice; we have no reports of the effectiveness of the new, very large snow-making installation. At La Croisette there is an all-day kindergarten. There are 16.5km of cross-country trails.

Tourist office ✆79082012. **Package holidays** Brittany Ferries (Sc), Club Med (Ht), Enterprise (Ht Sc), Hourmont (Ht), Global (Sc), Made to Measure (Sc), Snow World (Ht Sc), Tourarc (Sc).

Not just a pretty place

Valmorel France 1400m

Good for *Lift queues, sunny slopes, skiing convenience, family holidays, freedom from cars, resort-level snow, nursery slopes, Alpine charm*
Bad for *Mountain restaurants, not skiing, après-ski*

Linked resort St-François-Longchamp

If any purpose-built resort can claim to be villagey, it is Valmorel, a small new development not far from Les Menuires and Val Thorens – resorts from which it could hardly be more different in spirit. Ever-so-tasteful residential 'hamlets' of wood-and-slate chalets are grouped around a colourful, traffic-free, toytown shopping street, all laid out so ingeniously that there is no loss of convenience for skiers. In other respects Valmorel is typical of small modern resorts: it mainly appeals to self-catering families, and there is not much to do but ski.

Valmorel is linked to St-François-Longchamp, a bitty little resort to the south of the Col de la Madeleine. The resulting ski area – now to be known as Le Grand Domaine – is uncrowded and varied, and fairly *grand* except by the exalted standards of the Tarentaise. St-François-Longchamp's slopes are sunny and gentle, and include excellent

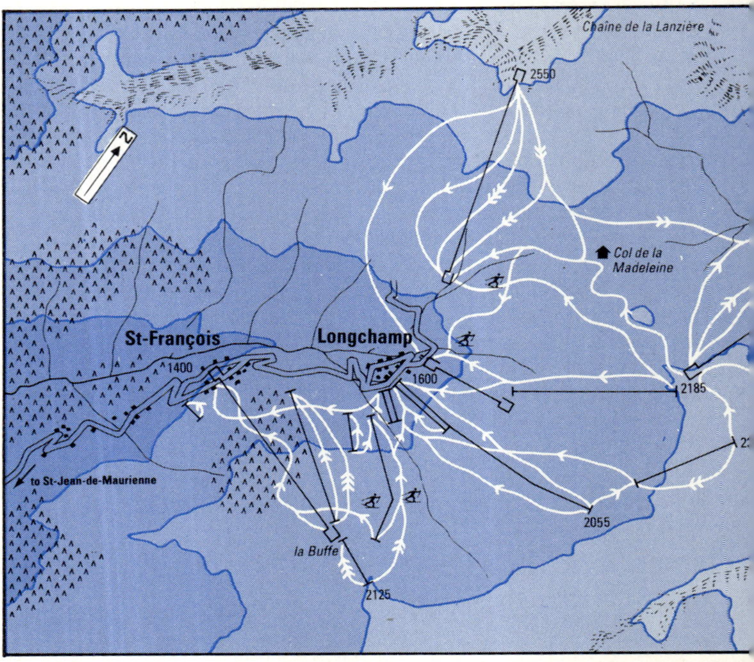

nursery slopes. Valmorel's side is more reliable for snow, more extensive and more challenging – many runs are more difficult than their gradings suggest.

Valmorel's charms have not escaped the attention of the British operators, who fill over a fifth of the beds, and a few reporters have been disappointed to find so many compatriots. But the majority of reports reaching us have been very enthusiastic.

The skiing top 2403m bottom 1250m

Valmorel sits at the foot of a horseshoe of ski-fields with slopes facing north, west and east.

Lifts from the top of Valmorel (Hameau du Mottet) give access to the Col du Gollet, the eastern extremity of the system. This is a fine open slope with off-piste or black and red runs, and is also the start of the Nine Valleys route, with an off-piste descent towards Les Menuires.

The main lift from the top of the village, the Pierrafort gondola, serves a broad slope with long blue runs which are not of trivial difficulty, and leads to the Col du Mottet chair-lift. This climbs to the highest point of the ski area over a wide, steep mogul-field (about 33°), and gives access to an excellent, long, less daunting black into the Celliers valley.

A long chair-lift from the centre of the village goes up to the rounded Tête de Beaudin, where drag-lifts serve long, very easy runs on top and down into the Celliers valley. The Montagne de Tête, on the morning-

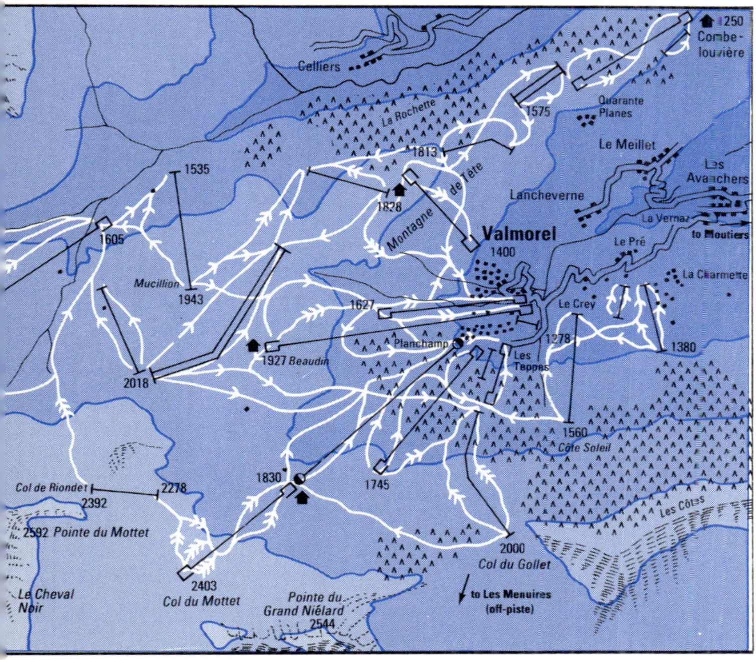

sun side of the resort, can be reached by drag-lift from here, or by chair from the resort. It provides good scope for off-piste skiing, a genuine black run and some tough intermediate ones down to the resort. There is also a very long green trail though the woods to Combelouvière.

From the Celliers valley an efficient stop-go three-seater chair reaches the broad ridge above the road pass (closed in winter). The two red runs beneath could well be black, with several pitches of nearly 30°, but there are blue alternatives. On the sunny side of the ridge the runs down to Longchamp are open and very gentle.

The west-facing slopes above St-François are little skied and include some wide, entertaining intermediate runs through light woods above the road and down to the village. The blacks are not very steep. The north side of the valley above Longchamp is now opened up by a new four-seater chair-lift to 2550m, with a blue descent of 900m vertical to Longchamp, and a varied trio of pistes beside the lift.

The area's **mountain restaurants** are few, and generally charmless. But the villages are easily accessible.

The area is generally free of **queues** except during school holidays, when St-François-Longchamp has suffered in the past.

Valmorel facts

Lift payment

Passes Cheval Noir pass covers all Valmorel and St-François-Longchamp lifts. Local pass also available.
Cost 6-day pass FF621.
Children 20% off, under 13.
Beginners Coupons or limited day passes. One free drag-lift.

Ski school

Classes 3hr morning (advanced) or afternoon (inexperienced).
Cost 6 days FF395. Special beginners' course including lifts FF736. Private lessons FF144 for 70min.
Children Flexible arrangements for children up to age 13, including play, ski school, lunch, tea as required, 8.45–7.15. Typical cost: 6 days with lunch FF850. All-day classes possible; 25% off adult prices, under 13.
Special courses Off-piste (various formulae), Nine Valleys tours via Méribel to La Plagne and Val d'Isère.

Cross-country skiing

Trails Totalling 20km, starting 4km from resort beyond Le Pré nursery area (transport provided free for those taking X-C ski school).

Not skiing

Facilities Organised snow-shoe outings, toboggan run, aerobics, fitness training, sauna.

Medical facilities

In resort Chemist and doctor.
Hospital Moûtiers (18km).
Dentist Aigueblanche (12km).

Getting there

Airport Geneva; transfer about 3hr.
Railway Moûtiers (18km); frequent buses.
Road Via Lyon/Chambéry; poor road from Aigueblanche; chains may be needed.

Available holidays

Resort beds 350 in hotels, 6,500 in apartments.
Package holidays Air France (Ht Sc), Blue Sky (Ht Sc), Enterprise (Ht Sc), Made to Measure (Ht Sc), Neilson (Ht Sc), Schools Abroad (Ap), Ski Lovers (Ap Sc), SkiSet (Ht), Snow World (Ht Sc), Snowbird Holidays (Ap), Sunmed (Ht Ch Sc), Thomson (Ht Sc), Tourarc (Sc)

Further information

Tourist office ✆79098555. Tx 980321.

The resort

Valmorel has runs and lifts reaching down into the very centre and down both flanks, and tentacles of road reaching up. At the base of the resort is Bourg-Morel, its commercial centre – a colourful arcaded pedestrian street full of restaurants, shops and bars, with café terraces at the foot of the main pistes. Nearby is the children's village, Saperlipopette – the spiritual heart of the resort.

Nearly all the **accommodation** is apartments, well liked by our reporters. Most of the 'hamlets' are served by a free shuttle lift (Télébourg) from Bourg-Morel. There are three hotels, rather expensive and functional. Skiers with cars can stay much more cheaply in the delightful hamlet of Les Avanchers, at the little Cheval Noir (✆79098190).

Valmorel is not suitable either for **cross-country** skiing or for **non-skiers**. There are few cleared walks, no swimming pool, and few excursion possibilities (though the newly opened air-strip offers joy-rides). **Après-ski** is also very limited. There are several satisfactory restaurants where you can get snacks or sophisticated cuisine, quite lively bars, and a disco. There is floodlit skiing once a week.

The dense network of pistes just above the village gives inexperienced skiers no easy options. But there are good, specially contoured **nursery slopes** with three lifts away, from the main pistes.

The resort claims that all staff speak English. The question raised by reports on both the **ski school** and children's village (which is very attractive) is whether they can be bothered to do so.

St-François-Longchamp 1450–1650m

Valmorel's partner is a succession of hamlets along the Col de la Madeleine road, linked by a free ski-bus. They attract few non-French visitors and the atmosphere is far from festive. The top hamlet, Longchamp, is an ugly group of modern buildings below the pass, surrounded by sunny slopes. It has a kindergarten, a natural ice rink and a couple of discos. St-François is a cluster of simple old hotels and *colonies de vacances*.

Tourist Office ✆75951056. **Package holidays** Quest (Ht).

All things in moderation

Valloire France 1400m

Valloire is an old village tucked away in a secluded bowl high up above the Maurienne valley, beside the road up to the very high Col du Galibier (closed in winter), where the *département* of Savoie meets Hautes-Alpes. It has developed gradually as a resort over the 60 years since skiing became popular with the local military. Although not a strikingly picturesque village, it has retained the spirit and looks of a real, typically French community, and offers a good combination of quiet village atmosphere, a fair amount of mostly intermediate skiing and moderate prices.

The skiing is spread over five sides of two neighbouring mountains and gives plenty of variations of terrain, with long runs of nearly 1000m vertical. There is no very difficult skiing (the black runs are not steep). Both areas are served by lifts only a few minutes' walk from the centre going up to almost 2500m, but most of the skiing is below 2000m. Each has a small nursery area beside a restaurant half-way up.

The major sector is Setaz, reached by a chain of lifts (now including an efficient gondola) over a narrow north-facing slope – more of a mountain-end than a mountainside. Various descents go through the woods to the resort or down the steeper sides of the mountain – easy ones from the restaurant, tougher ones starting higher up. The downhill race-course starts near the top – a 3.8km run for 920m vertical. The west-facing slope goes down to Les Verneys, beside the Galibier road (1563m); beyond it, on the Crey Rond massif, is a small nursery area and a chair-lift up to 1912m which opens up a very worthwhile expanse of off-piste skiing. The east-facing slope of Setaz is linked at Pragontier (1750m) to the Crey du Quart sector – a broad, open, sunny hillside, lightly scrub-covered lower down. There is some excellent easy skiing on the gentle, spacious top half; there may also be some more demanding slopes on the bottom half, but on our visits they were unskiable. Conditions are more reliable on the north-facing runs towards Valmeinier – again, satisfying length and varying difficulty from easy blue to toughish red, graded black.

Long and varied cross-country trails climb south from Valloire to Les Verneys and on to Plan Lachat (1961m), past several restaurants. The easiest loops are at Les Verneys, reached by bus from Valloire.

There are several modest, inexpensive hotels and unobtrusive apartment buidings. The most attractive hotel is the Christiania (✆79560057), simple but adequately comfortable and conveniently placed on the main shopping street. Although there is a fair range of bars and restaurants and two discos, the evening ambience is subdued. There are kindergartens and an artificial ice rink.

Tourist office ✆79560396. **Package holidays** Quest (Ht), Ski Club of GB (Ht), SkiBound (Ht Cl Sc), Sunmed (Ht Ch Sc), Thomson (Ht Sc), VFB (Ht Sc).

Priorité à droite

Val Cenis France 1400m

If you have spent time skiing around on the gentle glaciers above Val d'Isère you may have wondered what happens on the other side of the Col de l'Iseran. The answer is skiing, in the long upper valley of the Arc between the beautiful old village of Bonneval and the ugly old town of Modane, an area known as the Haute Maurienne. This quiet corner of the Alps, a dead-end in winter, has a number of unspoilt rural villages and plentiful skiing: an enormous extent of cross-country trails and unmarked itineraries between Bramans (1250m) and Bessans (1750m), and an excellent downhill area above Lanslebourg (1400m) and Lanslevillard (1450m), neighbours at the foot of the Mont Cenis pass and collectively christened Val Cenis.

New skiing above old French villages is an enticing recipe and Val Cenis works pretty well. The ski area is uncrowded, and larger and more interesting than those of most small resorts, and the new role of ski resort fits little Lanslevillard like a glove. Prices are generally low. But before booking, think hard about the implications of this kind of development. Apart from admiring the old churches and savouring the farmyard smells there is very little to do when not skiing. The villages attract a low-spending clientele of families and hostellers and give the impression that the habit of hibernation is not easily shaken off.

Lanslebourg is the larger of the two villages and the less appealing, having developed as a roadside travellers' rest at the foot of the pass, now closed in winter but one of the easiest and historically most important in the western Alps. The lift station is across the river from the long village, quite a walk from most of the accommodation. The village has a modest selection of bars and restaurants, a couple of discothèques, a gym and a natural ice rink. A couple of miles up the valley, Lanslevillard is more villagey and rustic, and has the most interesting church in the valley. More to the point, its old centre is on the same side of the river as the ski slopes, with access lifts from various places along the edge of the village and a row of hotels and apartment buildings ideally set beside piste and nursery slopes. Les Prais (✆79059353) is one of them, a simple, homely old chalet hotel with a good restaurant and a sunny terrace. Bedrooms are small and plain, but inexpensive.

Lanslevillard has the resort's kindergarten, catering for ages two to eight. A few buses a day run the full length of the valley between Modane and Bonneval; the service along the central section, linking the downhill and cross-country resort villages, is more frequent, and covered by the lift pass.

The ski area spreads across the broad north-west-facing mountainside above the two villages and offers a fine variety of long runs evenly split between woodland and open ground, with the top station high above Lanslevillard at 2800m. Several blacks and reds take the mountain straight, and include a splendid top-to-bottom black of nearly 1400m vertical, nowhere very steep but in places narrow and awkward. Blues and greens follow a more roundabout course, providing the links from one side to the other and plenty of piste crossroads, mostly well signposted. An unusual feature is a 7km stretch of the Route Nationale 6, otherwise known as the Escargot green run, from near the Mont Cenis pass to Lanslebourg, complete with road signs warning of hairpins and crash barriers to help you stay on course.

The local mountains are not particularly beautiful but there are fine views across the pass and into Italy from the top station, and an interesting long run over the back (shown as a black piste on the map, marked but not pisted in fact), ending up beside the pass (2083m) where it links up with the lifts above Lanslebourg. The run is fairly steep in places, south-west-facing (so likely to be in worse condition than the slopes on the other side of the mountain), and not easy to follow in poor light. One of the main drawbacks of what is not a small ski area is the scarcity of mountain restaurants. A seven-day lift pass entitles you to a free day in one of several other resorts in the region, including Valloire and Valfréjus.

We have neither experience nor reports of the cross-country skiing, but it is clearly very extensive. The higher village of Bessans claims 70km of trails and is the main centre. It has a few hotels. The Val Cenis tourist office produces a useful leaflet guide to the valley's cross-country itineraries and sightseeing attractions along the way.

Tourist office ✆79052366. Tx 980213.
Package holidays Quest (Ht), Schoolplan (Ht Sc), Sunmed (Ht Cl Sc).

A star is marketed

Valfréjus France 1550m Bardonecchia Italy 1250m

The two resorts on the Italian and French sides of the Fréjus road and rail tunnels are as different as the more famous pair separated by Mont Blanc and its tunnel (Chamonix and Courmayeur). There are plans for a lift link betweeen little, new Valfréjus and big, old Bardonecchia, but for the time being they are quite separate resorts, in their contrasting ways typical of the style of the two countries. Without doubt the skiing potential is enormous, although several big question-marks hang over the projected Italian side of the ski area. It seems more likely that the next expansion of the ski area will take place in France, towards Valloire and Valmeinier, with which Valfréjus hopes to be linked before 1992.

The brainchild of an Alpine entrepreneur who has had a lot to do with the development of Tignes, **Valfréjus** was launched a few years ago with all the hype usually reserved for new blockbusters of romantic fiction, and soon found its way into a number of UK package holiday brochures. Needless to say, the product does not live up to all the claims made and implied by its promoters. It is not yet a vast new international ski area to rival the biggest and best in the Alps – nor is it even growing significantly; it is not the favourite rendezvous of the ultra-chic and those smart enough to jump on bandwagons before they start rolling; and it is not super-reliable for the deepest and freshest of snow. So what is it? A very small, smartly and attractively styled modern resort with a small but tall, varied and uncrowded ski area. When compared with other small resorts of the southern French Alps, it emerges as a very worthwhile and interesting new development.

The resort stands in a narrow but not oppressively enclosed wooded setting at the top of a steep hairpin road from Modane, at the French end of the tunnels. There are two units, with a sensitive architectural style incorporating lots of new wood, balconies and colourful decoration. One unit is the so-called Chalet Club, a very clubby institution with small apartments modestly equipped and thus encouraging use of the two in-house restaurants. There are squash courts, a free swimming pool and jacuzzi, disco-aerobics sessions and some organised evening entertainment. It is quite a walk up the road to the main centre and lift station (Thabor) but a couple of lifts make it possible to ski across and have created short easy runs above the Club. Thabor is a larger precinct of similarly styled buildings, including some smart shops, framing the foot of the pistes and lift station; skiers pose quite a threat to pedestrians. Two hotels have opened recently; the Relais de Valfréjus (✆79053400) is attractive, comfortable (although rooms are not large) and fairly expensive.

The ski area is served by a long six-seater gondola, climbing in two stages over north-west-facing slopes from the resort to Punta Bagna (2737m), a panoramic peak with a smart new restaurant on top. The lower slopes are steep and wooded, with a difficult red run including a serious pitch of about 28° which we found in a dangerously icy and stony condition and causing widespread misery. There were no warning signs. The black is presumably more severe. A long track provides a gentle route down.

Around the mid-station (Arrondaz, 2200m) is a flat open area with an unenticing restaurant, some nursery lifts and steeper short drags. The gondola continues up a splendid steep coomb to Punta Bagna and offers the choice of the direct black run down the front, which is less awesome than it looks from below, or easier runs (blue and red) of about 400m vertical in the wide, beautiful and sunny bowl behind Punta Bagna, the Combe du Fréjus. The most roundabout run goes down via the Col du Fréjus (2540m), which will one day be accessible by lift from Bardonecchia and from where it is possible to ski down to Bardonecchia off-piste, returning by train and bus. The high peaks above the Combe du Fréjus are also scheduled for lift development (Pointe du Fréjus, 2934m, is next on the agenda).

The bottom of this back bowl (Pas du Roc, 2350m) is linked to the Arrondaz mid-station by a chair-lift up and over the Col d'Arrondaz (2500m), with a disembarkation point at the pass and short intermediate runs on both sides. The alternative way home is a long, beautiful and not difficult red run down from Pas du Roc ending up with a long track through the woods back to the resort. The top half of the run has some good off-piste variations.

Apart from the facilities in the Chalet Club, there is not much to do in the resort. Operators organise day trips to Valloire and evening excursions to Bardonecchia. There are nursery and ski-kindergarten facilities for children of three months upwards.

Bardonecchia is one of Italy's biggest ski resorts, and cannot be ignored, by us anyway. A sizeable town on one of the main routes into and out of Italy, it has neither charm nor character and is not convenient for either of its two ski areas. British skiers are present in considerable numbers, but they do not fill what is quite a large resort. Its main function is as a weekend outlet for Turin, which is only about an hour and a half's drive away, and outside peak periods it is very quiet (or at least empty – trains ensure that it is never too peaceful). The resulting lack of companions in the discos may be a drawback, but there is welcome compensation in a lack of crowds on the slopes, which are extensive and very entertaining, if snow conditions are good. On recent evidence, that 'if' is a big one. The ski areas seem outdated even by Italian standards, with old lifts, lunchtime closures, and very rudimentary piste marking and maintenance. This does not inspire confidence in the plan to link up with Valfréjus. There is no piste grading – though this is less of a problem than it might be, because most of the runs are obvious woodland trails and the slopes are unusually consistent in gradient, mainly of intermediate difficulty.

The modern town consists of a large grid of residential roads with a single long shopping street climbing from the station. Although not pretty, the station area is lively and the main street has a town-centre range of stylish and attractive shops, by no means dominated by sport. Bars and restaurants beside the station see most of the resort's nightlife, except at weekends and in peak season, when there is reported to be plenty of disco life. There are a few old and simple hotels by the station, and a row of more modern ones along the ring road between the station and the main lift departure, Campo Smith. The small Bucaneve (✆9892) is the pick of them – clean, modern, comfortable, and conveniently close, but not too close, to the station/centre. Ski buses do a circuit of the town and serve all the lift stations. Sports facilities on the western edge of town near Campo Smith include a natural ice rink and an indoor tennis hall.

There is an old part of town (Borgo Vecchio) to the north, at present very much a backwater where few skiers set foot, but destined to become the base of the new ski area. Apart from the attraction of being old, it has at least one good hotel, the large and simple Genzianella (✆9897), beside the church, whose bell is loud.

The main ski area stretches across a wide, wooded north-west-facing mountainside to the south of town, with three access points beside the road and river: Campo Smith (1300m), on the edge of the resort, with ski school, nursery slopes, restaurants and some apartments; Melezet (1370m), an attractive old village with a few simple hotels and restaurants about 3km from Bardonecchia; and Les Arnauds, a riverside hamlet between the two. A simple arrangement of chair-lifts and drags reaches the top of the mountain ridge in five places, between 2050m above Campo Smith and 2400m above Melezet, serving a large number of admirable but rather similar long, wide, fast undulating trails through the larch woods. Links across the mountainside between the different sectors exist but are complicated by river gullies and poor signposting. The Melezet end has the advantage of better off-piste and higher skiing (some of it above the trees); it is also less busy and, in our experience, has better snow. There are restaurants and nursery lifts at the half-way stations at both ends of the ski area.

On the other side of Bardonecchia, near the road tunnel entrance, Jafferau is a very different ski area, tall and narrow. A long series of lifts scales a west-facing mountain from 1350m to 2750m, with two drags serving an area of high open skiing above Pian delle Selle (2250m), and some long off-piste runs. Poor piste marking can be a real problem in bad visibility. The lower slopes are fairly steep and often bare.

There are long cross-country trails in the Valle Stretta, a thoroughfare closed in winter beyond Melezet, and down the valley to the town of Oulx.

Tourist offices Valfréjus ✆79053400. Tx 980150. Bardonecchia ✆(0122) 99137.
Package holidays Valfréjus: Enterprise (Ht Sc), Intasun (Ht Sc), Schoolplan (Ht). Bardonecchia: Club 18-30 (Ht Ch Cl), Schools Abroad (Ht), Skiscope (Ht), Thomson (Ht Sc).

Not a pretty pass

Sauze d'Oulx Italy 1500m

Good for *Après-ski, big ski area, mountain restaurants, sunny slopes, short airport transfers*
Bad for *Skiing convenience, not skiing, resort-level snow, late holidays, tough runs, lift queues, freedom from cars*

Linked resorts: Sestriere, Sansicario, Jouvenceaux

For many years Sowzy Doo has been one of the most popular, or at least one of the busiest, of Alpine resorts among young British skiers. Its simple recipe has been cheap hotel accommodation and cheap and extremely cheerful nightlife, combined with an entertaining area of intermediate skiing ideal for sunbathing and bombing through the woods working up a thirst for the evening action. The resort has its drawbacks: steep and icy walks around town, slow lifts and queues, and very unreliable snow. Lots of gregarious holidaymakers have nevertheless managed to have a good time; just as others have found Sauze, the Benidorm of the Alps, abhorrent even when snow conditions are at their best. The place does not change much from year to year, except in its luck in attracting snowfalls. After virtually snowless visits in 1984 and 1985, adequate cover in February 1986 allowed us to confirm old memories that the resort has plenty of good skiing to offer. For much of 1986–87, skiers were less fortunate. But Sauze didn't do particularly badly during last winter's early-season drought, when shortage of snow was the general rule.

As far as we can tell (and getting information out of the tourist office is not easy), the hike in lift pass prices in 1987 (which we attributed to the need to fund Sestriere's lift improvements) has largely been reversed, with the result that the pass shared by these two resorts is no longer one of the most expensive in the Alps.

Not many resorts would stand to benefit greatly from pulling down their main lifts, but that is what Sestriere did two years ago, dismantling the three pre-War cable-cars that launched the first purpose-built ski resort – a joint venture between Mussolini and Agnelli, hand-built by fascist robots. Only one new drag-lift was needed to maintain the size of the ski area, and Sestriere looks less of a period relic as a result. A new gondola has now improved the link with Sauze and makes Sestriere's artificial snow (of which it can produce a great deal) more accessible to Sauze-based skiers. Sestriere itself is not the most appealing of resorts – all-modern, and spread across a very high, wide and windy pass. Traditionally fashionable with Italian skiers, it still attracts smart weekenders and second-home owners from Turin, which is only a couple of hours away by car, but is pretty lifeless most of the time and especially so in low season.

Some of the smart crowd have forsaken Sestriere for neighbouring Sansicario, a stylish small modern development which is little marketed in Britain. It has a good small skiing area of its own, and although at present it shares a lift pass with Cesana and Clavière it has better skiing links with Sauze d'Oulx. A more sensible lift pass arrangement is under discussion.

The skiing top 2820m bottom 1390m

The **Sauze d'Oulx** ski area occupies a quarter-circle of mostly wooded mountainsides facing west and north. Lift departures are awkwardly sited, and the ski area is broken up by gullies. The main division is between the main Sportinia/Clotes system on the north-facing slopes and the west-facing Genevris lifts, only recently covered by the same pass as the bigger area, and still relatively neglected by skiers.

Several reporters have commented on the low standard of piste marking at Sauze d'Oulx. The woodland runs are quite similar and, considering how straightforward the layout of the slopes is, it is surprisingly easy to get lost. The ski map is not much help.

The sunny plateau of **Sportinia** is at the heart of the skiing. It has a couple of hotels, a small and crowded nursery area, and a circle of restaurants. Above it there is some good open skiing around the top of Triplex, with a couple of lifts behind giving access to Col Basset and the run down to Sestriere. The top of Fraiteve, a windy peak where the ski areas of Sauze d'Oulx, Sestriere and Sansicario meet up, can now be reached from Sauze d'Oulx via a new drag-lift, and the steep upper bowl on the Sauze side of the peak is now a black piste. This is the start of the famous Rio Nero off-piste run which follows a river gully down to the Oulx–Cesana road, 1600m below.

Below Sportinia there are excellent wide runs back through the woods – marked blue, red and black, steep in places but never really difficult. A green run traverses across the mountain and back, but is not entirely trivial skiing. Runs down to Jouvenceaux are graded blue and black, but are reported to be less different than that suggests.

The **Genevris** lift system starts (with a chair instead of the old bucket) a long way from most hotels and is usually approached via Clotes. From the Belvedere mid-station there are drag-lifts serving gentle runs below Monte Genevris; below Moncron are Sauze's most challenging pistes, where the difficulty is often accentuated by the effect of the sun and lack of maintenance.

Sauze is linked with **Sestriere** via Col Basset. The run (marked red) is wide and gentle but snow is often difficult or lacking as the slopes are open and face south-east. Most people ski down to Borgata, but it is possible to ski to Sestriere where chair-lifts return to Fraiteve with easy south-facing slopes on the Sestriere side, and runs from the top down to Sansicario and Sauze. The top is windswept and often short of snow, adding discomfort to the narrow red run down the shoulder to Sauze.

The bulk of Sestriere's skiing is on the other side of the resort, mainly north- and west-facing slopes on two mountains (Sises and Banchetta) separated by a deep valley. The lower slopes on this side of Sestriere and the very easy runs beside the road between Sestriere and Borgata

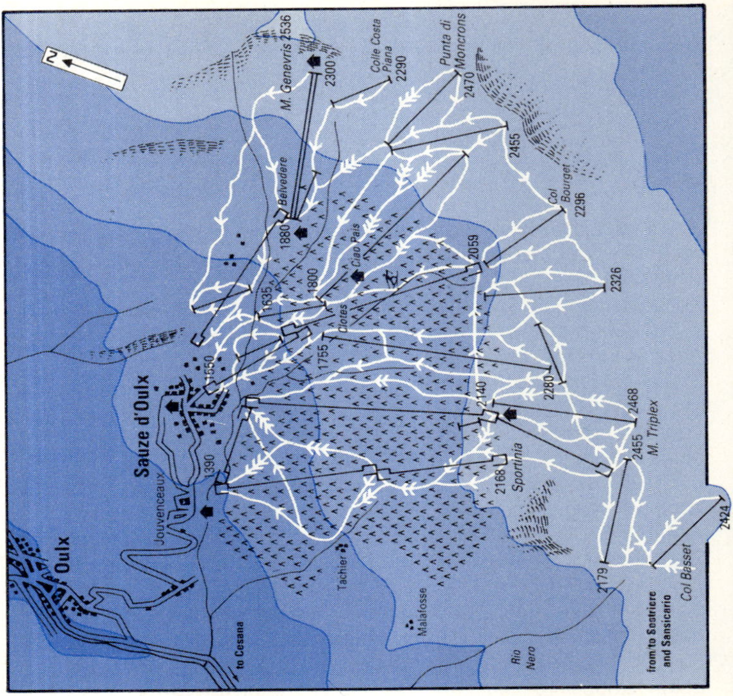

have been equipped with one of the biggest snow-making artillery in the Alps, covering 60km of pistes. This is not so vast an area as it sounds, but does make sure that early-season visitors can ski and improves the durability of the runs. Unfortunately there are no snow machines beside the runs over from Sauze.

Above Sestriere itself Sises is a good slalom hill, with short steep runs below Alpette. The top drag-lift may offer some good off-piste skiing, but the gorge between the two ski areas does not look hospitable. There are intermediate runs down to Grangesises and the Hotel Principi. Banchetta is a better holiday skier's mountain, with longer and more varied runs down to the roadside mini-resort of Borgata. The steep Motta drag-lift serves the highest and toughest of Sestriere's skiing, with slopes of about 30°, often mogulled, beside the lift. You don't have to tackle these to reach the wide and beautiful west-facing red run down into the dividing valley and on through woods.

Below Banchetta there is a wide expanse of red and blue pistes and some entertaining off-piste hollows and ridges above the sunny Amfiteatro. The wooded north-facing slopes above Borgata are steep, but beside the road there are drag-lifts up to Sestriere and very easy runs down – ideal for near-beginners.

Distribution of **mountain restaurants** is very patchy, with none at high altitude, and a general shortage (apart from two good restaurants

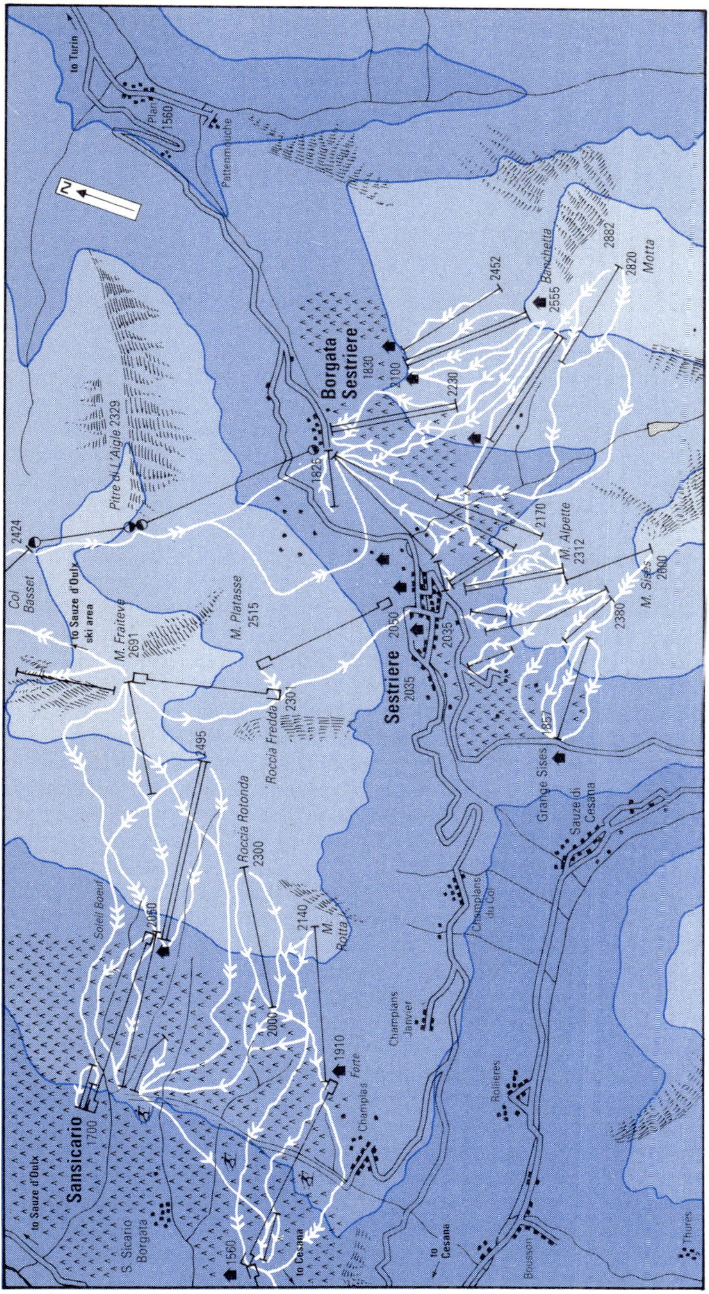
to Turin
Plan 1560
Pattenmouche
N
Borgata Sestriere
1830
2100
2452
Banchetta
2555
2882
2820
Motta
2230
Pitre di L'Aigle 2329
1826
2424
Col Basset
to Sauze d'Oulx ski area
M. Fraiteve 2691
M. Platasse 2515
2170
M. Alpette 2312
Sestriere 2035
2050
2035
2380
M. Sises
2301
Roccia Fredda
1857
Grange Sises
Sauze di Cesana
2495
Roccia Rotonda 2300
Champlans du Col
2140
M. Rotta
Soleil Boeuf
2050
2000
1910
Forte
Champlans Janvier
Champlans
Rollieres
Sansicario 1700
to Sauze d'Oulx
S. Sicario Borgata
1560
to Cesana
to Cesana
Bousson
Thures

above Borgata) at Sestriere. Sauze has some memorable restaurants, not all well plumbed: the old Capanna Kind at Sportinia; Ciao Pais tucked away below Moncrons; and the smart and expensive Capricorno at Clotes.

The main **queuing** problems are on the Sauze side of the mountain, with Sportinia being the main bottleneck. The best way to avoid queues at resort level is to use the Genevris access chair-lift.

The resort

Sauze stands on the sunny west-facing flank of a wide valley junction. It is built on a steep slope; it is also large, and growing, and almost everywhere seems to be a long, steep walk from everywhere else – including the three widely separated lift stations. A ski-bus covered by the lift pass does a circuit around the village and its lift stations until early evening. Perhaps surprisingly, there is a very picturesque old village backwater with a fine old church; but apart from this Sauze is an undistinguished mess of modern buildings. For much of the winter it is a British-dominated resort. People speak English and ski equipment is priced (and paid for) in sterling in several shops.

Accommodation is mostly in hotels, basic to simple, without charm, and cheap. By far the best location is around Piazzale Miramonti, between the Clotes and Sportinia lifts. The only attractive hotel in this area is the new and small Hermitage (✆85385), in a sunny open situation overlooking the village nursery slopes. The San Giorgio (✆85162) is far from luxurious and badly placed, but friendly and inexpensive. The Palace (✆85222) is the biggest, the most comfortable and the most expensive hotel, but not particularly stylish. There is a variety of high-altitude accommodation. The Capricorno at Clotes (✆85273) is expensive and attractive; you can be first on to the nursery slopes by staying at Sportinia – the Monte Triplex (✆85015) or even the old Capanna Kind (✆85206); the Ciao Pais (✆85280) also offers cheap, very simple accommodation.

Après-ski in Sauze is very lively ('Force 8 varying gale force 10 at times'), very British, and very inexpensive. It is not to everyone's taste – we have bitter reports of holidays spoilt by rowdiness. There is usually some organised après-ski every night of the week – disco nights, meals out, torchlit descents, tobogganing and Miss Sauze competitions. Favourite British haunts are the Derby hotel bar and neighbouring Moncrons cocktail bar, the Schuss disco and the Gran Trun pub in the old village (darts, bingo, burgers and sing-songs). The Simpaty is the most expensive and most Italian disco.

Sauze is not good for **cross-country** skiing or for **non-skiers**. Walking around is no great pleasure, and there are few non-skiing facilities. If it snows, the ice rink is apparently not cleared promptly.

Nursery slopes are adequate – the main slope is at Sportinia, open and very sunny but very crowded. There are also nursery areas at Belvedere on the Genevris side, and in the village (if there's snow).

We have very mixed reports on the standard of instruction in the two

Sauze d'Oulx facts

Lift payment

Passes Area pass covers all Sauze, Jouvenceaux and Sestriere lifts. Limited area day pass available.
Cost 6 days L130,000. 15% off in low season.
Children No reduction.
Beginners One free lift at Sauze and Sestriere; coupons.

Ski school

Two schools, at Sportinia and Genevris.
Classes 3hr mornings only (afternoon classes can be arranged).
Cost 6-days L95,000 (L75,000 low season). Private lessons L22,000.
Children Ski kindergarten from age 3, same timetable and cost as adult ski school. Non-ski kindergarten, age 6m–8yr, 9.00–5.00, L5,000/hr.

Cross-country skiing

Trails You can use the green run to Pian della Rocca (4km).

Not skiing

Facilities Natural ice rink, tennis, bowling.

Medical facilities

In resort Doctor, chemist.
Hospital Susa (29km).
Dentist Oulx (5km).

Getting there

Airport Turin; transfer 2½hr.
Railway Oulx (5km); frequent buses.
Road Via Chambéry/Fréjus tunnel; chains occasionally needed.

Available holidays

Resort beds 1,800 in hotels, 8,200 in apartments.
Package holidays Club 18-30 (Ht Ch), Enterprise (Ht), Neilson (Ht Sc), Pegasus (Ht Sc), Ski NAT (Ht Sc), Thomson (Ht)

Further information

Tourist office ✆(122) 85009.

Prices are approximate.

ski schools (one for each half of Sauze's ski area), but there is no shortage of English-speaking instructors. The Sportinia school quickly brings beginners off the nursery slopes on to real pistes, so they need a lift pass. Ski school races are a popular weekly event.

Jouvenceaux 1380m

This small and charming hamlet is just below Sauze d'Oulx, and is growing up the road from Oulx to meet it. At the bottom of the lifts that link the two villages is a delightfully unspoilt maze of crumbling alleys with old fountains and medieval paintings on the wall of the church. Most of the Jouvenceaux accommodation is quite a walk or a bus ride from its lifts, and does not share the charm of the old village.
Tourist office ✆(122) 85009.

Sestriere 2035m

Sestriere is a bleak and often windswept place, spread around the wide col with a scattering of thin larches around the bottom of the mountain flanks. The great landmarks are the tall, round towers of the Torre and the Duchi d'Aosta hotels (now occupied by Club Med), and the gothic turrets of the restored and newly re-opened Principi di Piemonte hotel, some way from the resort centre but with its own lift access to the Sises ski area. Buses run to and from Borgata, Grangsises and the end of the Rio Nero run (on the Oulx–Cesana road). Accommodation is in the form of hotels, apartments in large new complexes, and Club Med. Apart from the Principi, the most luxurious hotel is the new low-rise Sestriere (✆76576). The Savoy Edelweiss (✆77040) is simple and central. The Miramonti (✆77048) is not very well situated, but friendly, attractive and good value. Après-ski is moderately lively and stylish when the Italians are in residence at weekends and in holiday periods. An ice driving course can be included in the hotel-plus-lift-pass formula. The resort is not appealing for cross-country skiers or non-skiers. The wide Col de Sestriere provides excellent nursery slopes, and very easy runs between the resort and Borgata.

Tourist office ✆(122) 76045. **Package holidays** Club Med (Ht).

Sansicario 1700m

Sansicario has a sunny position half-way up a west-facing mountainside, well placed for exploring the Milky Way. It consists mainly of apartment buildings below a neat commercial precinct to which it is linked by a shuttle lift. Facilities are generally good for beginners, especially children (a good skiing and non-skiing kindergarten providing all-day care plus lunch if required). Cross-country skiers are reasonably well catered for, with a 10km loop across the hillside from the resort. Non-skiing and après-ski facilities are good, but there is little variety – a discothèque, a smart restaurant, a cheap restaurant, swimming, sauna, massage, gym, riding and even ski-jöring. Accommodation is of a high standard, mostly in apartments, but with a few comfortable, expensive hotels, of which the most attractive is the Rio Envers Gallia (✆811313), a bit of a walk from the centre.

The open slopes above Sansicario can be reached via Fraiteve from both Sauze and Sestriere. They are fairly steep at the top, and the run all the way down to Sansicario, starting off black or red, is a challenging and satisfying descent. Most of the rest of the west-facing skiing is wide, intermediate to easy woodland trails. There are some good long off-piste runs (including the Rio Nero) to points along the Cesana–Oulx road and an infrequent bus service back to the lifts at Cesana. Runs to La Combe, beside Cesana, get progressively steeper as they go down; the section below the bottom chair-lift is never easy and is often too bare to be skied. There are a couple of attractive mountain restaurants. The local lift pass covers the central section of the Milky Way – Sansicario, Clavière and Cesana. A supplement of about £5 a day covers Montgenèvre, but trips to Sauze and Sestriere cost more.

Tourist office ✆(122) 811212. Tx 211495.
Package holidays Hourmont (Groups) (Ht).

Relais Routier

Montgenèvre France 1850m

Good for *Big ski area, resort-level snow, easy runs, skiing convenience*
Bad for *Not skiing, après-ski, late holidays, mountain restaurants, tough runs, freedom from cars*

Linked resorts: Clavière, Cesana Torinese (Italy)

A border village beside a main road at a high pass is an unpromising specification for a resort, and Montgenèvre, just inside France on its border with Italy, looks unappetising as you drive through it. But around the church, just off the road, is an attractively unspoilt old village. Not surprisingly, Montgenèvre is popular with local weekenders from both sides of the border (Briançon and Turin). It often has the best snow conditions in the region, and at times of general snow shortage fills to bursting with skiers from large nearby resorts (Sestriere, Sauze d'Oulx and Bardonecchia). But most of the time it is very quiet, and by French standards it is inexpensive. There is cheap self-catering accommodation as well as good-value hotels, skiing and nursery slopes are conveniently arranged, and Montgenèvre would attract the 'family resort' label but for the main road (which is less main since the opening of the Fréjus road tunnel a few miles to the north) running between village and slopes.

Montgenèvre's local skiing is mostly easy but there are links with other resorts, providing a large and reasonably varied area whose worst aspect is the lift pass arrangements, a confusing tangle of supplements and extensions which threaten to make skiing expensive for skiers with itchy feet. Montgenèvre is the minority French sector of the Milky Way (Voie Lactée/Via Lattea), a long chain of linked skiing which makes it possible, snow and the customs permitting, to travel by piste and lift to and from Sauze d'Oulx or Sestriere, via Clavière, Cesana and Sansicario (all these resorts being in Italy). This is more of an occasional excursion than a single ski area ripe for sharing, especially since there is no longer a Milky Way lift pass. Current pass-sharing arrangements link Sansicario, Cesana and Clavière in the central section of the system, but the natural break in the chain is the valley floor at Cesana, which divides Sauze d'Oulx, Sestriere and Sansicario from the rest. Accordingly, we describe Sansicario and its skiing in the Sauze d'Oulx chapter.

It is often easier to make the most of the Milky Way resorts by travelling between them in a car rather than on skis. Montgenèvre is also well placed for day trips to a variety of French resorts, and this may involve less expenditure on lift passes than exploring the Milky Way. Serre Chevalier is only a few miles away to the west, and La Grâve, Les Deux Alpes and Alpe d'Huez are within reach. South of Briançon are Puy-St-Vincent, Risoul and Vars.

The skiing top 2600m bottom 1350m

Montgenèvre has ski slopes on both flanks of the pass. The south-facing side, Chalvet, is marginally higher (up to 2600m) and usually less crowded than the north-facing slopes (which form the main link with the Italian Milky Way resorts), but is expanding into what may soon be the more interesting of the two halves. It also provides an easy low-altitude route to Clavière.

A few minutes' walk east of the centre is the gondola for **Chalvet**, where two chairs and three drag-lifts now serve treeless, mostly easy runs with one or two more difficult runs and also some off-piste skiing down to Montgenèvre from the Bélier drag (2365m). There is a fairly easy red and a long green run back to the bottom. The blue run beside the drag-lift to the Col de l'Alpet (2430m) is very gentle, but the lift gives access to Montgenèvre's interesting new ski area. Already the north-east-facing slope behind the col has a chair-lift with black and red runs beside it and a long easy run round to Clavière. Future lifts up to 3000m will open up much more skiing, apparently challenging. This side of Clavière can also be reached by a long traverse from the top of the Chalvet gondola. Its lift, the Montquitaine chair, has an awkward short black beside it, but is mainly used for access to Montgenèvre, another very gentle traverse.

On the other side of the pass, a gondola from the Briançon end of the village and drag-lifts from the centre serve easy runs through woods opening out into wide nursery slopes above the road. From the top of the gondola there is a choice of three skiing areas. The wide, sheltered bowl of Querelay/Les Anges has eerie ruined fortress buildings around the crests and some red and black runs beneath them; but there is really no difficult skiing. The Brousset drag-lift serves some challenging skiing in the woods. The long dog-leg drag-lift through impressive rocky scenery to Rocher de l'Aigle has a red run beside it, awkwardly narrow in places, but is mainly used for access to Clavière. The Milky Way link starts with a poorly signed traverse around the mountain, easily missed in bad visibility. In other respects it is not at all difficult, and leads to a long Italian blue past the Gimont drag-lifts and down to Clavière, past two good restaurants. The more obvious run down from Rocher de l'Aigle is a splendid off-piste bowl which leads, via some scrub, to the Brousset drag.

The north-facing slopes above Cesana offer some of the best skiing in the Milky Way: fast sweeping trails through the woods (none of them easy) and some good off-piste skiing. The bottom section below Rafuyel is often bare, calling for a lift ride down to La Combe, just outside Cesana. The steep slopes opposite, where a long succession of lifts spans the Sestriere road on the way up to Sansicario and Fraiteve (the link with Sauze and Sestriere ski areas), are even less often in good condition and are little skied. Clavière's few lifts provide the necessary links to ski back to Montgenèvre, up and down along the steep wooded slopes beside the road and cross-country tracks. In good snow the runs are not particularly difficult, but there is no genuinely

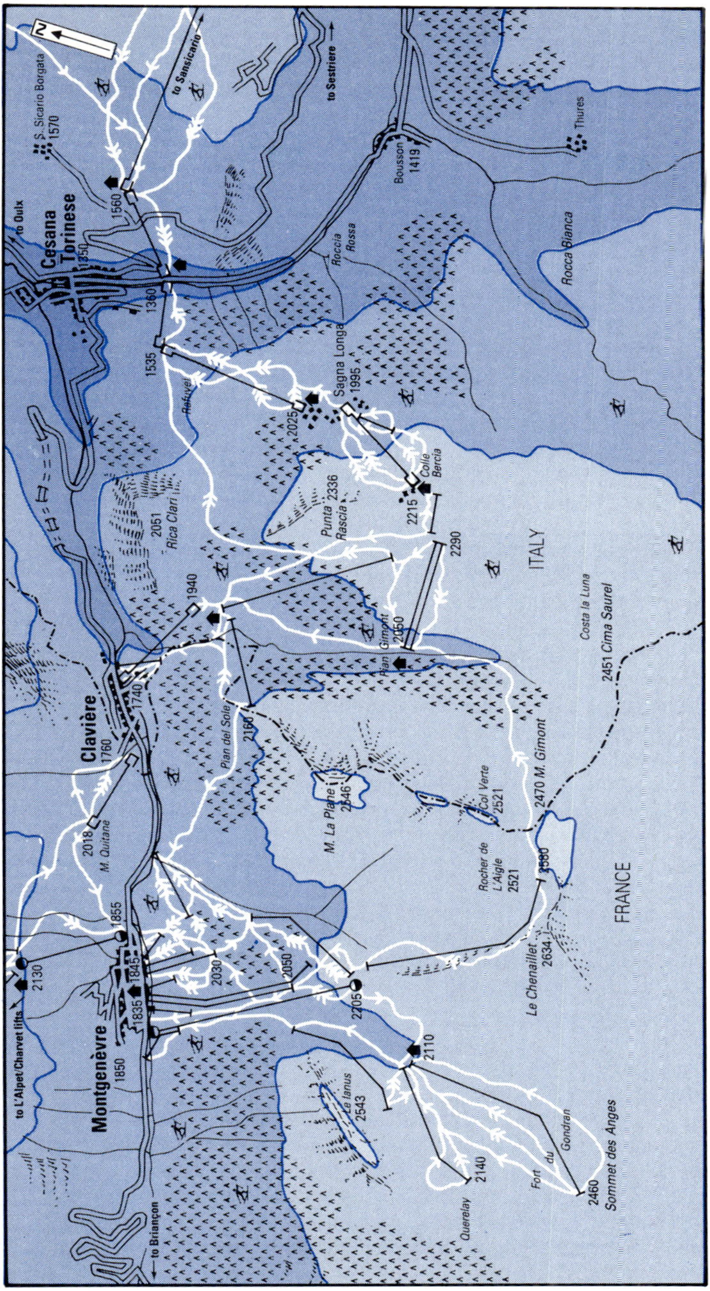

N
Cesana Torinese
1350
to Oulx
S. Sicario Borgata
1570
to Sansicario
to Sestriere
Thures
Bousson
1419
Roccia Rossa
Rocca Bianca
1560
1360
1535
Sagna Longa
1995
2025
Colle Bercia
2215
Punta Rascia
2336
2051
Rica Clari
2290
ITALY
1940
Pian Gimont
2050
Costa la Luna
2451 Cima Saurel
Clavière
1760
1740
Plan del Sole
2160
M. La Plane
2546
Col Verte
2521
2470 M. Gimont
2018
M. Quitaine
Rocher de L'Aigle
2521
2580
FRANCE
1855
2130
to L'Alpet/Charvet lifts
1845
2030
2050
2705
Le Chenaillet
2634
Montgenèvre
1850
1835
2110
Le lanus
2543
Querelay
2140
Fort du Gondran
2460
Sommet des Anges
to Briançon

easy way back except via Montquitaine, involving a long walk.

Montgenèvre is seriously short of **mountain restaurants**. The excellent and inexpensive bars and restaurants above Clavière (we have particularly mouth-watering reports of La Coche) offer some consolation.

Queues are bad only at weekends and when snow in nearby resorts is poor. In the past one of the worst bottlenecks for large groups of day-trip visitors to Montgenèvre has been in the lift pass office, getting passes validated.

The resort

The village is spread along the north side of the busy main road across the high col, now also the main street, with a customs hut at the Italian end of it. On the south side of the pass are open fields, with a row of lifts and a wide area of **nursery slopes**, admirable except for the amount of non-nursery skiing traffic and wind they receive. (Montgenèvre is itself more windswept than its main ski areas, which are relatively sheltered.) There are three supermarkets but shopping facilities are limited. Banks visit the village only a few times a week; hotels accept lire.

There is not much **après-ski** activity, especially during the week, but there is a good choice of inexpensive restaurants and three of them have nightclubs attached. The Ca del Sol is a popular bar in the centre. We have an enthusiastic report of Le Boom – a disco with fondues.

Montgenèvre is better than other resorts in the Milky Way for **cross-country** skiing, with a fair extent of easy trails beside the road to Clavière (more attractive than that sounds) and some more advanced runs in the woods on the Briançon side of the resort. There is very little for **non-skiers** to do in the village.

Accommodation is mostly in apartments widely spread along the road, in the old village and on the lower south-facing slopes. Access to skiing is easy from most places, but the Italian end of the village is the more convenient. A large new resort development is planned here, along with a new access lift for the south-facing side of the ski area. The pick of Montgenèvre's few and unluxurious hotels are the Napoleon (✆92219204), convenient and fairly comfortable, and the more attractively rustic Valérie (✆92219002) near the church.

Recent reports speak well of the **ski school** – 'friendly, helpful, good English' – for all grades of skier and for private lessons, including monoski.

Clavière Italy 1750m

Clavière is very much a border village, with the customs post in the middle, and a row of shops on the Italian side specialising in food and cheap Italian alcohol, with prices in francs and lire. There are a few quiet and not unattractive hotels along the road. The village is tightly enclosed by wooded slopes, and the nursery slope is small and steep. Lifts give access to the skiing above Montgenèvre and Cesana, with easy runs back from both. There is a cross-country trail up to

Montgenèvre facts

Lift payment

Passes Montgenèvre pass (5 to 15 days) valid for Montgenèvre lifts only, with two free days in Les Deux Alpes/ Alpe d'Huez. Daily supplements for Via Lattea Sud (Clavière/ Cesana/ Sansicario), Puy-St-Vincent, Serre-Chevalier. Grande Galaxie supplement to Montgenèvre pass gives one free day in each of Via Lattea Sud, Serre-Chevalier, Puy-St-Vincent as well as two free days in Alpe d'Huez/ Les Deux Alpes. Weekly Briançon area pass covering Montgenèvre, Serre-Chevalier and Puy-St-Vincent. Day pass available for lifts between Montgenèvre and Cesana.
Cost 6 days FF434. Grande Galaxie supplement FF100.
Children 25% off, under 12.
Beginners Day passes for limited area.

Ski school

Classes 2½hr morning, 2hr afternoon.
Cost 6 days FF540. Private lesson FF125/hr, 1 or 2 people.
Children Ski kindergarten, ages 3–11, 6 days without meals FF480. Non-skiing kindergarten, ages 1–4, 6 days without meals FF335.

Cross-country skiing

Trails Total 18km on either side of the pass, and at Les Alberts (5km away).

Not-skiing

Facilities Natural skating rink, open until 11pm, curling.

Medical facilities

In resort Doctor and chemist.
Hospital Briançon (10km).
Dentist Briançon (10km).

Getting there

Airport Turin; transfer 2½hr. Grenoble; transfer 3hr.
Railway Briançon (10km) or Oulx (17km).
Road Access via Fréjus tunnel or Grenoble/Briançon. Chains may be needed.

Available holidays

Resort beds About 140 in hotels, 5,900 in apartments.
Package holidays Bladon Lines (Ht Ch), Club 18-30 (Ch), Horizon (Sc), Schoolplan (Ht Sc), Sunmed (Ht Ch Sc), Thomson (Ch Sc)

Further information

Tourist office ✆92219046.

Montgenèvre and back. Clavière's après-ski is very limited, and it is no place for non-skiers. A recent report speaks of good snow in Clavière at a time when there was not much of it around, good food in the village and mountain restaurants, a quiet but pleasant local atmosphere, and a high standard of apartment accommodation. The lift pass covers Sansicario but not Montgenèvre. The ski school has some English-speaking instructors and, outside high season, mainly English-speaking pupils. Queues and weekend traffic are serious problems.
Tourist office ✆(122) 8856.
Package holidays Hourmont (Ht).

Cesana Torinese Italy 1350m

Cesana is an attractively dilapidated old village on a busy road junction at the foot of the Italian approach to the Montgenèvre pass. It is confined and sunless, and accommodation is limited. More holiday-makers go to the hotels and chalets dotted around the ski slopes (mainly at Sagna Longa, 2000m). The chair-lifts up to the skiing above Clavière and Sansicario are a long walk from the centre.
Tourist office ✆(122) 76698.
Package holidays Hourmont (Ht).

Auto suggestion

Serre-Chevalier France 1350m – 1500m

Good for *Big ski area, off-piste skiing, nursery slopes, cross-country skiing, lift queues*
Bad for *Mountain restaurants, skiing convenience, not skiing, Alpine charm, resort-level snow, freedom from cars*

The least international of France's major ski resorts seems likely to stay that way, despite a very large recent influx of British school groups. Our earlier editions expressed qualified enthusiasm for Serre-Chevalier and, although our return visits have been inconclusive because of weather conditions, one reporter who travelled with a 200-strong school party was very satisfied with everything except the restaurant prices (which are not in fact high by French standards).

Serre-Chevalier is not a village but a mountain, which stands above Briançon, the highest town in Europe, privileged in the amount of good skiing on its doorstep. The slopes have been a playground for local skiers for over half a century, and both resort and ski area have developed in a messy, unplanned way. It still has the atmosphere of a place for locals, and although the resort is not at all picturesque it does offer the chance to enjoy something of everyday provincial France. Lift pass arrangements are complicated and liable to change but generally allow visitors to divide their time between the many different resorts, participating in the Grande Galaxie arrangements. Serre-Chevalier and Briançon are a good base for exploring by car, being about at the centre of this region – with Montgenèvre to the east, Puy-St-Vincent to the south, Les Deux Alpes and Alpe d'Huez to the west.

The slopes of Serre-Chevalier and its neighbours drop down to the Guisane valley, where no less than 13 villages and hamlets make up the modern ski resort. There are three main ones, styled for skiers as Serre-Chevalier 1350, 1400 and 1500 but normally known by their proper names: Villeneuve, Chantemerle and Le Monêtier. The lower two share most of the accommodation, resort facilities and the larger half of the ski area. But Le Monêtier is the only one of the three with any village atmosphere, and it also has the most interesting skiing, for good skiers at least. Unfortunately it is the least convenient. All main villages suffer from traffic on the main Grenoble to Briançon road.

The skiing certainly deserves to be more widely known now that its two halves have been linked. As well as a large area of mostly intermediate pistes, there is a huge amount of unpisted, skiable north-facing mountain within striking range of the lifts. Serre-Chevalier cultivates a reputation as a resort for the connoisseur of off-piste skiing. In this sense, too, it is a place for locals (or skiers with local guides), for the best runs are not obviously visible. One excellent excursion is to the off-piste mountain at La Grâve, which has not in the past participated in the galactic lift-pass-sharing arrangements.

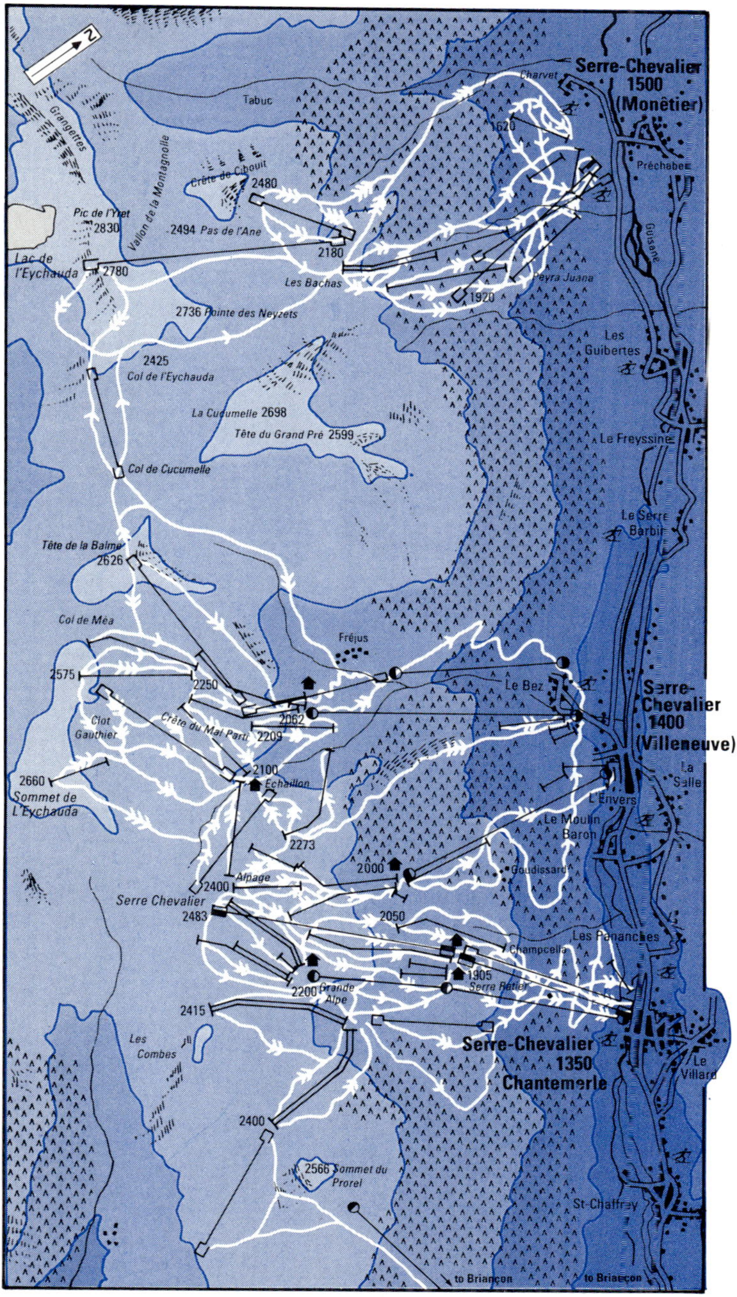
N
Serre-Chevalier 1500 (Monêtier)
Charvet
Tabuc
Grangettes
1620
Préchabert
Crête de Cibouit
2480
Vallon de la Montagnolle
Pic de l'Yret 2830
2494 Pas de l'Ane
2180
Guisane
Lac de l'Eychauda
2780
Les Bachas
Peyra Juana
1920
2736 Pointe des Neyzets
Les Guibertes
2425
Col de l'Eychauda
La Cucumelle 2698
Tête du Grand Pré 2599
Le Freyssinet
Col de Cucumelle
Le Serre Barbin
Tête de la Balme
2626
Col de Méa
Fréjus
2575
2250
Le Bez
Serre-Chevalier 1400 (Villeneuve)
Clot Gauthier
Crête du Mal Parti
2062
2209
2100
Échaillon
La Salle
2660
Sommet de L'Eychauda
L'Envers
Le Moulin Baron
2273
2000
Goudissard
2400
Alpage
Serre Chevalier
2483
2050
Les Pananches
Champcella
1905
Serre Ratier
2200
Grande Alpe
2415
Serre-Chevalier 1350 Chantemerle
Les Combes
Le Villard
2400
2566 Sommet du Prorel
St-Chaffrey
to Briançon
to Briançon

The skiing top 2780m bottom 1350m

Most of the lifts and pistes are concentrated above the neighbouring villages of **Chantemerle** and **Villeneuve** in a linked network covering two adjacent bowls of open, mostly intermediate skiing between 2000m and 2500m, with longer runs of varying difficulty down through thinly wooded lower slopes dotted with chalets and farm buildings and with rough roads that make easy alternatives to the direct descents to the valley floor. Le Monêtier's distinct but now linked sector is in many ways the most appealing (unless you want lunch on the slopes), with good red runs in the woods and the best of the off-piste skiing.

Above **Grand Alpe** is an open basin of rather featureless

Serre-Chevalier facts

Lift payment

Passes Grand Serre-Che pass covers all local lifts, entrance to Villeneuve pool and one session in the fitness centre, and local buses; available for all periods from half-day, also 8 non-consecutive days; passes of 6 days and over give right to one day in each of Les Deux Alpes, Alpe d'Huez, Puy-St-Vincent, Milky Way resorts from Montgenèvre to Sansicario, Bardonecchia. Various limited passes available.
Cost 6-day pass FF600. 20% off in low season.
Beginners Free lift at Chantemerle, beginners' day passes for valley lifts at Villeneuve and Monêtier.
Children About 40% off, under 13.

Ski school

Ecole du Ski Français in all three villages, Ski Ecole International in Villeneuve and Chantemerle.
Classes 3hr morning, 2hr afternoon; Le Monêtier, 2hr morning and afternoon.
Cost 6 days mornings only ESF FF350;, 6 days mornings and afternoon ESF FF545. Private lessons FF110/hr (1 or 2 people).
Children 20% off. Ski and non-ski kindergartens in all centres, typically for ages 2–6, 9.00–5.00, FF790/week.
Special courses Off-piste, freestyle.

Medical facilities

In resort Doctor, chemist and dentist.
Hospital Briançon (5km).

Cross-country skiing

Trails About 45km of trails along valley floor between Briançon and Le Casset (west of Le Monêtier).

Not skiing

Facilities (Most at Villeneuve). Natural ice rinks (all centres), riding, 20km cleared paths, ice driving, sleigh rides, fishing (from early March), swimming, hang-gliding, fitness centre.

Getting there

Airport Grenoble; transfer about 2½hr. Also Turin.
Railway Briançon (5 km); frequent buses.
Road Via Grenoble/Col du Lautaret or Chambéry/Fréjus Tunnel; chains may be needed.

Available holidays

Resort beds 30,000, mainly in apartments.
Package holidays Bladon Lines (Ch), Horizon (Ht Sc), Hourmont (Groups), (Ht), Hourmont (Schools), (Ht), Neilson (Ht Sc), Quest (Ht), Schoolplan (Ht), Schools Abroad (Ht), Skiscope (Ht), SkiSet (Ht), Snowbird Holidays (Ht), Thomson (Ht Ch Sc)

Further information

Tourist offices Villeneuve ✆92247188; Chantemerle ✆92240034, Tx 400152; Le Monêtier ✆92244198, Tx 244004.

intermediate runs with a good but congested nursery area at the top of the gondola. The double Prorel drag-lift serves quieter pistes and should, by the end of 1988, join up with a new lift system (a two-stage stand-up gondola and a chair-lift) starting in Briançon itself, with pistes back to the town, snow permitting. Serre-Chevalier itself is an unremarkable peak, but there are good views from the top and a fast race-course through the woods to Serre-Ratier.

The **Fréjus/Echaillon** sector above Villeneuve provides more interesting runs for good skiers, with short, fairly steep unprepared pistes beneath the crest of the mountain chain. There are splendid views southwards into the Vallouise and a beautiful run (L'Isolée, well named) along the narrow ridge from Eychauda towards Echaillon. In good snow conditions, inexperienced skiers can enjoy very long runs to the valley.

Le Monêtier's previously limited network of lifts is now linked to the Fréjus sector by a series of chair-lifts and has been extended upwards by the Yret chair-lift, the highest point in the lift system, giving runs of 1300m vertical to the valley. The link run itself is not difficult, but it is high and exposed – unpleasant or impossible in bad weather. The wide and beautiful east-facing bowl above Fréjus has now been opened to piste skiers; other favourite off-piste runs have simply been made more accessible, notably the steep descents from Yret. The steep (about 35°) face under the chair-lift is much skied and often a formidable mogul-field. Fortunately snow conditions are usually good, as they are not on the pistes down from Yret to the Col de l'Eychauda. Tabuc is a splendid long black run through the woods away from the main ski area, with one or two awkwardly narrow steep sections. None of the skiing above Le Monêtier is easy. The vast extent of larch woods, up to 2200m, makes good off-piste skiing.

Mountain restaurants, absent from Le Monêtier's ski area, are to be found at most of the other main lift stations. The old chalet-hotel Serre-Ratier is a welcome exception to the general mediocrity.

Lift **queues** are not a problem (except on one or two beginners slopes), provided runs down to the valley are skiable – Villeneuve and Chantemerle now have three access lifts each, and the resort as a whole can now shift over 10,000 skiers an hour from the valley floor. As a result, main pistes around Grand Alpe and Fréjus can be very congested. Streams and hillocks make it difficult or impossible to traverse across the natural balcony at around 2000m. At the time of going to press, it was thought unlikely that the new Briançon lifts would be covered by any Serre-Chevalier lift pass, or vice versa.

The resort

Chantemerle (1350) is only 5km out of Briançon and serves mainly as a service area for skiing commuters; space between main road and river is limited and parking facilities are inadequate. The new Briançon lifts will no doubt improve matters. **Villeneuve** (1400) is more spread out, with a narrow high street on one side of the river and more spacious resort development (commercial centre and apartment buildings) beside the main road at the foot of the slopes on the other side. If there is any centre of Serre-Chevalier, this is it. Near the Fréjus lifts, the old hamlet of **Le Bez** has been converted to serve as a resort community without losing all its charm. **Le Monêtier** (1500) is a quiet old rural spa village with some delightful huddles of old buildings between road and river. The lift departure is on the other side of the river, quite a walk from the centre.

Local transport consists of seven buses a day from Briançon along the valley and a more frequent (and free) shuttle bus, serving all main resort centres and lifts.

Accommodation consists of apartments and about 30 hotels, mostly small and simple, evenly distributed between the three resort centres, and in many cases run and staffed by British operators. Villeneuve is the best location for skiing convenience. The Christiana (✆92247633) is a simple, friendly and reasonably priced hotel between the two main lifts. On the other, quieter side of the village, La Vieille Ferme (✆92247644) is a long walk from skiing, but rewards the effort with interesting décor, a warm welcome and good food. The Aigle du Bez (✆92247224) is a clean and functional new woody hotel at Le Bez, very convenient for the Fréjus lifts. In Le Monêtier the simple Alliey (✆92244002) is very charming and central. Skiers with cars who are planning to explore other resorts to the south and east may prefer to stay in Briançon.

Après-ski is quiet except at weekends. There are plenty of restaurants (the Serre and the Marotte in Villeneuve are recommended) and a few discothèques, of which the Baita (Villeneuve) and Serre-Che (Chantemerle) attract most of the local young.

The **cross-country** skiing is good, especially west of Le Monêtier (the best base for this purpose) where the valley is less built up; long off-piste excursions towards the Col du Lautaret are possible.

Despite the various facilities (mainly in Villeneuve) and the charm of some of the old hamlets dotted along the valley floor, Serre-Chevalier is not appealing for **non-skiing** holidays.

Nursery slopes are good, with open areas at the foot of Villeneuve and Le Monêtier slopes, and higher up at the top of the Fréjus and Grand Alpe gondolas.

Our one recent reporter was impressed by his **ski school**, but hasn't told us which it was. The schools and guides are very active in organising day excursions.

Upward mobility

Alpe d'Huez France 1850m

Good for *Nursery slopes, beautiful scenery, big ski area, tough runs, off-piste skiing, late holidays, resort-level snow, family holidays, sunny slopes, easy road access*
Bad for *Not skiing, Alpine charm, easy runs, freedom from cars*

Linked resorts: Auris, Villard-Reculas

Alpe d'Huez is a big modern resort spread widely across a treeless hillside in an outstandingly open and sunny yet sheltered setting high up on the northern wall of the Romanche valley east of Grenoble. The skiing is well suited both to beginners, with green runs at low level, and to experts, with the world's longest black run and some very long, exciting off-piste runs; it caters less well for the intermediate majority, especially when the strong southern sun, of which the resort is so proud, has had its effect on the mainly south- and west-facing slopes. Already impressive and much the better for recent improvements to the lift system, Alpe d'Huez's ski area stands to benefit enormously from new lifts planned for the next few seasons. Development of a big area of north-facing slopes above Vaujany began last season and is due to be completed for 1988–89.

Like Les Deux Alpes (a close neighbour as the helicopter flies but emphatically separated by the deep, wide valley), Alpe d'Huez is an early post-War development, which means it has grown up piecemeal, and has hotels as well as apartments, and animated après-ski – at least at holiday times, when it has quite a chic French clientele. The foreign presence is still small – though the number of British firms offering package holidays in the resort has multiplied in recent years.

Again like Les Deux Alpes, Alpe d'Huez has limited lift-pass-sharing arrangements with several other resorts in the area – Les Deux Alpes is nearest, but Serre-Chevalier and Montgenèvre, close to Briançon, are within reach by car.

The skiing top 3320m bottom 1350m

There are three distinct areas, two of them accessible from the top of the resort. The third, Signal de l'Homme, is separated from the resort by the Sarenne gorge, but can be reached by catching a lift down and then up, or in a very roundabout way on skis.

Most of the skiing takes place on the **Grandes Rousses**, reached by a two-stage 25-person gondola followed by cable-car to Pic Blanc. The first section climbs only very gently over the enormous area of green runs and walks; above it the rocky massif climbs increasingly steeply. The second gondola serves little skiing of its own and if the top cable-car is not open the chair-lifts up to Clocher de Mâcle offer more interesting runs. These include a beautiful, long black run past Europe's highest disused coalmine (the Combe Charbonnière) and from there either round to the resort or down into the Sarenne Gorge. A more direct descent is the downhill race-course. The short run down from Clocher de Mâcle to Lac Blanc (for access to the cable-car) is steep (33°), but snow is usually good.

Behind the Pic Blanc cable-car station is the south-facing, crevasse-free Sarenne glacier, which starts with a steep, often stony and usually crowded mogul-field immediately below the lift station. The view is enormous and so are the runs – only blacks, of which two are notorious. One is the mogul-slope under the cable-car, reached via a tunnel through the mountain and an awkward path at the end of it; this is steep, but much less fearsome than it looks from below. The second is the 16km run all the way down the glacier and into the Sarenne Gorge, the longest black run and possibly the longest piste in the Alps, mainly thanks to the very long, almost flat run-out beside the river. It is a superb trail, wild and beautiful, of over 1800m vertical, but snow conditions below glacier-level are often difficult. A few black passages punctuate long, fast-cruising stretches. The Combe du Loup variant is a much more serious proposition than the main run.

Pic Blanc is also the point of departure of a number of very long off-piste runs. Some involve precipitous walks and very steep slopes, and most end up in valleys far from Alpe d'Huez. For all these adventures, guides are essential.

A new lift from L'Olmet (1350m) to the mid-station of the Grandes Rousses gondola (to be supplemented for 1988/89 by a lift from Vaujany to the Petites Rousses, just above the gondola top station) means that some of these runs can be tackled without having to arrange to be collected by helicopter. Already there are good long intermediate pistes down to L'Olmet, but the Vaujany lift is the most important part of this new area, which promises to be a very valuable addition for both experts and moderate skiers. On the other side of the Sarenne glacier, a chair-lift from Clavans (1400m) to the Col de Sarenne will ("soon") have the same effect, opening up new pistes and providing a way back from another popular off-piste area. The **Signal** climbs to a rounded peak not very far above the top of the resort with easy, open runs beside the numerous lifts. Behind Signal, longer runs drop down the open west-facing slopes above Villard-Reculas. There are gentle runs at the top but no easy way down. The main red piste includes an often very unpleasant mogul-field.

On the other side of the resort, the **Signal de l'Homme/Auris** sector is not very large, but offers plenty of variants on the wide open north-facing slopes above the river gorge (an easy path links up with the Sarenne runs and lifts back to Alpe d'Huez) and a splendid long red (Maronne) down to Le Châtelard. The return drag-lift and black run beside it are both steep, albeit briefly. The short intermediate runs served by chair-lifts above the new resort of Auris do not enjoy very reliable snow cover.

Mountain restaurants away from the resort itself are few and dull, notable exceptions being the chalet just above Villard-Reculas (which

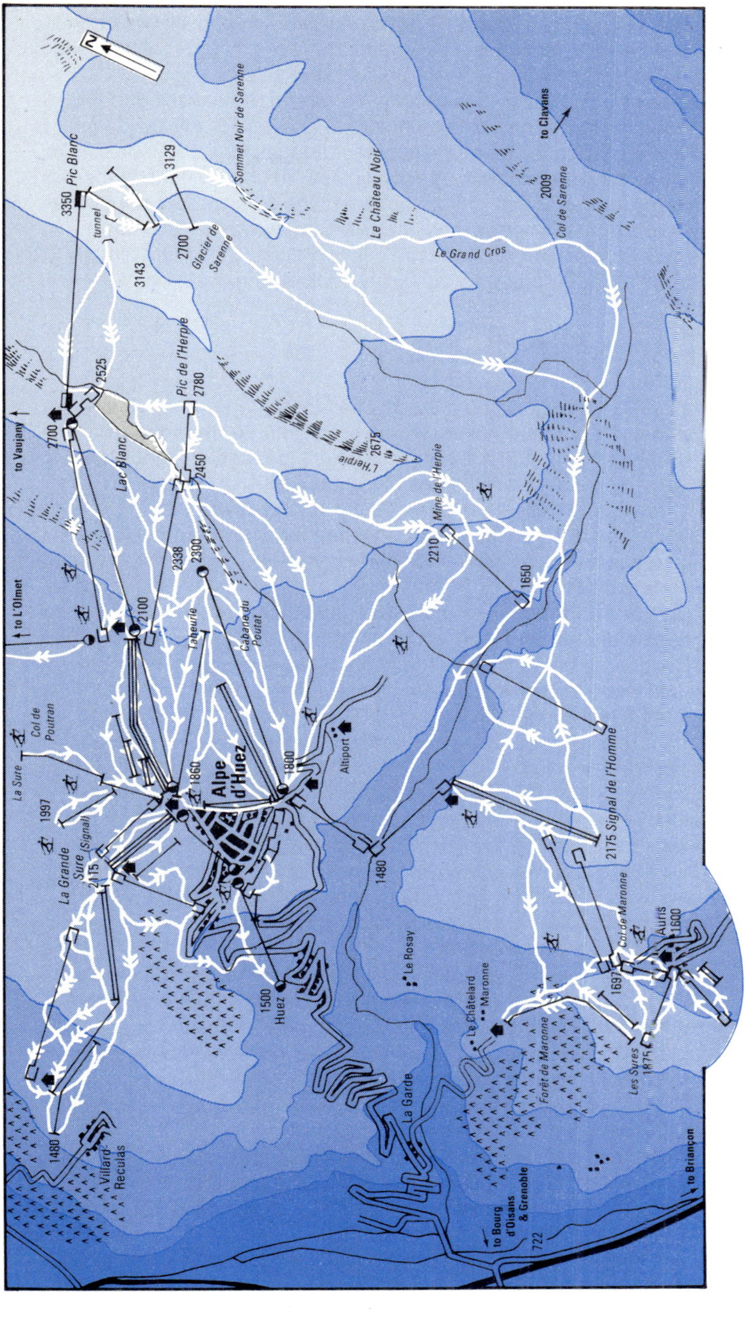

N
Pic Blanc
3350
tunnel
3129
Sommet Noir de Sarenne
Le Château Noir
to Clavans
2009
Col de Sarenne
Le Grand Cros
2700
Glacier de Sarenne
3143
2525
Pic de l'Herpie
2780
2700
to Vaujany
Lac Blanc
2450
L'Herpie
2675
Mine de l'Herpie
2210
1650
2300
2338
2100
to L'Olmet
Taburle
Cabane du Poutat
Col de Poutran
La Sure
1997
1860
Alpe d'Huez
1800
Altiport
La Grande Sure (Signal)
2115
1480
2175 Signal de l'Homme
Col de Maronne
Auris
1600
1697
1500
Huez
Le Rosay
Le Châtelard
Maronne
Forêt de Maronne
Les Sures
1875
La Garde
1480
Villard-Reculas
to Bourg d'Oisans & Grenoble
722
to Briançon

has a ski-in outdoor bar where you can sit down with skis on), and the Forêt de Maronne hotel at Le Châtelard. The restaurant at the gondola mid-station has waiter service and is expensive.

The main **queuing** black spot is the Grandes Rousses gondola. Thanks to the big new cabins the queue moves quickly, but it remains difficult to judge, as there are separate queues for those travelling to half-way and the top, with alternating flow. In holiday periods there are queues for the bucket lift from bottom to top of the resort, but the new gondola from the bottom has improved access to the Grandes Rousses. This is the first section of a two-stage lift leading directly to the Sarenne glacier, currently accessible only by the cable-car.

The resort

Alpe d'Huez has just celebrated its half-centenary. Although modern, the resort is not at all new or stylish architecturally (apart from its beautiful church) and has spread over a large area of steepish hillside in a triangular shape with the main lift departure at the top.

A daytime shuttle lift runs frequently up and down, with a stop in the middle. The bus service is no longer free, and non-skiers take priority. The roads form a complicated one-way system, often choked with traffic in icy conditions.

Accommodation is in apartments and plenty of small and medium-sized hotels, none of them particularly luxurious. The growing band of UK tour operators offer a range of both, and one or two have managed to find chalets. The best location for skiing purposes is right at the top of the large resort near the lift station. The Christina (✆76803332) is friendly and charming and one of the few attractive, chalet-style buildings at the top end of the resort. The nearby Chamois d'Or (✆76803132) is a bright, functional, comfortable modern hotel with a highly reputed, expensive restaurant. Après-skiers may prefer to be nearer the bottom of the resort. The comfortable Vallée Blanche (✆76803051) is well placed and has its own disco. Apartments in the resort vary considerably in age and comfort, and in shopping convenience. We have received reports from self-caterers expressing disappointment.

Après-ski is lively during the New Year, February and Easter holidays but relatively quiet at other times when the French, who dominate the resort's clientele, are not at play. The resort is generally reckoned to come second only to Courchevel for good restaurants. There are piano bars, and several hotels have live bands or discothèques. Also a few fast-food counters and one or two simple, inexpensive bars.

There are long **cross-country** trails and splendid walks high up in the main ski area, but despite these and other sports facilities Alpe d'Huez cannot safely be recommended for a **non-skiing** or cross-country skiing holiday.

Nursery slopes are exemplary: very spacious, very extensive, very gentle and adjacent to the resort. **Ski schools** meet at the top and bottom of the resort. The SEI offers *ski évolutif* for adult beginners and has a maximum class size of eight.

Alpe d'Huez facts

Lift payment

Passes Area pass covers all the lifts, pool and ice rink. Passes of over 5 days give a free day in Les Deux Alpes, Serre-Chevalier, Puy-St-Vincent, Montgenèvre/Sansicario, Bardonecchia, Sestriere. Passes of over 11 days valid for 2 days in each centre. Various day passes are available for more limited areas.
Cost 6-day pass FF625. 15% off for senior citizens.
Beginners 2 free lifts, coupons, and day passes for limited areas.
Children 15% off under 13.
Summer skiing On Sarenne Glacier, 2700m–3300m, 3 lifts.

Ski school

Ecole du Ski Français and Ski Ecole International.
Classes 2hr morning and 2½hr afternoon.
Cost 6 days, ESF FF580. Private lessons FF120/hr.
Children Under 13, 30% off adult ESF prices. Ski and non-ski kindergartens, age 2 up, 8.30–6.00, 6 days with meals and instruction FF900.

Cross-country

Trails Short beginners' loop, 6.3km and 8.2km blue loops, 16.4km red loop above resort.

Not skiing

Facilities 30km cleared paths, artificial ice rink (skating/curling), heated open pool, clay pigeon shooting, boules, hang-gliding, ice-driving.

Medical facilities

In resort Doctors, dentists, chemists.
Hospital Grenoble (65km).

Getting there

Airport Geneva; transfer 2½hr. Grenoble 1½hr.
Railway Grenoble (65km); daily buses.
Road Via Lyon/Grenoble; chains may be needed

Available holidays

Resort beds 25,000 in apartments and 36 hotels.
Package holidays Activity Travel (Ht Ch Cl Sc), Air France (Ht Sc), Club Med (Ht), Crystal (Ht Sc), Inghams (Ht Sc), Intasun (Sc), Made to Measure (Sc), Neilson (Ht Sc), Ski Sutherland (Ht), Skiscope (Ap), Skiworld (Ht Sc), Thomson (Ht Sc), Tourarc (Sc), Vacations (Ht Sc), VFB (Ht Sc)

Further information

Tourist office ✆76803541. Tx 320892.

Look to the future

Les Deux Alpes France 1600m

Good for *Tough runs, off-piste skiing, beautiful scenery, sunny slopes, après-ski, late holidays, resort-level snow, summer skiing*
Bad for *Alpine charm, mountain restaurants, not skiing, freedom from cars*

We reported favourably on this big modern resort in previous editions, and return visits (admittedly in good conditions) have not dimmed our enthusiasm for it. To sum up the summary: the resort is ugly, strung out and messy, but not too inconvenient; and it is young, lively, friendly and not necessarily expensive (there is cheap accommodation). The skiing is very high, with a magnificent easy glacier area, a row of challenging runs immediately above the resort and some skiing below it – though without the shelter of dense forest which makes the lower runs of resorts like Courchevel so valuable in bad weather.

Les Deux Alpes has not impressed all its visitors so favourably. Some have been disappointed not to find an all-French resort: Les Deux Alpes is now well and truly discovered. Others expected a ski area to compare in size with Val d'Isère/Tignes or the Trois Vallées, which it does not. Others have found that the easy runs are not very easy and that conditions on the difficult lower slopes make the last run of the day an unpleasant experience. The reservation that we endorse most wholeheartedly is that the narrowness of the ski area makes it difficult to escape people and pylons and limits the variety of the skiing. Les Deux Alpes offers a foretaste of what skiing may be like in the 1990s in many more big resorts: over-efficient lifts relieving queues but causing overcrowded pistes.

One sure way to escape the problem is to ski to La Grâve, a famous mountaineering resort to the north-east of the glacier with no pistes but long chain of lifts which by the 1988-89 season will go right to the top of the skiing. La Grâve's uncompromisingly wild ski area is almost unique, and the new management of the lift company is anxious to resist the obvious pressures to widen the resort's appeal. Keen off-piste skiers and local mountain guides will hope that they succeed.

Also planned for the coming season is a new funicular built in the rock beneath the glacier, as at Saas Fee. This will relieve the pressure on the existing heavily used drag-lifts at the top of the very efficient gondola up from Les Deux Alpes. Looking another two years ahead, there are plans to build a high-level cable-car to link Bons, on the north-west extremity of the skiing, to Auris, on the southern fringe of the Alpe d'Huez ski area. For the moment, Alpe d'Huez is easily reached by road (or helicopter), as is Serre-Chevalier to the south-east.

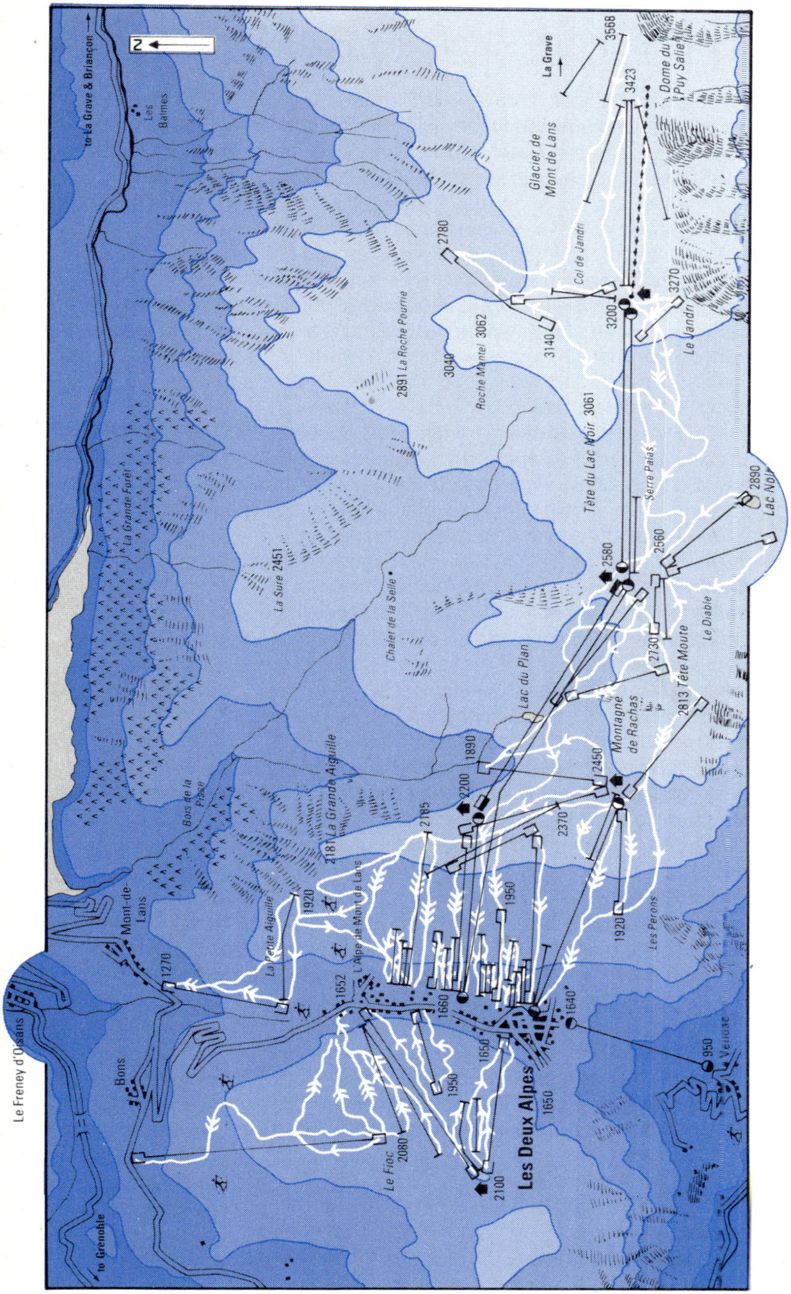
to La Grave & Briançon
Les Balmes
La Grave
Glacier de Mont de Lans
Dome du Puy Salie
Col de Jandri
Le Jandri
La Roche Pourrie
Roche Mantel
Tête du Lac Noir
Serre Palas
Lac Noir
La Grande Forêt
La Sure
Chalet de la Selle
Lac du Plan
Montagne de Rachas
Tête Moute
Le Diable
La Grande Aiguille
Bois de la Pisse
Mont-de-Lans
La Petite Aiguille
L'Alpe de Mont de Lans
Les Perons
Les Deux Alpes
Bons
Le Fioc
to Grenoble
Le Freney d'Oisans
Venosc

The skiing top 3568m bottom 1270m

As far as skiing goes, Une Alpe et Demie would be a more appropriate name. The western side of the skiing climbs only a few hundred metres above the resort and is not heavily used, despite the attraction of a long north-facing run down to the small village of **Bons**. This run is not maintained, and the snow may be difficult or lacking. The blue run down to the Venosc end of Les Deux Alpes is steep.

The skiing that matters is on the eastern side of the resort. The lower slopes are broad and steep, the upper ones on the glacier broad and gentle; between the two, from 2200m to 3200m, is a large area of narrower middle slopes where the ground is too broken up to provide a network of runs, although some good north-facing slopes have been opened recently. This area contains several bottlenecks, with congested pistes particularly in the afternoon.

The first section of skiing immediately above the resort, with main access lifts from the central complex and from Alpe de Venosc, is a broad, steep, open, west-facing mountainside, terraced for safety. There is little variety in the runs, but all are difficult except for a narrow path (graded green) along a road at the northern end of the mountain, from which it is possible to traverse to most parts of the resort. When crowded at the end of the day, this run is no fun at all. At the Venosc end, the black Diable run from the Tête Moute gives an uninterrupted 1200m vertical descent, and steep, icy/slushy moguls thrive all over it. At the northern end of this broad west-facing slope, the unbashed run down to **Mont de Lans** is similar to the one to Bons, and rarely tempting unless you want to notch up the longest on-piste descent (in vertical drop) in the Alps – 2300 metres from the top of the glacier.

The top of this broad mountainside is a spacious open ridge with very easy runs and a number of lifts along it. Behind the ridge and the Tête Moute, a deep coomb interrupts the ski area. The installation of the Combe du Thuit chair-lift has opened up some steep off-piste skiing here, and serves a long blue run with a steepish mogulled start. Taking this lift also provides an alternative to the narrow, crowded track around the bowl which is the main way home. From Tête Moute there is an easy run across to the top of the cable-car and steep north-facing runs between the rocks, down to the Lac du Plan and onwards to the Thuit chair.

The top section of the gondola to the Col de Jandri spans a slightly more open area of long blue and red runs with shorter, north-facing runs served by the Lac Noir and Toura chair-lifts. There are splendid views from the top of both these lifts, steeply down into the Vénéon valley. Although there is not a very wide network of lifts, the skiing in this area is long (over 1000m vertical).

Thanks to new lifts on the Glacier de la Girase, Les Deux Alpes and La Grâve now share one of the best summer skiing areas in Europe: a wide expanse of long, easy runs between 2780m and 3568m. This is a lot of open, easy skiing with magnificent views and totally reliable snow conditions. Naturally the glacier area is inhospitable in bad weather.

The new lifts and pistes should make it easier to ski across to, and possible to ski back from, the Col des Ruillans (3200m), near the top of the La Grâve gondola and the start of various long and very beautiful off-piste runs down to the village (1500m). The safe ways down are not obvious – there are neither signposts nor avalanche warnings – so you should not attempt the trip without a guide. The ski school takes groups regularly when conditions are good. Les Deux Alpes' very long and narrow lift system gives some other opportunities to go off-piste, but not many of the runs end up anywhere near the resort. Many come into the category of ski mountaineering, and guides are essential.

This is not a resort for lunchtime gourmands – **mountain restaurants** (at the main lift junctions) are few, uninviting, expensive and crowded. But they do have large terraces.

Thanks to the Jandri Express 20-person gondola, going up is now easier than finding space in the restaurants or on the pistes back down to the resort in the afternoon. There are **queues** for the Signal and Roche Mantel chair-lifts in fine weather and for the Combe du Thuit chair in late afternoon. The piste map is much less good than its predecessor, and in many places positively misleading; the resort authorities have no plans to improve it. Agreement has been reached with La Grâve for a shared lift pass.

The resort

The setting of Les Deux Alpes is a remarkably symmetrical one, with steep drops to the north and south of the flat col on which it sits, and steep walls climbing evenly to the east and west. Of the two parts, Alpe de Venosc is the more compact and lively, and is splendidly set on the ledge above the very steep Vénéon Valley. There is now a free resort bus service.

Accommodation is mostly in apartments, but there are also lots of small hotels, mostly simple and friendly – and UK tour operators' holidays employ a range of both, plus an increasing number of catered chalets. The best location is right in the centre near the main Jandri lift station. The Meije (✆76792087) is a welcoming small chalet-style hotel with an open fire in the sitting room. Le Cairn (✆76805238) has less charm and is marginally less convenient but is similar in style. Attractive hotels (also simple and inexpensive) at the Venosc end are the Chalet Mounier (✆76805690), Pied Moutet (✆76805021) and Neiges (✆76805202).

Après-ski is plentiful and lively, with a number of interesting and good restaurants, entertaining bars, a couple of discothèques at Alpe de Venosc, and one at Alpe de Mont de Lans.

Les Deux Alpes is not ideal for **cross-country** skiers but Venosc has a long network of peaceful cross-country trails in the Vénéon valley (below Les Deux Alpes at the low altitude of around 950m, reached by gondola). **Non-skiers** are likely to find the resort limited.

Nursery slopes are at the foot of the steep slopes on the west-facing side of the village beside Alpe de Venosc. Although not a very extensive

Les Deux Alpes facts

Lift payment

Passes Area pass covers all lifts, swimming pool and ice rink, and gives a reduction at the fitness centre. Available for all periods from half-day. Three other more limited passes are available. Passes of over 5 days give one free day in Alpe d'Huez, Serre-Chevalier, Puy-St-Vincent, Montgenèvre/Sansicario and Bardonecchia. Passes of over 11 days give two free days in each centre.
Cost 6-day pass FF630. Senior citizens 20% off.
Children 20% off, under 13 years.
Beginners Two free lifts, plus limited pass for 18 lifts near the resort.
Summer skiing Extensive area with 12 lifts, 2780m to 3568m.

Ski school (2 schools)

Classes 2½ hr morning or afternoon.
Cost 6 days (15hr) FF410 mornings, FF360 afternoons. Private lessons FF105/hr (1–4 people). FF120/hr (1–4 people) at midday.
Children 30% off in classes. Ski kindergarten, ages 3–6, 9.30–5.00, For 15 hr/wk FF295 mornings FF270 afternoons. Various non-ski kindergartens can provide all-day care for children from 6 months to 8 years. Typical price FF150/day. Evening babysitting also provided.
Special courses Day excursions, competition classes, weekly adventure courses.

Medical facilities

In resort Doctors, dentists, chemists.
Hospital Grenoble (75km).

Cross-country skiing

Trails 1km, 2km, 3km and 8km loops, northern end of resort (Petit Alpe and La Molière). 4km and 8km trails at Venosc (reached by gondola) with links to Bourg d'Oisans.

Not skiing

Facilities Skating (artificial rink), open-air heated pool, sauna, fitness centre with facilities for bodybuilding, dance classes and Turkish bath, squash, cinemas.

Getting there

Airport Geneva; transfer 3hr; Grenoble 1½ hr.
Railway Grenoble (75km); several buses daily.
Road Via Lyon/Grenoble; chains may be needed.

Available holidays

Resort beds 5,000 in hotels, 15,000 in apartments.
Package holidays Activity Travel (Ht Ch Sc), Bladon Lines (Ht Ch Sc), Crystal (Ht Sc), Horizon (Ht Sc), Intasun (Ht Sc), John Morgan (Ht Ch), Neilson (Ht Sc), Quest (Ht), Schoolplan (Ht), Schools Abroad (Ht), Ski Lovers (Cl Ap Sc), Ski MacG (Ht Ch Sc), Skiscope (Ht), Skiworld (Ch Sc), Snow World (Ch Sc), Snowbird Holidays (Ht), Sunmed (Ht Ch Cl Sc), Thomson (Ht Ch Sc), Tracer (Cl Sc), VFB (Ht Sc)

Further information

Tourist office (✆76792200. Tx 320883.

area, these serve the purpose well enough, and are well maintained when snow is poor. But the huge area of easy skiing on the glacier makes this very much a resort where beginners should be encouraged to get up the mountain at an early stage. (They can ride back down to the resort in the gondolas, avoiding the steeper slopes immediately above the village).

We have no reports on the quality of **ski school**. As well as basic instruction it provides a regular programme of off-piste excursions and visits to nearby resorts. A local ex-champion freestylist runs courses of adventure skiing, including freestyle, monoski and off-piste.

Hutch; not just for rabbits

Puy-St-Vincent France 1600m

Unlike most French Alpine developments well known in Britain, but like several other resorts in the southern Alps and most of the Pyrenean ones, PSV is small, cheap and unsophisticated. It was the first resort of its kind to be launched in Britain. It attracted a sizeable minority following, mainly because of low coach/self-catering prices, and became something of a British holiday camp complete with weekly drag beauty contests. Operators have now discovered other, less claustrophobic resorts in the region, and PSV has to some extent lost favour. It claims to be less unreliable for snow than most resorts in the southern Alps, and backed up its claim recently by staging races moved from Val d'Isère because of a lack of snow.

PSV is a split-level place with a split personality. At 1400m is the old community – just an attractively messy mountain village with a couple of simple hotels which is linked by lift with the new complex at 1600m. This isolated, unsightly, modern hulk of an apartment complex is what most brochures mean by PSV.

From upper PSV at 1600m the skiing extends up the mountain to 2750m, and down it to 1400m, giving a very respectable total vertical drop for a small resort. There is an attractive mixture of woodland skiing, on and off the piste, up to about 2000m, and a bowl of open snowfields above it giving occasional access to a long, initially steep off-piste run into the beautiful Vallon de Narreyroux. This is a good little skiing area, mostly facing north and east, with some tough runs near the top, and plenty of skiing to suit beginners and timid intermediates. Queues are rarely a problem, there are easy slopes around and between PSV 1400 and 1600, and the two ski schools usually feature some native English-speakers. But it is little, and offers less scope than its less well-known neighbours, Les Orres and Risoul/Vars. After a few days most piste-bashers will be keen for a change of scenery and should consider day-trips to nearby resorts (Serre-Chevalier and Montgenèvre are the most convenient) covered by the local lift pass.

The single building at 1600m consists mainly of flatlets, but there are also a few hotels. The complex has a single supermarket, which gets more crowded than the lifts at peak times, an occasional bank, some surprisingly smart ski and clothes shops, pinball machines, a few bars and restaurants, but no chemist. There is not much après-ski apart from organised parties and outings to restaurants. PSV is very convenient; the ski-lift is just in front of the complex, where there is also a kindergarten play area. At lunchtime or after skiing you pop straight out of your ski bindings into your flat. Cross-country skiers can tackle a reputedly difficult 15km trail in the woods beside the resort; there are no non-skiing sports facilities.

Tourist office ✆92233580. Tx 403404. **Package holidays** Sunmed (Sc).

Short-circuit skiing

Risoul, Vars France 1850m

Risoul and Vars are two very different resorts sharing the biggest linked ski area in the southern Alps (south of Briançon). Vars, which attracts a chic French clientele, is the longer established and larger of the two and has more skiing. Unlike most neighbouring resorts, it has more to it than ski-fields and apartments – varied shopping, lively après-ski, some attractive hotels, good walks and cross-country trails, and mountain restaurants. Its drawbacks are that it is ugly, set in a rather enclosed position in a narrow valley, and very strung out along the road up to the Col de Vars, between 1650m (Vars-Ste-Marie) and 1850m (Vars-les-Claux, the main resort). The most attractive hotel is Les Escondus (✆92455035), small, friendly and very convenient.

Risoul is a new resort in a beautiful open situation with splendid views over a once-strategic junction of valleys (complete with fortifications) towards the highest peaks of the southern Alps. It is built on a normal village plan, with large wood-clad buildings grouped loosely around a main street, and an annoying amount of traffic. At the top of the village is a broad, sunny plateau at the foot of the pistes, with an arc of apartment buildings and café terraces. The mountains above do not keep the sun out. Risoul is small but less claustrophobic and better equipped with bars and restaurants than many similar places. There is skating, and long cross-country trails around the mountain.

The Vars/Risoul ski area consists mainly of two broad bowls above the two resorts facing east and north respectively. They are nearly back-to-back, but the neighbouring peaks at the top of the two areas are separated by a saddle which is not equipped with lifts. This makes skiing from Risoul to Vars and back a roundabout business, but it can easily be done in a leisurely day. Neither area is very large, neither offers very much difficult skiing, and few of the runs are long – the top lifts approach 2600m; but, provided the links are open (when we visited, the top runs had been swept bare by wind), there is plenty of scope for energetic intermediate skiers. Most of the Risoul side is gentle and particularly suitable for inexperienced skiers, with an excellent sunny beginners' area out of way of the rest of the pistes. When snow is abundant it is possible to ski down to old Risoul (1071m) on a piste graded red which carries on from the beautiful run along the easternmost rim of the bowl. Vars also has some attractive woodland runs on the opposite side of the valley.

Skiers can choose between a pass covering both resorts (not available by the day) and a local pass for either resort with a supplement payable for excursions to the other. There are kindergartens in both resorts.

Tourist offices Risoul ✆92450260; Vars-les-Claux ✆92455131.
Package holidays Risoul: Bladon Lines (Ch Sc), SkiBound (Cl Sc), SkiSet (Ht), Sunmed (Ht Sc), Thomson (Sc); Vars: Quest (Ap), SkiSet (Cl), Snowbird Holidays (Cl).

Embrun solaire

Les Orres France 1600m

Les Orres is a small modern resort beautifully set above the handsome old town of Embrun and the Serre-Ponçon reservoir, east of Gap. Although the resort's facilities are limited and snow conditions unreliable, Les Orres is a good resort of its kind. The skiing is high, beautiful and varied, the resort is user-friendly without being a concrete blot on the landscape, and the people are unusually cheerful and welcoming. In good conditions there is plenty of scope for an entertaining week – and an inexpensive one if you travel by coach to a self-catering flat. Little known until recently, Les Orres now swarms with British skiers, mostly young.

The resort is a scattering of apartment buildings and chalets across a steep, lightly wooded hillside a few miles beyond the old hamlet of Les Orres. Although it's a long way up to the nucleus of the resort from its lower fringes, there are pistes through the resort and lifts from top and bottom. Most rented accommodation (flats) is in the buildings immediately surrounding the central concourse, a small plateau with a shopping precinct ('much wider choice than at Flaine or Avoriaz') and sunny café terraces at the foot of the pistes, pleasant and animated at lunchtime. Bar prices are reasonable, and the evening atmosphere is very chummy. There is one discothèque, and outings to restaurants in old Les Orres and Embrun can be arranged.

The ski area extends across a broad north-west-facing mountainside which rises to a crest between two peaks with a top lift station at 2720m and a top-to-bottom drop of 1170m. All the lifts are chairs or drags, so there is no escaping cold weather. All the skiing above 2000m is red or black, and one or two of the red runs ought to be black. A beautiful run drops behind a ridge into a wide neighbouring bowl, one day to be equipped with ski-lifts. Immediately above and beside the resort there is an area of gentler skiing served by chair-lifts, but the runs are short and used by other skiers speeding down to the resort. There are a few nursery lifts, but in general the terrain is not ideal for beginners. Queues are rarely a problem except over the February school holiday period. Even then, skiers neglect the lifts at the northern side where there is some good off-piste skiing in the woods as well as long red pistes.

There are two ski schools – a reporter was impressed by the attitude but not the linguistic ability of SEI instructors – and all-day ski and non-ski kindergartens. In the recent past most British ski school pupils in Les Orres have used instructors employed by their tour operator.

Les Orres has little to offer non-skiers, and the advertised total of 50 km of X-C trails includes a large proportion of 'itineraries'. There are a few hotels in the resort, and a greater range of accommodation, some of it very cheap, in Embrun.

Tourist office ✆92440161. **Package holidays** Schools Abroad (Ht), SkiBound (Cl Sc), Skiscope (Ht), Sunmed (Sc).

Not so splendid isolation

Isola 2000 France 2000m

Good for *Nursery slopes, skiing convenience, resort-level snow, sunny slopes, family holidays, freedom from cars*
Bad for *Alpine charm, not skiing, tough runs, après-ski, easy road access*

Isola 2000 is the most southerly major ski resort in the Alps, and one of the highest of the purpose-built, apartment-based, family-oriented resorts which are the French speciality. It claims an exceptional record of both snow and sunshine, and offers a 'Sun and Snow Guarantee' to back it up. And there are great attractions for families in the resort's basic formula: hotels and apartments looking directly on to a gloriously long, gentle, sunny nursery slope, with cars safely confined elsewhere. For most visitors, the other merits of the compact, thoroughly mechanised ski area are somewhat secondary.

In its original form, Isola was the ultimate purpose-built resort – designed so that you could step from the front door of your hotel or apartment block into your bindings and schuss off down the nursery slope, and in the afternoon reverse the process. Everything you might want access to during the evening was provided under the one roof, so that you didn't need to stray outside. This original concept was diluted some years ago by the construction of Le Hameau – a detached group of small apartment blocks, widening the range of accommodation available. And other developments have been added since – principally Les Adrets (between the two earlier units), completed in 1987. The majority of holidaymakers apparently still prefer to be housed in the main building, which is no longer tatty (having been refurbished outside in 1986 and inside in 1987) but remains irredeemably claustrophobic.

Isola does not rely entirely on self-catering families for its custom: on good weekends, there is a jet-set invasion from the Côte d'Azur (only one and a half hours' drive away) which fills the three hotels and ensures hefty queues for some of the lifts.

Despite its name, Isola is not entirely isolated. Skiers with a car may be tempted to a day in Auron (with skiing which is reportedly less convenient than Isola's, but more challenging).

The skiing top 2610m bottom 1800m

The resort's piste map employs a sensible division of the skiing into three areas, though all are linked – the south-west-facing slopes of Domaine du Levant, and the north-east-facing slopes split by the Tête de la Cabane into the Domaine du Pélevos, immediately above the resort, and the Domaine du Saint Sauveur, further west.

The **Pélevos** area is densely equipped with pistes and lifts, the major

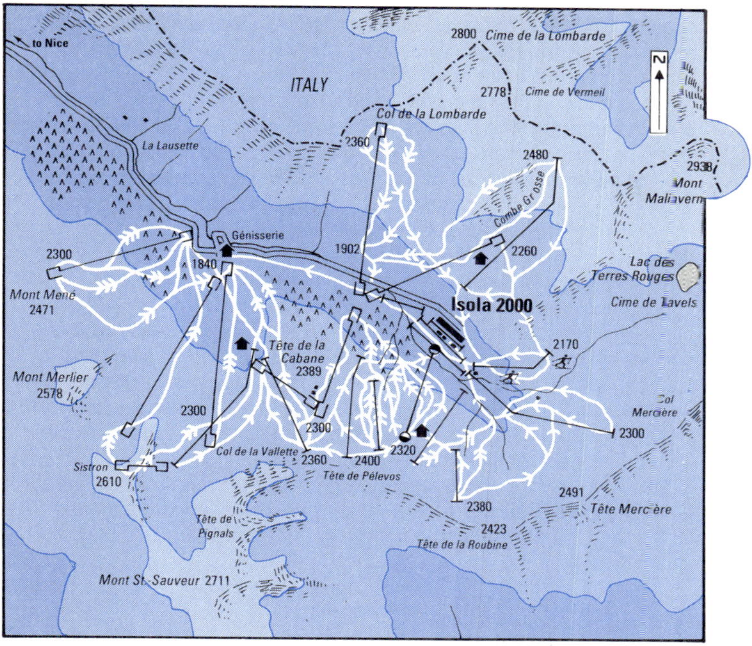

one being a gondola which departs directly from the resort building. From the top (2320m) there are satisfyingly varied easy and intermediate runs back down through the patchy trees, and links in both directions to drags which go slightly higher. If you go east, you can get to a long green run, well away from the lifts, which is splendid for near beginners in the right conditions, but hard work if there is new snow. If you go west, a drag gives access to further varied runs to the resort and makes the link with the Saint Sauveur area. Skiing down to the big car park at 1900m (the main way into the skiing for day visitors, below the resort) brings you to a chair which forms another link with the Saint Sauveur area as well as serving its own worthwhile red and black runs.

Saint Sauveur is the serious sector, with satisfying skiing for intermediates and experts. The skiing in this area has been modified in recent years, with existing lifts lengthened and shortened, new lifts added and pistes rearranged. A drag and short chair take you to the high point of Isola's skiing, the Cime de Sistron (2610m), on the flank of Mont Saint Sauveur. There are red and blue variants of the run back down, and off the back of the mountain is a short black (which we have not yet sampled) leading to a long red down and a return drag on a partly wooded slope which until recently accommodated three black runs and no lifts. Further across the mountainside is the chair-lift towards Mont Mené, which has now been abbreviated to cut out the problematic area at the summit, which was very exposed to wind. There are black and red variants of the run to the bottom of the chair, not greatly different in difficulty. The return from this whole sector to the slopes above the resort depends on the Génisserie chair, once a famous bottleneck but now tripled in capacity.

Once back up the Génisserie chair, a choice of lifts takes you back over la Cabane to the Pélevos slopes, and runs either to the resort or down to 1900m, where the main chairs go up to the Levant area – the Col de la Lombarde and Combe Grosse. These serve south- and south-west-facing slopes which are distinctly gentler than those opposite, mainly on open mountainsides above the trees. Easy traverses from this area link with drag-lifts at the head of the valley serving long, flat green runs which are an uphill extension of the nursery slopes.

The lift system works well enough, and **queues** are not usually a problem. Weekend queues in the Saint Sauveur sector (which is easily accessible to day visitors, as well as having the most challenging skiing) used to be serious, but the improvement to the Génisserie chair and the installation of the new drag behind Mont Mené have apparently transformed the situation. Two evenings a week the Belvedere slope immediately above the resort is floodlit.

Mountain restaurants are few, but adequate for a small ski area with good lifts out of the resort, permitting trouble-free lunching at base. The Génisserie restaurant (at the bottom of the Saint Sauveur skiing) is stylishly rustic.

The resort

The 'resort' consists mainly of a zigzag series of modern blocks linked by a meandering spinal corridor which will convey you to wherever you want to go within the main complex, including no fewer than 30 shops which are sufficiently flashy to betray Isola's second role as a venue for weekend sprees from the Côte d'Azur. Residents of Le Hameau have their own supermarket, ski shop and restaurant, but for other requirements are dependent on the mother ship. To get to and from it they are provided with something which no self-respecting convenience resort should need – a shuttle bus.

Accommodation is mainly in apartments, though there are three hotels spaced along the building, arranged in price order from up-piste, down-market Le Druos (✆93231220) via the Pas du Loup (✆93231171) to down-piste, up-market Le Chastillon (✆93231060) – and this winter will see the opening of a new five-star luxury hotel with all the trimmings. Reporters recommend paying the premium for south-facing balcony rooms. The resort brochure contains detailed plans of apartments in both the main building and Le Hameau. A handful of individual chalets have been built, and more are on the way.

Après-ski in the early evening revolves around bars, one or two crêperie-style restaurants and the supermarket, and is quite lively. Later on there are two discos; whether you will find them animated other than at weekends is another question. For dining out there are restaurants symbolically detached from the main building – the Cow Club in the middle of the nursery slope has been recommended by one reporter, and you can get to the Génisserie by car. There is a baby-sitting service.

It is not a good resort for **cross-country** skiers or **non-skiers** – though the facilities for non-skiing activities are being improved. The small swimming-pool has already been replaced by a larger one (though it remains outdoor) and this season there will be a new ice rink; we are not sure whether, like the old one, it is to be positioned, logically but depressingly, in the shade of the main building. Snow-scooters, officially allowed on the piste only after 5pm, are reportedly a day-time hazard.

The **nursery slopes** are superb, running the length of the resort, and the progression to real pistes is so gradual as to be imperceptible.

We lack recent reports on the two **ski schools**. As elsewhere, the Ski Ecole International sets out to capture non-French business – but the Ecole de Ski Français also claims that nearly all its instructors are bilingual, so there should be no language problems. The resort claims to be the first in France to offer heli-skiing. Advance booking is recommended for the kindergarten.

Isola facts

Lift payment

Passes One pass covers all lifts.
Cost 6-day pass FF496. 10% off in low season. 20% off for over 60s.
Beginners Coupons, or limited-area Mini-Pass (FF83/day).
Children 20% off, under 12.

Ski school

Two schools: Ecole de Ski Français and Ski Ecole International.
Classes ESF 2½hr, morning or afternoon. SEI 2hr to 3hr, morning and afternoon.
Cost 6 half-days ESF FF375. Private lessons FF122/hr.
Beginners *Ski évolutif.*
Children ESF classes, 2½hr/day, 6 days FF360. SEI 6 days FF420. Ski kindergarten, ages 3–8, 9.00–5.00, 6 days with lunch FF996. Non-ski kindergarten, ages 1–5.
Special courses Various, from both schools – including mono-ski, artistic, slalom skiing, ski touring, surf.

Not skiing

Facilities Natural ice rink (skating, curling, football), swimming pool (outdoor, from February), sauna, weight-training, yoga, aerobic and 'stretching' classes, cinema, hang-gliding, language school, ice driving, motor-trikes, snow scooters.

Cross-country skiing

Trails One, 4km long, above the village.

Medical facilities

In resort Medical centre with doctor and chemist. Ambulance helicopter.
Hospital Nice (85km).

Getting there

Airport Nice; transfer 2hr.
Railway Nice; two or three buses daily.
Road Via the Côte d'Azur (roads from the north-west which look more direct on the map are in practice very slow); chains often needed, 1½hr.

Available holidays

Resort beds 200 in hotels, 7,300 in apartments.
Package holidays Air France (Ht), Neilson (Ht Sc), Ski NAT (Sc), Snow World (Sc), Vacations (Ht Sc)

Further information

Tourist office ✆93231515. Tx 461666.

Pyrenean preamble

Reflections on the view that small is friendly

Early editions of the *Guide* provoked tourist offices, tour operators and readers alike to tell us that we had not done justice to the delights of Pyrenean skiing, more particularly French Pyrenean skiing. We had reports of enviably happy holidays in resorts plentifully supplied with snow and, to their mind, not short of charm either. They told us that any idea that Pyrenean snow is unreliable is quite unfounded, that the people are welcoming, and that the price is right. We duly returned for a Pyrenean tour of duty in early February 1987, and found snow conditions that gave us every incentive to reflect on these important matters while sitting in bars. Our coverage of resorts in the Pyrenees is as a result now more detailed, but we do not expect those with a stake in the matter to be thrilled by what it says. As a complement to the down-to-earth assessments contained in our resort reports, we offer here some more wide-ranging observations.

First, the contentious subject of snowfall. There is no evidence of less precipitation in the Pyrenees than in the Alps. If anything there is more, especially in winter. But there is plenty of evidence that the Pyrenean winter is significantly milder than the Alpine one, not because the region is further south, but because it is further west and nearer the warm Atlantic. As well as snow it sees plenty of rain and rapid thaw, and even in the depths of winter it is often mild.

The Pyrenees also have a more pronounced influence on the climate than the Alps. Simply stated, the ski resorts on the northern side of the chain (the French resorts, plus Spanish Baqueira-Beret) are much more reliable for snow than those on the southern side. Then, the Mediterranean side of the Pyrenees is much drier than the Atlantic side. The main French resorts are concentrated in a relatively small area at the centre of the chain. The Spanish resorts are more spread out and there may be a greater divergence between their snowfall, something which is hard to assess when there is little snow at any of them (except Baqueira). On the Spanish side the ski area closest to the Med is that of La Molina and Masella, a notoriously risky place for snow. Although nearly all of Andorra is on the southern side of the Pyrenees, and closer to the Mediterranean than the Atlantic, its main ski areas are high and straddle the mountain barrier. Good snow conditions are by no means exceptional.

Brochures make a big thing of how welcoming local people are in the Pyrenees. Sceptics may read between the lines and conclude that there are few good things to be said about more tangible aspects of Pyrenean resorts. But there is no denying the importance of the atmosphere in a resort in determining the success or failure of most people's ski holidays. It is what the enduring popularity of many small Austrian resorts is based on, and it is what counts more than anything else in the Pyrenees. People seem to be genuinely pleased to receive visitors and anxious to make sure that they enjoy themselves. This helps to compensate for the lack of the frills that adorn the well-wrapped Austrian tourist package, with its sleigh rides, ice-rinks, saunas, whirlpools, tea dances and Tyrolean evenings.

For many people the most important part of the Pyrenean welcome is ski school. Following the example of Andorra, where the British-run school has made a great success of ensuring that people enjoy learning to ski, schools in several of the French resorts are listening to what the British operators tell them. The instructors are being made to learn English and organise separate classes for British skiers, and are not too proud to mix with the tourists in the evenings. This is all old hat in the Tyrol, of course; perhaps for that very reason there seems to be an enthusiasm in these Pyrenean resorts that may be lacking in resorts where they have been going through the routine for decades.

Equally important is straightforward friendliness. In too many upmarket Alpine resorts, the skier with money to spend is clearly regarded as someone to be milked as speedily as possible, while the skier without money to spend is regarded as a waste of expensively furnished space. And there is no doubt in our minds that this is not true of the Pyrenees. People go to Spain in summer because they do not get this kind of reception; the atmosphere is usually relaxed and friendly. For skiing purposes this is almost as true on the French side of the Pyrenees as in Spain. Cheap-and-cheerfulness is an even greater part of the appeal of duty-free Andorra. Perhaps too many of us succumb to the temptation of cheap-skate holidays (self-catering) in expensive resorts where we are out of place and grumpy. In a cheaper resort we could relax, enjoy ourselves and perhaps find to our surprise that the limitations of the skiing weren't so intolerable after all.

Part of the reason that the Pyreneans are pleased to see the British is that we represent the only foreign business they can hope to attract. It may or may not be a plus point that in the resorts served by British operators almost all non-natives are British, apart from some Spaniards in France, a few French in Spain, and both in Andorra. Outside Andorra the British presence is small in absolute numbers, but it can still be quite dominant, especially out of season.

If your picture of a mountain village has the timbered prettiness of Switzerland and Austria, the Pyrenees may come as a bit of a shock. The usual building material is stone, and even the most handsome old villages are not colourful. In France you face an unappealing choice between grey spas (Barèges and Cauterets) and purpose-built resorts which are no more attractive than their Alpine counterparts (La Mongie, Piau-Engaly, Pla d'Adet). Only St-Lary has any charm as a village. In Spain the purpose-built resorts (Formigal and Baqueira) are more stylish, and the old village resorts (notably Cerler) are much more appealingly rustic. There are some beautiful old buildings in Andorra, but generally the Principality seems an architectural rubbish heap.

Pic of the Pyrenees

Barèges France 1250m

Good for *Big ski area, short airport transfers, sunny slopes, Pyrenean charm*
Bad for *Tough runs, resort-level snow, late holidays, not skiing, mountain restaurants*

Linked resort: La Mongie

Many a skier disillusioned by anonymous French ski resorts must have wondered where to go in search of somewhere combining the charm of a real unspoilt French country village with the sport of a large, varied ski area. Our shortlist of possible answers (and it would be short) would include a few Alpine resorts and Barèges, which is among the friendliest Pyrenean resorts and has a half share in the largest Pyrenean ski area. A dull-looking grey spa, it is not at all institutional and has a cheerful, intimate atmosphere, partly due to its very small size. There is very little to do apart from ski and soak up the sulphur in the spa-water pool. But for many skiers a simple hotel, a few bars and welcoming people are enough for a good, cheap holiday.

Barèges was one of the first ski resorts in the Pyrenees, with some famous long runs through the woods to the village. These now form only a small part of a long lift system following the course of a road which in summer leads over the Col du Tourmalet to the modern resort of La Mongie. Although hardly the Trois Vallées, the area offers plenty of variety of slope, scenery and, usually, snow conditions.

La Mongie is larger and higher than Barèges but has no more facilities to offer, apart from good nursery slopes. It has the less varied half of the ski area, and lacks the charm of Barèges. We have reports that La Mongie is much less unfriendly than it looks. It could hardly be more so.

The skiing top 2350m bottom 1250m

An approximately M-shaped arrangement of two hills immediately above Barèges offers the only woodland skiing, reached by any of the three access lifts from the resort. The **Ayré** funicular climbs steeply in two stages through the woods and serves fine red and black runs down to the Lienz clearing – about the most satisfying skiing in the area, especially when conditions are good all the way down to the resort. Although these sweeping runs are not terrifyingly steep there is no easy way down from Ayré; but inexperienced skiers can make their way easily across from the mid-station, mainly used by cross-country skiers, to Lienz. Of the runs from there down to Barèges, the green is a road starting with an uphill section; it is rarely used. Snow on the bottom of the run to the funicular station is unreliable.

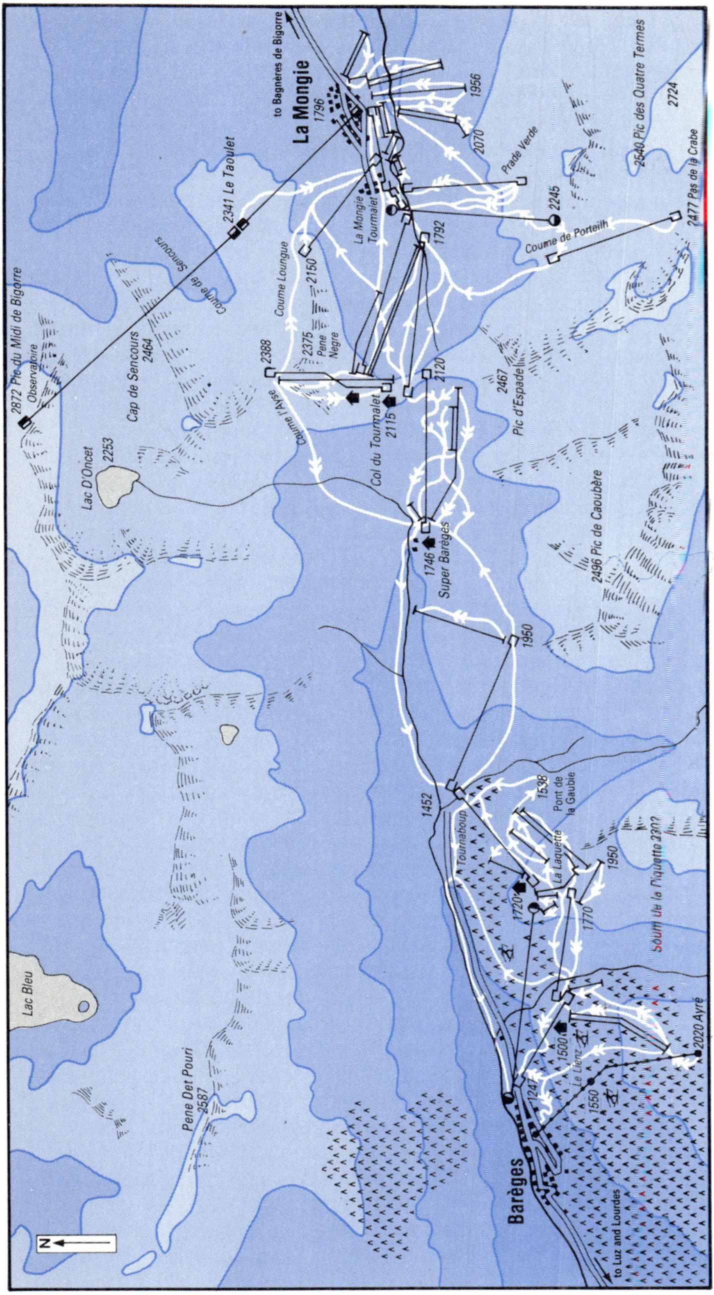
to Bagnères de Bigorre
La Mongie
1796
1956
2070
Prade Verde
2245
La Mongie Tournalet
1792
Coume de Porteilh
2477 Pas de la Crabe
2540 Pic des Quatre Termes
2724
2341 Le Taoulet
Coume de Sencours
Coume Loungue
2150
2375 Pene Negre
2388
2120
2467 Pic d'Espade
2872 Pic du Midi de Bigorre
Observatoire
Cap de Sencours 2464
Coume l'Ayse
Col du Tourmalet 2115
Lac D'Oncet 2253
1746 Super Barèges
2496 Pic de Caoubère
1950
1452
1538
Pont de la Gaubie
Tournaboup
La Laquette
1950
1720
1770
Lac Bleu
Pene Det Pouri 2587
1500
Le Lienz
2020 Ayre
1247
1550
Barèges
to Luz and Lourdes
N

The **Laquette** gondola is the busiest of the access lifts, being the most direct route towards La Mongie as well as the way up to the ski school meeting place, a congregation area on a knoll with restaurant and nursery area. A variety of short intermediate pistes, from green to red, covers the flanks of the hill, west-facing down to Lienz and east-facing down to Tournaboup, but there are no runs through the woods below the lift directly down to Barèges.

Tournaboup is where the Col du Tourmalet road ends in winter, and is also the end of the woods. There is a small nursery area and a long chair-lift over a wide, moderately steep west-facing mountainside, unpisted but tempting and much skied in good conditions. From the top of the lift an uncomplicated link run leads on to **Superbarèges**, a grand name for what is no more than an undistinguished restaurant in the pit of a wide theatre of snow-fields of which few are part of the ski area. The few are fairly steep west-facing slopes below the Col du Tourmalet, including some short, stiff mogul-fields, well worth avoiding in the morning. Below Superbarèges, the run back to Tournaboup and Barèges is a very long path beside road and river (and across both), a pretty enough way home into the sunset, but not very interesting skiing and often crowded. Being so flat, at least it holds the snow fairly well.

As the toiling Tour de France cyclists probably have little chance to appreciate, there are fine long views east and west from the ridge beside the **Col du Tourmalet**, although the mountains themselves are not particularly beautiful. The eastern slopes are gentler and all the runs directly down to **La Mongie** are wide and easy. The rocky slopes flanking the resort and road, facing north and south, are steeper and both have lifts, although the terrain does not allow a very wide network of skiing. The main lift on the north-facing side is a gondola serving a blue run down, a long gully which sees almost no sun. The 4 Termes chair-lift has added to this run and also gives access to a very long (and by all accounts beautiful) off-piste itinerary down the Aygues Cluses valley, ending up at Tournaboup. We found the steep runs beneath Prade Verde closed, and this is apparently far from unusual.

On the south-facing side of La Mongie the Pic du Midi cable-car is a ski-lift only as far as the first station (2340m). There are plans to allow skiers up to and down from the observatory on top (2877m), which would add an exciting new dimension. The slopes beneath the nearby Sud chair-lift are not gentle, and the single blue run down includes an awkward and unavoidable narrow section. On this sunny side of the mountains, the most interesting runs are reached from the top of the Coume Louque drag and chair, a splendid viewpoint. One run follows a valley back down to La Mongie, the other leads down a wide south-west facing coomb to Superbarèges; the start is exposed and followed by a sequence of pitches steep enough to be graded black. Here, too, morning ice is to be expected. A variant is another favourite off-piste itinerary, round to the Lac d'Oncet, a good place for spring snow (often in midwinter) and scheduled for development soon.

Mountain restaurants are adequate and inexpensive (by Alpine standards), but neither numerous nor particularly appealing, with the notable exception of the delightful Chez Louisette at Lienz. Among several sunny places for lunch in La Mongie, Le Yeti is recommended.

As usual in the Pyrenees, **queues** can be a serious weekend problem and a very serious Sunday one. Barèges itself cannot cope with many cars and the lifts from the top of the village and from Tournaboup are oversubscribed. At other times the main problem is queues at Superbarèges for access to La Mongie.

The resort

Barèges is a tiny village, little more than a single street climbing steeply beside a river, narrowly enclosed at the feet of wooded mountainsides. This is no place for a village, and none would have grown up had it not been for the hot springs, which became famous when in 1675 Madame de Maintenon brought the sickly infant Duc du Maine, natural son of Louis XIV, to Barèges. Napoleon later chose it as a recuperation centre for wounded war heroes, the waters being particularly beneficial for trauma. Until the 19th century, avalanches made the site uninhabitable in winter, and each spring a new village of makeshift shelters was built for the summer season. Avalanche barriers allowed the construction of more permanent buildings, which stand today grey and undistinguished

Barèges facts

Lift payment

Passes Half-day and longer passes for Barèges, with daily supplement payable for La Mongie.
Cost 6-day pass FF330. About 20% off in low season.
Beginners Limited area day pass.
Children 30% off, under 12.

Ski school

Ecoloski as well as ESF.
Classes ESF 2hr, mornings only (afternoon classes in school holidays). Ecoloski 3hr, mornings only.
Cost ESF 6 days FF269. Private lesson FF110/hr. Ecoloski 5 days FF275. Private lesson FF100/hr.
Special courses ESF: parascending, slalom. Ecoloski: slalom, monoski, surf, touring.
Children ESF: ages up to 12, timetable as for adults, 6 lessons FF198; ski kindergarten, ages 4 up, 6 lessons FF215. Non-ski kindergarten in village, ages 2–8, 9.00–5.00.

Cross-country skiing

Trails 15km near Lienz, reached by funicular.

Not skiing

Facilities Hang gliding, parascending, sauna, massage, spa bath.

Medical facilities

In resort Fracture clinic, doctors, chemist.

Getting there

Airport Tarbes, transfer about 1 hour
Railway Lourdes (37km). SNCF bus to resort.
Road Via Toulouse, Tarbes. The road up from Luz (6km) is narrow, but chains are rarely needed.

Available holidays

Resort beds About 1,500 in apartments, 500 in hotels.
Package holidays Bladon Lines (Ht Ch Cl Sc), Ski Club of GB (Ht), Ski Miquel (Ch), Thomson (Ht Sc)

Further information

Tourist office ☎62926819.

(except for the spa itself, a mixture of smart renovation and grand old church-like buildings at the top of the village). There are a few shops, and a bank on Tuesday mornings.

Having a car is of no great value in Barèges, and parking space is limited. A shuttle mini-bus service runs up and down the village street.

Accommodation is in simple, ordinary, old-fashioned, inexpensive hotels, none with more than two official stars. At least one has recently been given over to British use on a chalet basis. We have mostly enthusiastic reports on the Europe (✆62926804) and the Richelieu (✆62926811, with a sauna), neighbours not too inconveniently placed just below the funicular station and about five minutes' walk (uphill) to the main lift station. Self-caterers will find Barèges limited, both for shopping and eating out.

Après-ski consists of a few bars (including one run by the mayor, so behave), a couple of restaurants and two discos. Traumatised skiers can show off bruises in the warm and smelly spa pool, open every evening. The spa also has a sauna and massage. The main organised event is an evening, usually very jolly, at Chez Louisette (Pyrenean meal and torchlit descent). There is a cinema.

There are reasonable **cross-country** possibilities, on and off piste, in woods around Lienz. Barèges is not recommended for **non-skiers**.

Barèges has **nursery slopes** in all the main areas, except on the edge of the village itself. The main one is at the top of the Laquette gondola. There is no shortage of long green runs.

We have good reports of the commitment, enthusiasm and entertainment value of the small band of instructors at the Ecoloski **ski school**, the alternative to the ESF, who among other things organise mountain restaurant evenings, supplying tandem skis for an aperitif of slalom races and torches for the descent.

La Mongie 1800m

La Mongie is an all-modern but far from new roadside resort in a high, bleak, treeless setting. Two resort units are linked by a bucket lift (daytime only) and an expanse of almost flat nursery slopes, which suffer only from being a thoroughfare. The main centre is the lower one, its focus a south-facing semi-circle of restaurants, shops and hotel buildings with a car park in the middle, lift stations nearby and a large number of dogs on the scrounge. As a whole La Mongie is a styleless and messy place, but it has a greater variety of bars, shops and restaurants than most small purpose-built resorts. There is almost nothing for non-skiers to do, and La Mongie is no place for cross-country skiers. The upper resort, known as Tourmalet or La Mandia, is a long angular modern complex with a three-star hotel, a restaurant and apartments, mostly with south-facing balconies. There are ski school and lift pass offices at both resort centres, and a kindergarten at the lower one. The road up from Bagnères-de-Bigorre is extremely busy on Sundays, and may be closed when the resort is deemed full.

Tourist office ✆62919415. **Package holidays** Ski Falcon (Ht Ap Sc), Thomson (Ht).

French Pyrenees: the other contenders

St-Lary, Piau-Engaly, Cauterets

Note There are some general observations about skiing in the Pyrenees starting on page 426.

St-Lary (830m) is the most complete French Pyrenean resort, the only rival to Barèges and La Mongie in size of ski area, and free from the different limitations of those villages (described in the preceding chapter). It is less cheerfully informal than Barèges; more tangible disadvantages are the distance between the resort and its skiing, and some awkward links in the chain of lifts and runs.

The village lies in a spacious, sunny setting at the end of a broad and attractively pastoral valley which climbs more steeply from the village to the new resort of Piau-Engaly. The main street is a fairly busy thoroughfare, especially at weekends, but it has some beautifully restored old rough-stone buildings around the central crossroads, and new development is harmonious. The Hotel Mir (✆62394003) is a friendly family-run hotel with a good restaurant and a bar with a darts board. 'St-Lary nightlife is here,' we were informed by some British residents; exploration confirmed this depressing verdict, although there are a few discos, bars and restaurants. There is also a plastic skating rink and a sports hall with tennis and a gym.

The skiing extends over a long, up-and-down area, starting at Pla d'Adet (1680m), a sunny and windy belvedere reached by queue-prone cable-car (running until 11.30pm) or road. This is a modern mini-resort, an ugly collection of modest hotels, bars and restaurants grouped around a car park at the foot of the pistes, with a large colony of A-frame chalets nearby.

Pla d'Adet has a small area of sunny nursery slopes (with snow-makers) at the foot of east-facing runs, mostly intermediate but with a few steepish mogul-fields, down from 2263m, below the summit of Soum de Matte. A red run through shady woods (and an over-subscribed chair-lift back) links this area with Espiaube (1650m), a modern development with a couple of hotels and a ski shop beside the road up from St-Lary, and the base station of the main ski area. This mostly consists of fairly tough skiing (red runs and a moderate black) on the east-facing side of the Col du Portet (2215m), with lifts up to 2370m, and a splendid, very sunny, open bowl on the other side of the pass, with mostly gentle and short runs facing south and west. There are lifts up to 2450m, a restaurant in the pit of the bowl at 2000m, and a run down to a reservoir (Lac d'Oule, 1820m) with a restaurant by the dam. For good skiers the best runs are those above Espiaube, but the only easy way down these slopes is by gondola.

With a car you can start and end the day at Espiaube, missing the main lift bottlenecks and staying in the sun until late in the day. The only bus service links Pla d'Adet and Espiaube.

Piau-Engaly (1850m) is the latest skiing craze in the Pyrenees, and at weekends the car parks at the top of the long hairpin road up from St-Lary fill to overflowing. The style of the resort is most unusual: four low, semi-circular complexes hug the contours of the bumpy plateau without protruding above ground level. The layout is convenient, with a flat, sunny, open area of nursery slopes at the foot of the slopes and lifts. Apart from a few bars and restaurants there is not much to the resort, which is still developing. Inside, the buildings seem plain and in places unfinished. Accommodation is nearly all in flats.

The ski area is also small but, being a high and mainly north-facing bowl, relatively snow-sure. In good conditions it is possible to make a long run by skiing from the top station (2400m) down through woods to a roadside chair-lift station at 1420m, but most of the runs are above the resort, short and distinctly tricky. Two runs drop into a small valley away from the main lifts. Both are difficult, especially the red, which includes a 33° wall. There are plans to double the size of the ski area. Until it grows, its main appeal is as a day-trip from St-Lary.

In sharp contrast to nearby Barèges, **Cauterets** (930m) is a large resort (nearly 50 hotels) with a small ski area, a combination of limited appeal to keen skiers. A 19th-century spa with narrow streets of grey buildings, it lacks the charm of a small resort and has little of the sophistication and varied facilities of more fashionable large ones, although there is more to do than in other Pyrenean resorts. Also, its ski area has to be reached by cable-car or by road.

Cauterets does have attractions. Its ski area, the north-facing Cirque du Lys, has the most reliable snow in the Pyrenees and a fair range of blue and red runs. Five lifts fan out from the top of the cable-car (1850m) to various points around the rim of the circus, with a top station at 2350m. From the bottom of this area it is usually possible to ski down to Cambasque (1350m), a car park 5km by road from Cauterets, with a gondola up to the main bowl. A 6km off-piste run drops down from near the top station into the valley behind, also ending up at Cambasque.

Cauterets is also the best of the main Pyrenean resorts for cross-country skiing, with a network of wooded trails of up to 13.5km at Pont d'Espagne (1500m), a famous beauty spot and departure point for climbers, hikers and ski tourers, 7km from Cauterets.

The resort does not entirely lack everyday provincial French charm: it has a food market, plenty of ordinary cafés, tea rooms and shops. Evening outings to a restaurant above the resort are organised, with a torchlit descent if snow permits. There is already indoor skating; a new hotel-club with squash, pool, sauna and gym is planned for 1987–88, and one of the resort's thermal baths will be open to the public. The neighbouring Etche Ona (✆62925143) and Bordeaux (✆62925250) are good small hotels between the cable-car station and the resort centre, comfortable but urban in style (not very spacious and without views). The Bordeaux is said to serve the best food around.

Tourist offices St-Lary ✆62305081. Tx 520360. Piau-Engaly ✆62395269. Tx 531596. Cauterets ✆62925027. Tx 530337.

Package holidays St-Lary: Thomson (Ht Sc); Cauterets: Thomson (Ht Sc).

Andorra's box – duty-free-for-all

Soldeu, El Tarter, Pas de la Casa, Grau Roig, Arinsal, Pal, Arcalis

Note There are some general observations about skiing in the Pyrenees starting on page 426.

Andorra differs from the Spanish Pyrenees in being even cheaper (lifts, lessons and equipment are cheap, as well as meals and drinks), and in being very popular with British skiers and après-skiers, who have the benefit of a ski school run extremely well by the British, for the British. Throughout the principality the Anglo-influence runs deep, with lots of British and colonial expatriates living in retirement or running hotels, bars, restaurants, development companies and ski schools. Everyone seems to know everyone else and there is a very easy-going, friendly atmosphere which sets Andorra apart.

None of Andorra's ski areas is very large or challenging, but that doesn't seem to matter. You don't go there for tough skiing – or for comfortable accommodation, haute cuisine, charming surroundings, ice rinks, snowy paths, smooth-running bus services or comfortable sheltered gondola lifts. You go for sun, fun, and a cheap holiday. The recipe suits lots of young skiers (and lots of not so young ones) well.

Andorra is a small duty-free principality with French and Spanish co-rulers. Spanish language (Catalan) and currency prevail, except in the north-east around Pas de la Casa, where the skiing and the supermarkets serve French weekenders. The single main road (42km long) carries heavy traffic from the Spanish border (850m) through the capital, Andorra La Vella, over the Port d'Envalira (2408m) to the French border at Pas de la Casa (2095m). La Vella is towny, characterless and a permanent traffic jam, and the road is lined by a succession of very ugly, shoddy modern villages – 'all the same, like abandoned building sites,' wrote one reporter. One of them is Soldeu (1800m), a small roadside development at the foot of the main ski area. Most British operators send their clients to hotels there or in Encamp (which has no skiing), about 20 minutes down the road. The side valleys north of La Vella have been more recently developed, with less ugly results. The main skiing here is near Arinsal. There is some accommodation in the village, and apartments within walking range of the lifts, but most packages to Arinsal use accommodation in La Massana a few miles towards La Vella. There is also skiing at Pas de la Casa and at two new developments, in their own side-valleys – Pal, close to La Massana, and Arcalis, further away to the north.

For all skiers not staying in Soldeu, transport is vital. Those with a car can reach all the skiing from a single base, but most skiers rely on tour operators' shuttle services which do not allow much flexibility. There are public buses, but they are unreliable and infrequent and of most use to skiers based in La Vella. No lift pass covers all of Andorra, and skiers keen to explore have to use day passes.

The biggest and best of Andorra's ski areas is shared by **Soldeu** and its lower neighbour, **El Tarter** (1700m), a car park and lift station beside the road between Soldeu and Encamp, with a few hotels nearly. For those based in Soldeu, skiing starts with a tiresome walk across a rickety bridge from the village ('I was exhausted before I started'). It features a broad area of mostly easy open skiing between 2100m and 2560m, with some good though short off-piste runs in the basin beneath the rounded Tossa del Llosada. There are some longer and tougher runs, and some off-piste skiing, through the woods down to Soldeu and El Tarter. The slopes are mostly north-facing and in good conditions Soldeu provides excellent skiing for beginners and leisurely

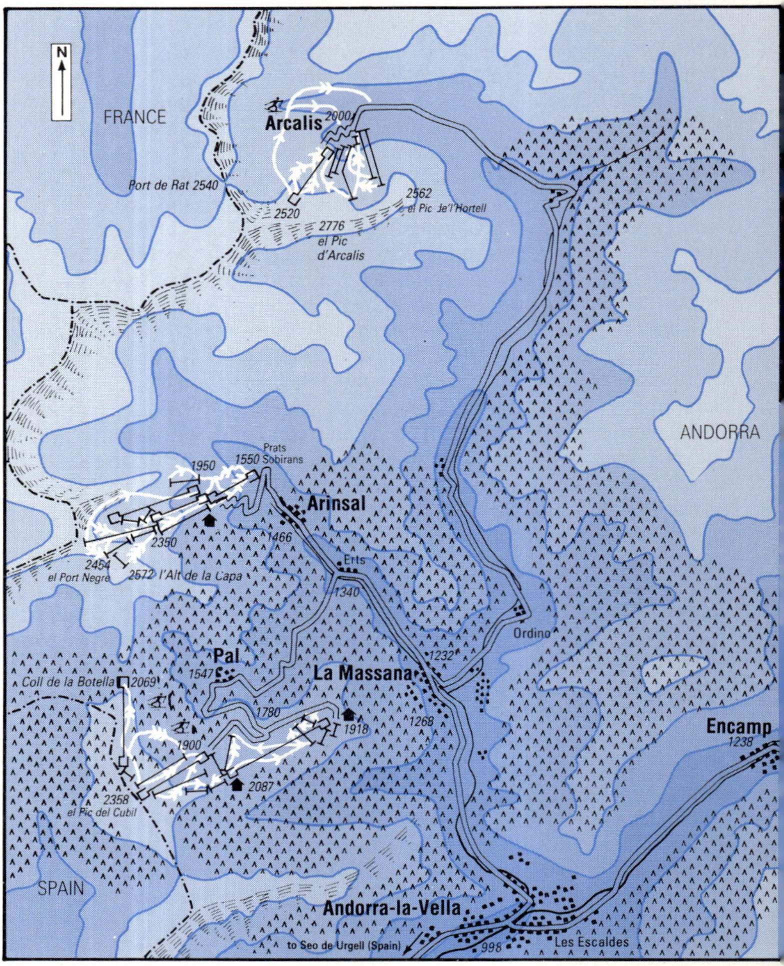

intermediates, including a 6km green run from top to bottom. There is a children's ski school and a good kindergarten. At the top of the main chair-lift is a wide, sunny nursery area and the only mountain restaurant: the main complaint seems to be that the plateau is too hot.

The most convenient access point for the **Pas de la Casa** skiing is Grau Roig (2040m), a collection of buildings near the main road. Ski-lifts climb up to the high ridge from both sides, providing a simple arrangement of open runs (about 500m vertical) facing west above Grau Roig, and north-east above Pas de la Casa (2095m). The scenery is bare, and very severe, and the terrain is not very varied, but snow is reliable and there is plenty of space.

Arinsal's skiing is at present much more confined, a narrow east-facing coomb with variants of a single descent from about 2500m to a congregation area with ski deposit and hire shops at 1950m, at the top of the chair-lift from the valley (1550m). There is also a black run under the bottom chair, and an indirect blue route down.

New **Pal** is a smartly equipped skiing area ('the only civilised skiing loos in Andorra, and a good restaurant') in prettier scenery than most, from 1810m to 2350m. There are attractive nursery runs on woodland clearings and a few gentle longer runs, most of them wooded. The area extends across a north-facing hillside, and involves a lot of traversing from lift to lift. In the far north **Arcalis**, difficult to reach even at the best of times, is in an even more embryonic state. It already provides some interesting skiing between 1940m and 2550m around a rugged north-facing bowl.

Après-ski revolves around bars, restaurants and discos. As well as ski-school celebrations, tour operators organise fancy dress parties,

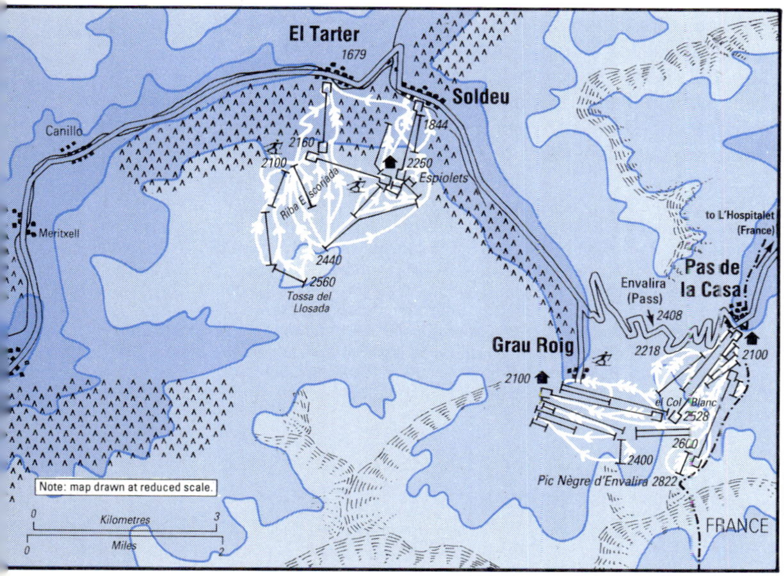

fondue outings, and bar crawls. Most of the quality restaurants are difficult to reach without a car, and in the resort hotels and restaurants food is cheap but indifferent. The Shangri-La just outside Encamp is recommended. Bar prices are very low, and skiers used to Alpine resorts, especially big French and Swiss ones, are amazed at how friendly and relaxed the atmosphere is, with free drinks flowing at the slightest excuse and lots of entertaining characters on both sides of the bar. Discothèques rarely get going much before midnight; entrance is often free, and the price of drinks not much higher than in the bars.

Shopping is Andorra's main industry and tourist attraction. La Vella is a supermarket city where well-known brands of gin and whisky can be found for about £5 a litre and less well-known ones for a lot less. Bargains in ski equipment depend on special offers and haggling.

Accommodation used by British operators is mostly very basic, and some of it primitive. We looked at most of the hotels and particularly liked the Rossell in La Massana, the Naudi in Soldeu, and the Prats Sobirans apartments close to the Arinsal lifts. We saw few preferable hotels not used by tour operators, except one in Encamp – the friendly Residencia Belvedere (✆31263), a simple guest-house run by a British couple, mostly for British visitors, with good food. Its disadvantage for those without transport is access to skiing. We have a very enthusiastic report of two hotels in El Tarter (much more convenient for skiing): the Sant Pere (✆51087), and its neighbour El Chalet, another small family hotel, 'extremely comfortable and well run' by a British couple. Hotels we liked least were the Encamp, Riu Blanc and La Mola in Encamp, and the Font in La Massana.

Most reports on **ski school** are favourable, with particular enthusiasm for the way the ski kindergarten is run.

Access for air travellers is most convenient from Barcelona. Twice-daily 'service taxis' cost about £10 a head between four. Transfer time is about 3½ hours. Transfers from Toulouse (about 4 hours) and coach trips from Britain are vulnerable to closure of the road from France; our inspector endured a 17-hour journey to Toulouse via a rail-only tunnel. There are overnight trains from Paris to L'Hospitalet, with connecting buses.

Tourist office Andorra Soldeu ✆51151 Encamp ✆31405 La Massana ✆35693.
Package holidays Arcalis: Ski NAT (Ht).
Arinsal: Andorra Holidays (Ht Ch Ap Sc), Beach Villas (Ch Sc), Blue Sky (Ht), Crystal (Ht Sc), Enterprise (Ht Sc), Horizon (Ht Sc), Intasun (Ht Sc), Neilson (Ht Sc), Ski Lovers (Ht Sc), Skiworld (Ht Sc), Snowcoach Holidays (Ht), Thomson (Ht Ap).
Encamp: Freedom (Ht), Ski NAT (Ht), Ski Young World (Ht), Skiworld (Ht).
Soldeu: Activity Travel (Ht Ch Sc), Andorra Holidays (Ht Ch Ap Sc), Crystal (Ht Sc), Freedom (Ht Cl Ap Sc), Global (Ht Sc), Ski Falcon (Ht), Ski Lovers (Ht Ch Sc), Ski Young World (Sc), Skiworld (Ht Sc), Thomson (Ht Sc), Top Deck (Sc).
Pas de la Casa: Blue Sky (Sc), Enterprise (Ht Sc), Global (Ht), Horizon (Ht Sc), Neilson (Ht Sc), Ski Lovers (Ht Sc).

Spanish Pyrenees

Formigal, Baqueira-Beret, Panticosa, Cerler, La Molina, Masella

Note There are some general observations about skiing in the Pyrenees starting on page 426.

Formigal (1500m) is the westernmost of the big ski resorts of the Spanish Pyrenees, set among bleak mountains above a reservoir and the old village of Sallent de Gallego. It is entirely modern, with one long main street of large hotels, shops and bars (apparently over 20) and a Romanesque-style church. The main lift station is about half a mile up the road up towards the French border at the Col du Portalet (closed in winter) but there is also a chair-lift to the slopes from beside the church.

The skiing covers a wide area of open mountainside, with some long gentle runs and a top altitude of 2250m. In good conditions it must be an enjoyable area for intermediates and inexperienced skiers. Its most famous problem is wind; when combined with poor snow, no enclosed lifts beyond the slow access gondola and lamentably inadequate restaurants, this can make skiing a pastime of rare unpleasantness. We encountered large expanses of windblown ice and frozen earth.

Formigal has good, expensive hotels in the large, comfortable and stylish Formigal (✆488000) and the very attractive Eguzki Lore (✆488075). Off the slopes, at least, ice is easily broken: in the hotel bars measures are large and prices low, an informal and friendly atmosphere prevails, and bruises are inspected at close range. There is very little to do apart from skiing. We heard good reports of ski school (three hours a day) and of a British-run ski repair/hire shop.

Baqueira (1500m) is genuinely exclusive – a small modern development without any cheap hotels, and with more than its fair share of Ferraris, furs and leather. It lies near Viella on the northern side of the mountains, which means easy access from France and more reliable snow than in other Spanish resorts. Its skiing is also interesting, but because it is not cheap Baqueira attracts few British skiers. The resort lies beside the road up to the very high Bonaigua pass, often but not always closed in winter. There is a handsome second-home development and a complex of tall modern buildings including the stylish hotel Montarto (✆645075). A tractor and trailer saves the short walk up to the lift station. The hotel Tuc Blanc is slightly cheaper and closer to the lift (✆645150). Nightlife is quiet.

There are two halves to the ski area, which as a whole is reasonably large and attractively varied: a mixture of wooded and open ground, with runs gentle and steep. The main hill is directly above Baqueira, with good intermediate runs (and a few genuinely challenging ones) of up to 1000m vertical down to the valley which separates this area from the wide and gentle open slopes going up to 2500m above Beret – no more than a car park and a large modern restaurant complex at 1850m.

Most of the slopes are west-facing, but some of the best and most challenging runs, from Cap de Baqueira towards Beret, face north. An entirely new area on the Cap will be opened up this season by the addition of three triple chair-lifts.

Panticosa (1184m) is an old village about 20 minutes' drive from Formigal; the two resorts share their lift pass but there is no bus between them. Panticosa's ski area is low and very small. The base station is a bus-ride down from the old village, which has no great charm and very limited facilities. There is some cross-country skiing at Balneario de Panticosa (8km), a dismal collection of spa buildings in an impressively severe setting.

Cerler (1550m) is a handsomely restored rustic village in a splendid remote setting, high above the larger and also interesting village of Benasque (1138m), which has some hotels. It is a long drive from anywhere (and anywhere else to ski, in case of snow shortage). Between old Cerler and its ski area is some much less attractive modern development including the large Hotel Monte Alba (✆551136), a short but steepish walk from the lifts. Some apartment buildings are closer to the village and further from the lifts. Although not huge, the ski area offers much more scope than Panticosa and more variety than Formigal, with a similar range of altitude (up to 350m). We have a report of good off-piste skiing. There is cross-country skiing in the beautiful Aneto valley, upstream of Benasque.

La Molina/Super Molina (1400–1700m) and **Masella** (1600m) are close neighbours looking out from thickly wooded mountainsides over the wide, high Cerdagne plateau. Dominating the plain is Masella's Tossa d'Alp, a magnificent ski mountain in all respects but one: snow is notoriously unreliable. The windswept peak commands huge views and the mostly wooded north-facing slopes below it give a large number of challenging trails between 2535m and 1600m, with a couple of nursery areas in sunny clearings. One of them is at the foot of the slopes, on the edge of the small modern resort, with a large, self-contained and very institutional modern hotel, used by tour operators. The nearby resort and ski-fields of La Molina/Super Molina are spread out over a larger area of what seem like foothills. The main slopes above Super Molina (which have some snow-making equipment) are not, or at least not easily, linked to a few lifts on the eastern side of Tossa d'Alp, which connect with Masella. La Molina straggles down the hill below Super Molina as far as the railway line at 1400m, but there are no lifts below 1600m. It attracts a large weekend influx of skiers from Barcelona. Although less claustrophobic than Masella, La Molina is neither villagey nor particularly stylish. Excursions are organised to Andorra and the border town of Puigcerda (which has an ice rink).

Tourist offices Formigal ✆(74) 488125. Tx 58885; Baqueira (Tourist reservations office) ✆(73) 645025. Tx 57707; Panticosa ✆(74) 488125; Cerler ✆(74) 551012; La Molina ✆(72) 892031; Masella ✆(738) 890053. **Package holidays** Formigal: Thomson (Ht Sc); Baqueira: Ski Miquel (Ht Ch Sc); Panticosa: Thomson (Ht); La Molina: Enterprise (Ht Sc), Neilson (Ht Sc), Ski NAT (Ht Sc), Masella Enterprise (Ht Sc).

White heather club

Scotland

Scotland has the only mechanised snow skiing in the British Isles. To those who are not satisfied with their annual week or fortnight in the Alps and who live close enough to the Highlands to make day-trips or weekend visits, the Scottish ski areas are of considerable value, and they offer Scots the chance to take up and practise the sport without going abroad. For the record, we think Scottish skiing is a good thing; and, for the Scottish Office, we think that more of it would not be too much of a good thing. But, despite the strong representations we have had from interested parties, we stick to the view expressed in earlier editions of the *Guide* that Scottish skiing does not represent an attractive alternative to an Alpine holiday; nor would it even if the ski areas were less crowded, more efficiently groomed and marked, and flanked by more convivial restaurants – although improvement in these respects would be welcome.

As our map shows, Scotland's largest ski area, on Cairngorm, is small. It cannot compete with the major Alpine ski areas which attract keen British piste-bashers. It perhaps could compete with the smallest Alpine resorts – its skiing is on much the same scale as that of Alpbach or Niederau, for example. But these are resorts that rely for their appeal on the traditional charm of an Alpine village. Compared with them, Aviemore, Scotland's only ski resort, looks a bleak and unwelcoming place in winter, and the coffee and cling-film sandwiches of Highland cafeterias are no match for the prospect of *Glühwein* and *Apfelstrudel* in an Austrian log cabin.

The greatest disadvantage of Scottish skiing is the weather. Our maritime climate gives a low proportion of the stable, dry, bright weather that contributes so much to the beauty of the Alpine winter, and a high proportion of wind and cloud. Skiing often takes place in extremely unfriendly conditions, with no shelter provided by trees, enclosed lifts or higher mountains. At other times skiing does not place at all, except on the dry slope at Aviemore. Storms not only close lifts but also affect the quality of the snow: conditions are rarely as consistent or flattering as Alpine piste skiers expect. The weather is the main reason not to book a holiday months in advance but to decide at the last minute on the basis of snow reports and the weather forecast.

Apart from easy and cheap access for those who live close to the Highlands, the main advantages of Scottish skiing are the advantages of not being abroad. A ski school staffed by native English-speakers has more than a head start over the foreign variety, as they have discovered in Andorra. Lift queues are as orderly as only British queues can be. Shop prices are much the same as at home and so is the cost of evening entertainment. There is a great sense of camaraderie, and the après-ski ambience is warm and friendly.

If you are a keen skiing Scot, you no doubt ski in all of the three main centres (Glencoe and Glenshee as well as Cairngorm) and most often in the one which is most easily accessible from home. You will probably have found that on weekends when conditions are good, you are not alone in wanting to exploit them. Skiers from south of the border should not disregard Scotland as a supplement to an Alpine skiing holiday: a weekend or week late in the season may provide some excellent skiing. In general, conditions are at their best in March, April and well into May. (Fences beside the pistes and lift tracks cause snow to accumulate there and to persist long after it has disappeared from most of the mountain.) Daylight hours are longer, and conditions on the mountain are more likely to be bearable than in the depth of winter.

Aviemore is the only developed resort. Glencoe and Glenshee are more often used by day-trip skiers (Glencoe is open only at weekends), and many skiers prefer these areas precisely because of the absence of modern development. Glenshee (between Braemar and Perth) now offers a ski area comparable in extent to Cairngorm, though it is not as high. A fourth area, the Lecht (between Grantown and Braemar), is of interest mainly to beginners.

Aviemore

Aviemore lies in the broad Spey valley between Perth and Inverness, about three hours by coach from Edinburgh or Glasgow. The main road along the valley is a very good one, but occasionally blocked. The Cairngorm ski area is nearly 10 miles away, to the east. There are several morning buses to the slopes, starting at 9.00, and several back in the afternoon, ending at 4.45. There are also daily buses from more distant villages in the Spey valley.

There is not much of an old village, just rows of shops, with a few hotels and guest-houses lining the road near the station; the resort largely consists of a modern development – the Aviemore Centre. The facilities available at the Centre include bars and discos, a dry ski slope, go-karting, swimming, skating and curling, squash, snooker, sauna and whirlpool, amusement arcades, a Santa Claus play park and a cinema. Undoubtedly these facilities do a lot, especially for children, to reduce the risk of boredom when skiing is not possible.

Reporters agree that Aviemore après-ski is very jolly, with live entertainment and reasonably priced drinks in hotel bars. There is a disco and skating disco in the Centre, a cinema, and several restaurants, from fish and chips to the Winking Owl's medium-haute cuisine. Après-ski shopping is limited.

Many people may prefer to be in a quiet hotel with a supply of whisky and good books. There are several other villages and towns in the Spey Valley, less obviously affected by tourism but offering good accommodation, ski school and hire shops. In good weather there are beautiful walks and excursions in the neighbourhood, including Loch-an-Eilean (with its picturesque ruin) and Loch Garten, where ospreys come to nest in spring. Other activities which can be combined with skiing in spring are pony-trekking, fishing, watersports, golf, reindeer-

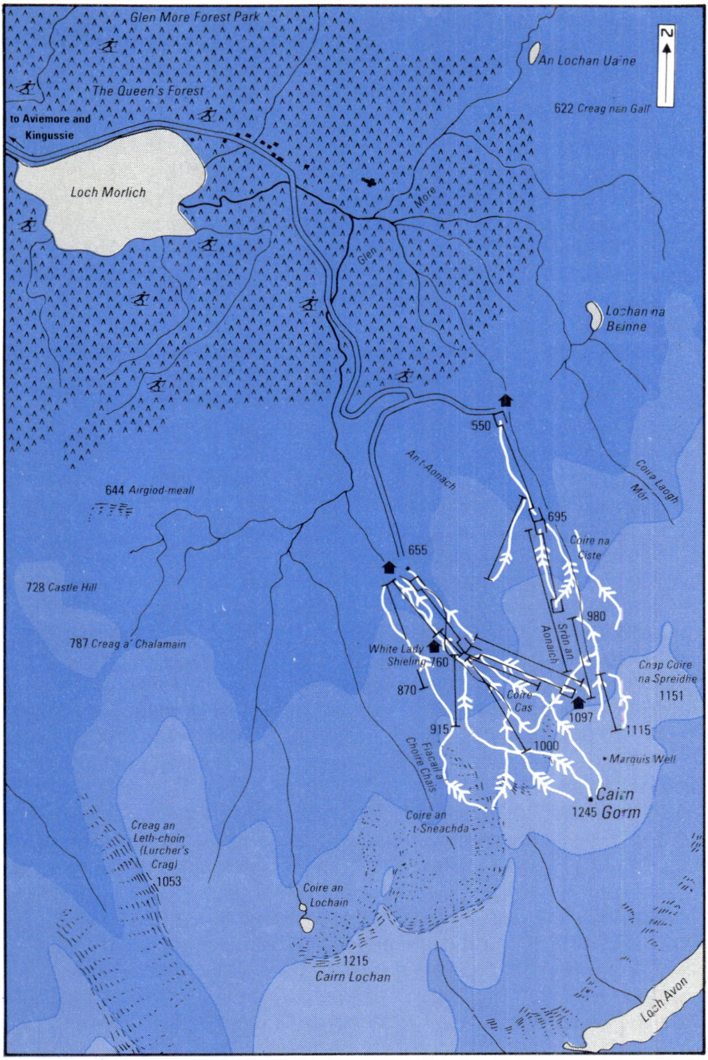

spotting, touring distilleries and a wildlife park.

There are several hotels and a self-catering chalet motel in Aviemore Centre itself; the Post House (✆810771) is comfortable in typical Trusthouse Forte style. There are several simple B&B houses in the village. The Coylumbridge (✆810661) is a large, comfortable and self-contained hotel with a holiday-camp atmosphere, outside Aviemore on the way to the ski area; it has a log-cabin bar and dancing in the evening, and its own ice rink, pool and tennis courts. Outside Aviemore, the Osprey in Kingussie (✆(05402) 510) and the Ard-Na-Coille in Newtonmore (✆(05403) 214) are excellent small family hotels.

The Cairngorm ski area consists of four chair-lifts and eleven drag-lifts serving a broad area of open mountainside with runs giving a maximum of about 450m vertical, or 600m for those prepared to walk up from the top station to the summit. There are two car parks at the bottom of the slopes, and four main access lifts. The runs offer reasonable variety; there are easy nursery slopes at the top, and easy longer runs down to Shieling and the car park and beside the Fiacaill tows. The White Lady chair and tow serve stiffer intermediate runs, often mogulled, and there are steep runs on either side of the Coire Na Ciste gunbarrel and below Headwall. In good conditions it is possible to ski down to the Coire Na Ciste car park.

Mountain restaurants which were inviting could add greatly to the appeal of the ski area in bad weather. They aren't. There is a small snack bar at the Coire Na Ciste car park and a larger one, with a bar (and TV display detailing lift closures and the latest wind speed at top station), at the Coire Cas car park. Higher up, there is only the Shieling picnic room and snack bar (with beer on sale if you buy food), and the unlicensed Ptarmigan snack bar at the top (refurbished for this season). A new Shieling restaurant is still on the drawing board.

Queues can be a serious problem at weekends and holiday times, particularly if the weather is good (thus attracting crowds) or bad (when the chair-lifts are closed) ; if all lifts are open, waits are not usually longer than 15 minutes (which is long, considering the length of the runs). Queuing is conducted in a uniquely orderly way – in ranks, so that piste-space is not wasted. On our last visit in April 1986, piste marking and maintenance were lacking, making it very easy to get lost in bad visibility. In general the runs are where snow lies; exposed rocks are not flagged and the snow fences beside runs and lift tracks are a further hazard.

There is a variety of different lift passes available, including a limited day pass designed to permit inexperienced skiers to ski around the Shieling and Ptarmigan areas, and vouchers which can be exchanged for five day passes over the course of several seasons. Day passes at about £10 (less in January) seem expensive compared with weekly ones at about £35, but the longer passes are risky because of the frequency of weather conditions not conducive to skiing.

There are several ski schools in Aviemore and many others based in nearby villages. We have a few reports, and they are generally very favourable. All the ski schools offer packages of equipment hire, tuition and lift pass. The Post House hotel has a nursery with resident nannies all year.

When there is a lot of snow, the forest land around Glenmore provides plenty of scope for cross-country skiing, as the mountains do for nordic ski touring and winter climbing. Dangers resulting from the unpredictability of the weather should not be underestimated. Access to the cross-country trails is at Inverdruie, just outside Aviemore.

Tourist office ✆(0479) 810363. **Snow report** ✆(0479) 811000 (updated three times a day); or ✆031-246 8031.

Orientation tour

Eastern Europe

Yugoslavia, Bulgaria, Romania

Downhill skiing on a serious scale – with established resorts served by extensive lift systems – can be found in many European countries other than the Big Four of Austria, France, Italy and Switzerland, and on many mountain ranges other than the Alps. Such skiing is often of no more than local interest, but it is not always so. Elsewhere in the Guide we describe the Pyrenean resorts of Spain and tiny Andorra, which from Britain tend to attract inexperienced skiers in search of a jolly holiday at keen prices. The other direction in which skiers on a budget tend to look is eastwards, to the Communist countries of Bulgaria and Romania, on the shores of the Black Sea, and to the neighbouring, more-or-less Communist country of Yugoslavia, which at its north-western extremity borders Italy and Austria – with resorts in the south-east Alps as well as ones much further south.

As you might expect, these countries have quite a lot in common with one another, and are in some ways quite different from the major Alpine countries – or, for that matter, from Pyrenean ones. The skiing can compete with that of minor resorts in Austria, for example, and the accommodation is built to match the expectations of foreign visitors, but in other respects eastern Europe – and particularly Bulgaria and Romania – can be disappointing. The heart of the matter is that, for a variety of reasons, these countries do not offer the opportunities for self indulgence that many skiers have become used to in resorts elsewhere. Although this matters a lot to some skiers, it matters much less to others – leaders of school parties, for example, may consider a shortage of tempting bars something of a blessing. Nowhere are the limitations more apparent than up the mountain. There are few mountain restaurants or ice bars, snacks are often limited (in the words of a reporter on Bulgaria, 'meatballs or meatballs'), and *Glühwein*, sumptuous cakes and good coffee are but a fond memory. English is widely understood in the major resorts, but service is at best unhurried, occasionally seeming to border on resentful.

There are restrictions on taking the local currency into or out of each country (which means that visitors should change money in small amounts, so as not to end up with a surplus), and few opportunities to spend heavily. In Bulgaria and Romania, shopping is restricted to the occasional souvenir shop and the special shops designed to extract precious foreign exchange from visitors.

Yugoslavia

Yugoslavia's best-known resort, offered by mainstream tour operators such as Thomson and Enterprise as well as the eastern Europe specialists, is **Kranjska Gora** (810m), on the south-east extremity of the

Alps, close to both the Italian and Austrian borders. The village is inoffensive – its chalets slightly more severe than their Tyrolean equivalents, and its setting in a flat-bottomed valley between craggy, wooded mountains a pretty one. But it is a difficult resort to recommend to any category of skier except dedicated ski school students who are content to perfect their turns on a limited range of pistes. There are wide and gentle nursery slopes right on the edge of the village, but the transition to real pistes is rather abrupt – the mountains rise quite steeply from the valley floor. There are lots of drag-lifts serving intermediate pistes on the Vitranc, but they go no more than half-way up what is in any case a small mountain – which means not only limited skiing but also a pronounced danger of poor snow. A two-stage chair-lift goes further, to 1570m, giving a fairly challenging descent of over 750m vertical to the valley; but that is all there is for the competent skier to enjoy. There are swimming pools and saunas in several of the slightly institutional hotels, and discos and bars in which a festive atmosphere can be made to prevail.

There are several other resorts in the Yugoslavian Alps which are accessible to the British package-holiday skier. From the skiing point of view the most interesting is **Bovec** (520m), south of Kranjska Gora; it does not have many lifts, but they include a three-stage gondola rising 1750m and serving some moderately challenging slopes. If and when there is snow down to the village (about the lowest resort in these pages), the run from top to bottom must be memorable.

Despite the eminence it achieved in hosting the Winter Olympics in 1984, **Sarajevo** (a long way to the south, about level with Florence) is not really a ski resort. Like Innsbruck, it is a valley town with skiable mountains nearby, and the accommodation for skiers is concentrated at the foot of the pistes in Jahorina (1530m) and Bjelasnica (1270m), a long way out of town (and widely separated). The lifts of the former go up to just over 1900m, those of the latter to almost 2100m, with runs of up to 800m vertical. Most of the skiing is of intermediate difficulty, on open slopes. Life revolves around the hotels, purpose-built for skiers. There are some simple non-skiing sports facilities at Jahorina, and very extensive cross-country skiing trails near Bjelasnica.

Bulgaria

The largest and best-known Bulgarian winter resort is **Pamporovo** (1620m); it is also the southernmost mountain resort in south-east Europe, so although the days may be sunny, snow conditions can be unreliable later in the season. This purpose-built resort is a fairly unattractive collection of modern hotels, lacking atmosphere but offering a surprisingly high standard of accommodation some five minutes' bus-ride from the slopes and lift network, consisting entirely of chair- and drag-lifts.

Pamporovo is well suited to the first-time skier, with several good nursery areas and a number of delightful confidence-building blue pistes down through the trees, including one from the top height of 1925m to the low point of the system at 1450m. There are two black runs, including the notorious 'Wall' which is used as a slalom race-course, but advanced skiers would probably find little to maintain their interest after the first two or three days. The lift system is adequate although there can be queuing at peak times, particularly weekends; ski schools take preference. Rental equipment is first-class, and the ski school excellent – the instructors take an obvious pride in their command of English, and instruction is reportedly clear, technically sound, and above all patient. Cross-country trails of 4km, 16km and 18km start in the resort, with instruction in cross-country techniques available. Après-ski is limited to a few 'folksy' restaurants and hotel discos, although there is a night club at the Hotel Smolyan some 45 minutes' bus ride away. An evening folk barbeque at the Cheverme restaurant is recommended. Non-skiing activities include indoor bowling and swimming at the Perelik – probably the pick of the hotels – together with tobogganning; there are also excursions to various local points of interest, including the capital, Sofia.

Borovets (1323m) is the other major Bulgarian resort popular with British tour operators. Spectacularly situated among pine forests high in the Rila mountains, the resort is more a scattered collection of hotels than a village, although the scenery is impressive. Because of its more northerly location, late-season snow conditions are better here.

With a highest ski point of 2430m, reached by the formidable three-mile Yastrebets six-seater gondola, Borovets' skiing compares favourably with that of many of the smaller Alpine resorts. It is less suitable for beginners than intermediate skiers, who have a choice of testing red and black runs; but there is little in the way of real challenge or off-piste scope for the expert. There is a series of fairly long parallel drag lifts between 2150m and 2540m, reached by the gondola, and a lower area above the resort including limited nursery slopes at the foot of the mountain and a range of modest runs served by a chair-lift up to 1790m and a drag up to 1550m. There is an easy blue meandering some 6km down through the forest, requiring a fair amount of pushing in places. Ski school and rental equipment reflect the same high standards as at Pamporovo, although lift queues can be an irritation at peak times (again, ski schools take preference).

Most of the hotels are within five minutes' walking distance of the slopes and lifts. The newly built Rila is situated right at the foot of the mountain opposite the main chair-lift and convenient for the gondola and nursery slopes. The twin hotels of Ela and Mura are also equipped to a high standard, offering comfortable if somewhat subdued accommodation close to the lift network. Après-ski relies almost entirely upon the hotel discos and floor-shows, with the Rila acting as the principal entertainment centre. Apart from a few excursions there is little for the non-skier. Three short cross-country trails commence 2km outside the resort, accessible by bus.

Romania

Sinaia (800m) is a small town stretching along the main road through the mountains from Bucharest to Brasov, its role as a ski resort relatively minor. A two-stage cable-car from the town (its top section duplicated by a chair-lift) serves long intermediate runs down the front of the mountain which are quite challenging (particularly in poor visibility, as they are poorly marked), but for most skiers the main area is the exposed, treeless slopes behind the mountain and on subsidiary peaks beyond – short intermediate runs with some variety, and plenty of scope for skiing off-piste. The town is quiet, and although there are one or two bars and restaurants, in practice après-ski life depends on what is happening in the tour operators' hotels.

Poiana Brasov (1020m) is a quite different and more satisfactory sort of resort, and an unusual one. It is purpose-built, with its hotels and other facilities dotted around a wooded plateau at the foot of the skiing, rather like an enormous holiday camp, and not at all like a village. This is no doubt an excellent arrangement in summer, when walks in wooded surroundings are what people go for. In winter it means that life for many skiers revolves around buses. The main ski area is reached by gondola or cable-car up to 1775m and consists of three main elements: satisfying intermediate runs approximately following the line of the lifts from top to bottom; a good, open nursery area at altitude; and a longish roundabout run away from the lifts, graded black only because it is not prepared, it has one moderately steep pitch towards the end, and it is used as a downhill race course. There is also a separate gentle nursery area down in the resort. Non-skiing and après-ski facilities here are more impressive than at Sinaia. There is a big public pool (as well as pools in some hotels), other sports facilities including skating, bowling, sleigh rides and horse-riding, and a range of nightlife from discos through family cabarets to very carefully contrived traditional-style restaurants. Excursions are organised.

In both resorts there is no shortage of ski school instructors who speak excellent English.

Package holidays Kranjska Gora: Enterprise (Ht Sc), Global (Ht), Inghams (Ht), Intasun (Ht Sc), Neilson (Ht Sc), Phoenix (Ht Sc), Ski NAT (Ht Sc), Thomson (Ht), Yugotours (Ht Sc). Bovec: Intasun (Ht), Phoenix (Ht), Yugotours (Ht). Sarajevo: Phoenix (Ht). Pamporovo: Balkan Holidays (Ht), Enterprise (Ht), Global (Ht), Phoenix (Ht), Schools Abroad (Ht), Ski Falcon (Ht), Skiscope (Ht). Borovets: Balkan Holidays (Ht), Enterprise (Ht), Global (Ht Sc), Inghams (Ht), Phoenix (Ht), Ski Falcon (Ht Ap Sc), Ski Travelaway (Ht), Skiscope (Ht). Sinaia: Blue Sky (Ht), Schoolplan (Ht), Snow World (Ht). Poiana Brasov: Blue Sky (Ht), Enterprise (Ht), Hourmont (Ht), Inghams (Ht), Intasun (Ht).

MAKING THE MOST OF YOUR SKIING

Up to this point, the *Guide* has been devoted more-or-less to one end: helping you decide where to go skiing. But there are other considerations involved in arranging a skiing holiday, and we deal with them in this final section of the *Guide*.

A Skiing Primer

Going on a skiing holiday isn't like taking a conventional summer holiday or winter break. For a start, choosing the holiday itself is only half the battle, and accounts for only half the bills. You've still got to arrange special clothes and equipment, special insurance, skiing lessons and a pass or ticket for transport uphill so that you can concentrate your efforts on sliding back down. Then there's the risk that you'll hate the whole business – that after a couple of days the pain of your boots, the ferocity of the weather, the unpleasantness of the lift queues, the indifference of your instructor, the impossibly slippery surface of the ski-runs or the frustration of your own incompetence will drive you off the slopes and into the bars, never to set foot on skis again.

That risk is very small. What's much more likely is that you'll be hooked – that you'll develop a perennial craving to be in the mountains. By December each year you may find yourself irresistibly drawn to spending Saturday mornings stretching your credit limit in ski shops and Sunday afternoons glued to BBC2's *Ski Sunday*, eager to gain some second-hand sensation of being back on snow.

The addictive power of skiing holidays is only partly explained by the exhilaration of skiing itself. What's just as important is that to go skiing is to be transported from the damp greyness of winter at home to a quite different world. It isn't only that the snow turns all but the most desperate of resorts into a magically sparkling place. It's also a world where you can dress as colourfully as you like without risking ridicule; where, for the price of a cable-car ride, skiers and non-skiers alike can get to places and see panoramas which were once the province of a few mountaineers; where the sun can toast your face even if the air is so cold that you have to be kitted out as for a moonwalk; where indulgence in food and drink is made respectable by your exertions on the slopes; where you can enjoy the rare treat of immersing yourself for weeks at a time in learning or polishing skills of no practical value; where the business of making new friends or rubbing along with old ones is lubricated by the common interest in skiing; and from which you return looking (and possibly feeling) wonderfully healthy. You have been warned.

If you haven't been skiing, there's a lot to learn about the kinds of resorts you can go to, about the kinds of holiday to be had in them, about the equipment you'll need – and of course about skiing itself. Even if you now go by the name 'intermediate' (that is, you're neither beginner nor expert), you're unlikely to have amassed a very wide range of skiing experience. This chapter covers the basics. Later chapters look in more detail at the choice of equipment, clothing, insurance – and, of course, the choice of a resort.

The season

One thing that virtually all skiing holidays have in common is that they happen in winter – though there is such a thing as summer skiing, which takes place on the permanent snowfields and glaciers found in the Alps at heights above sea level of over 3000 metres or so.

In most ski resorts, the season starts with Christmas – the first big holiday period of the winter. That's not to say you can't go skiing before then, but if you do you must choose your resort with care to be confident of finding the lifts open and a good covering of snow on the runs. Christmas and (particularly) New Year in the Alps can be very jolly – but are not a good time for serious skiing, because of the crowds.

January is low season and not traditionally a Continental holiday time. Although there should be plenty of snow on the runs, the blizzards that often bring it can also mean skiing without being able to see where you're going, and getting miserably cold. Resorts popular with package holiday-makers from Britain are half-alive, populated only by people taking advantage of low package prices. Other resorts may be practically deserted until a bright weekend follows a week of snow, when the nearby city dwellers come out to play. The other side of the coin, however, is that queues are minimal, so you can get a lot of skiing in – and the weather can often turn out surprisingly well. It's simply that it's more of a lottery than later in the season.

February sees the beginning of the high season, with correspondingly high prices. It's the best compromise between winter and spring: snow should have accumulated on the runs, and the weather should be improving to the point where the chances of a bronzed face are pretty good. As spring approaches, sunshine becomes more reliable and snow less so – and even in March some of the more vulnerable resorts are regularly in danger of losing much of their skiing. Easter, whenever it falls, is the final peak in the skiing season, but if it's late in the spring the number of resorts able to capitalise on it may be very few.

Purely from the skiing point of view there is something to be said for each of the periods of the season *except* Christmas and Easter, and in any large group of skiers you will find advocates of every particular week in the skiing calendar. If we had to come off the fence with a recommendation for beginners it would be for early March, when the odds are against consistently bad weather; everyone skis better in sunshine, but novices can be transformed by it – and if you throw in the towel you can at least hope to revel in the intense spring sun.

The strength of the sun catches many first-time skiers off-guard; at high altitudes the sun's rays have to penetrate less air than they meet on the way to lower spots such as London or Liverpool, with the result that less of their original strength is lost in the process. And their effect is greatly intensified by the reflected glare from snow. As the season progresses, skiers need to take more careful precautions against getting burnt or blinded *and* against finding themselves on unskiable slopes as the sun begins to affect the snow.

Ski resorts

The range of places in which you can base yourself for a skiing holiday is vast. Neither the ancient city of Innsbruck in the Austrian Tirol nor the pair of buildings called Super Nendaz in the Swiss Valais can properly be called ski resorts, but you can have a skiing holiday in either. Even within the narrower range of places which *are* thought of as resorts, there is chalk and cheese. Many of the differences are explained in our chapter on 'The skiing phenomenon', which identifies three broad 'generations' of resort – the long-established railway-based resorts, where skiing began; the smaller village resorts, stemming from the period between the two World Wars when skiing began to expand, but developed most spectacularly since the second War; and the entirely new resorts, purpose-built since World War II. The three generations of resorts are classically (though not exclusively) to be found in Switzerland, Austria and France respectively.

Resorts vary in how much skiing terrain they offer, and how much charm. These are perhaps the two most basic variables, but there are many others. Some resorts are built on main roads, while others are car-free; some are small and tightly knit, while others are big and sprawling; in some you can expect snow on the streets (though there are no guarantees), while in others it would be a bit of bonus; some have few visitors from other countries, while others are over-run by incomers (and some resorts are dominated by the British); some resorts are the province of dedicated skiers, while in others ankle-length mink coats outnumber anoraks; some are deserted in the daytime because the skiers quit the village to spend the day up the mountain, while others are the hub of activity.

You might with some justification expect that one thing ski resorts would have in common is altitude; but you'd be wrong. There are a lot of resorts (in Austria, particularly) which are in or close to major valleys, at heights above sea level of no more than 600m (2000ft). The skiing around these places is largely on clearings through the forests, and may go no higher than 1800m or 2000m (6500ft). At the other extreme are resorts where even the 'village' – the point from which the skiing goes up – is higher than that. Val Thorens at 2300m (7000ft) is the highest resort in Europe; there are quite a few over 1800m. These resorts have most or all of their skiing on open slopes above the tree-line (the altitude above which trees can't survive the cold).

Altitude is an important consideration when choosing a resort. All other things being equal, you get more snow falling at higher altitudes; and because the air generally gets cooler the higher you go, the snow stays longer, and stays in good skiing condition longer. But, of course, all other things are not equal. The 600m-high resorts of Austria, for example, get much better snow than communities at that same altitude in France, where virtually all resorts are above the 1000m mark.

Even if you count the queuing for lifts and the riding on them, the time you spend actually skiing is unlikely to amount to half your waking hours in the resort. If you mould your skiing to ski-school hours you may do no more than two hours in the morning and two in the afternoon. If on the other hand you ski from when the lifts start to when they stop you could probably double that.

But to do that you'd have to miss out lunch. One of the delights of skiing – indeed, one of its main attractions for some people – is lunch 'on the mountain'. It may come as a bit of a surprise to discover that (in many but not all ski areas) the mountains are dotted with hostelries of one sort and another where food and drink can be had in abundance. In many resorts some of the restaurants are accessible to non-skiers, too. You won't find *haute cuisine*, but you won't care. The simplest of meals becomes intensely satisfying when consumed on a sun-terrace at 2500m after a morning's skiing; or in an atmospheric mountain hut while a blizzard rages outside. (If, like many skiers, you lubricate lunch with beer, wine or schnapps, you may find you ski better afterwards. This isn't necessarily self-deception: some skiers do indeed benefit from an artificial boost to their confidence. But moderation is vital: there is increasing concern in the ski world about accidents – to themselves and to others – caused by drunken skiers.)

The skiing day ends with sunset – most lifts will stop running at around 4pm to 4.30pm in the depths of winter, perhaps as late as 5.30pm in spring. And when skiing ends, après-ski begins – at least in theory. Resorts vary widely in what après-ski activity they provide – and it's not always very much. But after a long, hard day's skiing you may find the key question is not whether there is life in your resort, but whether there is life in your legs.

Perhaps because fatigue tends to set in so early, it is traditional for skiers to combine the evening's musical entertainment with tea, one of the most important meals of the day. The clomping ski-booted tea-dance is still alive, and kicking, whether it be to the accompaniment of yodelling tunes, Edelweiss and the March of the Mods on the concertina, zither and rhythm machine or to old pop songs pumped out just as mechanically by Brylcreem-and-leather live bands. In more sophisticated traditional resorts the tea-dance has evolved into tea with background music, or simply tea. Hotels in many long-established Swiss resorts may organise chess and bridge games.

Later evening entertainment ranges from further live music (in many places the same band continues after a break of an hour or two) with higher prices, to discothèques (much like discothèques anywhere) and bars, sometimes styled (especially in France) as pubs or piano bars. Some of the latter do have live piano players, but often the musical background is pre-recorded. Most resorts have a cinema (films in English are rare); a few have casinos.

In a resort popular with package holiday-makers, the chances are that organised evenings out on the town, or out on the mountain, will be offered by the tour operators' local representatives. Typical activities include meals in restaurants or fondue parties, meals or drinking sessions in a mountain restaurant followed by toboggan rides, disco evenings with specially negotiated prices, Tyrolean evenings (local dances and costumes), and bowling (the last two typical of Austria). In some resorts, especially where accommodation is in staffed chalets, the personnel may organise drinks parties and, if the clients give the nod (Heaven help them if they don't) real parties. The livelier club-chalet operators organise fancy dress and drag beauty contests and so on, much as they do in summer.

In these popular package resorts the beat goes on through the peaks and troughs of the season – and whatever else you may think about organised nightlife, it does have the advantage that you can count on a lively atmosphere in at least one establishment, even in low season. In contrast, the resorts with a reputation for chic, which do undoubtedly pull in the sophisticated night owls at certain times, can be entirely lifeless in low season.

Many resorts come to life at weekends, when discothèques are packed and charge much higher prices than during the week. This is particularly true of Italian resorts, even ones which are remote from big towns; those which aren't much used by tour operators wake up from apparent mid-week hibernation, and those which are, such as Sauze and Cervinia, take on a different atmosphere.

With a handful of exceptions, French ski resorts tend to be particularly short on commercial nightlife. There isn't much of the traditional cheek-to-cheek live music that provides an alternative to discothèques in many Austrian and Swiss hotels. Discothèque prices are higher than most skiers care to pay, and people staying in apartments and chalets are inclined to stay in at night. The fact that most people are not staying in hotels, coupled with the fact of being in France, means that there is normally a reasonable range of restaurants, whereas in all but the biggest Swiss and Austrian resorts eating out means eating in hotel dining rooms – or indulging in a typical Alpine evening with fondue in an old (or 'old') chalet/barn.

Skiing and après-skiing aren't the only things you can do in a ski resort. Many skiers (particularly those on holiday for a fortnight or more) like to take a day off now and again and do other things; or they like to mix skiing with other activities – perhaps swimming or skating in the early evening; and not everyone who goes to a ski resort is a skier. So resorts normally parade a long list of sporting and other activities you can do. Swimming and skating are pretty standard, though not universal. There may be curling, tobogganing, horse-riding, sleigh rides, hot-air balloons, cleared paths for mountain walks, and so on. From some resorts there are excursions to nearby (or not so nearby) places of cultural or commercial interest; naturally, the location of the resort determines above all else what is available.

Cross-country skiing (from which downhill skiing evolved) is enjoying a distinct revival, and most resorts now have prepared tracks on which you can practise the basic skills required. Cross-country skiers use much lighter equipment than downhill skiers, and travel over (that is, up as well as down) gentler hills, or across completely flat countryside. Serious cross-country skiers in your party will want to consider their choice of resort just as carefully as the downhillers; a few Alpine resorts offer a reasonable small-scale simulation of the real Scandinavian thing, but most do not approach it, offering little more than a flat or gently undulating loop a few kilometres long.

The skiing

For downhill skiing you need snow, and slopes. Not all mountain **slopes** are suitable for skiing. In the early days, skiers roamed over areas which in summer were pasture for cattle – generally undulating slopes, smooth and grassy, and needing only a thin covering of snow to be skiable. A great many resorts still depend on pasture-land for their ski-fields – and it can be something of a surprise to go to such a resort in summer to find cattle contentedly munching on your favourite run, to the cacophony of their huge necklace-bells. But that surprise is nothing compared with the shock of seeing in summer the rocky terrain which forms the ski-fields of the higher resorts – and the obvious extent of the bulldozing which often goes on in order to form skiable runs.

Virtually every resort has nursery slopes in or close to the village itself, where beginners spend their first day or two coming to terms with the treacherous new extensions to their anatomy. Ideally, a nursery slope should slope very gently indeed, finishing up in a part which is completely flat; many come close to this ideal, but some fall a good way short. In some resorts, the nursery slopes are not at the village level but higher up the mountain; this may be dictated by the lie of the land – some resorts sit on a completely flat valley bottom enclosed by ferociously steep valley sides – or it may reflect a general lack of snow at village level, particularly if that level is low. Some resorts have village nursery slopes *and* higher slopes, to which beginners can be taken if the snow lower down is too poor.

The main runs of the resort, similarly, may reach down to the resort or stop short, or may depend on snow conditions. If the valley sides close to the village are steep, runs which go down more-or-less directly will be fairly (or even very) difficult. In these circumstances beginners will usually be able to get a lift down the mountain as well as up it, or they will be able to wend their way down a gentle but narrow zig-zag track through the forest. These woodland paths are thought by many to have little appeal, being boring, often dangerously overcrowded, hazardous if icy, and (at least for a beginner) surprisingly hard work. There are exceptions, but generally this is not skiing for fun, it is skiing to get home. Skiing for fun happens mainly on two kinds of run – on broad swathes cut through less precipitous areas of forest or on wide open mountainsides above the tree-line.

In the beginning, skiers just found a suitable piece of mountainside and skied down it. People still do much the same, and are said to be skiing 'off-piste'; 'piste' is the French for trail, and has worked its way into skiing English. It's used slightly differently from the word 'run', which simply indicates an identifiable route which skiers take, whereas a piste is a run which is marked and patrolled; it is thus possible to speak of an 'off-piste run'.

Pistes have several advantages for inexpert skiers. They are staked out, so that you know you're following a recognised route to somewhere – particularly important in poor visibility; they're identified, so that you should be able to work out whether a particular piste goes where you want to go; they (usually) have defined edges, which should mean that you don't stray on to ground which is unsuitable for skiing; their surface is normally kept fairly smooth and unbroken by piste-bashing machines, making the skiing easier; they're patrolled by safety monitors who should mark any dangerous parts and if necessary close the piste altogether in poor conditions or if there is a danger of avalanche; and they're almost always graded, so that (in theory at least) you can predict how difficult each run is.

Most resorts grade their runs by means of a colour-code which is used (with varying degrees of clarity) on signposts and maps of the ski area. Most use three colours: black for the most difficult, red for medium-difficult and blue for easier ones; some add a green category, at the 'easiest' end of the scale. The precise definition attached to the three or four gradings varies from resort to resort – red will be described as 'difficult' in one resort (and black 'very difficult') whereas it will be described as 'medium' in another. These discrepancies might be of some concern were they not completely overwhelmed by the much more pronounced variations in *real* meaning. The sad fact is that you cannot rely on a resort's piste gradings to indicate more than relative steepness within that resort – the black will be steeper than the red, and so on. When it comes to judging how easy or difficult one ski area is and comparing it with another, the piste gradings are of very little use. Every resort will contrive to have at least one black run, regardless of the unalterably horizontal tendency of its skiing terrain; and every resort will be sure to show on its piste map a sprinkling of both blues and reds, even if the runs are indistinguishable in practice. It's important to remember that any one piste can be considerably more or less difficult to ski at different times. Crowds of people, for example, can make a moderate slope distinctly tricky; but what matters above all else is the state of the snow. Good snow on a black run, for example, may make it easier to ski than a blue run in an icy condition.

The first requirement of the **snow** is that it should entirely cover the slopes. This may sound elementary, but it is a lucky pair of skis which spend a week on the slopes without encountering grass, earth or rocks poking through the snow at least once. Because a good covering of snow is the first essential, and because many skiers who live in the Alpine countries (and a few who live elsewhere) can tailor their skiing plans to suit the conditions, most resorts measure the depth of snow lying on the lower and upper slopes, and the results are widely published. To the innocent eye the figures look very impressive. Recorded depths of between one and two metres are common, at least on the upper slopes, and depths of below 50cm (or about 20 inches) are cause for concern. Surely that's enough to ski on? Well, yes it is – more than enough, on a perfectly smooth piste. But in practice, even when the tourist office is quoting a measured depth of snow in excess of a metre, there will be uneven areas where the scraping action of hundreds of skis has exposed some of the bumps in the ground.

The other key thing about snow is what condition it's in. The state of the snow can vary enormously, requiring different levels of skill and effort for safe and dignified progress. The easiest sort of fresh snow to ski is the tiny light flakes which fall in very cold conditions, called powder. Experienced skiers dream about powder – the expert will dream of skiing off-piste, skis hidden in deep powder, the less expert of skiing on-piste in a shallow layer of powder in which the most incompetent and half-hearted turns will work perfectly. Most of the time, you have to dream, and ski on something else.

The something else may be heavier fresh snow, which can be murderously tiring and even dangerous for the average skier; or older snow which will have been compacted either by skiers or by bashers. It is now standard practice for fresh snow on the pistes to be 'bashed' by caterpillar tractors towing rollers and/or blades. This is partly to prolong the life of the snow, but also because skiers these days are accustomed to skiing on snow which has already been flattened by the passage of other skiers, and many can't cope with virgin snow if it's more than a few inches deep. The bashing is designed to give the first skiers of the day as smooth a ride as the last.

In fact, the first skiers of the day often get a smoother ride than the last, because they get a uniformly flat surface; later in the day, slopes which are steep and long enough to cause skiers to do lots of turns on the way down become covered with *moguls* – mounds of snow created by skiers themselves in the simple process of following in one another's tracks. Where the skis run and turn, the snow is compacted and to some extent scraped away; in between, it accumulates in uncompacted piles. Some steep runs in a resort may be bashed rarely or not at all, partly because they're difficult to bash, and partly because some skiers prefer to ski unprepared snow – either deep fresh snow or the moguls which eventually form.

Bashing apart, the snow's condition will depend above all else on what the weather has done since it fell. If it's consistently fairly cold, snow can maintain a pleasant powdery surface for some time, even though it is firmly compacted. If it's very cold the snow will tend to go hard; if the air becomes warm during the day or if the sun is strong (not always the same thing) the snow will tend to soften – and if this is followed by low temperatures at night the result the next morning will be very hard indeed; at the extreme, and as a matter of routine when winter gives way to spring, the snow at lower altitudes does actually melt and become slush – and in that case what you get the next morning is not very hard snow but rock-hard, rutted ice. This is at best unpleasant and at worst highly dangerous. At higher altitudes, off-piste skiers hope to find 'corn' or 'spring' snow – a thin layer of sugar-like crystals on a hard base, which gives excellent pre-lunch skiing.

Late in the season, at least, in most resorts there are sharp variations in the snow conditions on different runs, according to how high (and therefore cold) they are, how much sun they get (and when they get it), and how much they get skied. An additional variable is the extent of artificial snow-making arrangements. In a growing number of resorts dotted across the Alps, when temperatures are low but precipitation is lacking, water can be sprayed into the air above the lower slopes to fall to the ground as white, snow-like crystals. (See the Introduction to the *Guide*.)

The lifts

What comes down must first go up. Although a few people like to get up their chosen mountain under their own steam, and some people can afford to be deposited on the summit by helicopter, most skiers use lifts built on the mountainside (or, increasingly, built within it).

Most resorts have a variety of types of lift, though individual resorts, and indeed whole countries, display bias towards particular forms. The study of lifts is an important discipline for serious skiers and resort managers alike. You may very well want your choice of resort to be influenced by the kinds of lift you'll be required to use; if you're keen on skiing you'll certainly want to be alert to the competing merits of the different lifts, so as to spend as little time as possible queuing and riding, and as much time as possible skiing.

Lift queues are a fact of skiing life – a resort with sufficient lift capacity to eliminate queues at peak times would be hopelessly uneconomic for most of the season. But there are at one extreme resorts where serious queues are exceptional, and at the other extreme resorts where they are the norm. Bad queues normally arise where a lift is a bottleneck in a haphazardly constructed system. Often, this comes about where the main way out of a substantial resort is either a **funicular railway** or a **cable-car**. In concept, the two are very similar – two cars or small trains linked by a wire, so that the one descending helps to pull the other one up. The rate at which either sort of lift can get a crowd up the mountain depends on the capacity of each car and the duration of the ride. The big cable-car at Courchevel, for example, can shift over 1,500 people an hour; 500 would be more normal.

What distinguishes the cable-car is that the fixed cable along which the car runs may be suspended at a spectacular height above the ground. This makes all the difference to the sensations given to passengers, and some difference to the safety record: neither is very reassuring. On the other hand, neither should put you off; the safety record is rather like that of aircraft – too patchy to make any statistical sense. There is a widespread feeling that cable-cars in Italy are more suspect than those elsewhere – perhaps because there are quite a lot of elderly ones springing from Mussolini's era. It is true that the most serious crash happened in Italy (at Cavalese, in the Dolomites) in 1976, when 42 people died. But there have been serious accidents in France and Switzerland, too.

For certain sorts of job – lifting moderate numbers of skiers over precipitous ground – the cable-car is still the right tool; the big Caron cable-car at Val Thorens is a good example. But for getting skiers out of their resort and up on to the main slopes the modern solution is a **gondola**, more graphically described by the Americans as a bubble lift. The basic characteristic of the gondola is that a fast-moving wire carries a series of small cabins which are detached from the wire and brought to a snail's pace at each end of the ride, so that you can easily get in or out. Some older cabins seat only two people; many more seat four, and most modern ones seat six, and may shift over 2,000 people an hour.

They go at a fair speed – so not only does the queue move quickly but also you are transported to the top quickly.

Railways, cable-cars and gondolas are generally big-time lifts, for major uphill leaps in major resorts. In such resorts they are almost always supplemented by smaller-scale lifts – chair-lifts and drag-lifts – and small resorts are often equipped entirely with such lifts. **Chair-lifts** transport you in mid-air, but without the need to take your skis off. Most are slow-moving, and offer little or no protection against the wind – which can be appreciably more biting a few metres above ground level. Most chairs take people two at a time, but there are single chairs, which on a cold day are pure misery; and there are 3- and 4-seaters (usually with special mechanisms – see below).

Drag-lifts propel you along the ground on your skis. The simplest form of drag-lift is the rope tow, which has a continuously moving rope to which handles are firmly attached. You grab a handle as it goes by, at considerable risk to your arms and shoulders. Fortunately, the tow is used only in a few resorts, and on very gentle, short slopes. The two more common forms of drag are physically less taxing because they don't so much pull you as push you along from behind – the **button** lift, taking one person at a time (sometimes called a Poma, after the main maker); and the **T-bar**, taking two.

Drags are standard equipment on nursery slopes – because they're cheap to build, not because they're easy for beginners to ride. On the contrary, drags can be something of a nightmare for beginners, who find that skiing uphill requires a set of skills quite different from those they're starting to develop for skiing down. In your first few days and weeks of skiing, falls on drag-lifts are only to be expected. On the nursery slopes you're unlikely to injure anything more than your pride; but some longer drags take you over hilly terrain, well away from any piste, where you can get into considerable difficulties if you fall. As we explain on the facing page, the T-bar is generally reckoned to be the greater of the two evils; and it is not surprising that many skiers (especially those brought up in France, where nearly all drag-lifts are buttons) reckon that the abundance of T-bars is a major drawback to skiing in Austria, where they are the norm. At least one Austrian resort now grades its drag-lifts as well as its pistes, in a laudable attempt to deter inexperienced skiers from taking unnecessary risks.

The distinctions between these types of lift are becoming more and more blurred. It is now common in French resorts to find gondola-style lifts where each of the cabins holds 10 or 20 people, standing. A number of resorts now have chair-lifts which employ a gondola-style mechanism to detach the chairs from the wire while you waddle on and off. This does away with problems of skiing away at the top – great for beginners; more importantly for the rest of us, it also allows the chairs to travel at a much higher speed, shortening the time you spend dangling in freezing mid-air and boosting the normally modest carrying capacity of the lift to a level which matches all but the most capacious gondolas – theoretically, as many as 2,800 people an hour. Sadly, no resort has yet found a way of forcing skiers to fill the available seats – so this capacity is not achieved in practice.

chair-lift

To get on to a **chair-lift**, you shuffle into position ahead of a moving chair and sit down as it thumps the back of your calf. As the chair proceeds to lift you into the air you pull down a protective bar and heave your ski-laden feet on to a foot rest. (Some old single-seat chairs have a chain instead of a bar, and no foot rest.) At the top, you're delivered on to a gently sloping ramp and accelerate away from the chair on your skis.

A **button** lift propels you by means of a plate-sized disc on the end of a pole which is attached (via a shock-absorbing spring) to a moving wire. Riding a button is not difficult, once you learn to relax and overcome the tendency to sit down. You learn soon enough to steer round the hazards of the track – dips, bumps, rocks, bends, fallen skiers – and before long you may even find that you enjoy the ride.

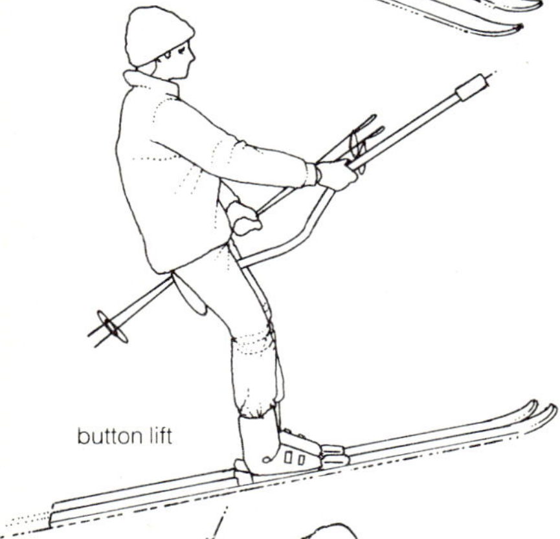

button lift

Riding a **T-bar** is quite a lot trickier: unless the two of you are physically well matched, the ride will be tiring and uncomfortable; when obstacles arise, there's immense scope for confusion about how to avoid them; even without obstacles, it's a bit of a struggle to prevent your skis crossing or your boot clips from getting locked together; if the duet loses its collective balance, recovery is impossible. Travelling alone on a T-bar is very uncomfortable.

T-bar drag-lift

normally use two or three of the possible means. Most skiers who have graduated from the nursery slopes will use a **lift pass** – a 'rover' ticket allowing unlimited rides for the duration of its validity, which may be anything from the whole season downwards. Some resorts don't issue passes for less than a day; many which issue half-day passes do so only for the afternoon. A welcome development in a few resorts is the pass on which you can get a refund depending on what time of day you hand it in (and what time you bought it). Normally, you cannot get a refund on a lift pass by handing it in, or if you lose it. The circumstances in which you *can* get a refund will be defined in small print on the pass, or the form you fill in to get one, or in the ticket office; usually, all the lifts in the ski area have to be closed – a state of affairs which the lift companies naturally strive to avoid. Buying a lift pass for more than a day, therefore, is in principle a bit of a gamble. But in practice, prices are such that a week or a fortnight's pass is normally a worthwhile buy in spite of the risk that you may not get full use out of it. If the weather forecast is a week of blizzards, that's different. A pass is also much more convenient than the alternatives.

But it would clearly be unreasonable to expect beginners to buy full-price passes. On your first day you may not use a lift at all, and in the first week as a whole you may use very few if you have a cautious instructor. Different resorts deal differently with this. A common arrangement is to sell **coupons** or **points-cards**; each lift has a 'value', and to use it you hand over so many coupons or get so many points punched off your card. This is a good arrangement not only for beginners but also for skiers who want to stray widely over the mountain but not to do a great deal of skiing on any one day. The other possible arrangements aren't nearly so good for that sort of skier. One is to have a cheap beginner's pass, which gets you on to certain lifts serving easy pistes, but not others; and the other is to have some lifts which are free. Paying **cash** for individual rides is normally possible for major lifts – particularly for long cable-cars, gondolas and railways which non-skiers might like to go up for the view, or to meet skiers for lunch. In some resorts you can pay cash for smaller lifts, too.

In many resorts there is a further choice of lift passes even when you've decided on the duration you want. Normally the choice will be between a pass for the local lifts only and a more expensive one also covering the lifts of neighbouring resorts. These are usually resorts you can get to on skis: there are now a number of areas in the Alps where the skiing of different resorts has been linked together so that you can ski a huge variety of interconnected runs – sometimes crossing national boundaries. Where you face this kind of choice, inexperienced skiers need to take advice – and find out whether you can buy a basic pass and get an extension for the one day you decide to go over the other side of the hill. Anyone joining ski school should find out where their instructors are likely to take them.

In Italian resorts the choice may be between different passes within the one resort, because different sets of lifts are operated by different companies; if they're on speaking terms there will be a joint pass available, but that isn't always how it is.

Equipment

Skiers take any amount of equipment with them up the mountain to deal with this or that eventuality. But there are three items (or rather pairs of items) which are indispensable: ski boots – monstrous plastic affairs which make walking a comical misery; skis, fitted with bindings to secure them to the boots; and poles, which have all sorts of uses.

In the beginning, skiers used **boots** not unlike those used by mountain walkers. Modern ski boots are designed specifically for skiing; as a result they give much better control of the skis, but are useless for anything else, including walking. A boot consists of a rigid outer shell made of plastic, and a padded inner lining. The inner is designed to cushion the rigid support of the shell and spread the pressure comfortably over your ankle and foot. The boot must fit well enough to anchor your heel firmly in the back of the boot but allow free movement of your toes. Ski boots are no longer tightened with laces; although there are lots of fancy alternatives, most modern boots employ buckles or clips instead – so they're sometimes called clip boots. Comfortable yet effective boots are vitally important if you want to enjoy your skiing.

The first thing a **ski** has to do is slide on the snow, so it has a smooth plastic sole. This sole is easily damaged by skiing over things other than snow, and substantial gouges in it will make the ski slide much less easily; so it's important to keep the sole in good repair. To make it really slippery, the sole should also have a very thin layer of wax applied. You may think that slippery skis are the last thing you want, since your main problem is keeping your speed down rather than keeping it up. But a smooth, waxed ski makes turning less effort; and on many runs there are level sections where slippery soles make the difference between coasting along and having to walk.

But the ski spends very little time flat on its sole. The most frequently used techniques in skiing – traversing, turning and slide-slipping – all involve tilting the ski so that its edge bites into the snow, and so controls your speed and direction. The steeper the slope, the more the ski is being used on its edge; and the harder the snow, the more important it is that the metal strip which forms the edge should present a clean, sharp right-angle.

The condition of the ski's sole and edges is all the inexperienced skier needs to worry about. More expert skiers may be sensitive to other aspects of a ski's performance; the outline shape of the ski and the subtleties of its internal construction will determine how the ski bends and twists, and what snow conditions and styles of skiing it suits. General-purpose skis are a compromise which will cope adequately with all conditions.

The length of ski you should use is a matter of continuing debate, in which fashion holds as much sway as logic. For many years, the 'proper' length of ski for an individual to use, beginner or not, was defined by how high you could reach with your hands. A few years ago there was a big drive to put beginners on short ('compact') skis, which are easier to turn; many more advanced skiers joined them – the cry was that skiing is for fun, and short skis give more fun for less effort. More recently, the view has gained ground that compact skis are slow, and difficult to control in a straight downhill run – so intermediate skiers are now encouraged to buy 'mid-length' skis. Compact skis are still the best bet for first-year skiers and are still available in rental shops, but are not normally found on sale.

The most important function of **bindings** is not to bind the boots to the skis but to separate them automatically when your legs are in danger. A good pair of modern bindings, carefully adjusted, will give you excellent protection from leg injury in most falls. But not in all falls: there are still some kinds of accident with which existing bindings do not deal safely – see 'Even safer skiing'.

The bindings will need adjusting to suit the length of your boot; this setting must be exactly right – too tight and the boot will be dangerously jammed, too far apart and the boot will wobble on the ski. There's another adjustment to cope with slight variations in the thickness of the boot's front and back flanges. Once the bindings have been adjusted to accommodate your boots, they must be set to release under appropriate forces. The mechanism and springs inside a binding are designed to 'sense' the forces on your leg while you're skiing and absorb any safe shocks that occur during a normal run – you shouldn't eject from the binding unless you really need to. If you fall, and a leg is subjected to twisting or pulling forces, the binding should let you out before there is any chance of injury.

It sounds simple enough, but it's not. Obviously, a frail skier could be injured by a fall which would not harm a stronger one; vigorous skiers will want to stay in their bindings in circumstances where timid skiers would welcome a release. The binding manufacturers have come up with elaborate charts which you can use to work out your 'ideal' setting taking into account the size of your boots, your skiing ability, your age, and either your weight or the thickness of your leg bones – a dimension which only a few shops are equipped to measure, but which is a much better guide than your weight.

When you come out of your bindings it's essential that your skis don't career off down the mountain on their own. They could do a lot of harm to anyone who got in the way, and the walk down the mountain wouldn't do you any good. The traditional precaution was to have safety straps linking your ankles to your heel bindings. But they're a real nuisance to put on and off, and mean that you stay in uncomfortably close touch with your skis when you have a fall. On modern bindings, the traditional straps have been replaced by brakes, which spring into action as soon as your boot is released. Usually, the ski comes to a halt further up the hill than you do. But brakes alone are inadequate when skiing in soft, deep snow, where a loose ski can nose-dive and prove extremely hard to find – or be lost altogether until spring.

It is possible to ski without them, but almost any skiing movement is more easily executed if you have **poles** to help you balance or to lean on. There's more about poles, and the other items of equipment, in the 'Getting equipped' chapter.

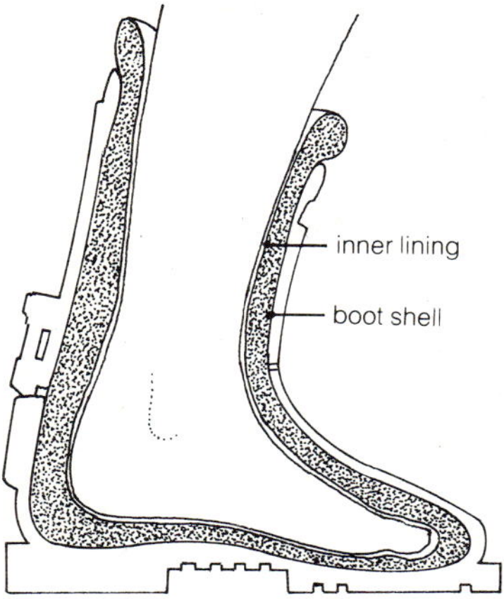

The **boot** helps you control and steer your skis by preventing sideways movement of your ankle joint. As you push your knee to the left or the right the ski tilts on to the same edge – a fundamental part of the techniques of turning and stopping. The boot also resists the forward and backward bending of your ankle. When you push your knee forwards or backwards, your shin or calf presses against the boot, and your weight is transmitted to the front or back part of the ski.

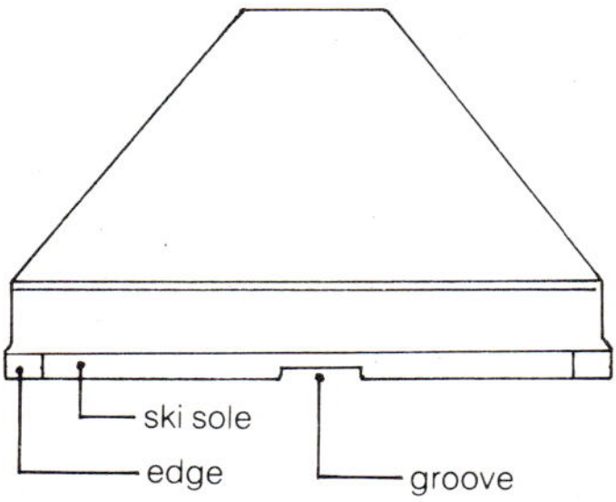

The **ski** has a core (often of wood or foam plastic) sandwiched between various layers of glass-fibre and other materials. The sole often has a groove along its length, meant to help straight running. To make the edges bite on really hard snow, they're made of steel, and are ground or filed to form a clean, sharp right-angle.

Most **bindings** hold your boots between separate toe and heel units which you step into (they're sometimes called 'step-in' bindings). Boots have projections front and back specially shaped to fit. Either unit can release your boot, according to the kind of tumble you take. In a forward fall the heel unit should open. In a twisting fall (which means most falls) the toe unit should open – particularly important because strains and breakages will otherwise result.

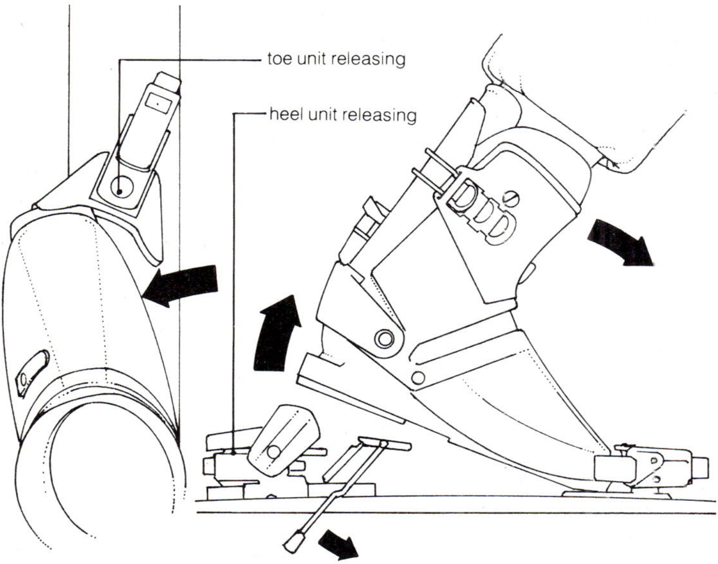

Clothes

Like most outdoor sporting activities, skiing is undoubtedly a more comfortable business when done in clothes designed to deal with the conditions, which can be savage but vary widely. You may be sitting motionless on a chair-lift for half an hour in temperatures ten or twenty degrees below freezing and in winds which make the effective temperature even lower (the wind-chill factor); you may be skiing energetically in strong sun and air temperatures ten degrees above freezing; you may get drenched in wet snow (either because it is falling or you are) or even (horror of horrors) rain. What sets skiing somewhat apart from otherwise comparable activities – sailing or mountaineering, say – is that the clothing industry it has spawned is in general much more concerned with fashion than with function. The result is that the unwary can easily spend a small fortune on ski clothes which look wonderful but which are not particularly effective.

Most people find specially made **trousers** well worth having. They provide much better insulation against the cold than normal trousers, and even if they're not really waterproof (which most are not), they won't get soaked by wet snow – and subsequently frozen solid – in the way that jeans do (for example). There are two main sorts of trousers – fairly loose-fitting, padded dungarees called salopettes, and tighter-fitting ski-pants (sometimes called racing pants) which may reach well above the waist and be supported by braces (just like salopettes) or may have an elasticated waistband.

Special skiing **jackets** are just as widely used, despite the fact that most of the ones sold at moderate prices do a mediocre job. They'll generally keep you warm in fine weather, and allow you to brush off snow as long as it's dryish. But few jackets offer more than token resistance to rain or wet snow, or deal particularly well with the sweat you produce when working hard, or have effective arrangements for sealing your wrists against snow. In other words, they offer little practical advantage over an ordinary anorak, worn over sweaters. Some people find a padded **waistcoat**, or 'gilet', a useful garment – if you are skiing in very cold weather a waistcoat can go on top of a jacket, while in hot weather you can simply wear it over a sweater; but since you're still going to need a jacket it has to be seen as an extra expense, and not one to which we would give a high priority. If you want to buy only one outer garment, but like the idea of a waistcoat, you can buy a jacket with sleeves which are attached by zip and are easily removed to produce a waistcoat.

Instead of a separate jacket and trousers, you can get a **one-piece suit**. There's nothing like it for keeping out the snow around your middle, but there are drawbacks: you can cope with differing weather conditions only by adding layers to it – you can't remove a layer, unless the suit actually consists of a jacket and trousers which zip together (and most do not). Even if the suit is of the zip-together variety, the top bit is unlikely to make much sense as a jacket on its own – so it won't be much use when you're not skiing.

There are all sorts of styles of ski clothing in the shops – and we give some guidance on choosing in the 'Getting equipped' chapter. One of the main things to consider is how you're going to keep your waist warm and dry despite repeated falls in the snow.

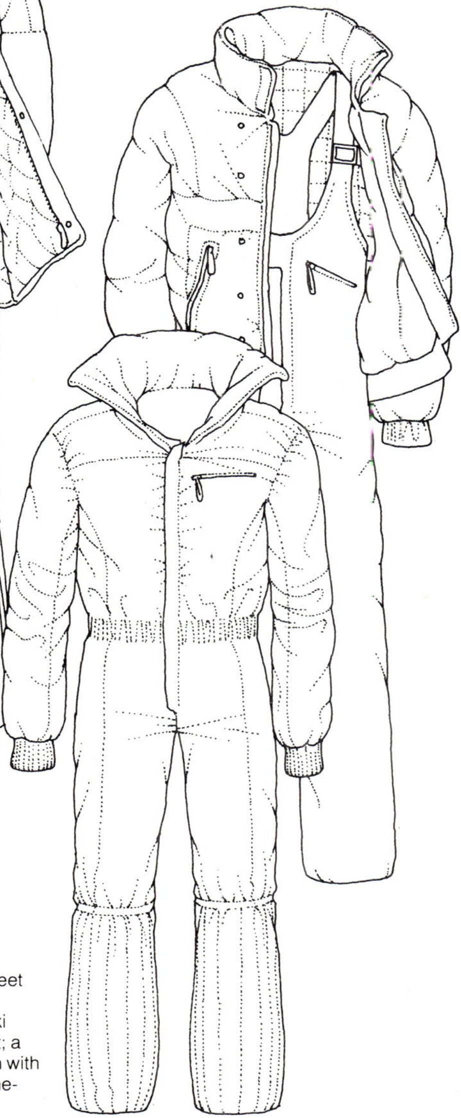

These are three outfits which meet the basic requirement – a long, anorak-style jacket worn with ski pants reaching only to the waist; a short, blouson-style jacket worn with chest-high salopettes; and a one-piece suit.

Ski clothes have traditionally made very full use of the spectrum of colours. These days they are by no means uniformly bright in colour – pastels and military drabs are just as popular. Followers of fashion must look elsewhere for guidance, but there are some practical considerations. The first is safety: the brighter the clothes you wear, the more easily you'll be seen by others. This can be important in all sorts of circumstances, but is particularly relevant if you have an accident or get caught in an avalanche. White is to be avoided absolutely – it makes you invisible against the snow. Secondly, bear in mind that if you have to wear the same clothes for two weeks (and many people do) they can get very dirty if they're a pale colour: lifts can be oily – and brightly dyed new leather gloves tend to stain everything they touch when they get wet.

In cold weather, all but the warmest jackets need supplementing by one or more **sweaters**. Ski shops sell smart, bright ones at very high prices, but (except for the very fashion conscious) any old sweater will do. A stock of several thinnish sweaters is more versatile than one or two very thick ones. And you'll need sweaters for the evening, too (again, how dressy and fashionable depends on the resort – and to a degree on the weather).

Opinions differ in the matter of **shirts**. The 'proper' equipment – except in hot weather late in the season – is a cotton polo-neck shirt, which will keep the chill wind from your neck. But many people ski in ordinary shirts; one advantage of this arrangement is that your tan is less likely to terminate abruptly just below the chin (though you can now get polos with a zip-up neck).

You can of course make adjustment to the thermal insulation of your outfit by installing **underclothes** under your clothes. There's no particular reason why you should, if your 'over' clothes are chosen carefully. But it certainly is true that a pair of trousers which are adequate in March may be not up to the challenge of January, when warm tights/long johns would be a sensible addition.

Racing aces, we are told, do without **socks**, which would impair the precise control they have to exert over their skis by introducing a spongy layer between the foot and the boot. Even for ordinary skiers the trend is towards having socks as thin as possible; very thick socks are neither necessary nor desirable in a modern boot. You can buy special ski socks, usually with a smooth outside and a fluffy inside, but any socks will do, as long as they reach above the top of the boot – otherwise you may find the top digging into your shins. You can get special thermal socks, meant to be warmer than ordinary ones. Using identical socks throughout the holiday will make it easier to get your boot adjustments consistently right.

On the other hand, special ski **gloves** or **mittens** are a luxury you can't do without. They are expensive, and easily lost, and they wear out; but they don't fall apart half as quickly as ordinary gloves, and they do a reasonable job in difficult circumstances of keeping your fingers warm – an important matter. Insulating inner gloves can be worn if you find one layer isn't enough. Mittens are warmer than gloves; but you're more likely to have to take them off to do up your jacket or get out your lift pass, which rather defeats the object. Leather lasts longer than plastic and is generally to be recommended; but it is not waterproof unless treated with some water-repelling agent (spray or goo).

You will need a **hat**. It's advisable to carry one with you even in good weather because the weather can change very quickly – and sitting on a long chair-lift, particularly late in the afternoon or in the shade, can be cold even on a sunny day. Ears can get very cold, so make sure your hat pulls down over them and keeps out the wind; alternatively, you can get special headbands which fit snugly over the ears. A **scarf** is useful to give protection to your neck or chin – which you're likely to need on a very cold day unless you have a jacket with a high collar which zips right to your nose (but don't wear a long, dangling scarf which could get caught on a ski-lift). A balaclava isn't a bad idea.

In most resorts you will need very little in the way of special **après-ski** clothes. Few hotels or night-clubs impose jacket-and-tie rules, and you're unlikely to feel out of place when dressed casually. A ski jacket will normally do for trips out in the evening – but if you take only one bear in mind that the exertions of the day may leave it damp and/or smelly. Most people wear special après-ski boots – often huge, highly insulated ones known (after one of the brand leaders) as Moonboots, or furry ones which give the impression that the occupant is being assaulted by two small dogs. In cold, dry conditions such boots are fine – they usually have soles which grip as well as can be expected on icy roads, and they'll keep your feet warm (though possibly sweaty, too). But not all such boots deal happily with water and slushy snow, for which there is nothing to beat wellingtons (provided they're big enough for thick socks).

Bits and pieces

Whenever you go skiing it's almost certain that you'll need some form of protection for your eyes. Cold air alone may make your eyes water when you're on the move, and glare from snow can be uncomfortably strong even when the sun's not out. When the weather's bad the wind and snow can be blinding unless you are able to retreat behind **goggles**, usually with yellow or pink lenses. There's a fair chance that you'll have trouble with goggles misting up on the inside – although there will be some ventilation of the space inside the goggles, it is necessarily limited. Misting is a lot less of a problem with goggles equipped with double-glazing – two lenses instead of one, with a small air gap between. Spectacle wearers have a particularly miserable time with goggles – keeping four surfaces free of snow and mist is a constant struggle. Contact lenses are worth buying for skiing even if you've no inclination to use them for anything else – provided you get a type which you can easily adapt to in a few days before each holiday.

You can get goggles with much darker lenses meant for skiing in sunshine, and many makes of goggles come with interchangeable lenses so that you can use the same basic pair in different conditions. But in good weather most people prefer to use **sunglasses** to cut out glare from the snow – particularly late in the season when it's sunny most of the time, and the glare off the snow is very strong. Run-of-the-mill sunglasses that you use at home can be used, but they may not be strong enough for snow glare. Make sure sunglasses fit tightly or are tied on with elastic or string – they're easily lost in a fall in fresh snow. If possible, always use plastic rather than glass lenses – in a fall you could not only cut your face badly but also severely damage the eye.

Any bits of skin which this assembly of paraphernalia leaves exposed will need protection from both the cold, dry air and the sun's rays. You'll need a **sun-screen** with a high protection factor, and **lip salve** to prevent your lips cracking.

If you keep to a minimum the bits and pieces you take with you on the mountain, you may be able to cram it all into your jacket pockets. But the stuff mounts up, particularly if you (very sensibly) travel prepared for any change in the weather; and jackets are all too rarely equipped with decent-sized pockets. The alternative is to use a small pack. **Bumbags** go round the waist, like a belt; they don't hold much and if you fall over a lot, or travel on chair-lifts, the contents are liable to get squashed, unless you wear the bag in front of you. **Back-packs** alleviate some of these problems; you can get special small ones for skiing. There are now some small bumbags on the market which convert into a back-pack when needed.

Rent or buy?

The major items of equipment and clothing don't have to be bought – they can be hired from a shop at home or in the resort, or through a tour operator – who will probably have a deal with a local shop.

Expert and frequent skiers invariably conclude that they're better off from most points of view owning their own **skis** and **boots** – even if snow conditions sometimes lead them to hire another pair of skis for one reason or another. For the absolute beginner, on the other hand, it's equally clear that buying is folly – and that renting at home doesn't make much sense either. When you're just starting, it's impossible for you to judge in the shop whether a boot is the right size and shape for your foot, so you're quite likely to have to change the boots you first accept; if you take to skiing quickly you may want to progress to more 'advanced' skis and boots; if on the other hand you don't take to it at all you'll want to cut your losses by handing in what you hired.

It's for the people in between – 'intermediate' skiers, particularly those who don't do much skiing in a year – that the decision to rent or buy is less straightforward. The first consideration for most people will be the **cost**. Whether buying or renting is cheaper depends on a number of things. If you managed to keep a single set of cheapish kit for ten years, and spent only a small amount each year on maintenance, the cost would be lower than that of renting in all but the very cheapest resorts – assuming you do a fortnight's skiing each year. But can you expect to keep it that long? You may come to believe that you've 'outgrown' your skis, or that your boots no longer give the support they once did (or the support the latest designs promise). You may be encouraged to trade up by the belief that your old gear has a second-hand value; no doubt it does, but it won't be much. If in the ten years you get through three pairs of boots and two pairs of skis instead of one, your average annual cost can climb to the point where it exceeds the cost of renting in all but the poshest resorts.

Many skiers buy their own equipment not because of cost but because of **convenience**. The shorter your skiing trips, the more this matters: with your own equipment there's no time wasted in ski shops when you could be skiing; no going back in search of boots you can live with. But carrying skis and boots does make travel more of a hassle.

The **quality** of what you get enters into the equation, too. In most major resorts you can expect to find a choice of shops offering well maintained, modern equipment. But you can't bank on that everywhere; in high season, the better equipment may run out and an unscrupulous hire shop may be tempted to retrieve old skis from the scrap-heap rather than start adding new ones to their hire stock. If there's a choice of shop, you can go elsewhere; but if you've pre-paid through your tour operator, or if you're in a tiny Italian village, there may be no choice. Buying your own equipment or hiring in the UK gets around these worries.

Good well-fitting boots are such a priority for an enjoyable ski holiday that many skiers buy a pair before they even think about buying skis. Buyers get a lot more attention in ski shops than renters and once you've found a comfortable pair of boots you can look forward to agony-free skiing for years to come. There are two ways to go about finding such boots: buy a pair that you've tried out by renting, or buy from a UK shop which offers a 'comfort guarantee'. If you rent boots in the resort, do not hesitate to change them if you experience cramp or pressure points in the first day or two; don't put up with pain in the hope that things will improve. If the shop is unsympathetic, or has run out of alternatives, call the deal off and go to another shop.

Pay particular attention to the condition of rented skis and bindings. The soles should be smooth and the edges should be reasonably sharp. It's very important to be sure that your binding adjustment has been carried out properly. See 'Getting equipped'.

You can also hire ski **jackets** and **trousers**. Once you're hooked on skiing holidays, the idea of renting clothes doesn't have much appeal. Your main problem is likely to be that of resisting the temptation to splash out on completely unnecessary additions to your skiing wardrobe every winter. But the first-timer who buys lots of special clothes risks wasting money. You may decide that once is enough, and your special clothes – designed to keep you warm in sub-zero temperatures – won't be much use in the warm, wet climate of home.

An alternative strategy for beginners is to concentrate on choosing a jacket for which you can envisage some use other than skiing, and a pair of trousers which are cheap. But the best thing to do is beg or borrow as much as you can from skiing friends. You (and they) may be surprised at how much cast-off ski clothing their wardrobes contain.

Learning

Every skier has to learn to ski; but you can approach learning in a variety of ways. For some holiday skiers, skiing and learning are one and the same – they check in to ski school year after year, and rarely go skiing except with an instructor. Other people regard learning as a process to be got out of the way so that they can then get on with actually skiing; others again regard it as yet another extra expense, to be cut out at the first opportunity. Neither extreme is to be recommended. Eternal pupils probably do less skiing than independent skiers, and may never learn to find their own way around the mountains. Skiers who go without instruction after year two, on the other hand, run the risk of finding that their skills never develop beyond the level necessary to ski good pistes in good conditions. Resolve, then, to steer a middle course.

Every ski resort worthy of the name – and certainly every resort covered by this *Guide* – has a ski-school. Traditionally, resorts have had just one – generally an 'official' school, administered by the resort authorities, and either affiliated to or actually a part of a national ski-teaching organisation. It's now increasingly common, particularly in French resorts, to find two schools. The second may be much like the first, or it may adopt some distinguishing attitude or practices – it may claim to make learning more fun, or may work with smaller class sizes, for example; or it may aim at visitors from abroad, calling itself International and providing instructors with appropriate languages. Choosing between two schools is not easy unless you can get some evidence locally about what actually goes on in each school.

Classes work on a weekly cycle, and usually last six days. In some places they're mornings only, in others both morning and afternoon. The general idea is that you join a class at the beginning of the week and stick with it. You turn up at the school meeting point at the appointed hour, and first of all get sifted into the right group. If you're a complete beginner, that may be all the school needs to know. If not, slotting you into the right class is trickier, and really requires a test. Some schools apply a test of aptitude (or perhaps attitude) even to complete beginners. With or without a test, mix-ups can occur – but if you're wrongly classified at first you can move later.

In a resort with a substantial British trade, you should be able to join a class consisting entirely of English-speaking pupils, and you can expect an instructor with a more than basic grasp of English. Of course, you may judge that your French/German/Italian is good enough for you to seek integration with the locals instead. In other resorts you may have no alternative, and if your grasp of the local language is not good this is very undesirable; even an instructor who can speak English will get bored with repeating everything, and you will miss the often useful observations made on other people's technique.

The basic idea of ski classes is that everyone in the class carries out the same exercises one after the other. Some things you do in turn, each person performing under the gaze of the instructor, witnessed in superior calm by those who have already done it and in increasing anxiety by those still to come. The obvious drawback is that the more people there are in the group, the less time you spend actually skiing (and, more importantly, getting feedback on your skiing). When everyone in the group has grasped the basics of a particular movement, the instructor will lead the whole group down the slope in a continuous snake; the idea is that the whole snake follows exactly the route and pace of the instructor, and learns to mimic him. In practice, it's usually only the one or two skiers immediately behind the instructor who get much out of this – so it's important that everyone takes turns at the front (although everyone in the snake benefits from the confidence of knowing that the terrain ahead holds no unseen terrors).

The class process as a whole suffers from the further disadvantage that the quick learners are held up by the slow, and the slow feel shown up by the quick. The instructor should be prepared to move people out of the class into other classes as the week progresses; if you think this is necessary (particularly if you think you're too good for your present class) be prepared to insist on a move – it may be in the instructor's financial interest to keep the class as big as possible. But classes do have two great attractions. They're cheap – the cost should not put anyone off. And they can be great fun – particularly if you're not skiing with a party of friends, your ski-class can become the focus of your holiday.

Individual lessons, with an instructor all to yourself or shared with one or two friends, are of course much more expensive. They are also more purposeful – not simply because the smaller group means less time spent watching others, but because you tend to sense the francs/schillings/lire clocking up if any time is wasted fooling around or stopping for a schnapps. But you can make real progress in an hour, particularly if you hit upon an interested instructor. Unfortunately, in some resorts your hour may have to be squeezed into the instructor's schedule before the morning classes (which from experience we wouldn't recommend) or during the lunch break.

You don't have to go to a proper school in order to learn to ski. If you have friends who are competent, patient and willing, you can get the benefit of personal tuition at zero cost; but unless you're very lucky, the tuition is unlikely to be of the first quality, and there is a risk that it may on the contrary be highly unreliable and misleading. There is the further possibility of buying instruction from an unofficial source. In many resorts there are good English-speaking skiers who tout around the resort for skiers dissatisfied with the ski school. Although they don't come free, these 'ski-bums' do cost quite a lot less than individual lessons with an official instructor; like friends, they may lack teaching skills, but at least most of them ski well enough to be worth mimicking, and you don't have to devote half your energy to preserving good relations as you may have to with a friend.

A great deal of effort is these days put into the business of standardising ski tuition – which means not only ensuring that instructors know how to ski and how to teach, but also that what is taught in one place is consistent with what is taught in another. Skiers who spend one holiday in Méribel and the next in St Anton should not now find, as they once did, that they are asked to do quite different things to achieve the same result. You will still find variations in emphasis, but these are as likely to be variations between individual instructors as they are to be the result of different regional or national philosophies of ski teaching.

The most fundamental departure from convention in ski teaching is the now well-established method of *ski évolutif*, known in the USA as the Graduated Length Method. It carries to extremes the widely accepted notion that beginners should not be encumbered with skis as long as those used by experts: you start on very short skis indeed, and having mastered them move on in stages to longer and longer ones. The French resort of Les Arcs is the home of *évolutif*, and the only place where it is (almost) universally employed – though it is available in some other French resorts and a few Swiss ones. We sent a researcher out to try it; on the facing page are some extracts from her diary. As you'll see, *évolutif* doesn't take the misery out of learning to ski; but if, like her, you end your first week starting to feel like a real skier, skiing long runs and experimenting with steep slopes and off-piste skiing, you're not doing badly.

Preparation

If you want to practise skiing before you get to the snow, you can do so on a number of artificial or **dry ski slopes** dotted around Britain. The slopes are covered with a mat of plastic bristles – some of them fairly fine, like a scrubbing brush, others much coarser and stiffer, like the teeth of a comb.

If you wanted to, you could learn enough on a dry slope to become a competent piste skier without ever seeing snow; and if you were to do so you would find most varieties of snow a good bit easier to ski on than plastic. But there's the rub: plastic isn't easy to ski on, and learning on it can be a demoralising business – not helped by the fact that falls which might be amusing on snow become distinctly painful. You run the risk that far from arriving in the Alps skilled and confident you'll arrive there convinced of your own incompetence – or with a thumb in plaster.

This is not to say that you should not try dry skiing – you should. Complete beginners generally find that a session or two with an instructor at a dry slope gives them a very valuable head start on their first skiing holiday. You become familiar with the boots and skis, and get used to standing and walking with them on; and if you persevere you can acquire the basic skiing skills. But don't be surprised if you don't enjoy it much; console yourself with thoughts of real snow.

One thing you can't expect to get out of a few hours' dry skiing is **fitness** for skiing – for that you have to do exercises. Skiers are very good at convincing themselves that they don't need to get fit before going skiing, and most people have very happy holidays without doing so. But there's no doubt (as we explain later) that getting fit pays dividends in a number of ways.

Ski évolutif: the diary of an evolving skier

Day 1

Struggle with unyielding boots, and then a few precarious slides down the nearest slope on our stunted, metre-long skis. It's quite easy to fall over backwards, because they stop just behind your heel. We assemble to be grouped into classes by making a trial run down a gentle slope towards a wall of instructors. We end up in five or six groups of about a dozen.

PM Our instructor, Jean-Paul, shows us the basic stance to adopt – skis and knees together, bent knees. First exercise – side-slipping; facing across a slope, keeping your skis together, slip down sideways and stop. Lots of uncontrollable sliding downwards and frantic digging of sticks into the snow.

Next, cautious wide turns, after JP demonstrates how to do it with exaggerated movements. In the middle of the turn you are meant to change your weight on to the outer ski, theoretically without the skis parting company. At first it is very difficult to keep the skis together and prevent the points colliding as you make the turn. As you lean into the turn it's easy to lean over too far and topple over sideways. We all do.

JP starts to add an elegant little jump at the end of the turn to bring the weight back equally on to each ski. We try to copy his neat jump; hopeless – we fall over continually. But never mind: if at first...

Day 2

Higher up the mountain for more side-slipping and turning practice. JP plants his sticks in the snow and skis off without them. We follow suit with flailing arms – and soon fall down as our legs begin to flail too. Convinced that sticks are vital for balance, we are now taught how to plant them properly as part of the turn, not as a last resort to avoid falling.

Day 3

Getting up isn't easy; we ease tender feet into lumpy boots and limp towards the slopes like weary commuters. Is this really a holiday? Going through the familiar turning routines we are now relatively steady on our skis; but JP takes us on to short turns, for which you need to have much tighter control. One by one we grotesquely imitate JP, looking as if we're trying to keep an invisible hula hoop in motion, and land one after another near his feet.

PM We change to longer skis (1.3 metres), and confidence wanes as we struggle to control them. We follow JP on longish runs and several people have difficulty keeping up. One girl sits down, removes her skis and starts to trudge down the hill until JP cajoles her into persevering.

Day 4

We explore new pistes, with breaks when JP makes each of us perform a series of turns for him to comment on. The pace quickens and JP expects us to follow him from the top to the bottom of long runs. When it goes well it's exhilarating – the better skiers jockey for a place at the front of the line and people dashingly cut across each other. But others are still rather nervous and cautious, anxious not to fall over and hold the rest of the class up – one man is demoted to the class below because he's doing just that.

Day 5

On to even longer skis – 1.6 metres This time the adjustment doesn't take so long. We just carry on skiing long runs, tackling different and steeper pistes and beginning to experiment with moguls. We feel like real skiers, at home on our skis – not able to go fast on steep and icy slopes, but at least able to try them.

Day 6

Heavy snow overnight. JP takes us through woods for some off-piste skiing, more for his own amusement than for our benefit. In the deep soft snow we fall over constantly, tumbling over snow drifts and each other. But at least it's fairly comfortable.

Day 7

Time to go home. Looking back, for the last three days of the course most of us had been skiing quite competently and enjoying it. Sometimes we could even reach the end of a piste without having fallen over once, and most of the aches and bruises of the first few days had worn off. It's been hard work – we rarely felt fit enough to go out in the evenings and certainly not to stay out late. But no one in our group gave up.

The risks

Skiing can be a hazardous sport: some of the people who do it get hurt, and some seriously. But the risks are often exaggerated – only a small percentage of those who go skiing suffer any injury at all, and (contrary to popular belief) few of them have broken legs. Improvements in release bindings and boots have reduced the number of broken lower legs and ankles very considerably (though not injuries to arms, knees and heads). See 'Even safer skiing'.

Most mishaps on the slopes are unlikely to prevent your getting back to the resort under your own steam. But of course skiers with broken limbs or other serious injuries are in need of **rescue**. If you're skiing on a recognised piste this shouldn't present too many problems. First, stick a pair of skis upright in the snow so as to form an X; this is a recognised sign to alert other skiers and routine safety patrols to the fact that someone is hurt. Patrols should cover all the pistes at the end of the day in any resort, and periodically during the day in a well-organised one. If a patrol happens along, they will be able to summon help by radio: otherwise, you'll need to get someone to go and make contact with the rescue service. In some resorts this will involve looking out for an SOS phone, which you're likely to find at the bottom of a major lift or run; in others, all the lift attendants are equipped with phones with which they can summon help. In due course the injured skier will be loaded into a stretcher-sledge (which British skiers with characteristic delicacy tend to call 'the blood wagon') and steered down to the resort or to a lift giving access to it. There will be a charge for such a rescue in some resorts, but it will not be large.

Most major resorts have a clinic or small hospital where fractures, sprains and other injuries can be diagnosed and treated. In smaller resorts you may have to be taken to a nearby town.

When skiing in Scotland, the UK's National Health Service will provide treatment, regardless of the fact that your injuries are self-inflicted. Abroad, you can often call on reciprocal medical care deals in which the UK is a partner. But, as *Holiday Which?* never tires of observing, the bureaucracy surrounding that system (even in its recently simplified form) is a big hurdle to have to get over – and most ski-resort clinics are in any case privately run, which means that reciprocal care deals are worthless. Also, medical attention isn't the only cost which can arise on a skiing trip. Some of the risks you run may be covered by a policy you have already taken out – loss of luggage, for example – but others are most unlikely to be covered. Your travel plans may have to be changed; you may break or lose your skis; and as we've said you may have to pay for a rescue. As a result, you need winter sports **insurance**.

Most tour operators have their own policies arranged direct with an insurance company. Many insist that you take out their policy (so making life easier from an administrative point of view – both in the office and in the resort when claims arise) and its cost is often included in the package holiday price. This means that if you don't like the policy, you have to buy another and effectively pay a second premium. All tour operators publish insurance details in the brochure but they are often rather scanty. The only way to find out what you're actually covered for is to ask for a copy of the actual policy before you book your holiday.

If your tour operator's policy is not compulsory or if you are not travelling with a tour operator, you can take out an independent policy through your travel agent, or through a source of insurance in general – an insurance company or a broker. There are a few specialist ski insurance policies, but most of those offered by travel agents are simply variants of regular holiday policies. These normally exclude winter sports but payment of a higher premium – usually double the normal one – gets you the extra cover.

When you have bought your insurance, keep the policy (or confirmation of booking) in a safe place and take it with you when you go on holiday. This can save time and complications should you, or one of your party, injure yourself. The procedure when a claim arises will vary with the circumstances.

How to go

When Henry Lunn hit on the idea of organising holidays to the Alps, in the last winter of the nineteenth century, he ran into the problem that his market was not too keen on the idea of packaged tourism. So he called his operation the Public Schools Alpine Sports Club, which proved immediately acceptable. The package tour has since come to dominate the British winter sports market, and although a few operators still style their wares to woo skiers who normally would not dream of taking organised holidays, most of them sell on price.

The arguments in favour of the package are compelling; for the great majority of skiers the package offers the same holiday you might arrange for yourself, at a significant saving of money, time, and worry. Most skiers are happy to stay in one place for the duration of their holiday, and don't really need their own transport. The number of highly recommendable resorts where you can't get a package is small. Going on a package doesn't mean you're confined to a single style of large characterless hotel, providing monotonous food: in most resorts packages cover most of the range of accommodation – from b&b to Ritzy, from places entirely taken over by UK tour operators to places mainly used by individual visitors. Tour operators will normally lay on organised activities during the holiday, but you're not obliged to take part in them. The resort representative can in theory give valuable help when things go wrong. And a growing number of tour operators are helping their clients to get the most out of their skiing by providing ski-guides to give conducted tours of the slopes.

Accommodation

When choosing skiing accommodation priorities are not exactly the same as for other holidays. The most important thing for many skiers is location; ski-boots are not made for walking, and a long walk morning and afternoon is a very unpleasant routine. Nearly all resorts produce street plans with hotels and apartment blocks marked on them, obtainable by post from the local tourist office if the national tourist office in the UK can't provide one. From these maps, even the crudest of them, it is usually possible to get an idea of how conveniently placed any hotel really is (very wiggly streets indicate a hill, straight ones are probably flat, and so on).

The **hotel** holiday, whether it be in a winter palace or a simple guest-house, is the norm in all but the most recently built resorts. Hotels in the Alps are not fundamentally different from hotels elsewhere. There are straightforward package hotels which, particularly in parts of Italy, may be best thought of mainly as a dormitory. There are a few exceptionally good places, and a great many pleasant, middle-of-the-road hotels. Austria and the Italian Dolomites deserve special mention in this respect, because of the great many modern hotels and guest-houses which have been built to high standards with traditional trimmings. Even the simplest places in these areas are generally reliable.

Board terms vary from full board to bed and breakfast. Half board (breakfast and an evening meal) is the usual arrangement, and suits most skiers best – particularly in resorts well equipped with mountain restaurants. Full board usually represents very good value (it's usually only about £15 to £25 a week more than half board), and in the right sort of resort it may not be too inconvenient. Most hotels will offer their full-board residents packed lunches, but these can be more trouble than they're worth. Bed and breakfast usually costs £20 to £50 a week less than half board for comparable accommodation; the attraction is not that you save money, but that you're free to eat in different places every night – more fun in some resorts than others. Some operators offer half- and full-board terms in the form of meal vouchers valid in specified mountain and resort restaurants.

Baths are a vital ingredient of a skiing holiday, and everyone wants to bath at the same time. Money spent on a room with private facilities, even if it adds significantly to the cost of a holiday (usually about £2 to £4, sometimes £5 a day), is money which few skiers will regret spending. A bath to yourself is one of the great advantages of the hotel holiday over most chalets and apartments – provided the hotel hot water supply is up to the demand.

In all Alpine resorts there are second homes (flats and chalets) which are let out for much of the winter season through an international letting agency (eg Interhome) or through local ones (information from local tourist offices). **Self-catering** packages are offered by British operators to a much more limited number of places, principally new French resorts where there are plenty of 'compact studios' (ie cramped flats) and very little other accommodation.

Saving money is one of the main attractions of the self-catering holiday – you can get a week in a top-rate resort for as little as £100, travel included. Local shops and supermarkets, especially in the high resorts which have the most self-catering accommodation, tend to be very expensive; but eating costs will still be modest by hotel/restaurant standards, especially if you self-cater as a group. If you drive out to ski, which doesn't exclude taking a package holiday, you can fill the car up with provisions to cut costs even further.

The other great attractions of a self-catering holiday are the privacy and freedom it offers. You can eat what you like, when it suits you and where it suits you; if your children are a nuisance they inconvenience only you; if you want to eat out on the town at night you can simply use the flat as a cheap dormitory; if you take with you no clothes other than ski clothes, no one need ever know. The drawbacks are obvious (you have to cater for yourself) but perhaps easily underestimated. After a day's skiing, not many people feel like trudging round the supermarket and then cooking and washing up. Less enthusiastic skiers and non-skiers may be quite happy to do this, and indeed there may be little else to occupy their time in many self-catering resorts.

It is very important to establish not only how conveniently situated an apartment is (in many new resorts the main problem is having to queue for the lift to and from the umpteenth floor), but also what its dimensions are. This information is usually easy to get hold of, and should be studied carefully; if 20 sounds quite a few square metres, take a moment to think it through. Do not assume if the flat is described as being for six that it would be extravagant not to fill it with six people. The additional cost per person of sharing such a flat between only four people will not be enormous – perhaps £20 or £40 per week – but in terms of enjoyment can make the difference between success or failure of the self-catering idea, and of the holiday as a whole. It can be the difference between friends and ex-friends.

Living space is in very many flats made to serve as sleeping space for (at least) two people. This means that two people have to get up first and go to bed last, and that anyone going to the bathroom may have to climb over them. Their privacy suffers and the living space inevitably does as well. If a hotel room is poky you can usually go and sit in the hotel bar or sitting room, and do no more than sleep in your bedroom. If a flat has inadequate living space you'll be driven out into the bars and restaurants of the resort, where you will spend money.

Stacking time for access to bathroom facilities, morning and evening, is very important; four is really the largest number of people who can happily share a ski holiday bathroom, and that is far from ideal. Think about how you'll want to lie and soak as soon as you get in from skiing. Think about how you'll want to be out on the slopes early in the morning, and how frustrated you may be if you have to wait for 20 minutes before you can shave; it often means the difference between strolling on to the cable-car and a half-hour scrum.

The packaged **chalet** holiday is a peculiarly British phenomenon: tour operators rent all or part of a house for the season, and staff it with British or colonial girls who clean up and cook and turn the chalet into a home. It all started as a swinging '60s London thing, combining the delights of metropolitan cocktail gatherings and country house-parties. Gals who were more used to being waited on than waiting boned up on Cordon Bleu cookery and dashed off to spend a winter or two in resorts such as Méribel, Verbier and Val d'Isère. To underline the excitement of the venture, the young socialites in charge decreed that no one should be allowed over the threshold under the age of consent or past the distant milestone of one score years and ten that defines the natural course of man's life.

Although there may still be a hint of social exclusiveness about chalet holidays, they reach a much wider public these days, and the girls are as likely to come from New Zealand as from Knightsbridge. The bosses themselves have found that there is life after thirty, and that the arrival of children does not preclude the possibility of enjoying the chalet formula. There is still a flexible rule that senior citizens and young children are not welcome except as part of a whole-chalet group. But there are now chalets which cater especially for families with young children. A real sign of the times is that Thomson and other mainstream operators are now offering chalet holidays.

The term 'chalet' indicates the style of holiday more precisely than the style of building. Though you are normally accommodated in small-scale buildings in traditional Alpine style, similar holidays are now offered in ordinary modern flats – in which case the inhabitants of several flats will be herded together under one roof for meals. Chalets are rarely to be found right in the centre of a resort, as a hotel might be, and many are on the outskirts. On the other hand, some are very well placed for skiing from and to the front door.

A big chalet will normally be marketed as several separate units – often on separate floors. These units normally take from 8 to 20 people, mostly in the upper end of that range. You can take over a whole unit and fill it with family or friends, and make yourself very much at home. Or you can go on your own or in small numbers and join other such people to fill the place – the operators claim to strive to make up compatible groups, though they are clearly not in a position to guarantee success. Chalet life pivots informally around the living/eating room, where you can relax, drink your duty-free Scotch and play cards or whatever. There's rarely more than one 'common' room, and so no prospect of escape from being sociable. This may involve tolerating invasions by the residents of other chalets or the friends of your chalet girls, as well as the inmates. You should not bank on retreating to your bedroom, which as often as not will be cramped and poorly furnished – and have paper-thin walls. Bathroom facilities, too, are often inadequate in one way or another – even if there are enough baths and showers, you'll be lucky to find constant hot water.

You are usually well fed, and heartily – from eggs and porridge at breakfast, through bread and jam (and cakes if you're lucky) at tea-time to a three-course dinner with wine included. The budgets on which the girls cook are not large, but most seem to manage to construct appetising meals in an anglicised bistro/trattoria style. Most people reckon the meals one of the plus-points of a chalet holiday.

Naturally a lot depends on the temperament and competence of the chalet girls. At best they can be extremely good cooks, very useful guides to the skiing and resort life, sympathetic to whatever style of holiday you want to adopt, and fun. Not all chalet girls are such paragons, and it's important to be alert to the possibility that some will consider their social lives more important than your holiday.

Some operators have developed the chalet idea into something rather different – the 'club' chalet. These are sizeable hotels or other holiday institutions run in chalet style – that is to say with English-speaking staff cooking and cleaning up. These jumbo chalets typically suit small groups, couples or individuals looking for a gregarious, sociable holiday, but really haven't got much to do with the original chalet idea. The large numbers of staff in these places usually keep themselves to themselves much more than chalet girls do. The accommodation – particularly the bedrooms – is often markedly better than that of the typical chalet.

Travel

Most people get to the Alps by **air**. The flight to Geneva, Milan, Munich or wherever generally takes only an hour or two, but is of course preceded by three or four hours' struggle at this end and is followed by anything up to eight hours on a coach winding its way into the Alps. Door to door, you rarely get much change out of a day – only if your flight leaves before dawn are you likely to get any skiing in on day one. The journey is not only long, but also fragmented – and the transitions from one stage to another are wearying, particularly if you're lugging skis and boots with you as well as a normal amount of holiday luggage.

Despite all the hassles, air travel is the most common means of transport from Britain to the Alps, and usually the quickest. If you live far from London (or, rather, far from Gatwick Airport) the availability of holidays from a convenient UK departure airport is bound to be a consideration when choosing a holiday – a number of tour operators use midland, northern and Scottish airports as well as London ones. You should also look carefully at the destination airport, especially when travelling to Italy, because operators don't always use the most convenient one. For Sauze d'Oulx and other Milky Way resorts, for example, some operators use Milan instead of Turin, which means a much longer transfer than is necessary.

If you are taking equipment with you, wrap it up well – a ski bag and boot bag are well worth investing in for protection and ease of carrying; don't wear your ski-boots (or après-ski boots unless you know your feet can take a Turkish bath). A few operators charge extra to carry skis, but most allow you a pair in addition to the usual baggage limit.

Travel by **coach** has only recently been offered on a large scale by operators. It has proved very popular, and it's not difficult to see why. For one thing it is very cheap – about £40 less than going by plane. For another, you get on the coach in London (or Birmingham or Manchester) and apart from the Channel crossing you don't have to move until you are in the resort; what's more, your luggage doesn't have to move from the coach at all. It takes longer than flying, but many people find it much less of a strain. Then there's the fact that the travelling is usually arranged so that you get one more day's skiing (7 days on the slopes for a week, 14 for a fortnight) than holiday-makers going by air. The disadvantages are that you have to put up with 24 hours on a coach, and that you may have to take all or part of Friday off work (especially if you're starting from the north). Most of the coaches used are reasonably comfortable for short people, and loos and videos are usually provided; but the arrangements (where there are any) for transforming the coaches into double-decker dormitories do not suit everyone.

Not so long ago air travel was reserved for the privileged few, and the Snowsports Special **train** from Victoria to Austria was the way everyone else went on their winter-sports packages. Now that flying is cheaper than going by train, few tour operators even offer rail travel as an option. But it has its attractions – it's more restful than flying, particularly if you're going to a resort which is on a main line (St Anton is the classical example). Many operators give their clients the option of driving out, and these arrangements can in most cases be tailored to include rail travel instead.

Getting to the Alps by **car** can work out cheaper than flying, and for self-caterers there is the added saving of being able to take cheap coffee and cans of beans. Naturally the economics of driving out depend on how full you fill your car; but they also depend on the extras involved in travelling out (motorway tolls, overnight stops, meals and drinks en route), and whether you count the cost of the essential service and preparation of the car for winter conditions, wear and tear from salty Alpine roads (not to mention wear and tear from encounters with post buses and snowploughs), snow chains, ski racks, breakdown insurance for the car, and a Green Card to extend your ordinary insurance for Continental use. It's far too simple to take the cost of a ferry and the cost of petrol over 650 miles and think that driving looks a cheap way to go.

But there are non-economic advantages too – principally that if you have a car you broaden the possibilities of a ski holiday enormously. You can meander out and back and enjoy the pleasures of travelling through France or Germany; a night in Paris perhaps, or an afternoon's wine-tasting in Burgundy. If your accommodation isn't ideally placed in the resort, you can be free of the overcrowded bus service and save leg-work. You can take off for some sightseeing or shopping in the local town, to ski in another resort, or to have a evening out in different surroundings. There's no doubt that taking a car is also the most convenient, least exhausting way of getting your luggage to the resort.

The disadvantages are basically the effort and the worry. Driving can be very tiring, slow and difficult, in April as well as January. Anything going wrong with the car is very time-consuming even if you're insured to the hilt. And there's no denying that driving on snow is hazardous and tricky – though there are plenty of resorts where snow on the access roads is the exception rather than the rule. In general front-wheel drive is better than rear, except in cars (old VW, Porsche) with the engine weight over the driving rear wheels. A major part of our 'Travel facts' chapter is devoted to information for motorists.

The skiing phenomenon

Skiing is a leisure phenomenon without equal – a huge, many-sided industry based, apparently, on a simple passion for sliding down snow-covered slopes on long, elaborately constructed plastic planks. Apparently; in reality the sliding downhill, exhilarating though it can be, is only a part of the appeal of a skiing holiday – and often a smaller part than many skiers will readily admit.

Whatever it is that sells skiing holidays, their sales are huge and so is their impact. In Europe alone, millions make an annual two-week pilgrimage to the Alps. In their name, forests are felled, mountainsides reshaped and draped with machinery to provide easy and efficient skiing; where skiable terrain exists but villages do not, resorts are created from nothing; restaurants are built in impossible positions, so that the creature comforts we're used to on holidays by the sea can also be enjoyed two vertical miles above it; come winter, shepherds and students are transformed into uniformed armies of ski-school *maestri* and *moniteurs*, of fabulous seductive power; come snow, fleets of snow-cats work through the night on the ski-runs to smooth the path of the morning's skiers.

Of course, it was not always so. Although skis have been used for thousands of years as a practical means of travel over snow-bound country, it's only in the past hundred years that skiing has become an end in itself; only in the last fifty that it has become a holiday activity for the British and other lowlanders; and only in the last thirty years that skiing has developed into a multi-billion-pound industry.

As skiing has changed, so have ski resorts – which makes it essential for any would-be connoisseur of resorts to have an appreciation of the evolution of the sport. That evolution is charted here by *Mark Heller*, who in 60 years of skiing has witnessed a good many of the most important developments, and in 40 years of writing has been able to reflect on all of them.

The origins of skiing

The late 1920s and early 1930s have often been called the 'Golden Years' of skiing. Golden they were for the few bright, gifted young British who dominated the sport in their exclusive hideouts of Wengen, Mürren and Villars. They brought to an obscure and exotic activity the gay abandon of the playing fields and often a monumental insensitivity towards the bewildered mountain farmers over whose pastures they flung themselves with unbounded daring. They defied all who opposed them; as far as they were concerned, they were the only skiers in the world and the only skiing worthy of the name was downhill racing.

In fact, they were only the highly visible public blooming of an activity which, as far as anyone can determine, has its roots in the ending of the

Würm Ice Age some ten thousand years ago. Who invented skis, and when, will probably never be known. The earliest hard evidence is the prehistoric ski remains found in Scandinavia, reliably dated at around 2500 BC, by which time skis had evolved into all three possible forms – two long, two short, or one long and one short. In AD 700 the Chinese described them in detail and called them 'Wooden Horses' (MuMa), a fact that thoroughly confused the scholars of the Middle Ages and later.

Although the legends of Scandinavia are full of skiing deeds, skiing raised no wider interest until the great labour migrations from Scandinavia to North America and Australia in the early and middle 19th century. In California they staged some heroic speed skiing races and John A. Thomson (born Jon Thorsteinson Rue) carried the mail over the Sierras from Placerville to Carson Valley – about 145 km – for many years, from 1856. A Norwegian introduced skiing to the gold-mining community in the Snowy Mountains in Australia and in 1861 formed the first ski club in the world, the Kiandra Club. In 1868, Konrad Wild tried to imitate Norwegian friends by skiing in Mitlödi in Switzerland. But none of these isolated incidents did more than cause local surprise and amusement.

But at about this time, in Norway, an unknown, semi-literate cottager from Morgedal called Sondre Norheim instinctively redesigned the traditional ski. He gave it a waist, reduced the length and invented a binding that held the foot on to the ski. As a result, skis became fully manoeuvrable for the first time, with the help of techniques we would now call the Telemark turn and the Christie stop. Norheim dominated the local ski scene; in 1868 he competed in Oslo in the annual gentlemen's ski competition (now the Holmenkollen championships) and won everything.

The birth of Alpine skiing

The next haphazard step was the Great Exhibition in Paris in 1889. Here an unknown Finnish exhibitor showed and sold skis. How many pairs were sold is unknown, but among the buyers were a number of Germans from the Black Forest and two visitors from the Swiss mountain resort of Davos: a Dr Paulcke (a German physician working there) and a young apprentice called Branger who bought two pairs – one for himself and one for his brother and sister to share.

The instruction leaflet was primitive and incomprehensible – it was, of course, written in Finnish. Dr Paulcke employed a Norwegian valet who was expected to teach his master how to ski. But Paulcke's presumption that all Norwegians are born skiers proved incorrect, and the skis were thrown into the attic where they were eventually discovered by his son, subsequently to become one of the the great Alpine ski pioneers.

The Brangers, however, realised that their skis would be a lot better for sliding downhill than the beer barrel staves they were accustomed to using, and set about teaching themselves secretly, at night, how to turn and stop. The Brangers became the ski pioneers of Davos and in 1894 achieved fame by taking Conan Doyle over the pass to Arosa.

The Black Forest skiers were even more influential. An eccentric poet, failed artist and visionary, one Mathias Zdarsky, discovered skis there (and later again on the Semmering hills outside Vienna) and by the turn of the century had opened the first real ski school in the world on his derelict farm property in Lilienfeld near Vienna. He invented the modern stem turn, devised means of skiing steep Alpine ground and laid the foundations for Alpine skiing as we know it today.

It's in the early years of this century that, with hindsight, we can now see the outline of a burgeoning new industry. At first, skiing was still very much a novelty, pursued by eccentrics. But before long it began to take root in the first generation of ski resorts. They were all well-established summer resorts – which meant they had plenty of accommodation, and were easily reached by railway; and they all had easy undulating terrain nearby on the high summer grazing meadows – slopes the skiers could handle with their crude techniques. Several of these resorts had built up a thriving winter tourist trade before the advent of skiing; some of these adapted to the new sport much more readily than others.

Davos was already patronised by several hundred tuberculosis sufferers and a further thousand or so relatives and friends. There was skating and lugeing, and there quickly grew up a very active skiing fraternity. With the primitive guidance of the brothers Branger and friends, British and Dutch visitors (and a few Germans and Argentinians) explored much of the terrain around Davos that is skied today, including the famous Parsenn run to Küblis (accidentally discovered by two English skiers looking for the pass to Arosa – a little error of 180 compass degrees). In the Bernese Oberland, skiing became accepted in Wengen and Mürren, and Vivian Caulfeild's teaching and writing enjoyed a wide following. Elsewhere in Switzerland, the Ski Club of Lucerne boasted ski lessons under Norwegian tutors.

In Austria, skiing was taking hold of visitors to Kitzbühel, and a ski school was established under Colonel Bilgeri at St Christoph, above St Anton. In Italy, Adolfo Kind set up a school at Sauze d'Oulx. Meanwhile, Duhamel fought a losing battle to establish a school at Grenoble, on the fringes of the French Alps.

By 1921 there was no skiable Alp – no pass, no summit which today is equipped with lifts and is skied by thousands daily – which did not carry ski tracks. But the higher tracks were predominantly those of mountaineers of one sort or another. The visitors to the comfortable resorts still found they did not need to go beyond the gentle slopes of the upper grazing meadows to find sport which was more than sufficiently strenuous and sometimes dangerous.

The Golden Years

During the twenties, skiing tightened its grip on the first-generation resorts. The trio of resorts below the Jungfrau became British enclaves which the Swiss claimed they needed a passport to enter. In Wengen, the skiers persuaded the Jungfrau railway to run up from both Wengen and Grindelwald as far as Kleine Scheidegg, the col between the two villages, and thus created the concept of 'downhill only' skiing. The idea of downhill racing was only a small step further, and a great rivalry developed between Wengen's Downhill Only Club and the Kandahar Club across the valley in Mürren. Meanwhile, over the hill in Grindelwald, the Eagle Club took a different direction, concentrating on skiing the remote passes and glaciers. In Austria, St Anton combined social smartness with improving technique: the Schneider brothers – pupils of Bilgeri – perfected the stem christie turn and crouch, and thus opened up the really steep slopes to continuous, controlled ski-turning.

The British upper crust travelled out to their chosen spots under the auspices of Thomas Cook, Sir Henry Lunn and the Ski Club of Great Britain. They went for three weeks or a month at least, and many for the whole season from December to March. Resorts published weekly guest lists which were eagerly scanned for news of friends, rivals and the grand folk. There was a distinct pecking order of hotels and, within those hotels, of the styles of accommodation; bathrooms were a rarity, and even running water something to be advertised. There were fancy-dress evenings and gala evenings, and luggage was swollen by the extra clothes which these essential events demanded. There were excursions by horse-drawn sleigh, barbecues, ice-rink jollities and the daily fashion parade up and down the village main street for those – still in the majority – who were bent on a mixture of 'winter sports' rather than skiing.

The growing enthusiasm for the new sport was by no means confined to the British, or to the famous resorts which they dominated. At weekends in the 1920s the skiers of Switzerland, Austria and Germany began to cram the railway stations and bus depots on their way to invade sleepy mountain villages surrounded by 'good skiing ground' – the gentle pasture which skiers sought out. Almost overnight these villages, unknown to tourists and rarely visited by outsiders other than farmers or commercial travellers, found themselves catering for the strange needs of the even stranger skiers – and found, too, a welcome and unsuspected new source of income. These were the villages which before long were to develop into Europe's second generation of ski resorts.

For the skiers whose ambitions went beyond the railways and funiculars of the established resorts (or whose purses would not stretch that far), the day was long and tiring. They left early in the morning; carrying their lunch (packed by the hotel according to an invariable formula) in uncomfortable rucksacks alongside the necessary skiing paraphernalia – sealskins, ski wax, spare gloves, sweaters, bits of string and wire for emergency repairs. After a climb of three, four or even five hours, the food would be consumed on some freezing col or in the shelter of a rock or tree, before the downhill run was started – not without some trepidation.

A run which is today completed by a first-year skier in a matter of minutes could be long, tiring and testing when tackled with the primitive equipment and techniques of the day. It could be wildly exciting and exhilarating – swoop after swoop of unblemished snow, schuss after schuss; or bitterly frustrating, on crusty snow or on the last run of the day, down steep narrow passages until the final, painful, icy woodland path brought into sight the still-distant village, half-hidden in the misty valley, the lights just beginning to show.

The romantic sight of the village – and the prospect it offered of thawing out frozen toes in welcoming hostelries – erased any doubts about the wisdom of having made the climb in the first place. The exertions of the day gave a special tang to 'five o'clock tea' – hot, fuggy rooms crammed with damp skiers, flush-faced and clumpen-booted, shouting, laughing, singing, dancing to a rustic three-piece band, supping hot chocolate or *Glühwein* and devouring cream cakes, united in adventures shared.

Skiing for everyone

With the close of the 1920s, Davos enters the story again. In 1931, the first funicular designed specially for skiers was built there; it went from the town to the Parsenn Weissfluhjoch, thus opening up the huge snowfields of the Parsenn to anyone who cared to take the ride. But the real revolution was still to come. The Parsenn railway, like those of Wengen, Grindelwald, Mürren and Villars, was fine for the experienced skier; but the novice still faced weeks, possibly years of drudgery, plodding repeatedly up the nursery slopes in order to acquire the skills necessary to tackle the longer Alpine runs.

Erich Konstam, an engineer from Zurich, calculated that in every hour on the slopes the average pupil spent only six minutes sliding downhill, and set about devising something to improve matters. What he came up with was the T-bar drag-lift; the first one in the world was opened for business on the Bolgen nursery slopes in Davos on the last day of 1934. The T-bar took half a minute to haul skiers up slopes that had previously taken twenty minutes to climb. Other resorts were not slow to see the potential of ski-lifts, and before long they were being installed not only on the nursery slopes but also on the treeless higher slopes: the peaks and passes that had once been the reward of half a day's climbing could now be skied five times in a morning. What's more, uphill transport now became affordable for villages which would not have dreamt of building a mountain railway.

The stage was thus set for an explosive increase in the number of people skiing, in particular of people learning to ski. Major Ingham and Erna Low started running skiing parties to Austria from Britain, signalling the beginning of the end of the socially exclusive nature of British skiing. It was a very small beginning, to be sure – skiing still required an affluence which was narrowly distributed in those days. But the hills heard the unfamiliar accents of the Midlands and the North; and the Ski Club of Great Britain shuddered.

The expansion of skiing was interrupted, to say the least, by the annexation of Austria and the World War which followed not long afterwards. But the War in its way gave the industry new impetus. In Switzerland, virtually isolated by the hostilities, skiing became much more popular as a result of a campaign to conserve fuel by encouraging outdoor sports; the slogan was *Ein ganzes Volk fahrt Ski* – 'A whole nation skis'. The impact on Austria was quite different but more profound. Under the Marshall plan, designed to finance the reconstruction of Europe's devastated industries, Austria chose to refurbish and develop its tourist villages. Before the War, places such as Söll, Sölden and Saalbach had responded slowly to the demands of skiers, despite their evidently plentiful supply of 'good skiing country'. The post-War plan was to install ski-lifts and build hotels, and to set about capturing the European ski market. The butcher, the baker and the farmer's boy could ski, and were prepared to teach others how to. And when they weren't skiing they would turn their hand to devising après-ski amusements to match anything seen in the grander resorts before the War.

In Britain Thomas Cook, Lunn, Ingham, Erna Low, Clarkson and others stood ready to package these wares and sell them to an entirely new generation and (more importantly) new class of skier – the ordinary inhabitants of Britain, liberated from the confines of a summer week in Blackpool or Margate, and no longer afraid of foreign places. Not surprisingly, the established skiing fraternity didn't go along with any of this, but returned to its traditional haunts and travelled to them by traditional means. The idea grew that the ski-fields of Austria – which certainly were in the main lower and less extensive than those of Switzerland – were also easier, and less worthy of the real skier's attention. This mattered not at all to the new generation, who wholeheartedly took to the uninhibited hospitality of the Austrian villages and have never looked back.

Against this background, France stepped in with the next and probably final revolution in skiing habits and skiing ambience. There had been very little skiing development before World War II – Megève was the principal exception – and the French Alps were thus a clean canvas awaiting bold strokes. Under the patronage of President de Gaulle and the uncompromising dictatorship of Engineer Michaud, an old dream became reality. On ski-fields of an immensity hard to envisage, M Michaud constructed Courchevel and the incomparable 'Three Valleys' ski-drome. It was closely followed by La Plagne, Val d'Isère, Les Deux Alpes, L'Alpe d'Huez, Les Arcs and a dozen more 'green-field' ski sites. This was the birth of the third generation of ski centres, where the 'village' was no more than a service station for skiers. There were few hotels but many apartments (a neat financial twist to make the owners finance their own ski resort) and the lifts left from the apartment door. Après-ski, a term originally coined by the French fashion press to sell a new kind of leisure wear, died – the skiers retired to their self-catering apartments and only resort staff crowded the ridiculously expensive discos and bars. Covered arcades replaced village streets, boutiques took the place of the village shop and the ambience was uniform and grey. But the skiing, around which everything was planned, was magnificent. The runs were laid out where no skiers had been before, their surface engineered and graded, difficulties categorised and designed for every level of performance, nursery areas carefully segregated from the hurly burly of piste life. These new resorts presented the old ski villages with a dangerous challenge which, on pure skiing terms, they were quite unable to meet then and which all but a few are still unable to meet now.

Developments elsewhere

The story of Alpine skiing is seen unfolding most clearly in Switzerland, Austria and France, but it is of course not confined to those countries. What of the Italians, who absorb a good proportion of Britain's skiers each year? Before World War II they had, from time to time, made some heroic appearances on the scene, but to no great effect. In 1934 the Agnelli family, the Fiat founders, had built the world's first 'green-field' resort, a futuristic little village near Turin called Sestriere. There were two daring cable-cars and, on paper, the skiing was magnificent. For reasons defying logic, it failed totally to capture the ski world's imagination. Cervinia, then still called Breuil, was developed in order to fulfil Mussolini's dream of building the highest, longest cable-car in the world. Three links from the newly-built village to the 11,000-foot col, called variously the Theodul Pass or Plateau Rosa or Testa Grigia, were completed with surprising speed by 1939 and linked Cervinia with Zermatt. Zermatt was not amused and, war intervening, the cable-car was not publicly opened until 1946.

Cervinia was created for the Italians, in particular for the weekend entertainment of the inhabitants of Turin and Milan – and so have been most Italian ski resorts. In the years after World War II, all along the Italian face of the Alps, resorts sprang up and flourished at weekends while on weekdays they were deserted except for the bored Italian grass (snow?) widows and their offspring, banished to these massive apartment blocks and residential grand hotels until their husbands returned for their Friday to Monday weekends. But some resorts – notably Sauze d'Oulx – played unashamedly to the British tour operator market. At the other end of the Alps, the resorts of the Dolomites were and are conveniently placed for invasion by car-borne Germans – and linguistically suited to receiving them, having been part of Austria until 1919. In a bold move to underline their appeal, a mass of Dolomite resorts combined to form what was in 1970 and remains today the largest single lift-pass area in the world, the Super-Dolomiti. This was a considerable achievement: Italian resorts have traditionally suffered from having several distinct lift companies, each requiring the skier to hold a separate pass.

Spanish skiing resorts, on the other hand, were a pure exercise in speculative development. Apart from La Molina there was no serious ski development (not least because of the uncertain snow cover and very moody weather) until the massive financial investment in the Spanish coastal areas began to show healthy profits. Parallel investment was then available for the grudging development of such subsequently popular resorts as Formigal. Today there are about thirty ski centres, ranging from the tiny two-lift one-hotel Picos de Europa ski 'region' to the super-smart Baqueira on the French frontier.

Both Italy and Spain, though suffering from poor ski planning and even poorer trail maintenance and haphazard ski instruction, have profited greatly from a weak currency and comparatively cheap ski holiday prices. Andorra, a tiny independent state on the Spanish side of the Pyrenees has also made low prices a sure part of its appeal by managing to levy no taxes – and Soldeu in particular has benefitted by encouraging British instructors to operate there.

Surprisingly, perhaps, the vast mountain territories of North America contributed little to the early Alpine ski development except for one technical innovation that has swept all ski countries – the chair-lift. It was invented in 1936 at Sun Valley in Idaho. Here the Union Pacific company created a ski resort, based by Hollywood architects on second-hand accounts of Austrian villages. It became the model for all succeeding North American ski centres when, after World War II, serious attempts were made to propagate the European ski success story. The problems were very different from those of the Alps. Not only were distances immeasurably greater, but also there were no convenient farming villages upon which the ski resort could be grafted. The emerging pattern has remained unchanged. A 'mountain' was leased from State or Federal Forestry Agencies, permits were obtained to clear trees to make ski trails and planning permission obtained to construct a base service area which might or might not include residential facilities. The mountain and the 'village' or real estate are mostly separate financial entities. On account of the very much higher tree-line of the West Coast's Rocky Mountain areas (where the bulk of the development has taken place), the runs are down very wide clearings and, with the very special consistency of West Coast snow, the skiing surface is a revelation to the European skier. And so, for that matter are the discipline, lift queuing (if any), piste preparation, marking and maintenance and the friendly, polite ambience. Whether by accident or design, American ski centres seem to have taken note of all the errors and unpleasantnesses to be found in Europe and eradicated them. The result may well be, to our eyes, almost synthetic, but there is no denying that the experience, even allowing for the relatively short runs and high altitude, is a revelation and dangerously addictive. Regrettably, there is little or nothing that can be imported to the Alps without simultaneously requiring quite unattainable alterations in law, custom and circumstances.

There has, however, been one North American development which, inevitably, will find its way into the Alps. A few years ago, a skier sued a ski resort for massive damages for injury sustained while skiing one of its trails. He claimed that the trail was ill-prepared and not in accordance with the publicly advertised snow conditions. He won. Now all American ski resorts have had to carry massive third-party insurance against future similar claims while, at the same time, spending further millions on extra special 'snow farming' (rolling, grooming, mogul bashing and covering with man-made snow).

The strangest recent development in both the Alpine countries and in North America is the re-emergence of cross-country skiing as a major recreation, paralleling the spread of fitness cults. It is the latest headache to irk the resorts. Quite apart from the cost of planning, preparing, maintaining and marking the special trails (for which payment can not easily be extracted from the skier), they are now faced with such strange problems as the control of dogs fouling the tracks, the rescue of overweight incompetent participants who collapse far from base, and the organisation of a complete teaching service for a recreation which, in theory, is supposed to be a simple, individual, back-to-nature occupation.

Visitors to Norway are very soon put to rights about the how and why and where of this earliest, simplest, most athletic and most enjoyable form of skiing. Despite the growth of 'slalom skiing' in Scandinavia, only two Norwegian resorts offer much in the way of downhill runs – Geilo and Voss. The other hundred or more tiny, well-appointed mountain hotels are still faithful to the old traditions; the guests depart after an ample serve-yourself breakfast to ski the hundreds of miles of marked routes that take them through wondrous forests or out on to the highlands where horizon and sky meet seemingly at the end of the world. The evenings are restful and quiet and 'old-fashioned', with talk of trails travelled, animals seen and tomorrow's expedition. Once you have experienced the freedom of the true, ancient ski sport, the boredom of plodding along machine-prepared tracks up and down a valley becomes unacceptable.

Two other ski areas deserve a little more than a passing reference. Scotland, the only practical venue for skiing in the British Isles, has in its own and not always quiet way paralleled the British interest in skiing in the Alps. The detailed history is convoluted, fraught with local and national politics and prejudices and a continuing, unwinnable fight against weather and poor snow cover. Three principal areas have survived (and new ones are being planned) since the earliest skiing efforts in Scotland in 1892. Glencoe was the private dream and development of Philip Rankin who, despite every obstacle deliberately put in his way, produced what many consider the best skiing venue in Scotland – even if access is not easy and the lift system discontinuous. Aviemore in the Cairngorms is a serious, all-season holiday centre which is today the nearest in scope and facilities to a serious, although minor, Alpine ski resort (a comparison they deeply resent!). Glenshee, largely the work of enthusiasts from Dundee, is a friendly club-orientated ski area of considerable potential but suffering from inadequate accommodation. But just as important as the problems of weather and distance from metropolitan England is the fundamental and inescapable fact that Aviemore and Glenshee and Lecht and Glencoe are not the Alps; and, silly as it may be, skiers prefer their thirst to be quenched by *Glühwein* in a *Stube* rather than tea in a cafeteria.

Skiing in Eastern Europe also suffers from a comparable psychological disadvantage. In Poland, Czechoslovakia, Romania, Bulgaria and Yugoslavia they too have known skiing for as long as have the Alps and, by 1939, there was every sign that it was to become a major tourist attraction. But, unfair as it may seem, it would appear that Alpine skiing is not considered a 'serious' occupation in Eastern Europe and the sport still carries with it overtones of an anti-social, suspect activity.

On the other hand, for anyone willing to accept slightly haphazard ski organisation and a lengthy journey, the enthusiasm, friendliness and cheapness to be found in Eastern Europe may be worth the possible disadvantages of slightly limited ski terrain, often primitive uplift and (in Zakopane, for example) inordinate waiting time for the quite inadequate capacity of the cable-car. It still remains to be seen how far the very successful Olympic games in Sarajevo in 1984 will produce a renewed interest in skiing in any of the more than 40 ski centres that are available.

Looking forward

A mere 80 years since modern skiing first tentatively made its appearance in Switzerland, there are now more than 3,000 ski resorts catering for a world-wide market of more than 30 million skiers. They may not all be skiing at the same time, but the ski area open to them is finite and the crowding is becoming such that the future must inevitably look somewhat bleak. There is little more that can be invented or developed that will extend the available ski-fields, or reduce the queues and the collisions on pistes which now accommodate ten times the number of skiers they were designed for, skiing twice as fast.

In many ways the skiing circle has almost closed. Once again the downhill skiers are discovering the pleasures of the slow climb, the deserved rest on a sun-dazzled summit and the savoured, well-earned run home. Soon the new converts to cross-country skiing will be demanding the untamed trails of Norway. If there is a fourth generation of resorts to come, perhaps it will be the composite ideal – the Austrian hamlet with ski-fields like those in Aspen or Vail, a lift system of French thoroughness, and the après-ski life of the Oberland of the late 1920s. An impossible dream? Probably. But then so was Alpine skiing to Mathias Zdarsky, and look where that dream led to.

Competitive edge

Ski racing champions in Austria and Switzerland are gods. Even in Britain, millions of non-skiers spend their Sunday afternoons watching ski races from the Alps. A few of them are armchair experts, well versed in the intricacies of pre-jumps, tucks and compressions, but most are simply revelling in the brilliant spectacle of the mountains in winter and of athletes competing at considerable risk to limb, and even to life. The results rarely give cause for national celebration: like the history of so many sports, the story of Alpine ski racing is one of Great British invention (in this case in the early 1920s) followed by consistently greater foreign achievement in performance. But, considering that we are a predominantly snowless and non-mountainous nation, this is hardly a matter for despondency: after all, the Swiss and Austrians don't turn out champion yachtsmen. And in recent years two outstanding British skiers have given *Ski Sunday* fans something to cheer by proving that they can compete on equal terms with the best racers from the Alpine countries and North America in the most exciting of the Alpine disciplines, the downhill. In this chapter we have brought them together to illuminate the ski racing scene.

Konrad Bartelski, now retired from racing but still very active in promoting the sport in Britain, earned the respect of the skiing world and a place among the top seeds when he took second place in a World Cup race in 1981. As in earlier editions of the *Guide*, he explains the differences between the Alpine disciplines and how the world of ski racing works.

Martin Bell is Bartelski's successor as the torch-bearer of British skiing – with great things expected of him in the wake of his splendid eighth place in the 1988 Olympics at Calgary. He gives us his own analysis of what it takes to ski and win, and talks us down the world's most exciting downhill courses.

Bartelski: the background

Ski racing has come a long way since the days when racers set off all at once (the expressively named geschmozzle start) in a first-past-the-post race with no prescribed course, and plenty of spills for winners as well as the also-rans. For obvious reasons of safety, the old horse-race soon gave way to the lesser excitement and greater precision of individuals competing against the clock down a narrowly defined course – planned within internationally agreed guidelines, landscaped for variety, groomed for safety and, yes, watered for speed. The three main alpine races are downhill, slalom and giant slalom. In all of them, skiers compete one by one down a set course, and the man or woman with the fastest time wins. The different disciplines use different kinds of course, which test different qualities in the racer.

The longest, straightest and fastest race is the **downhill**. Men's courses are set on hills giving a vertical drop of between 800m and 1000m, women's between 500m and 700m. The course length is two to three miles for men, up to two miles for women. Racers take about less than two minutes on the course, which means average speeds of 50 to 60 miles an hour for women, and 65 to 70 miles per hour for men. Skiers are allowed a series of practice runs before each race, which consists of a single descent. The first 15 to run, in randomly selected order, are the seeds, based on recent performance.

Courses for **slalom** races are set on short, steep and usually (indeed preferably) icy slopes, giving only about 200m vertical drop for men, 180m for women. In this relatively short space men have to ski through 55 to 75 gates, women through 45 to 60; they are laid out on the hill in such a way as to test turning ability and control more than speed alone. No practice runs are allowed, and the race is run over two legs on different courses (in the early days of racing it used to be one leg on hard snow the other on soft). Experimental changes have been made to the rule that skiers run the second leg in the order they finished the first, except that the first five go in reverse order.

The **giant slalom** consists of about the same number of gates as a slalom, but spaced out more widely over a course of about a mile, giving a vertical drop of 300m to 400m for men, and 300m to 350m for women. The race is run like a slalom, with each leg taking about 90 seconds. For reasons to do with the organisation of ski racing competitions, another discipline has recently been introduced; this is the **super giant slalom** or super-G, where gates are spread over an even longer, wider course designed to give the downhill racers more of a chance of winning. Having been coolly received at first, and even boycotted by some skiers, the super-G seems to have established itself as a worthwhile and exciting event.

The circuit

All the course regulations are laid down by the FIS (Fédération Internationale du Ski) which organises a circuit of races every winter, starting in Europe in December, ranging from Bulgaria and Sweden to Furano in Japan, before finishing in North America several long, hard months later. Racers score points for finishing in the first fifteen of any race, and these points over the season decide placings in the annual **World Cup** Championship. At the end of the season the highest scorer in each discipline wins the World Cup for that event. There is an overall World Cup title for the best performer in all disciplines, with a limit placed on the amount of points which can be amassed in any one, and extra points for combined performance in downhill and a slalom event at a particular race meeting. It's an extremely complicated scoring system which is often changed, usually to the disadvantage of specialists like Sweden's Ingemar Stenmark, and the advantage of all-round skiers who enter and score points in downhill races as well as winning slaloms.

So far as men's skiing is concerned, the giant slalom has proved to be much closer to the slalom than to the downhill, and since skiers have become specialists it's the slalom skiers, notably Stenmark, who have dominated the giant slalom. This has given them a commanding advantage in the overall competition, designed to reward all-round achievement, even if, like Stenmark, they don't compete in downhill races; so the super-G was conceived to suit downhillers and redress the balance. In the early days of the World Cup, when Killy and Schranz walked off with all the prizes in all the events, things were much simpler! Killy won the first overall World Cup in 1967 with maximum points – three victories in all of the three disciplines. It's hard to imagine any skier doing that now – though the outstanding achievements of the Swiss racer Pirmin Zurbriggen in the World Cup and World Championships in 1985 immediately led some people to brand him a second Killy, and in the 1988 Olympics he took the giant slalom bronze as well as the downhill gold.

Specialisation hasn't been so pronounced among women. A number of downhill racers have been consistent giant slalom winners, outstandingly Austria's Anne-Marie Moser-Pröll, who dominated women's racing in the 1970s. Liechtenstein's Hanni Wenzel and the German Rosi Mittermaier each won two golds and a silver medal in the 1980 and 1976 Winter Olympics respectively.

So every year the World Cup produces several champions based on consistent performance throughout the season. These aren't the only champions around, though. Every Leap Year, attention shifts from the World Cup circuit to the **Winter Olympics**, where all the laurels go to the best skier on the day in a single race in each discipline. The **World Championships** are an Olympic-style race meeting organised by the FIS, and are now to be held every two years. The gold medallists in each discipline reign as World Champions for two seasons. So it can happen that a skier who hasn't won a race for two years and who hasn't done at all well in the World Cup is still the World Champion in a particular discipline. One odd feature of the World Championships is the Alpine Combined title, which goes to the best performer in a shortened downhill and one of the slalom events. At the Schladming World Championships in 1982 none of the three combination medallists finished in the first ten places of any of the three races, which shows how specialised men's racing has become, and arguably makes rather a nonsense of the combined and overall titles. Skiers compete to win races, not accumulate points, and that's why the Olympics and World Championships mean more to many skiers than the World Cup.

The business angle

World Cup racers are technically amateurs, and most fulfil the requirements of the Olympic Committee, but all the top racers earn a living from the sport out of commercial sponsorship; so-called 'broken time' payments are allowed, enabling the athlete to be compensated for not having the time to work because of competition and intensive training. Rules of eligibility for the Olympics, or at least the interpretation of them, are in practice stricter than for the World Cup and

World Championships, which has meant that a few of the world's top skiers have been unable to compete for Olympic medals. It happened to Karl Schranz at Sapporo in 1972, and in 1984 at Sarajevo the absentees included the near-invincible Ingemar Stenmark and Hanni Wenzel – ruled out because of their semi-professional status.

There is some professional racing, mostly in North America, where the parallel slalom is the great spectator sport. Two racers battle it out together side by side on parallel courses, swapping sides for the second leg to even out the inevitable differences. Ironically, the prize money for pro racing isn't as good as the money the top World Cup racers can attract, and as a result the pro circuits tend to attract the less successful amateur racers.

Racing skills and thrills

Among Alpine ski races downhill is the ultimate test of commitment, guts and, some would say, sanity – that's what makes it so exciting to watch and to perform, especially at Kitzbühel. In the downhill it's man against mountain, rather than man against contrived difficulty. Within the two minutes of the race, skiers accelerate up to 90 miles an hour; they fly off ridges for up to 50 yards in the air, and their legs have to contend with crushing forces in a compression (where the course flattens out), and through every inch of a tight bend. There's no need to be an expert technical observer to enjoy watching this kind of race, and it comes across well on television, where you benefit from cameras positioned at different points on the mountain, although you'll never really appreciate the speed until you stand on the sidelines and watch the racers flashing past. Downhill racing, of course, is also the discipline which sees the most spectacular crashes, and although we racers like to think that people don't watch for that reason, there's no doubt that the spills add to the thrills.

The appeal of the slalom is rather more subtle. Unlike the downhill racer, who can hardly hope to win if he doesn't push himself right up to and even beyond his normal capabilities, the slalom skier has to make the tactical judgement about when to ski with a safety margin, hoping others will force too hard and miss a gate, and when to let rip. Where many skiers would choose to go all out on the first leg, in the hope of establishing a margin for a safety-conscious second run, Ingemar Stenmark made a speciality of skiing unspectacularly in the first leg and then coming from behind to annihilate the field with a blistering second run. The slalom can be a dramatic struggle in its own way, and for the spectators on the hill it's much easier to follow the race as a whole than it is with a downhill race on its much longer course. On television the dominant impression is of an indecipherable maze of red and blue poles. What never seems to come across is how steep slalom courses are, and what an achievement it is simply to hang on to the icy mountain and negotiate the awkward, twisting course.

The modern style of slalom skiing gives the impression that racers devote more energy to knocking down poles than to controlling their skis. This is because all they have to do is make sure that both their skis pass on the required side of the pole; from the hips up, the body takes a much straighter line down the hill than the feet, which means that poles get knocked all over the place. Fortunately, they are flexible and unbreakable these days, and the risk of skewering yourself on a broken slalom pole isn't great.

While the two extreme disciplines of downhill and slalom make greatest demands on a skier's resilience and courage on the one hand, and his agility and lightning reflexes on the other, the giant slalom is a test of the precise application of technique at high speed, and demands a combination of smoothness and strength.

Behind the scenes

Of course, there's much more to ski racing than what you see on the hill on the day, although the racer gets all the glory for a victory. Each national squad has its back-up team of technical experts who have the great responsibility of cooking up the right blend of ski-wax for snow conditions on the course; these can change hour by hour, and usually vary over different parts of the course. Just as important is the fact that during training (for downhill) there are groups of coaches and technicians stationed all the way down the mountain to amass as much information as possible about the racer training on the course – the Austrians and the Swiss will have up to 15 observers on the hill, giving them a big advantage over smaller teams. Because each racer gets only three or four training runs, this in-depth analysis is essential to establish the fastest line and select the optimum equipment. The big teams have video cameramen filming all the top racers, as well as lines of electronic timing equipment to establish who is gaining time at which point on the course.

Ski racers train long and hard. As soon as one season is over in April, preparation for the next one begins with the racers hardly having time for a breather before they have to head off to the weight training rooms, wind tunnels (to perfect aerodynamic posture), running tracks, and snow – some of them to the summer snow-fields on Alpine glaciers, others crossing to the other end of the world to ski in Australia and New Zealand. Long hours of race training are designed to simulate, wherever possible, true racing conditions. As well as building up agility, strength and stamina for the duration of a race, the skier has to be prepared mentally to maintain form through the long winter with all the travelling it involves. So when you're reaching for your beach towel, think of the poor World Cup skiers loading their huge ski bags into vans and aeroplanes for another heavy summer's training!

If ski racing still sounds attractive, the best way to approach it is to join one of the racing clubs at your nearest dry ski slope, or to sign up with one of the long-established race training clubs which organise trips to the Alps in the winter holidays; the Ski Club of Great Britain can give information about these. Either way gives you the opportunity to compare your ability with others of your age and, equally important, to enjoy a new aspect of skiing – you don't have to be a World Cup champion to get an enormous amount of fun out of ski racing. If you do aim for the top then you'd better grit your teeth and start working hard right now. But don't forget still to enjoy your skiing!

Bell: downhill only

People have the idea that the main requirement of a downhill racer is to be a daredevil, but that's wrong. What you need, first and foremost, is to be a technically good skier. The basic skill in skiing is turning, and that goes for downhill as well as slalom, giant slalom and super-G. It's on the turns that races are won and lost – on good courses, at least. On a tight turn which slows most racers down from 80mph to 40mph, the winner is the man who comes out of the turn at 45mph. The best skiers around are probably the giant slalom specialists. In special slalom you can get by with quick reactions and a lot of aggression, but take a good skier from GS and put him into the downhill, and his technical ability will stand him in good stead (once he gets used to the speed, which takes a couple of years). Zurbriggen is the obvious example of this; but people often forget that even Klammer was a very good GS skier before he started specialising in downhill. He'd be the first to admit that his downhill performance started to deteriorate when he allowed his GS technique to slip. There's a growing trend for downhillers to spend their summers practising the same basic skills as slalom skiers. Of course, downhillers do have an extra problem to contend with: jumps.

. . . the art is to 'suck' the jump up . . .

The most important thing about a jump is that it must have a steep landing. A flat landing is much harder on the body, and more dangerous. Look at nordic ski jumping: if anyone flies too far and lands beyond what's called the critical point of the slope, they lower the start.

Basically you can't gain or lose much time on a jump, and the main thing is to stay in control. The worst you can do is be totally stretched in an unaerodynamic position for two or three seconds, losing you perhaps half a second. On the other hand, you don't accelerate in the air, and if you land on the flat you won't accelerate there either – the art is to 'suck' the jump up well, land high up and use the steep slope to gather speed for the flat. Sucking or squashing is where you go over the lip of a jump with a downward movement of your body to absorb the kick it gives you. The trickier alternative is pre-jumping, where you actually take off before the lip – a risky business, but useful on jumps with a very clearly defined lip.

Some jumps are combined with a turn. The toughest recent example of that was in the 1987 World Championships at Crans-Montana, a very tight turn off a ridge with very little room to set up before the turn and a jump just as you were finshing it. In a turn you usually have a lot of pressure on the edge of the ski, and if you still have that pressure on the edge when you go off the lip it catapults you a long distance. The trick is to get the turn finished and depressurise the ski before you go off the lip – easier said than done! I was in difficulties on that jump, always too worried about making a nice turn instead of slamming on the edges really quickly and getting off them again. I was still turning when I went off the lip, and did a lot of waving to the crowd in the air. I don't think it lost me a lot of time, but if I'd been in a much worse state I'd have crashed like Michael Mair.

The most common way people fall off jumps is getting wind under the tips of their skis, which at speeds of 70mph act like wings. If you're leaning slightly back when you come off a jump the wind catches the ski tips and you land on your back. If you think forward and make the right move off a jump, it's no problem. But if you allow it to come up on you and make no move, you'll crash. It happened to me at Val Gardena with the Camel Humps. I pride myself on that being my only fall on a jump.

. . . he had a one-in-a-million pair of skis . . .

Apart from turning and jumping, the other art is gliding – a very elusive skill. Some people don't even believe there is such a thing, and argue that it's the skis that make the difference; it certainly is hard to explain why two racers in exactly the same position standing flat on their skis can have different times over a straight section of course. But there is a skill: it comes down to a good aerodynamic position and also being soft on the skis – if you're going over small bumps, being able to suck them all up. They say that if you listen to a good glider going along a bumpy flat section his skis will make less noise than a bad glider. Noise is energy being wasted.

People are always talking about a secret new wax, but in fact waxing is much less important than it used to be. Provided you don't get the wax drastically wrong, the skis themselves are more important. Amazingly, they still don't really know what makes a ski fast, so it's a simple question of using ski-testing to find out which is your fastest pair and doing what you can to save them for race day. A downhill racer will have about 15 pairs of skis of the right stiffness and flex for him. They will have different bases: some with a black graphite base – supposed to cut down on static – others with the traditional clear base; some very smooth, others ground to give them a very rough texture, generally better for warm snow. Bill Johnson will be the first to admit that in 1984 he had a one-in-a-million pair of skis that gave him a great advantage over the flat. Strangely they subsequently just went off the boil; after a summer on the shelf, fast skis may no longer be fast. But if you save a good pair of race skis you can use them for two or three seasons. Franz Klammer won about twenty races on one really fast pair. Fischer have still got them, and test them from time to time on their track to see how they compare with the skis they're making now.

. . . man-made snow is just about the ideal surface . . .

For a good race it's important that the snow should be hard. At the Sarajevo Olympics they had 200 soldiers shovelling snow off the course as it fell. In the Alps they tend to spray water on the courses; the most extreme place for this is Garmisch – you can be sure it'll be icy there, even after days of blizzard. This may sound vicious, but it definitely makes for a better race. New snow favours later starters and generally makes the course easier. On ice you have to be much more precise, and the guy with the most skill wins. Above a certain temperature it becomes unfair to hold downhill races because the snow's so soft it cuts up for later starters. This is often a problem at Aspen in Colorado – quite far south and really hot when the sun is out in March. Downhills can be run if it's snowing, provided it isn't foggy – but not in the rain, which sticks to the goggles much more than snow.

Man-made snow is a recent addition to the European racing scene, and very valuable. The main advantage is fairly obvious: it guarantees that you can have races in December. Not long ago, when early-season races were repeatedly being cancelled or moved from snowless venues, pressure built up for a later start to the racing season. But some of the big backers of the circuit are ski manufacturers, and their biggest selling time is just before Christmas, so they demand races on TV at that time. Now everyone's happy. The other point is that man-made snow is just about the ideal surface for racing – if made properly, it turns out not as slippery ice but as very hard snow, grippy not shiny, uniform in texture and durable. Part of the reason late starters tend to do so well at Val Gardena – as Konrad Bartelski did a few years ago and Rob Boyd two years ago – is the man-made snow, which doesn't deteriorate as the race goes on, and so gives later guys a fair chance. The main drawback is that when the only snow is the man-made stuff on the course, you may not be able to ski at all except on the training runs.

. . . you should go flat out in training . . .

When you arrive in the resort several days before the race, the first thing is the inspection, where you take about half an hour to slide down beside the course trying to memorise every contour. Then there are training runs before the race – between two and five runs, depending on weather and how many they can fit in. Training times have no effect on the starting times for the race itself, but they can be psychologically important. Some racers feel that good training times put pressure on them, and you often see people making a couple of turns before the finish to lose time – though the effect is actually very slight. To my mind, if you know a course well you should go flat out in training to see how well you can ski it. The other tricky decision, especially when there are rocks around, is whether or not to use your fast skis. Even if you know a poor training time was a result of using slow skis, you'll always be a little bit unsure when it comes to the race. My problem has often been that I ski well in training but not in the race. A couple of seasons back at Garmisch, for example, I had an 8th in training, then 30th in the race; at Wengen I was 12th in one training run and 30th in the race; at Kitzbühel I was 9th and 10th in the last two training runs and nearly crashed in the race. Happily, I managed to reverse this pattern more recently at the Olympics, where my best result in training was 19th but I managed 8th in the run that mattered.

Most races are shown live on local television so if you are some way down the starting order and there's a mountain restaurant with a TV you may be able to watch the early starters to see how the course is running on the day. In the combined downhill at Crans-Montana I had start number 15 so I was able to watch the first five. The last guy I saw before I left the restaurant to ski down to the start had a really bad crash – not a very good send-off!

On the course, you get a good idea of how you're doing in comparison with training, and if you're quicker in the race you might hope for a good result. That's fine if the conditions haven't changed, but quite often you find that after a cold clear night the course firms up and gets faster.

. . . the mountain has to be steep . . .

World Cup downhill courses fall into three categories. Kitzbühel and Wengen are out on their own – the two great classics that every racer dreams of winning. Next come the minor classics, with a race just about every season: Val d'Isère, Val Gardena, Garmisch and Aspen. Then come all the other courses that hold races from time to time.

There are very few courses outside the main Alpine countries, mainly because the rules require a minimum vertical drop of 800 metres. Furano in Japan, for example, only just scraped in and at for the 1984 Olympics at Sarajevo in Yugoslavia they had to build a new restaurant on top of the mountain and have the start on a ramp on top of that. The mountain also has to be steep, so that good turns can be set without making the race too slow. The course at Las Lenas in Argentina the summer before last had a lot of good, difficult turns in it but wasn't very fast or hair-raising; it was more like a super-G course than a downhill, in fact. Part of the problem is that the organisers of the World Cup have always wanted it to be a world-wide competition, so although the Japanese course didn't come up to standard by a long way, they're guaranteed a World Cup race every other year. A lot of the courses in Europe have long flats in them, but they always have some steep turny sections.

. . . louder cheers for me than for the French . . .

The first big race of the downhill season is in early December at **Val d'Isère**, one of the few places where they have men's and women's downhill courses side by side. In 1986–87 I got my only good result here (sixth, and less than a second behind the winner). I used to think 'Piste OK' on the results sheet referred to the snow conditions but it's the name of the run, the initials of two great local champions Henri Oreiller and Jean-Claude Killy. It's like a home race for me because there are so many British tourists around – there are louder cheers for me than for the French racers! Also I know the course really well: they used to hold the British championships there, and it was the first downhill I ever did when I was 14. In 1992 it'll be the Olympic course.

In general it's what you might call a motorway course – very fast, with long turns not at all like the tight ones at Kitzbühel where you just slam on the edges. At Val d'Isère you have to be very slow and smooth in your movements in the turns. Fast skis count for a lot at the top, which is pretty flat and straight.

There are two really tough sections. The Collombin jump is never shown on TV, which is rather a shame as it's one of the trickier jumps around because of the very high speed. It's not a real kicker but a long convex roll, which makes it very difficult to judge where you actually take off. The ground just drops away from you and suddenly you're five feet up in the air. The steep section to land on is actually quite short so if you fly too far you land on the flat and lose a lot of speed for the long flat section that follows. The Swiss racer Roland Collombin fell two years in succession there. The first time he had a really bad crash but was all right; the next year apparently he just froze – had a mental block – and didn't make a move as he went off the jump. He crashed, broke his back and never raced again. The other trouble spot is the Compression, where I once crashed. It comes just after the tunnel jump where the piste goes under the course. It's a bit of a misnomer – not so much a compression, where your body really comes under pressure, as an S-bend with a small compression in the first turn of the S, a left-hander. As you turn out of it your body gets light, and with no weight on your skis it's very difficult to turn. You float out wide, which makes you late going into the right-hander, where there's very little space because of the nets. It's this second turn that catches you.

. . . you've got to take the first jump just right . . .

Val Gardena almost always comes after Val d'Isère. It's the first really tough course, much harder on the body than Val d'Isère and a real test of physical fitness. Lots of racers end up with sore backs from all the jumps and bumps. The most famous section consists of three jumps in a row – peculiarly called the Camel Humps. The first jump is a little way away from the second and third which are the tricky ones because they're so close together – though you've got to take the first jump just right to stand a chance with the others. What you can do is suck up the first bump to fly as little distance as possible, then spring off the second like a ski jumper and land just on the far side of the third bump. The classic thing is that someone who jumps over the camels gains maybe half a second; then he's so relieved that he managed to clear the third jump that he totally loses concentration for the turns that follow and loses two seconds on those!

The turns on the course after the Camels, called the Meadows, are incredibly bumpy. I think they must be bumps in the ground, but it might have something to do with the way the man-made snow piles up overnight – every year the bumps seem to be in different places. One day I'll go there in summer and check! I already mentioned that the man-made snow holds up well and gives late starters a good chance. Another factor in their favour is a huge Dolomite peak which shades the course until about start number 20. After that the sun moves round and hits the course just on these bumpy turns after the Camels, and the good visibility makes this section quite a bit easier to ski.

Garmisch is the next of the great courses, with a race held there virtually every year. As I said before, they water the course so it's always icy, and the top is very technical: it has steep, icy turns, quite like Kitzbühel except that you have a lot more room at Garmisch, which makes a big psychological difference. Make a mistake at the top of Garmisch and you'll lose a couple of seconds; make a mistake at the top of Kitzbühel and you'll probably crash, and certainly come very close to it.

. . . weird things that wouldn't be allowed . . .

What with the wonderful scenery, the peace of the car-free village and the little train that takes you up to the start of the course, **Wengen** has a very special atmosphere – and its race, the Lauberhorn, is one of the two great classics. The main thing about it is the length of the course – about half a minute longer than most of the others. It doesn't have a lot more turns, but there are long straight sections between them so if you mess up a turn and carry less speed into the straight you really pay for your mistake. The course includes some weird things that wouldn't be allowed in a new course, like going under the railway bridge.

From the start you pick up a lot of speed on long sweeping sections before coming to a 180° turn where you slow down (fortunately!) from about 80mph to about 30mph before going over the Hundschopf, which must be one of the most dramatic sections on any course: a 20m vertical drop between two cliff faces. Then comes Canadian Corner, where a lot of Canadians crashed one year, then the bridge, then Austrian Hole, named after another national débâcle, and finally the S-bends and a jump into the finish, site of Peter's Müller's famous crash. Müller was risking a lot through the S's, using the full width of the piste like a Grand Prix driver using the curb stones – letting it run out, we call it. But if you only just squeeze through the gate before the jump you don't have time to squash it, so he flew a long way, landed hard and his legs just gave way and he sat down. They still had hay bales in those days, and Müller ended up in one.

Recently they've held the Lauberhorn race the week before the Hahnenkamm at Kitzbühel. I much prefer it the other way round because then you can enjoy Wengen without knowing you've got to go to Kitzbühel the next week! That sums up the difference between them.

. . . it makes you wonder how anyone can do it . . .

At Wengen you almost have time to sit back and enjoy the scenery; **Kitzbühel** is probably the only course that frightens most experienced downhillers, which includes me. Even in a year when a lot of the courses aren't really stimulating enough, at Kitzbühel you know if you make a slight mistake you've got a very good chance of crashing. On the other hand, if you're aggressive and don't let the course get you down, Kitzbühel is the supreme thrill to ski. When I'm getting it right here I have virtually no fear of it.

The start is the steepest of any downhill. You hardly need to push out of the start – it's almost a free fall. Inspecting the course for the first time, you think the first couple of turns are steep, then you come to an edge where it gets even steeper. That's the Mausfalle: virtually one in one. It's really frightening, but not that difficult once you know you can do it. You fly about 20m over it, land on it and go straight down. Every year you get the butterflies because you've forgotten that it's actually possible. I never like to watch the racer before me disappear over that cliff; it makes you wonder how anyone can do it.

The really difficult bit is about ten seconds after the Mausfalle – the Steilhang (which just means steep slope). A compression leads into a 180° turn, technical but not that steep, then you dive down to the

Steilhang with a left-hand turn down into it. This is definitely the hardest turn in any downhill because it goes on for so long and because the slope runs away from you as you try to turn. I made a mistake here in 1987. In the middle of the turn I was doing really well, carving cleanly and high, then I got too aggressive: I moved my weight back too much, started to sit back and also got twisted – the dreaded rotation. I found myself heading straight for the net and had to do a slalom turn at 60mph, which killed off all my speed and probably lost me a couple of seconds. But at least I stayed out of the net, just!

You never see the long flat road on TV. This is where the skis and gliding ability come into it. If you're not a very experienced racer you just sit on the road and thank God you made it. Once you get more experienced you wish you hadn't messed up the turns before the road, because you seem to be going so slowly at this point. Still travelling very slowly, you come round the mountain, see the village a long way below, and realise it's going to take all of 20 seconds to get down to that level – the hill just drops away. You're tired by then and, what's worse, you've had time to think about it, and to wonder how your legs are going to cope with the compression below.

The finish is really steep again, not as technical as the top, but incredibly bumpy: you just hang on. Anyone could catch an edge on those bumps; Todd Brooker's fall last year was probably one of the worst I've seen. Sometimes I think they deliberately don't make it as smooth as they could, just to keep their reputation going. But that's how it should be – demanding. Even more than Wengen, Kitzbühel is a course which couldn't be introduced to the circuit today – trainers would throw up their hands in horror and say 'too dangerous'.

At Wengen and Kitzbühel they usually have the downhill on Saturday and the slalom on Sunday. The best place for setting warm-up courses for the slalom is on the downhill just after it's been used, so the national slalom trainers have their own race to secure the best piece of piste. Literally as the last racer is going through the finish the trainers dash out on to the course with their drills and poles; it's a free-for-all.

One of the funnier aspects of Kitzbühel is the sight of all the spectators climbing over the fence after the race. The course becomes an absolute madhouse, with hundreds of people sliding on their bums down the steep sections, which are unskiable if you don't have razor-sharp edges. Once, when my ski pre-released at the top after about five seconds (despite special springs and the top release setting of 20 DIN) I had to wait until the race was over before I could ski down the course. It was definitely more dangerous than doing the race itself, trying to avoid people skidding out of control.

One thing you notice in Austria and Switzerland compared with the other countries is the huge numbers of supporters: they have to run special trains into places like Kitzbühel, which gets incredibly full for the Hahnenkamm race. Generally the Austrian supporters are very knowledgeable, and generous with their applause. In Italy and especially Yugoslavia, foreign racers get a really hard time. The French don't go to watch ski racing at all, but then they don't have much to cheer these days!

. . . all the racers like going there . . .

The US race is always at **Aspen** – Ruthie's Run. It's a pretty good course, very flat and straight at the top, which is where your skis count. The second half is steep and turny; a couple of years back it was set by the American coach, who put the gates much tighter than normal so it was even more difficult on the turns – some of the gates were very hard to make. In training I had about number 20, came back up and watched the guys in the 40s and 50s: about half of them were missing Aeroplane Turn, as Müller did in the race. By race day most people had worked out how to make the gate, but obviously Müller just pushed a little bit too hard. It's called Aeroplane Turn because of the way the way the hill banks, the opposite to the Steilhang where the ground slopes away from you, which is much more difficult. The bank in the turn helps you to turn, but when you hit the bank you do get a compression effect.

Aspen is a really lively and (unlike most American resorts) compact town, with more restaurants and bars than I've ever seen in any other ski resort – all the racers like going there. The organisers treat us very well and have a unique deal whereby the ski teams can eat free at about 30 or 40 restaurants – Chinese, Japanese, Mexican, you name it. Some of the Alpine nations could learn a lot from American hospitality.

Of the other courses, the best are probably **Whistler**, near Vancouver – a better course than the Olympic one on Mount Allan – and **Are** in Sweden. Before we first went there to race, the idea of a downhill course in Sweden was a bit of a joke, but it turned out to be quite a surprise – very well designed by the famous Swiss racer Bernhard Russi. There are a lot of jumps, and when you land from a jump there are plenty of smaller bumps to throw you. After the first training run the trainers were unanimously horrified at the size of the jumps, but in the end it was just right and the camera positions were excellent.

. . . you can be doing 90mph and it won't feel bad . . .

For the 1987 World Championships, **Crans-Montana** created a new women's downhill course, a very exciting one, definitely the Kitzbühel of the girls' circuit. Our course was not that tough, but full of jumps – I think there were about 13. The toughest was the one I mentioned before, where you turned off the ridge, but the biggest was the last one, just before the finish. It had quite a flat landing as well, so it was easy to collapse on landing if your legs were beginning to go.

Schladming has the fastest average speed of all downhill courses, but that doesn't mean it's tough – in fact quite the opposite: on a smooth piste like that you can be doing 90mph and it won't feel bad at all. Schladming also has the record attendance for a ski race – something like 70,000 for the 1982 World Championships. **St Anton** has a race every few years. It's not a particularly exciting course, but quite technical, with lots of turns; they've improved it recently, adding a really tough turn and a big jump near the finish, but unfortunately you no longer do the Krazy Kangaruh jump – over the road near the restaurant – which was the fun part.

Morzine was the last race in the Alps in 1987–88. I wouldn't say it's one of the classics, but it's a good course with some interesting terrain.

You start off along a ridge above Avoriaz then turn off it on to a road with a really long turn of over 180° that seems to go on and on. The lower section is straighter but has a couple of really big jumps.

Japan has a race only every other year – it alternates with Scandinavia. Everyone agreed in 1987 that the course was far too easy. The hill is too flat: to keep the speed going at 60 to 70mph they had to set the course straight, which makes the race more a test of skis than skiing. Two guys from the top group crashed on a jump, but I put that down to a false sense of security. You don't really get keyed up or tense before the start. Once the word spread that the jump was causing problems, everyone else handled it OK.

I'd always heard that the skiing in Japan was really crowded but there was hardly anyone there. Furano is up in the northern island and all the Japanese who live around Tokyo use resorts in the south, so skiing in Furano is a bit like going to the Outer Hebrides. The mountains are very spaced out and gentle. The best thing was one really nice powder run at the top of the course, where it was actually quite steep and the snow was waist-deep – more exhilarating than skiing the downhill!

. . . the main danger at the Olympics is nerves . . .

Last season all eyes were on **Mount Allan**, the Olympic downhill course near Calgary in Alberta, Canada. It's a course of two halves, like Aspen in reverse and quite similar to the 1980 Olympic course at Lake Placid. The top is very steep, so they have to set turns in; you have to ski well to get through them with any speed. The bottom is flat and would be very slow if it weren't straight, so it's more a test of gliding and skis. My only criticism is that in new snow you can get away with skiing quite badly on the turns. But I can't really complain about the course on which I achieved the highest Olympic placing by a British skier!

Have a little respect

The *Guide*'s consultant editor **Adam Ruck** reflects on the impact of skiing on the mountains, and the impact that conservation measures are having on the development of skiing.

For environmental nuisance value there can be few sports to rival skiing, at least in the form it has taken as a holiday industry. Mountains are mechanised and electrified, their peaks cluttered with pylons, cables and restaurant buildings. The natural contours of the mountain are bulldozed and flattened, and underground pipelines are laid so that the slopes can be sprayed with artificial snow whenever the real stuff is in short supply. The skier demands that there should be apartment buildings, supermarkets and discothèques at the foot of the slopes. Visit a ski resort in summer when the skiers are on the beach, and you will see the full ugliness of the scars inflicted on the mountain landscape in the name of their sport.

The delicate equilibrium of the Alpine environment sets the city-dwelling conservationists against the commercial interests of the local people. For about 30 years after World War II the developers were given a free rein, and many Alpine regions have prospered as never before. In remote and inhospitable parts of the high French Alps, huge tracts of empty, open mountain have been mechanised for skiers, and grand plans have been hatched, promising more and more lifts spanning the gaps between resorts until the entire Alpine range resembles nothing so much as a single uninterrupted motorway network, with multiple exits and entrances and no traffic lights.

Over the last few years the pace of development has slackened, partly for financial reasons, partly because the balance of power has shifted in favour of conservation. Austria, more dependent on tourism for its prosperity than any of the other Alpine countries, has taken the strongest line. 'We have effectively put a stop to all development,' explains Werner Fritz, National Tourist Office director in London. 'In the western province of Vorarlberg it has actually been made a law and, to take one example, the project of building a summer ski area in the Silvretta has been blocked. In the other provinces the situation is a little more flexible, but even here you won't see any major new development. All we are doing is replacing inefficient lifts with efficient ones to improve the quality of the ski areas that already exist. There is a general feeling in the population that nothing must be done to damage nature. That is our resource.'

In France, predictably, the authorities are less unbending. Over the last five years the development argument has raged most fiercely around Mont Blanc and the Chamonix valley, one of the most spectacular natural beauty spots in the Alps, and safeguarded since the early 1950s by protection orders on all the land above 2000m. As the valley's skiing has become more and more popular, the problem of imbalance between plentiful accommodation and very limited ski-lift capacity has become more and more acute. In 1982 the government authorised new lifts at the head of the valley, but local conservationists persuaded a tribunal in Grenoble to reverse the decision. It was re-imposed and re-reversed several times before the lifts were finally opened two years ago. Developers will have noted with interest the ruling that the Minister was right to take account of 'economic considerations' when deciding on authorisation to build. So will the Cairngorm lift company in Scotland, which has been fighting a similar battle over a Site of Special Scientific Interest, a snowy gully ideal for skiing and also favoured by nesting dotterel. Myrtle Simpson, chairman of the Scottish National Ski Council, is quoted as saying that a quarter of a million Scottish skiers won't be fobbed off because of a couple of bird's nests. But so far they have been. In France, one of the boldest proposals is for a lift link between Val d'Isère and Bonneval-sur-Arc in the Haute Maurienne valley, on the south side of the Col de l'Iseran, which would inevitably mean more building in the Vanoise National Park, where there are already some lifts. The Val d'Isère lift company is not over-optimistic about the project. 'Getting permission for anything in the Park is very difficult now,' we were told. 'As it is, the small refreshment hut inside the Park had to be built like a shepherd's mountain hut with a traditional stone roof.'

In 1980 Giscard d'Estaing, himself a keen and adventurous skier, courted the green vote by banning all helicopter drops for skiers. Mountaineers deplore the use of remote peaks as helicopter landing pads for idle rich skiers, but French professional guides resent the loss of income that heli-skiing brings to their fellows in the other Alpine countries, and complain that there is no broad environmental logic in what is no more than a 'not in my back yard' ban – French skiers can be helicoptered across borders to nearby Swiss and Italian mountains. The Savoyards are confident that the ban will soon be lifted, although there are sure to be strict controls on permitted helicopter-drop areas. The Austrians take a pragmatic approach to heli-skiing, allowing it in a few places, where helicopters are used for mountain rescue, as a way of cutting rescue costs. The Swiss show no reluctance to profit from wealthy skiers' willingness to pay for the ultimate ski-lift.

The French have learnt to style their new projects in what is fondly imagined to be an environmentally respectful way, something the Austrians decreed 40 years ago. In the 1960s, new resorts such as La Plagne, Tignes and Les Menuires were constructed in a style that declared unashamedly their nature – new, functional service areas. In the latest generation of resorts, such as Valmorel and Valfréjus, gaily painted timbers and carefully aged stone roofs have been substituted for the bare concrete. These muesli resorts may not be any less disruptive to the environment, but they certainly look more attractive. No resort shows the change of style more clearly than La Plagne, which consists of half a dozen separate units built at different stages over the last 25 years. The most recent units are Belle Plagne (with a restaurant significantly called Au Vieux Tyrol) and Plagne Lauze (which means rough-stone Plagne).

However pretty a new resort may be, the pylons and cables of its ski-lifts remain an eyesore. The latest fashion, for the few resorts with budgets lavish enough to afford it, is for lifts discreetly buried in tunnels cut in the living rock of the mountain. Saas Fee and now Les Deux Alpes employ these lifts under glaciers, where other high-capacity lifts would be impracticable. But Zermatt's Sunegga Express would have been a major surface lift if built a few years earlier – as would the more recent Funival in Val d'Isère. This lift goes from the edge of the resort to the top of the mountain nearly 1000 metres above. Its efficiency is very impressive – about 3,000 skiers an hour and a journey time of under five minutes, matching the speed of a cable-car and improving on the capacity of the most efficient gondola – but so is the cost. The new lift cost about 75 million francs (about £7 million). A new gondola lift to do the same job, albeit less efficiently, would have cost about half as much. 'Of course, the environmental argument is one of the reasons that the funicular was preferred to the alternatives considered,' says Marty Nasso, one of the financial managers of the Val d'Isère lift company. 'There is no ugly terminal building at the bottom of the lift and we even agreed that the metal pillars supporting the viaduct for the short overground section at the bottom of the lift would be clothed with stone.' Another of Val d'Isère's recent projects has been installing artificial snow-making machines on the lower slopes of its famous downhill racecourse. In summer the nozzles fold down into unobtrusive plastic discs, coloured green, snug with the grass.

The concerns of the Swiss conservation lobby are less cosmetic. The message from foresters is that worrying about pylons and helicopters defiling the beauty of nature's unspoilt Alpine countenance is as relevant as suicide bombers worrying about their pensions. The forests are in danger, and when the forests are in danger we are all in danger; people living in the mountains are particularly threatened because of the role of woodland in preventing avalanches. According to the Swiss Forestry Office, one Swiss tree in three is diseased, with a ratio nearer one in two in the mountainous southern half of the country. The Davos Avalanche Institute is currently making a study of 200 recent avalanches that started below the possible treeline. According to Martin Mayer, who is running the project, 'the problem is as bad as it's made out to be. Skiers are often blamed but really there are three main causes: air pollution, game and bad forestry management.'

Perhaps surprisingly, trees were a controversial aspect of the 1986 World Championships at Crans-Montana. The resort directors made no secret of their delight in being selected as hosts to the Championship, because it would help them win permission for new development which would otherwise have been refused. The key issue was a small area of woodland to be cleared for a new downhill course and piste. They were right: having been denied them for years, permission came forth and the trees came down. The conservationists digested the implications and immediately started campaigning against Swiss candidacy for future Olympic and World Championships which, they claim, are no more than a Trojan horse for unwanted new tourist development.

Pollution and disease is a new problem, but the loss of forests is not. In the last 200 years the amount of vegetation in the Austrian Tyrol has declined by half, the tree-line has fallen by 400m in places, and the area of avalanche paths has quadrupled. Forestry experts estimate that, of the several thousand avalanches that descend into inhabited areas of Austria each winter, about two-thirds start below the possible tree-line but in places where there is now no timber. Skiers may also be concerned that the declining forest coverage is one of the reasons for increasingly patchy snowfall in the Alps.

The Austrians have already moved faster than the rest of Europe on air pollution and car exhaust emission controls. All new cars with engines of over 1500cc have to be fitted with catalytic converters, and there are big tax advantages if you convert an old car. Lead-free petrol is subsidised and on sale everywhere, and filling up with leaded petrol earns you nasty looks from the pump attendant. Similar rules for new cars have now come into force in Switzerland.

Throughout Austria and Switzerland skiers are being urged by conservation groups not to ski off-piste in the woods, because of the damage that sharp ski edges do to young trees hidden below the surface of deep snow. Off-piste skiers are also being told to keep silent because of the distress they cause to wildlife. When rushing around in panic, the animals themselves do more damage to the saplings than usual. There is also some evidence that animals frightened by off-piste skiers may be dying of exhaustion. If you've ever tried off-piste sprinting, you won't be surprised by this.

An increasing number of resorts are backing up the exhortations by roping off large areas of woodland in an attempt to keep skiers out. The Austrian resort of Lech was one of the first in the Alps to do this. 'For years now we have had signs on every main lift and beside every lift queue telling skiers in German, English and French that it is forbidden by order of the Mayor of Lech to ski off-piste in the trees,' explains Hubert Schwarzler, Lech's Tourist Office director. He prefers not to emphasise the legal and punitive aspect of what he describes as a campaign of persuasion. After all, Lech is a holiday resort. 'I attended a meeting with the University of Vienna and the Forestry Commission to discuss how to stop people skiing in the woods. The general view was that you can put up as many ropes and signs as you like, but that the only effective method is men with machine guns. I was able to tell them that at Lech we have succeeded, thanks to a long and gradual process of educating people. We have noticed an enormous change in attitude. Now if someone drops a sweet paper on the mountainside there is someone behind who says, "Excuse me, I think you have lost something." Ten years ago no one cared.'

The question that many less advanced resorts should perhaps be asking themselves is whether they can afford a 'long and gradual process' to tackle a problem which demands a response within years rather than decades.

Getting equipped

As anyone bitten by the skiing bug finds out all too soon, kitting yourself out for skiing is something of a nightmare. Not only is the equipment and clothing expensive, but also it's virtually impossible to know which brands or models will meet your needs; or whether the new, improved product that everyone else seems to be using is actually any advance on what you're using at present; or whether your apparent inability to make any progress towards perfect parallel turns can be attributed to your inferior skis/boots/thermal underwear.

It's tempting to spend huge amounts of money rather than have doubts like these gnawing away at the few shreds of confidence you possess. In this chapter, we aim to help you find a cheaper strategy. We assume you're familiar with the basics of ski equipment and clothing; if not, turn first to 'A Skiing Primer' – which includes a section on the important question of whether to rent or buy.

Choosing boots

Beginners, intermediates and experts require different things of their boots. Racers, who want the ultimate in control, often use traditional boots (frequently out-of-date models) with stiff shells and custom-moulded inners to get a tight grip on the foot: the stiffer the shell and the firmer the inner padding, the more directly any leg movement is transmitted to the ski. If you're an advanced skier, you might well use boots much like the ones racers use. But for most skiers, precise transmission of leg movements is not so crucial, and it's worth sacrificing some control in exchange for comfort; and in the very early stages some movement within the boot is positively desirable.

So boots for ordinary skiers are 'de-tuned' versions of the ideal ski boot; the further down the makers' ranges you look (which normally means the further down in price), the more you will find boots designed to be comfortable and accommodating. They will have shells which are more flexible at the cuff, they will flex forward more easily as you bend your ankles, and the inner padding will be softer.

It isn't easy to find a boot which will be comfortable throughout a seven-hour skiing day and at the same time give you the degree of control you need. A particular snag is that there are now boots on the market which seem to be designed entirely for comfort, and are far too spongy for anyone but an absolute beginner – and, as we explain in 'A Skiing Primer', absolute beginners should be renting, not buying. There is in the end no substitute for trying boots out on the slopes; but you make success in picking a boot in the shop more likely if you understand the different parts of the boot, and how they vary between

Boot features

front-entry boot

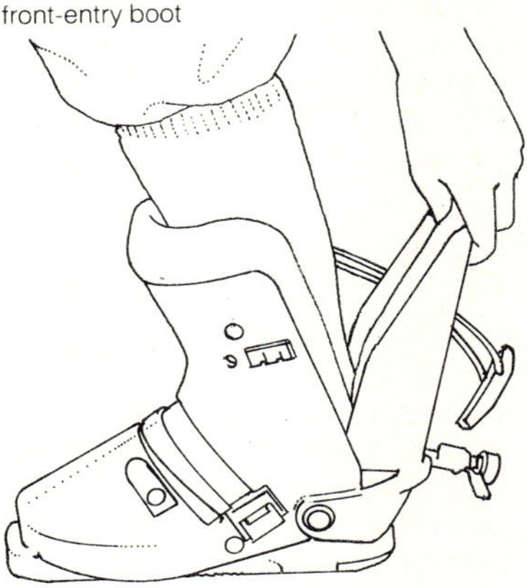

rear-entry boot

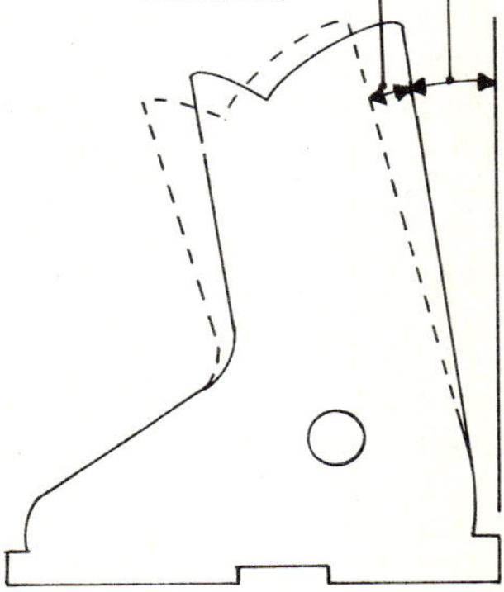

Boot shells vary in **height**. Experts' boots reach high up the leg; beginners' boots should not reach nearly so high.

Front-entry boots have a tongue, and open like an everyday laced boot. They are normally closed and tightened with a row of three to five clips. **Rear-entry** boots have a hinged flap behind the calf which opens to let you get your foot in, and pushes the foot forwards into the shell when closed. There are no hard and fast rules as to which type provides a better fit. Rear-entry boots are easy to get into. But the majority of ski racers, who need a particularly close fit, continue to ski in front-entry boots.

The boots you choose must fit your foot comfortably to start with. But when you're skiing it's equally important that you're able to **adjust** the boot, reducing its volume around the foot. On a front-entry boot, there will usually be two, three or four clips to tighten the fit around the foot, ankle and lower leg. The fit of a rear-entry boot is normally tightened by an internal plate, cable or inflatable air bladder which presses against the instep. There may be only one such device, or more.

All boots have a built-in **forward lean**, which means that the shell above the ankle is angled forwards (usually by 10 to 15 degrees from vertical). Avoid boots with the most pronounced forward lean unless you want to ski aggressively. Some boots can be switched from forward lean to vertical to make walking easier. Some boots for experts allow adjustment of the forward lean.

Boots are also designed to **flex**, so that you can press your shin forwards without a great deal of force. Ideally the shell should be hinged at the ankle. Some boots have a flex control so that you can adjust the boot's flexibility to suit your weight and strength and the amount of forward pressure you want to apply to the ski – useful for advanced skiers.

Some boots now have a built-in **cant control** to alter the angle of the upper boot to the sole, thus compensating for bow-legs or knock-knees.

A **non-skid heel** makes boots safer for walking; they wear out – buy replacements when you buy the boots.

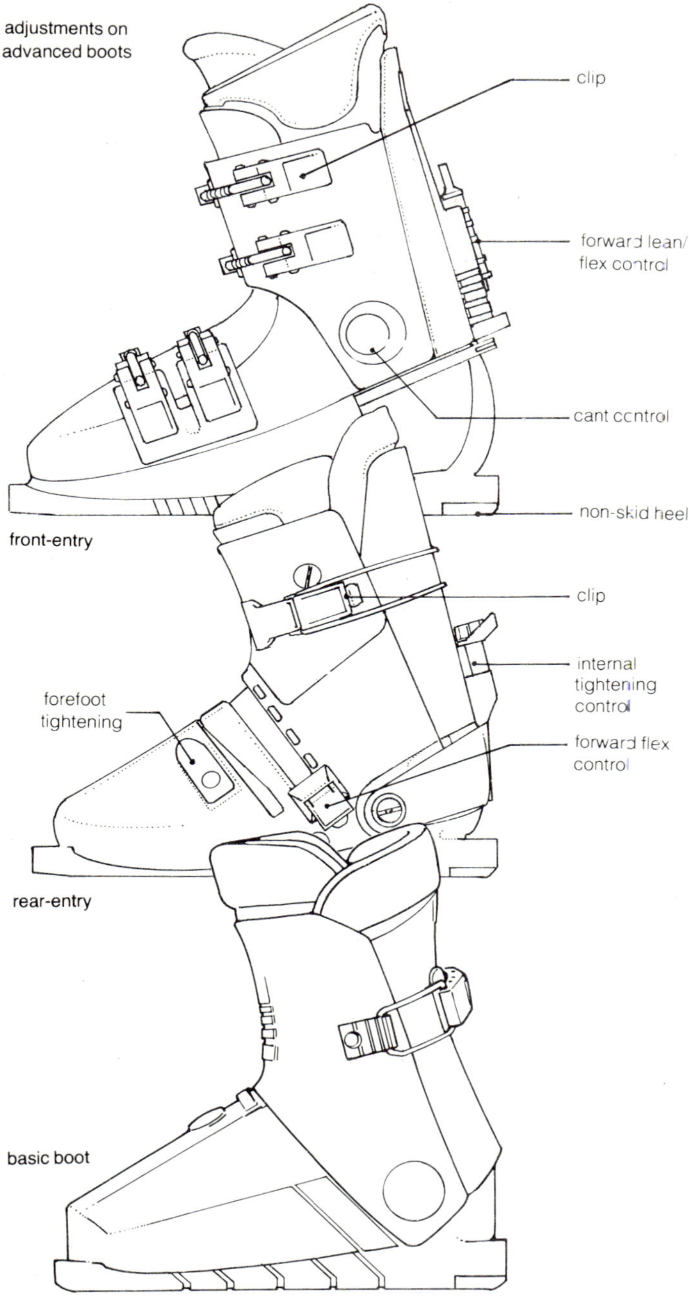
adjustments on advanced boots
clip
forward lean/ flex control
cant control
non-skid heel
front-entry
clip
internal tightening control
forefoot tightening
forward flex control
rear-entry
basic boot

models. These days there are two basic types of outer **shell** – the conventional *front-entry* type, and the newer *rear-entry* sort – and a wide range of **adjustments** to give a close fit to your foot. There are some variations in type of **inner** boot, too.

The comfort, convenience and simplicity of the rear-entry design has won the approval of around 80 per cent of boot buyers recently. But, for the moment at least, front-entry boots seem to be resisting extinction: many expert skiers and racers have rejected the rear-entry concept, arguing that the plastic shells do not fit closely enough. For the great majority of recreational skiers, rear-entry boots have a lot to be said for them; but it's still important to distinguish between good rear-entry boots and bad rear-entry boots. The important thing to consider is what goes on inside the outer shell.

Most rear-entry boots, unless they are very basic beginners' models, have some means of clamping the foot inside the shell. The mechanisms fall into three basic types:

- a cable which is looped over the instep and is pulled tight by a clip or dial at the back of the boot;
- a plate over the instep which is screwed down to hold the foot firmly;
- an air bladder between the inner boot and outer shell which is inflated by a small pump built in to the boot and fills out the boot to tighten the fit.

Experience suggests that the first type of mechanism is best for most skiers. It provides an immediate positive fit and the closest effect to that achieved by a traditional boot. If the cable is controlled by a clip (as featured on all Salomon, most Raichle and some Nordica models) the tightness of fit is 'memorised' from day to day. Air boots have their followers. They are usually quite comfortable, but the pump usually has to be worked repeatedly to achieve a tight fit, and there is no way of knowing precisely how tight you have 'set' the boot; it's all too easy to spend your time veering from too sloppy to too tight.

The efficient working of a ski binding depends on the boot's ability to slide out of the binding with the minimum of friction. The boot should have a DIN/ISO standard sole shape (boots made before 1980 may not conform and should probably be replaced – check with a good binding technician). Boots made from soft, rubbery *thermoplastics* – mainly beginners' or childrens' models – are potentially dangerous because of the friction they generate. (You can test a boot by trying to use it as a pencil eraser – if it works, it's thermoplastic.)

Choosing your size

Although ski shops often have UK shoe sizes marked on the boots they're selling (or at least on the boxes containing them), up to now boots have basically conformed to Continental or American shoe sizes. But this winter sees the introduction of a new international system of sizing, called Mondopoint, which is meant to replace the existing systems. So far, the new system has been adopted by four major boot manufacturers – Nordica, Dynafit, Caber and Lange. Salomon seem likely to stick with their unique sizing system, which uses the foot length and width and the instep height to determine an overall volume for your foot. The new system, like the tradtional shoe sizes, relates only to the length of your foot; in fact, in the new system your size *is* the length of your foot, measured in centimetres – a blissfully simple arrangement which deserves to spread to shoe sizing in general. A men's size 9 converts to 28 on the Mondopoint scale, and a women's size 5 converts to 24. It's important to realise that getting the length of the boot to match the length of your foot is only half the battle – see below.

Getting the fit right

Finding a good comfortable pair of boots should be your clear priority when buying equipment. A hurried purchase could be a disaster, so allow plenty of time to try different models in different shops. Here are some guidelines to help you.

- Try boots at specialist ski shops where there are likely to be staff who can help with specific fitting problems – first by working out what your problem is and then if necessary making modifications to the shell or inner boot. Ask whether these services are available. Avoid Saturdays and the busy pre-Christmas rush if you can.
- Consider going to one of the larger ski shows held around Britain in October or November (mainly London, Birmingham, Manchester and Glasgow), in order to draw up a short-list of boots. You can visit a number of retailers, all under one roof, with a large selection of boots – though it's rather too hectic to evaluate a boot thoroughly. Go on a weekday: weekends are much too busy to get good service.
- Take along the socks you will be skiing in, and wear them (one pair only) when trying out boots. (See 'A Skiing Primer' for advice on socks.)
- Start with your normal shoe size but expect to move up or down a half size or more, as necessary. The new international size scale (see above) may or may not simplify matters – you still have to convert your normal UK size into the international size. Your toes should be free to wiggle inside the boot. Lean back in the boot (get someone to hold the front down) and your toes should lightly touch the front of the boot if the size is about right.
- Ask to try the boots out with some skis, or bindings fixed to dummy skis. Then you'll be able to ensure that your heel is firmly held down: put all your weight on one foot, and push that knee forwards and downwards, with your shin pressed against the front of the boot. There should be no upward movement of your heel. If you find the pressure on your shin painful you may be better off with a softer boot.
- The boots should also hold you firmly around the calf and around the instep but without causing cramp, numbness or pressure.
- If a pair of boots seem comfortable at first, walk around and flex your ankles for a further 20 minutes to check for discomfort.
- Try boots from different manufacturers. They can vary appreciably in fit since the inner boots are modelled to different lasts. Try different boots on your left and right feet to compare fit.
- Try operating the clips and other fitting controls while you wear the boots – and preferably while wearing gloves. Are they convenient and easy to use?
- Once you've bought the boots, wear them at home or ski in them at a

plastic slope to identify any problems before your holiday.

• Be careful not to buy boots that are too large. There is a natural tendency for inner boots to 'stretch' in use, so a boot which is comfortably loose when new may end up a half or full size too large.

Some shops offer a 'comfort guarantee': if the boots turn out to be uncomfortable when you actually go skiing, you get a credit note for the price you paid, less a rental charge – around a quarter to a third of the original price. Whether this represents good value will depend on how much skiing you get out of the boots: if you manage to use them for three weeks you'll have done quite well; but if you have to hire replacements in the resort you'll effectively have hired two pairs for the duration of your holiday. Some shops take a different approach, and undertake to modify the boots you buy so as to make them fit comfortably – or to exchange them for another pair. Again, this arrangement is fine if you don't find the boots too painful to use.

If you are nervous about commiting yourself to a pair of boots and possibly wasting the cost of two weeks' hire, the thing to do is to wait until you get to the resort, and find a hire shop which has new or nearly new equipment on hire. Ask if they are prepared to sell you boots that you have hired, and if so at what price (taking care to get clear whether this does or does not cover the hire period as well). This arrangement allows you to do what no other deal does: try out the boots on snow with the option of buying them at a fair price if you like them or returning them without paying any penalty if you don't.

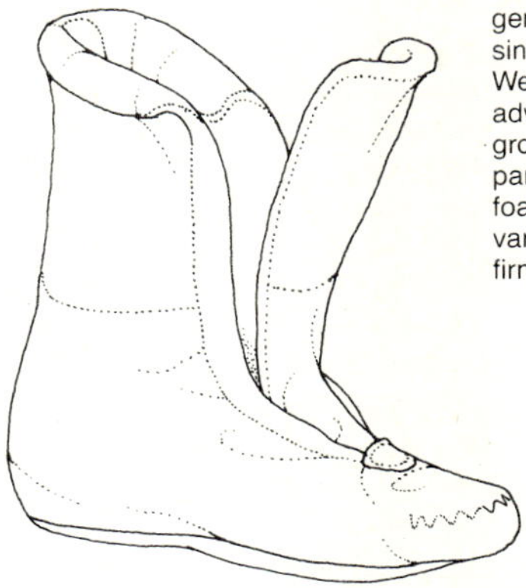

Within the stiff outer shell of a ski boot is the foam-padded **inner boot**. There are two varieties. Shown here is a *stitched* inner, made of several pieces of foam-backed fabric or leather or plastic, sewn together in much the same way as a conventional shoe. A *moulded* inner generally has no seams, but is made of a single piece of synthetic foam, like a Wellington boot; this type has the advantage that it can be shaved or ground to relieve pressure on the foot at particular points. The hardness of the foam padding in either type of inner varies from soft, for beginners' boots, to firm, for experts' boots.

Warmer feet

In low temperatures it is the extremities of the body – feet and hands – that suffer first; for some skiers, keeping fingers and toes alive and well is a real and persistent problem despite the fact that modern plastic ski boots, lined with foam, have proved a lot warmer than the old leather boots that they have replaced.

If you have trouble with cold feet, start by ensuring that your boots are as dry and warm as possible in the morning. If the ski room is a cold and damp basement, take them into your bedroom, taking precautions to prevent damage to the carpet. Remove the inner boots if they are damp, and place them near (but not directly on) a radiator.

To get your boots even warmer before you set out – or to warm them up at lunch-time – you can get chemical heating packs which can be inserted in the inner boot. These can be used only once and are not controllable – so there is a chance of overheating unless you keep a close eye on the temperature. You can improve the insulation of your boots by installing reflective insoles, which reduce the amount of heat lost through the sole of the boot.

If money is no object, you can trade up to specially warm boots. Some ski boots have higher insulation standards – a spin-off from the design of ski mountaineering boots – through the use of new thermal lining materials. Goretex Thermo Dry padding, featured on some Dynafit models, has proved to be warmer than average. But probably the most effective solution is the electrically heated boot, powered by rechargeable batteries mounted in the boot which can provide a number of bursts of heat during the day by way of an element in the inner boot insole. Heated boots are made by Lange, Raichle and Nordica. They do a good job of keeping even the coldest feet alive, though early models were not entirely reliable.

Problem feet

The majority of skiers find boots that fit 'off-the-shelf', and you should certainly try out all available brands and models before concluding that you're a special case. If and when you reach that conclusion, you can have a pair of standard boots specially modified – either by having the inner or shell of a standard boot altered, or by fitting orthopaedic insoles moulded to your feet. The most common problems are these:

Wide foot If you find your boots exert pressure on the bones at the widest part of the foot, the first thing to try is modification of the inner boot. A moulded inner can be ground away at the pressure points; with a stitched inner you can try padding the area around the pressure points – a less sure remedy. In more extreme cases the shell of the boot can be stretched by heating the plastic to soften it – though there are limits to how far this can be taken.

Flat foot Various problems can arise if your feet don't have the normal arched instep. If you feel pressure on the back of the heel, try fitting arch supports or heat-moulded orthopaedic insoles. If the pressure is on the ankle bones, you can fit C-shaped pads to the inner boot, ahead of the outer bone; a moulded inner can be ground away at the pressure point if pads don't solve the problem.

High instep If the arch of your foot is exaggerated, you may feel pressure on top of the instep or underneath the arch. First, try removing any arch-support insole from the boot. If the problem remains, a moulded inner can be ground away over the instep.

A good ski shop will be able to carry out the modifications. Orthopaedic insoles, made by Sidas or Formthotics, have helped many people gain extra support and comfort in their boots. They are moulded to the shape of the foot when heated. The cost ranges from around £15 to £30, and many specialist ski shops now offer the service.

The alternative to modifying standard boots is to buy boots which are specially designed to cope with difficult feet. Some models made by Dachstein, Dynafit and Koflach have an inner which can be filled with foam to fit your foot. The process involves standing inside the boot while bladders inside the inner boot are injected with a rubbery plastic foam. This sets to shape around the foot. If done well this can be a useful way of dealing with unusual bone protrusions and so on, but successful foaming requires considerable expertise on the shop's part. Foaming also has the disadvantage that the process is irreversible: the foam sets solid inside the boot, and is difficult to remove if the boot proves to be too tight in practice. Raichle have tackled this problem by introducing a new material called 'Flo', which is similarly injected to fill the space between the inner boot and the shell but does not set solid – it retains a putty-like consistency. This means that the amount of the filling in the boot can be adjusted up or down in the light of experience. At present, this feature is available on only one boot, the RX 979.

Problem legs

People with bow-legs or knock-knees tend to encounter special difficulties in skiing. If you have either problem (and it shows up as uneven wear of your normal shoe soles) you will probably find it hard to keep your ski soles flat on the snow and turn with a good parallel technique. If you have bow-legs, you'll tend to catch the outside edge of your skis on the snow in a gentle turn, with disastrous consequences.

When this problem was first tackled in the 1970s the cure was to fit angled wedges between the bindings and the skis, so that the soles of the skis were parallel to the snow even if your boot soles weren't. Although some shops still undertake this work, it's more common now to try to compensate with the boot. Many expensive boots now have a cant control which changes the angle of the boot's upper part relative to its sole. In most boots it is also possible to fit an angled plate under the inner boot. And some compensation can be introduced if you have a boot foamed to fit your foot (see above).

The latest idea comes from Salomon, and sounds as though it may be attractive for someone who needs more than a slight correction to the angle of the lower leg. On the new SX82 and SX92 models, the whole sole of the boot can be removed and replaced by a wedge-shaped sole which alters the angle of the upper boot to the ski.

Choosing skis

When choosing skis it's all too easy to be blinded by choice and pseudo-scientific jargon. Well over a hundred models are available in British ski shops and the more shops you visit the more brand names you'll find. Unfortunately, once you put the names, graphics and other gloss to one side, there are few immediately apparent differences between models. Boots you can to some extent evaluate in the shop; it's not so simple with skis. You can easily find yourself at the mercy of a very enthusiastic salesman who probably skis much better than you and has very firm ideas on what is This Year's Ski.

So how do you avoid buying the wrong ski, and make some attempt at narrowing the choice towards one which will suit your needs? The first step is to resolve to spend as little as possible. It's easy to spend a lot of money on skis in the hope that they'll transform your skiing technique; but they won't – a course of good instruction would be a better buy. While it's worth spending on boots and bindings, which can markedly affect your control and safety, the best that an expensive pair of skis can do is to make your skiing a little faster, a little more stable and a little more accurate. (Expert skiers, capable of appreciating subtle differences in ski performance, may well want to choose skis which are not only expensive, but specially designed for particular sorts of skiing – moguls, or powder; what we are concerned with here is the intermediate skier who wants a compromise ski for all sorts of skiing.)

The next thing is to make sure you're looking at skis that will suit your standard of skiing. Ski manufacturers produce different models for different groups of skiers, according to ability. Beginners' and intermediates' skis are deliberately 'de-tuned' to cope with imperfect technique on the part of the user and to handle easily at low speeds. Experts' skis are designed to give precise control at high speeds, when the pressure being exerted on the ski in turning is very high; an inexpert skier going more slowly would find such skis hard work.

Sorting out which skis will suit you isn't always easy. Standard 'target groups' of skiers were devised some years ago by the German and Austrian standards institutes, and on some skis you'll find a symbol which identifies the target group(s) the ski is made for – see below. But on most skis you won't, and your best bet then is to try to get hold of catalogues produced by the ski makers or by retailers (which draw on the makers' ones).

Using the definitions below you can easily assign yourself to one of the three target groups. (This will help you to determine what length of ski you need as well as in finding the right models.)

Target Group L – Beginners or those who can ski parallel on easy slopes only, and at slow speeds.
Target Group A – Intermediates who can ski parallel on moderate gradients and easy snow conditions at medium speeds.
Target Group S – Experts who can ski all types of slope, snow and gradient at higher speeds.

What length of ski?

Once upon a time, the length of skis you used was determined by how high above the ground you could reach – the 'hands-high' formula. The rule has a certain common-sense appeal – a very short person would certainly have trouble manoeuvring very long skis – but it is fundamentally wrong: it doesn't take account of the way skis work, which is by bending in response to the forces the skier subjects them to. These days, it's recognised that factors other than height need to be taken into account – that is, your weight and your standard of skiing; but height still receives more attention than it deserves.

It's easy to get confused by the apparently simple matter of the length of a ski. The confusion arises because different skis of a given length – 185cm, say – are designed to suit various sorts of skier. If designed for a big, heavy skier, a 185cm ski will be called a short or compact ski; if for a small, light skier, it will be called a full-length ski. Thus it is possible for one person's 'short' ski to be longer than another's 'full-length' one.

Short skis were all the rage a few years ago, when their advantage of easy turning attracted all the attention – not surprising, because the alternative then was the much more unwieldy full-length ski. Short skis are still the best bet for beginners, but ski makers now flatter intermediate skiers by insisting that they need something which is quicker and holds its direction better – the mid-length ski. Manufacturers have coined all sorts of names for their mid-length models: sport, stretch, Elite, Lite and Performance, for example.

Some manufacturers, recognising that height alone is not a good guide to the correct length of ski, have made length selection easier by marking on their skis a tiny chart which shows the length you need according to which of the L-A-S target groups you fall into (see previous page). But the lengths these markings give still relate to your height; for example, the marking shown below means that a skier in group A should use that ski in a length which reaches 15cm to 25cm above head height, a skier in group L in a length which reaches 5cm to 15cm above head height.

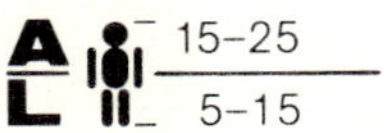

This is an improvement on going by height alone, but it still ignores the important question of weight. Two skiers of the same height would be led to buy the same length of ski, but a relatively heavy skier may overload the ski and bend it too much, making it slow and difficult to keep running straight, while a relatively light skier will find it difficult to turn. The formula on the next page gives ski lengths for all sorts of skier, based almost entirely on weight and style of skiing – taking height into account only as a final modifying factor.

Expert skiers can be expected to have learnt from experience what type and length of ski suits them and their style of skiing. At the other extreme, beginners can safely concentrate on persuading the ski hire shop to give them relatively short skis which will be easily managed in the slow, clumsy manoeuvres they'll be doing at first; for them, choosing skis by reference to height is quick and convenient, and should cause few problems – aim for skis reaching to eye height or lower.

But for the rest of the skiing population, deciding on the right length of ski isn't easy. The length of ski you need depends basically on the amount of force you're going to apply to the ski when executing turns; and that depends on your weight and the way you ski.

The calculation set out below gives most emphasis to these two factors. But it also takes account of the kind of slope you plan to spend your time on – recognising that moguls, for example, are more easily skied on a shorter ski than motorway pistes.

The choice of ski length cannot be separated from the choice of ski type. The 'target group' system explained on the previous two pages is becoming more widely accepted as a standard way of matching skiers to appropriate skis, and the calculation below will help you select your own group if you think you're on the borderline between two of the groups.

Categorise yourself

Under each of the following three subheadings, decide which category you fall in and write down the corresponding number of points.

A: How well do you ski?

category	*points*
You're among the best around	45
You're fast, smooth, confident and can keep pace with a top ski class	42
You're concentrating on traverse-free mogul skiing with some success	38
You like to ski black runs regularly but you haven't yet 'tamed' them	34
You're quick and safe on red runs	27
You like to keep it slow and easy	22
You've just achieved parallels	18
You're a keen learner	14
You're still scared stiff	10

B: Where do you like to ski?

category	*points*
On fast, open slopes	15
On all slopes	13
In bumps or powder	10
On soft red pistes	8
On soft blue pistes	5

C: What do you weigh?

category	*points*
4 to 4½ stone	27
4½ to 5 stone	30
5 to 5¾ stone	33
5¾ to 6½ stone	35
6½ to 7¼ stone	37
7¼ to 8 stone	39
8 to 9½ stone	41
9½ to 12 stone	43
12 to 14 stone	45
14 to 15½ stone	47
15½ stone plus	49

Find your target group

Add together your A and B points, and consult the table below.

A + B points	*target group*
15 – 26	DIN group L
27 – 51	DIN group A
52 – 60	DIN group S

Find your ski length

Add together all your points – A, B and C – and add 100 to the total. The result is your theoretical ideal ski length in centimetres. In practice, you will usually have to go for a ski slightly longer or shorter because skis lengths go up in jumps of 5cm or so. You may also wish to take account of your height at this stage: if you're unusually tall for your weight, you could go for a ski 5cm longer than the calculation indicates, if unusually short you could go for one 5cm shorter.

If you're very short for your weight you may find that this way of calculating ski length prescribes skis much longer than you're used to; if you're happy on 180cm skis but the calculation says you should be on 195cm ones, you ought not to feel obliged to change – but you might find it worth hiring some longer ones to see how they feel.

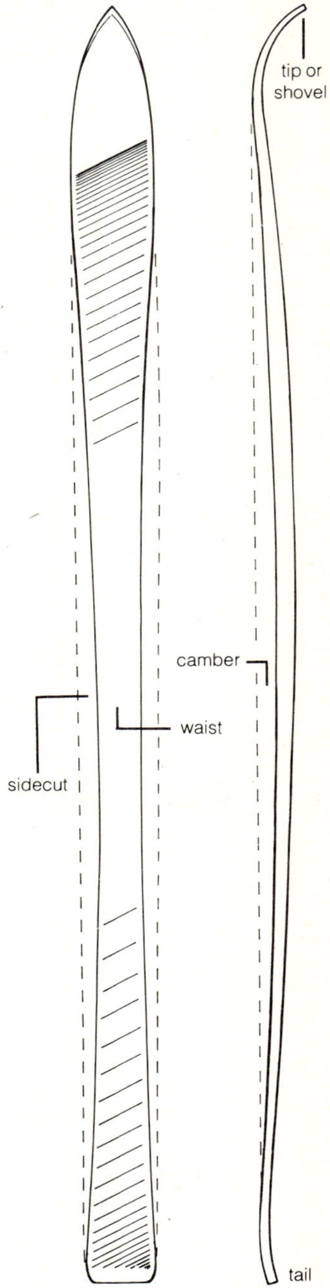

Ski characteristics

As we've stressed elsewhere, what's most important when choosing skis is not to get carried away by the glossy brochures and the sales pitch. You may find it easier to see through all that if you understand a bit about the theory of ski performance – and you'll also be better able to evaluate skis as you use them.

A top-down view of a ski shows that it is not the same width all the way along. The ski's *sidecut* – the degree to which it is waisted in the middle – affects its turning ability: the more pronounced the sidecut, the more the tip of the ski will tend to bite when the ski is tilted on to its edge, and the more easily the ski will perform a turn.

A side view shows that the thickess of the ski varies, too – it's thicker and stiffer in the centre than at the tip and tail – and that it has a definite curved shape. When put on a flat surface, the centre of an unweighted ski stands higher than the tip and tail; the purpose of this *camber* is to distribute the skier's weight along the length of the ski.

To show how a ski responds to the loads put on it, we've shown a ski on the facing page supported by a set of springs, like the springs in a mattress. The natural shape of the ski is visible only when the ski is unweighted (1). On hard pistes, a uniform distribution of weight (2) is what you need to keep the whole edge of the ski in contact with the snow – and this means you need a relatively stiff ski. When skiing deep, soft snow, contact is not the problem since the whole ski will be immersed; what you need then is a softer-flexing ski so that the tip tends to float (3). If you use a ski which is too short and too flexible, it will be inclined to flex too much; your weight will be concentrated beneath your boots, and the ski will not turn properly on hard snow (4). If on the other hand you use a ski which is too long and stiff, your weight will be concentrated at the tip and tail, making it difficult to swivel the ski on the snow (5).

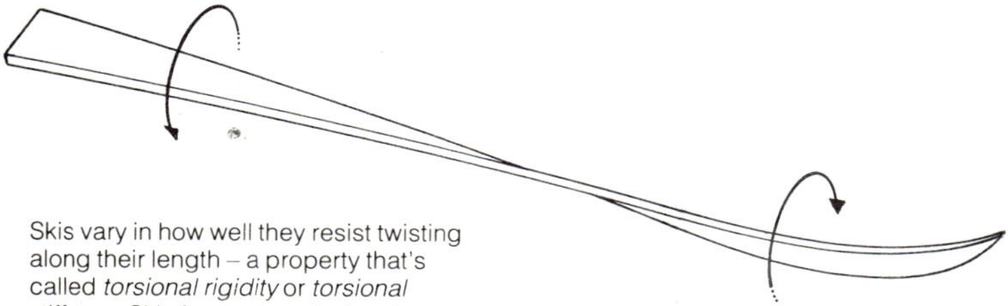

Skis vary in how well they resist twisting along their length – a property that's called *torsional rigidity* or *torsional stiffness*. Skis for experts don't twist easily. The result is that the skis' edges are biting just as hard at the tip and tail as they are under your foot. With a less rigid ski the tip and tail will tend to flatten on the snow the harder you turn – not much good for the experts' 'carved' turns, but fine for the vague skidding turns that most skiers produce.

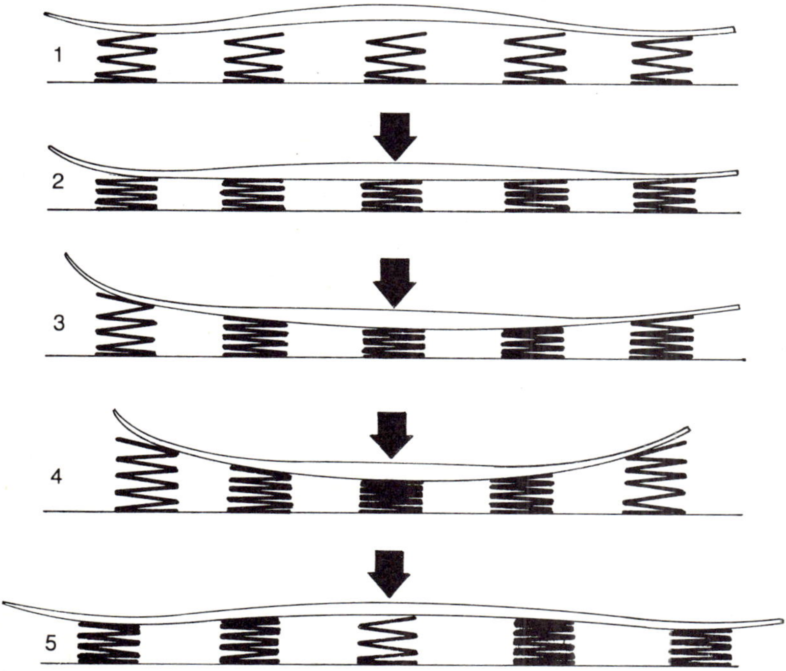

Looking after skis

Skis will perform at their best only if the soles and edges are kept in perfect condition. Unfortunately, it's all too easy to damage a ski by hitting the occasional exposed rock. You can often avoid the worst of them by keeping to the side of the piste. If you see a rock ahead and can't avoid it, try to take it straight rather than skidding across it – a groove cut down the sole is easier to repair than a gash across the edge. If the snow is wearing really thin, it's best to rent skis, in spite of the cost. Any serious damage you do to your skis may be irreparable or involve re-soling – an expensive business.

The ski's **edges** need to be sharp in order to give you control on hard snow or ice – though at the extreme tip and tail of the ski it's advisable to have slightly dulled edges. Check your edges regularly for sharpness by drawing the face of a fingernail across them. A well sharpened edge will produce wide shavings. Edges should be sharpened to a right-angle (or a little more acute). This is a possible DIY job – a special edge-sharpening tool from a ski shop is best but if you have an appropriate file already you can make do with that.

Shallow notches down the middle of the ski's **sole** don't markedly affect the performance of the ski, but are easily repaired. You can repair them yourself using a special 'candle' of plastic material (the common brand is P-tex) which drips molten plastic into the notch; once it has set you scrape the repair smooth with a rectangular steel scraper. On the new, harder 'sintered' soles it is better to weld or patch the repair material into the sole. Any deep holes which expose the layer underneath the sole, or notches along the edge of the ski, should be repaired professionally. The latter can seriously affect the turning power of the ski in some circumstances.

Even if you manage to avoid conspicuous damage to the soles of your skis, in time they will wear down in the middle, and become concave. The middle of the sole cannot be built up (unless you have the ski completely re-soled); the edges of the sole must instead be reduced until they are level with the middle. A slightly concave sole can be filed flat by hand using a single-cut file – get one around ten inches long, with a handle. Hold the file in both hands flat against the sole, with your thumbs pressed downwards over the ski edges; file in one direction, from tip to tail. The grooves of the file will become clogged with plastic; clear them regularly with a fine wire brush or a special file 'card'.

For flattening more seriously worn soles most shops use a large belt-sanding machine, but it is not a wholly satisfactory approach. Unless the ski is drawn smoothly over the belt by a skilled operator, uneven grinding takes place. A belt also tends to grind the sole rather coarsely to a slightly lower level than the edges – it's then vital that the edges be cut back by hand filing. A better result is achieved with a high-speed stone grinding wheel. Regrettably, few shops have these – look for grinding machines made by Montana or Wintersteiger.

Skis run best with a thin film of **wax** on the soles. This also helps protect the soles. You can apply wax by rubbing a solid block along the sole, or you can buy it in aerosol or paste form – more convenient, but more expensive. But the best solution is to apply hot molten wax which will form a bond with the sole and last much longer.

Most ski shops use a special machine for this job: the ski is pushed over a roller which picks up molten wax from a small reservoir and leaves a fairly even coating along the sole. Some shops carelessly leave it at that; but the wax coating should then be scraped down and the centre groove cleared – most of the wax should end up on the workshop floor. If the wax film is proud of the steel edges, the effect of the edges will be reduced. The soles should be smooth and polished, with the film of wax no thicker than paper.

You can hot-wax your own skis satisfactorily with a few pieces of uncomplicated equipment. You can get special waxing irons, heated by a small butane gas cylinder, but an ordinary non-steam electric iron is fine for the job – provided you take a socket adaptor with you or fit a local plug to the flex. The wax is melted and dripped on to the ski by holding a block against the surface of the iron. You then spread it quickly over the sole with the iron, taking great care to avoid overheating the sole, which is easily damaged. You'll need a rectangular steel scraper to smooth the wax down. Unfortunately it's not always a practical proposition to tackle this work in a hotel or chalet – be prepared to clear up a fairly messy residue of wax shavings.

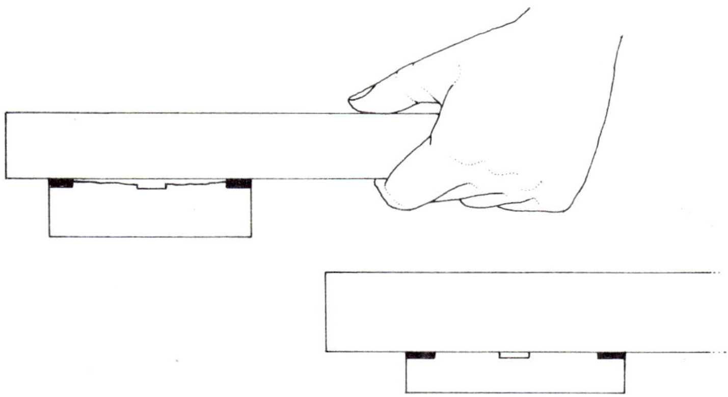

Check that your ski soles are flat from edge to edge by holding a ruler across the sole. If you can see light under the ruler (apart from the groove, of course) the sole needs filing, sanding or grinding flat – a concave sole will make the ski difficult to pivot on the snow.

Choosing bindings

You'll find that buying a pair of bindings is pretty straightforward after searching for a boot that fits or a ski that suits. Most bindings are suitable for most people – they have a wide range of adjustment. If you weigh between 45kg and 90kg (7st and 14st), more-or-less any binding sold for adults will do; but check the recommended weight ranges for specific models before you buy.

Satisfy yourself that a binding has been tested and approved by one or more of the Continental test or standards institutes. If it has been approved, the manufacturer is entitled to use the appropriate institute's logo on its products or packaging – look out for the initials TUV, IAS or GS (Germany), BFU (Switzerland), ISO (International) or ONORM (Austria).

Bindings of the following brands are generally approved and available in the UK: Ess, Geze, Look, Marker, Salomon and Tyrolia. Each manufacturer produces a range of models with varying degrees of mechanical sophistication. The advantages of buying the top models are usually over-stated, even for advanced skiers. Anyone except a racer or very aggressive skier will get satisfactory performance from one of the cheaper models.

What all bindings have in common is some way of triggering the release by hand (or with your ski pole) – it's worth finding out how convenient this is – and screw controls to set the point at which the toe and heel units will release in a fall. Modern bindings show the setting on a scale which is supposedly calibrated to an international standard. Ski brakes are now a standard feature of bindings.

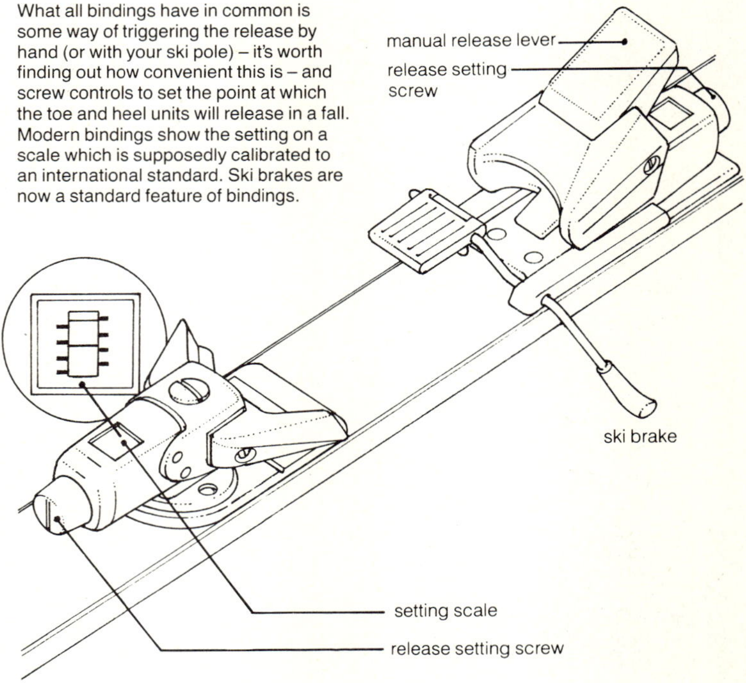

Most bindings have very much the same overall form, though there are occasional departures – for example, the Ess VAR binding (not shown here) has toe and heel units connected by a flexible steel band, and the whole assembly can be shifted back and forth along the ski to alter the way the ski behaves.

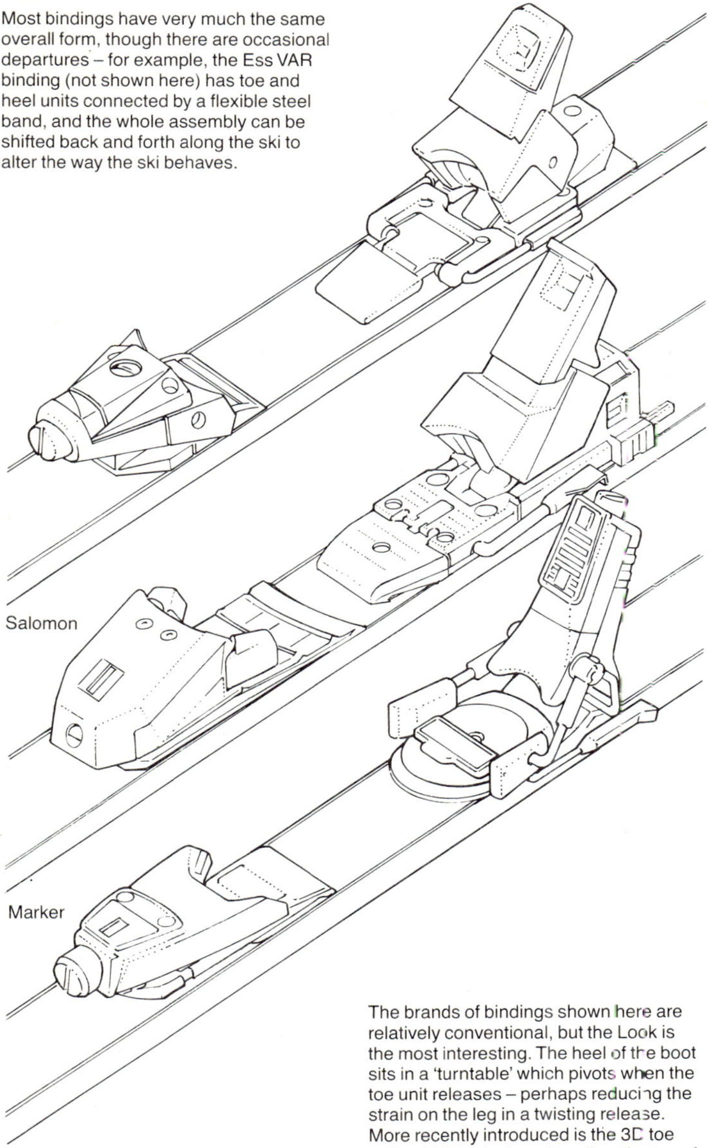

The brands of bindings shown here are relatively conventional, but the Look is the most interesting. The heel of the boot sits in a 'turntable' which pivots when the toe unit releases – perhaps reducing the strain on the leg in a twisting release. More recently introduced is the 3D toe unit, which is designed to allow the toe of the boot to move upwards as well as sideways. The aim is to release the boot in a backward fall in the same way that the heel unit releases in a forward fall. Some kinds of knee injuries may be reduced as a result.

Bindings safety

It's very important that bindings are properly set to suit you and your boots. In principle, the best way to make sure of this is to leave it to a competent, conscientious ski-shop mechanic. But not all mechanics fall into that category, and there is a lot to be said for understanding how to adjust your bindings yourself.

- Get your supplier to demonstrate the adjustments and (if you're buying) give you a detailed instruction leaflet.
- Check that the bindings are adjusted to the size of your boots – if they're not, the boot may wobble in the bindings, or be jammed dangerously by excessive friction. The heel unit will incorporate an indicator to show whether the two units are the right distance apart, and the toe unit must be set at a height above the ski which holds the toe-piece of the boot precisely but not tightly.
- Mark your skis left and right and ensure that each set of bindings is adjusted to suit the correct boot – there may be slight differences between the soles of your two boots.
- Check that the release settings are right for you. If the bindings have the new internationally agreed setting scales, you should be able to work out from the instructions what setting to use; ideally, you should then have the bindings tested to see that the scale setting is accurate. The alternative (which you'll have to resort to if you don't have information on what the scale means) is to adjust the settings by trial and error. You can start out on the slopes with low release settings and gradually adjust them upwards until you're no longer coming out of the bindings when you don't want to; or you can set the bindings before you start out. Put your boots on and follow the steps set out below for each ski. In each case, start with the release settings at the minimum, so that the binding will open easily; turn up the release setting a bit and try again; repeat the exercise several times, turning up the release setting each time, until it takes all your strength to open the binding.

To check heel release Put the skis on the floor with their tips against a wall. Step into one set of bindings; get someone to stand on the back of the ski; simulate falling forwards by leaning towards the ski tip, pressing your knee forwards and pulling up at the heel.

To check toe release Step into one set of bindings on a carpeted floor (not one that's very precious). Lean forwards, pushing your weight down at the ball of your foot; grip your knee with both hands and tip the ski on to its outside edge (right edge on right ski, left edge on left ski). Twist your whole body towards that same edge (clockwise on right ski, anti-clockwise on left ski) while putting your weight on the ski.

- Whenever your skis have been left exposed to the elements, check by hand that the bindings are not iced up.
- Before stepping into the bindings, always scrape snow, ice or dirt from the soles of your boots. They can dangerously jam up the toe unit.

Choosing poles

The most important thing about ski poles is that they should be the right length. Poles for adults vary from 110cm to 135cm, in 5cm steps. When choosing a pole in the shop you have to allow for the few inches of shaft which digs into the snow when skiing – see drawing. If you are unsure which of two pole lengths to choose, always take the longer one. If necessary, a pole can be cut down to size by removing the handle and cutting off an inch or two of the shaft with a hacksaw.

The quality of alloy used in making a pole's tubular shaft is crucial to its strength. Look for poles conforming to DIN 7884. Avoid heavy poles, which can be tiring.

Handles vary widely in design. It's important that you're comfortable when gripping the handle. Moulded finger grips help a lot as does a good platform under the hand for support. Most handles come with a strap, which not only makes it less likely that you'll lose the poles but also allows you to put weight on the pole without having to grip the handle tightly. Strapless or 'swordgrip' handles have a flexible shield around the back of the hand which holds the pole on to your hand in normal circumstances but allows it to be pulled away in a fall. They were developed originally for racing; they have the advantage for ordinary skiers that they're less fuss to get in and out of – but most people seem to prefer handles with straps.

If you're buying handles with straps make sure that they are of the type which releases in an emergency. This will ensure that your arms and wrists don't suffer if your pole gets caught in something and you continue moving, or if you get seriously tangled up in a fall.

When you plant your pole in the snow, your forearm should be just about horizontal. To check the length of a pole in the shop, you have to allow for the two or three inches at the bottom which will be sticking in the snow. Do this by holding the pole upside down, with your hand immediately under the basket.

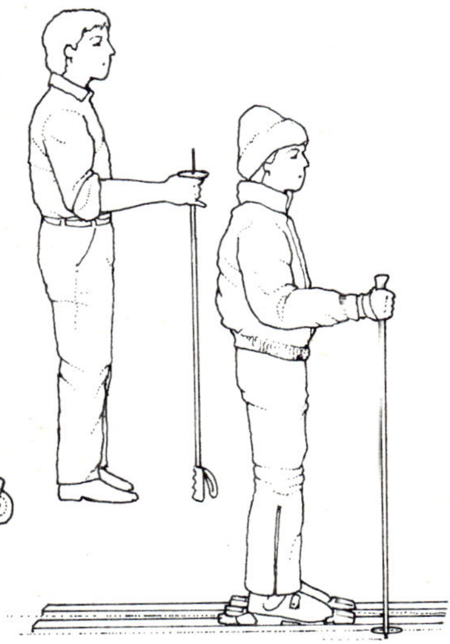

Be sure that you're happy with the way the straps are adjusted, and that they are designed to release in a serious fall.

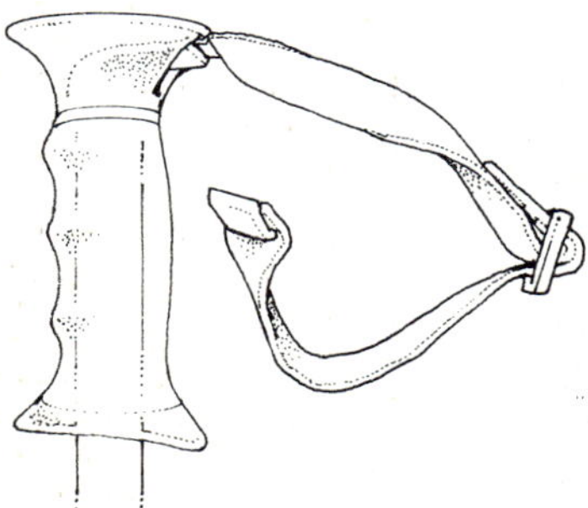

Choosing clothes

As we explain in 'A Skiing Primer', ski clothes are more often designed to look good than to work well. It's difficult to give clear guidance on what to buy, when the effectiveness of a garment can depend on small details of its construction – and when fashion demands that each season's range should be different from the last. But there are definite practical considerations to be borne in mind as you grapple with the temptation to junk last year's boiler suit for this year's parka; and even quite experienced skiers might be grateful to be reminded of those considerations – and for some demystification of the 'miracle materials' you'll find in the shops.

Insulation

The basis of insulation is trapped air; the more air that's trapped in the material of a garment, and the less that air is able to move around, the warmer it will keep you. Jackets are usually padded with either an artificial fibre filling or natural down. These fillings vary both in thickness and weight; and there are now special versions of fibre meant to give better thermal insulation for the same amount of material.

Ordinary artificial *fibre* filling is the cheapest and most common, and works adequately provided there's enough of it; it doesn't absorb water, so even when wet it retains much of its insulating power. The new improved fibres trap air more effectively in two different ways. *Thinsulate* is made up of microfibres that are one tenth the thickness of typical synthetic fibres; the result is that air trapped within the filling has more difficulty moving around. *Dacron Hollofil* is made up of hollow fibres which trap air within themselves as well as in the spaces in between.

Down is the fluffy, not-quite-feathery undercoating of birds, usually waterfowl; it puffs up in use, making the garment bulky. When not in use, the garments can be squeezed up into small bundles. Down is light and very warm when dry, but can become heavy and lose some of its effect when wet. You need to make sure that it's encased in a water-resistant material.

Fabrics

Most materials of which ski clothing might be made are either impervious to water (in which case you get moisture evaporating from the body condensing on the inside of the garment) or not (in which case you get soaked by rain or wet snow). Fabrics can be waterproofed, which in theory means that big drops of water will be kept out, while water vapour will be allowed to escape; but it is rarely completely successful. There are now several materials which have been specially developed to tackle this problem, which skiing shares with mountaineering and other similar pursuits. Some of the main brands are listed below – but new developments are in the pipeline which may put these in the shade.

Gore-Tex The original 'hi-tech' fabric: it's a laminate, with a membrane sandwiched in the middle of the fabric to do the essential job of discriminating between water drops trying to get in and water vapour trying to get out. Having used a Gore-Tex jacket for two seasons we are unconvinced of its practical value: the membrane certainly seems to do its job, but in wet weather the outer layer of fabric becomes sodden, particularly towards the bottom of the garment. Materials which shed water entirely seem to us a better bet.

Stormbeta Fabric coated with a special 'synthetic wax treatment'. The makers claim a waterproof and highly flexible finish, high tear strength, increased wind and abrasion resistance, plus a surface which repels dirt and grease. This process has been applied to polyester/cotton materials which, in the past, have not proved receptive to coatings.

Mecpor Another fabric with a special surface coating – in this case a layer of resin.

Entrant A Japanese fabric coated with polyurethane and also available in a 'Hi-Resist' version with a Goretex-like membrane. This may represent the best compromise between waterproofing and breathability at present available.

Silmond A non-coated fabric, less water-resistant than some competitors but with better 'breathability'.

Seams and stitching are extremely important and you need to look at these aspects carefully. No matter how waterproof the actual fabric is, if the seams are loosely stitched or made from a non-waterproof fabric there's always the possibility that water will get in through them. The same thing applies to wind – a garment will not be windproof unless all the seams are airtight.

It's important that your ski clothes should not be too slippery – when you fall on a steep slope, you want to come to a halt as soon as possible rather than sliding until you hit something or somebody. Some years ago, ski clothes were made which were dangerously slippery; once the lesson had been learnt, fabrics which weren't so slippery appeared on the market with the tag 'anti-gliss'. As the slippery fabrics have disappeared, so has the need to label other fabrics in this way.

Jackets

Insulation Ordinary fibre filling is the norm, and there's no particular reason to pay for the more expensive alternatives unless you particularly want to look slim (when the fancy fibres are what you need) or fat (when down will achieve the desired effect).

Room to move? Does it give you plenty of room to move around and stretch, particularly round the shoulders? Jackets which come with either stretch inserts or pleats in the shoulders provide a greater range of movement. When you raise or move your arms, the bottom of the jacket should stay at (or below) the waist, and sleeves should stay at the wrist. A close-fitting waist prevents snow going up your back, and close fitting cuffs do the same for your arms.

Durable shoulders? How will the shoulders stand up to the wear and tear of carrying skis? It's a good idea to have extra protection on the shoulders, preferably in a dark colour so that the dirt won't show.

Effective collar? Will the collar be any good for keeping the wind and

snow at bay on a cold day? A high collar that you can zip right up to your nose is best.
Good hood? Some jackets have an attached hood zipped into the collar, which is particularly useful if you find yourself skiing in a blizzard; a drawstring is needed to pull the hood tight around your face, leaving only your eyes, nose and mouth exposed.
Window pocket? A window pocket, usually on the front or the sleeve, can save you digging in your pockets for your lift pass every time you have to produce it – unless you have to put the pass through a computerised machine to get on the lift (which is now quite common).
Zips Does the zip look as if you could work it with your thick ski-gloves on – not only unzipping but engaging the two bits?
Warm waist? You need to consider jackets along with trousers – one or other of them must take responsibility for keeping you warm and dry around the middle.

Trousers

Insulation Fibre filling is the norm in salopettes. You don't need as much insulation as you do in a jacket, and pants made of other, less well-insulating materials are worth considering if you don't like the baggy look of fibre-insulated ones – stretch nylon and cord pants are usually much more close-fitting, but cord is not always waterproof. You can buy loose, and light, water- and wind-proof overtrousers to wear over ski pants and they will keep you warmer.
Room to move? Can you squat and touch your toes without distressing either the garment or yourself?
Warm waist? Dungaree-style trousers are what you need if you plan to wear a short jacket.
Warm ankles? It's important that the trouser leg has an effective arrangement (usually an elasticated cuff) to go over the top of your boot and keep the snow out.
Durable ankles? The part of your trouser leg which goes over the top of your boot gets a lot of wear on the inside from the other ski; it needs a patch of tough material which won't be cut or easily worn by the ski edge.

One-piece suits

Most of the same considerations apply. Suits with the jacket attached to the trousers by a zip are more practical than those which are indivisible; but unaccountably they are very rare in the shops. The most important part of these suits is the zip; make sure it's sturdy and easy to use. It's very important to have plenty of room to manoeuvre – it will be uncomfortable if your suit is too tight and there's always the possibility that it will rip when you fall over. You can buy suits without any insulation, called 'shells'. They can be very useful if you are likely to go skiing at different times of the year and don't want to buy more than one outfit – they enable you to wear several extra thin layers underneath when the weather's cold.

Surviving the experience

Going skiing is a bit different from most other ways of spending a holiday – and from most other outdoor activities that the averagely indolent person gets up to. First, it's physically quite demanding. Downhill skiing can be a relatively relaxed business if you ski well and gently; but the less well you ski, the more effort everything takes, and the better you ski the more you're likely to want excitement out of your skiing – which means speed, and harder work. More importantly, skiing taxes muscles which at other times may barely be used – in particular, of course, in the legs. It uses those muscles for long periods each day; and it imposes all sorts of sudden shocks and strains on the body. Preparing for all these unusual demands on your body by doing exercises beforehand makes very good sense.

Skiing is also different because it exposes you to dangers which are unfamiliar, and easy to ignore. You could ski for years without appreciating quite what these dangers are – thinking of snow simply as friendly white stuff, of cold winds as no more than an irritant when you're standing in a lift queue. It may take a shock – perhaps a scare in bad weather, or a real tragedy witnessed at close quarters – to bring home the fact that the mountains in winter are basically a hostile place, where you need to have your wits about you. Once off the nursery slopes, every skier needs some understanding of snow and of mountain weather in order to keep the risk of a mishap to a minimum, and some idea of how to react if the worst comes to the worst.

Getting fit to ski

It's easy to convince yourself that going out of your way to get fit before going skiing is a waste of time. After all, you say to yourself, the skiing itself will soon loosen up any reluctant muscles; and, in any case, those twice-weekly sessions of squash/swimming/darts are already keeping you in good shape. And it is certainly true that many skiers have happy holidays without doing any training beforehand. But it is equally true that to get the most out of your skiing you need to prepare for it. If you don't, you risk:

- wasting valuable (and expensive) skiing time getting fit
- feeling stiff and achey while you're on holiday
- being too weary to ski as many runs as you would like
- finding that your skill deteriorates as your muscles get tired
- being unable to build up a rhythm because of too-frequent rests
- not having the muscle power to put in as many turns as you should
- being more prone to injury.

What sort of exercise?

Being fit for squash, tennis, rugby, football or whatever is not the same as being fit for skiing. Different sports make different demands on the body, and skiing is no exception – so to be really fit for skiing you have to train specifically for skiing. But there's no denying that other forms of exercise do help in some ways.

One of the main requirements of skiing is **stamina** – the ability to keep on exerting yourself. As your muscles get tired you become increasingly unable to use your skills and perform the movements involved. Stamina is one aspect of fitness which can be improved by any form of exercise. By exercising regularly and for an increasing length of time, you will develop your muscle fibres and increase the efficiency of your breathing and circulation. Jogging (either on the spot or over a distance) is simple and effective – do it for a short time at first, gradually increasing the minutes as your system becomes more efficient. When five minutes is easy, run faster but for only three minutes, then increase the duration again as your stamina continues to improve. Other forms of strenuous exercise – cycling or swimming, for example – make good substitutes if jogging doesn't excite you. The kind of exercises we explain later in the chapter will help with stamina, if you work at them; aim to do several exercises consecutively. As it gets easier, take shorter rests and increase the length of each exercise.

Your muscle **endurance** determines how many times you can repeat the same movement, or how long you can maintain a given position.

The **strength** of your muscles is important too. You need strong muscles to make powerful turns, and to react to the unexpected or the undesirable – 'fighting the fall'. And strong muscles give good support to the bones if fighting the fall has failed. Training for strength is to do with increasing the number and efficiency of muscle fibres, so that they can work harder for longer.

Increased **suppleness** of your joints and muscles – an increased range of movement – helps to cut down the risk of injury to either muscles or bones. You encourage this by using your joints through their full existing range of movement, and stretching your muscles.

When to exercise

Start exercising at least six weeks before your holiday, doing a 15-minute session each day – after all, you'll be skiing every day. If you normally lead a very inactive life, start earlier. If you need to break yourself in gently, regard four sessions a week as a minimum. Do your exercises at whatever time of the day suits you. Maybe you can spare a quarter of an hour at lunchtime; or you might choose to exercise when you finish work – although initially this takes some self-discipline at the end of a long day, lots of people find that it gives them quite a boost for the evening. If you prefer to get your exercises out of the way by doing them first thing in the morning, it is particularly important that you warm up properly when you start – remember, your body has been on a go-slow for several hours.

You don't have to jump around in a leotard to do your muscles some good – and you can minimise the amount of time you need to devote specifically to exercising by working exercises into your daily routine. You can make valuable use of those vacant minutes during the day – when the iron is heating, the watched kettle not boiling, the bath running or even when making a telephone call. And you can build exercise into other activities – for example by doing five knee-bends every time you pick something up off the floor.

Spare-moment exercises should never be strenuous – leave the hard work for the serious sessions when you have time to warm up first. Over the page we show several gentle exercises that can be done any time, any place (though some are perhaps better not done in public).

One useful exercise that can be done absolutely anywhere is simply to tighten up your muscles without moving. It is particularly valuable to work your thigh muscles in this way. Nobody in the bus queue will ever know you're shortening your quadriceps (front thigh muscles) to pull up your patellae (knee caps). This is an excellent exercise for those with knee problems. Another not-too-strenuous exercise, although slightly more likely to attract attention, is to rotate your joints (particularly wrists, shoulders and hips) through the biggest circles you can manage.

Never do difficult and energetic exercises until you have done a series of gentler, easier ones first, to work all the parts of your body through their natural ranges of movement. We show a set of suitable **warming-up exercises** over the page. Do these exercises (mixed up to give a bit of variety) for at least four minutes; some people may need longer to loosen up. After the initial warm-up it's good to get the heart pumping a little faster by running on the spot. Aim to do three minutes, starting with a minute's very relaxed jogging, then start to raise your knees further – about half as far as the highest you could manage. Every 20 seconds vary the height of your knees and/or the speed at which you run. Revert to the gentle jogging when you need to.

After the spare-moment and warming-up exercises we explain and illustrate 11 individual exercises which can form the basis of **serious exercise** sessions. If you're going to embark on this or any other series of serious exercises, bear these points in mind:

- if you are in any doubt about the wisdom of starting an exercise programme, consult your doctor first
- don't eat for an hour before your exercise sessions
- put on your favourite music with a beat to exercise to
- before you do any exercise, pull in your stomach muscles
- never do more exercise than you feel you want to do; it is *not* true that if it hurts it must be doing you good
- similarly, never do any individual exercise which you can't manage without hurting yourself; train, don't strain
- after you've done something energetic take in some good deep breaths; your muscles need a good oxygen supply
- as you get fitter, increase the number of times you do an exercise in a single session.

Spare-moment exercises

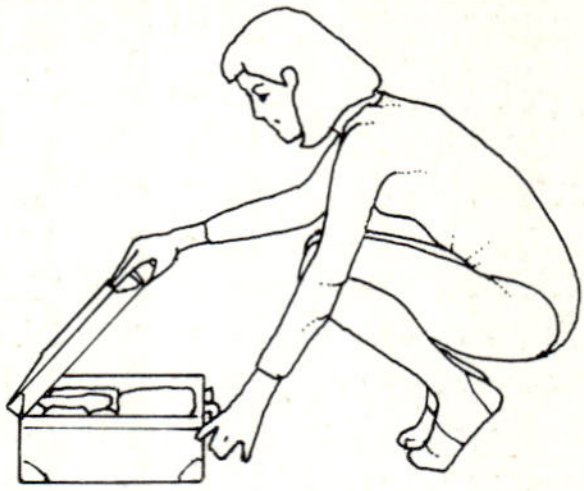

Knee-bends Whenever you pick something up from the floor, squat down several times in quick succession

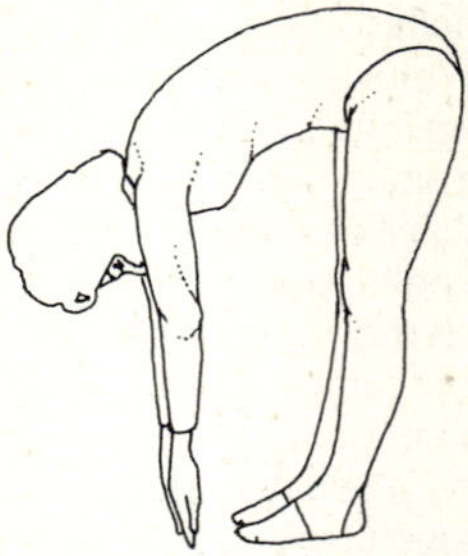

Stretch A Feet apart, stomach in and chin lowered towards chest, relax forward towards the floor and gently bounce

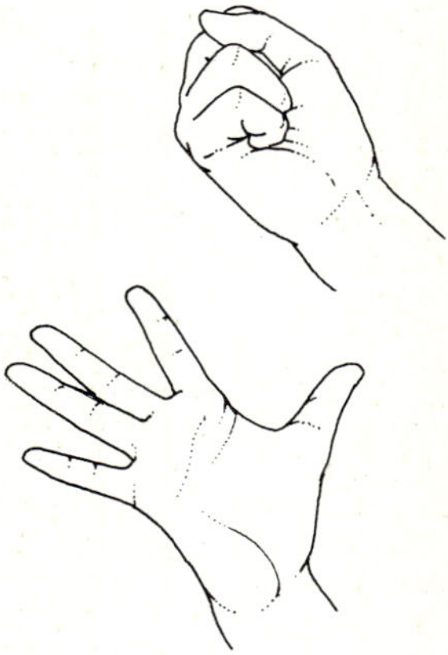

Finger-flicking Clench your fist, then flick your fingers open and stretch your palm as far as you can

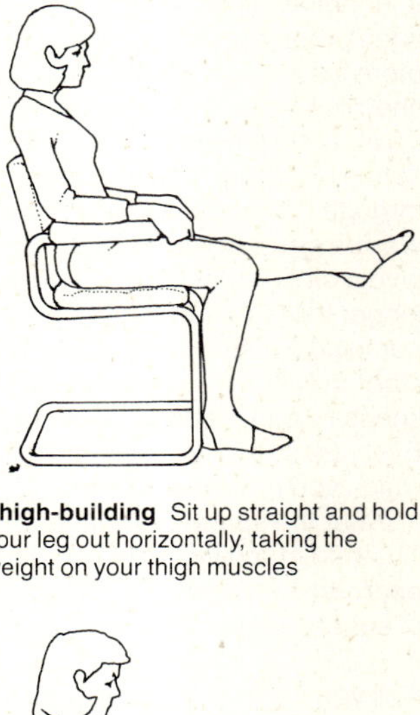

Thigh-building Sit up straight and hold your leg out horizontally, taking the weight on your thigh muscles

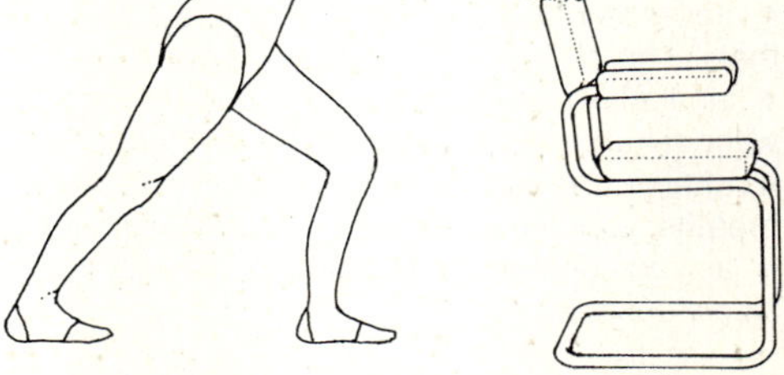

Stretch B Stretch one leg out behind you and bounce the heel of that leg towards the ground, stretching your calf

Warming up exercises

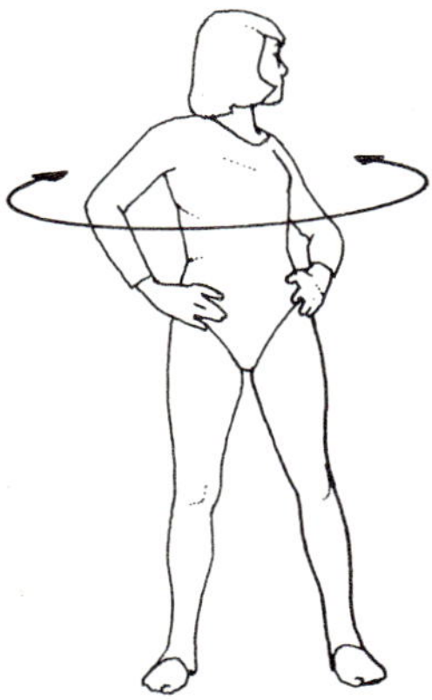

Start by swinging your arms and legs forward and back in opposition – ie left arm and right leg at the same time. Swing them out to the sides as well as to and fro. Follow the swings by:

1 circling your ankles
2 pulling your knees to your chest
3 circling your arms
4 bouncing gently with feet flat, pushing knees over toe line
5 stretching as high as you can
6 bending to one side then the other
7 twisting at the waist

After a gentle warm-up, and before going on to the main exercises, do some jogging on the spot to get your heart pumping – see main text.

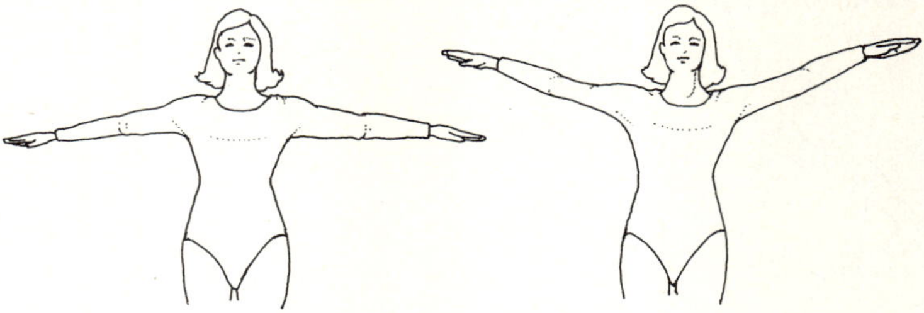

Arm circles Good for strengthening your arms and shoulders and, like all standing exercise, good for your abdominal muscles. With your arms straight to the sides at shoulder level, palms up, do 10 quick, football-size arm circles each way. Repeat with palms down.

Knee bounces Not only excellent for strengthening your thighs and calves but also for building up your endurance. Stand with your feet parallel and hip-width apart. Hold your arms in a ski-pole position – elbows in, forearms horizontal. Bend your knees forward over the line of your toes, then straighten, keeping your weight on the front of your feet. Do 10 of these quick knee bounces. Crouch. Keeping your heels off the floor come up half way, hold this semi-crouch for the count of 4, bounce twice then stand straight. Use your arms to help you balance.

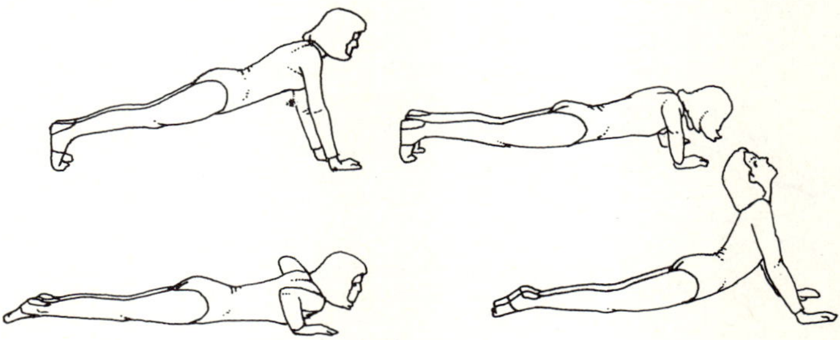

Press ups Particularly good for the pectorals and abdominal muscles. The exercise should be adapted to suit your strength. Lie face down, with your hands flat on the floor next to your shoulders. If you lack strength in the shoulders, upper arms and abdomen, keep your legs and hips on the floor and push only your chest off the ground. Start with 5, gradually build up to 20. When that's easy, try a couple of real press-ups: tighten your stomach and bottom muscles and straighten your arms to lift your whole body, pivoting on your toes and keeping your body and legs in a straight line; then lower to the floor again.

Lean backs Especially good for the inner side of the knees but they must not be over-done. You will be able to feel your thighs working. Kneel with your feet together and knees hip-width apart. Squeeze your bottom muscles, pull in the paunch. Lean back for the count of 2, pull forward. It is important to keep your body, from your knees to your head, absolutely straight.

Side leg flings Will improve the flexibility of your hips and help strengthen some of the muscles involved in side-stepping. Lie on one side, head supported by your hand, other hand on the floor. Point both feet, and raise your upper leg towards the ceiling 8 times. Pull up the toes of both feet and repeat the exercise. Point both feet again, take the top leg back about a foot, turning your upper hip in towards the floor, and repeat the exercise again (you won't be able to get the leg quite so high this time). Finally, bring the top leg forward until almost at right angles to your body, pull up your toes and repeat the exercise again. (Don't do this last part of the exercise if you have back trouble.) Roll over and do the other side. Don't forget to pull in your stomach muscles all the time.

Twisty jumps Will improve your stamina while strengthening your calf and thigh muscles. Put your feet firmly together, go up on your toes; put your arms in a ski-pole position. With your shoulders forward (down the mountain) all the time, jump a couple of inches off the floor, twist from your waist so that your knees go to the left and then the right. These are quick jumps – aim to do 20, on the spot. Then, with the same lower body twist, bend your knees a bit more and jump higher. These jumps are half as quick as the little ones so do half the number.

Burpees A quick series of movements that builds up your stamina whilst strengthening your calf, thigh, abdominal, shoulder and arm muscles. Quite an exercise! You may have seen the Superstars doing these on TV. They're really two exercises in one – squat thrusts with a jump up in between. Start with the squat thrust and when you feel fit enough add the jump. From standing, crouch down. Put your hands flat on the floor; taking your weight on your hands, thrust both feet straight back behind you, and then immediately pull them back in, and jump up. Repeat this for 10 seconds at first and aim for 30 seconds; count how many you do, and try to do more each time.

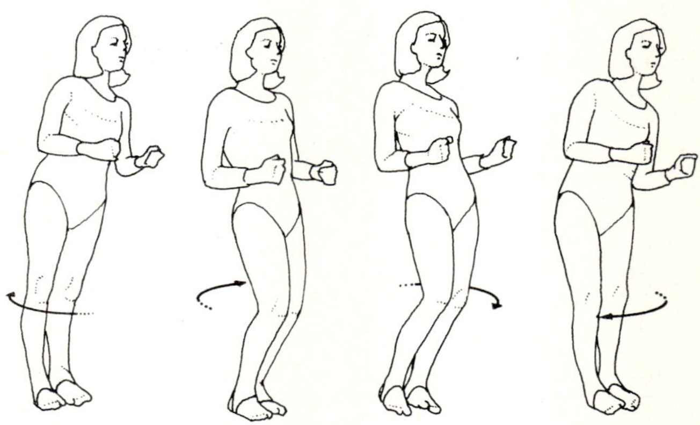

Knee circles Good for the whole leg, especially for extending the movement of your knee and hip. Do these as often as possible. Stand with your feet flat and together, arms in a ski-pole position. Roll over on the sides of your feet to start the knee circle, push your knees forward and circle them round to the other side. Do 5 of these smooth circles each way before repeating with your legs shoulder-width apart. These circles come from your hips.

Shoulder rolling Obviously good for the flexibility of your shoulders. Stand with a firm base for your feet and your hands on your shoulders. Quickly rotate your shoulders to make very large circles with your elbows – start with 10 and aim for 50. Repeat the same number in the opposite direction.

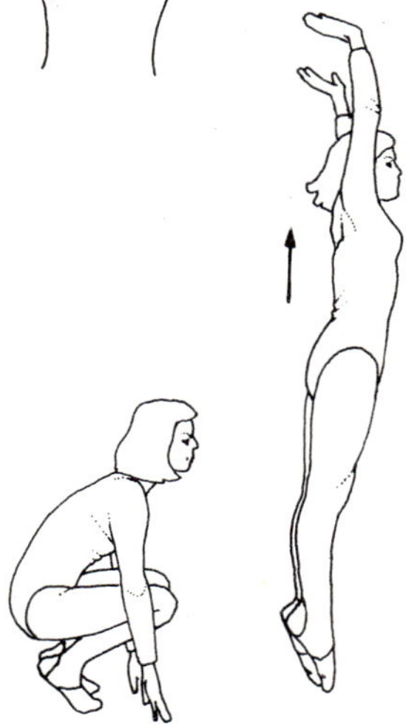

Power jumps Will improve your stamina and strength, not to mention endurance. They are particularly good if you intend skiing off-piste but you should include them anyway. First, make sure the room has a sound floor and a high ceiling. Crouch down. Spring up off the floor, straightening your legs. Fling your arms up in the air as you jump. Land on your toes as you return to the crouch. Jump up again straight away. Do them for, say, 10 seconds and after the last jump come up half way from the crouch, heels off the floor, your thighs close to the horizontal, and hold for as long as you can.

Snowplough sequence Very good for calf and knee strength and movement. It will also work your thighs. If you are at all doubtful about the strength of your knees don't do the last part of the exercise. Stand with your heels shoulder-width apart and toes turned in, arm's in a ski-pole position. Push your knees forward over the line of your toes and don't let your feet roll over or your knees knock; your weight should be on the front of your foot. Straighten your legs. Do 8 of these knee bounces. Finish with your knees bent. Push them as far forward as you can. Keeping your feet flat, straighten your left leg; count to 8. Shift your weight on to the right leg, bending that one while keeping the left leg straight. Lift the left leg a few inches off the floor. Hold this position for the count of 4. Straighten then bend that knee twice (as you get fitter, increase this number to a maximum of 8). Now start again on the other leg.

Staying safe on the mountain

Skiing isn't the 'dangerous sport' that it once was. Modern boots and bindings, properly adjusted, make it very unlikely that you'll come back from your holiday with a broken leg. And, in a properly organised resort, serious accidents of any kind are kept to a minimum by close monitoring of snow and weather conditions. But the evident efforts of the resort authorities – the constant ski patrols and piste grooming, the closure of the top lifts in bad weather, the detonation of avalanches – are not a guarantee of safety, even for the skier who sticks entirely to the piste. It's well worth acquiring a grounding in what the dangers of the mountains are, and how to deal with them.

Weather and exposure

Skiers are interested in weather not only because it determines the quantity and quality of snow available to ski on, but also because (to one degree or another) anyone out on a mountain in winter is at the mercy of the elements.

The mountains themselves greatly influence the conditions. They tend to generate their own weather, or at least to exaggerate the weather that is being experienced in the lowlands – if rain is expected in general, there'll be snow (or rain) in plenty in the mountains. If high winds are forecast, they will be much stronger at 3,000m than at lower altitudes – much stronger, even, than at ski-resort altitude. Temperatures are almost always lower the higher you go, and by appreciable amounts – as much as a degree Celsius for every 100m of altitude. Thus, the higher lifts in a resort can be closed because of hundred-mile-an-hour winds and temperatures of twenty degrees below freezing, when in the valley there is little more than a frosty breeze blowing.

Although it is hard to predict weather patterns accurately weeks in advance, day-to-day forecasting is not the black-magic art many people take it to be. Weather follows patterns which, when understood and recognised, produce reasonably accurate forecasts.

The better-organised resorts display daily (or even twice daily) a local weather forecast including a **synoptic chart**. These charts use lines (similar to contour lines on a map) called *isobars* to show variations in atmospheric pressure over a region. As a general rule, a low-pressure area (a 'depression') indicates bad weather and a high-pressure area (an 'anti-cyclone') good weather. The spacing between the isobars gives an indication of wind speed – isobars close together mean high winds, isobars far apart mean calm weather.

These charts also show *fronts* – junctions between moving masses of warm air and cold air. An approaching front can often be recognised by characteristic and definite changes in the clouds in the sky; a warm front normally brings rain clouds.

The impact the weather has on skiers exposed to it depends on the temperature, the wind speed and the precipitation (weatherspeak for rain or snow). For many skiers, the most important direct result of bad weather is poor visibility, either because of mist or blowing snow. But it's also mostly – though by no means only – in circumstances like these that the effects of cold on the body are likely to become serious. The rate at which you lose heat from the body rises considerably with the speed of the wind. (Not for nothing do car engines have cooling fans.) This effect is known as windchill, and the measure of it is the chill factor – the difference between the actual air temperature and the lower temperature you sense; this difference can amount to tens of degrees Celsius. If your clothes get wet through, heat loss will again be increased considerably. So it's important to have on clothing which is both wind- and water-resistant. Exposure to cold and hostile climates can be more than just unpleasant – if protracted it can result in frostbite or hypothermia.

Frostbite is the excessive cooling of small areas of the body – usually of the fingers, toes, nose, cheeks or ears; it can be the result of extremely low temperatures, or of ordinarily low temperatures coupled with inadequate clothing – if you lose a glove, say. The affected tissue first goes white and numb; this first-degree frostbite can be dealt with simply by immediate re-warming – by putting your hands under your armpits, for example. Warming should be gentle, not involving anything hot or rubbing the skin – least of all with snow. It's only in the most extreme conditions, rare in skiing, that frostbite develops to its second or third-degree stages, which can eventually result in tissue loss.

Hypothermia is the condition resulting from a drop in the temperature of the body as a whole. It is a result of exposure to cold, wet weather with insufficient food and clothing. It is difficult to diagnose, as the symptoms are often similar to those of exhaustion, and indeed it is by no means certain how much of the condition is in part due to tiredness. But the distinction between the two is important: tiredness can't kill, hypothermia can.

Some of the more obvious symptoms of hypothermia are out-of-character behaviour, physical or mental lethargy, slurring of speech, sudden unexpected spurts of energy, and abnormality of vision. It is important to realise that not all of these symptoms will manifest themselves; and that if one member of a party is hypothermic, the rest of the party are also probably suffering to some degree as well.

Hypothermia is better prevented than treated. In very cold conditions, as well as wearing proper clothing, you need to eat lots of high-energy food throughout the day. If you're feeling cold, it may be that all you need do is put a hat on – in doing so you may be reducing by as much as a half the total heat loss from your body. If someone does show signs of hypothermia, the obvious priority should be to get them out of the weather into somewhere warm, preferably with a supply of warm drinks. Until then they should be kept as warm as possible – add more warm clothes (don't remove those already being worn). Do not give alcohol, which will simply increase the rate at which heat is lost. If for some reason the person is unable to carry on skiing, remember that you can conserve a lot of body warmth by huddling together. In extreme conditions, evacuation by stretcher may be essential. In any case, seek medical help as soon as possible.

Accident procedure

When an accident occurs, it's important to know how to act quickly and efficiently in order to preserve life and minimise suffering. If you are armed with some basic knowledge of first aid and with common sense, you can accomplish a great deal at the scene of the accident – and to do so may be vital if the accident is serious.

Someone whose injury is clearly superficial should be helped to carry on skiing down the mountain and then to seek medical help. If the injury is too serious or painful for the casualty to move, first of all mark the accident site by placing crossed skis about ten metres uphill of the casualty; this will warn others of the obstruction, and so prevent multiple pile-ups, and will attract help either from other skiers, ski instructors or ski patrols.

If the bindings have not released, you can usually help to make the casualty comfortable by carefully removing their skis. If the injury is to the lower leg *do not* remove the ski boot – it has the effect of a splint, and leaving it on will generally help to minimise discomfort until the breakage can be given proper attention. Keep the casualty warm, comfortable and set about contacting the ski patrol, who will effect the evacuation. Send a *competent* skier down the piste in search of the nearest SOS point or lift station, armed with all the relevant information – what sort of injury the patrol will have to treat, as well as the precise location of the casualty (referring to piste marker numbers if they exist). Expect a wait of around half an hour, and devote yourself to keeping the injured person cheerful and warm, and watching for signs of deterioration in their condition. Anyone who shows signs of shock – going pale, cold and faint – should be encouraged to lie with their head lower than their feet; don't give any food or drink.

Although it's unlikely, except after an avalanche or a very long fall, it's not impossible that the injured skier will be in a more serious condition. The first priority is to check that the person is breathing, and if not to administer artificial respiration – the kiss of life, or whatever other method you know about. More lives can be saved by attending speedily to breathing than by any other single measure. If artificial respiration is necessary, make sure that no foreign bodies are lodged in the mouth or throat – for example vomit, broken teeth or, in the case of avalanche victims, snow. Continue with respiration until the patient breathes normally again, or until medical help arrives, or until the casualty is presumed to be dead (a very serious presumption for unqualified people to make). Someone who is breathing but unconscious (or seems likely to become unconscious) can vomit and choke, so it is best to turn them on to their side. But first it's important to try to establish the extent of their injuries: a fractured limb will need to be protected against movement, while an injury to the back or spine makes any movement extremely risky.

The next priority is to deal with any severe bleeding. Bleeding is best stopped by applying direct pressure to the site of the wound, using some sort of cloth pad if possible. If bleeding continues, do not remove the pad but place another pad on top of the first and continue applying pressure to the wound.

Safety on the piste

As we explain in our review of skiing safety in the next chapter of the *Guide*, the risks that are traditionally associated with skiing – basically, broken legs resulting from falls – have declined as equipment has improved. But as pistes become more crowded and as more skiers become capable of skiing quickly there is an increasing risk which is no less serious: the risk of collision with other skiers.

A set of rules for skiers has been drawn up by the Fédération International du Ski (FIS), with the aim of keeping skiing accidents to the minimum. Not only do these rules offer worthwhile guidance, but they are increasingly forming the basis of legal judgements in both civil and criminal actions in Continental courts. If you cause an accident while in breach of these rules, you could find yourself in trouble.

The FIS Rules are reproduced over the page. Three other rules which increase your own chances of avoiding accidents are these:

- don't assume that the snow ahead of you will necessarily behave like the snow you're on – particularly late in the season, when the effects of sun and shade can be profound
- don't start skiing without doing some gentle exercises to warm up cold muscles – see the earlier part of this chapter for some ideas
- don't be tempted to have 'just one more run' when you finish your 'last' run of the day and find the lift is still going; you'll be tired, and liable to make mistakes; and deserted pistes can be very lonely places once the sun has gone down.

Safety off-piste

Most people start skiing off-piste in a small way – maybe even accidentally – by straying on to virgin snow next to a piste. The main thing to be wary of then is having to ski in very heavy, sticky snow: a fall in such snow is likely to be a slow, twisting affair which even the best bindings don't deal with reliably.

When soft snow develops a hard crust on its surface – usually as a result of wind, or snow during the day and extreme cold at night – it can provide a very good skiing surface, provided it can support the skier's weight. But it may support only a flat ski, not a ski on its edge. Every time a turn is made on this *breakable crust*, the ski punches through the surface layer and sinks into the softer layer beneath. This again makes unpleasant falls likely. The best solution is to try to ski with both skis evenly weighted or to resort to slow snowploughs.

But serious off-piste skiing, well away from the beaten track, can have many dangers – avalanches, crevasses on glaciers, the possibility of losing your way, for example. If you lack experience, don't go far off-piste without a guide. In any event:

- never go alone
- always ski in control; an injury no more serious than a twisted ankle can have very serious consequences when off-piste
- use safety straps or tapes when skiing in deep snow, otherwise it may take hours to find a lost ski after a fall – if you find it at all

- always assess the risk of avalanche – and if it's significant, be sure that you know how to minimise the risk on particular slopes
- if possible, carry an avalanche cord and an avalanche transmitter to steer rescuers towards you if you are buried
- carry a map and compass *and* know how to use them; navigation is a skill which takes time and practice to master, and it is the only way to find your route in bad visibility
- be wary of slopes where the run-out is not obvious from the start.

If an accident happens off-piste, the first aid priorities are exactly the same as on-piste, but evacuation is usually a much more difficult, serious and lengthy procedure. If possible the ski patrol should be summoned, but you should remember that they are not responsible for the help and rescue of off-piste skiers. You may have to be rescued by helicopter. This can be very costly, and so it is essential that you have adequate insurance. Since the rescue is liable to take much longer, it is particularly important that the casualty is kept warm to reduce the chances of hypothermia (see 'Weather and exposure'). It is also best to send two skiers for help, and they should ideally have a map grid reference giving the exact site of the accident. A casualty who is in a dangerous position, exposed to avalanche for example, should if possible be moved to a safer location.

Avalanches

To most skiers, snow is simply the solid, low-friction material on which you ski; it's sometimes hard, sometimes soft, sometimes light and dry, sometimes heavy and sticky, sometimes wet and sloppy. Whatever condition it's in, you necessarily adapt to it and think no more about it. But ask a mountaineer about snow and he will paint a different picture, because he knows that snow can hold all kinds of dangers and that he has to rely on his own judgement of those dangers. What the mountaineer is worried about, above all else, is the risk of avalanche – the sudden movement down the mountainside of a huge mass of snow, sweeping away anything and everything in its path. Off-piste skiers obviously need to be similarly concerned; but avalanches are not dangerous only to off-piste skiers, they can sweep down pistes as well – as incidents in recent winters have served to demonstrate. Never disregard avalanche warnings signs; see our 'Skiing vocabulary', at the back of the book, for translations of the vital words.

Whatever the truth of the claim that no two snow crystals are alike, there is certainly a great variety of types of crystal, and their properties vary widely. Perhaps the two clearest examples are the perfect Christmas-card star crystal and the hailstone – the one mainly air, the other mainly ice. The type of crystal is dependent upon atmospheric conditions prevailing at the time of formation – and upon subsequent weather. Falls at different times will accumulate as a series of layers of snow which may or may not be easily distinguished. What determines the chances of avalanche is the degree to which these layers remain separate, rather than bonded together.

In cold, still conditions snow falls as a dry powder which lies on the

FIS Rules for the conduct of skiers

The rules are reproduced below exactly as published in English by the FIS; the *Notes* are our own observations, drawing on the FIS Commentaries which accompany the rules and on other evidence about the interpretation of the rules.

Rule 0
Skiing is a sport and as all other sports, it has a risk element and certain civil and penal responsibilities.
Notes Skiers are expected to know the FIS Rules and to follow them. If you do not, you lay yourself open to legal action in the event of an accident.

Rule 1 – Respect for others
A skier must behave in such a way that he does not endanger or prejudice others.
Notes The FIS Rules apply to all skiers, including ski school pupils and racers. Instructors must respect the rules, teach them, and enforce them.

Rule 2 – Control of speed and skiing
A skier must adapt his speed and way of skiing to his personal ability and to prevailing conditions of terrain and weather.
Notes Speed should take account not only of the need to stay in control, but also of the prevailing speed of skiers on a run. It is normal to go fast on a run generally used by accomplished skiers – a black or a red run – and slow skiers must not obstruct such runs. It is normal to go slowly on an easy run generally used by beginners – a blue or a green run – and fast skiers must allow for inexpert skiers. All skiers must go slowly in narrow passages and at the bottom of runs and near lift departures. You must be able to stop or make a turn within your range of vision.

Rule 3 – Control of direction
A skier coming from above, whose dominant position allows him a choice of path, must take a direction which assures the safety of the skier below.
Notes Skiers are expected to allow for those ahead of them to stop suddenly, but are not expected to allow for sudden turns to right or left. There are no 'rules of the road' (such as keeping to the right or left); skiers must decide responsibly for themselves how to handle situations as they arise. You must take account of skiers alongside you on a run as well as those in front.

Rule 4 – Overtaking
It is permitted to overtake another skier going down or up – to the right or to the left, but always leaving a wide enough margin for the overtaken skier to make his turns.
Notes An overtaking skier must not cause any difficulties for the skier being overtaken, whether stopped or moving.

Rule 5 – Duties of a skier crossing the course
A skier wishing to enter a course or passing a training ground must look up and down to make sure that he can do so without danger to himself or others. The same applies when starting again after a stop on the course.
Notes Any manoeuvre on a ski run other than normal skiing down it can be dangerous, and implies the need for special care.

Rule 6 – Stopping on the course
If not absolutely necessary, a skier must avoid a stop on the course, especially in narrow passages or where visibility is restricted. In the case of a fall, a skier must leave the course free as soon as possible.
Notes If you stop, do so at the side of the run. Adding to the danger of skiing difficult slopes (for example, narrow passages with bad visibility from above) by obstructing the run could be considered an offence.

Rule 7 – Climbing
A climbing skier must keep to the side of the course and in bad visibility keep off the course entirely. The same goes for a skier who descends on foot.

Rule 8 - Respect for signals
A skier must respect the signals.
Notes Signs indicating that runs are closed or marking dangerous points must be respected.

Rule 9 – Conduct at accidents
At accidents, everybody is duty-bound to assist.
Notes The FIS hopes that irresponsibly leaving the scene of a skiing accident will be considered equivalent to leaving the scene of a road accident.

Rule 10 – Identification
All witnesses, whether responsible parties or not, at an accident must establish their identity.
Notes The reports of witnesses to an accident can be of great importance.

ground (if it is the first fall of the winter), or more probably on the surface of the existing snow pack. If the existing snow surface is hard and icy, any slope steeper than about 20° presents ideal conditions for an avalanche: the new snow will build up until the mass is too great for its grip on the slippery mountainside, and then it will slide, starting at a point and spreading in a fan shape. Powder-snow avalanches are usually easy to predict – they follow heavy falls (more than 20cm) of light, dry snow, usually on a hard base. ('Sunballs' may be apparent – naturally occurring snowballs caused by snow melting in the sun, which leave trails in the snow as they run off.) Only a rise in temperature, allowing the new snow to settle and bond with the old, will render the slope safe. If the weather stays cold and dry, the danger of avalanche will remain. North-facing slopes may be dangerous for many weeks.

If a wind is blowing when the snow falls, the result will be quite different. The wind picks up the falling snow and sweeps it across the ground to be deposited on lee slopes – slopes which are sheltered from the prevailing wind. This snow then forms a slab, which is very dangerous; it gives the appearance of being firm and safe, but it is not – it is liable to break off across the whole width of the slope, and this breaking off is particularly likely to be triggered by the slicing action of a skier's traverse. This 'windslab' has a characteristic chalky appearance and tends to squeak when walked on or when a ski stick is pushed into it. The wind strength at the time of deposit will determine the hardness of the slab formed. Strong winds can strip the snow from windward slopes and deposit it on lee slopes as windslab in much the same way as they do falling snow.

There is a third type of avalanche, which occurs particularly in spring – the wet-snow avalanche. This is triggered by a pronounced rise in temperature, usually in the afternoon. Wet-snow avalanches often follow well defined tracks, and are most common on south-facing slopes, where the snow faces the midday sun.

So basically the danger periods for avalanches are: after heavy snow falls; after strong cold winds; and on warm afternoons. The old rule of thumb, that snow is safe 24 hours after it has fallen, is not true.

If you are caught in an avalanche, current theory says that you should discard your skiing equipment to make movement easier; attempt to move to the side of the avalanche; try to stay on your feet for as long as possible – the more snow that passes by, the less there is to bury you; once swept off your feet, keep your mouth shut and save your strength for the the last few seconds of the avalanche, as the snow is coming to rest – and then attempt to get as near the surface as possible and try to maintain an air space around your face. The difficulties of translating this theory in practice seem considerable.

If you see someone else being buried by an avalanche, mark the spot where they were hit by the avalanche and the spot where you last saw them; then make an immediate search below that point – the longer a person is buried, the less their chance of survival. Use a ski-pole with the basket removed to probe the snow. Only after this initial search has been completed should you go off in search of help (unless of course there are enough of you around to divide these tasks).

Even safer skiing

As we are reminded every autumn by various interested parties, skiing is no longer the dangerous sport it once was – thanks mainly to vastly improved boots and bindings. Insurers tell us that now only one injury in ten is a broken leg and only one skier in thirty claims under the medical expenses section of their insurance policies – not an alarmingly high rate, considering how many people go skiing every year physically underprepared (if we and our skiing friends are anything to go by, that is). But, to look at it another way, keen skiers taking two skiing holidays a year can expect to have to call on their medical insurance (normally as a result of an injury) four times in a skiing lifetime, all other things being equal. Of course, other things are not equal. Skiers, slopes, snow, weather, equipment and the maintenance of it are variables. Is there any way of manipulating these variables so as to enjoy sixty years' skiing without the expectation of four injuries?

During winter 1985–86 we contacted skiers who made claims for medical expenses on insurance policies provided by two of Britain's biggest winter sports insurers (Fogg and Norwich Union, to whom we are very grateful), and asked them to tell us about their injuries and the accidents that led to them. To the 200 who took the trouble to answer, we are equally grateful.

We heard of a rib injury inflicted by a bottle of sun-cream carried in an anorak pocket, a septic toe caused by kicking steps in an icy piste on the way up to collect a ski discarded in a fall, a deep cut in the lower back from a plastic bumbag clip, and a mountain rescue operation to assist a skier who had blacked out from low blood sugar. There are lessons to be drawn from all these cases, including the easily overlooked matter of cutting your toenails. There are other lessons to be drawn from more typical skiing injuries, of which we had many more reports – people injured in collision with other skiers (13 per cent of the injuries reported to us), and an impressive number of knee injuries (41 per cent of the total). We have used the results of the survey to illustrate a more general analysis of various aspects of skiing safety. We refer also to a survey of skiing injuries conducted by the Swiss Bureau de Prévention des Accidents (BPA) in 1984, where over 2,000 injured skiers in three major Swiss resorts were questioned at length, and submitted their equipment to inspection; and to research into Scottish skiing injuries carried out over several years by Graham Stewart, Senior Registrar in Orthopaedics at Dundee Royal Infirmary.

Knees

All the improvement in the risk of injury has taken place below the knee. The frequency of injuries to all parts of the body above and including the knee has not changed very much, so these knees-up injuries now account for a much higher proportion of the total, with the knee itself now the major injury black spot: 26 per cent of all injuries in the BPA survey and a much higher proportion of our own sample. The modern ski boot is often blamed for these injuries, but in general the boot does not cause knee injuries: it simply does not protect the knee.

Nor does the binding. 'It does not appear that safety bindings offer any protection against knee injury,' was the stark message Graham Stewart gave the Commonwealth Conference on Sport in 1986. Bindings manufacturers are concentrating their research on improvements in this area, but Stewart is sceptical of what can be achieved, at least in a binding that is not extremely expensive. 'In lots of knee injuries, for example when you fall forwards between your skis on to the insides of your knees, there is boot-to-ground contact and the ski and binding cease to be relevant.' So is there anything you can do to save your knees, apart from not falling over?

We put the question to Jenny Brown, honorary physiotherapist to the British Alpine ski team. 'Any exercise that improves the strength and flexibility of thigh muscles and hamstrings will help protect the knees,' she told us. 'Bicycling is ideal, since it doesn't load the knees at all. If possible use toe clips: that way you exercise both front and back of the thigh by pulling the pedal up as well as pushing it down. The other obvious exercise is to use the stairs.' What about the idea that swimming is positively bad for skiing? 'Swimming is good exercise for just about everything and especially skiing, because it helps build up stamina. But it is true that breast stroke can cause wobbly knee joints: better to do crawl or back stroke.'

Bindings

Even if our knees will always be at risk when we ski, there is no doubt that many of us are not making the most of the very considerable protection current bindings can offer. The BPA inspections of injured skiers' equipment found that of the heel bindings 36 per cent were set too high and 8 per cent were jammed; 70 per cent of the toe bindings were set too high and again 8 per cent were jammed. In no less than 64 per cent of cases there was no vertical play between the toe binding and the flange on the toe of the boot (a vital factor in the correct functioning of a binding in the case of a twisting fall), and in 14 per cent of cases the binding exerted strong downward pressure on the boot. In our own survey 67 per cent of the victims of knee injuries in falls (and 62 per cent of all fallers with leg injuries) reported non-release.

It is tempting to react to this information by recommending that skiers make sure they get an expert technician to set their bindings by going to a good ski shop. But the majority of skiers (certainly the majority of British skiers in Europe) already get their bindings set by ski shop technicians. In the BPA survey, 87 per cent of the injured skiers reported that their bindings had been set by a specialist, and the result of our survey was almost identical: 86 per cent of the skiers who injured a leg in a fall without binding release had had their bindings set by a ski shop technician. And how do you tell a good ski shop and a good technician from a bad one, before you injure yourself?

The short answer is that you can't. But you can look for clues, particularly when hiring equipment, in the general appearance of the shop and its stock. Are the ski edges rusty and the soles full of unrepaired scratches and holes? Does the technician expect people to accept an uncomfortable boot or one missing a clip? Does he set bindings without bothering to ask how much people have skied before and how much they weigh? If the answer to any of these questions is yes, take your custom somewhere else.

It does not make sense to pre-pay for hire of equipment, however attractive the brochure price looks, unless you have very good reason to believe in the high quality of the equipment offered. In some areas notorious for the low standard of rental equipment (notably Eastern Europe) British tour operators have done a lot to improve their clients' safety by supplying their own equipment. But in most cases pre-payment simply locks you into a contract with a local hirer who has little incentive to give you good service. Large numbers of British skiers arrive in the same ski shop all at once, and fitting them with skis and boots is a rushed job. Whatever the quality of the equipment, this is a raw deal from the hirer's point of view. David Wooden described his arrival in Söll on a Sunday in January 1986, having pre-paid for hire of equipment: 'Long queues, very poor equipment, no binding adjustment. Most of us would have gone elsewhere but for UK purchase of hire contract.' They accepted what they knew to be poor equipment poorly adjusted; the next morning Mr Wooden's wife fell over, her binding did not release and she ruptured knee ligaments. Two months later, when we heard from Mr Wooden, she was still in plaster and off work.

The French equivalent of *Which?* magazine, *Que Choisir?*, concluded from the BPA survey that it is a waste of time and money to get a ski shop technician to set your bindings. We would not go so far, but we do urge all skiers to find out for themselves how their bindings work, beyond simply knowing how to tighten the setting – with bindings this is the little knowledge that is a dangerous thing. Whether you're buying or hiring equipment, take careful note of the section on bindings safety in our 'Getting equipped' chapter. Check that your bindings will release at the beginning of each skiing day, and at intervals during the day. And remember that however well a binding is set, it won't work properly if you have snow, ice, earth or grit on the sole of your boot when you step into the binding.

Piste-wise skiers commonly argue that pre-release of bindings is as dangerous as non-release, but surveys have consistently shown it to be a negligible contributory factor to skiing injuries.

Upper body injuries

Men have more arm and shoulder injuries than women, and shoulder dislocation is a common male skiing injury. We asked Jenny Brown to recommend specific exercises. 'Press-ups are fine for men, although lots of women can't do them. One good stretching exercise racers use a lot is to place your hands in front of you on something at about shoulder height – someone else's shoulders, for example – and drop your head down between your arms.'

Collisions

Like others who have researched the subject, we found that the overwhelming majority of accidents resulted not from a collision (13 per cent of the injuries in our survey and 7 per cent in the BPA survey) but from a fall involving no other skier (81 per cent and 88 per cent respectively). But 13 per cent is large enough to be worrying, and collision injuries are important, because they are probably increasing, they are certainly avoidable and they can be very serious.

None of the skiers who reported to us was involved in legal proceedings following the accident. But it can happen, as we heard from Christine Wilson, who in March 1983 collided ('while traversing slowly across a piste' during a ski class) with a German skier who twisted her knee as she fell. The German skier walked away from the accident, but three days later Mrs Wilson was summoned to the police station with her ski instructor to make a statement, after which both were told to consider the matter closed. On her return home Mrs Wilson found a lawyer's letter claiming damages, which she passed on to her insurance company. A few weeks later she learned that an Austrian district court had found her guilty of causing serious bodily harm by disregarding right of way, and fined her about £250, which she paid.

In an age of litigation and crowded pistes, it is an unwise skier who ventures out on to the slopes without an understanding of the highway code. At the end of our 'Surviving the experience' chapter we set out the rules (which are not laws, but guidelines for those interpreting local laws) as formulated by the International Ski Federation. The rules are deliberately general, so as not to impinge unduly on the skier's freedom. But they are not so vague as to be meaningless, and there is plenty of legal precedent to demonstrate the practical legal implications of accidents. The fundamental principle is that every skier is responsible for his or her own actions. There might seem to be a world of difference between the culpability of a boy racer who roars far too fast round a blind corner on a crowded piste and that of the skier who falls over and slides down a slope, but in terms of responsibility for a collision there is none. Two aspects of the rules are not widely known. One is that the slower or downhill skier does not have absolute priority – on red and black runs, slow skiers have an obligation to keep out of the way of fast skiers for whom the runs are intended. And the other is that the slower skier's priority covers only 'normal manoeuvres': if judged to have made abnormal ones, such as sudden changes of direction, you have no priority.

To judge from the reports we have received, most British skiers seem to regard being seriously hurt in collisions as bad luck to be endured with stoicism. Only one collision victim, who fractured her spine when a skier crashed into her while she was standing with her ski class, and missed three months' work, intended to seek compensation. 'I'm afraid that the person will have to be informed of the damage he caused,' she wrote, as if reluctant to contemplate so unsporting a course of action. Not following things up is a sure way to encourage dangerous skiing.

What should you do in case of a collision? The procedure is not very different from what happens after a road accident. As a victim, you may be in no position to stop a skier deserting the scene, but as a witness you probably are. As a victim or a victim's companion, you should collect details of the other skier and of witnesses, and take note of as many precise circumstantial details as you can: location, temperature, visibility, snow conditions, crowd density on the slope and even tracks in the snow. You should then contact the police as well as your insurance company. Bear in mind that injuries, even serious ones, are often not obvious immediately.

The resort's role

Our survey was not intended as an exercise to gather ammunition to throw at individual resorts or countries, although a small number of the skiers we heard from did feel that the resort was in some way to blame for their injury. A skier in Kitzbühel had to take sudden evasive action when confronted by an advancing piste-basher, and ended up off-piste with a torn ligament. Another was injured while trying to back out of a steep deep-snow slope at La Plagne having lost the piste in poor visibility. A skier who injured a knee in heavy fresh snow on a red piste in Avoriaz blamed her injury on the failure to bash the snow. About half a dozen skiers blamed piste grading for their fall and injury.

Snow conditions and warnings

Logic suggests and statistics confirm that bad snow conditions – ice, rocks and slush – cause injuries. There is some concern that immaculately groomed pistes may cause an increased number of high-speed collision injuries, but there is not much evidence to support that idea, and in general the message is clear: you are much more likely to fall over on ice and rocks than on snow, and they are much more likely to cause you an injury – specifically an upper-body injury; heavy snow is particularly dangerous for knees. A few years ago 17 skiers slid to their death in a week in the Pyrenees when rain was followed by a deep freeze. Two years later eight skiers died in one day at Courmayeur, sliding down icy gullies in a series of separate incidents. A survey of skiing head injuries at Chur in eastern Switzerland found that of 16 fatal head injuries over an eight-year period, six occurred in one season of bad snow conditions. The poor snow cover in early 1988, resulting in icy and rocky pistes in many Alpine resorts, reportedly led to a noticeable increase in head, arm and body injuries.

Resorts have a duty to ensure that open pistes are safe. In America, litigation has led resorts to spend so much money on snow-making that lift passes cost far more than in Europe, and to close pistes the moment a stone appears. In European countries the obligation on resorts to save skiers from all potential hazards has not been taken to such lengths, and skiing is a freer and more varied sport as a result. But fear of litigation may lie behind St Anton's decision to declare many of its most famous runs off-piste (although their existence and approximate location is shown on the map and they are routinely skied by large numbers of skiers). This disclaiming attitude (which is not exclusive to St Anton) does nothing to advance the cause of skiing safety.

Piste grading and marking

Resorts should provide information about the nature of the risk with colour grades to give an idea of how difficult a run is in normal conditions, more temporary signs warning when conditions are not normal and, at times, signs that the run is closed. And there should be markers to indicate where the run is. Although in many respects a nonchalant nation, the French are generally much more helpful in providing information and warnings about difficult pistes and off-piste runs. Unlike the Austrians, they recognise that the best way to deal with the modern problem of inexperienced skiers with a taste for dangerous skiing is to provide them with more information, not less.

We looked in some detail at the question of piste grading in the Introduction to last year's *Guide*. There is little evidence to prove that inconsistent grading of pistes contributes to accidents, but common sense suggests that it is likely to.

Systems and standards of piste marking vary enormously throughout the Alps, and often within a single ski area. While it is not beyond the wit of most skiers to come to terms with local customs, some attempts to harmonise them would be helpful. We think markers should be placed along both sides of a piste, not in a single line down one side or down the middle – the approved system in Switzerland, where the standard of piste marking is generally very low. The red and green globe markers used in many Austrian resorts have the great advantage of showing clearly which side of the post is piste – often vitally important in bad visibility. Many resorts use decreasing numbers to indicate how much of a piste remains to be skied, a useful aid to orientation and the location of accidents. The use of luminescent orange discs or bands on the marker poles is recommended by the Swiss anti-accident commission, but rarely employed.

In a few resorts there is information at the bottom of all lifts about the runs they serve, a system of which we greatly approve. At Obertauern, where all runs are ungraded, we found a chair-lift serving only a single steep run with no warning and only a notice in German that riding down by lift was not allowed.

Road crossings, drag-lift crossings and piste intersections are obvious accident black spots, and all too often signposts giving advance warning about them are either inconspicuous or non-existent. Most resorts could do more to encourage skiers to slow down as they approach a piste crossroads. The Courmayeur accident illustrated tragically the importance of nets on the edges of pistes crossing steep slopes where falls are dangerous.

The contribution of resort organisation to the safety of skiers is an area which seems to us neglected by comparison with the research that goes on into other aspects. We should be glad of readers' help in building up evidence about resort practices both good and bad. Write to the Editor at the address given on page 599.

Variations on the theme

This *Guide* concentrates on skiing as most people in Britain understand it – skiing downhill, using heavy, stiff boots attached firmly to heavy, stiff skis. But downhill (or Alpine) skiing is only one form of the sport. Cross-country skiing (or Nordic skiing, *langlauf* in German, *ski de fond* in French) is very different: you use long, light skis and relatively light boots which are barely attached to the skis at all, and you ski downhill only as much as you are prepared to ski uphill.

Cross-country developed as a sport about a century ago in Scandinavia, where skis had long been used as means of everyday travel across snow-covered fields and woods. They are still a standard way of getting around in winter there, whether for shopping, going to school or hunting. More recently, cross-country has seen explosive growth in other European countries and in North America. There are now millions of cross-country skiers in Europe's Alpine countries alone.

Cross-country skiing naturally evolves into ski-touring, in which you may travel considerable distances on ski, often going from hut to hut or from hotel to hotel, and possibly skiing off the beaten path, in untracked snow. However, Alpine skis are also used for ski-touring of a rather different sort, with special boots and bindings and detachable 'skins' to enable the skis to grip going uphill. They come into their own on the steep terrain and fast descents encountered in the high mountains, though suitable Nordic skis may also be used there. Alpine ski-touring has about it an air of intrepid mountaineering; but, as we explain later in this chapter, you don't have to be a mountaineer (or an exceptionally good skier) to go touring, and enjoy it.

Cross-country skiing

Cross-country skiing should appeal to anyone who likes snow, walking or jogging, and is not exclusively addicted to downhill skiing. It is easy to learn to a reasonable standard (though in its more advanced form it is just as technical as Alpine skiing); it is less hazardous than Alpine skiing, and less expensive (because the gear costs less and lift tickets do not have to be bought); and many people who live near moorland or hilly country can practise it not far from home for at least some days each winter.

Its essence is its freedom and grace of movement, using the glide of the skis to maximum effect. It is not like plodding along on snow-shoes; and it often requires a varying rhythm as your route takes you up and down over undulating terrain. The downhill sections are usually gentle, but give an exhilarating sensation of speed; a good sense of balance, and elementary techniques like the snow-plough and the stem and skating turns will see you through.

Skiing cross-country you rely very little on artificial help such as ski-lifts, and get a marvellous sense of being close to nature and of peace and quiet. It is also a very healthy sport, involving the use of legs and arms, and also lungs and heart, though not in any excessive way except during competition. It gives well-earned enjoyment through your own efforts; and for its devotees it is a way of life, leading them to health and fitness year-round – if you're to be really fit when the snow arrives, you have to do some training in the summer (for example with roller skis).

Photographs of cross-country skiers often show an advanced racing style, giving the impression that you really need to be in hard training if you are to ski properly. But, like walking, jogging and running, cross-country can be done at any speed, depending on your own inclination; it can vary from the equivalent of a gentle stroll on a Sunday afternoon to that of a marathon run or longer.

Like downhill skiers, most cross-country skiers these days stick to prepared trails; these are not simply flat paths, but have distinct grooves in which you aim to keep your skis – like tramlines. In Scandinavia, these tracks range for many miles; from your mountain hotel or chalet you might do a 10km trek in the morning and perhaps a shorter one in the afternoon; if you're more energetic you might do the 20km or the 50km track instead. In Alpine ski resorts, the tracks may be as short as 3 or 5km (some are even shorter), so that it would become repetitive to go too far.

It is thus a sport for all the family, with both the youngest and the oldest well able to enjoy it at whatever pace suits them best – though teenagers may prefer Alpine skiing, with its greater speed and excitement. But there's no doubt that you will enjoy cross-country most if you are reasonably fit – for example if you also enjoy hill- or mountain-walking. Fitness means that you can keep going without tiring; and this in turn helps you to ski better and with less effort, and in turn to get more enjoyment out of your skiing and your surroundings.

Many of the people who ski cross-country do so to avoid the technicalities and the general hurly burly of Alpine skiing; it gets them out and about on the snow when the other members of the family are skiing downhill, for example. It is perfectly possible to combine the two sports in a single holiday. Many Alpine resorts now cater for cross-country, and in some the terrain lends itself well to cross-country tracks – for example in Pontresina or St Moritz in Switzerland, or Seefeld in Austria. Some people even find it pleasant to ski Alpine for half of the day and Nordic for the other half.

You can hire the equipment you need for cross-country skiing, and it would be normal to do so if you are combining cross-country with a downhill skiing holiday; this is probably the best course anyway until you have decided to commit yourself to the sport. But when you are clear that you will want to continue with cross-country skiing, it would be best to buy at least shoes or boots, and preferably also skis and sticks, so that you have equipment which really suits you and so that you can take any opportunities to go skiing near your home.

Equipment

You will need shoes or **boots** specially made to fit into the bindings on the skis. The weight of the shoe or boot will depend on the type of cross-country skiing: very light shoes are used for racing, but quite heavy and robust boots for mountain skiing off-piste, where a strong control is needed to give the necessary stability and edging in icy conditions. For everyday recreational skiing, you need something which comes between these extremes.

As the drawings over the page show, there are three main types of **binding**; each connects only the toe of the boot to the ski, in a fairly flexible way. Each of them also comes with a heel grip, to help control the skis when turning – either a serrated plate or a plastic fitting which slots into the heel of the boot.

Your sticks (or poles) are an important means of propulsion. They need to be longer than Alpine ones – they should come up to your armpits, or to between your armpits and your shoulder for an extra long push. They need a sharp point for gripping on ice, preferably inclined forwards so that it comes out from the snow easily when you have moved ahead of it.

Cross-country **skis** are rather longer than Alpine skis – 190cm to 210cm is the normal range. The length helps to give the even spread of pressure on the snow necessary for a good glide (compensating for the narrower width of the skis), and also improves your stability in bumps and dips. For track skiing, the edges may be quite straight, but some waisting will help them to turn when off the track. They are made in three widths: 48mm (at the centre) for racing; 52 to 55mm for normal use; and 58 to 65mm (possibly with metal edges) for wilderness skiing, off the track (including mountain ski-touring). The narrower skis, combined with lightweight boots and narrow bindings, give the best glide on tracks if only because there is the least friction against the sides of the track.

The skis need to glide well so that you can travel with the least effort and most grace; but they also need to grip, without sliding back, when you drive forward off your foot – so that you transmit all your energy to the forward movement. The ability to both glide and grip has traditionally been obtained with Nordic **waxes** applied to the sole of the ski, to suit the particular snow conditions and temperature. It may sound surprising but it is in fact quite possible, within a fairly narrow temperature range, for a wax to be soft enough to let the snow grip into it when stopped for the forward drive, yet glide over the snow as it moves on. The question of temperature is particularly important around the melting point as the hardness and crystalline strength of the snow reduces when it warms, and it needs correspondingly softer waxes to match it.

For the novice, in particular, waxing is a bit intimidating, and a welcome development in recent years has been the various 'waxless' skis, which get the necessary grip and glide from a textured sole. They don't work quite so well as a really good waxed ski, but are fine to start with and get the feel of cross-country. You can then progress to waxing if you think that the rather better performance justifies the bother.

The two main movements in cross-country skiing are the double-pole push, in which you use both poles and your arm strength to drive the skis forward (most useful when you are already travelling at speed) and the alternating or **diagonal step**, shown (not very athletically executed) below, in which the drive off one foot is counterbalanced and assisted by a swing forward of the opposite arm and stick.

Cross-country skis, like Alpine skis, have an arch or **camber** to spread your weight along the whole length of the ski. The fastest skis have an arch which is deep and rigid, so that the section under your foot presses on the snow only as you drive forward off that ski – it is this centre section which gives the grip needed for the forward drive, while the rest of the ski sole can be smooth to give the least friction for gliding.

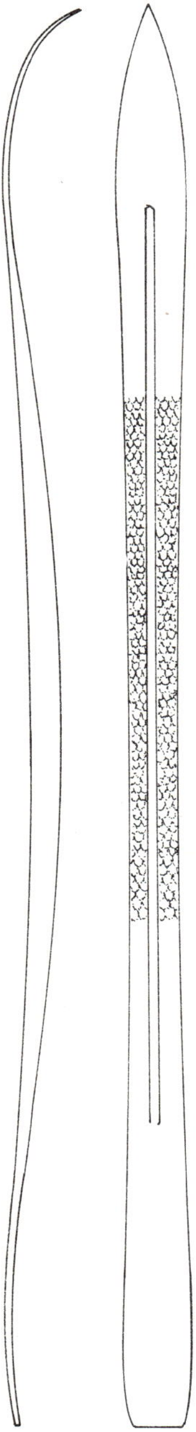

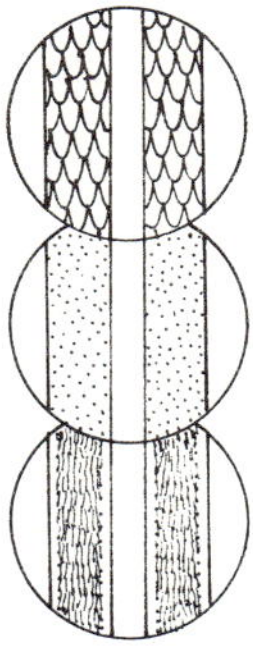

There are several different types of **waxless skis**:

- stepped or fishscale, where the sole has slight but distinct sloping 'teeth' to grip the snow one way but not the other – the best all-rounder
- mica-sole, in which slivers of mica are embedded at an angle in the plastic base material – a microscopic version of the fishscale sole, giving excellent grip, but a bit slow
- mohair strips stuck to the sole – also a bit slow, and the most easily damaged.

The three sorts of **bindings** you're likely to come across are these:

- the 'Nordic norm' – a three-pronged binding on the ski and a boot with a matching extension on the toe; there are variants of different widths, so make sure boots and bindings match
- narrower bindings designed to minimise friction with the snow at the side of the ski – the link between boot and binding tends to vary from make to make, so it's vital to be sure that the two are compatible
- the traditional cable or Kandahar binding, which is still used by some ski-tourers.

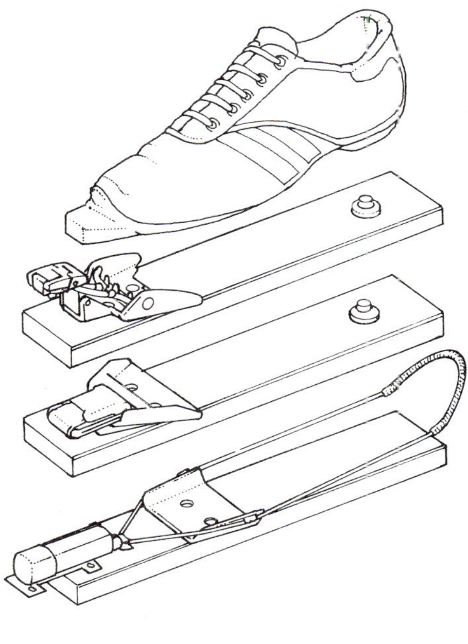

There is a considerable range of waxes (both hard waxes in sticks and klister waxes in tubes) to suit the range of temperatures and types of snow; but to start with the complexities can be avoided by using the two wide-ranging waxes now available, one for below-freezing and one for above-freezing temperatures. You rub the below-freezing one on to the soles of your skis and get the best possible spread and smoothness with a rubbing cork. Then, if the weather turns warm and you find that the skis are not gripping, you add some of the above-freezing wax (being softer, it will hold on to the other wax), increasing the area of the ski sole covered by this new wax until the ski grips satisfactorily. When it gets colder, you reverse the process by scraping off the above-freezing wax which may otherwise tend to ball up as the snow gets stronger and sticks in it.

Clothing

The cross-country skier wears clothes rather similar to those of a walker or jogger – free-moving and wind-resistant, but not heavy or bulky. They must both conserve heat when moving slowly and allow you to get rid of heat when going strongly; hence plenty of zips are needed. It will pay to have several thin layers, rather than one or two thick ones, so that you can adjust the amount more readily.

Your jacket should be windproof. Below it have a thin sweater and a thin thermal vest, with possibly a shirt as well. Generally, you should not expect the clothes you ski in to keep you warm when standing still, and should carry an extra sweater for this purpose. A scarf can help to keep you warm before you have really got into your stride. A wool hat, or a peaked cap, may sometimes be needed. For your hands, anything from windproof mittens (with thermal pile inside) to lined leather gloves will do; but they should not have any rough internal stitching, as this would cause discomfort when gripping your ski sticks hard in order to push yourself along.

It's normal to wear breeches, often supplemented by thermal long johns; but any loose fitting wind-proof trousers will do. Knee-length stockings complete the outfit, preferably with some form of cloth gaiter to protect them (and the boots) from snow.

How to do it

It is easy to learn to ski cross-country to a moderate standard, since the basic techniques are not at all difficult – most of the movements will come fairly naturally once you get moving on cross-country skis, and develop the necessary balance, agility and rhythm on which everything else depends.

But you can now get tuition in many resorts, including ones very much dominated by Alpine skiing, and it's worth having some instruction in the early days if at all possible. There is quite an art in transferring your weight from one ski to the other in the most efficient way – with the aim of keeping your skis really gliding. These movements can best be developed by imitating a good Nordic skier; but a worthwhile trick is also to ski without sticks for half an hour or so in order to get your foot positions correct.

Where to do it

Cross-country skiing is best done in Scandinavia, where virtually everyone learns to ski as a child, and where most families go to the open country for cross-country skiing, especially at Easter. The Norwegian uplands to the west and north of Oslo have hundreds of miles of ski-routes, giving plenty of scope for day trips from mountain centres; for example from the British lodge at Kvitavtn Fjellstuge which has a very extensive programme (and would be a good place to start cross-country). There is also enormous scope for long journeys from hut to hut, possibly even with dog sledges. And there are vast areas suitable for cross-country in Sweden and Finland too.

For a normal cross-country holiday, you would be based in one place, either a hotel or a mountain lodge (sometimes it is difficult to tell the difference as the lodges are so comfortable). You then do day trips out from there, or may even return for lunch and go out again. This has the advantage that you ski lightly laden and do just as much or as little as you wish. You also have all the other attractions of a comfortable hotel, including possibly some nightlife.

As cross-country skiing can be done wherever there is rolling terrain with good snow cover, the scope elsewhere in Europe is also very considerable. And with the increasing popularity of the sport the number of places where it is practised is correspondingly growing. Areas with extensive cross-country skiing include many parts of Austria, the Dolomites (eg the Trento area) and other parts of northern Italy (eg the Aosta valley), Bavaria (eg Mittelberg and Oberammergau), the Black Forest, the Jura and many other parts of France including the pre-Alps, the Massif Central and the Pyrenees.

While a number of the Alpine resorts have cross-country ski-schools and tracks suitable for learning the techniques, few give sufficient scope for the long journeys which are the particular attraction of cross-country skiing. Instead they may be short circuits of only about 3km or 5km, sometimes with steep sections, strenuous at that altitude. So if you want to enjoy some cross-country as an adjunct to an Alpine skiing holiday, it is necessary to choose your resort carefully. There should be extensive tracks and, to ensure a reasonable chance of good snow in the period December to March, these need to be at about 1000m altitude. They are most likely to be found in wide valleys running east–west, where the south side will be in shadow; or alternatively on plateaux off the main valleys. Avoid steep-sided narrow valleys with a lot of habitation if you want to get the true feel of cross-country. Examples of Alpine resorts with good potential for cross-country are St Johann and Seefeld in Austria; Pontresina/St Mortiz, Klosters/Davos, Kandersteg and Lenk in Switzerland; and La Clusaz in France. There is very extensive cross-country in North America, notably throughout the eastern states of the USA and in Canada.

In Britain there are usually quite a number of days each winter when it is possible to take cross-country skis on to moorland or hilly country, such as the Pennines (sometimes even the South Downs!); while in Scotland there can be good possibilities, for example in the Cairngorms and Glenshee.

Cross-country touring

Cross-country touring, involving a continuous journey lasting several days or a week, with nights in different hotels or cabins, is a natural extension of cross-country skiing. It gives a challenge, as difficult or easy as you wish according to the choice of tour; and the opportunity to get away from one area and feel that you have achieved a real journey. To enjoy touring, you need to be able to ski cross-country without fatigue and to be able to carry a rucksack with essential gear, weighing perhaps 10kg to 15kg – food and spare clothing, and possibly a sleeping bag. For anything but the simplest tours the party must include someone who is experienced in map-reading and navigation and who has an understanding of winter survival in case something goes wrong. The alternative is to join an organised tour, with an experienced leader and possibly a guide.

A good plan when starting touring is to spend some of the first week at a fixed base, getting to know each other, and improving fitness and skill, before starting your tour from hut to hut.

In Norway, excellent touring may be found in the whole upland area between Oslo and Trondheim. Areas with good chains of huts include the Hardangervidda and areas to the north of Finse (on the Oslo–Bergen railway); the Jotunheim; and the Rondane. Sweden has Lappland (notably the Abisko-Kebnekaise area) as well as areas further south. Tours are possible in the other areas of Europe which lend themselve to cross-country, of which perhaps the best are those in the Jura, with its very attractive combination of hills, farms and quiet, peaceful villages.

Organised holidays

A few of the major tour operators include cross-country holidays within their programmes. The main specialist operators Britain are Waymark, who have a wide range of holidays, including tours and competitions. (Waymark are included in the Package holidays section of the 'Travel facts' chapter.)

Organised tours are arranged by some of the clubs (particularly the Eagle Ski Club) and national organisations (notably the DNT – the Norwegian Touring Federation – and the Club Alpin Français).

Competition

At top international level, Nordic racing is one of the most demanding of sports. But there is also plenty of competition at Citizen, regional or club level which is there to be enjoyed by those who like to test and improve themselves in this way.

The shortest distance is 5km and the longest international distance is 50km (taking only about 2 hours), but the Citizen races may go up to 85km or 90km. The Citizen races may be likened to the marathons for runners or joggers; and attract thousands of participants of all ages and standards. The most famous, forming the world Loppet series, are: Dolomitenlauf; Marcialonga; König Ludwig Lauf; Gatineau; Transjurassienne; American Birkebeiner; Finlandia Hihto; Vasaloppet; Engadin Skimarathon; and Birkebeinerrennet. But there are many other

Loppets, including even one in Iceland. To enter, you will normally need to be a member of a club within the national ski organisation and may have to have a racing licence and a medical check-up. Waymark Holidays organise parties to train for and race in some of these competitions.

A particularly demanding variation is the Biathlon where cross-country racing is combined with rifle shooting. This tends to be a military preserve because of the standard of training required – both physical and with weapons.

Clubs and associations

In Britain, in addition to the touring clubs mentioned above, there are many cross-country ski clubs, particularly in the Midlands and north of England and in Scotland. It would be worth joining one in order to meet fellow cross-country enthusiasts and find out about cross-country skiing opportunities; to share transport; and possibly to enter competitions. Lists may be obtained from the English Ski Council or the Scottish National Ski Council respectively.

Alpine ski-touring

Quite apart from Nordic or cross-country ski-touring is the much less widely practised sport of Alpine ski-touring, which takes place on the steeper ground of the Alps, the Pyrenees and other mountains. Although it bears some similarity to cross-country touring, this form of touring derives from Alpine skiing (using very similar equipment) and may be linked also with Alpine mountaineering. It involves travelling over steep mountains on skis, using bindings which allow the heel of the boot to lift for walking uphill, and fabric 'skins' on the soles of the skis to grip the snow.

The really good tourer, or ski-mountaineer, will be able to climb big mountains on skis, such as the Wildspitze in Austria, Monte Rosa in Switzerland and Mont Blanc in France; but much of the fun of ski-touring comes from travelling over cols and on glaciers well below the summits, or even at much lower levels, near the tree-line. A main attraction of Alpine ski touring is just to travel through such high mountain country, and experience the magnificent solitude and beauty of the mountains, with their steep faces and glaciers, which it is normally impossible for anyone else, other than Alpine mountaineers, to know. Although you do not have to be a mountaineer, for the easier tours at least, you do need some love of the mountains to get the most satisfaction from it. And unless your party includes really experienced mountaineers you will probably need a guide.

From many resorts, it is possible to undertake day-tours, usually starting from the top of a lift and involving some climbing uphill to a col or ridge to get access to fresh country outside the scope of the piste system. There is a great deal of pleasure to be gained from such excursions – the technical satisfaction of using skis whatever the snow conditions, ranging from good spring snow to breakable crust or icy snow; and there is the physical pleasure of climbing uphill on skins, and the health and fitness which come with it. But the best touring comes from travelling from hut to hut, over the high cols and glaciers, and including suitable peaks from time to time. Then there is the comradeship of the group, where everone relies on each other to some degree, and you share a communal life 24 hours a day. A particular pleasure is the long, lazy afternoon at the hut, following a good ski-tour that morning – working out and savouring the prospects for tomorrow, or just reading or sleeping.

The main qualification you need to go touring is the ability to stay upright on your skis in all conditions. Falling is physically tiring, delays the party and can also of course cause injury in the normal way; falling in the wrong place (eg near a crevasse or above an icy slope) can be dangerous. Ski-tourers therefore tend to ski very steadily and reliably, often forsaking parallel turns for stem-swings where these are more effective – for example in difficult snow or where it is important to save energy (eg with a heavy sack or at high altitude). But it also helps if you're a good enough skier to be able to concentrate on the route-finding and on enjoying the day, rather than on skiing technique.

Ski-touring can be physically demanding, but is rarely exhausting. It is much more a question of rhythm and steadiness than of dashes of speed and lung-bursting activity. You will need to be fit enough to walk uphill with skis, skins and a pack; and to ski downhill without getting tired. You must be acclimatised to the altitude for the higher tours; but otherwise the question of just how fit you need to be really depends on how strenuous the tour is. For a first tour, it should be possible to find something which has a gentle first few days, without excessive uphill climbing, which will allow you to acclimatise.

You must have the right equipment to go touring. In some resorts where ski-touring is customary, you can hire skis with touring bindings and skins; and this would certainly be advisable for day tours. But for serious touring – going from one valley to another, which may be some distance away – it's more convenient to own your equipment.

Equipment

Ski-tourers need **boots** which are a cross between conventional ski boots and mountaineering boots – with a ridged rubber sole, and some flexibility for the ankle to move forward without discomfort; but for a short tour, ordinary ski-boots can be used, with the top clips undone for going uphill. Most of the main manufacturers make touring **skis** which are flexible in the tip, light in weight, easy in difficult snow, grip well on ice, and may have a groove in the heel to take the rear clip of the **skins**. For ease of carrying, lightness and manoeuvrability, you may wish to choose rather shorter ones than you would use for downhill skiing. The **bindings** need to have all the normal release functions since it is particularly important not to hurt yourself when far from help.

For steep, icy ground, or on summit ridges, it may be necessary to climb on foot, possibly even roped up. An **ice-axe** may then be a considerable help, and a necessary safeguard against falling; it's important to know how to use it. **Crampons** (sets of spikes which fit

Uphill progress when ski-touring depends on having fabric *skins* (so called because sealskins were originally used) strapped or glued to the sole of the ski to give grip on the snow; for icy snow you need snow blades (*harscheisen*), which may be part of the touring binding or clipped into special fittings on the side of the ski, below the boot.

Touring *bindings* allow your heels to lift from the ski when going uphill – and some have a special device to make climbing more comfortable by supporting the heel at an angle to the ski. When skiing downhill, the boot is clamped on to the ski in the normal way. Safety straps are better than brakes, since it's important not to get separated from your skis if your bindings release in a fall.

beneath your boots) will also give you a very much better footing than boots alone. Before going on an alpine ski-tour, check with the leader as to whether you are likely to need them.

Clothing

Clothing needs to be warm and windproof, but it is important also to be able to get rid of excess heat: so good ventilation (plenty of zips) is vital. Ski-tourers tend to use mountaineering clothing (breeches, gaiters over the boots, an anorak or cagoule, and a warm hat, possibly supplemented with a down jacket); but for a day tour in good conditions, or for a moderate longer tour, ordinary Alpine ski clothing would be satisfactory, provided it can be ventilated.

Touring skills

Touring on moderate ground (for example below the upper tree-line), like cross-country touring, requires little more than common sense and the ability to move on skis without falling. Most ski resorts have gentle untracked terrain nearby, often on summer paths away from the main pistes, and there is everything to be said for starting to find your way around on these as early as possible – provided they are genuinely moderate, there is no avalanche risk and you always go with someone else. But any more difficult terrain requires both care and skill; for example anyone starting to tour at moderate altitudes away from resorts would need the ability to:

- ski reliably off-piste, carrying a rucksack; this requires a sound stem Christie (or stem swing) turn
- walk up-hill on skis, using skins
- halt a fall by rolling over or by using ski sticks
- read a map and compass
- recognise avalanche conditions and know the main rescue procedures.

To safely embark on high Alpine ski-touring you would need, in addition, an adequate understanding of:

- use of *harscheisen* – blades fitted beneath the boot to give grip when walking uphill on hard or icy snow
- glacier touring technique including simple rope handling, crevasse formations and crevasse rescue
- elementary snow and ice climbing, including the use of ice-axe and, if possible, crampons
- elementary rock scrambling or climbing, including methods of belaying
- Alpine weather.

An introduction to these skills can be obtained on various touring meets of the main British clubs (see below). The leaders of touring parties, especially ones without guides, bear a heavy responsibility and must have not only these skills but also the more general skills of mountain leadership, which come only with considerable experience.

Where and when to do it

There are quite a number of regular tours such as the round tours of the Stubai or the Oetzal, traverses of the Silvretta or Ortler, or the Haute Route of the Valais (Chamonix to Saas Fee) or the Bernese Oberland (Les Diablerets to Meiringen). In addition there are many single day tours, for example in the Bernina, or the Vallée Blanche on Mont Blanc.

In deciding what to undertake, the main considerations are:

- the competence, experience and fitness of the party
- the availability of guides
- the time of year – the lower areas tend to be in condition early (March) while the higher ones come in later (April or May)
- the recent and forecast weather and snow conditions, with their implications for avalanche risk
- the technical difficulty and magnitude of the tour, taking account of the state of the glaciers
- the intervals between huts; their dates of opening; whether or not they have a guardian; and whether or not they provide food and fue
- rescue arrangements.

It is essential to get to know the route as accurately as possible before embarking on it. You can do this by studying very closely the various guidebooks and maps, from reading accounts in journals and other publications, and by talking to club members and others who have done it. Allow plenty of time in case of bad weather or other problems.

Clubs and associations

The main ski clubs with Alpine ski-touring activities are the Ski Club of Great Britain, the Eagle Ski Club, and the Scottish Ski Club. The Ski Club of Great Britain runs and subsidizes several tours each year including some for beginners, in addition to arranging day tours at certain centres, through the SCGB resort representatives. The Eagle Ski Club has a major touring programme, which includes a high Alpine training course.

The Association of British Mountain Guides can provide details of guides specialising in Alpine ski touring.

Waymark and other specialist tour operators arrange parties for the Haute Route, in addition to their cross-country tours.

The Alpine countries have their own national Alpine clubs which own huts, publish guidebooks, journals and newsletters and arrange many other facilities for their members. These facilities usually include preferential treatment in almost all the Alpine huts, cheap rates on the mountain railways and cable-cars in each club's own country and, usually at extra cost, insurance against the often very high cost of a rescue party. The British Ski Federation, in association with the British Mountaineering Council, runs a ski-touring leaders' course – as do some of the Continental clubs. The British ski clubs sometimes award scholarships to assist British skiers to attend courses.

Most British ski tourers undertaking high mountain tours join one of the Continental clubs, though of course this is not necessary for lower level touring. It is not only pleasant to be a member, but also, over a fortnight or so, it may save you more than the cost of the subscription through the preferential rates in huts. The UK branch of the Austrian Alpine Club (OAV) is the most popular, and has ski-touring activities for its members. Alternatively, the British Mountaineering Council can provide a reciprocal rights card which entitles the holder to reduced rates in huts. The Council also runs training courses.

Travel facts

In this final major chapter of the *Guide* we bring together all the names and numbers you're likely to need when you get down to arranging the practical details of your holiday – whether you take your car, buy a package or travel independently by public transport. It isn't just facts; in particular, the major section on insurance has clear buying guidance, and that on motoring has advice on how to deal with the extreme road and weather conditions you'll meet in the mountains. The chapter is broken down into the sections (some quite short, some quite substantial) listed below.

Insurance

As we explain in 'A Skiing Primer', if you're set on a particular package holiday you may not have much choice about the insurance you get. And these days the obvious differences between one policy and another may not seem huge. But the less obvious differences are not trivial – they may matter enough to steer you away from the tour operator you first thought of, or to make you decide to buy your insurance independently. In this section we outline the variations, so that you can weigh up the policies which are thrust at you. We take in turn each of the kinds of cover you can expect to find.

First, a bit of key terminology. Under many sections of a policy, the amount that's paid out in settlement of a claim will be less than the amount you've lost. The difference, called an *excess*, varies between policies and between sections, but is often £25 per claim. Every separate incident is considered as a separate claim. For example, if your ski bag is damaged on the journey out and you lose your ski poles at a later stage of the holiday, you will be making two claims, and you will have to bear two excesses; if your ski bag is damaged and your ski poles are lost as a result, it's considered to be one incident, so you will pay only one excess.

We divide policies into those offered by tour operators and those sold separately – 'independent' policies. Where we say 'all policies', we mean all those we've looked at, which strictly speaking is not all but a great many. It's unlikely that you will come upon policies which do not follow the usual pattern, but it's vital to check that the policy you're about to buy suits **you**.

As well as setting out the reasons for which you'll be able to claim, a policy will have *exclusion clauses* – these tell you about circumstances in which the insurance company won't pay up. You should carefully check these exclusions before buying a policy in case there are any which might catch you out. You'll often find that you won't be covered if you take part in very risky sports – for example, ski-jumping, racing in major events, ice hockey or bob-sleigh riding. Other things to watch out for are exclusions relating to illnesses you've suffered from or for which you've been treated recently.

Although everyone should read policies carefully, there are two groups who should be particularly wary – those who are over 65 and those for whom pregnancy is a possibility. Some policies have an age limit, usually 70 or 75 years; others have an age exclusion in respect of medical and cancellation expenses only. Where pregnancy is concerned policies vary a lot. Some have no exclusions at all, others provide cover only if the pregnancy starts after the policy is taken out or is in the early stages when the holiday is to be taken. A few exclude all claims.

You should tell the insurance company about any health problem you have when you take out the policy. If you don't, a subsequent claim could be turned down.

Claims involving expenditure should always be supported by receipts. And claims must always be submitted within a reasonable time of your return.

In most countries UK citizens are entitled to treatment by the local national heath service, either free or at reduced cost. DHSS leaflet SA30 has details. Do *not* take this to mean that you can manage without insurance.

Cancellation

What it's for To repay money you've paid in advance for a holiday you're unable to go on.
Do you need it? Yes, unless you're making no advance bookings.
Who offers it? All policies.
When it applies Most policies pay up if you are prevented from travelling by your own illness, or the illness or death of a close relative of yourself or of another member of your holiday party. Most pay if any member of the party is called for jury service or is required to appear in court as a witness. Many policies will pay out if you decide to cancel your holiday after a delay in departure of at least 12 hours (sometimes 24 hours). Some pay if you have to cancel because a close business associate or someone you plan to stay with while on holiday is ill, if you're made redundant or if your home is made uninhabitable by fire, flood or burglary. Look for a policy giving the widest possible cover and the fewest worrying exclusion clauses.
What you can claim Whatever amounts you have paid out that you can't get back.

An excess will usually be deducted – it may be lower than usual if you claim only the deposit. (You don't get your insurance premium back of course.)

How much cover? Tour operators' policies generally cover the cost of the holiday; others set a limit – usually between £1,000 and £3,000. Obviously you need to make sure that the limit is high enough to meet the full cost of your holiday.
Watch out Some policies won't pay out if you cancel your holiday because of an injury while taking part in a 'hazardous activity' – eg mountaineering or parachuting.

Curtailment

What it's for To repay a proportion of money you've paid for a holiday you have to cut short, and extra costs arising from an early return home.
Do you need it? Yes, unless you're making no advance bookings.
Who offers it? All policies.
When it applies If you have to come home early for the kinds of reason set out under Cancellation.
What you can claim A proportion of the pre-paid cost of the holiday, according to the length of time on holiday you've lost, and reasonable additional expenses for travel and accommodation to get you home. Most policies have an excess.
How much cover? Generally, the same limits apply here as under Cancellation. With tour operator policies, a limit equal to the cost of the holiday may be too low if you have to fly back soon after you arrive. Narrow cash limits may be similarly inadequate – look for a limit of at least twice the holiday cost.

Medical expenses

What it's for To meet costs arising from illness or injury.
Do you need it? Yes, even in countries where there are good reciprocal health care agreements (see over the page).
Who offers it? All policies.
When it applies If you fall ill or injure yourself during the holiday, either on or off the slopes, or require emergency dental treatment.
What you can claim All treatment expenses – doctors' fees, hospital bills, prescription charges etc – plus any additional accommodation and travel costs resulting from your illness or injury, including mountain rescue in normal circumstances (see over the page). Many policies will pay to bring you back home (by air ambulance if necessary) for medical treatment if it would be better for you (or cheaper for the insurance company). Most policies will not pay the additional cost of private-room accommodation in hospital unless your doctor thinks it is necessary.

Some policies will not cover surgery or treatment which can reasonably be delayed until you return to the UK, where you can be treated under the NHS or your own medical bills insurance. Other policies provide for any expenses incurred up to 12 months after the time when you are injured or fall ill.

In the event of death all policies will meet 'reasonable' costs for burial or cremation locally or for reasonable cost of transport of the body or ashes to the place of residence in the UK.
How much cover? Anything from £10,000 to an unlimited amount. The smaller amounts of cover on offer will deal with the great majority of cases in Europe, but may not be enough for the few really nasty ones involving air ambulances staffed by high-powered medical teams. To be on the safe side (which is, after all, what insurance is about) we would recommend cover of at least £50,000. If you're going to North America you should have at least £500,000 – but since unlimited policies are available, why not take one? If you have insufficient cover, you will become personally liable for any costs incurred.

The limit on claims in the event of death may be only £1,000 or £2,000.
Watch out A claim may be refused if you were under the influence of drink or drugs at the time of the accident.

Hospital benefit

What it's for To cheer you up.
Do you need it? Not really.
Who offers it? Several policies.
When it applies If you have to spend at least 24 hours in hospital as a result of an injury or illness outside the UK.
What you can claim A specified amount (usually £10, sometimes more) for every 24-hour period in hospital.
How much cover? Most policies set a limit to what they will pay – often £200.

Personal accident

What it's for To compensate you for disablement, or to compensate your heirs for your death.

Do you need it? Not as part of a skiing policy. If you think you need insurance against disability or death, you should have a year-round policy (probably at a much higher level of cover).
Who offers it? Most policies, although with some it's an optional extra.
When it applies If you are killed or suffer a specific injury, eg loss of a limb or an eye, or permanent total disablement. Most policies will pay compensation for disablement occurring up to twelve months after the date of the accident. Some also offer a weekly benefit for temporary total disablement.
What you can claim A fixed lump sum, according to the injury you suffer.
How much cover? The size of the lump sum varies considerably; it's usually at least £5,000 but can be as much as £25,000. Compensation for children (and in some policies, for elderly people) is much lower.

Personal liability

What it's for To meet claims made against you by others for damage to themselves or their property for which you are legally liable.
Do you need it? Yes and no: this sort of insurance is valuable at any time, so you really should have a permanent policy. Household contents insurance normally provides it.
Who offers it? All policies.
When it applies If an individual successfully makes a claim against you for damages. Many policies won't cover claims made by members of your own family or by someone you employ. And watch out if you hire a car – a skiing policy won't cover you for liability arising out of the use of a vehicle, so you must make sure you are adequately covered under the insurance you get with the rented car.

Mountain rescue

If a rescue team judges it necessary for you to be transported off the slopes by helicopter you don't have much alternative, even if your policy won't cover the cost (of around £10 a minute). They are used fairly frequently in Switzerland, less often elsewhere because of environmental laws. You can buy helicopter insurance in most Swiss resorts if your own policy excludes it.

What you can claim Any damages awarded against you (and legal costs of disputing the claim), but not the costs of defending yourself in criminal proceedings.
How much cover? Usually £500,000 but sometimes £250,000 or £1,000,000. We recommend that you have at least £500,000 of cover (and £1,000,000 for North America).
Watch out A few policies exclude claims made in overseas courts – these are not recommended.

Personal money

What it's for To replace lost or stolen money, and other things which can be used in exchange for goods or services.
Do you need it? Yes, unless you have an existing policy which covers you all the time for such risks.
Who offers it? All policies – though some include it within the Baggage and personal effects section.
When it applies If your cash, travellers' cheques, credit cards are stolen, lost or destroyed. Such things as air and other travel tickets, petrol coupons and vouchers will also be covered. Some specialist winter sports insurance policies specifically cover the loss of your lift pass, but this would otherwise be dealt with as a specialised form of travel ticket.
What you can claim The value of whatever you have lost.
How much cover? The limit of cover varies from £100 to £500, but most are in the £150 to £250 range. While this may not sound much, remember that there are special arrangements to replace travellers' cheques or credit cards if you lose them, so they should not need to be taken into account.
Watch out Claims for loss or theft of money (sometimes belongings as well) will normally be met only if the incident has been reported to an appropriate authority (usually the police) within 24 hours.

Baggage and personal effects

What it's for To replace lost or damaged belongings.
Do you need it? Probably, though many of your possessions may be already covered if you have a house contents and/or an all risks policy.
Who offers it? All policies.
When it applies If any of your

possessions are lost, stolen or damaged – with certain exceptions. Contact lenses and documents are excluded by virtually all policies, as are fragile things (eg binoculars, souvenirs) which get broken. **What you can claim** Usually the actual value of what you lose (ie its second-hand value, not the cost of replacing it with something new).
How much cover? Often £1,000, though it could be as low as £75 or as high as £2,000. It's important to work out how much it would cost to replace your belongings should the whole lot be lost – it may be more than you think, particularly if you're relying on the holiday policy to cover such things as your jewellery and cameras as well as clothes and suitcases. And many policies also cover ski equipment in this section. Most policies have a limit on what will be paid for any one item, often somewhere in the £200 region. A pair of skis and ski sticks is usually counted as one item as is a camera together with its lenses, flash unit and so on. Some policies also have a limit to what they will pay out in total for valuables such as jewellery, watches, cameras and so on – £200 or £300, say.
Watch out All policies expect you to take 'reasonable care' of your possessions. Some specifically say they won't pay if unattended belongings go missing.

Delayed baggage

What it's for To tide you over until your delayed bags turn up.
Do you need it? It can certainly help.
Who offers it? Most policies.
When it applies If your baggage is delayed for 12 hours or more.
What you can claim The cost of essential items. If you have a tour operator policy, the rep should give you the necessary cash; if your baggage never turns up, the money you've been given will be deducted from your claim for the loss. If you have an independent policy, you will have to use your own money and claim it back on your return to the UK. If your skiing equipment is delayed you will be entitled under some policies to the cost of hiring replacements until it shows up.
How much cover? The limit on what you can claim ranges from £50 to £100.

Ski equipment

What it's for To replace lost or damaged ski equipment.
Do you need it? Yes, if ski equipment is excluded from cover under Baggage and personal effects; hired equipment is likely to be excluded from that section, even if your own equipment is not.
Who offers it? Some tour operators and specialist skiing policies; some have a separate ski equipment section, others include it as a subsection of Baggage and personal effects.
When it applies If your skis, ski sticks, bindings or ski boots are lost, stolen or damaged. Some policies which cover loss or theft of hired equipment will not cover *breakage* of hired skis.
What you can claim Some companies pay the cost of replacement, or repair if that is practicable, others pay only the market value, allowing for wear and tear. Although some companies say they will pay only for the one broken ski, in practice this is often not the case – you will be covered for the pair. If it's your own equipment that's lost or broken, some policies will cover the cost of hiring replacements for the remainder of your holiday (as well as paying for a replacement set); if not, you have to bear the cost of rental yourself – or buy new equipment immediately out of your own pocket.
How much cover? Cover is usually limited to between £200 and £300. This is more than enough for a cheap set of equipment, but not for a flashy set. If you're taking your own skis it's worth looking for a policy which will pay for hire of replacement skis. If you're hiring skis make sure you won't have to pay for any damage or loss yourself.
Watch out Some companies insist you bring broken skis home with you so that they can satisfy themselves that they are beyond repair.

Ski pack

What it's for To repay a proportion of what you have paid a tour operator in advance for a 'ski pack' (a package of equipment hire, lessons and lift pass) if you become unable to make use of it.
Do you need it? Worth having if you're buying a ski pack.
Who offers it? Some tour operators.
When it applies If you fall ill or are injured during the holiday.
What you can claim A proportion of the cost of the ski pack, depending on how long you spend out of action.
How much cover? Look for cover of at least the cost of the ski pack.

Travel delay

What it's for To compensate you for big delays in your journey.
Do you need it? It's less fuss than seeking compensation in other ways.
Who offers it? Most policies, although with some it's an optional extra.
When it applies If you're delayed for more than twelve hours – often only if the delay is for a specified reason – usually including strikes, mechanical breakdown and bad weather.
What you can claim A specified daily amount during the delay or, if you wish to cancel your holiday, the total cost of it.
How much cover? Usually £20 for the first 12 hours, £10 for each subsequent 12 hours, up to a maximum of £60. If you cancel your holiday, the limit of cover in the Cancellation section will apply.

Missed departure

What it's for To meet the costs which arise if you miss the outward flight.
Do you need it? Seems worthwhile.
Who offers it? Mostly tour operator policies, and a few independent ones.
When it applies If public transport fails to deliver you to the airport or other departure point in time to join the booked trip – provided you allowed a reasonable time to get there. Some policies also cover you if you miss the flight because of a car accident or breakdown.
What you can claim The cost of extra transport to get to your resort, and accommodation if necessary.
How much cover? It varies a lot and could be from as little as £150 to £500.

Interruption of transport

What it's for To compensate you if you're marooned in your resort.
Do you need it? Doubtful; it's the tour operator's responsibility to get you home once they've got you out to a resort.
Who offers it? Several policies have variations on the same theme.
When it applies There are policies which will cover you for hi-jacks, avalanches, landslides, riots, strikes or civil commotions provided that they occur within the period of insurance. Some tour operators have a *weather extension* which covers you only if the difficulties are attributable to the weather. Several tour operators include something under other policy sections.
What you can claim What you have to spend while marooned, up to a limit.
How much cover? The cover limit varies from £100 to £300.

Tour organiser failure

What it's for Refund of advance payments if your operator goes bust.
Do you need it? No. The insurance applies only to circumstances in which you would get your money back anyway – though you may get it back more promptly from an insurance company.
Who offers it? A few independent policies.
When it applies If the holiday you've booked has to be cancelled or cut short because the tour operator goes out of business – provided that you've booked with an ABTA member or an otherwise bonded operator.
What you can claim Whatever you have paid out – or a proportion if you are already on holiday when the collapse occurs.
How much cover? Up to £1,000.

Withdrawal of services

What it's for To compensate you for a lack of services in your accommodation.
Do you need it? It's less fuss than suing your tour operator (though suing may get you more money).
Who offers it? A few policies.
When it applies If there is no water or electricity in your room; or no waiter service at meals; or no hot meals are served; or no chambermaid services.
What you can claim A daily amount, usually of £20, for as long as the services are missing.
How much cover? There is usually a maximum total payment of £100 or £200.

Snow guarantee

What it's for To meet the cost of getting to snow or lifts if your resort lacks either, or to compensate you for their absence.
Do you need it? Not essential. You can claim only in extreme conditions.
Who offers it? Only a few policies, but many tour operators now have a separate snow guarantee.
When it applies If all the lifts in the resort are shut and it's impossible to ski – either because of the weather or because of a shortage of snow.
What you can claim The cost of getting to a nearby resort – in practice your operator will probably arrange for transport, ski school (where appropriate) and lift pass for a nearby resort, and no money changes hands. If that's not possible, some will pay compensation – often £15 a day, though you may get no money for the first two days.
How much cover? Unlimited.

National tourist offices

The national tourist office of a foreign country may be able to give you a lot of information, or only a little. The best will have full lists of accommodation, and detailed literature on individual resorts.

Andorran Delegation in Great Britain
63 Westover Road, London SW18 2RS; ✆01-874 4806.
Austrian National Tourist Office
30 St George Street, London W1R OAL; ✆01-629 0461.
Bulgarian National Tourist Office
18 Princes Street, London W1R 7RE; ✆01-499 6988.
Canadian High Commission
Canada House, Trafalgar Sqare, London SW1Y 5BJ; ✆01-629 9492.
French Government Tourist Office
178 Piccadilly, London W1V OAL; ✆01-491 7622.
German National Tourist Office
61 Conduit Street, London W1R OEN; ✆01-734 2600.
Italian State Tourist Office
3rd Floor, 1 Princes Street, London W1R 8AY; ✆01-408 1254.
Norwegian Tourist Board
20 Pall Mall, London SW1Y 5NE; ✆01-839 2650.
Romanian National Tourist Office
29 Thurloe Place, London SW7 2HP; ✆01-584 8090.
Scottish Tourist Board
23 Ravelston Terrace, Edinburgh EH4 3EU; ✆031-332 2433.
19 Cockspur Street, London SW1Y 5BL; ✆01-930 8661.
Spanish Tourist Office
57 James's St, London SW1A 1LD; ✆01-499 0901.
Swiss National Tourist Office
Swiss Centre, New Coventry Street, London W1V 8EE; ✆01-734 1921.
United States Travel and Tourism
22 Sackville Street, London W1X 2EA; ✆01-439 7433.
Yugoslav National Tourist Office
143 Regent Street, London W1R 8AE; ✆01-734 5243.

Public transport

Going by rail

You can travel to quite a number of ski resorts by rail – mostly long-established resorts; some in Austria are on a direct line from Calais, so you can get there without leaving the train, except to cross the Channel. The French high-speed TGV trains make it possible to leave Paris after an early breakfast and get to many French resorts in time for lunch.

We list major resorts with railway stations, and give approximate journey times from London and the number of changes of train involved excluding that for the Channel crossing.

Andermatt 20hr, two changes
Arosa 21hr, one change
Aviemore 10hr, direct
Badgastein 24hr, direct
Chamonix 21hr, one change
Davos 19hr, one change
Grindelwald 19hr, two changes
Gstaad 18hr, two changes
Kitzbühel 23hr, one change
Klosters 19hr, two changes
Les Arcs 21hr, two changes, then cable-car
Mayrhofen 24½hr, two changes
Mürren 19hr, three changes
St Anton 20hr, direct
St Moritz 20½hr, one change
Verbier 18½hr, three changes, then cable-car
Wengen 19hr, two changes
Zell am See 24hr, one change
Zermatt 19hr, one change

Going by coach

International Express, the Continental arm of National Express, offer scheduled through routes all over Europe, using a number of European coach operators. Services start from London Victoria with UK services timetabled to connect with European departures. Their Eurolines service 131 runs three times a week to Chamonix with stops at Grenoble, Chambéry, Annecy, Annemasse and Geneva. Total journey time is 22 hours.

Tickets (£45 single, £79 return, children half-price) are available from International Express reservation centres in London, Birmingham, Bristol, Cardiff, Edinburgh, Exeter, Glasgow, Leeds, Manchester, Newcastle and Peterborough, and from any of the 3,300 National Express outlets throughout the UK. Further information on ✆01-730 0202.

A quicker service to Geneva, taking about 15 hours, operates every Saturday night and combines coach travel with the TGV. Tickets are £95 return (no single fares available).

Going by air

Quite apart from the fact that most package holidays employ air transport, there are many ways in which an independent traveller can fly out to ski. There are scheduled air services to many airports within striking distance of the skiing regions, and provided you look for 'promotional' fares (which have inconvenient conditions attached – advance booking for example) the cost need not be prohibitive. But it will almost always be cheaper to buy a seat on a charter flight from a tour operator – many firms listed in the Package holidays section of 'Travel facts' sell seats on their flights with no accommodation strings attached, making use of loopholes in the regulations which are meant to prevent this. Some of these firms offer what amounts to a scheduled service, with several flights a week to their major destination airports.

UK airports

When departure day arrives, it's always worth giving your departure airport a call to check that your flight is not delayed. We give the phone number of the information service. Provincial airports are all served by buses from the centre of nearby cities; for London and Birmingham airports we outline the public transport links.

Belfast Aldergrove ✆(0232) 229271
Birmingham ✆021-767 5511
Passenger transit system links airport with Birmingham International railway station.
Bristol ✆(0272) 5874411
Cardiff–Wales ✆(0446) 711211
East Midlands near Derby ✆(0332) 810621
Edinburgh ✆031-333 1000
Glasgow ✆041-887 1111
Leeds/Bradford ✆(0532) 509696
London: Gatwick ✆(0293) 28822 Fast trains from Victoria, slower ones from London Bridge. Greenline coaches from Victoria. Buses from many points in south.
London: Heathrow Terminal 4 (KLM, NLM City Hopper, Air Malta, BA Intercontinental and BA Paris, Amsterdam flights) ✆01-745 7139; Terminal 1 (other BA flights, all Sabena, SAA, ELAL and domestic) ✆01-745 7702; Terminal 2 (other European airlines) ✆01-745 7115; Terminal 3 (other inter-continental flights) ✆01-745 7412 arrivals, ✆01-745 7067 departures. On the London undergroud system (Piccadilly Line) with separate station for Terminal 4. Railair coach link from railway stations at Reading, Woking. Airport buses from central London railway station - Victoria (A1) Euston (A2). Greenline buses from Victoria coach station.
Luton ✆(0582) 36061
Manchester ✆061-489 3000
Newcastle ✆(0632) 860966

Foreign airports

We list the transport links you're likely to want to use if you're travelling independently. On a package you'll normally be transferred to the resort by your operator. Even going independently, you may be able to arrange a seat on a package transfer coach going to your resort.

Bern Bus connection to Bern railway station.
Geneva: Cointrin Airport buses to Geneva and Lausanne stations. Bus links with several ski resorts in Savoie.
Lyon Airport buses to Lyons Perrache station, and buses to Tarentaise towns and resorts.
Milan Airport buses from Linate, buses from Malpensa; both to town centre.
Munich Airport bus to Munich railway station, and buses to Kitzbühel, Innsbruck and the Dolomites.
Nice Airport buses to Menton, Monte Carlo, Nice, Cannes, and buses direct to Isola 2000 and other resorts.
Salzburg Airport buses to Salzburg railway station, and buses to Kitzbühel.
Turin Airport buses to town centre.
Venice Airport buses to town centre.
Zurich Train to Zurich railway station, and buses to western Austrian resorts.

Taking a car

Whenever you're planning to take your car on the Continent there are a number of things to bear in mind:

- always carry official documents including driving licence, vehicle registration document, insurance certificate and passport
- make sure you are fully insured; to be sure that you are covered as fully abroad as at home, you need a Green Card from your insurance company
- display an approved GB sign on the back of your vehicle
- remember that seat belts are compulsory in many countries on the Continent, and that children are not allowed in front seats in many countries
- carry an advance warning triangle – either compulsory or recommended for most Continental countries
- adjust or adapt your headlights for driving abroad
- carry a good map or road atlas
- get your car serviced well in advance of departure
- carry a first aid kit (in Austria it's compulsory)
- fit an exterior rear view mirror on the left hand side of the car – valuable anywhere on the Continent, compulsory in Italy.

Preparations

When going to the mountains in winter, the weather and road conditions you're likely to meet make special preparations necessary:

- if your car engine is water-cooled, make sure the anti-freeze is strong enough; this is particularly important if the car is going to be left outside at night, when the temperature may drop as low as –30°C
- don't forget you'll need a strong solution of winter screenwash, too
- if you have any doubts at all about the condition of your battery, have it tested before you set off; and consider equipping yourself with 'jump leads' so that you can start your engine from another car's battery
- check the car handbook to see whether thinner oil is recommended for very low-temperature conditions, and whether you need to adjust the engine air intake
- if you can arrange it, get some experience on a skid pan before you go – on snow-bound roads in the Alps your car will spend a good part of its time skidding in one way or another
- if your car's headlights throw a lot of light upwards (rather than having a very sharp top edge to their beam) consider fitting special fog lamps – night driving in falling snow is a nightmare without good lights
- take a small shovel for getting out of roadside drifts; if you have a tow rope, take that, too.

Snow-chains

If you expect to find snow on the pistes in your resort, it's reasonable to expect snow on the roads as well. And if there is snow on the roads you'll need chains for the car's driving wheels – not only to keep going on hills but also to satisfy the local laws. (In Austria, the police have a habit of obliging chainless motorists to buy chains from them, at punitive prices.) Chains tend to be expensive in Britain; in and around the Alps they're easy to find at much lower prices (at least in common car sizes) in hypermarkets and service stations. You can hire chains from the AA, among others.

You should put your chains on before they become absolutely necessary; if you wait until the car slithers to a standstill you may find yourself putting them on in an acutely inconvenient and dangerous place, perhaps blocking the road. It helps if you practise putting them on as soon as you buy them – not only to make sure that you know how, but also to make sure that you've got all the bits.

You can keep chains on while driving on ordinary roads, but only for short periods and at very low speeds – the limit should be specified in the instructions. People who live in or near the Alps avoid the tedious and messy business of repeatedly applying and removing chains in one of two ways. The first is by fitting special winter tyres with chunky treads and often with metal studs; these are meant to be used at higher speeds on normal roads, but aren't a practical (or economic) proposition for a trip across the Continent. The second is by owning a four-wheel-drive car (normally also fitted with chunky tyres); four-wheel-drive is a huge advantage, making chains unnecessary in all but the most extreme circumstances and giving much more control when going downhill, where chains don't help all that much – particularly on a rear-wheel-drive car. If you have a choice of front- and rear-wheel-drive cars, take the front-wheel-drive.

In the mountains

Once you've arrived there are several ways in which you can diminish the risk that you'll be caught out by the cold or the road conditions:

- when parking the car overnight, try to leave it in a place where it (or at least the engine) will be sheltered from the wind, and where you can safely leave the handbrake off (so that it doesn't get frozen on); leave the car with first or reverse gear engaged
- pull the wipers away from the windscreen so that they don't get frozen in position
- don't disregard road closures: a closed road which looks passable may be closed because of avalanche danger
- don't be tempted to drive in après-ski boots unless your car has agricultural pedals
- drive at about half the speed you reckon would be safe – especially downhill
- when starting off or going uphill on snow, use the highest possible gear to minimise the risk of the driving wheels spinning.

Alpine passes

Many Alpine passes are blocked by snow during the winter months, but some are kept open by snow-ploughs; we list below major passes which are normally kept open.

Aprica (Italy), Bayard (France), Bracco (Italy), Brenner (Austria–Italy), Brunig (Switzerland), Bussang (France), Croix-Haute (France), Faucille (France), Fern (Austria), Forclaz (Switzerland), Fugazze (Italy), Gerlos (Austria), Ibaneta Roncesvalles (France–Spain), Jaun (Switzerland), Julier (Switzerland), Katschberg (Austria), Loibl (Austria–Yugoslavia), Maloja (Switzerland), Mauria (Italy), Mendola (Italy), Monte Croce di Comelico (Italy), Montgenèvre (France–Italy), Mosses (Switzerland), Ofen (Switzerland), Peyresourde (France), Port d'Aspet (France), Potschen (Austria), Resia (Italy–Austria), Restefond (France), Seeberg (Austria–Yugoslavia), Semmering (Austria), Sestriere (Italy), Somport (France–Spain), Tenda (Italy–France), Thurn (Austria), Tonale (Italy), Toses (Spain), Turracher Hohe (Austria), Wurzen (Austria–Yugoslavia) and Zirer Berg (Austria).

Tunnels

There are several tunnels which help you avoid making a detour or travelling over a mountain pass. Some, but not all charge a toll which varies according to size of car. We give one-way tolls based on average family saloon where they are charged.

Fréjus France–Italy FF95.
Mont Blanc France–Italy – wheel chains are occasionally required for the approaches in winter. FF95.
Grand St Bernard Switzerland–Italy – wheel chains may be needed in winter. SF22.50.
St Gotthard Switzerland – wheel chains for approaches, but not permitted in tunnel. Free.
San Bernardino Switzerland. Free, but requires toll disc.
Arlberg Austria AS140.
Felbertauern Austria AS100 (AS180 in summer).
Glenalm Austria AS120.

In addition there are the following rail tunnels; cars are transported through the tunnel on a train.

Lotschberg Kandersteg–Goppenstein SF15.
Simplon Brig–Iselle SF22.
Lotschberg + Simplon Kandersteg–Iselle SF42.

Motorway tolls

You have to pay tolls on most motorways in France. Italy and Spain, and on sections in Austria and Yugoslavia. These can add up to quite an amount over a long journey so it's worth doing your sums. Calais to Chambéry adds up to FF217; the Brenner Pass motorway south from Innsbruck costs AS120. It may be cheaper (but take longer) to drive on non-toll roads and stay the night on the way. If you are using the toll roads make sure you have some of the local currency – toll booths don't accept travellers cheques; but in France Visa and Access cards are sometimes accepted. In Switzerland, foreign motorists using motorways must display a toll disc (valid 14 months, from 1 Dec to 31 Jan) which costs SF30 at the border (or £13 from the Swiss Tourist Office, AA or RAC in the UK.) The AA Overseas Routes department have information on tolls ✆0256 20123.

Continental ferries

When planning winter crossings to the Continent, bear in mind the possibility of bad weather. If there are heavy seas hovercraft services are more liable to interruption than conventional ferries; while long ferry crossings can seem (or even be) interminable. Winter return fares in the 1988 brochures for two adults in a typical saloon are £90 to £140 on the short and medium length crossings to France and Belgium. We list addresses, phone numbers and routes for companies operating ferry and hovercraft services to the Continent.

Brittany Ferries The Brittany Centre, Wharf Road, Portsmouth PO2 8RU; ✆(0705) 827701. Poole–Cherbourg, Portsmouth–St Malo; Portsmouth–Caen; Plymouth–Roscoff; Plymouth–Santander.
Hoverspeed Maybrook House, Queens Gardens, Dover, Kent CT17 9BR; ✆(0304) 240241. Dover–Boulogne; Dover–Calais.
Norfolk Line Atlas House, Southgates Road, Great Yarmouth, Norfolk NR30 3LN; ✆(0493) 856133. Great Yarmouth–Scheveningen.
North Sea Ferries King George Dock, Hedon Road, Hull HU9 5QA; ✆(0482) 796145. Hull–Rotterdam Hull–Zeebrugge.
Olau Line Olau Terminal, Sheerness Docks, Sheerness, Kent ME12 1SN; ✆(0795) 666666. Sheerness–Vlissingen.
P&O European Ferries Channel House,Channel View Road, Dover, Kent CT17 9TJ;✆(0304) 203388. Dover–Calais; Dover–Oostende; Felixstowe–Zeebrugge; Portsmouth–Cherbourg; Portsmouth–Le Havre.
Sally Line Argyle Centre, York Street, Ramsgate, Kent CT11 9DS; ✆(0843) 595522. Ramsgate–Dunkerque.
Sealink UK Ferries Charter House, Park Street, Ashford, Kent TN24 8EX;✆(0233) 47047. Dover–Calais; Folkestone–Boulogne; Harwich–Hoek; Newhaven–Dieppe; Portsmouth–Cherbourg; Weymouth–Cherbourg.

Motorail services

You can get your car to the Alps by putting it on a car-carrying train, although getting to the starting point of the service may involve quite a bit of driving.

French railways run several services from Paris – destinations include St-Gervais (between Megève and Chamonix), Moûtiers (for Tarentaise resorts – Valmorel, Méribel, Courchevel, La Plagne, Les Arcs, Tignes, Val d'Isère), Grenoble (for Les Deux Alpes, Serre-Chevalier and neighbours), Nice (for Isola and neighbours) and Narbonne (for the Pyrenees). There is also a service to Milan. For further information contact SNCF ✆01-409 3518.

German railways run a service from Cologne to Munich, and services from Hamburg (in northern Germany) to Innsbruck (Austrian Tirol) and Chur (south-east Switzerland). For further information contact DER Travel Service ✆01-408 0111.

Second-class return fares for a family plus car range from about £200 on the shortest routes to over £400 on the longest – plus supplements for couchettes or sleeping berths (practically all services are overnight). Some services run daily or several times a week, others only once a week. It's advisable to book as early as possible – up to six months in advance – to be sure of getting on.

Road maps

We list below the maps recommended by *Holiday Which?*, with scales.

THE ALPS
Kummerly + Frey: Alpine Countries 1:1 million, Alpine Roads 1:500,000

FRANCE
National maps (all 1:1 million)
Recta-Foldex, Michelin, IGN, Geographia International, Hallwag
Regional maps
Michelin 1:200,000, Recta-Foldex Cart'Index 1:250,000, IGN Red Series 1:250,000

ITALY
National maps
Michelin 1:1,000,000, Freytag & Berndt 1:650,000, Shell-Mair Special 1:750,000, TCI Carta Stradale 1:800,000, Kummerly + Frey 1:500,000

AUSTRIA
National maps
Michelin 1:400,000, Freytag & Bendt 1:500,000
Regional maps
Freytag & Berndt: Grosse Strassenkarte 1:300,000, Touring Atlas 1:250,000

SWITZERLAND
National maps
Kummerly + Frey/Swiss Touring Club 1:300,000, 1:250,000

Breakdown insurance

The two main motoring organisations – the AA and RAC – offer various services to members (eg advice on route-planning and road conditions). They and several other organisations also offer insurance against some of the cost and inconvenience of breakdowns and accidents abroad.

Breakdown insurance is an expensive way of buying peace of mind, but you may feel it's worthwhile – particularly in winter, when roads are at their most dangerous and cars at their least reliable. Some of the deals on offer can (or must) include personal insurance for medical expenses and so on.

Most of the following types of cover are included in all the policies we looked at, though the amounts you can claim vary from company to company:

- assistance if you break down either in the UK or abroad including towing to, and storage in, a garage
- emergency labour charges
- the cost of despatching any spare parts, including communication expenses but not the cost of the parts themselves
- additional hotel and travel expenses
- hire of replacement vehicle
- all necessary costs to bring your vehicle home but not including cost of repairs or sea passage
- chauffeur to drive vehicle home if only driver is medically unfit
- legal cover, including bail bond

In addition, both the AA and RAC offer emergency credit vouchers.

Below we give addresses and phone numbers of companies offering breakdown cover, with premiums.

Automobile Association (AA) ✆(0256) 20123; Fanum House, Basing View, Basingstoke, Hampshire RG21 2EA. Their 5 Star service costs £34.75 for 31 days. There's an extra charge of £3 for non-members.

Royal Automobile Club (RAC) ✆01-686 2525; RAC House, Lansdowne Road, Croydon, Surrey CR9 6HN. Their Travellers Bond Vehicle Protection costs £34 for standard cover (31 days), £5 per week extra thereafter. There's an extra charge of £3 for non-members.

Europ Assistance ✆01-680 1234; Europ Assistance House, 252 High Street, Croydon, Surrey CR10 1NF. Their Premier Continental Service costs £27.50 for 1–17 days. Additional medical and personal travel cover costs an extra £14 per person.

National Breakdown Recovery Club ✆(0274) 671299; Cleckheaton Road, Low Moor, Bradford, West Yorks BR OND. They offer members vehicle protection as part of a package – you have to take out their medical insurance as well. Two adults in a car, both going skiing, pay £71 for 10–17 days.

Mondial Assistance ✆01-681 2525; Church House, Old Palace Road, Croydon, Surrey CRO 1AX. Their Motorists Emergency Service costs £27 for 11–17 days, with an additional cost of £13.75 for personal and medical cover.

Autohome Limited ✆(0604) 28730; 202/204 Kettering Road, Northampton, Northants NN1 4HE. Their Autohome Continent policy costs £54.50 for 10–17 days for car and two adults.

The Caravan Club ✆(0342) 26944; East Grinstead House, East Grinstead, West Sussex, RH19 1UA. Their Red Pennant Foreign Touring Service is available only to members and costs £49.50 for 31 days for 2 adults, a car and caravan or trailer.

Almost all these organisations charge more, between £8 and £10, if you are towing a caravan or trailer.

Package holidays

The resorts section of the *Guide* contains lists of companies offering package holidays to each resort. The lists fall under the 'Available holidays' heading, towards the end of the fact-box in major resort entries, and at the very end of minor resort entries. Our lists are based on the latest information available to us in April/May 1988; some operators were able to tell us about their 1988–89 programmes, but in many cases the information relates to the 1987–88 season.

After the name of each operator is a list (in brackets) of the kinds of accommodation the operator offers in that resort. We use the following abbreviations:

Ht: hotels and hotel-like guest-houses
Ch: catered chalets
Cl: 'club' or 'jumbo' chalets
Sc: self-catering apartments
Hm: rooms in private homes
Ap: catered apartments.

The operators are listed here in alphabetical order. Where possible we have resisted the use of the word 'Ski' on the front of major operators' names – Enterprise is under E, Global under G. As well as summarising the package holidays the operators sell – what resorts, accommodation and travel arrangements they offer – we say whether they provide ski guides.

We have listed only those operators whose holidays are bonded, so that the money you pay for the holiday before you go is protected in the event of the financial failure of the company. The letters ABTA after the name and address signify that the operator is a member of the Association of British Travel Agents. In most cases this means that the operator's holidays are available through high-street travel agents, but some ABTA operators sell most or even all of their holidays direct to the public. The letters ATOL signify that the operator has a licence from the Civil Aviation Authority to run air-travel package holidays using charter flights; we have not included companies who package holidays under the 'umbrella' of another company's ATOL – a practice of which neither the CAA nor *Which?* approves and which does not provide reliable protection. (Bear in mind that an ATOL gives no protection for holidays based on coach travel, self-drive or scheduled airline flights – and that an operator may offer unprotected and protected holidays in the same brochure.) The letters PSA signify membership of the Passenger Shipping Association's bonding scheme.

If buying a holiday from one of the many small-scale operators who are not bonded and so not listed here, make your payment by credit card direct to the operator. Then, if the operator goes under you can claim your money back from the credit card company. Note that American Express and Diners Club are charge cards and not credit cards, and do not offer this additional protection.

Many operators sell charter flight seats without the other components of a package holiday, and we note this where appropriate. Such deals formally count as packages, which means that they can be sold at low prices, undercutting government-approved fares on scheduled airlines. Some operators do not sell proper packages at all – their whole business is selling flight seats. Such operators are listed separately under 'Flight-only operators'.

There are many agencies which have self-catering accommodation to let independently rather than as part of a package holiday. We list the major ones in the ski market after the tour operators.

Future editions

We aim to include in the *Guide* all package holiday operators who offer bonded holidays. Any operators missing from this edition should send two copies of their brochure to the Editor at The Old Forge, Norton St Philip, Bath BA3 6LW.

Activity Travel

19 Castle Street, Edinburgh EH2 3AH
✆031-225 9457.
Tx 728290 ATT ACTIVITY.
ATOL, ABTA
Started operating holidays in Scotland but now offer the Alps too. Sell flight seats as well as packages. **Resorts** Six in France, Cairngorm and Glenshee in Scotland, plus Verbier in Switzerland, St Anton in Austria and Soldeu in Andorra. **Accommodation** Hotels, self-catering apartments, catered chalets. **Travel** Air, coach. UK airports: Edinburgh, Gatwick, Glasgow. Coach departures: Scotland. **Ski Guides** Yes.

Air France

Georgian House, 69 Boston Manor Road, Brentford, Middlesex TW8 9JQ
✆01-568 6981. Tx 8953196 AFHOLS.
ATOL, ABTA
Tour operating arm of the French national airline. **Resorts** Eight, all in France. **Accommodation** Hotels, self-catering apartments. **Travel** Air, self-drive. UK airports: Heathrow. **Ski guides** No.

Alpine Activity Club

91 Wembley Park Drive, Wembley Park, Middlesex HA9 8HF
✆01-200 6080/ 903 4444.
Tx 929394 SKIVAL.
ATOL, ABTA
Off-shoot of Ski-Val, operating summer activity holidays including skiing. Prices include instruction. **Resorts** Only one: Tignes (Le Lavachet) in France. **Accommodation** Club chalet, self-catering apartments. **Travel** Air, coach. UK airports: Gatwick. Coach departures: Bristol, Edinburgh, London, Manchester. **Ski guides** No.

Alpine Tours

16A High Street, Ashford, Kent TN24 8JG
✆(0233) 34382.
ATOL, ABTA
Sell individual and schools' packages. **Resorts** Three in Austria's Tirol. **Accommodation** Hotels, self-catering apartments. **Travel** Air, coach. UK airports: Gatwick, Glasgow, Heathrow, Manchester. Coach departures: Dover, London. **Ski guides** No.

Andorra Holidays

PO Box 2, Dalbeattie DG5 4NT, Scotland
✆(038778) 684. Tx 776146 BAREND.
ATOL
Specialists in Andorra. Sell flight seats as well as packages. **Resorts** Two, both in Andorra. **Accommodation** Hotels, chalets, self-catering apartments, catered apartments. **Travel** Air, coach, self-drive including ferry and/or hotel en route. UK airports: London, Manchester. Coach departures: London. **Ski guides** Yes.

Austro Tours

5 St Peters Street, St Albans, Herts AL3 5EG
✆(0727) 38191. Tx 298822 AUSTRO.
ATOL, ABTA
Sell flight seats as well as packages. **Resorts** 24, all in Austria. **Accommodation** Mainly hotels. **Travel** Air. UK airports: Birmingham, Gatwick, Heathrow, Jersey, Manchester. **Ski guides** No.

Balkan Holidays

19 Conduit Street, London W1R 9TD
✆01-491 4499. Tx 262923
ABTA
Specialists in Bulgaria. **Resorts** Pamporovo and Borovets. **Accommodation** Hotels. **Travel** Air. UK airports: Gatwick, Manchester. **Ski guides** No.

Beach Villas

8 Market Passage, Cambridge CB2 3QR
✆(0223) 311113. Tx 817428 BCHVLA.
ATOL, ABTA
Established operators of summer villa holidays who have been offering skiing holidays for several years. Sell flight seats as well as packages. **Resorts** Arinsal in Andorra, Méribel and Morzine in France, Verbier in Switzerland, and Arabba in the Italian Dolomites. **Accommodation** Hotels, staffed chalets, and self-catering apartments. **Travel** Air, self-drive. UK airports: Gatwick, Manchester. **Ski guides** Yes.

Best Skiing

31 Topsfield Parade, London N8 8PT
✆01-444 3366. Tx 25302 GRECIA.
ATOL, ABTA
Part of the Grecian Holiday group. Sell flight seats as well as packages. **Resorts** Four in Austria, three in Switzerland. **Accommodation** Hotels, rooms, self-

catering apartments and catered chalets. **Travel** Air. UK airports: Edinburgh, Gatwick, Glasgow, Manchester. **Ski guides** No.

Bladon Lines

56 Putney High Street, London SW15 1SF
✆01-785 2200. Tx 295221 SKIBLT.
ATOL, ABTA
Sell 'á la carte' tailored holidays and flight seats as well as ready-made packages. **Resorts** 24, mainly in France, Switzerland and Austria, plus Courmayeur and San Vigilio in Italy. **Accommodation** Mainly catered chalets, club-style hotels, budget chalets; also hotels, pensions, self-catering apartments. **Travel** Air. UK airports: Gatwick, Glasgow, Luton, Manchester. **Ski guides** Yes.

Blue Sky

Broadway, Edgbaston, Five Ways, Birmingham B15 1BB
✆021-632 6282. Tx 335641 HORIZON.
ATOL, ABTA
Now part of the Horizon group. **Resorts** Ten in Austria, others in Italy, France, Andorra and Romania. **Accommodation** Hotels, self-catering apartments. **Travel** Air. UK airports: Gatwick, Glasgow, Manchester. **Ski guides** Yes.

Brittany Ferries

The Brittany Centre, Wharf Road, Portsmouth PO2 8RU
✆(0705) 751833.
PSA
Channel ferry operator selling packages based on Portsmouth–Caen crossings. **Resorts** Six, all in France. **Accommodation** Self-catering apartments. **Travel** Self-drive. **Ski guides** No.

Club 18–30

Academic House, 24 Oval Road, London NW1 7DE
✆01-485 4141/267 4311.
Tx 295440 CLUBA.
Bradford: ✆(0274) 760077.
ATOL, ABTA
Part of the International Leisure Group; operate cost-conscious holidays for 18- to 30-year-olds. Sell learn-to-ski weeks as well as ordinary packages. **Resorts** Seven in Austria, two in Italy, plus Montgenèvre in France. **Accommodation** Hotels, pensions, catered chalets. **Travel** Air, coach. UK airports: Belfast, Birmingham, Bristol, Gatwick, Glasgow, Luton, Manchester. Coach departures: Birmingham, Leeds, London, Luton, Manchester, Sheffield, Stoke-on-Trent. **Ski guides** Yes.

Club Méditerranée

106 Brompton Road, London SW3 1JJ
✆01-581 1161. Tx 299221 CLBMED.
ATOL, ABTA
A French-owned company, based in Paris. Holidays are all-inclusive, covering most things from full-board accommodation to lift passes and ski instruction. **Resorts** Six in France and eight in Switzerland, plus Sestriere in Italy, Copper Mountain in USA, and Sapporo in Japan. **Accommodation** Hotels. **Travel** Air. UK airports: Gatwick, Heathrow. **Ski guides** No (but instruction included in cost of holiday).

Crystal

The Courtyard, Arlington Road, Surbiton, Surrey KT6 6BW
✆01-399 5144. Tx 265284 CRYHOL.
ATOL, ABTA
Major independent operator. **Resorts** Many in Austria, plus France, Andorra and Switzerland. **Accommodation** Hotels, self-catering apartments. **Travel** Air, coach. UK airports: Birmingham, Bristol, Gatwick, Glasgow, Luton, Manchester. Coach departures: London. **Ski guides** No.

DER Travel Service

18 Conduit Street, London W1R 9TD
✆01-408 0111. Tx 21707 DERLDN.
ATOL, ABTA
Sell flight seats in addition to packages, and 'tailor-made' holidays. **Resorts** Four in Germany. **Accommodation** Hotels, pensions, private houses. **Travel** Air, rail. UK airports: Heathrow. **Ski guides** No.

Edwards Ski Holidays

861 Green Lanes, Winchmore Hill, London N21 2QS
✆01-360 7135. Tx 27606 EDWARD.
ATOL, ABTA
Sell coach and air seats as well as packages. **Resorts** Four in Austria, two in Italy. **Accommodation** Hotels. **Travel** Air, coach. UK airports: Gatwick, Luton, Southend. Coach departures: Birmingham, Coventry, Dover, London. **Ski guides** No.

Enterprise

Groundstar House, London Road, Crawley RH10 2TB
✆(0293) 51951 (for Gatwick, Luton, Heathrow and Ski-Drive departures).
Tx 878791 WING G
Glasgow: ✆041-204 2552 (for Edinburgh/Glasgow departures).
✆061-926 9000 (for Manchester departures).
ATOL, ABTA
Now operated by Redwing Holidays. Sell flight seats as well as packages. **Resorts** Many in Austria and France, plus Italy, Spain, Bulgaria, Yugoslavia, Romania and Andorra. **Accommodation** Hotels, self-catering apartments. **Travel** Air, self-drive (using Sealink), fly-drive. UK airports: Birmingham, Bristol, East Midlands, Edinburgh, Gatwick, Glasgow, Heathrow, Luton, Manchester, Stansted. **Ski guides** Yes.

Freedom

224 King Street, London W6 ORA
✆01-741 4471. Tx 892928 FREDOM.
Manchester: ✆061-236 0019.
ATOL, ABTA
Sell flight seats as well as packages. **Resorts** Encamp, Soldeu in Andorra, Châtel in France. **Accommodation** Hotels, self-catering apartments, catered chalets. **Travel** Air. UK airports: Gatwick, Heathrow, Manchester. **Ski guides** Yes.

French Travel Service

Francis House, Francis Street, London SW1P 1DE
✆01-828 8131/9152.
Tx 919354 FTSLON.
ATOL, ABTA
Resorts Only one: Chamonix in France. **Accommodation** Hotels, self-catering apartments. **Travel** Air, rail, self-drive. UK airports: Gatwick. **Ski guides** No.

GTF Tours

182 Kensington Church Street, London W8 4DP
✆01-229 2474. Tx 263696 GTFL.
ATOL, ABTA
Sell flight seats to Bern, Geneva, Innsbruck, Munich, Salzburg, Zurich as well as packages. **Resorts** Three in Germany, two in Austria.
Accommodation Hotels, boarding houses. **Travel** Air. UK airports: Gatwick. **Ski guides** No.

Global

26 Elmfield Road, Bromley, Kent BR1 1LR
✆01-464 7515. Tx 8953010 GLOBALLANAIRS.
Reservations: ✆01-464 6666.
Belfast: ✆(0232) 248908.
Birmingham: ✆021-454 6677.
Bradford: ✆(0274) 736633.
Cardiff: ✆(0222) 377086.
Glasgow: ✆041-332 1727.
Newcastle: ✆091-281 8131.
ATOL, ABTA
Part of the International Leisure Group. Sell flight seats as well as packages. **Resorts** Many in Austria, Italy and France, plus Switzerland, Bulgaria Spain, Yugoslavia and Andorra.
Accommodation Hotels, pensions, self-catering apartments. **Travel** Air, coach, self-drive. UK airports: Belfast, Birmingham, Bristol, Gatwick, Glasgow, Luton, Manchester. Coach departures: Pick-up points throughout country. **Ski guides** In some resorts.

Horizon

Broadway, Edgbaston, Five Ways, Birmingham B15 1BB
✆021-632 6282. Tx 335641 HORIZON.
London: ✆01-680 1184.
Manchester: ✆061-833 0322.
Bristol: ✆(0272) 277213.
Nottingham: ✆(0602) 476601.
ATOL, ABTA
Sell flight seats and various special holidays as well as ordinary packages. **Resorts** 17 in Austria, 12 in France, plus Italy, Switzerland and Andorra.
Accommodation Hotels, self-catering apartments. **Travel** Air. UK airports: Birmingham, Bristol, East Midlands, Gatwick, Luton, Manchester. **Ski guides** In selected resorts.

Hourmont Total Ski

Brunel House, Newfoundland Road, Bristol BS2 9LU
✆(0272) 426961. Tx 44817 HOURMT.
ATOL, ABTA
Operate two programmes – one for school parties, the other for adult groups (normally 10 people or more). Instruction, equipment hire and lift passes included in the cost of all holidays. **Resorts** Many in Austria, Italy and France, plus Switzerland and Romania.
Accommodation Hotels, catered apartments. **Travel** Air, coach. UK airports: Gatwick, Glasgow, Luton, Manchester, Newcastle. **Ski guides** No.

Inghams

Gemini House, 10-18 Putney Hill, London SW15 6AX
✆01-785 7777. Tx 25342 INGHAMS.
ATOL, ABTA
Part of Hotelplan – the tour-operating subsidiary of giant Swiss company Migros. Sell flight seats as well as packages. Also special packages for first-time skiers, in separate brochure. **Resorts** Over 50, half in Austria; several in Switzerland and France, three in Italy, two in USA, plus Bulgaria, Romania and Yugoslavia. **Accommodation** Luxury hotels (in a separate brochure), hotels, pensions, self-catering apartments. **Travel** Air, self-drive, rail. UK airports: Birmingham, Bristol, Edinburgh, Gatwick, Glasgow, Heathrow, Luton, Manchester, Newcastle. **Ski guides** No.

Intasun Skiscene

Intasun House, 2 Cromwell Avenue, Bromley, Kent BR2 9AQ
✆01-290 0511. Tx 896089 INTASN.
Reservations: ✆01-851 3321.
Bradford: ✆(0274) 736633.
Reservations ✆(0274) 736403.
ATOL, ABTA
Part of the International Leisure Group. Sell flight seats as well as packages. **Resorts** Over 40, half in Austria, plus America, Andorra, Italy, France, Switzerland, Yugoslavia and Romania. **Accommodation** Hotels, pensions, self-catering apartments, private houses. **Travel** Air, coach, self-drive. UK airports: Belfast, Birmingham, Bristol, Gatwick, Glasgow, Heathrow, Luton, Manchester. **Ski guides** No.

John Morgan

Meon House, College Street, Petersfield, Hampshire GU32 3JN
✆(0730) 68621. Tx 86181 MEON.
London: ✆01-499 1911.
ATOL, ABTA
Now part of the Meon Travel group. **Resorts** Six in France, four in Switzerland, plus Austria and Italy. **Accommodation** Catered chalets, hotels. **Travel** Air. UK airports: Gatwick, Heathrow, Manchester. **Ski guides** Four days a week in some resorts.

Kuoni

Kuoni House, Dorking, Surrey RH5 4AZ
✆(0306) 881002. Tx 859445 KUODK.
ATOL, ABTA
An established Swiss-owned company which has only recently entered the winter sports market. Sell flight seats as well as packages. **Resorts** 17, all in Switzerland. **Accommodation** Hotels, self-catering apartments in Wengen and Lenzerheide. **Travel** Air. UK airports: Birmingham, Gatwick, Guernsey, Heathrow, Jersey, Manchester. **Ski guides** No.

Made to Measure

43 East Street, Chichester, West Sussex PO19 1HX
✆(0243) 533333. Tx 869205 MTMHOL.G
ATOL, ABTA
Originally specialists in tailor-made holidays, now offering ready-made packages too. Programme includes special ski mountaineering and powder courses, guided ski tours and ski clinics. **Resorts** Over 50 in Switzerland, France, Austria. **Accommodation** Hotels, pensions, self-catering apartments. **Travel** Air, coach, rail, self-drive. UK airports: Gatwick, Heathrow, Manchester. Coach departures: London. **Ski guides** No.

Mark Warner

20 Kensington Church Street, London W8 4EP
✆01-938 1851. Tx 24304 SKIMWT.
ATOL, ABTA
Established chalet operator. **Resorts** Two in Austria, two in France, Italy and Switzerland. **Accommodation** Club-style hotels, catered chalets. **Travel** Air. UK airports: Gatwick, Heathrow, Manchester. **Ski guides** Yes.

Neilson

Holiday House, Leeds, LS12 6HR
✆(0532) 420420. Tx 557453.
London: ✆01-446 2134.
Scotland: ✆041-221 6725.
ATOL, ABTA
Specialists in low-cost holidays. Sell flight seats as well as packages. **Resorts** Over 40, mainly in Austria and France, plus Italy, Switzerland, Andorra and Yugoslavia. **Accommodation** Self-catering apartments, hotels, pensions, private houses. **Travel** Air, coach, rail, self-drive. UK airports: Birmingham, Bristol, Edinburgh, Gatwick, Glasgow, Heathrow, Luton, Manchester, Newcastle. Coach departures: Dover, London, Manchester, Midlands, Yorkshire. **Ski guides** In many resorts. Neilson ski schools in Isola, Les Arcs, Livigno, Sauze d'Oulx and Kolsass Weer.

Pegasus Ski Italy

River House, Restmor Way, Hackbridge Road, Wallington, Surrey SM6 7AH
✆01-773 2323. Tx 918635 PEGASUS.
ATOL, ABTA
In addition to their regular holidays, Pegasus have separate programmes for schools and adult groups, and also sell flight seats. **Resorts** 12 in Italy. **Accommodation** Hotels, self-catering apartments. **Travel** Air. UK airports: Gatwick, Luton. **Ski guides** No.

Phoenix

16 Bonny Street, London NW1 9PG
✆01-485 5515
Manchester and Glasgow departures: ✆(0706) 356611.
ATOL, ABTA
Specialists in holidays to eastern Europe. **Resorts** Seven in Yugoslavia, two in Bulgaria and one in Italy. **Accommodation** Mainly hotels, some self-catering apartments. **Travel** Air. UK airports: Gatwick, Glasgow, Heathrow, Manchester. **Ski guides** No.

Quest

43 Belsize Lane, London NW3 5AU
✆01-794 0427
Payments are held in trust by solicitors until holiday completed. Specialists in highly supervised school holidays. Prices include equipment hire, lift pass, instruction, evening activities. **Resorts** Seven, all in France. **Accommodation** Hotels, catered apartments. **Travel** Coach. Coach departures: from schools. **Ski guides** Yes.

Ramblers

Box 43, Welwyn Garden City, Herts AL8 6PQ
✆(0707) 331133. Tx 24642 RTOUR.
ATOL, ABTA
Sell holidays for cross-country skiers and walkers. **Resorts** Kandersteg in Switzerland, Bad Aussee and Kössen in Austria, Megève and the Vercors in France. **Accommodation** Hotels, pensions. **Travel** Air. UK airports: Gatwick, Heathrow. **Ski guides** Yes.

Sally Tours

Argyle Centre, York Street, Ramsgate, Kent CT11 9DS
✆(0843) 595522.
ABTA
Sell packages based on Sally Line Channel ferry services. **Resorts** Five in Austria. **Accommodation** Self-catering apartments. **Travel** Self-drive. **Ski guides** No.

Schoolplan

Europe House, East Park, Crawley, West Sussex RH10 6AS
✆(0293) 517566. Tx 87374 SCHPLA.
ATOL, ABTA
Specialists in schools parties – instruction, equipment hire and lift pass are included in the cost of the holidays. **Resorts** Italy, Austria, France, Switzerland, Andorra, Romania. **Accommodation** Hotels, pensions, self-catering apartments. **Travel** Air, coach. UK airports: Belfast, Gatwick, Glasgow, Luton, Newcastle, Manchester, Teeside. Coach departures: from schools. **Ski guides** No.

Schools Abroad

Grosvenor Hall, Bolnore Road, Haywards Heath, West Sussex
RH16 4BX
✆(0444) 441300. Tx 877156 SCOARD.
ATOL, ABTA
Part of Grosvenor Hall Leisure Group. Specialists in holidays for school groups; prices include equipment hire and instruction. **Resorts** Many in Italy, Switzerland, France, Austria; also Bulgaria. **Accommodation** Hotels, catered apartments. **Travel** Air, coach. UK airports: Belfast, Gatwick, Glasgow, Heathrow, Luton, Manchester, Newcastle, Stansted. Coach departures: from schools. **Ski guides** No.

SkiBound

Meeting House Lane, 26 North Street, Brighton, East Sussex BN1 1EW
✆(0273) 728462. Tx 877658.
ATOL, ABTA
Sell individual packages and group and school holidays. **Resorts** Six in France, two in Austria and one in Italy. **Accommodation** Hotels, club chalets, catered chalets, self-catering apartments. **Travel** Air, self-drive. UK airports: Belfast, Gatwick, Manchester. **Ski guides** No – but own ski schools in all French resorts.

Ski Club of Great Britain

118 Eaton Square, London SW1W 9AF
✆01-245 1033. Tx 291608 SKIDOM.
The Ski Club of Great Britain does not sell package holidays, but in conjunction with ATOL-holding tour operators it organises 'Skiing Parties' for members. All parties have at least one leader per 8–12 members, and they often hold BASI

(British Association of Ski Instructors) qualifications. The parties fall into specific categories; for instance you can learn to ski off-piste; take British ski tests; ski with groups of your own age; go with other families; or send your children on one of the special teenage parties. They also offer cross-country and touring groups. **Resorts** Mostly in France and Switzerland, a few in Italy and Austria. **Accommodation** Mostly hotels, some catered chalets. **Travel** Mostly by air. UK airports: usually Gatwick (occasionally Heathrow) though on certain dates Manchester and Glasgow are available at a small extra cost.

Ski Esprit

Austen House, Fleet, Hants GU13 9PE
✆(0252) 616789/625175.
ATOL, ABTA
Specialists in holidays for families, with British nannies and babysitters in all resorts. **Resorts** Four in northern France, three in western Switzerland. **Accommodation** Catered chalets. **Travel** Air, self-drive. UK airports: Gatwick. **Ski guides** No.

Ski Falcon

33 Notting Hill Gate, London W11 3JQ
✆01-229 9484. Tx 883256 WESELL.
Birmingham: ✆021-233 3131.
Edinburgh: ✆031-447 9015.
Glasgow: ✆041-248 7911.
Manchester: ✆061-831 7000.
ATOL, ABTA
Sell packages for cost-conscious skiers, with tuition, equipment and lift pass included. **Resorts** Five in France, three in Italy and Austria, three in Bulgaria and one in Andorra. **Accommodation** Self-catering, hotels. **Travel** Air, coach, train. UK airports: Gatwick, Glasgow, Manchester. Coach departures: London, Manchester. **Ski guides** No.

SkiGower

2 High Street, Studley, Warwickshire B80 7HJ
✆(052785) 4822. Tx 8950511 ONEONE ref 14312001.
ABTA
Specialists in holidays for school groups; prices include instruction and equipment hire. **Resorts** Ten in Switzerland. **Accommodation** Hotels, youth centres. **Travel** Coach, rail from schools. **Ski guides** No.

Ski Lovers

11 Liston Court, High Street, Marlow, Bucks SL7 1ER
✆(06284) 76991. Tx 848717 SKILOV.
ATOL, ABTA
Sell all types of ski holiday – individuals, sharing and groups. **Resorts** Several in Austria, France and Andorra. **Accommodation** Hotels, club-style hotels, pensions, catered chalets, catered and self-catering apartments. **Travel** Air, coach, rail and self-drive. UK airports: Birmingham, Gatwick, Glasgow, Manchester. Coach departures: Dover, London, Manchester. **Ski guides** In some resorts.

Ski MacG

37 Uxbridge Street, London W8 7TQ
✆01-221 0166. Tx 24632.
ATOL
An established name in the chalet business, recently revived under new ownership; sell direct to the public. **Resorts** Three in France, two in Switzerland. **Accommodation** Catered chalets, hotels, self-catering apartments. **Travel** Air, self-drive, coach. UK airports: Edinburgh, Gatwick, Heathrow, Manchester. **Ski guides** Yes.

Ski Miquel

244 Deansgate, Manchester M3 4BQ
✆061-832 2737/3773.
Tx 667664 SHARET.
ATOL
Sell packages and flight seats direct to the public. **Resorts** Mainly in the Pyrenees: Barèges in France, Baqueira in Spain; also Hinterstoder in Austria and Lauterbrunnen in Switzerland. **Accommodation** Hotels, catered chalets, self-catering apartments. **Travel** Air. UK airports: Gatwick, Manchester. **Ski guides** Yes.

Ski NAT

Holiday House, Leeds LS12 6HR
✆(0532) 422333. Tx 557435 NATUK.
Glasgow: ✆041-221 6725.
ATOL, ABTA
Specialise in low-cost holidays by express coach, but also offer other formulae. Programme includes all-inclusive learn-to-ski weeks. **Resorts** Over 20, half in Austria, plus Italy, Spain, Andorra, France, Switzerland and Yugoslavia. **Accommodation** Hotels, pensions, self-catering apartments, private houses. **Travel** Air, coach, self-drive. UK airports: Birmingham, Bristol,

Edinburgh, Gatwick, Glasgow, Heathrow, Luton, Manchester, Newcastle. Coach departures: 20 different points. **Ski guides** No.

Ski-Plan

30-32 Cross Street, Islington, London N1 2BG
∅01-359 3500. Tx 935628.
ATOL, ABTA
Sell various special holidays as well as ordinary packages. **Resorts** Six in Austria, one in France. **Accommodation** Hotels, rooms in private houses. **Travel** Air, coach. UK airports: Birmingham, Gatwick, Manchester. Coach departures: from Dover, London. **Ski guides** No.

Skiscope

Grosvenor Hall, Bolnore Road, Haywards Heath, West Sussex RH16 4BX
∅(0444) 441300. Tx 877156 SCOARD.
ATOL, ABTA
Part of the Grosvenor Hall Leisure Group, selling holidays both for individuals and groups, direct to the public. Sell flight seats as well as packages. **Resorts** In Italy, Austria, France, Bulgaria and Switzerland. **Accommodation** Mostly hotels, some self-catering apartments (breakfast provided). They stress the fact that their hotels are sometimes modest. **Travel** Air. UK airports: Belfast, Gatwick, Glasgow, Luton, Manchester, Newcastle, Stansted. **Ski guides** No.

SkiSet

Grosvenor Hall, Bolnore Road, Haywards Heath, West Sussex RH16 4BX
∅(0444) 441300. Tx 877156 SCOARD.
ATOL, ABTA
Offers low-cost ski-course packages for schools. **Resorts** Eight in France, six in Austria, four in Italy, two in Switzerland. **Accommodation** Hotels and club chalets. **Travel** Coach. Departures from schools anywhere in Great Britain. **Ski guides** No.

Ski Sutherland

Church Gate, Church Street West, Woking, Surrey GU21 1DJ
∅(04862) 70383/ 70696.
Tx 859397 EIGER.
ABTA
Sell 'personalised packages' plus inclusive school packages. **Resorts** 15 in Switzerland, 14 in Austria, plus Norway and France. **Accommodation** Hotels. **Travel** Air, coach, rail. UK airports: Birmingham, Gatwick, Heathrow, Manchester, Newcastle. Coach departures: from school gates. Trains: Dover, London (Victoria). **Ski guides** No.

Ski Team

41 High Street, Langford, Bedfordshire SG18 9RU
∅(0462) 700038
ABTA
Sell cheap-and-cheerful packages to popular resorts; they will also tailor-make packages. **Resorts** Three, all in Austria. **Accommodation** Hotels and rooms in private homes. **Travel** Air, coach, self-drive. Coach departures: London. **Ski guides** No.

Ski Total

10 Hill Street, Richmond, Surrey TW9 1TN
∅01-948 6922. Tx 94013570 TOTA.
ATOL
Small company in eighth year of operation. **Resorts** Three in France, one in Austria. **Accommodation** Hotels, catered chalets, self-catering apartments. **Travel** Air, coach, self-drive. UK airports: Edinburgh, Gatwick, Manchester. Coach departures: London. **Ski guides** Yes.

Ski Travelaway

Grosvenor Hall, Bolnore Road, Haywards Heath, West Sussex
RH16 4BX
∅(0444) 441300. Tx 877156 SCOARD.
ATOL, ABTA
Specialists in holidays for school groups – part of the Grosvenor Hall group. Sell flight seats as well as packages. **Resorts** Five in Italy, three in Austria, plus Switzerland, France and Bulgaria. **Accommodation** Hotels. **Travel** Air, coach. UK airports: Belfast, Gatwick, Luton. Coach departures as arranged. **Ski guides** No.

Ski-Val

91 Wembley Park Drive, Wembley Park, Middx HA9 8HF
∅01-200 6080/ 903 4444.
Tx 929394 ADLIB.
ATOL, ABTA
Sell holidays mainly direct to the public. **Resorts** Four in France. **Accommodation** Catered chalets and club chalets, hotels and self-catering apartments. **Travel** Air, coach. UK airports: Edinburgh, Gatwick, Manchester. Coach departures: London. **Ski guides** Yes.

Ski West

Eternit House, Felsham Road, London SW15 1SF
∅01-785 9999. Tx 927900 WESTRA.
ATOL, ABTA
Sell holidays for groups as well as ordinary packages. **Resorts** Many in France, plus Verbier in Switzerland, Courmayeur in Italy and St Anton in Austria. **Accommodation** Self-catering apartments, catered chalets, hotels, pensions. **Travel** Air, coach. UK airports: Gatwick, Glasgow, Manchester. Coach departures: Dover, London. Birmingham, Manchester can be arranged for large groups. **Ski guides** No.

Ski Whizz

Crescent House, Angell Hill, Bury St Edmunds, Suffolk IP33 1UZ
∅(0284) 750505.
London: ∅01-244 7333
ATOL
Chalet specialists selling direct to the public (incorporating Ski Bonne Neige). **Resorts** Four in France, two in Switzerland. **Accommodation** Catered chalets, club chalets, self-catering apartments. **Travel** Air, self-drive. UK airports: Gatwick. **Ski guides** Yes.

Skiworld

Skiworld House, 41 North End Road, West Kensington, London W14 8SZ
∅01-602 4826. Tx 946240 CWEASY.
ABTA, ATOL
Sell flight seats as well as packages. **Resorts** Seven in France, plus Austria, Andorra and Italy. **Accommodation** Hotels, self-catering apartments, catered chalets, club chalets. **Travel** Air, coach, self-drive, air. UK airports: Gatwick, Manchester. Coach departures: Birmingham, Dover, London, Manchester. **Ski guides** No.

Ski Young World

PO Box 99, 29 Queens Road, Brighton BN1 3YN
∅(0273) 202391. Tx 877593 ASLINK.
London: ∅01-651 4090.
ATOL, ABTA
Sell flight seats as well as packages geared towards cost-conscious skiers; also sell flight seats. **Resorts** Encamp, Soldeu in Andorra, Livigno in Italy and La Toussuire in France. **Accommodation** Hotels, self-catering apartments. **Travel** Air, coach. UK airports: Gatwick. Coach departures: London. **Ski guides** No.

Small World

Old Stone House, Judges Terrace, East Grinstead, Sussex RH19 1AQ
∅(0705) 210510. Tx 95224 YCAINT.
ATOL, ABTA
Specialists in catered chalet holidays, selling direct to the public. **Resorts** Five in Italy, four in Switzerland, two in Austria and one in France. **Accommodation** Catered chalets. **Travel** Air. UK airports: Gatwick. **Ski guides** In some resorts.

Snowbird

Grosvenor Hall, Bolnore Road, Haywards Heath, West Sussex RH16 44X
∅(0444) 441300. Tx 877156 SCOARD.
ATOL, ABTA
Part of the Grosvenor Hall Leisure Group, selling holidays for individuals and families directly and through travel agents. **Resorts** Eight in France, two in Austria, plus Italy, Canada and USA. Ski weeks for all grades. **Accommodation** Hotels, self-catering apartments. **Travel** Air. UK airports: Birmingham, Gatwick, Glasgow, Luton, Manchester, Newcastle. **Ski guides** No.

Snowcoach Holidays

Holiday House, 146 London Road, St Albans, Herts AL1 1PQ
∅(0727) 66177/ 33141.
Tx 8814162 CANTAB.
ATOL, ABTA
A subsidiary of Club Cantabrica, selling low-cost holidays. **Resorts** Ten in Austria, four in Italy, and Arinsal in Andorra. **Accommodation** Hotels pensions. **Travel** Air, coach, self-drive. Coach departures: many points around the country. **Ski guides** Yes.

Snowtime

23 Denmark Street, London WC2H 8NA
∅01-836 3237. Tx 267707 SNOWT.
ATOL
Sell packages and flight seats direct to the public. **Resort** Méribel in France. **Accommodation** Catered chalets, self-catering apartments, hotels (two exclusive to Snowtime). **Travel** Air, coach, self-drive. UK airports: Gatwick; limited availability from Glasgow, Manchester. Shuttle bus in resort. **Ski guides** Yes.

Snow World

34 South Street, Lancing, West Sussex BN15 8AG
✆(0903) 765581. Tx 877437.
ABTA, ATOL
Sell packages tailored to groups and families. **Resorts** Six in France, two in Italy, three in Austria, plus Switzerland and Romania. **Accommodation** Hotels, catered chalets, self-catering apartments. **Travel** Air, coach, self-drive. UK airports: Gatwick, Glasgow, Manchester. Coach departures: London. **Ski guides** In some resorts.

Sunmed

Groundstar House, London Road, Crawley, West Sussex RH10 2TB
✆(0293) 560777. Tx 878791 WING.
ATOL, ABTA
Now part of Redwing Holidays. Specialists in French Alps. **Resorts** Eleven, all in France. **Accommodation** Hotels, catered chalets, self-catering apartments. **Travel** Air, coach. UK airports: Gatwick, Manchester. Coach departures: Dover, London, Manchester. **Ski guides** Yes.

Supertravel

22 Hans Place, London SW1X OEP
✆01-584 5060. Tx 263725 SUPTVL.
ATOL, ABTA
Specialists in chalet holidays. Sell flight seats and à la carte holidays as well as packages. **Resorts** Seven in France, four in Switzerland, two in Austria. **Accommodation** Catered chalets, hotels, self-catering apartments. **Travel** Air. UK airports: Edinburgh, Gatwick, Heathrow, Manchester. **Ski guides** In some resorts.

Swiss Travel Service

Bridge House, Ware, Herts SG12 9DE
✆(0920) 3971. Tx 81633 BRIDGE.
ATOL, ABTA
Resorts Switzerland only – a good cross-section. **Accommodation** Hotels. **Travel** Scheduled air. UK airports: Birmingham, Gatwick, Heathrow, Manchester. **Ski guides** No.

Tentrek

152 Maidstone Road, Ruxley Corner, Sidcup, Kent DA14 5HS
✆01-302 6426/ 7828.
Tx 897497 TENTRK.
ATOL, ABTA
Sell holidays geared towards the cost-conscious skier. They also sell flight and coach seats. **Resorts** Five, all in Austria. **Accommodation** Hotels, pensions, private houses. **Travel** Air, coach. UK airports: Gatwick. Coach departures: London; some connecting regional departures. **Ski guides** Yes.

Thomson

Greater London House, Hampstead Road, London NW1 7SD
✆01-387 9321. Tx 261123 THGLH.
Birmingham: ✆021-236 3624.
Bristol: ✆(0272) 297744.
Cardiff: ✆(0222) 21041.
Glasgow: ✆041-221 6707.
Leeds: ✆(0532) 441318.
Leicester: ✆(0533) 559655.
London North: ✆01-439 2211.
London South: ✆01-771 5131.
Manchester: ✆061-833 9611.
Newcastle: ✆(0632) 611716.
ATOL, ABTA
The market leader. Sell flight seats as well as packages. **Resorts** Over 70, in Austria, France, Italy, Spain, Switzerland, Andorra and Yugoslavia. **Accommodation** Hotels, pensions, private houses, self-catering apartments, chalets. **Travel** Air. UK airports: Birmingham, Bristol, East Midlands, Gatwick, Glasgow, Leeds, Luton, Manchester, Newcastle. **Ski guides** In selected resorts; also Ski Safaris and Learn to Ski weeks in many resorts.

Top Deck Travel

133 Earls Court Road, London SW5 9RL
✆01-373 8406/ 5095.
ATOL, ABTA
Specialise in 'action-packed holidays for younger people'. **Resorts** Two in Andorra, two in Austria. **Accommodation** Hotels, club chalets, self-catering apartments. **Travel** Air, coach, self-drive. UK airports: Gatwick, Glasgow, Manchester. **Ski guides** No.

Tourarc

197B Brompton Road, London SW3 1LA
✆01-589 1918. Tx 269710 ARCS.
ATOL, ABTA
UK representatives of Les Arcs, but also sell packages to other French resorts. **Resorts** Eight, all in France. **Accommodation** Self-catering apartments, hotels. **Travel** Air, self-drive, coach. UK airports: Gatwick, Manchester. **Ski guides** No.

Tracer

5 St Andrews Road, London W14
✆01-385 6146. Tx 265871 MONREF ref MAG95313.
ATOL, ABTA
Sell packages and flight seats direct to the public. **Resorts** Five in France. **Accommodation** Self-catering apartments, catered chalets. **Travel** Air, coach. UK airports: Gatwick. Coach departures: London. **Ski guides** Yes.

VFB

(Vacances Franco-Britanniques)
1 St Margarets Terrace, Cheltenham, Glos GL50 4DT
✆(0242) 526338. Tx 43574 VFB.
ATOL
Sell packages direct to the public. **Resorts** Five in France. **Accommodation** Hotels, self-catering apartments. **Travel** Air, self-drive. UK airports: Gatwick, Manchester. **Ski guides** Yes.

Vacations

60 Charles Street, Leicester LE1 1FB
✆(0533) 539100. Tx 347111.
ATOL, ABTA
Recently formed by ex-Neilson directors. **Resorts** 11 in Austria, three in France. **Accommodation** Hotels, catered chalets, self-catering apartments. **Travel** Air, self-drive. UK airports: Birmingham, Gatwick, Glasgow, Manchester, Stansted. **Ski guides** Yes.

Waymark

295 Lillie Road, London SW6 7LL
✆01-385 5015/ 01-385 3502.
ATOL
Specialists in cross-country skiing, both from centres and on tour. **Resorts** in Austria, Germany, Norway, Switzerland, Italy, France, Canada, Scotland, Czechoslovakia. Also tours in Finland, France, Germany, Norway and Switzerland. **Accommodation** Hotels, pensions, huts on tours. **Travel** Air. UK airports: Aberdeen, Gatwick, Heathrow, Manchester, Newcastle. **Ski guides** Yes.

Yugotours

150 Regent Street, London W1R 6BB
✆01-439 7233. Tx 263543.
Birmingham: ✆021-233 3001.
Glasgow: ✆041-226 5535.
Manchester: ✆061-228 6891.
ABTA
Specialists in packages to Yugoslavia. Some prices include beginners' lessons. **Resorts** Eight in Yugoslavia, one in eastern Austria. **Accommodation** Hotels, self-catering apartments. **Travel** Air. UK airports: Gatwick, Glasgow, Heathrow, Manchester. **Ski guides** No.

Letting agencies

The companies listed here are major agencies for the letting of self-catering accommodation independent of package holidays.

Interhome

383 Richmond Road, Twickenham TW1 2EF
✆01-891 1294. Tx 928539 IH.
A Swiss company which is Europe's biggest holiday-home and hotel agency. They have properties in hundreds of ski resorts in Austria, Switzerland, Italy, and France. You can book direct with them or through a travel agency. It's mainly accommodation only but they also offer 'skiing holidays by car'.

Perrymead Properties (Overseas)

55 Perrymead Street, London SW6 3SN
✆01-736 4592/ 5331.
Tx 943763 CROCOM REF PER.
Self-catering chalets and apartments to let in eight resorts in Switzerland and Italy. Travel arrangements can be made.

Flight-only operators

The main list of operators contains many who sell flight seats without accommodation; some operators specialise in flights only, and they are listed below in alphabetical order.

Cresta

Six Acre House, Town Square,
Sale, Cheshire M33 1SN
✆061-962 9226. Tx 667171 CRESTA.
ATOL, ABTA
Sell flight seats to Basel, Geneva, Lyons, Milan, Munich, Nice, Rome, Turin, Venice, Zurich. **Travel** UK airports: Gatwick, Heathrow, Manchester.

Falcon Flights

33 Notting Hill Gate, London W11 3JQ
✆01-221 0088. Tx 22535 WESELL.
Manchester: ✆061-831 7000.
Glasgow: ✆041-204 0242.
ATOL, ABTA
Specialists in flights to Zurich and Geneva. **Travel** UK airports: Gatwick.

Intasun Skyworld

Intasun House, 2 Cromwell Avenue,
Bromley, Kent BR2 9AQ
✆01-290 6677. Tx 896089 INTASUN.
Belfast: ✆(0232) 320340.
Bradford: ✆(0274) 760055.
Bristol: ✆(0272) 214503.
Cardiff: ✆(0222) 45121.
Glasgow: ✆041-332 4466.
Midlands: ✆021-454 6677.
Newcastle: ✆091-281 8131.
ATOL, ABTA
Sell flight seats to Geneva, Barcelona, Ljubljana, Milan, Munich, Salzburg, Turin. **Travel** UK airports: Belfast, Birmingham, Bristol, Gatwick, Glasgow, Luton, Manchester.

Pilgrim-Air

44 Goodge Street, London W1P 2AD
✆01-580 2831 Tx 267752 SPESER.
Bristol: ✆(0272) 606787.
Manchester: ✆061-798 8228.
ATOL
Sell flight seats to Milan, Turin, Venice, Verona, Treviso. **Travel** UK airports: Gatwick, Heathrow, Luton, Manchester.

Slade

Slade House, 15 Vivian Avenue,
London NW4 3UT
✆01-202 0111. Tx 23425 SLADE.
ATOL, ABTA
Sell flight seats to Barcelona, Bern, Geneva, Lyon, Milan, Munich, Nice, Rome, Turin, Venice, Zurich. **Travel** UK airports: Birmingham, East Midlands, Edinburgh, Gatwick, Glasgow, Heathrow, Luton, Manchester.

Swiss Airtours

61 Notting Hill Gate, London W11 3JS
✆01-727 1370. Tx 295356 BRITAV.
ATOL
Sell flight seats to Geneva, Innsbruck, Milan, Munich and Zurich. **Travel** UK airports: Gatwick, Heathrow.

Valuair

Academic House, 24–28 Oval Road,
Camden Town, London N1 7DE
✆01-267 4311, 01-482 2228
Tx 295440 CLUBLG.
ATOL, ABTA
Sell flight seats to Geneva, Milan, Munich, Salzburg, Turin. **Travel** UK airports: Birmingham, Bristol, Gatwick, Luton, Manchester, Belfast, Glasgow.

What to pack

We have listed on this page all the things you *might* want with you on a skiing trip – not all the things we think you should take. So your first step should be to go through the list crossing out the things you don't possess or don't want with you; you're then left with a checklist that you can tick off as you do your packing. There's space at the end for you to add your own clothes list. (In 'A Skiing Primer' we give advice on what sort of clothes first-timers should think of taking.)

Packing checklist

GENERAL
- ☐ hip-flask (and funnel)
- ☐ passport
- ☐ travel tickets
- ☐ accommodation papers
- ☐ foreign cash (for lift pass)
- ☐ British cash (to get home)
- ☐ cheques
- ☐ credit cards
- ☐ first aid kit
- ☐ sewing kit
- ☐ Swiss Army penknife
- ☐ lip salve
- ☐ sun-screen
- ☐ après-sun cream
- ☐ camera (and film)
- ☐ detergent (for clothes)
- ☐ sunglasses
- ☐ contact lenses (and kit)
- ☐ alarm clock
- ☐ small torch
- ☐ GSG resort checklist

FOR SKIING
- ☐ skis
- ☐ boots
- ☐ socks
- ☐ poles
- ☐ ski repair kit
- ☐ tools for bindings
- ☐ gloves
- ☐ inner gloves
- ☐ hat
- ☐ scarf
- ☐ goggles
- ☐ ski trousers
- ☐ ski jacket
- ☐ shirts
- ☐ pullovers
- ☐ warm underclothing
- ☐ bumbag/rucksac
- ☐ photo (for lift pass)
- ☐ personal stereo/tapes
- ☐ compass
- ☐ avalanche bleeper

FOR NOT SKIING
- ☐ swimsuit
- ☐ moonboots
- ☐ wellingtons
- ☐ slippers/house-shoes
- ☐ corkscrew
- ☐ books
- ☐ games
- ☐ jewellery
- ☐ make-up
- ☐ hairdrier
- ☐ iron
- ☐ clothes (write your own list)

Skiing vocabulary

We translate words and expressions of particular value on a skiing trip. Many are also included in our Glossary and Index.

English	French	German	Italian
ambulance	ambulance	Krankenwagen	ambulanza
ankle	cheville	Knöchel	caviglia
antifreeze	antigel	Frostschutz	antigelo
area	région	Gegend	zona
avalanche danger	danger d'avalanches	Lawinengefahr	pericolo di valanghe
back (body)	dos	Rücken	schiena
bandage	bandage	Verband	benda/fasciatura
bindings	fixations	Bindung	gli attacchi
– toe-piece	– butée	– Zehenteil	– pezzo della punta
– heel-piece	– talonnière	– Fersenteil	– pezzo posteriore
blanket	couverture	Decke	coperta
blister	ampoule	Blase	vescica
blizzard	tempête de neige	Schneesturm	tormenta
blocked (road)	barré	blockiert	bloccato
blood wagon	traineau	Rettungsschlitten	slitta
bone	os	Knochen	osso
bruise	contusion	blauer Fleck	ammaccatura
bumbag	banane	Gürteltasche	borsa-marsupio
burn	brûlure	Brand(wunde)	scottatura
cable-car	téléphérique	Seilbahn	funivia
caution	attention	Achtung	attenzione
chains (snow)	chaines	Schneeketten	catene
chair-lift	télésiège	Sessellift	seggiovia
clinic	clinique	Klinik	clinica
clip (on boot)	boucle	Schnalle	clip
closed	fermé	geschlossen/ gesperrt	chiuso
col	col	Sattel	valico
cold	froid	kalt	freddo
collision	collision	Zusammenstoss	scontro
compass	boussole	Kompass	bussola
cornice	corniche	Wächte	cornice
crampons	crampons	Steigeisen	ramponi da ghiaccio
crevasse	crevasse	Gletscherspalte	crepaccio
cross-country	ski de fond	Langlauf	sci di fondo
crutches	béquilles	Krücken	grucce
cut (on skin)	plaie	Schnittwunde	taglio
danger	danger	Gefahr	pericolo
dangerous	dangereux	gefährlich	pericoloso
descent	descente	Abfahrt	discesa
downhill ski	ski aval	Talski	ski a valle
drag-lift	téléski	Schlepplift	skilift/traino
edges (of skis)	carres	Kanten	gli spigoli
exit	sortie	Ausgang	uscita
first aid	premiers secours	erste Hilfe	pronto soccorso

English	French	German	Italian
fog	brouillard	Nebel	nebbia
forbidden	interdit/ défendu	verboten	vietato
fracture	fracture	Bruch	frattura
freestyle	ski acrobatique	Freestyle	stile libero
gaiters	guetres	Gamaschen	gambali
glacier	glacier	Gletscher	ghiacciaio
gloves	gants	Handschuhe	guanti
goggles	lunettes protectrices	Skibrille	gli occhiali
gondola	télécabine	Gondelbahn	telecabina
guide	guide	Führer	guida
gully	couloir	Schlucht	canalone
helicopter	hélicoptère	Hubschrauber	elicottero
helmet	casque	Schutzhelm	casco
herring-bone	montée en ciseaux	Grätenschritt	salita a spina di pesce
hill	colline	Berg	collina
hire, for	à louer	zu vermieten	da noleggio
hospital	hôpital	Krankenhaus	ospedale
hut (mountain)	cabane	Hütte	rifugio
ice	glace	Eis	ghiaccio
icy road	chaussée verglacée	Glatteis	strada ghiacciata
information	renseignements	Auskunft	informazioni
instructor	moniteur	Skilehrer	maestro/istruttore
jacket	veste	Jacke	giacca
knee	genou	Knie	ginocchio
left (hand)	gauche	links	sinistra
leg	jambe	Bein	gamba
lessons, ski	leçons de ski	Skistunden	lezioni da sci
lift pass	forfait/ abonnement	Liftausweis	abbonamento
lift coupons	coupons	Punktekarte	abbonamento a punti
ligament	ligament	Band	ligamento
map	carte	Karte	carta
mittens	moufles	Fausthandschuhe	manopole
mogul	bosse	Buckel	gobba
mountain	montagne	Berg	montagna
mountain restaurant	restaurant d'altitude	Berggaststätte	ristorante del rifugio
muscle	muscle	Muskel	muscolo
neck	cou	Hals	collo
no entry	accès interdit	kein Eintritt	vietato accesso
nursery	garderie d'enfants	Kindergarten	asilo
nursery slope	piste pour débutants	Ubungshang	pista 'baby'
off-piste	hors piste	abseits der Piste	fuori di pista
open	ouvert	offen/geöffnet	aperto
out of order	derange	ausser Betrieb	guasto
overtrousers	surpantalon	Überhose	sopracalzoni
pass	col	Pass	passo
pelvis	bassin	Becken	bacino
piste	piste	Piste	pista
plaster	plâtre	Gips	gesso
pool, indoor	piscine couverte	Hallenbad	piscina coperta
queue	queue	Schlange	coda
rent (verb)	louer	mieten	affittare
repair	réparer	reparieren	riparare
rescue service	service de secours	Rettungsdienst	servizio soccorso
rib	côte	Rippe	costola
ridge	arête	Kamm/Grat	spigolo
right (hand)	droite	rechts	destra

English	French	German	Italian
rucksack	sac à dos	Rucksack	zaino
safety strap	lanière	Fangriemen	cinghia di sicurezza
salopettes	salopette	Lifthose	tuta
screwdriver	tournevis	Schraubenzieher	cacciavite
skating rink	patinoire	Eislaufplatz	pista di patinaggio
ski (noun)	ski	Ski	sci
ski (verb)	faire du ski/skier	skilaufen	sciare
ski boots	chaussures de ski	Skisschuhe	scarponi da sci
ski brake	stoppeur	skistopper	freno
ski-flying	vol à ski	Skifliegen	volo da sci
ski instructor	moniteur	Skilehrer	maestro di sci
ski-jumping	saut à ski	Skispringen	salto da sci
ski lift	téléski	Ski lift	ski lift
ski pants	pantalon de ski	Skihose	pantaloni da sci
ski patrol	pisteurs	Pistenwart	pattuglia sciistica
ski pole	bâton de ski	Skistock	rachetta da sci
ski resort	station de ski	Wintersportort	localita sciistic
ski run	piste	Abfahrt/Piste	pista
ski school	école de ski	Skischule	scuola sci
ski-touring	ski de randonnée	Skitour	sci alpinismo
skier	skieur	Skilaufer/ Skifahrer	sciatore
skins (touring)	peaux de phoque	Felle	pelli
slide (verb)	glisser	rutschen	scivolare
sling	écharpe	Schlinge	bendaggio ad armacollo
slope	pente	Hang	pendio
slush	neige fondue	Schneematsch	neve sciolta
snow	neige	Schnee	neve
snow-blindness	cécité des neiges	Schneeblindheit	accecamento da neve
snow-drift	congère	Schneeverwehung	cumulo di neve
snowfall	chute de neige	Schneefall	nevicata
snowplough	chasse-neige	Schneepflug	spazzaneve
snow-slabs	plaques de neige	Schneebrett	lastre di neve
splint	attelle	Schiene	stecca
sprain	entorse	Verstauchung	storta/strappo
stop (noun)	arrêt	Haltestelle	fermata
stop (verb)	arreter	anhalten	fermare
strained	froissé	gezerrt	teso
stretcher	brancard	Tragbahre	barella
summer skiing	ski d'été	Sommerskifahren	sci estivo
sun	soleil	Sonne	sole
suncream	crême solaire	Sonnencreme	crema da sole
ticket	billet	Fahrkarte	biglietto
toboggan	luge	Rodelschlitten	toboga/ slittino
tourist office	office de tourisme/ syndicat d'initiative	Verkehrsbüro	ufficio turismo/ turistico
traverse (verb)	traverser	traversieren	traversare
turn (verb)	tourner	wenden	girare
turn (noun)	virage	Drehung	girata/curva
twisted	foulé/tordu	Verrenkt	slogato
uphill	en amont	bergauf	a monte
valley	vallée	Tal	valle
visibility	visibilité	Sicht	visibilita
waistcoat	gilet	Weste	panciotto
wax	cire/fart	Skiwachs	sciolina
wedel	godille	wedeln	serpentina
weight	poids	Gewicht	peso
wind	vent	Wind	vento
X-ray	radio	Röntgenbild	radiografia
zip	fermeture éclair	Reissverschluss	chiusura lampo

Reporting to the Guide

The first editions of the *Guide* have been greatly strengthened by the hundreds of reports we have had from people about their own skiing holiday experiences. We hope you will help future editions, too, by sending in further reports on the resorts you visit; whether or not you agree with what we've said in this edition, this is your opportunity to influence what we say in future. New arrangements are being made from now on to encourage reporters – see the introductory pages of the *Guide*.

Rather than provide cramped tear-out report forms, we've prepared the checklist below. If you use the items in the list as headings for your reports, the job of analysing the reports will be greatly simplified. You'll also be sure to cover subjects on which we need help, and not subjects which are more easily covered by other means. Under *Prices*, please aim to be general in your judgements ('wine outrageously expensive by French standards') but specific in your evidence ('ordinary Cotes du Rhone FF32 a bottle in most places, FF45 at Le Dahu'). Be sure to distinguish mountain restaurants from village restaurants and bars.

Send reports to Dept HM, Consumers' Association, FREEPOST, 2 Marylebone Road, London NW1 4DX. No stamp is needed. Please write as clearly as you can, or type your reports if at all possible. Include your name, address and phone number, and give us some idea of your skiing skills and interests.

BASICS
- ☐ Resort name
- ☐ Date of visit

SKIING
- ☐ Snow and weather
- ☐ Weather information
- ☐ Piste maintenance
- ☐ Piste grading (for difficulty)
- ☐ Piste marking/signposting
- ☐ Ski patrols
- ☐ State of nursery slopes
- ☐ Lift closures
- ☐ Lift queues
- ☐ Ski schools
- ☐ Ski kindergartens
- ☐ Ski hire shops
- ☐ Mountain restaurants
- ☐ New lifts or runs
- ☐ Planned lifts or runs

RESORT
- ☐ Road access
- ☐ Non-skiing activities
- ☐ Restaurants and bars
- ☐ Après-ski
- ☐ Non-ski kindergartens
- ☐ Shopping
- ☐ Medical facilities
- ☐ Accommodation
- ☐ Clientele / atmosphere
- ☐ New facilities

PRICES
- ☐ Restaurants
- ☐ Bars
- ☐ Nightclubs / discos
- ☐ Ski / boot hire
- ☐ Ski / boot purchase
- ☐ Food shopping

Glossary / Index

This combined glossary and index covers general skiing terminology, and a few people who figure prominently in the general chapters of the *Guide*.

Resort reports have their own index following this one, and are not included here.

Italic type is used throughout for cross-references to other entries.

A

Aerials *Freestyle* discipline involving acrobatic jumps
Air travel 481, 576
Alpine skiing Skiing downhill (as opposed to *cross-country*) 484
Altitude Height above sea level: key factor in determining quality of *snow* 453
Angulation Zigzag posture necessary for *carved turns* and in a *traverse* on a steep *slope*
Anticipation Positioning of upper body to assist ensuing *turn*
Anti-friction pad Slippery pad behind toe-piece of *binding* to ensure efficient release of *boot*
Anti-gliss Type of fabric used in ski clothing, designed not to be too slippery in case of fall 531
Après-ski Late-afternoon and evening ski resort entertainment 454
Artificial slope *Dry slope* 474
Avalanche Slide of *snow* down a mountainside, often extremely destructive 546
Avalement *Compression turn*

B

Ballet *Freestyle* discipline involving dance-like movements
Banana *Bumbag* 470
BASI British Association of Ski Instructors
Basic swing Long-radius *parallel turn* taught by *BASI*
Basket Disc near bottom of *pole* to limit penetration into *snow* 529
Biathlon Competition combining *cross-country* racing and target shooting
Binding Means of attaching *boot* to *ski*, designed to release in fall 464, 526, 557, 564
Bird's nesting *Off-piste* skiing among trees (deliberately)
Black run Steep, difficult marked *run*, usually left unprepared 457
Bleep Signal-emitting device carried by *off-piste* skiers to assist rescue after an *avalanche*
Blood wagon Stretcher-sledge used by *ski patrol* for carrying injured skiers down mountain 476
Blue run Easy marked *run*, in some resorts the easiest there is 457
Bob sleigh Armoured toboggan for teams of two or four riders
Boot Instrument of torture not made for walking 463, 511, 557, 564
Brake Spring-loaded prongs attached to *binding* which prevent runaway *ski* after fall on piste 464, 526
Breakable crust Hazardous *off-piste* snow condition 545
Bubble *Gondola* 459
Bucket Cage-like *lift* with no seat and no advantages
Bumbag Small pack worn as belt around waist 470
Button lift One-person *drag-lift* 460

C

Cable binding Simple kind of *binding*, obsolete and dangerous
Cable-car Lift with large cabin without seats, suspended from cable 459
Camber Arched shape of *ski* when no weight on it 522
Canting Altering angular relationship between *boots* and *skis* to compensate for knock-knees or bow-legs 518
Car, taking a 482, 577
Carved turn *Turn* in which *ski* cuts a clean, curved track in *snow*, with minimal skidding
Chair-lift *Lift* with series of chairs suspended from cable, each carrying one to four skiers 460, 490
Chalet Uniquely British style of skiing accommodation 33, 479
Chalet girl One who cooks for and cleans up after holiday-makers staying in a *chalet* 479
Chicane Narrow passage in *downhill* race-course

Chill factor Apparent drop in temperature resulting from cooling effect of wind 543
Christie Original name for *parallel turn*
Circus Series of linking *lifts* and *runs*, permitting small tours
Clip boot Modern ski *boot* 463, 511
Clothes 466, 530
Club chalet Giant *chalet*
Coach travel 481, 575
Compact ski Short, easily manoeuvrable *ski*, usually about head height 463, 520
Compression Passage of downhill race course where ground flattens 496
Compression turn Advanced *turn* for use when skiing at speed through *moguls*
Corn snow *Spring snow* 458
Cornice Potentially dangerous wind-blown *snow* overhanging a ridge
Couloir Steep, narrow descent
Coupons Tickets exchanged for individual rides on *lifts* 462
Crampons Grid of metal spikes attached to *boot* (or between *boot* and *ski*) for icy climbing when *ski mountaineering* 564
Crevasse Crack in fabric of *glacier*, often veiled by *snow* cover
Cross-country Skiing over snowy countryside without recourse to *lifts*, and using different equipment from *Alpine skiing* 455, 555
Crud Heavy, broken, difficult *snow*
Crust Brittle surface of *snow*, found *off-piste* – hazardous if 'breakable'
Curling Sport akin to bowls on ice rink

D

DIN German standards organisation, very influential in skiing equipment design
Downhill *Alpine skiing*; and racing discipline involving few *turns* 494
Drag-lift Any *lift* which pulls skier uphill on *skis* 460, 487
Dry slope Hill covered with bristly plastic carpet for skiing with normal *Alpine skiing* equipment 474

E

Edge Metal strip along edges of *ski sole* 463, 524
Egg Aerodynamic posture adopted by speed skiers and *downhill* racers; or *gondola*
Exercises Highly desirable but often neglected preparation 534

F

Fall-line The steepest, most direct line down a *slope*
Fasching Lenten carnival; crowds and revelry (on and off the slopes), especially in Austria
FIS Fédération Internationale du Ski – the International Ski Federation, organisers of international racing
FIS Rules Skiers' Highway Code 547
Flo-fit Kind of *inner boot* whose padding disperses itself naturally round anatomy of foot
Flying kilometre *Speed skiing*
Foam injection Technique of customising *inner boot* for exact fit 517
Föhn Warm wind which leads to rapid deterioration in *snow* conditions
Freestyle skiing Competitive variant of *Alpine skiing* involving acrobatic jumps, *ballet* and *mogul* skiing
Frostbite Loss of sensation in fingers etc, through cold 543
Full-length ski *Long ski* 520
Funicular Mountain railway with two cars linked by cable – one goes up as the other goes down 459

G

Gaiter Waterproof tube, elasticated at each end, to keep *snow* out of boot
Gate Pair of poles through which *slalom* racer must pass, either planted across the hill 'open' or down it 'closed' **Giant slalom** Alpine racing discipline with well-spaced *gates* 494
Gilet Padded waistcoat 466
Glacier Slowly moving mass of ice formed by accumulation of *snow* on high ground, where skiing takes place in spring and summer
GLM Graduated Length Method of teaching beginners to ski; American version of *ski évolutif* 474
Gloves 468
Glühwein Spicy hot wine; minor national variations – vino caldo, vin chaud
Goggles Essential aid to vision 469
Gondola Lift with series of small cabins, traditionally with seats but increasingly without 459
Grading Categorisation of *runs* for difficulty 457
Grass skiing Skiing with special caterpillar-tread *skis* on grassy *slopes*
Green run The easiest grade of ski *run*; not used by many resorts 457
Gun barrel Narrow descent, rising at the edges

H

Harscheisen Blades fitted beneath boots
designed to provide grip on icy *slopes* when *ski-touring* 565
Heli-skiing Skiing with the aid of helicopter uphill transport
Herringbone Method of climbing on *skis*, like *snowplough* in reverse
High season Opposite of *low season* 452
Hockey stop *Uphill christie*
Hot-dogging *Moguls*
Hotel holidays 32, 478
Hypothermia Dangerous lowering of body temperature 543

I

Ice bar Mountain bar serving naturally chilled drinks
Inner boot Usually detachable, cushioned lining of *boot* to ensure insulation and snug fit 463, 518
Inner glove Silk or similar glove worn inside glove for extra warmth 468
Inner skiing Unconventional teaching method which aims to exploit natural learning ability
Insurance Don't go without it 476, 570
Intermediate Skier who is off the *nursery slopes* but neither happy nor expert on the most difficult *runs*

J

Jet turn *Parallel turn* initiated by sharp braking action
Jumbo chalet Giant *chalet*
Jump turn *Parallel turn* in steep or difficult conditions

K

Kangaroo turn Trick *turn* involving exaggerated sitting position
Kick turn *Turn* executed at a standstill; invaluable in moderately awkward spots; impossible in really awkward ones

L

Langlauf *Cross-country* skiing 555
Learning 472
Lift Normal means of access to top of a *run* 459
Lift pass 'Rover' ticket giving unlimited rides on *lifts* for period of validity 462
Loipe *Cross-country* ski *run*
Long ski *Ski* of full, orthodox length – roughly 10cm to 20cm above head height, depending on weight 520
Low season Periods of winter *season* in which package holidays are cheaper than in *high season*, and other prices may or may not be 452
Luge *Skeleton toboggan*
Lunn, Henry Key figure in development of skiing holidays 477, 486

M

Mid-length ski *Ski* meant to be ideal compromise for *intermediate* skiers between *long* and *compact* skis – usually just above head height 464, 520
Mogul Large bump in *run* caused by skiers being sheeplike 458
Mogul-field Section of *run* consisting entirely of moguls
Moguls *Freestyle* discipline involving acrobatic skiing through *mogul field*
Monoski Single broad *ski* with room for both feet side by side
Moonboots Fat, warm, snow-proof après-ski boot (major brand)
Motorway Broad, easy *piste*

N

Nordic skiing *Cross-country* skiing and *ski jumping* 555
Nursery slope Gentle *slope* used by beginners 456

O

Off-piste Area and technique of skiing away from marked, prepared and patrolled *runs* 456

P

Package holidays 477, 581
Parallel slalom *Alpine racing* discipline
Parallel turn *Turn* executed with *skis* parallel throughout
Piste Ski *run* marked, patrolled, usually prepared, and virtually always graded according to difficulty 456
Piste basher Tracked bulldozer used to compact and smooth *snow* on *runs* 458; derogatory term for someone who displays apparent competence on the *piste*, but never ventures off it
Piste map Printed plan of *lifts* and *runs* in a resort
Pisteur Member of resort *ski patrol*
Plastic slope *Dry slope* 474
Points card Similar to *coupons* 462
Pole Essential aid to balance 464, 529

Poma *Button lift* (brand name) 460
Porridge Sticky, lumpy *snow*
Powder Light, newly-fallen *snow* 458
Public transport 575

Q

Queues Necessary prelude to riding many *lifts* in *high season* 31, 459

R

Racing pants Tight-fitting elasticated skiing trousers 466
Rail travel 575
Ratrac *Piste basher* (major brand)
Red run Medium-tough *run* 457
Rent or buy? Key question for early intermediate skiers 470
Rescue Sequel to skiing accident 476
Roller skiing Simulation of *Cross-country* skiing on tarmac, using roller-skate-like *skis*
Rope tow Primitive form of *drag-lift* 460
Rotary binding *Turntable binding*
Rotation/counter rotation Shoulder movements once fashionable as ingredients of *parallel turns*
Run Identifiable path followed by skiers – usually a *piste* 456

S

NOTE Many terms normally prefaced by 'ski' are to be found not here but under their own initial letter – eg 'ski pole' is under 'pole'

Safety strap Leash attaching *boot* to *ski* to prevent runaway ski after fall 464
Salopettes Skiing dungarees 466
Schuss Straight descent down *fall-line*
Season Winter period when ski resorts are open for business 25, 452
Self-catering Accommodation which in theory permits preparation of meals 32, 478
Short ski *Compact ski* 520
Short swing Short-radius parallel *turn* taught by *BASI*
Shovel Front *tip* of *ski* 522
Sidecut Narrowing of *ski* between *tip* and *tail* 522
Side-slip Controlled sideways slide down *slope*, invaluable on steep slopes
Side-step Stepping sideways up or down ski *slope*
Skating turn *Turn* involving exaggerated transfer of weight from one ski to another, as in ice skating
Skeleton toboggan Basic frame toboggan for single rider
Ski Expensive plastic plank 463 519, 557, 564
Ski birding Skiing with wing-like flaps for extra uplift
Ski bob Small bicycle-like conveyance with skis instead of wheels
Ski bum Person (m or f), usually good-looking and young, who will do anything for a season in a ski resort 473
Ski Club of Great Britain 486, 586
Ski de fond French term for *cross-country* skiing 555
Ski évolutif Method of teaching beginners using gradual progression from short skis to longer ones and immediate learning of *parallel turns* 474
Ski flying Competition judging ski jumps according to length alone
Ski guide Tour operator employee, meant to show you the *pistes* but not how to ski 477
Ski jumping Competition judging length and style of ski jumps
Ski-lift Any form of *lift*; more specifically, a *drag-lift* 460
Ski-mountaineering Climbing up mountains and skiing down them 563
Ski pass *Lift pass* 462
Ski patrol Team employed to supervise safety of *pistes* 476
Ski route Ski *run* marked on mountain but not prepared or patrolled
Ski school Most common and most reliable source of skiing tuition 472
Ski stopper *Brake* 464, 526
Ski-touring *Alpine skiing* without recourse to *lifts* 563
Skins Artificial fur stuck or tied to base of *skis* for walking uphill on *snow* (when ski-touring or mountaineering) 565
Slalom/special slalom *Alpine racing* discipline with tightly-spaced *gates* 494
Slopes Basis of *Alpine skiing* 456
Snow Atmospheric vapour frozen into ice crystals and falling to earth in light white flakes, or spread on it as a white layer after falling (Concise Oxford Dictionary 6th edition) 35, 457, 553
Snowboard Cross between *ski* and surfboard
Snowcat/Snowmobile Vehicle capable of negotiating snowy mountain terrain
Snow-chains Means of keeping cars going on snow-bound roads
Snowplough Basic method of controlling speed and turning by forming *skis* into a V, *tips* together
Snow shoes Broad, round webbed footwear for walking on soft *snow*
Sole Smooth base of *ski*, which slides on *snow* 463
Speed skiing Pursuit of speed records

Spring snow Hard but granular crust formed by thawing of *snow* by day and freezing overnight 458
Star turn Turning round on flat ground
Stem Half-snowplough used in transitional *turns* (stem turn/stem christie) between *snowplough* and *parallel turns*, and in difficult *snow*
Step-in binding Typical modern *binding*
Step turn Parallel *turn* initiated by step uphill
Studio/duplex Small compartments to let in large blocks in French Alps, in which you can eat and sleep but not live
Sunglasses 469
Sun-screen 470
Super-G Alpine racing discipline coming between *downhill* and *giant slalom* 494

T

T-bar Two-person *drag-lift* 460, 487
Tail Back part of *ski* 522
Target group Classification of skiers and skis to simplify *ski* selection 519
Telemark Method of turning when skiing downhill with *cross-country* equipment
Tip Front part of *ski* 522
Touring binding Adjustable *binding* enabling heel to be secured to *ski* for skiing downhill and detached from it for climbing 565
Tourist offices 575
Trail North American terminology for *piste* 456
Transfer Journey (usually by coach) from airport to ski resort 28
Transformed snow *Spring snow* 458
Travel 481
Traverse Skier's course across *slope* of hill, terminated by a *turn*
Tuck *Egg* position
Turn What learning to ski is all about
Turntable binding *Binding* with rotating heel piece 525

U

Unweighting Method of briefly taking pressure off *skis* as an aid to turning
Uphill christie Method of turning uphill and stopping with *skis* parallel

W

Waist Narrow part of *ski* 522
Wall Steep, wide descent
Wax Applied to *sole* of *ski* for lubrication and protection 524, 557
Wedel German term for succession of linked short-radius *turns*
Wedelkurs Package of intensive ski instruction and accommodation offered at beginning of season 25
Wedge *Snowplough*
Wedging *Canting*
White-out Skiing conditions in which falling *snow*, fallen snow and cloud merge, and all sensation of direction is lost; not to be confused with black-out (après-skiing conditions)
White week Package offered by resort, usually in *low season*, including accommodation, *lift pass* and instruction
Windslab Dangerously unstable and invisible patches of *crust* caused by wind over surface of *snow*
Winter Olympics 495
World Championships 495
World Cup 495

X

XC American term for *cross-country* skiing 557

Z

Zdarsky, Mathias Father of *Alpine skiing* 485

Resort index

Resort descriptions are grouped into chapters, usually because they share a skiing area, and are arranged in a geographical sequence. First, north-east Italy is taken east to west; then the sequence goes through the Alps in an anti-clockwise sweep from eastern Austria to southern France; then come other skiing areas. The page references given here take you to the start of the chapter in which the resort is described or mentioned.

The contents of the resorts section of the *Guide* are listed in chapter order on page 22; that's where you should look if you know roughly where you want to go, but don't know the names of the resorts in that region. A comparative summary of all the major resorts in the *Guide* starts on page 37; that's where you should look if you know what your holiday needs are but don't know which resorts will meet them. (For help in getting your needs clear, see 'Choosing your resort', page 25.)

Resort names starting with Le, La or Les are indexed not under L, but under the initial of the main part of their name.